COLONEL ALEXANDER W. DONIPHAN
[From portrait in possession of Mrs. L. M. Lawson, of New York.]

★ War ★
with Mexico
1846-1847

Doniphan's Expedition
and the
Conquest of New Mexico
and California

—Portraits, Maps, and Illustrations—
Includes a reprint of the work of Col. John T. Hughes

by
William Elsey Connelley

Author of Memoirs of the late Senator John J. Ingalls, The Provisional Government of Nebraska Territory, Wyandot Folk-Lore, Kansas Territorial Governors. The Heckewelder Narrative, etc., etc.

HERITAGE BOOKS
2008

HERITAGE BOOKS
AN IMPRINT OF HERITAGE BOOKS, INC.

Books, CDs, and more—Worldwide

For our listing of thousands of titles see our website
at
www.HeritageBooks.com

A Facsimile Reprint
Published 2008 by
HERITAGE BOOKS, INC.
Publishing Division
100 Railroad Ave. #104
Westminster, Maryland 21157

Copyright © 1907 William Elsey Connelley

— Publisher's Notice —
In reprints such as this, it is often not possible to remove blemishes from the original. We feel the contents of this book warrant its reissue despite these blemishes and hope you will agree and read it with pleasure.

International Standard Book Numbers
Paperbound: 978-0-7884-1461-9
Clothbound: 978-0-7884-7348-7

PREFACE.

THIS book is an account of the most remarkable military campaign in American history. In many respects Doniphan's Expedition was the most wonderful of which history tells. And it was not only marvelous—it accomplished much, few campaigns having ever accomplished more. For one thing, it saved Buena Vista and averted disaster to the American arms on that bloody field. For Colonel Doniphan not only had no help from Generals Taylor and Wool, but by dividing the Mexican forces he saved them from destruction. Had they done one-half as well at Buena Vista as did Colonel Doniphan at Sacramento, Santa Anna's army would have been destroyed the first day, with plenty of time to spare. And what a strange thing it is that Colonel Doniphan got no promotion for his brilliant achievements! Colonel Price was made a Brigadier-General. This gross injustice to Colonel Doniphan I believe it my duty to point out. The State of Kansas honored him by naming a county and a town for him, and the State of Missouri named the seat of Ripley County in his honor.

The battle of Sacramento was the most wonderful ever fought by American arms. Dewey's battle in Manila Bay may be set down as its only rival. The only land-battle at all approaching it was that of New Orleans; but in that battle the Americans fought at home, on their own soil, behind fortifications. The battle of Sacramento far outranks it. Colonel Doniphan's men attacked a fortified position held by troops outnumbering them nearly five to one. They were in a strange land, thousands of miles from home. They were in rags, suffering from starvation. They were seemingly abandoned by their Government and left to their fate. In case of defeat there was no hope of succor, no help,—nothing but inevitable destruction. But all these discouragements did not daunt the Missourians. They made their arrangements for battle as coolly as they would have planned the reaping of a field at home. They would not be hurried by the tactics of the enemy, but stood under fire a long time carrying out their preliminary movements to the minutest details. They even had their jokes. A shot from the enemy's cannon carried away part of the cap of a Missourian, and he remarked with apparent unconcern: "I want to tell you they shoot mighty d——d close in this country," and went on with the preparations for the battle. And when the Americans were finally ready to begin to fight they charged with the force of the thunderbolt. They were irresistible. They never halted. They poured over the fortifications of the enemy and routed his forces from the trenches. They overwhelmed the Mexicans by their audacity and furious courage.

That charge was as gallant and heroic as any ever made in the world. It was as resistless as the avalanche, grim as death, inexorable as fate. It has never been equaled in all the annals of the world's warfare.

To those heroic Americans, Missourians by birth or adoption, we accord honor and fame and glory. They stand the peers of any soldiers that ever shouldered arms. Their achievement is worth more than a thousand battleships and ten thousand armies with banners. Their triumph declares that the American arms in a righteous cause can never be successfully resisted.

It is strange that so little is known of this great victory. Even Missourians, descendants of the men who won it, know little about it. They seem to have no proper conception of the fame won for them by their fathers. The victory of Sacramento—the success of Doniphan's Expedition—is a heritage more valuable than kingdoms and powers and principalities. It ought to be the theme of the poets, the song of the daughters, the boast of the sons of Old Missouri. It should become the pride and inspiration of the people of Missouri. And some day it will.

In order that I might put into this work incidents connecting with the present time the events of the remarkable campaign, I have sought all sources of information. That this book might be a living narrative I have cast about for accounts of those things which light up the scenes of those times with human interest and individual action. I have endeavored to have these incidents picture the men as they marched footsore and weary over desert wastes, as they bivouacked shelterless on the frozen ground under the cold and silent stars, as they starved and their hair and beards ran riot and their clothing fell to pieces, as they appeared on the battlefield fighting like demons for their country which neglected them, and as citizens of a great State returning to the pursuits of peace and pleasures of home. It is a picture worthy a great painter who will one day spring from the soil of Old Missouri.

An army is a community under arms. Human ambitions are there more active and persistent than in times of peace in the quiet country-side. As these men marched there occurred humorous incidents and tragedies as dark as midnight. Some cursed, and others prayed. Some carried in their hearts fidelity to home and wife, while others were captivated by fair women encountered by the way. And it requires mention of these things to round out the record and make a picture upon which shall stand the proper lights and shades. I have done my best to secure and write them down.

Those official reports omitted by Colonel Hughes have been supplied by the War Department at the request of Hon. Chester I. Long. I found in the library of the Missouri Historical Society, St. Louis, Mo., the original letter-book of General Stephen W. Kearny; from it I secured the letters, orders and proclamations set out herein. The Rolls I copied from the records in the office of the Adjutant-General of Missouri. I visited the survivors of the Expedition, and secured from them accounts of the many incidents mentioned in this work. And of these it is but just to say that Meredith T. Moore, Esq., of Cedar City, Mo., was of greater aid to me than any of the others.

No attempt to preserve the pagination of the work of Colonel Hughes was made, as it was deemed unnecessary, two forms of the work having been printed, with page-numbers different in each. References are as often to one as to the other, and it was impossible to preserve the page-numbers of both.

The notes in the original work written by Colonel Hughes have been preserved to him by placing his name after them. All other matter and notes of every kind were written by me.

PREFACE.   vii

In gathering material for a History of Eastern Kentucky I made inquiry of Captain John C. Collins, of the Fourteenth Kentucky Infantry, concerning the battles fought at Paintsville and the Meadows of Licking. He directed me to write to Colonel E. F. Clay, Paris, Kentucky, who commanded the Confederate forces in those battles. This I did, and he referred my letter to Mr. James R. Rogers, who wrote me satisfactory accounts of those conflicts, he having been in them both. Afterwards I mailed him a prospectus of my *Doniphan's Expedition*. We know not how the world is entangled and intertwined, nor what trains of thought and recollections a little thing may bring forth. Mr. Rogers wrote me as follows in response to my prospectus:

PARIS, KY., R. R. No. 3, March 27, 1907.

MR. W. E. CONNELLEY—*Dear Sir:* The accident by which we became known, in a way, is not unusual, but when you mail me a prospectus of the Life of Colonel Doniphan, which you are preparing for publication, my mind reverts to a scene of forty-nine years ago, and it becomes impressive. A. W. Doniphan, Jr., the only living son, in 1858 was my room-mate at Bethany College, now West Virginia. In the spring of that year, with some others, we were foolish enough to brave the swollen waters of a stream near by, for a bath, a perfect mill-race. I entered the stream first, and with great difficulty landed upon the opposite bank some hundred yards below. Doniphan, on the eve of leaping into the stream, used the familiar quotation, "Darest thou, Cassius, leap with me into this raging flood and swim to yonder point?" In the full current of the stream, a distance away, an exclamation of some words escaped him, which I failed to catch, but the turning-point of the quotation was applied by his friends who never entered the stream—"Help me, Cassius, or I sink." His remains were recovered a month later in the Ohio, nineteen miles away. When recovered, one foot was gone, and only by means of the other could I alone identify the body. It was distinctly a model foot, and was the only feature of the body unchanged. The elder brother's death was still more harrowing—he was ill, and by accident was given a deadly poison.

I am under obligations to the following persons, and I make my acknowledgments here: W. Boone Major, Secretary Missouri State Association Mexican War; General Odon Guitar, Columbia, Mo.; General DeArmond, Adjutant-General State of Missouri, and his chief clerk, Mr. D. F. Thompson; Captain William H. Gregg, Kansas City, Mo.; Judge James Peacock, Independence, Mo.; Hon. D. C. Allen, Liberty, Mo., for interviews and correspondence covering the life of Colonel Doniphan and his men, for the use of his *Life of Colonel Doniphan*, for assistance in tracing Dr. Josiah Gregg, and for aid in every department of this work. Mr. Allen is the greatest living authority on the history and traditions of western Missouri. To Mrs. John H. Rothwell, Liberty, Mo.; Mrs. Andrew Loughrey, Randolph, Mo.; George L. Boone, Medford, Oregon; Colonel Max Frost, Editor of the *New Mexican*, Santa Fé, New Mexico; W. H. Woodson, Liberty, Mo., for information relating to Colonel Doniphan and the family of Major Samuel C. Owens; R. P. C. Wilson, Platte City, Mo., for letters concerning the Platte County Company and Colonel Doniphan; D. P. Thompson, Kansas City, Mo., for photographs of Colonel Doniphan and Dr. Josiah Gregg; The *Annals of Platte County*, Mo., by W. M. Paxton, Esq., for information about everything connected with the history of western Missouri; the Missouri Historical Society, St. Louis, Mo., and its officers, Hon. Cyrus A. Peterson, President, Charles P. Pettus, Esq., Secretary,

PREFACE.   ix

Judge Walter B. Douglas, Director, and Miss Mary Louise
Dalton, Librarian; Peter Connelly, Kansas City, Mo., for
information relating to his father, Dr. Henry Connelly,
and to Mrs. Sallie Stone Lewis, Taylorsville, Kentucky,
for information relating to the early history of the Connelly
Family in America; Mr. Milton Moore, Kansas City, Mo.,
for interviews and letters giving information of Colonel
Doniphan and his men; Hon. Roland Hughes, Kansas
City, Mo., son of Colonel John T. Hughes, for aid in all
departments of this work; Dr. W. A. Curry, Kansas City,
Mo., for information about Captain W. Z. Angney; Mrs.
Carrie Westlake Whitney, Librarian Kansas City Public
Library, for general assistance in the preparation of this
work; the Kansas State Historical Society, Topeka, for
the use of its great library; James L. King, State Librarian, Topeka; Charles M. Harvey, of the St. Louis *Globe-Democrat;* Edward J. Glasgow, St. Louis, Mo., for much
valuable information about the Traders' Battalion, about
Dr. Henry Connelly, and about northern Mexico and its
conditions in 1846; Mrs. Mildred P. Standish, Matron
Missouri Institution for the Blind, St. Louis, Mo., for material for sketch of the life of Captain M. M. Parsons;
Clark Brown, of the *Franklin County Tribune*, Union, Mo.,
material for a sketch of the life of Captain John D. Stephenson; Mr. E. S. Link, Jefferson City, Mo., for photographs of the old cannons about the Missouri Capitol
Building; P. B. McCord, of the *Newark Evening News*,
Newark, N. J., for the portrait of "Joe Bowers"; Mrs.
Rush Campbell Owen, Springfield, Mo., for information
for the sketch of her father, Major John P. Campbell;
Judge Thomas J. C. Fagg, Louisiana, Mo., for information

concerning authorship of the song "Joe Bowers"; Hon. Champ Clark, Bowling Green, Mo., communications relating to "Joe Bowers"; John Smith Story, Liberty, Mo., for information concerning Company C; Colonel Henry S. Kearny, New York city, son of General Stephen W. Kearny; the sons of Willard P. Hall, Kansas City, Mo.; Michael McEnnis, Kirkwood, Mo., for material for a sketch of his life; Miss Eleanor Glasgow Voorhis, New York city, for much assistance and many favors in the preparation of this work; Charles R. Morehead, El Paso, Texas, for sketch of his life and information of William H. Russell, also sketch of adventures on the Plains and in the Rocky Mountains; Judge Joseph Magoffin, El Paso, Texas, for material for sketch of his life and that of his father, the late James Magoffin; Hon. D. W. Wilder, Hiawatha, Kansas; E. N. Hopkins, Lexington, Mo.; Hon. E. F. Ware, Topeka, Kansas, for information concerning General Sterling Price and other Missourians prominent in both the Mexican and Civil wars; to L. M. Lawson, New York city, for the portrait of Colonel Doniphan, from which was made the frontispiece of this work. And I have consulted the files of the following newspapers:

St. Louis Globe-Democrat,   Kansas City Star,
St. Louis Republic,   Kansas City Journal.

WILLIAM ELSEY CONNELLEY.

Topeka, Kansas, May 7, 1907.

TABLE OF CONTENTS.

	Page.
Preface,	iii
I. PRELIMINARY,	1
1. Missourians,	3
2. Colonel Alexander W. Doniphan,—His Life and Character, by Hon. D. C. Allen,	15
3. Major-General Sterling Price,	40
4. John Taylor Hughes,	46
5. Diary of Colonel John T. Hughes,	60
II. THE HUGHES REPRINT,	113
1. Preface to,	117
2. Chapters and Contents of,	120
3. Map of,	122
4. Memoir of Colonel Alexander W. Doniphan,	123
5. Beginning of the Work,	129
III. OFFICIAL ROSTERS,	525
1. Remarks Upon,	527
2. Regimental Field and Staff,	529
3. Company A, (Jackson County,)	530
4. Company B, (Lafayette County,)	534
5. Company C, (Clay County,)	542
6. Company D, (Saline County,)	547
7. Company E, (Franklin County,)	550
8. Company F, (Cole County,)	553
9. Company G, (Howard County,)	556
10. Company H, (Callaway County,)	560
11. Laclede Rangers, (St. Louis,)	563
12. Infantry:	566
1. Cole County,	566
2. Platte County,	568
13. Artillery:	570
1. Captain R. H. Weightman's Company,	574
2. Captain Woldemar Fischer's Company,	577
14. Field and Staff, Colonel Price's Regiment,	580
15. Field and Staff, Santa Fé Battalion,	581
16. Field and Staff, Separate Battalion,	581
IV. APPENDICES,	583
1. Appendix A,—Interview with Colonel Doniphan,	585
2. Appendix B,—Address of Major Gilpin,	592
2. Appendix C,—Narrative of Chas. R. Morehead,	600

4. Appendix D,—Thomas Hart Benton, ... 623
5. Appendix E,—Michael McEnnis, ... 625
6. Appendix F,—Francis Xavier Aubrey, ... 628
7. Appendix G,—The Santa Fé Trail, ... 630
8. Appendix H,—General Stephen Watts Kearny, ... 636
9. Appendix I,—Meredith T. Moore, ... 639
10. Appendix J,—General Odon Guitar, ... 644
11. Appendix K,—Edward James Glasgow, ... 645

ILLUSTRATIONS.

	Page.
Albuquerque, Plaza at,	231
Albuquerque, Scene Near,	78
Bent's Fort,	206
Brazito, Plan of the Battle of,	376
Cannons Made from Guns Captured at the Battle of Sacramento,	542
Cart, Mexican,	320
Cover of the Paper Edition of the Work of John T. Hughes, photographic reproduction of,	50
Cross by the Wayside,	482
"Cut the Rope, or Pull Up the Picket," (on Title-page of the Hughes Reprint,)	115
"D——n a Mule, Anyhow,"	471
Deer, Black-tailed,	316
Frontispiece.	
Guerrilla, Shooting of, by Texan Rangers,	489
Jornada del Muerto, the American Army Crossing,	368
Los Angeles, Plan of the Battle of,	346
MAPS:	
1. Los Angeles, Plan of the Battle of,	346
2. Presidio, Plan of,	96
3. Reproduction of that in Work of John T. Hughes,	122
4. Reproduction of that in Work of Dr. Wislizenus,	649
5. Sacramento, Plan of the Battle of,	412
6. Sacramento, Preliminary Movements of Americans at,	105
7. San Gabriel, Plan of Battle of,	345
8. Santa Fé and Its Environs, Plan of,	210
Mexicans, Group of,	212
Mexican Woodman,	449
Monument to Colonel Alexander W. Doniphan, Liberty, Mo.,	30
Music, that of the Joe Bowers Song,	12
PORTRAITS:	
Allen, D. C.,	17
Bledsoe, Colonel Hiram,	539
Bowers, Joe,	6
Connelly, Dr. Henry,	277
Doniphan, Colonel Alexander William,—	
1. Frontispiece.	
2. From Hicks Photograph,	16
3. From the Work of John T. Hughes,	112
4. From Painting in Missouri Historical Society,	526

xiv   ILLUSTRATIONS.

Gilpin, Major William, ... 145
Glasgow, Edward J.,—
   1. At the present time, ... 100
   2. At the age of twenty years, ... 645
Gregg, Dr. Josiah, ... 162
Guitar, General Odon, ... 644
Hall, Hon. Willard P., ... 582
Hughes, Colonel John T., ... 47
Kearny, General Stephen Watts,—
   1. From Old Print, ... 225
   2. From Miniature in possession of his son, ... 636
MacLean, Lachlan Allan, ... 118
McCord, P. B., ... 13
McEnnis, Michael,—
   1. At the age of eighty-one, ... 625
   2. At the age of thirty, ... 626
Magoffin, James, ... 196
Morehead, Charles R., ... 600
Moore, Meredith T., ... 639
Narbona, Chief of the Navajos, ... 293
Patton, J. W., The Volunteer, ... 114
Price, General Sterling,—
   1. In the Civil War, ... 41
   2. In the Mexican War, ... 112
Russell, William H., ... 601
Weightman, Captain Richard Hanson, ... 361
Presidio, Plan of the, ... 96
SACRAMENTO:
   1. Captain Reid's Charge at the Battle of, ... 413
   2. Plans of the Battle of, ... 412
   3. Map of Preliminary Movements of Americans at, ... 105
   4. Topography of Land at the Battle of, ... 417
SANTA FÉ:
   1. National Cemetery at, ... 71
   2. Old Palace of the Governors at, ... 2
   3. Plans of the Environs of, ... 210
San Gabriel, Plan of the Battle of, ... 345

ERRATA.

Page 27. "Silas H. Woodson" should be "Samuel H. Woodson;" there was no Silas H. Woodson.

Page 420. In the account of the actions of John Rice in the Battle of Sacramento, in note, eighth line from bottom of page, "banished" should be "brandished."

Page 441. "40,000," eighth line from bottom of page, should be "4,000."

PRELIMINARY.

THE OLD PALACE OF THE GOVERNORS, AT SANTA FÉ.

DONIPHAN'S EXPEDITION.

MISSOURIANS.

MANY great Missourians had part in the conquest of the American Southwest. The roll contains such names as Doniphan, Sterling Price, Gilpin, Dr. Gregg, Dr. Connelly, Francis Preston Blair, Kit Carson, Benton, Hughes, and Willard P. Hall. It will be necessary in this work to notice them individually, but before doing so it will be well to view Missourians generally and obtain a perspective of their achievement as a people. They heard that "call of the wild" which is one of the primal instincts of man. It will be profitable to note what particular work these people were given to do, the manner in which it was performed, and to see if they shall have a place on the eternal scroll of glory.

Missouri is a great State. She has done her full share of great things in the Union. The statesmanship of her Senators gave us the Oregon country. An army of her citizens marched thousands of miles over desert and plain without a commissary, penetrated to the heart of the enemy's country, defeated and routed an entrenched army nearly five times its size, and added an empire to our borders. The controversy over her admission to the Union and the repeal of one of the stipulations enacted at the time were among the potent and immediate causes of the Civil War. Missouri was the temporary resting-place of the English-speaking people in their conquest of the wilderness. Here they gathered, overspread the land, took root, turned the soil, built towns, grew prosperous and waxed strong, developed a unique commerce, and erected a great Commonwealth as a base from which to make the final assault upon the endless stretches of mountain and plain that went out to the Pacific Ocean.

Opportunity is not everything. The men to whom it comes are factors, and often count for as much as the opportunity itself. Let us see what manner of men this original stock of Missourians embraced. In such numbers were they pioneers in the country westward of them that California, Oregon, Montana, and Colorado were for years little more than Missouri colonies, and in some of them the characteristics of a Missouri community predominate to this day; the political institutions of all (and of other Western States) were modeled after those of Missouri. Missourians wrote the first Code of New Mexico. When New England statesmen were opposing the establishment of mail routes to the Columbia and wishing the Mississippi river a stream of flaming lava to mark our western bounds forever, Missourians, with the true genius of the Anglo-Saxon, were scaling the Rocky Mountains and walking to and fro in the valleys which led down to the western sea. From Missouri there set a rising tide. It rose and surged and flowed over a great part of the New World. Neither snowy mountains, nor raging floods, nor waterless plains, nor wastes of burning sand, nor hordes of savage warriors could turn them from their way. Into their hands was given the destiny of the world. Through all the shiftings of the ages, the mutations of time, the uncertainty of all human affairs, the erection and fall of governments and powers and principalities, there had come to them the honor of closing the gap completing the migration of the human race westward around the globe.[1]

The Missourian is massive of frame, stalwart, kindly of heart, shrewd and forceful in business, enterprising, adventurous, patient, conservative, fearless, and daring. He is sanguine and full of resource. In 1849 one conceived the idea of hauling a large sawmill overland from the Missouri river to the Sacramento valley. He would have accomplished it, too, but for the enormous profit he was paid on his venture at Fort Kearny on the Platte, to which point men had hesitated for years to attempt to bring even a small mill. The old fur-traders established trading-posts more than a thousand

---

NOTE 1.—The Spaniards discovered and occupied the west coasts of North and South America. It is not intended to say here that the Missourians discovered California or the Pacific Ocean. The occupation of the West by the Americans was the establishment there of modern civilization—something Spanish occupancy did not accomplish. And the Spaniards were thrust out, but the Americans will never be displaced.

miles out from civilization among savage and hostile tribes that could have destroyed them and their forts in a single day. There developed in the Rocky Mountains a class of frontiersmen who looked with loathing contempt upon the demoralizing luxury of the effete civilization of St. Louis in the thirties! They were self-reliant. They depended upon themselves alone. They slew the buffalo, trapped the beaver, fought the grizzly, and outwitted the wild Indian. They had little fear of God and none at all of the devil. And yet they were true men—great men. They were moved by the emotions common to the human heart. Their eyes were not satisfied with seeing nor their ears with hearing. They were charmed with the view of a snow-capped range bound about with the green forests growing on its lower slopes. The bright valley with a silvery stream winding through it appealed to them. As descried from the shoulder of some projecting mountain, the plain spotted with the leathern lodges of barbarous bands afforded them pleasure. A view of the slow-heaving masses of buffalo rolling northward gave them supreme satisfaction. These pioneers guided the succeeding generation of Missourians through passes, down gorges, up and over mountains that rose to the stars, and along golden valleys down to the uttermost limits of the New World. And when they were stopped by the ocean, the next country to the west was the East of old, from which the human race set out in the morning of the world to girdle the earth.

In the achievements of the Missourians there were of necessity men of every stamp. In the intercourse among themselves there arose every human passion. When the history of America comes to be adequately written it will deal chiefly with the events which transpired west of the Appalachians, and the petty annals of New England will become local lore. And when a truly American literature shall arise some hundreds of years hence, it will be the flower of the heroic actions of the pioneers of the West—beyond the Mississippi, largely of Missourians by birth or adoption. And there are not lacking examples foretelling this. Whether Joe Bowers[2] was

---

NOTE 2.—Many people believe Joe Bowers was a real character of that name, and that he went to California as a forty-niner, where the ballad-maker had before him a genuine living Argonaut when he wrote the immortal song giving an account of his misfortune in love because of the fickle course of heartless Sally Black. But it is not likely that Joe Bowers was a man of flesh and blood. William Kincaid, of Bowling Green, Mo., told Champ Clark that the character of Joe

(From a drawing made by P. B. McCord.)

JOE BOWERS,
The Folk-Hero of the Argonauts.

> My name it is Joe Bowers,
> And I've got a brother Ike:
> I came from Old Missouri—
> Yes, all the way from Pike.

Bowers was drawn after a man named Abner McElwee, "Who lived in Pike county, on Noix creek, about midway between Bowling Green and Louisiana, many of whose relatives reside in that vinicity to this day. He was born in North Carolina, as were many of the pioneer settlers of Pike county. In 1849 Abner McElwee went to California with a company of Pikers, in which, among others, were two of his nephews named Massey, one of whom, Tom Massey, is the 'Brother Ike' mentioned in the song. Mr. Kincaid says that the plot of the song was imaginary, and thinks that the reason the poet took Abner McElwee for his hero was that he was a tall, big-hearted, big-bodied, jolly old bachelor who was always going into mock heroics about a girl of ravishing beauty he had left behind in Pike."

man or myth matters not. If man, he is immortal; and if myth, his fame is more lasting than if he were in very truth a man of flesh and blood. He is the typical man who has gone out into the world in all ages to make his fortune: some by conquering other kingdoms, as told in the relations of Homer; some to discover and plunder new countries, as we may see in the chronicles of Mexico and Peru; and others, the just, normal, immortal ones ,as Joe Bowers, to earn enough to start in life with those the love for whom inspired the voyage. Only the last were moved by proper and the noblest of impulses, and their voyages are replete with romantic possibility. In the interim between the outsetting and return tides of the venture there might develop experiences revealing every emotion of the human heart. The strolling singer who wandered up and down the Coast had no other idea than to get bread; or, it may be in addition, rum. And what should he sing? Clearly, something to please; for men in the passive mood contribute little to strollers of any ilk. To please whom? Those to hear. Then it must be something to please the Missourians, something to appeal to them, for they were everywhere. In some places there were no other people.[3] Bret

NOTE 3.—Missourians all are destined to be called "Pikers" as are the Kentuckians "Corncrackers," the Kansans "Jawhawkers," etc. The growth of this term is easily traced. It was formerly "Pikes," and referred to the inhabitants of Pike county only. That term was not euphonious, and in its broader application it has come to be "Pikers," and it will so remain. The name has not attached to Missourians generally, but in time it will do so. The origin of the name is well told by Noble L. Prentis, in his *Pike of Pike's Peak*, an address delivered before the Kansas Historical Society, at Topeka, February 19, 1877:

"Those who happened to be on the Plains in the old days, when the 'star of empire' was on wheels—(wagon-wheels), when California was known as the land of gold, the North-American El Dorado, must have noticed on the broad, white, sun-baked highway, the passage of a team, the beasts being called, by a construction of the plural peculiar to their owner, 'oxens.' The wheelers were known as 'Buck' and 'Bright;' the leaders as 'Tige' and 'Golden'—the former as an allusion to his supposed-to-be ferocious and untamable disposition; the latter possibly out of compliment to the destination of the outfit, or their prospects, but probably on account of the dull-yellow color of his hide, which was supposed to resemble the metal which had led his human friends to undertake the long and toilsome journey.

"To these people thus described, and to all who bore to them a family resemblance, and who in 1849 and in subsequent years crossed the Plains to California, came to be applied, by whom originally I know not, the general name of 'Pikes.' Various explanations have been given of the origin of the name. The most reasonable one is, that there are in Missouri and Illinois two large counties named Pike, and separated from each other by the Mississippi river. In 1849 an immense emigration set in from these counties to California. In consequence the traveler bound for the States, meeting teams, and asking the usual question

Harte understood those times, and when he would ridicule the pretensions of the Pliocene skull his apostrophe embraced the geologic ages, but the reply carried the matter of antiquity to no remoter time than the days of the Argonauts:

"'Speak, thou awful vestige of the Earth's creation,—
Solitary fragment of remains organic!
Tell the wondrous secret of thy past existence,—
Speak! thou oldest primate!'

"Even as I gazed, a thrill of the maxilla,
And a lateral movement of the condyloid process,
With post-pliocene sounds of healthy mastication,
Ground the teeth together.

"And, from that imperfect dental exhibition,
Stained with expressed juices of the weed Nicotian,
Came these hollow accents, blent with softer murmurs
Of expectoration:

"'Which my name is Bowers, and my crust was busted
Falling down a shaft in Calaveras County,
But I'd take it kindly if you'd send the pieces
Home to old Missouri!'"

And so, indeed, must the stroller have been familiar with the conditions which required the subject of his song to be one with which every Missourian was of necessity familiar from experience—the trip from home and loved ones across the Plains to the Mecca of the gold-hunters. It must relate what might be true of each and all—not necessarily true of any. And this embraces the genius of literature.

So, a simple ballad was written along the lines of necessity. It made no pretensions to literary merit, for it had none; and it was doubtless the best the stroller could do. The lines scrawled as like as not on some rum-puddled bar-counter must have appeared stale

---

'Where are you from?' was answered, frequently, with 'Pike county,' meaning in some cases one Pike county and in some cases the other. This led to the general impression that everybody on the road was from Pike county, or that the inhabitants of Pike had all taken the road. Hence the general name of 'Pikes,' as applied to emigrants, especially to those traveling from Missouri, and, generally, those migrating from southern Illinois and southern Indiana. Thus the popular song—the only poetry I ever heard of applied to this class of 'movers'—commences:
"'My name it is Joe Bowers,
I've got a brother Ike;
I'm bound for Californy,
And I'm all the way from Pike.'"

and flat enough.[4] And no great composer of music would have tolerated for an instant the simple tones of the tune or air devised to accompany them. Any assembly of competent literary and musical critics would have condemned the whole production at once. How fortunate that the world has not had to depend upon "competent" persons for the creation of those things that are worth most and that live longest! The music that has moved the world was never the production of the great musical composers, but it is that of the simple folk-songs that sink into the heart and stir the soul. When

NOTE 4.—Champ Clark insists that it was written by "Mark Twain," but Mr. Clemens did not cross the Plains early enough to have written it; "Joe Bowers" had been sung in California for years before he arrived there. Meredith T. Moore, Cedar City, Mo., crossed the Plains in 1849 and again in 1852. He heard the song at least as early as 1854, and perhaps long before that time. He thinks it possible that a man known to the miners as "Squibob" (true name unknown) may have written it. He furnishes me a statement by a friend of his, which is to the effect that the song was written by a Piker, "Joe Bowers," whose name is not remembered, who went to Mexico with Doniphan, and that it was sung by the soldiers; that it was carried to California by some Missourians who went on there with Kearny; that afterwards one English, of New Jersey, rewrote the poem, changing it to suit him, and appropriated the old tune that Bowers had used. This statement further says that the man known as Joe Bowers is buried at Chillicothe, Mo.; but inquiries I have made there brought no response. Mr. Moore says that in California in the early days Missourians were called "Pikers" indiscriminately and generally.

It is not known who wrote the song. Judge Thomas J. C. Fagg, of Louisiana, Mo., "went to California a few years ago and sought to trace the Joe Bowers ballad to its source. In San Francisco he found a man who declared himself to have been well acquainted with the author of the ballad. This man said that a variety actor and singer named John Woodward was the author. Woodward, he averred, wrote the lines and first sang them in San Francisco, and later, all up and down the coast. For years, according to this authority, Woodward sang the song as his own. Hundreds of others took it up and the song soon spread all over the United States."

Judge Fagg wrote me under date of October 5, 1906, as follows:

"I have the sworn testimony of an old actor connected with 'The Melodian,' one of the oldest theaters in San Francisco, showing that the song, 'Joe Bowers,' was written by John Woodward, who was connected with Johnson's Minstrels in 1849 and the early fifties. He says the song was written by John Woodward, a member of that company, and first brought out by that company at the old Melodian Theater in San Francisco in 1850. I got exactly the same statement from another man in San Francisco in 1898, who was at one time connected with the same company. This latter was a seedy specimen who called himself 'Joe Ratler'—his real name I could not find out. Who John Woodward was I was also unable to find out. He went to California from Kentucky in 1849, and just simply dropped out of sight when the minstrel company dissolved. 'Joe Bowers' was simply a model Piker."

It is probable that Woodward wrote the song. If not, then some one of his

the miserable stroller combined his ungrammatical lines and his soft and simple notes, what a change! There was a song! There was in it that indefinable quality that the heart recognized as a part of itself! The stroller intended it to be humorous; and men may have laughed at the misfortune of Joe Bowers—may yet do so; but tears go with such laughter, and a lesson by which every man may interpret his own life. We may safely conclude that many a stalwart Missourian turned aside to conceal his emotion and hide his streaming eyes as the stroller sang the simple story of Joe Bowers. And more! He stood again in the green fields of the home-land; he kissed his wife and child or mother or "Sally Black" an affectionate farewell; he toiled beside his oxen over plain and mountain under burning sun and amid eternal snows to descend into the golden valleys of California. Fortune, it may be, had been kind to him. Perhaps biting adversity had been rendered doubly bitter by a letter from "brother Ike," and a barrier ten thousand times higher than the Sierra Nevada shut him out from home forever. And the song became the chronicle and the interpretation of his life. Such ex-

---

profession wrote it and sang it in the cheap shows common in California in the early fifties.

I have examined many versions of "Joe Bowers." There are slight differences in them. The following is believed to be the best form of this immortal song:

My name it is Joe Bowers,
  And I've got a brother Ike;
I came from Old Missouri,
  And all the way from Pike.
I'll tell you why I left there,
  And why I came to roam,
And leave my poor old mammy,
  So far away from home.

I used to court a gal there—
  Her name was Sally Black;
I axed her if she'd marry me;
  She said it was a whack.
Says she to me, "Joe Bowers,
  Before we hitch for life,
You ought to get a little home
  To keep your little wife."

"O Sally, dearest Sally,
  O Sally, for your sake,
I'll go to California
  And try to make a stake."
Says she to me, "Joe Bowers,
  You are the man to win;
Here's a kiss to bind the bargain"—
  And she hove a dozen in.

periences and such emotions sink into the soul to grow and ripen into ruling influences of action.

Such is the true office of song. The effects of a true song crystallize into elemental principles of character, and this is true of nation as well as of individual. If it were possible to trace the strains to which the simple ballad of Joe Bowers is set, we might find that they were chanted by moving hordes of barbarians riding across the steppes of Asia bent on bloody conquest. Or we might find that they were sung by those ancient Argonauts in their search for the Golden Fleece. Or the Huns or Scythians, Tartars or Arabians, Goths or Vandals, Franks or Gauls, Moors or Spaniards may have marched and fought to their inspiring melody. They may have originated on the Euphrates, on the Indus or the Ganges, on the Tiber, the Danube or the Neva, on the Rhine, the Thames, the Shannon, or the Spey. Certain it is that our stroller did not make them,

> When I got to that country
>   I hadn't nary red;
> I had such wolfish feelings,
>   I wished myself 'most dead;
> But the thoughts of my dear Sally
>   Soon made those feelings git,
> And whispered hopes to Bowers—
>   I wish I had 'em yit!
>
> At length I went to mining,
>   Put in my biggest licks;
> Went down upon the boulders
>   Just like a thousand bricks.
> I worked both late and early,
>   In rain, in sun, in snow;
> I was working for my Sally—
>   It was all the same to Joe.
>
> At length I got a letter
>   From my dear brother Ike;
> It came from Old Missouri,
>   And all the way from Pike;
> It brought to me the darndest news
>   That ever you did hear,—
> My heart is almost bursting,
>   So pray excuse this tear.
>
> It said that Sal was false to me,
>   Her love for me had fled;
> She'd got married to a butcher,—
>   And the butcher's hair was red;
> And more than that, the letter said—
>   It's enough to make me swear—
> That Sally has a baby,
>   And the baby has red hair!

12   DONIPHAN'S EXPEDITION.

nor did he know where he got them. That they are hoary with antiquity we may safely conclude. That they have flowed through the human heart a living stream from time immemorial there can be little doubt. And they have been recovered by a new people to be carried about the world, and so, can never die.[5]

Joe Bowers is more than the true type of the Missouri Argonaut. He is the hero of the final era of the migration of the human race. He will ever remain such. It is meet that he should. No guile

---

NOTE 5.—The music, copied and arranged for this work by Miss Edith Connelley, is as follows:

was in him found. Sally Black played him false, and it caused him such grief as like calamity might cause any true man, but for her no word of resentment rose to his lips. We may safely conclude that such a man bent to his task, whatever it may have been, and did a man's work in building the empire beyond the Snowy Mountains. He is the type of the soldiers who fought, Missourian against Missourian, brother against brother, father against son, in the Civil War in Old Missouri. Braver men nor better soldiers ever marched or fought or died on a battle-field than these Missourians, without regard to the side upon which they were found.

Whether he ever lived or not, as a character in the history of the West Joe Bowers is the greatest Missourian. And to those to whom the history of folk-heroes is a familiar matter it is not at all improbable that in this capacity he may become the greatest American.[6]

NOTE 6.—The picture herein published has come to be the accepted portrait of Joe Bowers. It was made hurriedly for Hon. Champ Clark's article on that hero, published in the *Globe-Democrat*, by Peter B. McCord, then an illustrator

P. B. McCORD.

for that paper. Since its publication it has been reproduced hundreds of times. It is the recognized and standard portrait of Joe Bowers. It is a typical picture. The artist caught the true spirit of the Missouri gold-seeker. It was an inspira-

tion, and will live as long as Joe Bowers; both will live as long as Missouri or California or America or Anglo-Saxon civilization.
I found Mr. McCord at work for the Newark (N. J.) *Evening News.* He furnished the drawing from which this picture was made, and at my solicitation sent me a photograph of himself, a cut from which is published herein. McCord is a native Missourian; born at Linn, Osage county, January 31, 1871; attended the schools of the town only; at the age of twenty went to work as illustrator for the *Globe-Democrat;* all he knew of drawing and illustrating was self-taught; and he says the only remarkable thing in his life is that for seven years that great paper published his productions. He did commercial drawing and book illustrations for two years after leaving the *Globe-Democrat;* then he was on the Philadelphia *North American,* from which he went to the *Evening News,* Newark. He was married September 2, 1905. Under the heading, "My Habits," he sets down this, and this only: "I chew tobacco, as every true Missourian should. And I vote for William Jennings Bryan at every possible opportunity."

COL. ALEXANDER W. DONIPHAN—HIS LIFE AND CHARACTER.

BY D. C. ALLEN,[7] OF LIBERTY, MO.

Alexander William Doniphan was born in Mason county, Kentucky, July 9, 1808. His father, Joseph Doniphan, was a native of King George, and his mother of Fauquier county, Virginia. His mother's maiden name was Anne Smith, and her paternal ancestor was among the original colonists at Jamestown, Virginia, in 1607. His first ancestor in America of the name of Doniphan came from England to Virginia near the middle or latter part of the seventeenth century, and settled near what is known as the Northern Neck. The given name of that ancestor was Mott.

It is a tradition in the Doniphan family (a tradition which I neither avouch nor deny), traceable and fully believed by its mem-

---

NOTE 7.—Hon. D. C. Allen was born in Clay county, Mo., Nov. 11, 1835. His father was Col. Shubael Allen, a native of Orange county, N. Y., who settled in Clay county, Mo., in 1820. Col. Allen and Miss Dinah Ayres Trigg were married in Howard county, Mo., in 1822. She was born in Estill county, Ky., and was a daughter of Gen. Stephen Trigg, of Bedford county, Va., who emigrated to Kentucky in 1794, and thence to Missouri in 1818.

Mr. Allen's father died in 1841, and he was reared by his mother. He graduated at William Jewell College, with the first honors, in 1855, and occupied the position of principal of the Preparatory Department in Masonic College, Lexington, Mo., during the succeeding year. His purpose was to become a lawyer, and so, under the advice of his friend Col. Doniphan, he devoted himself to a special course of reading and study for a year.

In 1858 he entered the law office of Richard R. Rees, at Leavenworth, Kansas, where he remained two years in the study of law under the direction of that eminent jurist, appearing occasionally in court, with his teacher, to secure a practical knowledge of litigation. In May, 1860, he returned to Liberty, opened an office, and has continuously practiced his profession since. He was elected Circuit Attorney in November, 1860, for the Fifth Judicial District, composed of Clay, Clinton, Caldwell, Ray and Carroll counties, and his administration of the affairs of that responsible position was able, vigorous and satisfactory. He was general attorney for the Kansas City & Cameron Railroad Company for the years 1866–67, and its prompt completion was due in large measure to his untiring efforts to that end. Mr. Allen was elected without opposition a member of the Constitutional Convention which formed the present Constitution of Missouri, and in that able body he took high rank.

Mr. Allen is a man of many accomplishments. He is a student in the best

ALEXANDER W. DONIPHAN.

(Photograph by Hicks, Liberty, Mo.)

Colonel First Regiment Missouri Mounted Volunteers, Mexican War. Commanded the American forces at the Battle of Sacramento. One of the greatest American lawyers. Was the idol of western Missouri. Born in Mason County, Kentucky, July 8, 1808. Died at Richmond, Missouri, August 8, 1887.

---

sense of the term. In addition to the law, which has his supreme devotion, he is a ripe scholar in general literature, especially in history, philosophy, criticism, poetry. He is a fine orator. He is a writer of great power, and his productions bear a charm rarely found in these times. His style is chaste and elegant, equal to that of the old masters. As a conversationalist he is brilliant and fascinating. His manner is charming, and he has the most delicate sense of honor. In Mr. Allen we have the able lawyer and the polished gentleman. During his whole life, he has been an ardent advocate of education, and he is in the foremost rank

bers for more than a century, that it is of Spanish origin. According to the tradition, their ancestor, who separated himself from the parent stock in Spain, was a young Castilian, of noble blood, who

of those gentlemen of Missouri who urge the higher or university education. He is noted as most strongly favoring the continuance of the study of Greek and Latin in the courses of academies, colleges and universities.

Mr. Allen married, May 18, 1864, Miss Emily E. Settle, daughter of Hiram P. Settle, of Ray county, Mo. They have had three children, of whom two survive. She is a native of Culpeper county, Va.

D. C. ALLEN.

Mr. Allen knew Colonel Doniphan long and intimately. Their friendship was broken only by the death of the Colonel. No other man is so well qualified to write a sketch of the life of that great soldier, lawyer and statesman as Mr. Allen. His paper is a masterpiece, and he has kindly given consent to its use in this work. It was first read before the Kansas City Bar Association, Dec. 5, 1895.

served under Ferdinand and Isabella in the conquest of Granada, and was knighted by King Ferdinand for gallantry on the field. Afterward and during middle life he indicated a preference for Protestantism, and to escape the terrors of the Inquisition and enjoy the freedom of religious belief he abandoned his native land and took refuge in England. There he married an English lady named Mott, and from that union have descended the Doniphans of America.[8]

The name—so speaks the tradition—of the young cavalier was Don Alfonso. This name, in English use, was insensibly corrupted into Doniphan.

A lineage which is traceable to the chivalry of the battle-field and the highest devotion to conviction, will always command the respect and admiration of men. The seven hundred years of battle between the Spaniards and the Moors left the impress of supreme courage, undoubting faith and unconquerable will on the former, which easily made of them the foremost men of all Christendom four centuries ago. Perhaps the tradition is true. If, so, I can explain without looking further, the tinge of old romance in Col. Doniphan's character, his wonderfully delicate respect for women, and his stern adherence to sentiments of honor; as if he were bound to these things—

> By the dead gaze of all his ancestors;
> And by the mystery of his Spanish blood,
> Charged with the awe and glories of the past.

All of the members of the Smith and Doniphan families in Vir-

---

NOTE 8.—This tradition is a degeneration from that of the true origin of the family. There can be no doubt that the name is a corruption of the Celtic Donovan or O'Donovan. Rooney says (Genealogy of Irish Families): "The O'Donovan family is descended from Milesius, King of Spain, through the line of his son Heber. The founder of the family was Carmac, King of Munster, A. D. 483. The ancient name was Donnaghadh, which signifies 'Destroying.' The title of the chief was Prince of Carbery and Lord of Cathal, and the possessions of the sept were located in the present counties of Cork and Limerick. The O'Donovans had their chief castle at Bruree, in the latter county. Their chief seat in the County of Cork was Castle Donovan, in West Carbery."

It is said that for some reason, unknown at this time, Colonel Doniphan abhorred the thought and scouted the idea that his family was of Irish extraction. But he was himself a typical Celt—of immense stature, noble appearance, brilliant parts, fearless, of great moral courage, sanguine, faithful, just, poetic in temperament, the champion of the down-trodden, eloquent beyond description, and without doubt entitled to be classed among the greatest orators that ever lived.

COL. ALEXANDER W. DONIPHAN. 19

ginia were Whigs during our Revolutionary War, and those families contributed an unusually large proportion of their men to the Continental army. Joseph Doniphan was with Washington at Yorktown, and his brother, George Doniphan, died for freedom at Brandywine.

Joseph Doniphan had gone to Kentucky prior to 1779, and remained there a year or more. While there he was engaged in teaching school, and he was the first man who "taught the young idea how to shoot" on the "Dark and Bloody Ground." Returning to Virginia prior to the siege of Yorktown, he entered the Continental army and remained in it until the conclusion of the Revolutionary [struggle. Marrying Anne Smith, he returned to Kentucky in 1790, and made his home in Mason county. Miss Smith was a lady of extraordinary mental powers and brilliant wit. She was an aunt, I may add, of the late Gov. William Smith, of Virginia.

Joseph Doniphan was for a great many years prior to his death, the intimate friend of the famous Simon Kenton. It will be seen, therefore, that the subject of this sketch was born during the generation immediately succeeding the conclusion of the struggle for independence by the colonies and the wresting of the soil of Kentucky from the savages. He was born amid the odors of the forest. The first tales poured into his ears when he was old enough to be intelligent, were those of stern conflicts for liberty and civilization. The first names by him lisped were those of Washington, Wayne, Marion, Light-Horse Harry Lee, and the whole immortal host of the Revolution. He was born when American manhood was at its acme, and the same profound feeling of patriotism thrilled every bosom from the Atlantic coast to the deepest recesses of the Western wilderness.

Joseph Doniphan died in the year 1813, and the subject of this sketch was left to the watchcare of his mother. She was adequate to the rearing of the young eaglet. At the age of eight years she placed him under the instruction of Richard Keene, of Augusta, Kentucky, a learned though eccentric Irishman, who was a graduate of Trinity College, Dublin. Mr. Keene was of that very considerable body of educated Irishmen—ardent followers of Robert Emmet—who found their safety in emigration to America at the conclusion of the Irish Rebellion in '98. Ardent, enthusiastic, boiling with courage, entertaining the most romantic ideas of freedom, they were a dynamical process in the history of every young mind brought in contact with them. An examination into the family history of our country will develop the fact that these young Irish teachers were an intellectual power and blessing all over the then settled portion of the United States. Col. Doniphan never ceased the expression of his gratitude to Mr. Keene.

One who was familiar with the absolute ease and accuracy with which Col. Doniphan wreaked his thoughts upon expression would be astonished at the declaration that he ever lacked for words. He said, however, that in his youth his vocabulary was limited and his expression clumsy and difficult. Mr. Keene assured him that only through acquaintance with the great poets could exact, powerful, brilliant expression be acquired. Through knowledge, said he, of the poets could alone come the precise meaning of words, the perfect pronunciation of them, the melody of speech, and the majestic declamation of the orator. By Mr. Keene's advice he carefully studied the poets, and results in the pupil went very far to prove correct the theory of the master.

At the age of fourteen years he was entered a student at Augusta College, in Bracken county, Kentucky. For many years it was an institution of very high repute, but, as I understand, it has not been in existence for quite a length of time. He graduated there at the early age of eighteen years, with great distinction, particularly in classics. While at Augusta College, he had the benefit of the training and molding influences of several very able instructors. I mention, as being among them, Drs. Durbin and Bascom. He constantly through life expressed his deep sense of obligation to those two gentlemen. Dr. Durbin was a very accomplished man—suave and refined—and was the author of a scholarly and elegant book of travels in the Levant. Dr. Bascom was, in his day, the greatest pulpit orator in the Union. Though a Methodist in creed, the stern theology of John Knox was much nearer his nature. In the time of Cromwell he would have been a Fifth-Monarchy man. He was ever as if in his great Taskmaster's eye. He seemed to hear the last trumpet and to see the smoke of the Pit ascending forever and forever. Sixty years ago "Young's Night Thoughts," a book now unread, was on every parlor table. Dr. Bascom seemed to have absorbed its profound melancholy. There were in his eloquence a sombre magnificence and a distant roar as if of the gathering storm.

In Dr. Durbin Col. Doniphan admired the man and loved the friend, but in Dr. Bascom he saw the orator and felt his seizure upon the soul. A reading of the sermons of Dr. Bascom will show that his influence on the pupil was greater and more lasting than that of Dr. Durbin. It is true that in Col. Doniphan's oratory there was nothing gloomy. There was often, however, a severe magnificence which could claim kinship with the terrors which peopled the imagination of Dr. Bascom. There were times in that oratory when men felt as if they lay helpless on some lofty, naked peak, where the lightnings flashed in their midst and the thunders rolled around them.

In lingering thus on the teachers of Col. Doniphan, it is because I clearly recognize the influence through life of an able teacher on his pupils, and for the further reason that he himself most distinctly saw and appreciated it. Besides, all men are, in a way, chameleons, and take on color from their environments.

In his youth the predilection of Col. Doniphan was for the law as a life-profession, and this was largely through the influence of his mother, who was a woman of great and far-reaching mind. Upon quitting college, therefore, for the purpose of legal study he entered the law office of the Hon. Martin P. Marshall, of Augusta, Kentucky. In the opinion of the pupil, his legal preceptor was one of the most learned and able of all the members of the famous Marshall family. In the course of study recommended by Mr. Marshall and required by him of his pupil is to be discovered the first instance within my knowledge, in this country, of the strictly historical method in the study of the law. First of all he required his pupil to read and carefully study portions of the classical authors of the English language. In this occupation he expended six months. It was, as Mr. Marshall phrased it, to fructify and chasten the pupil's imagination and give him wings for more arduous flights. Secondly, he required him to read the histories of England and America and cognate works, so that he might see, historically, the evolution of our system of law. And, thirdly, he required of him a most careful study of those text-books of the law which were then considered necessary in order to admission to practice. These studies consumed near three years, and were under the eye of and with recitations to the preceptor. The progress of the pupil was great; and where the preceptor is learned and skillful and the pupil brilliant, we must measure progress in study by genius and not by time.

Toward the close of the year 1829 Col. Doniphan was licensed to practice law in the States of Kentucky and Ohio. In March, 1830, he emigrated to Missouri, and in the forepart of April of that year he was licensed to practice in this State by our Supreme Court, then in session at Fayette, in Howard county. On April 19, 1830, he made his home at Lexington, Missouri, and was enrolled a member of the Lexington bar on the 26th of the July succeeding. He became at once, heart and soul, a Missourian, and ever after so remained.

It was at Lexington, therefore, he began his long, successful and brilliant legal career. The practice of the law was then in the West far more laborious than it is now. Law libraries were few and limited, and the day of legal blanks had not arrived. At the age of twenty-two he was placed in collision with Abiel Leonard, Robert W. Wells, Peyton R. Hayden and others, gentlemen eminent for ability and legal attainments, all of them much older than he, and already thoroughly expert in the management of causes. His maiden speech at the bar was made in 1830, and in defense of a man indicted for murder. He assisted Mr. Leonard. This was the first trial for murder that he had ever witnessed. His conduct in this trial was modest, and gave clear evidence of the dawning of the reputation as a criminal lawyer which he very soon afterward acquired.

In 1833 he removed to Liberty, Missouri, where he made his home for the succeeding thirty years. There he found, already established in the practice, those eminent lawyers, David R. Atchison, Amos Rees, James M. Hughes, and Gen. Andrew S. Hughes. His experience at Lexington had been preparatory; at Liberty his reputation attained its zenith. Nor was the state of society there at the time unfavorable to the development of any of the manly, social or mental qualities.

I feel sure that I will be excused if, in the briefest manner, I rend the veil of the past and portray—imperfectly indeed—the environment, characteristics, origin, condition and social life of the men and women of Liberty and Clay county sixty-five years ago. From the standpoint of art, such a portrayal is germane to my subject. Every picture should have its background. The facts stated by me, when not taken from records, and all of the opinions expressed, were derived from the distinguished gentleman whose life and character I am feebly sketching, or from other lips, yet older than his, whose accuracy and truth were beyond all doubt.

Clay county was organized in 1822, and reduced to its present limits in 1833. Settlements began there in 1819, and the immigration constantly increased in numbers for five or six years thereafter. In 1830 its population was 5,338, which was, in the main, located on the territory comprised in its present area. Hence, in 1830, the county was not a wilderness. The population, drawn from Virginia, North Carolina, Tennessee, Kentucky, Maryland, and in lesser numbers from the other States, was purely of American birth. The customs, manners and modes of thought of colonial days still prevailed to a very marked degree. The influence of old, well-known, leading families was strong. In the larger proportion of cases public offices were filled from the ranks of the men of the higher classes. For instance, its first circuit clerk was William L. Smith, a man of education and a gentleman of distinguished bearing and princely elegance of manners. Population emigrated in those days by families in a much larger degree than now. A man of wealth in the older States would emigrate West, bringing with him not only his family, but all of his movable property—his flocks and herds, his men-servants and maid-servants. Some locality in Virginia or elsewhere would be almost exactly reproduced in Clay county. That was prior to the acerbities in political feeling which developed into civil war. It was immaterial from what State in the Union a man came. All were sons of the sires of the Revolution, kinsmen of the heroes of New Orleans and Lundy's Lane—all were Americans—and universal good feeling and brotherhood prevailed.

Several of the chief men of the county were from the East. Of the leading merchants of Liberty at that time, one, Cyrus Curtis, was from New York, and another, Hiram Rich, was from Vermont. Liberty was a little village of a couple of hundreds of inhabitants, but its business was enormous, and ramified all over northwest Missouri. The business and leading men of town and county were beyond the average in capacity. They were generally young men, of high social station in their native localities, educated, chivalric, generous, and had come to the Far West—the verge of civilization—to make their homes and fortunes. The county was, indeed, on the verge of civilization. From its borders the explorer could track his uncertain and dangerous route only through the domains of savages, who were as fierce and terrible as their ancestors a thousand years ago, until his halting and feeble steps were checked by the roar of the waves beating on the western coast of America.

For the little town of Liberty, almost a hamlet then, a fortunate circumstance occurred. In 1827 the post of Fort Leavenworth was established. At that post there always has been a greater accumulation of troops than at any other in the Union. Liberty was the nearest town to it. To relieve the tedium of station life there resorted to Liberty for many years the choice and prime young officers of the army—the Rileys, the Kearnys, the Johnstons—who from time to time were stationed at that post. The wives and daughters of officers went there for shopping purposes. The sons of officers were often sent to Liberty for academic education. The officers of the Fort and their wives and daughters were almost as much a part of the social life of the town, as freely united in public amusements, balls, parties and the like, as its inhabitants themselves. From the union of local intellect with the brilliance of the army the society of Liberty became exceptionally charming and elegant.

Into such a society and into the midst of such people Col. Doniphan went from Lexington in 1833. He was young, ambitious, highly cultured, and his mind expanded with ease to meet the magnitude of each new occasion. The faculty of ready, powerful and tempestuous speech, the flashes of brilliant thought, had come to him. Already the people of the State had recognized in him the orator. The people of Clay county received him with open hearts.

From 1830 to 1860 he continued in the active practice of his profession. His fame was greatest as a criminal lawyer, and during that period there was no criminal cause of magnitude in northwest Missouri in which he was not retained for the defense. He never prosecuted. The reputation of a great advocate usually absorbs that of the counselor. And this was true to a greater degree, perhaps, sixty years ago than now, because then the jury was more often demanded. He was employed to make the great, the decisive argument on the side by which he was retained. No client would think for a moment of excusing him from speaking. He was employed.

and paid to speak—he must speak. A silent Doniphan in a cause would have meant defeat anticipated. As a natural result of this, the work and labor of the cause, the preparation of the pleadings, the gathering of the testimony, the interrogation of the witnesses, etc., devolved on his associate counsel. Occasionally, in examining the witnesses, he would interject some far-reaching question. In the councils of war which precede great trials, his view of the line of defense or attack was always adopted. He saw by a flash of intuition the strong points.

Not one of his oratorical efforts as a criminal or civil lawyer has been preserved. Opinion, therefore, of their power and splendor can only be formed from old tradition. All traditions and opinions concur as to their singular brevity, wonderful compression, vast force and dazzling brilliance. I will merely call attention to two of his orations in criminal actions, and give one opinion in each. They are that in defense of Thomas Turnham, indicted in the Clay Circuit Court for the murder of Hayes, and tried in November, 1844, which resulted in his conviction for manslaughter in the fourth degree, with a fine of $100; and that of John H. Harper, indicted in the Jackson Circuit Court for the murder of Meredith, and tried in Platte Circuit Court in November, 1847, (whither the case had been taken by change of venue,) which resulted in Harper's acquittal. There can hardly be a doubt that Turnham's case was one of murder. After great pressure, he was admitted to bail and his bond fixed at $8,000, an enormous amount in those days. Col. Doniphan was constantly afraid that his client would disappear.* The prisoner's father, the late Maj. Joel Turnham, of Clay county, was a stern, old-fashioned man, "more an antique Roman than a Dane," plainly educated, well advised, however, as to all current events, of strong, penetrating sense, familiar with the great speakers of Missouri and Kentucky, possessed of a will and courage of adamant; but none the less, not at all conscious of the fact that his was the only name in the State which could be found among the paladins of Richard Cœur de Lion when he charged the Paynim hosts on the plains of Palestine. Everything melted away before the force of Col. Doniphan's oratory. At the conclusion of the speech Maj. Turnham was asked what he thought of Doniphan's speech, and his answer was: "Sir, Aleck Doniphan spoke only forty minutes, but he said everything."

The case of Harper more easily admitted of defense. Meredith had—

"Loved not wisely, but too well."

Harper believed, whether with or without good reason, that Meredith had invaded the sancity of his home. Such a circumstance in the hands of a genius like Col. Doniphan's was sufficient to enable him to stir to the uttermost all of the passions and to "call spirits from the vasty deep." The occasion was great. He had returned only a few months before from his wonderful Mexican campaign, and the whole country was full of his glory. Everybody—lawyers and all—had gathered in Platte City (where the case was tried) to hear him, and expectation of his eloquence was on tiptoe. By universal agreement he even surpassed expectation. The late James N. Burnes, of St. Joseph, (then of Weston,) heard it, and declared that it determined him to become a lawyer. He also declared that he had never heard or read any speech in defense of a criminal which equalled Col. Doniphan's in that case.[9]

NOTE 9.—As this was one of the greatest criminal trials of Missouri, some account of it is given. Fanny Owens, daughter of Colonel Samuel S. Owens (killed at the battle of Sacramento), married John H. Harper. Harper was a lawyer, probably from Georgia. He had an office at Independence, Mo., and is said to have been a bright fellow without character. He paid court to Fanny Owens, then very young and very beautiful. His attentions were discouraged by Mr. and Mrs. Owens. Believing herself imposed upon by her mother in a certain matter, she went to the office of Harper and said she was ready to get married. He took her in a buggy, intending to go to the office of James Bean, Justice of the Peace, at or near Blue Springs. They met Bean on the way and were married in the road without alighting from the buggy, no license being necessary at that time. The Owens family were deeply chagrined and humiliated, and some efforts were made to have the rash act undone, but they came to nothing. Mr. and Mrs. Harper took up residence in the Owens home.

The following spring a young man named Meredith came from Baltimore to make a trip across the Plains with Colonel Owens, for the benefit of his health, he being a sufferer from consumption. The journey could not begin until the grass was grown enough to furnish subsistence to the teams, and in the mean time Meredith was an inmate of the Owens home. A flirtation arose between him and Mrs. Harper. Harper became very jealous and determined to kill Meredith, and laid plans to that end. He placed cards on a table in his office, which was on the second floor of a building fronting on the public square. He provided himself with two pistols, and waited for Meredith to pass along the street. As he came by, Harper invited him into his office. A shot was heard immedi-

Anyone who did not know Col. Doniphan intimately, and who saw him in his prime, or even in his latter years, would have supposed, from the largeness of his frame, the freshness of his complexion, and his erect bearing, that he was a man of vast physical strength and endurance. The exact reverse was true. He was physically one of the most delicate of men, and least able to endure exposure or excessive or protracted strain. His whole life was one long struggle against bodily infirmity, and the world knew it not. As a consequence, the prodigious strain on the brain in the delivery of his argument in each of the Turnham and Harper cases, causing excessive cerebral excitement,—a flame of thought, scorching his nervous system,—threw him into a dangerous fever, from which he could not be released by the skill of his physicians for several weeks. The same result occurred in others of his great oratorical efforts. I am perfectly satisfied his consciousness of his physical delicacy acted as a detersive on his ambition and prevented him from seeking those advancements which his friends wished and expected, he fearing that

---

ately after he went into the room, and men rushed up to see what was the trouble. They found the cards in disorder on the table, Meredith lying dead on the floor and a pistol by his side, and Harper standing over him with a smoking pistol in his hand. He said that he and Meredith had been playing a game of cards, over which they disagreed; that one word brought on another until a fierce quarrel resulted; that Meredith drew his pistol, and he, Harper, shot him dead. Harper's story was not believed. There was no time for a quarrel between the time that Meredith entered the room and the report of the pistol. Harper was arrested for murder and cast into jail. His wife stuck to him and aided him to escape; some say she furnished him saws and files; but Meredith T. Moore says she secured admittance to the jail and there changed clothes with him. He went down into New Mexico and was gone a year or two, but finally was apprehended and brought back. In those days the law allowed a criminal more than one change of venue. Harper secured a change to Henry county, and from thence to Platte county, where he was tried.

The trial was in November, 1847. Harper's attorneys were Colonel Doniphan, John Wilson, and Silas H. Woodson, all great lawyers. They believed that it would be necessary to show criminal intimacy between Meredith and Mrs. Harper, the theory of self-defense having been pretty well abandoned. In this matter the judge made a strange ruling. He held that the prosecution might show this criminal intimacy, but that the defense could not show it as a justification for the murder. All the attorneys were surprised at the ruling, and Colonel Doniphan is reported to have said that if this ruling was to stand he feared that it meant that Harper would hang. When all the witnesses for the defense but one had been examined, the attorneys requested that court adjourn until the following day, as they desired to consult upon certain matters. It was then

on great and momentous occasions,—occasions demanding extraordinary and prolonged mental effort,—his physical man would yield to the pressure, and he be rendered incapable of meeting expectation.

Before 1836, the lines between Whiggery and Democracy (or "Locofocoism") had been clearly drawn. Col. Doniphan came from Kentucky an ardent Whig. He had been politically trained in the school of Harry of the West, of whose vast genius he was, throughout life, a most unqualified admirer. Politics in those days had warmth as well as now. Every foot of ground was fought over by the contending parties. In 1836 the Whigs of Clay county demanded that he should become a candidate for the Legislature. He acceded to their demand, and was elected. The same facts occurred in 1840,

---

about four in the afternoon, but had the judge known that but one witness remained to be examined for the defense he would have insisted that the case go on; however, he adjourned.

In those days lawyers made the rounds of the circuit, and it was customary for them to visit about at night with the local attorneys. When court adjourned Woodson said to Wilson that it would be necessary for him to make a night of it with the leading attorney for the prosecution. This Wilson did, and neither closed an eye in sleep; both appeared in court the following morning just about worn out. The defense put on the remaining witness, the only one by whom it was expected to show the matter of criminal intimacy. This was the only thing expected to be proven by him, and under the ruling of the court it was impossible for them to show that—a desperate situation. Woodson conducted the examination; he questioned the witness at great length, leading up to the point he wished to make. When right at the point, and where the next question would have been the one and only one he really desired an answer to, he said to the prosecution, "Take the witness."

The court and audience had hung breathless on the examination, and there was disappointment that it resulted in nothing. When the sleepy attorney for the State took the witness his first question was the very one the defense desired to ask but could not. But he saw his mistake instantly and said excitedly, "Do not answer that question!" Then there was a scene. The defense insisted that the witness be allowed to answer the question, while the prosecution protested that as no answer had been given it had the right to say none should be given. The jury was removed, and the remainder of the day was consumed in arguments pro and con. The defense took the ground that by the ruling of the court it could not ask the question but that the prosecution could ask it, and the prosecution having done so, it was the right of the defense that the question be answered,—that the ruling of the court gave them that right. The court held that the question must be answered, which was done, and the criminal relations shown.

Colonel Doniphan made the principal speech for the defense. He was suffering from jaundice at the time, and was physically in bad condition for a great speech. But such an address has rarely been heard in any court as he delivered.

and yet again in 1854. In the Legislature of 1854 he was the Whig nominee for U. S. Senator, and received their unbroken vote.

On December 21st, 1837, Col. Doniphan was married to Miss Elizabeth Jane Thornton, of Clay county. It was a perfect union of heart and intellect. She was a highly intellectual, cultivated woman, and her grace of manner and charm in conversation made her the delight of society. Save when public duty or business imperatively demanded it, he and she were constantly united. At home or abroad they were together. They were both insatiable readers, and their evenings in literature will always stir delightful thoughts in the memories of their friends. He knew and loved no place like home, and neither the mystery of lodges nor the joviality of clubs had any power to draw him thence. Heaven withdrew her from him in 1873, but it was decreed that he should remain a pilgrim many years thereafter before he felt the stroke of the invisible specter—

"And sought his love amid the Elysian field."

Of his marriage there were born only two children—both sons.

He said afterwards that he was not satisfied with it. Hon. R. P. C. Wilson, son of John Wilson, in a letter to the writer thus describes it:

"I was well acquainted with Col. Doniphan all my life, nearly; for his having married a kinswoman of mine, I was much thrown in his company.

"He was a remarkably attractive man, and when he attended court here, which he did pretty regularly, he attracted marked attention, and being one of the most companionable of men, his stay in town was one continued ovation and levee. Missouri or the West never before or since had, and possibly never will have, a man of such surpassing eloquence. He was simply and literally invincible before a jury or in an address anywhere or upon any subject.

"His greatest triumph at the bar in Platte county was in the successful defense of Harper for killing Meredith, on change of venue from Jackson county. Harper was a son-in-law of Col. Sam Owens, of Independence,—a renowned and wealthy Mexican freighter and trader, and with his train fell in with Doniphan on the march to Chihuahua, and on the morning of the battle of Sacramento organized his trainmen into a company, and at its head went into the battle, and was killed immediately in front of the Mexican breastworks. Harper being his son-in-law, and Owens being a dear friend of Doniphan, and having fallen under his own eye in battle, the Colonel entered the defense with his whole heart, and his matchless and impassioned address to the jury so wrought up the jury itself and the immense crowd in attendance inside and jammed outside the courthouse, that both the jury and the people gave way to incontrollable cheers. It is needless to say that Harper was promptly acquitted. And Doniphan was seized by the people, taken upon their shoulders, and, attended by the shouting multitude, borne to his hotel. Nothing like it has ever occurred before or since in upper Missouri. This is merely one of the many triumphs of this rare and gifted man."

On the 29th day of June, 1906, being in Liberty, Clay county, Missouri, I visited the cemetery for the purpose of viewing the monument erected there to the memory of Colonel Alexander W. Doniphan. The monument is of gray granite, and is about twenty-five feet in height. It is situated in a fine lot about

They were youths of rare intellectual promise, and their father might well hope to prolong his life and fame in those of his children. One of them died from accidental poison, at Liberty, in 1853, and the

forty feet square, and is near the center of the burying-ground. I copied the following inscriptions from the monument:

MONUMENT TO COLONEL DONIPHAN, AT HIS GRAVE IN THE CEMETERY AT LIBERTY, MISSOURI
(Photograph by Hicks, Liberty, Mo.)

[North face.]
GENL. ALEXANDER WILLIAM DONIPHAN.
Born in Mason Co., Ky.,
July 9, 1808,
And Died at Richmond, Mo.,
Aug. 8, 1887.

An Orator, Jurist, Statesman
Soldier, and a Christian.

other beneath the angry waves of a West Virginia brook, in 1858. From blows so severe as these, it can be well understood why the life of Col. Doniphan, during more than thirty years before its close, was void of ambition.

Of the Mormon War in 1838, I will simply state that Col. Doniphan was present, in command of a brigade of State militia, at the surrender of Joe Smith, the so-called prophet, at Far West, in Caldwell county, and afterward defended him in the criminal proceedings which were instituted against him and other Mormons.

In 1846 the War with Mexico began. In May of that year, Governor Edwards requested Col. Doniphan to assist him in raising troops, in the western counties of the State, for the volunteer service. He acceded to the request. The enthusiasm of the people was extremely high, and in a week or so the eight companies of men had volunteered,

[East face.]
Colonel Commanding the United
States Troops at the Battles of
Sacramento and Brazito
In the Mexican War.
A Member of the Peace Congress
of 1861 from Missouri.
A Lawyer for Over Fifty Years,
And a Life Without Reproach.

DONIPHAN.

[South face.]
ELIZABETH JANE,
Eldest Daughter of
Col. John and Elizabeth Thornton,
Born in Clay Co., Mo.,
Dec. 21, 1820.
Married to A. W. Doniphan
Dec. 21, 1837,
And Died
July 19, 1873.

As a Child, Wife, Parent, and a
Friend of the Poor and Humble,
She Discharged a Christian's Duty.

Blessed are the Dead which
die in the Lord.

[West face.]
JOHN THORNTON DONIPHAN.
Born Sept. 18, 1838.
Died May 9, 1853.

ALEXANDER W. DONIPHAN, JR.
Born Sept. 10, 1840.
Died May 11, 1858.

which, upon organization at Fort Leavenworth, formed the famous First Regiment of Missouri Mounted Volunteers. The counties which furnished those companies were Jackson, Lafayette, Clay, Saline, Franklin, Cole, Howard, and Callaway. Col. Doniphan volunteered as a private in the company from Clay. The desire to volunteer was so great among the counties that each of the companies was much overfull. That from Clay numbered 118 men, rank and file. The subject of this sketch was elected colonel of the regiment almost by acclamation. There never was in the service of the United States a regiment of finer material. It was composed of individuals from the best families in the State, and they were young men in the prime of life, equal, physically and mentally, to every duty of the soldier. They were, mainly, the sons of the pioneers of Missouri, and had the courage and manliness, and possessed the endurance and virtues of their fathers. This regiment formed a portion of the column known as the Army of the West, commanded by that chivalric soldier, Gen. Stephen W. Kearny. All of the troops of the column rendezvoused at Fort Leavenworth. The volunteers having undergone a few weeks drilling, the Army of the West commenced its march to Santa Fé on June 26th, 1846.

It would be impossible to express in words the feelings, apprehensions and hopes of the people and of those volunteers when Gen. Kearny's army moved to the conquest of northern Mexico. The knowledge of the American people then of Mexico was very limited. The people of Missouri knew more than any others, for their traders, at least, during over twenty years previously, had laboriously tracked and retracked the dangerous trail from Independence to Santa Fé, and thence to Chihuahua. The geographies of that day—old Olney and Mitchell—showed little beyond outlines delineating Mexico and the countries west of Missouri. They indicated, however, very clearly, the Great American Desert, extending long and wide between Missouri and Mexico. The regions between our State and Mexico were Indian country, and dangerous, and those beyond were Indian and Mexican, and still more dangerous. Our volunteers must have felt that every mile of their march would reveal surprises and wonders. And we may liken their expectation of encountering the marvelous to that of Sir Francis Drake, when, three hundred years ago, he weighed his anchors at Portsmouth and turned the prow of his ship towards the South Sea.

On August 18, 1846, Gen. Kearny's army entered Santa Fé without firing a gun. In November, 1846, Col. Doniphan, with his regiment, was ordered into the country of the Navajo Indians, on the western slope of the Rocky Mountains, to overawe or chastise them. He completed this movement with great celerity. His soldiers toiled through snows three feet deep on the crests and eastern slope of the mountains. Having accomplished the object of the expedition, concluding a satisfactory treaty with the Indians, he returned to the Rio del Norte, and, on the banks of that stream, collected and refreshed his men, preparatory to effecting what was then intended to be a junction with Gen. Wool. He was here reinforced by two batteries of light artillery. In December, 1846, he turned the faces of his little column to the south, and put it in motion towards Chihuahua. In quick succession followed his brilliant and decisive victories at Brazito and Sacramento, the capture of Chihuahua, the plunge of his little army into the unknown country between Chihuahua and Saltillo, and its emergence in triumph at the latter city.

After his arrival at Saltillo, inasmuch as the period of enlistment of his men would soon expire, his regiment was ordered home. Its march, therefore, was continued to Matamoras, where it took shipping to New Orleans. The men of the regiment, having been discharged at New Orleans, arrived at home about July 1st, 1847. The march of this regiment from Fort Leavenworth to Santa Fé, Chihuahua, Saltillo and Matamoras—a distance of near 3,600 miles—is called Doniphan's Expedition.

On his return from Mexico he at once resumed the practice of his profession.

In 1854 a fact occurred which fully illustrates the belief of the people of Clay county—a belief which extended all over the State—in his universal ability and fitness for any station, high or low. On February 24th, 1853, the act was passed by our Legislature, which provided for the organization, support and government of the public schools, and which thereafter set apart twenty-five per cent., annually, of the State revenue for their support. In November, 1853, it became necessary for the county court of Clay county to appoint a "commissioner of common schools" for the county. By a singular unanimity and without thought of anyone else, the people asked Col. Doniphan to accept the position, and petitioned the county court to appoint him. He accepted the appointment, saying he ought to do so because the people of the county had done everything they could for him. He retained the position near a year, and gave, by his energy and encouragement, an impetus to the public-school system in the county which was never checked. During his incumbency, and through his inspiration, a teachers' institute was organized and held in the county, which was the first one ever held in Missouri.

In January, 1861, he was appointed a member of the peace conference, which assembled at Washington with a view to the prevention of civil war. During his absence in attendance on that body he was elected a member of the State convention called by the Legislature, January 21st, 1861. In the convention he maintained the position of a conservative Union man, and did not permit himself to lose sight either of the supremacy of the Constitution or the reserved rights of the States. In 1863,—during the heat of the civil war,—he removed from Liberty to St. Louis. Family reasons compelling, in 1868 he removed from St. Louis to Richmond, Missouri, and resided at the latter place until his death.[9½]

The oratory of Col. Doniphan at the bar constitutes only a part of the basis of his fame as an orator. From his immigration to Missouri until the close of 1860, in every canvass he responded to the wishes of the political party to which he was attached, and on the hustings in various parts of our State he advocated and defended his party's principles in addresses of surpassing logic and flaming eloquence. Enormous crowds met him wherever he spoke, and the people would never weary of listening to his accents. And this was

NOTE 9½.—The Directory for 1864 gives "Doniphan & Field, Lawyers"; no residence given. Office was at 5 Kennett Building.

The Directory of 1865 says Colonel Doniphan boarded at Olive street, S. W. corner Eighth. Doniphan & Field, Lawyers, 76 Chestnut street.

In 1866 Colonel Doniphan lived at 262 Olive street. Doniphan & Field, Lawyers, 5th, S. W. cor. Chestnut.

In 1867 Colonel Doniphan lived at Fifteenth street, S. E. cor. Olive street. Doniphan & Field, Lawyers, Fifth street, S. W. cor. Chestnut.

The Directory of 1864 contains the following as a display advertisement:

"Doniphan & Field, Attorneys and Counselors at Law. Room 5, Kennett Building, south side Chestnut street, bet. Third and Fourth. Government Claims Prosecuted, Bought and Sold."

not all. His addresses on various public occasions, educational, social and patriotic, from his arrival in our State until 1872, were numerous. And yet of all his magnificent orations, so far as I know, but two remain complete, and they were delivered on occasions social or festive. In so far as the records of time—the gravings of history and legislative proceedings—extend, his name is secure. But what of the power and magnificence of his oratory? It rests only in tradition.

It must always be a matter of regret that not in equal degree are the efforts of genius transmitted to after times. The mighty historians and poets are secure in their immortality. Homer, Virgil, Milton, Thucydides, Tacitus, Gibbon, will always be read. The great Greek historian, in sixty pages of moderate size, sketched the Athenian expedition against Syracuse, the embarkation, the passage of the sea, the debarkation, the beleaguering of the city, the assault, the repulse, the retreat, the overthrow and capture, with an amazing clearness and power which have made his place in the temple of fame as stable as the world itself. The sculptor, secure in his marble, may reasonably hope that the visions of loveliness, or majesty, born of his brain, may transmit his name some thousands of years. Even the painter is assured that the divine conceptions which he has limned may be admired and judged by the eye—and his name repeated—for a few centuries after he has passed away. It is said:

"The actor only, shrinks from Time's award."

After the revolutions of eighteen centuries, we know the name of Roscius, and but little more.

"The grace of action—the adapted mien,
Faithful as nature to the varied scene;
The expressive glance—whose subtle comment draws
Entranced attention and a mute applause;
Gesture that marks with force and feeling fraught,
A sense in silence and a will in thought,
Harmonious speech whose pure and liquid tone
Gives verse a music, scarce confessed its own,"—

How can these be conveyed to the mind of another by the force of words? In so far as action is concerned, what is true of the actor is equally true of the orator. Who would attempt to paint Alexander W. Doniphan in the torrent of his eloquence on some momentous occasion? Who would attempt to convey an idea, by language, of his grand person, towering above all the people—his eyes burning with tenfold the lustre of diamonds—the sweep of his arm when raised to enforce some splendid conception—his pure and flutelike voice, thrilling every bosom like electricity—his rapid, explanatory sketch of preliminary matters, each word a picture to the life—his conclusions, remorseless as death—his flaming excursions into every realm of fancy—his wit, his humor, his pathos, his passionate energy of utterance? All this must forever remain unknown, save only to those who were so fortunate as to have heard his oratory when he was in his prime.

In the absence of mental efforts preserved—which can be studied and meditated—in order to a proper measurement of the intellect of Alexander W. Doniphan, and a due appreciation of his genius, some one is needed who was familiar with him in his prime, that is to say, from 1835 to 1855, and who was himself of mature mind during that period. I heard none of his great efforts in criminal causes. I heard a few of them in civil cases. My opinion of his intellect and genius is formed from a copious and sure tradition, a few of his political and public efforts, worthy, in my judgment, of the reputation of the greatest of American orators, the expressions of men of high intellect themselves, and familiar and intimate observation of the action of his mind since my earliest recollection.

Great men only appear after long intervals. Eight centuries prior to the Saviour of men, the mightiest poet of the antique world sang the tale of Troy; more than seven centuries elapsed before the Mantuan bard sang of Æneas; and sixteen centuries must then roll away ere time was prepared for the birth of Shakespeare. Three hundred years intervened between the great Macedonian conqueror and imperial Cæsar; and eighteen hundred between Cæsar and Napoleon. Between Thucydides and Tacitus are near five hundred, and between Tacitus and Gibbon near seventeen hundred years. From Demosthenes to Cicero were three hundred years, and from Cicero to the majestic line of Chatham, Sheridan, Burke, Fox, Clay, Webster, Calhoun and Doniphan were eighteen hundred years.

The genius of Col. Doniphan can only be estimated, in all its height, depth, breadth and splendor, by one who had known him in his prime, and under all circumstances and conditions. He must have known him in the field of Sacramento, when, six hundred miles in the enemy's country, he led his little army of Missourians to the assault of works manned by four times their number; when, in the defense of some prisoner, charged with the greatest offense known to the law, in order to succeed he called into action all of his intellectual powers, and thundered and lightened in addressing the jury; when, before a great audience of his fellow-citizens, assembled to hear him on some momentous occasion, he brought into play the whole range of his stores of thought,—sentiment, eloquence and wit,—transported his auditors from grave to gay, from tears to mirth, with a certain divine ease and rapidity, and molded their opinions and hearts to his will with a thoroughness only possible to the greatest orator; and when, the cares of the forum and politics laid aside, at his own or a friend's fireside, or, beneath the spreading branches of some monarch of the forest, he relaxed his gigantic intellect to the needs and uses of social converse, and charmed all listeners with a flow of wisdom, humor, anecdote—strong, yet airy and graceful—so rich, so varied, so flashing, that it would have made the literary fortune of a dozen writers.

It is and has been the clear opinion of all who have known him well, that, in all the qualities of the loftiest intellect,—breadth of vision, foresight which could farthest in advance discern matters that would come to pass,—intuitive perception, rapidity of determination, sharp analysis, precision of judgment, corroding logic, subtilty of thought, richness and variety of fancy, aptness of illustration, powerful and unfailing memory, compression of words, ease in mental action, and intense, nervous, crystalline and electrical language,—indeed, in all the elements of genius,—he has never had a superior in America. This opinion I will accentuate by that of a man well able to judge, and whose opportunities to form a safe judgment were better than those of any man, living or dead,—I mean the late Gen. David R. Atchison. Gen. Atchison was a man of education, of strong, judicial intellect, trained thought, had been senator from our State from 1843 to 1855, and his observation of and experience among men had been of the largest. A few years prior to his and Col. Doniphan's death, he said to me: "I was familiar with the city of Washington in my early manhood. I knew all the great men of our country in the earlier days—Clay, Webster, Calhoun, John Quincy Adams, Clayton, Crittenden and others. I have presided in the United States Senate when Clay, Webster and Calhoun sat before me. I knew Aleck Doniphan familiarly, intimately, since 1830, and I tell you, sir, when he was in his prime I heard him climb higher than any of them."

But higher than Col. Doniphan's gifts of mind were those of his heart—his marvelous humanity.

A Roman said:

"Victrix causa Diis placuit, sed victa Catoni."

The gods loved the victors, but Cato the vanquished. The nobility of this sentiment is the more to be admired because of the rarity of expressions of sympathy by victors for the vanquished in the classic world. He knew that Roman conquest meant the march of the legions to the devoted country—the overthrow and slaughter of opposing armies—the siege and sack of cities—the desecration of temples—the capture of spoils of silver and gold and men—captives following at the chariot-wheels of the triumphant general—the sale of men and women into slavery—the prætor and tax-gatherer, following the sword—the exactions and extortions; and his great, compassionate heart overflowed with pity for the enslaved, the feeble, and unhappy. Like Cato, Col. Doniphan had this wonderful compassion for the weak, defenseless and miserable,—only that it was broadened and made more tender, gracious and personal by Christian culture. To compassion, he united, in the highest degree, courtesy and modesty, and therefore he was accessible to all alike,— the rich, the poor, the high, the low, the statesman and the peasant. No one who knew him will fail to remember with what charm he drew all to him, nor how a child, a humble slave, a modest woman, a poor laborer in the field or shop, could address him with as much ease and as free from embarrassment as the proudest potentate in the land. There was no oppression in his presence. The great man was forgotten in the genial friend and faithful counselor.

In the varied circumstances of his life, Col. Doniphan exerted a very great influence. In parliamentary bodies he did this mainly through social impress and personal contact. He was wonderfully fascinating in conversation, and his society was sought with the greatest eagerness wherever he went. The people all over Missouri thronged around him when he was among them, and it seemed they could never sufficiently drink in his utterances. Perhaps there never was a more delightful or instructive and amusing conversationalist. His faculties of generalization, perception and analysis were very remarkable. His temperament was poetic, even romantic, but guarded by fine taste and the most delicate sense of the ludicrous. Indeed, his mind was so well organized, so nicely balanced, its machinery so happily fitted, its stores of information so well digested and so completely incorporated into his every-day thought, that its riches, without effort, apparently, flowed or flashed forth on all occasions, and placed all it touched in a flood of light.

His personal appearance was truly imposing and magnificent. His was of the grandest type of manly beauty. A stranger would not have failed to instantly note his presence in any assemblage. In height, he was six feet and four inches. His frame was proportioned to his height, and was full without the appearance of obesity. His face approached the Grecian ideal very closely, the essential variance being in the nose, which was aquiline without severity. His forehead was high, full and square; his eyes of the brightest hazel; and his lips symmetrical and smiling. When young, his complexion was extremely fair and delicate, and his hair sandy.

At the peace conference in 1861, when introduced to Mr. Lincoln, the latter said to him: "And this is the Col. Doniphan who made the wild march against the Navajos and Mexicans. You are the only man I ever met who, in appearance, came up to my previous expectation."

Col. Doniphan died at Richmond, Missouri, August 8th, 1887, and was buried at Liberty, Missouri, with his wife and sons.

He united with the Christian Church in 1859, and died in its faith.

MAJOR-GENERAL STERLING PRICE.

Sterling Price was born in Prince Edward county, Virginia, September 14, 1809. His family claimed a close relationship with that of Lord Baltimore, the founder of Maryland, but the exact degree of kinship is not known to the writer.

There is little information accessible relating to the early life of Sterling Price. He attended the schools in the vicinity of his home, and at the age of nineteen graduated from Hampden-Sidney College. Upon his graduation he accepted a position in the office of the clerk of the County Court of his native county, which he filled for two years with credit; and in this place he acquired a knowledge of legal forms which was ever after very valuable to him. He had relatives living in Missouri with whom he was in constant communication; and being possessed of a bold and enterprising spirit, he determined to make that State his future home. He arrived in the Boone's Lick country in 1830, and spent some time in looking over that region, settling finally in Chariton county, where he lived until the commencement of the Civil War.

He soon became known as a man of sterling qualities, with an interest in the political questions uppermost in the public mind of the time. He was appointed Brigadier-General of the State Militia. He was a Democrat, as were others of the Prices (relatives) in Missouri; and in 1836 he was elected to the Legislature. He was not an orator, but was one of those quiet, forceful men who saw quite through the motives and actions of men and parties. He possessed a great capacity for hard work and exerted a large influence on the action of the General Assembly. He became a potent factor in the politics of Missouri. He was returned to the Legislature in 1840 and in 1842; and in the latter year was elected Speaker of the House. In 1844 he was elected to Congress from his (the Third) District. In Congress he was an ardent supporter of President Polk in all matters pertaining to the Mexican War. He resigned his place in Congress to accept one in the army. He raised a regiment of cavalry, the Second Missouri Mounted Volunteers, which was mustered into the service of the United States early in August, 1846, at

Fort Leavenworth, with himself as Colonel. He marched at once to New Mexico over the old Santa Fé Trail.

Colonel Price was assigned the duty of holding New Mexico while

GENERAL STERLING PRICE.
(By courtesy of Lafayette County Historical Society, Lexington, Mo.)

Colonel Second Regiment Missouri Mounted Volunteers, Mexican War. Governor of Missouri. Major-General in the Confederate Army. Statesman and soldier. Born in Prince Edward County, Virginia, September 14, 1809. Died at St. Louis, Mo., September 29, 1867.

General Kearny went on to California and Colonel Doniphan to what is now northern Mexico. In January, 1847, there was an uprising of Indians and Mexicans in New Mexico. The outbreak began with the murder of Governor Charles Bent, at Taos, January 19. Intelligence of this rebellion against the authority of the United States reached Colonel Price at Santa Fé on the 20th of January, and he immediately marched upon the rebels with three hundred and fifty men and four twelve-pounder pieces of artillery. On January 24 he fought the battle of La Canada, killing thirty-six of the rebels, wounding a large number, and dispersing the remainder. In this engagement Colonel Price was wounded. At El Embudo, on the 29th, he defeated and dispersed another force of insurgents, after which he continued his march up the Rio Grande, and arrived at Taos February 3, where he found the rebels strongly fortified. On the 4th he attacked the enemy, and during the day pressed in upon the main position; at night he succeeded in occupying some houses commanding this position. The rebels were defeated and forced to surrender the conspirators and murderers, whom Colonel Price hanged after trial and conviction. His prompt action and vigorous measures put an end to all disorders, and there was little further trouble in the Territory. Colonel Price was commissioned a Brigadier-General, July 20, 1847.

The first general election in Missouri after the close of the Mexican War was in 1852, and in that year General Price was elected Governor. The term was four years, and the administration of Governor Price was fair to all, was strong and just, and it was satisfactory to the people of Missouri. Afterwards Governor Price served the State in the office of Bank Commissioner, performing his duties in that capacity with the same fidelity that marked all his official acts.

In all the movements preliminary to the Civil War, General Price was a strong and earnest advocate of the preservation of the Union. As a Union man he was elected a delegate to the convention called by the State of Missouri to take into consideration her relations to the Federal Government. He was regarded as the foremost Union advocate of the State, and for this reason the convention selected him as its president. In all the negotiations between the State and Federal authorities in the dark days of the early part of 1861, General Price strove to make effective the Missouri policy of neutrality. But events and their consequences made this impossible. He was made

Commander of the State Guards, and in this position he did everything in his power to uphold the course of the State Government. And this compelled him finally to come forward openly in favor of resistance to the Federal Union. But he fought in the beginning of the war under the Bear Flag of Missouri.

There is no space in this paper for a review of the military career of General Price in the Civil War. His great ability as a military man seems never to have been appreciated by the Confederate Government, although he was made a Major-General. The simplicity and honesty of his character made him impatient of the red tape and circumlocution of the War Department. His services were mainly in Missouri and Arkansas.[10] He led his army with great skill and immortal courage in the battles of Wilson Creek and Pea Ridge. He crossed the Mississippi and fought at Farmington. September 20, 1862, he fought the battle of Iuka, and in the early days of October was in the battle of Corinth. He and his Missourians were the heroes of every battle-field. Their courage and splendid qualities amazed the West-Pointers in the Confederate Army, who praised them in official reports. But petty jealousies incident to all systems kept General Price inactive much of the year 1863. In the beginning of 1864 he was in command of a considerable army in Arkansas, but not to exceed three thousand of his troops were of the Old Guard who followed him out of Missouri. The rest were scattered abroad or in their graves, the great majority having been killed in battle or died from wounds. In August, 1864, he began his last invasion of Missouri. He displayed the same sublime courage and skillful generalship, but the campaign ended at Newtonia in disaster. He retreated into Arkansas, never to return to Missouri as a soldier.

The close of the war found General Price a man without a home, and he believed himself without a country. It is said that his heart was broken. With ineffable sadness he turned his face towards

---

NOTE 10.—General Price was a man of fine proportions and of noble bearing. The following description of him was written during the war:

"He is over six feet in height, with frame to match, full, but not portly, and straight as an Indian. His carriage is marked with dignity, grace, and gentleness, and every motion bespeaks the attitude and presence of the well-bred gentleman. He has a large, Websterian head, covered with a growth of thick white hair, a high, broad, intellectual forehead, florid face, no beard, and a mouth among whose latent smiles you never fail to discover the iron will that surmounts all obstacles."

Mexico, where he sought service under Maximilian. He also attempted to form there an extensive colony of his countrymen, but without success. Word came back that his health was broken, and his people called him to return home to Old Missouri. And he came again to dwell in that State, the country of his adoption, the land that had been given the devotion and strength of his manhood. He engaged in the commission business in St. Louis, for it was necessary that he earn his daily bread. But the world was slipping away from him; he died in that city at two o'clock P. M., September 29, 1867.

Sterling Price was a great man and a great General. No other man in the Civil War had to contend with the discouragements and difficulties which daily confronted General Price. He seems to have been a man who accepted conditions, doing under them every thing mortal man could do, and making no complaint.[11] There is no more

---

NOTE 11.—General Price seems to have been often neglected and left to shift for himself. Only a man of wonderful resources could have sustained an army under the circumstances surrounding General Price during most of his service. The fact that he not only maintained good discipline, but secured the warm personal devotion of every man in his army, when it was composed of such varied elements and divergent nationalities, is proof positive that he was eminently just and wholly unselfish, and that the care of his men was his first and chief care. The following is an account of his army at one period of the war:

"The army of General Price is made up of extremes. It is a heterogeneous mixture of all human compounds, and represents in its various elements every condition of Western life. There are the old and the young, the rich and the poor, the high and the low, the grave and the gay, the planter and laborer, farmer and clerk, hunter and boatman, merchant and woodsman,—men, too, who have come from every State, and been bronzed in every latitude, from the mountains of the Northwest to the pampas of Mexico. Americans, Indians, half-breeds, Mexicans, Frenchmen, Italians, Germans, Spaniards, and Poles,—all mixed in the motley mass who have rallied around the flag of their noble leader. It is a 'gathering of the clans,' as if they had heard and responded to the stirring battle-call.

"It has been a puzzle to many how Price, without governmental resources, has managed to subsist a considerable army in a country almost desolated. His system is not known in the 'regulations.' He never complains of a want of transportation, whether he is about to move ten miles or a hundred miles. He pays for what he takes, in Missouri State scrip. His men go into cornfields, shuck the corn, shell it, take it to the mill, and bring it into camp, ground into meal. Or, should they have no flour, they take the wheat from the stack, thresh it themselves, or with horses or oxen, and as with corn, ask the aid of the miller to reduce it to flour. Such an army can go where they please in an agricultural country. His troops not only loved him, but were enthusiastically devoted to him. His figure in the battle-field, clothed in a common brown linen coat, with his white hair streaming in the wind, was the signal for wild and passionate cheers; and there was not one of his soldiers, it was said, but who was willing to die, if he could only fall within sight of his commander."

perfect example of devotion to duty in American public life than that of Sterling Price.

Perhaps the strongest feature of the military discipline of General Price was his care and consideration for his men. It was not in his heart to erect barriers between himself and his fellows. He loved men and loved their presence and company. He was accessible at all times to the humblest private in his army. He trusted his men because of his faith in them. And they idolized him. They said they would rather die under his command than fight under any other man. His Missouri army partook largely of the nature of a family, and survivors of it yet speak of their chief as "Old Pap Price." And to-day in Missouri the memory of this strong man of kindly heart and honorable life is sacred.[12] And not only in Missouri, for in the Rocky Mountains and the green valleys of Oregon I have seen tears in the eyes of battle-scarred veterans when they spoke of their campaigns in Old Missouri under "Pap Price." Who may say that the fame of this great citizen, this just statesman, this magnificent soldier should not survive as long as man shall love truth and worship liberty? Not one. In many respects he towers to the height of the greatest Missourian.

NOTE 12.—In a recent conversation on the characters of the Civil War in the West, Hon. E. F. Ware said that prisoners returning to the Union lines from Price's army always came with praises for General Price; and that those who had been wounded or sick were especially loud in his praise. They said that General Price came often to see them, and that he never failed to inquire closely as to the treatment they were receiving and the food they were getting; and that such orders as "Get this man something more to eat," or, "This man must have different treatment," or, "This man must have a different diet," were always given by General Price when going through the sick wards where Union soldiers were confined. To him a sick soldier was a sick soldier, without regard to the side upon which he was enlisted. No wonder his men were willing to die fighting under his command! He was more than their commander: he was their personal friend; "Old Pap" was their father indeed.

JOHN TAYLOR HUGHES.

John Taylor Hughes was born near Versailles, Woodford county, Kentucky, July 25, 1817; killed in the battle of Independence, Missouri, August 11, 1862. His father was Samuel Swan Hughes, the descendant of Stephen Hughes and his wife Elizabeth Tarlton Hughes. Stephen Hughes came to Maryland from Wales, probably from Carnarvonshire, but possibly from Glamorganshire. The date of his arrival in America has not been preserved. His son Absalom moved to Powhatan county, Virginia, where he intermarried with the daughter of a planter whose name was also Hughes, and whose Christian name was either David or Jesse—most probably Jesse. He lived on Hughes creek, in that county, and was a man of character and influence; many of his descendants live yet in Virginia and West Virginia, and some of them live in other parts of the United States. Joseph, the son of Absalom Hughes, married Sarah Swan. He moved to Kentucky about the year 1790, and settled in Woodford county. There his son, Samuel Swan Hughes, married Nancy Price, daughter of Colonel William Price, a Virginia soldier of the War of the Revolution. Colonel Price was of that family which has furnished so many men of the name famous in the history of the West, especially in Missouri. His wife was a Miss Cunningham, who claimed direct descent from Robert Bruce, King of Scotland.

In 1820 Samuel Swan Hughes moved with his family to Howard county, Missouri. He settled some five miles from Fayette, on the road leading to Old Franklin. There, on a farm, his son, John Taylor Hughes, grew to manhood. There were but meager educational facilities in Missouri in those days, but young Hughes availed himself of the best he could secure. To one of his teachers, a Mr. Cunningham, a man of culture, he owed his taste for classic literature and much of his proficiency as a writer of correct English. In 1840 he entered Bonne Femme College, a Baptist institution six miles from Columbia, Boone county, Mo., from which he graduated in 1844. In the next two years he taught school in Missouri, first at Richmond, Ray county; then at Huntsville, Randolph county; and at Liberty,

Clay county. He took a lively interest in public affairs, and was a frequent contributor to the newspapers published in Missouri at the time.

COLONEL JOHN T. HUGHES.

(From old daguerreotype in possession of his son, Hon. Roland Hughes, Kansas City, Mo.)

Private in Company C, First Missouri Mounted Volunteers, Mexican War. Became the historian of Doniphan's Expedition. Was Brigadier-General in the Confederate Army. Born in Woodford County, Kentucky, July 25, 1817. Killed in the battle of Independence, Missouri, August 11, 1862.

It was while Hughes was teaching at Liberty that war with Mexico was declared. The causes of this war were well understood in Missouri, for many of her citizens had taken an active part in the war between Texas and Mexico. It is evident from his review of the events immediately preceding the war, and which justified the course of the United States, that Hughes was a firm believer in the righteousness of the American cause. He enlisted as a private in the Clay county company (C), of which O. P. Moss was captain. He served in that capacity during the term of his enlistment. The company was one of those which composed the First Regiment Missouri Mounted Volunteers, of which Alexander W. Doniphan was the Colonel. Doniphan and Hughes were congenial, and nothing ever occurred to mar their friendship. Hughes made known his intention to become the historian of the regiment if he survived, and he was given every facility to secure material for his contemplated work. There is little to tell of his military record; for he was a modest man and severely refrained from any mention of himself. That he was a good soldier we may safely declare from the esteem in which he was held by the officers and men with whom he served. Colonel Doniphan never failed to speak of him in the highest terms, and after the death of Hughes, in a conversation with Hon. James H. Birch, said of him: "I am not surprised at his death, nor at the manner in which it occurred. As a fighter there was none better. When he joined my regiment he was a young man of great nervous vitality, and had just graduated from some Baptist college. During his entire service he occupied himself in making notes from which to write a history of the expedition, which he afterwards wrote and published. He was in the expedition against the Navajos, and while out had an opportunity to show himself. After crossing the great Jornada the Lipan Indians, the most desperate savages in that country, took advantage of our natural distress and annoyed us so greatly that I had to organize a party to chastise them. Hughes was of this party, and killed a noted chief in personal conflict in the open field. When I reached Chihuahua and made up the party to carry dispatches to General Wool at Saltillo, seven hundred miles through an unknown country of the enemy, he was the first one I selected from those who volunteered to go."

Hughes must have labored industriously at his book from the day of his discharge. The preface is dated at Liberty, Mo., September 25, 1847, his company having been mustered out at New Orleans

June 21, 1847. The title is a long one, as was the custom of that time, and is as follows:

"*Doniphan's Expedition; Containing an Account of the Conquest of New Mexico; General Kearny's Overland Expedition to California; Doniphan's Campaign against the Navajoes; his Unparalleled March upon Chihuahua and Durango; and the Operations of General Price at Santa Fé. With a sketch of the Life of Col. Doniphan. Illustrated with Plans of Battle-fields, a Map, and Fine Engravings. By John T. Hughes, A. B., of the First Regiment of Missouri Cavalry.* Cincinnati: Published by J. A. & U. P. James, Walnut St., between Fourth and Fifth. 1848."

Hughes went to Cincinnati to arrange for the publication of the book, and upon his return stopped at Jefferson City and visited friends and comrades, among them Meredith T. Moore. Since the day of its publication the work of Hughes has been the one great authority on the Expedition. There are a number of other books of value on the subject, but the final appeal is always to the work of Hughes. In the closing paragraph he declares that his reward is ample if he has succeeded in furnishing "entertainment for the curious, truth for the inquisitive, novelty for the lover of romance, instruction for the student of history, or information for the general reader." He certainly did all these things, and in doing them left an enduring monument, not to his regiment alone, but to himself also. The work went through a number of editions, and it was issued in two different forms. One was bound in cloth, and is a 12mo volume of 407 pages. The other was paper-bound, with two columns to the page, containing 144 pages. There was no difference in the text. The price of the first was one dollar; and of the second, twenty-five cents. The illustrations are the same in both (though differently arranged), except that the steel engravings, portraits of Colonel Doniphan and General Price, were omitted from the paper-bound edition, as was also the map. It is not known whether the book brought him any financial remuneration, but it is known that he furnished many a comrade with a copy and refused pay therefor. The book made him one of the best-known men in Missouri, and gave him reputation in the country generally. Its value as a contribution to American history has grown steadily, and there is now an increasing demand for it. Copies of the cloth edition have sold for as much as twenty

PRICE TWENTY-FIVE CENTS.

DONIPHAN'S EXPEDITION.

BY JOHN T. HUGHES.

OF THE FIRST REGIMENT OF MISSOURI CAVALRY.

ILLUSTRATED.

CINCINNATI:
PUBLISHED BY U. P. JAMES,
No. 167 WALNUT STREET.

(Photographic reproduction of front cover of the paper-bound edition of the Hughes work.)

dollars each, and it is rare that one in good condition can be obtained for less than four dollars. Colonel Doniphan recognized its fidelity and worth, and he saw the need of a new edition even in his day. He realized that it was not complete in some respects, and pointed out the requirements for the new edition.

Hughes continued to live in Liberty after the Mexican War. He married there Miss Mary Lucinda Carpenter, August 8, 1848. She was the daughter of Thomas Dudley Carpenter, who married at Paris or Versailles, in Kentucky, Miss Paulina Dale, sister of Timothy Redding Dale and Weekly Dale. Of this marriage three children were born—Mrs. Hughes, Noah Paley Carpenter, and Paulina Carpenter. All came to Clay county, Missouri. Noah P. never married; died in California, in 1870. Paulina lived in Plattsburg, in the home of Mr. Hughes, until her marriage to his brother, James E. Hughes, in 1854.

In 1849 Hughes was appointed by President Taylor Receiver of the United States Land Office at Plattsburg, Missouri, and immediately moved to that town, then a mere village. There was no bank in the town, nor even a safe in which to keep the money of the Government. He was in the habit of keeping the money in shot-bags and small boxes. Sometimes he stacked it on a table in his house, often covering a table with tall stacks of gold double-eagles, eagles, and half-eagles; other tables would contain stacks of silver dollars, half-dollars, and quarters. This money he would count carefully into bags, which he would seal and throw under the bed, there to remain until enough had accumulated to justify a trip to St. Louis. Then it was hauled by ox-wagon to Liberty Landing, four and a half miles south of Liberty, and taken thence to St. Louis by steamboat. At St. Louis it was turned over to the Government treasury-agent in settlement for lands sold.

Hughes, in height, was five feet eight, and weighed about a hundred and sixty pounds; was of ruddy complexion, had dark-brown hair and gray-blue eyes; his features were strongly cut, and his expression of countenance grave. "Notwithstanding the fact that he was a serious man," says Col. Birch, who knew him well, "he was a man whom all delighted to meet. He was a scholar, and it pleased him to illumine his conversation with rich thought. He seemed to know everything, especially on grave subjects. He was a great reader, and his memory was marvelous. He was recognized as authority on the subjects of science and general history." His library contains many works on mathematics and astronomy, written in Greek. As a public speaker he appealed to reason alone, never to feeling, and was strong and convincing in argument. By nature he was not severe, but sociable and sympathetic, and held firmly the friendship and respect of those who knew him. He sought the companionship of good men, and avoided that of all others. He was chaste in manner and language, and, being something of a fatalist, was without fear. He was a Baptist, and lived a consistent member of that denomination to the end of his life. He was one of the organizers of the Baptist Church in Plattsburg, and he contributed largely to the endowment fund of William Jewell College, the great Baptist school of Missouri. He took a serious view of life and its duties and obligations.

Hughes was elected to the Legislature in 1854 as a Whig, and in the session of 1854–55 he labored for the election of Colonel Doniphan as United States Senator from Missouri. He secured the passage of a law establishing a State road from Liberty Landing directly north to the south line of Iowa; and it was surveyed and located by his wife's uncle, Timothy Redding Dale. This road was the main artery of commerce from the Missouri river to Iowa for many years. His interest in the subject of popular education was great, and he was one of the founders of the splendid system of public schools of Missouri. He was one of the moving spirits in the establishment of a college at Plattsburg. He was even in favor of educating the slaves, especially along industrial and mechanical lines. His great interest in public schools caused his election to the office of County Superintendent of Clinton county, in which capacity he rendered good service in organizing the schools of the county.

Hughes was a man of untiring energy. He owned a number of slaves and was engaged in numerous enterprises. He acquired a large amount of land in northwest Missouri, upon one tract of which, containing eighteen hundred acres, lying ten miles north of Plattsburg, he intended to make his future home. He lived in the town of Plattsburg, where he owned much property, including a block of brick business buildings. He operated the plantation north of Plattsburg with his slaves, going there frequently to give instructions to his overseer. His treatment of his slaves must have been just and kind, for they were obedient and respectful in their demeanor, and while he was in the army they were loyal to his family. For long after they were granted their freedom they did not leave the plantation; some of them never did move away, remaining there and dying on the place of old age. When, in that community, it became necessary to sell slaves to settle estates, they often entreated Hughes to purchase them, knowing that their treatment would be just and humane. He would not permit the separation of his slave families even temporarily. He favored the gradual emancipation of slaves, freedom to be granted them as rapidly as they were capable of maintaining themselves, a condition which he believed education along industrial lines would enable them to attain rapidly.

In Missouri before the Civil War the elections for State and county officers were held in August. At the August election in 1860 Claiborne F. Jackson, Democrat, was elected Governor of Missouri, and there was elected also a Democratic majority in the Legislature. Presidential electors were chosen at an election held in November, and they were for Stephen A. Douglas, Missouri being the only State to cast its entire electoral vote for him. Upon the election of President Lincoln many Southern States passed ordinances of secession, and the people of Missouri had their full share of excitement. Hughes held a commission as Colonel in the militia organization of the State, by authority of which he mustered into that service the troops from Clay, Platte, Clinton, DeKalb, and other counties of northwest Missouri.

In the Legislature, George G. Vest, the member from Cooper county, introduced a resolution calling a convention to take into consideration the relation of the State of Missouri to the Federal Government. The resolution was adopted, and it inaugurated the contest in Missouri between those in favor of the Union and those in favor of secession. Hughes was outspoken for the Union. He canvassed northwest Missouri in the interest of delegate-candidates in favor of the Union. He published a paper at Plattsburg called the *Northwestern Recorder*, and in this paper he advocated the election of Union delegates. The overwhelming triumph of the Union party in his portion of the State was, in large measure, due to his efforts. Sterling Price was made President of the Convention, defeating the secession candidate for that position. James S. Green, who was in favor of secession, was defeated for United States Senator by Waldo P. Johnson, who favored the Union. These events demonstrated that Missouri was not in favor of secession, but desired to remain in the Union. But war could not be averted by any action taken by Missouri. Her efforts to prevent it from invading her own borders were futile. The State militia was assembled to no purpose. Events which occurred in St. Louis placed it in opposition to the Federal Government. Hughes believed in the justice of the cause of the State, and he threw himself into the conflict with a feeling that overshadowed every consideration of family, friends or fortune. He wrote from the camps of the Missouri troops the most vehement denunciations of the Provisional Government established in Missouri with Hamilton R. Gamble as Governor.

When the army was reorganized at Lexington, Hughes was made Colonel of the First Regiment, Missouri Infantry, Fourth Division of Price's Army, and was in all the important engagements in which it participated. At Carthage, in command of Thornton's Battalion, he occupied the center of the line of battle, and by hard fighting pressed Sigel back from his first and second positions. His third position was in the town of Carthage, in houses, behind walls, and sheltered by other protecting objects. Hughes secured some reinforcements and drove Sigel from the town to his fourth position, about a mile to the east; and this position was charged by Hughes, and Sigel forced to retire.

The first shell from Totten's battery at Wilson Creek awakened Price's sleeping army. This battery had been placed on a hill where it commanded the whole of Price's camp. It was superbly served and was supported by troops under the immediate direction of General Lyon. General Price saw at a glance that its position was the key of the Federal position and that the battle would turn upon its possession. He said to Col. Hughes, "Can you take that battery?" "If you will reinforce me on both the right and the left I will try," replied Hughes. The reinforcements were brought up, and around this hill surged and roared the storm of battle. All were finally drawn into the conflict around this, the "Bloody Hill." Col. Hughes led seven charges up that hill. Six times he was driven back. He had three horses shot from under him. In the seventh charge the lines approached to within thirty feet of each other. General Lyon fell in front of his men, and soon the battle was over. Major Sturgis assumed command and drew off the Federal troops.

In the winter of 1861-62 General Price sent Colonel Hughes with a column of men with orders to cross the Missouri river at Camden and cut off St. Joseph, Leavenworth and Kansas City by destroying the Hannibal & St. Joseph Railroad, and bring out of that part of the State as many recruits as possible. Colonel Doniphan, who lived then at Liberty, learned of this intended expedition; and to prevent it and the consequences he knew would follow it, he rode to Plattsburg through a snow-storm and laid the facts before Col. James H. Birch, who was a member of the Provisional Government of Missouri, urging him to go to St. Louis as quickly as possible, inform General Halleck, and induce him to take steps to prevent the crossing of the Missouri by Hughes. In order to impress upon Col. Birch the importance of securing quick action, Colonel Doniphan said to him: "Colonel, I have reliable information that John T. Hughes intends to cross the Missouri river at Camden, six miles west of Lexington, and after crossing, to tear up the Hannibal & St. Joseph Railroad from Macon to St. Joseph and burn the bridges. He will then recruit a brigade and recross the river with it before the Federal troops can be brought in. Now this alone would not trouble me, for he would take out of northwest Missouri hundreds of men the absence of whom would tend to give us a greater degree of peace. But the force of Hughes would doubtless commit some depredations, and when the Federals came in again the devil would be in supreme command in this particular country. I know John T. Hughes well; he was in my regiment in Mexico; and he is the most ambitious and daring officer in Price's army, and if effective steps are not taken at once he will execute his purpose, and you know as well as I do what will follow." Colonel Birch hurried to St. Louis and laid this information before General Halleck, and when Colonel Hughes reached the Missouri river he found on the opposite bank a superior Federal force. He saw that his movement was checked, and after exchanging shots across the river turned again to the south and rejoined Price in time to participate in the battle of Pea Ridge. Colonel Hughes never knew that Colonel Doniphan prevented the success of his expedition. He was intent on doing his duty as a soldier, and Colonel Doniphan shuddered at the thought of suffering that would result in the warfare between neighbors which he knew would certainly follow.

At Pea Ridge Col. Hughes, in the first day's fighting, commanded the cavalry on the extreme right of Price's line, on the eastern slope of Sugar Mountain or Pea Ridge. With Gates, Little and Slack he charged the Federal left under Carr, Vandever, and Dodge, pressing the Federal line back to Elkhorn Tavern, where Slack fell mortally wounded. Col. Hughes assumed command on the field. About two o'clock in the afternoon he again led the advance of the right, conducting his men up a hollow through brush and small timber. To check Hughes, Vandever advanced masses of infantry, and a desperate conflict ensued, resulting in the advance of the Confederate line to the position held by the Federal troops earlier in the day. Further reinforcements of the Federals did not stop the Confederate advance, and they were forced to fall back from Elkhorn Tavern with the loss of three guns of Hayden's Battery. Col. Hughes slept with his men on the field, waiting for the dawn and orders to renew the battle, confident of his ability to continue to advance. But during the night it became known that both McCullough and McIntosh had been killed and their forces scattered. Col. Hughes was placed with Raines in the rear of Van Dorn's retreating columns to beat back the troops under Curtis. Raines fell mortally wounded, and Hughes fought back the Federals and saved the army, then drew off his men, leaving the dead on the field.

After the battle of Pea Ridge it was seen that the operations of the Missouri State Guard were restricted by its position, and that to continue as an army it would have to be under the direction of the Confederate Government. General Price assembled his men at Des Arc, and there those of the Missouri State Guard who remained in the service entered the Confederate army.

Col. Hughes went with the army to Mississippi, and after the battles of Corinth and Iuka returned to Missouri to recruit a brigade, having been made brevet Brigadier-General. His purpose was to cross the Missouri river at Wayne City, or possibly at Blue Mills, raise his brigade in northwest Missouri, and march south, crossing the Missouri as near Kansas City as possible. He did not deem it wise to cross the Missouri river and leave a Federal force in his rear, and to prevent this, fought the battle of Independence as a part of his general plan. In company with Col. Gideon W. Thompson, he repaired to the recruiting camp of Col. Upton Hays, on the Cowherd farm, near Lee's Summit, Jackson county. There he planned the battle of Independence. The town was held by Union troops under command of Col. James T. Buel, of the Seventh Missouri Cavalry. Buel arrived at Independence June 7, 1862, and his force consisted of three companies of his own regiment and three companies of militia, two of which belonged to Nugent's Battalion, and were commanded by Captains Axline and Thomas. Buel decided to break up the Confederate recruiting station, which, it is said, contained but two hundred and fifty men all told. August 10 (Sunday) Buel searched Independence and seized all the firearms to be found, to prevent residents in sympathy with Hays from attacking him in the rear. The officers of the recruiting camp were promptly notified of the search and seizure at Independence, and they decided to strike first. Sunday night Quantrill arrived at the camp with about thirty men.

Buel, with one hundred and fifty men, was stationed in buildings at the southwest corner of the Independence public square; the remainder of his force, about three hundred men, was camped in a pasture half a mile west, between the present Union and Pleasant streets, immediately south of Lexington avenue.

The Confederate attack was directed by Col. Hughes. He assigned to Quantrill two things to do: the first was to guide the attacking force to Independence; the second was to cut off Colonel Buel and hold him in the town, which it was believed he could do, as Col. Hughes was to follow him closely with the main force and would be himself between the different bands of the Federal force. The Confederates dashed through the town and surprised the Federal camp, opening a heavy fire at close range. Though thrown into confusion, the Union soldiers returned the fire. The town was captured and Buel and about half his force surrendered, most of the men in camp escaping to Kansas City. Near the close of the battle Col. Hughes received a musket-ball in the right temple and died immediately. Credit for the victory belongs to him. Thus died John T. Hughes, on the eleventh day of August, 1862, in his forty-sixth year. Had he survived he would have become the historian of General Price's Army, as he had already been that of the army under Colonel

Doniphan. At the time of his death he had been in the service about a year and a half.

His untimely death left his estate much involved. Because of his various enterprises he had contracted debts; but he had laid the foundation for a large fortune, and but for the coming of the war his plans would have worked themselves out and made him a rich man. The war destroyed values. The business property which he owned in Plattsburg was burned. The estate had to be settled during the war, and all the property except his library went to pay his debts. His widow retained his library and her dower in the homestead ten miles north of Plattsburg.

Colonel Hughes was survived by a widow and five children, all living at this time (1906).

(1) Paley Carpenter Hughes; born at Liberty, Mo., in August, 1849; married Mary E. Burr, daughter of John Burr and Willie Wiltshire Burr; Mrs. Burr was the daughter of John Wiltshire, foreman of the jury which condemned John Brown to death for his attack on Harper's Ferry. The marriage of Paley Carpenter Hughes to Miss Burr was May 19, 1881; he now lives on a farm ten miles north of Plattsburg; of this marriage have been born—(1) Mary Edna, September 2, 1887; (2) Inez D., November 23, 1889; (3) Byron Burr, May 14, 1896; (4) John Dudley, May ——, 1901.

(2) Roland Hughes; born March 31, 1852, at Plattsburg, Mo.; attended the public schools in Plattsburg, also in the country after the family moved to the farm in the spring of 1861; attended William Jewell College; after teaching for a time studied law in Plattsburg, where he opened an office and practiced his profession; was twice elected Prosecuting Attorney of Clinton county; formed a partnership with General Byron Sherry and moved to Kansas City, Mo., in 1887; after the dissolution of the partnership with General Sherry, formed one with Hon. Thomas A. Witten; was elected Prosecuting Attorney of Jackson county, Mo., and served two years, the term ending January 1, 1905. Has been retained in much litigation of great importance, and is recognized by the bench and bar of Kansas City as an able lawyer; at Uniontown, Kansas, in 1880, married Maude Steele, second daughter of Count Sobieski Steele and Chloe (Collins) Steele; two children—a son who died in infancy; (2)

Ethel Llewellyn. Roland Hughes lives in Kansas City, where he is engaged in the practice of his profession.

(3) Thomas Edward Hughes; born at Plattsburg, in 1855; never married; now living with the widow, his mother, on the farm ten miles north of Plattsburg.

(4) Henry Clay Hughes; born at Plattsburg, in 1857; educated at William Jewell College and State University; twice elected Collector of Clinton county; read law and was admitted to the bar, but preferred banking as a business; now living at Richmond, Mo., and is connected with the Hughes Bank there; married at Plattsburg, January 29, 1889, Aimee Radell; one son, John Taylor Hughes, born July 8, 1890.

(5) Tyre Clifton Hughes; born at Plattsburg, in 1860; educated at the Missouri State University; is a civil engineer and mining expert and mineralogist; married, and lives in Denver, Colorado.

In the spring of 1861 John Taylor Hughes was at home on his farm. There one ideal day the teams were driven afield and the mellow furrows turned. Cattle contentedly grazed among the clumps of pasture trees. Peace and happiness reigned in the home beneath the oaks well back from the public way. As the sun swung low a man in the prime of life came out upon the great bluegrass plot before his open door, to prune and clip and beautify. Rising yonder swell dashed a rider, his horse weary and foam-flecked. He halted at the hospitable gate and summoned the man in the dooryard. A message was delivered. The man read it. He turned to a slave and ordered his saddle-horse made ready forthwith. He hung his pruning-hook upon a tree, entered his home, kissed his wife and children, came forth again, and as the sun went out he flung himself upon his horse and rode away in the gathering gloom of night, to return no more forever. We saw him die upon a battle-field. Glorious death, meet and fitting for the heroic scion of a brave and patriotic people.

Colonel Hughes lies buried at Independence, near his last field of glory. By him lie Colonel Boyd and Major Hart. They fell with him on the same battle-field.

DIARY OF COL. JOHN T. HUGHES.

[The following is a portion of the diary kept day by day by John T. Hughes from which to write his history of Doniphan's Expedition. Its existence was brought to my attention by accident. I spent an evening with Roland Hughes, Esq., of Kansas City, son of Colonel Hughes, for the purpose of going over the copy of this work. While we were engaged in going over the copy and discussing the sources of information from which I had written my part of the work, Mrs. Hughes spoke of having seen in the home of "Mother Hughes," the widow of Colonel Hughes, an old diary. Mr. Hughes had never seen any diary among his father's papers and could scarcely believe any existed, but Mrs. Hughes insisted that what she had seen was an old diary written by Colonel Hughes. Mr. Hughes immediately wrote to his mother to inquire about the diary. She sent him this, and said it alone escaped a fire which broke out in the office of Colonel Hughes, it having been brought to his home and there left.

This diary was hurriedly written on the march and by the feeble blaze of the camp-fire, often by fingers stiffened with cold. Colonel Hughes did not always stop to spell the words correctly, and he wrote only enough to recall the incidents when he should want to set out the account in due order. It is written in a small blank book, and it is printed here as written, with its quaint expressions and capitalization. It will be seen that Colonel Hughes was a true Southerner. Many of the provincialisms used in this diary I heard fifty years ago in the mountains of eastern Kentucky, where they are used to this day. The diary is a valuable addition to this work, and it is here because of the quick perception of its true character and worth by Mrs. Roland Hughes, to whom the author here writes his grateful acknowledgment.]

DIARY.

MONDAY, 17TH AUG., 1846.

To-day we expect to have an engagement with the Spanish Gen. Salasar, the murderer of the Texan prisoners—3 Spanish spies taken last night by the picket Guard—Marched at 7 A. M. Among the prisoners is the son of the Spanish Gen. Salasar—He reports that there are disputes between his father & Gov. Armijo for the command —that yesterday there were three thousand men at the pass 15 miles from Santa Fé—but a Spaniard being bribed by Kearny, reported our army as being 5500 men & so many cannon that he could not count them—this Rumor spread dismay among their ranks & they dispersed, some of them to their homes, some of them are with their respective leaders—Only one man still raised his voice for war, a Congress-man—The Pueblo Indians did not unite with them, in consequence of an ancient tradition that at a certain period of time succor would come from the east to deliver them from the Spanish oppression & restore the kingdom of Montezuma. They regard the Americans as the long expected succor—1000 to 1300 are said to be well armed—the rest indifferently—10 miles we came to the castle of the Pagos, a very ancient ruin on the Puerco or Pecos—this palace is said to have been built 200 or 300 years ago, and soon after the death of Montezuma, for the purpose of burning incense to [him] until his return—this practice of keeping up the Vestal fires on the Altar was instituted by his daughter—the Pagos tribe being exhausted about 3 to 6 years ago, the fire became extinguished—the palace is much dilapidated—the palace is 111 feet long, 30 wide & 50 high—it has fine fancy carved, & flowered work inside—doors 12 ft. high, 6 wide, & the walls are 6 ft. thick, built of adobies—it has a garret, & an Altar, & various private Rooms. I dared to ascend the Altar & stood in the very spot where the Vestal fire had blazed for ages & wrote my name upon the white-washed wall near & in rear of the sacred altar. Within this ruined city there is a castle or citadel furnished with cisterns & store rooms for the purpose sustaining a siege—the wall is of stone & must have been 8 or 10 ft. high & 4 thick,—this wall extends quite round the town—Some say that Montezuma died here & that he was a perbleau [Pueblo]. The Spanish are indolent & poor. They sell their onions, melons, fruits, grain, flour, meal, milk, cheese, &c. to the soldiers—they run along the lines for this purpose—this money will be drained out of their hands to pay the priests—Saw 50 men in a cornfield, on half Rations, & not one man pulled an ear. Salasar's son was taken by Thos. McCarty & James Chorn. Marched 13 miles and encamped in the valley of the Puerco near the finest spring I almost ever saw. Camp No. 46.

Tuesday, 18th.

The Spaniards have fled in every direction. Gov. Armijo has left with 200 to 400 regulars for El Paso. Part of the citizens of Santa Fé have left and fled into the mountains—Some Dragoons sent at 1 a. m. to reconnoiter the pass—Rain—good grass—the country is timbered from Bagas to Santa Fé—Marched 8 or 9 miles up one branch of the Puerco & down another, hedged in on either hand by a very high range of mountains & at the Canyon or breach through the rocks. Here it was that Gen. Salasar & Armijo prepared to oppose our march —the position was well selected; but they had neither the harmony nor the bravery to defend it—the camp exhibited the appearance of about 2500 men—the cedars were hewn down to clear a way for the cannon. 3000 men were here, but not all at once—it was agreed that they would not fight the Americans before they left Santa Fé.

Armijo fled for fear of assassination by his own people. Country remarkably dry & sterile 5 or 6 miles before you get into the town, & covered by a dwarf cedar—The day was cloudy until evening, when the sun broke out just as we entered Santa Fé. Gen. K. came in advance & entered the town with ten companies, in fine array & banners streaming in the breeze, behind them the Artillery, which halted on the hill, and the Volunteers under Col. Doniphan marched next in order through the various crooked streets of the town; their banners gaily flown to the breeze, while the batteries fired a salute of near 20 guns. The American flag was erected in the public square so as to wave over the Palace Royal or Gov. Armijo's Residence. We encamped on a perfectly bare spot of sand, after a travel of 29 miles, not having halted to eat a bite—the men were very hungry & much fatigued—the horses are almost perished to death—neither man nor horse had anything to eat; nor did they get anything until the next morning—some few got a piece of bread or cheese from the Spaniards. My own adventures at night with W. P. Hall & Maj. Going.

WEDNESDAY, 19TH.

Gen. K. took up his headquarters in the Palace or Royal Palace on the night of the 18th—the flag waved about the public square—at 9 A. M. I was invited to go down in town to hear Gen. K.'s speech to the Spaniards & to see them take the oath of allegiance to the Govt. of the U. S.—fight on hand—Gen. K. called together the Governor adinterim, the Secretary of State, the Alcalde, & other civil officers, & made the following address to them through his interpreter, A. Rubideau. [See the speech in full in Chapter III, and the account of the fight in Chapter IV, *Doniphan's Expedition*, by Hughes. The Diary has another entry on the 19th, in which the fight is mentioned and the speech given in full. The additional entry follows.—W. E. C.]

WEDNESDAY, 19TH.

(Took breakfast—invited to go down into town by Col. Doniphan—While sketching the public square a fight occurred & Gen. K. ordered me to arrest the parties.)

"Spaniards, citizens of N. Mexico: I have come amongst you to take possession of New Mexico in the name of the Govt. of the U. S. I have come with peaceable intentions & kind feelings towards you. We come as friends to better your condition & to make you a part of the Republic of the U. S. We wish not to murder you or rob you of your property. My soldiers will take nothing from you but what they pay you for—in taking possession of N. Mexico we do not mean to take away your Religion from you—our Govt. has no connexion with Religion—all Religions are equal—the one has no preference over another, the Catholic & Protestant are esteemed alike. Every man has the right to serve his God according to his own heart. When a man dies he must render to his God an account of his acts here on earth, whether good or bad. In our Govt. all men are equal. We esteem the most peaceable man as the best man. I advise you to attend to your domestic concerns—cultivate industriously; be peaceable and obedient to the laws—do not resort to violence to correct abuses. I do hereby proclaim that I am in possession of Santa Fé, & therefore virtually in possession of all of New Mexico. Armijo is no longer your Governor—his power is gone—but he will return & be as one of you. I am your Gov. Look to me for protection. You are not to molest him. You are no longer Spanish subjects. You are now become American citizens, subject to the laws of the U. S. You no longer owe allegiance to that Govt., & I do hereby proclaim that you are to be governed by the same Rulers as formerly except the Governor, & I am your Governor. Look to me for protection." He then asked them if they were willing to take the oath of allegiance to the Govt. of the U. S.—to which they responded (*ci*, yes). The General then administered to the officers of state the following oath: "Do you swear, thro' faith, that under all circumstances you will bear allegiance to the Govt. of the U. S., & that you will be obedient & faithful citizens to the laws of the country, in the name of the father, & the Son & the Holy Spirit, Amen."

When the Genl. finished his address the Spaniards shouted & many of them shook his hand & called him Governor. One aged man (92 years old) embraced him & wept. The Gen. passed through very nearly the same ceremonies with the Purbleau [Pueblo] Indians & promised them some presents—they professed to be well pleased—the Spaniards are also pleased at the idea of becoming citizens of the U. S. They had nothing to lose by the change of Govt. & every thing to gain. Houses built of adobies — 1 story high — flat roofs — 6 churches.

Camp No. 48.

THURSDAY, 20TH.

Remained in camp—Rambled through town. Visited private houses. American Residents expected to be murdered before we came in.

FRIDAY, 21ST.

Remained in camp—Attended to camp duties.

SATURDAY, 22.

Visited Santa Fé & went into many private houses—Women not handsome, rather more intelligent than the men—phandangoes almost every night. Courtmartial sat to try a Mr. I. Herkins, of the Saline Company.

SUNDAY, 23D.

Visited the Catholic church—Great many women—all kneel down —no seats—Governor Kearny's proclamation to the inhabitants of Santa Fé, that those who remain peaceably at home should be protected in their lives & property—that they were to all intents and purposes citizens of the United States—that those who remained in arms against him, or who should take up arms to incite others to rebellion, should be considered as traitors, & treated as such & their property confiscated to the Government of the United States.

MONDAY, 24TH.

Lieut. Oldham, of Company A, arraigned before a courtmartial for disobedience of orders in leaving Balistea for some provisions for his men—Lt. Jas. S. Oldham was broke of his commission & dismissed from the service.

TUESDAY, 25TH.

Express left for Fort Leavenworth—5 men, 3 Dragoons & 2 Volunteers. R. W. Fleming & W. C. Gunter—A priest came in to-day & submitted to Gen. K. & took the oath of allegiance to the U. S.

WEDNESDAY, 26TH.

Priest came from Tous to hold a parley with Gen. K. Gen. Sallasar took Gen. McClure & 287 prisoners near San Miguel & 3 of them were put to death near that place & 4 near Balistea—Gen. McClure gave into the hands of Gen. Sallasar 4000$ & other property to feed the prisoners, which he converted to his private ends & starved the prisoners—When Gen. S. arrived at El Paso the prisoners were given into the charge of Otese of Santa Fé & treated well. The sensible young Purbleau chief told Gen. K. he had heard of him & came to see him & know what his intentions were—if he intended protection or not—that the priests had told him the Americans would plunder & kill—take their women & brand them on the cheek with the American brand—rob them of their daughters, & drive the men into the fastnesses of the mountains—he would not suffer this—that Armijo had been up to see them, but their wise men told Armijo that there was no end to the American people—that if he whipped Kearny millions more would keep coming—that he, Armijo, would run & then the Americans would whip the Purbleaus—General K. asked what other Rumors he had heard, to which he replied, that it was useless to tell a man of K.'s sense about the tales that came like the wind & had no responsible source—Gen. K. gave them some money, which they accepted by way of compliment.

Thursday, 27th.

Cannon drill—10 pieces, 2 howitzers & 4 iron & 4 brass pieces—each battery lacks one howitzer—7 pieces taken from the Spaniards—mostly 4-pounders—2 four-pound howitzers with Col. Price—The Texan Piece is a 6-pounder made of brass.

Friday, 28th.

The Gen. is having the laws & constitution of the U. S. [translated] into the Spanish language—& also the Mexican constitution into English—Printing Press.

Saturday, 29th.

Gen. Kearny abolished the "stamp paper" of the Government of New Mexico—8 dollars per sheet.

Sunday, 30th.

Made out Muster Rolls & Pay Rolls—Church—Wagoner Frazier died in Santa Fé.

Monday, 31st.

Col. Doniphan left as Governor of the Territory of New Mexico—the Col. & Willard P. Hall preparing a Code of laws for the Department—Gen. K. intends to start south with 700 men on the 2nd (Wednesday) of September—500 Vols., & 100 Dragoons, & 100 Artillerists—

He has been informed the Armijo party & the malcontents are concentrating to give him battle—Regiment Mustering for Pay.

TUESDAY, 1 SEPT., '46.

Nothing of moment occurred—the usual business of the camp going forward—The men preparing for the Southern Campaign.

SOUTHERN EXPEDITION.

WEDNESDAY, 2ND SEPT., '46.

On Wednesday morning, Sept. 2, Gen. Kearny left Santa Fé with the following troops on a Southern Campaign—(viz)—

6 companies of Vol., com'd by	L. B. Sublette	(C)	
"	Capt. Walton	(B)	
"	Capt. Reid	(D)	
"	Capt. Waldo	(A)	
"	Capt. Rodgers	(H)	
"	Lt. DeCourcy	(G)	500 men
"	Capt. Weightman, Art.		100 men
"	Hudson & Burgwin		100 men
			700 men

& a full Staff of Aids—We passed through S. Fé with our banners flying to the breeze—The Ladies looked intently from the housetops as we passed—We were soon out of the suburbs of the town & on the broad road that leads to Chihuahua. We pursued our way over a sandy barren soil, covered with neither grass nor shrub except the Dwarf Cedar, the Wild Sage, & the "cactus a cutus" or prickly pear, & a few spears of the Grama-Grass. Water is very scarce—the creeks & even the rivers are but a bed of dry sand—The valley of the Santa Fé River is poor, & possesses but little interest after you get below the confines of the town—it becomes much narrower & the fine stream of water that irrigates the Capital sinks into the sand. At night camped on the Galesteo, where we were badly supplied with water & grass after a tiresome day's march of some 25 miles.

Camp No. 1.

THURSDAY, 3RD.

Pursued our way down the Galesteo—the Sierra Nevada to the right & high ridges on the left—Sandy barren country—Flint & Sandstone—Gen. K. went by Santo Domingo to receive the submission of the inhabitants—The Chief with 60 men and a white flag came out to escort him—they went through various evolutions, charges, &c. The Gen. was received cordially. The Vol. Regt. went a direct route to San Filipe, on the west side of the Del Norte—it contains a church & several other buildings. Here we enjoyed the first sight of the Rio Grande Del Norte—We were thirsty, and enjoyed the stream much—About two miles below San Filipe we encamped—Abundance of the fine Oporto Grape, the finest in the world. Good grass and shade under the cottonwoods.

Camp No. 2.

FRIDAY, 4TH.

Took up the line of march early & proceeded down the valley of the Rio Grande—the valley is about 2 miles wide, & is perhaps the finest fruit country in the Department—it is cut into various channels for the purpose of irrigation—fine vineyards and peach orchards— Timber scarce, clumps of cottonwood—grass fine in places—The Rio Del Norte is 2000 miles in length, & at this point is 200 yds. in width —The water is clear & good, as most of the water is furnished by the Springs in the mountains—The Valley is hedged in by lofty mountains on the east & West—They appear blue in the heat of the day & are shrouded in mists and clouds—look quite dazzling in the rays of the setting sun—6 miles, came to the town Algodones, containing near a thousand inhabitants—fine fruit—walls around the gardens— cactus on the walls—The people submitted willingly and received us kindly—they offered us all kinds of fruit, melons, bread, &c.—hundreds of Spaniards & Indians follow along with the Army. They seem to be well pleased with the change of government & the idea of being considered as citizens of the American Republic—They say that Armijo has gone to the D—l. 10 miles, to Bernalillo—population 500— lofty mountains on the east—15 miles, came to Sandea—population 3 or 400—These towns are inhabited by Pueblos & Mexicans—in fact, the houses & villages & Ranches are scattered thickly up & down the Great River of the North—it resembles perhaps the settlements on the St. Lawrence between Kingston & Montreal, except that the houses here are built of mud & flat-roofed—Excitement still prevails in camp in consequence of an order at Galesteo to wear "coats" in hot weather & that those who had none would be dismissed—Capt. Reid's Remarks.

Camp No. 3—23 Miles.

Saturday, 5th.

By daybreak we were on the line of march, the Clay Company in front of the Vol. Regiment, with the flag bravely waving. Albuquerque stretches about 7 or 8 miles up & down the River—The settlement is thick—fine gardens, orchards, cornfields & truck-patches—8 miles, came to Albuquerque proper. Here the command halted near the church—A salute was fired from the top of the church—the Gen. halted here to spend the Night & Lt. Col. Ruff took the command—Grass good—2 miles below Albuquerque, grazed—Melons, grapes, apricots, &c.—cranes, geese, brants, & other water fowl in the Rio Del Norte—Reptiles, frogs, turtles, as in the Missouri bottoms—Burrs and Spanish-needles—Soil good, but sandy; irrigated by aqueducts—no rain in this country—crowds of Spaniards & women follow the Army to sell fruits, &c.—crowd around the Gen. About 8 miles below Albuquerque we encamped on a piece of ground totally destitute of wood & very scarce of grass—Mountains on the east Bank of the Rio Grande—16 miles march to-day.

Camp No. 4.

Sunday, 6th.

Proceeded on the march 5 miles, came to the town Isleta—Placeres on the Southwest side of the river—This appears to be an Indian village—quantities of Melons, grapes, Apricots, &c., for sale by the Indians—A deputation of well-dressed, intelligent-looking Spaniards came to meet us & submit themselves to the General—Grazed at a cottonwood grove 8 miles from camp. Sand drifts on the east—bottom sandy—grass moderate—blue pink—no timber on the mountains. This grove has the appearance of being artificial. The grass is fine. Here we camped to spend the day, as it was the Sabbath—Peralta or Placeres is just below us—Gen. K. took his dinner in the town—Phandango at Palesta or Peralta, & my adventures in the vineyard.

Camp No. 5.

Monday, 7th.

Many of the sons of the wealthiest men are educated in the U. States—3 miles, we passed the little town of Placeres containing about 2 or 300 inhabitants—Sand hills—vegetation same as hitherto described—The Valley heightens in interest & in variety as you descend the Rio Bravo. Crowds of Spaniards & women follow the General—3 miles more came to the town of Tomé (named after San Tomé). Here the people were assembling for the purpose of celebrating the anniversary of the Inception of the Virgin Mary—There were at this commemoration at least 2000 persons—The Army pitched the tents about an hour before Sundown—The city was illuminated by pine faggots placed on the walls of the town & the church. The illumination was brilliant—About 8 P. M. the Salute to the General was given from the top of the church—for 3 hours in succession the sky-Rockets & fire balls were streaming in the air in zigzag motion 100 feet high—The women & men promiscuously mingled in the crowd, ran to & fro & shouted & yelled tremendously—when this part of the ceremony was concluded the people seated themselves on the ground in the Square in front of a porch & here a kind of Theatrical show was exhibited—Men & women speaking at the same time—Many of the Vols. left the camp to see the town & make observations—Lt. L. B. Sublett, being officer of the Guard, was sent up to town by order of Lt. Col. Ruff to bring all the Vols. to camp & put them on extra duty—This order was executed—70 or 80 men were taken & put on extra guard—They kept the camp in a continual uproar during the night—The 8th was the celebration—it commenced about 9 A. M. on the 8th.

Tuesday, 8th.

The Army remained in camp—The celebration began at about 9 A. M. The church was crowded with a sea of heads—The house was lighted up with candles—The Gen. & his Staff were present—each one as he entered in went & worshiped the Infant Saviour in the manger, then the Holy Virgin, then the Saviour on the Cross, &c. I was particularly struck with a very aged and decrepit lady who went to the Saviour & prayed before him & wiped her streaming tears on the robes that clothed the image—The firing of guns & circular rockets was kept up during the ceremonies—3 or 4 priests officiated, preaching from the pulpit—Singing & instrumental music—They play the same tunes in serving God as they do in the phandango—They keep good time—Horse racing after meeting—The whole is a pompous, unmeaning show, & a gross mockery of the pure religion of the meek & humble Jesus whom they pretend to serve. The little village of Tomé was the terminus of our Southern Campaign—At 4 P. M. received orders to return to Santa Fé—Gen. & part of his Staff remained to attend a feast or Phandango at night—We return by the same route we came.

WEDNESDAY, 9TH.

On the return—and the same on Thursday the 10th and Friday the 11th.

SATURDAY, 12TH.

Got back to Galesteo Spring.

SUNDAY, 13TH.

Left horses on the Galesteo under the charge of Major Gilpin & one-third of the detachment, & walked into town.

MONDAY, 14TH.

Wrote back home by H. Carson.

TUESDAY, 15TH.

An Express sent back to the States by the Gen.

WEDNESDAY, 16TH.

News from Col. Price & the Mormon troops on the Arkansas.

THURSDAY, 17TH.

Lt. Col. Ruff resigned his office & accepted a commission in the Regular Army—In consequence of this resignation an order was issued by the Col. to supply said vacancy by an election—There were three competitors for the station, Maj. Gilpin, Captains Reid & Jackson. The camp was in great excitement—the election was ordered at 6 A. M. on the 18th—Candidates had but little time to make their calculations, as a detachment of 3 companies were ordered to march to Ceballeta & 2 to Abequeu on the morning of the 18th—The privates were anxious to defeat Maj. Gilpin. West Point men do not suit the Western men—Col. Kearny has appointed Capt. Hudson to command a Company of Volunteers to California. A very lamentable circumstance occurred at 9 P. M. An aged man, Wm. Bray, of the Franklin Company, being in liquor, & raving about in camp, made an attempt to rush upon Capt. Stephenson; the latter drew a pistol & snapped at him twice. Mr. Bray still rushed on him with his knife drawn—the Capt. shot him through the breast—he fell dead with the knife clenched fast in his hand—Mr. Bray was an old soldier, was in the

NATIONAL CEMETERY AT SANTA FÉ.

battle at New Orleans, was a man of family, was 63 years old, & now lies buried on the hill to the north of Santa Fé in the American Burying Ground.

Resolutions were adopted to run no man who was not a private in the ranks—carried, though not acted upon—(here insert the resolutions). [These resolutions have not been found.—W. E. C.]

Friday, 18th.

The election for Lt. Col. took place this morning—the vote stood as follows:

        314 for Capt. Jackson.
        221 for Maj. Gilpin.

        93 majority for Jackson.
        446 for Jackson.
        263 for Gilpin.

        183 maj. for Jackson.

Saturday, 19th.

Copying the laws—building the fort—Nothing of interest transpired.

Sunday, 20th.

A deputation of Eutas came in to hold a council with the General—Major Gilpin with 2 Companies left for Abiqui, viz., Waldo and Stephenson—Under Lt. Col. Jackson, three Companies under Captains Parsons, Reid, & Lt. De Courcy—Express from Col. Price—Bob Laten [or Later] came in as express bearer.

Monday, 21st.

Finished the laws for the territory—Grand Council with the Euta Chiefs—The Gen. told them to be peaceable, not because he feared them, but it was best for them—he wished to be friendly, but if they misbehaved he would send his soldiers & make them submissive—he gave them some presents to secure their good behavior; consisting of blankets and calicos.

Tuesday, 22d.

The Apache Chief, Chian, came in with about 30 of his tribe to have a friendly talk with Gen. Kearny—The Gen. told them that he had come amongst them with peaceable intentions—that he was disposed to be their friend—that the President had sent him for that purpose—that if they would not be friendly he would march his army amongst them & thus scourge them from the face of the earth;—if he had any bad young men amongst them he must bring them in to him, or punish them as they deserve—or if they continued unruly he must keep them under his eye—stake them out as the Mexicans do their pigs, with a lariat—that they must be industrious, & not Rob or steal; that if there was not game enough in their country to subsist upon they must cultivate the soil as the Christians do—plant corn, beans, & other vegetables—that the Great Spirit will not feed them if they do not work—that they must not lie upon their beds idle & inactive & expect the Great Spirit to feed them, but must produce, out of their mother earth, a subsistence—that all mankind must procure a livelihood by labor—that he must not allow his young men to rob the Mexicans; if they did so he must deliver [them] up to justice or he would hold the nation responsible for their conduct—that the President loves his red children as well as his white children—that they are all brothers—all Americans—that war exists between the U. S. & Mexico; but the whites are on friendly terms with the people of New Mexico—that if any disputes occur between the Apaches & the Mexicans, or the Apaches & the Eutas or Arapahoes or Comanches, he must come to Governor Bent, who will do justice to his red children—I have now given you good advice, & will give you some presents as a memorial of the friendship subsisting between us—I am going away, & may never return again, but I leave Mr. Bent as your Governor—obey him—To all these things the Chief replied alternately with a spirit & resolution worthy of his tribe—he promised obedience, & said that the Apaches were poor, that he must speak a good word to the Eutas, Arapahoes & other tribes & permit them to hunt buffaloe wherever they could find them—that he did not lie—that the Great Spirit had given him an honest heart & a straight tongue—that he had not two tongues that he should speak forked—that though his skin was red, & that he was a poor Indian, a dog, he did not fear to stand before him & look him in the face—there is no guilt there (putting his hand upon his heart)—the Council ended by making some presents to the Chief and his people.

Thursday, 24th.

A train of 17 wagons arrived—one men, a Mr. Cooke, was shot by accident, but is not yet dead—Don Manuel 'emasculated—first act of the New Administration—John Franklin sentenced to stoppage of 10$ & to pack 60 lbs of rock for 2 hours out of 12 for 10 days.

Friday, 25th.

This morning Gen. Kearny departed for the far-off shores of the California, with the following companies (viz): Captains Sumner, Cooke, Moore, Burgwin & Lt. Noble—300 in all, with directions for Capt. Hudson's company & Col. Allen's Regiment of Mormons to follow him as soon as practicable.

Saturday, 26th.

Lt. Col. C. F. Ruff left for the States—Fandangoes every night &c.

Sunday, 27th.

Attended the Catholic Church—senseless mockery of Religion—evil effect of the Catholic System—Rumors that the Navahoes have killed 5 Spaniards & driven off 10,000 head of sheep & cattle.

Monday, 28th.

This evening Col. Price of the 2nd Regiment arrived in quite a feeble state af health—nothing of interest occurred.

Tuesday, 29th.

Some part of the Staff of the Col. arrived.

Wednesday, 30th.

Stewart, Sargent Major, & others came in—also Albert Wilson, the Sutler, came in.

Thursday, 1st October.

Some few of Col. Price's Regiment dropped in.

Friday, 2d.

The first Battalion, consisting of the St. Louis, St. Genevieve, Benton & Boone companies, arrived under the command of Maj. Edmondson—53 days from the fort—Horses in moderate [condition] —Lost one or two men on the Route.

THE HUGHES DIARY. 75

SATURDAY, 3D.

Visit to Galesteo & thence to the grazing Encampment 50 miles from Santa Fé—Travel by moon-light, &c—The encampment is in a beautiful elevated prairie, about 10 miles from San Miguel—in this lovely undulating plain there is a glassy lake of fine fresh water, while the whole prairie is covered with a tall gramma grass, resembling a rich meadow—The whole plain is most beautifully skirted with cedar & pine of beautiful size—Even the solitude is beautiful & the scene romantic—The days are bright.

SUNDAY, 4TH.

Remained at the grazing Encampment.

MONDAY, 5TH.

Returned from the Grazing Ground to Galisteo & lodged in a Rico's plaza—cannot drink Goat's milk.

TUESDAY, 6TH.

Examination of the method of making molasses of the corn stalk, pounded as we do apples or peaches & then pressing the juice from them & boiling it down to "miel."

WEDNESDAY, 7TH.

Adjusted our pay Rolls—Captain Giddings, of Monroe, arrived with his company.

THURSDAY, 8TH.

Wrote home to Col. Switzler—3 companies extra Battalion came in from Ray, Polk, & Marion counties.

FRIDAY, 9TH.

Town full of Americans. Three companies of Mormons arrived under command of Lt. Smith, U. S. A. The companies are respectively commanded by the following Captains. [Names of the Captains are omitted in the diary.—W. E. C.]

SATURDAY, 10TH.

Five companies came in under command of Lt. Col. Mitchell, forming the 1st Battalion, 2d Regiment. The companies are from Randolph, Capt. H. Jackson; Polk, Robinson; Ray, Hendley; Marion, Smith.

Sunday, 11th October—1846.

A Mr. Wilhoit, Com. E, 2 Regiment, died this morning—also on the 10th, Samuel Blunt of Boone Company—both interred on the morning of the 11th—Express from California—Capt. Frémont, Governor of California—American flag in Monterey—Commodore Stockton—Gen. Kearny with 1000 men pushing foward. The rest will return to Santa Fé.

Monday, 12th.

The Platte Company, Capt. I. Morin, arrived, & also 1 company of Mormons—nothing new.

Tuesday, 13th.

Express to Fort Leavenworth—Eutaw chiefs came to hold a council with Col. Doniphan—50 in number.

Wednesday, 14th.

The Chiefs of the Navahoes sent Col. Doniphan word that they would come in and make a treaty of peace—Moved to the "Grazing Encampment"—ordered to march against the Navahoes on the 20th—12 Provision wagons arrived & 12 more expected to-morrow (15th).

Thursday, 15th.

Completed our trip to the Galesteo Encampment.

Friday, 16th.

Remained in camp—cold & windy—at night went over into the tall forest with Thomas McCarty—built a large fire & spread our blankets on the ground.

Saturday, 17th.

Remained in camp—hunted horses—shot ducks—amused ourselves.

Sunday, 18th.

Remained in camp—Provisions arrived, 40 wagons—about this time Mormons left for California.

Monday, 19th.

Nothing new—under marching orders—Man killed in bed with another person's wife—horribly mangled.

THE HUGHES DIARY.

TUESDAY, 20TH.

Remained in camp—commissary trains arriving every day—Campbell has 900 head of cattle on the Mora. [Col. John P. Campbell, founder of Springfield, Mo.—W. E. C.]

WEDNESDAY, 21ST.

[No entry made on this day.—W. E. C.]

THURSDAY, 22D.

Edmond Hopper, of the Polk company, died.

FRIDAY, 23D.

Daniel Jacobs, of Benton, died—18 new graves in the American Burial Ground.

SATURDAY, 24TH.

A train of 11 wagons came into Santa Fé—A Mr. Lane like to die—I & Neally stayed in Galisteo.

SUNDAY, 25TH.

Twelve Provision wagons came in—found oxen at Galisteo—night spent at Galisteo—domestic habits of the New Mexicans.

MONDAY, 26TH.

Left the Grazing Encampment for our excursion against the Navahoes—Camped near Galisteo—3 companies, H, B, & C.

TUESDAY, 27TH.

Marched 7 miles & encamped on the west side of the Rio Galisteo.

WEDNESDAY, 28TH.

Cold & snowing—horse lost—marched 15 miles to the spring on the Chihuahua Road—news that our traders are taken by the Mexicans.

THURSDAY, 29TH.

Marched 12 miles into the bottom of the Rio Grande, 6 miles below Santo Domingo.

FRIDAY, 30TH.

Marched 8 miles down the Rio Grande to Sandico & encamped. Rain during the night. News that Gen. Wool has taken Chihuahua with 6000 men & no fight.

Saturday, 31st.

Marched about 12 miles & encamped on the Rio Del Norte, 8 miles above Albuquerque—cold—Election for 3rd Lt. in Company C—Thos. Ogden elected—Thos. McCarty 2nd Sargent—nothing of interest.

SCENE NEAR ALBUQUERQUE.

Sunday, 1st Nov.

Marched 8 miles to Albuquerque & crossed the Rio Del Norte, & encamped in a rich bottom on the west side. Lt. Noble of the U. S. A. with 20 men left here—the rest under Bogwin gone to El Paso—news that the Navahoes have worsted Major Gilpin.

Monday, 2d.

Col. Doniphan & Staff left for Cibolleta—10 miles, came to La Pueblo—Ladies look fairer & politer—Grass good—sand hills—horses exchanged for mules—geese & swans—health of the Army good—2 of Col. Price's men died in Santa Fé—At Isleta the Pueblos had a war dance over the scalps of 2 Navahoes.

Tuesday, 3d.

Moved camp 2 miles down the river—went over to the little town Peralta—laid by.

Wednesday, 4th.

Moved down the river 6 miles & camped in a cottonwood grove—Teams in bad condition—was sick.

THURSDAY, 5TH.

A singular kind of bird was taken on the west side of the Rio Del Norte by the soldiers, called by the Spaniards Guianetta—it is speckled, has a top-not, long tail, straight black legs, is about the size of a crow, & is remarkably swift on foot—the soldiers took a fine chase after it—Remained in camp on the river.

FRIDAY, 6TH.

Moved on slowly down the River 8 miles & encamped opposite San Tomé—Wood is a great object with us—Difficulties occur between the Spaniards & American soldiers for fuel—wood, water, &c., are the gifts of Nature—these are the only things we take without money.

SATURDAY, 7TH.

Cannon firing last night. Day warm—heavy frost—Layed by in camp—Quartermaster at Albuquerque procuring flour, Beef, sheep, &c.—Prospect of a treaty with the Navahoes.

SUNDAY, 8TH.

Rain, snow, &c.—deep snow in Sierra Blanco—cold—lying by.

MONDAY, 9TH.

Fair weather—marched 8 miles & encamped near Rico's on the Del Norte, where there were a marriage & then a Fandango—Bought wood of the Rico—this put a stop to the hooking process—Spaniards are very friendly—furnished with various articles of food—chickens, cheese, molasses, melons, corn, meal, Flour, &c.—Fared well.

TUESDAY, 10TH.

Marched 5 miles & encamped in a beautiful cottonwood grove—Saltpetre flows on the surface of the earth, a sure indication of rich soil—weather fair—heavy frosts—sunny days—most of the timber on the west side of the river.

WEDNESDAY, 11TH.

Remained in camp—Traded my horse for a mule—fair sunny weather—waiting the return of Col. Doniphan.

THURSDAY, 12TH.

Made a march of 15 miles & overtook the commissary Teams—

Saltpetre on the surface of the ground—news that the Spaniards are forming Companies to rebel against us under pretense of fighting the Navahoes—La Hoya & Hoyeta on the east side opposite to this camp—weather fair, River low—fordable.

Friday, 13th.

Remained in camp—cartridges distributed—orders to sleep on our arms—fear of an attack by the Spaniards.

Saturday, 14th.

Remained in camp—The regulars passed up to Albuquerque under Capt. Bogwin—on their march down the river at or near Isleta they charged upon 60 or 70 Navahoes & killed 2 of them & took an immense quantity of stock from them—They however took off one Spanish woman & 5 children. This was near the 1st November.

Sunday, 15th.

Remained in camp—fair—news that 2 Mexican Gentlemen had formed an agreement to rob the Traders.

Monday, 16th.

Some part of the mail arrived late at night—various rumors afloat of Taylor's Army.

Tuesday, 17th.

Very cold and disagreeable—still in camp—tents a poor protection against inclemency of the weather.

Wednesday, 18th.

Morning fair—left camp & pursued our march down the River 12 miles, over lofty sand hills, & across a great many Jornadas or sand creeks—encamped for the night in the finest grove of cottonwood I had beheld since leaving Missouri—here the bluffs close in on either side almost to the water's edge.

Thursday, 19th.

Remained in camp—fair—Drew provisions for 11 days to commence on the 20th—Manlius Branham, one of the Traders, came into camp to inform the commanding officer of the state of the Traders—They have thrown their wagons together, forming a corral or kind of breastwork—1500 men are said to be on their march to meet the traders & take possession of their goods & persons—They sunk their wagons in the sand.

Friday, 20th.

To-day 2nd Lt: Jas. G. Snell, of Company H, died in a little town 8 or 9 miles back. Capt. Rogers, Lt. Snell, & 2 other sick men were left at La Hoya de Cibolleta some 4 or 5 days ago—it is hard enough to die at home where all the attentions of friends can be bestowed; but it is truly hard to die thus, away from all comfort & solace in hour of utmost need—A great uproar took place in camp at supper; two fights on hands at the same time; Co. B.

Saturday, 21st.

Most of the officers in all of the Companies & the whole of Co. H went back [to] La Joya to attend the funeral of Lt. Snell—he was buried with the honors of war—Capt. Rogers is still unwell—About 50 of the Mormons on their way back to Santa Fé or Ft. Pueblo on the Arkansas—they have some sick with them.

Sunday, 22d.

Moved off for Soccorro, which is about 15 miles, & encamped in a fine bottom below the town—fared well—Soccorro is situated on the west side of the River & east of a lofty Range of mountains that overlook the town & is covered with perennial snows—This is a peak of the Sierra De Mimbres. Above town there is a rich bottom of considerable extent.

Monday, 23d.

Marched 12 miles & encamped in a fine cottonwood grove—we passed Gentry's Train of wagons to-day—he has the largest train ever brought from the U. S.—here we have plenty of grass & water & wood. About tattoo we were aroused from our repose by the sudden appearance in camp of a Spaniard sent by the Traders, with a letter addressed to the Captain Grande requesting that we would march as quick as possible to the relief of the Traders—they expect to be attacked by a hostile force of 1500—early next morning 2 white men came in announcing the same fact—The traders are in the greatest consternation—The Volunteers began to clean up their guns, &c.

Tuesday, 24th.

This morning we put off in hot haste, wound up to the highest expectation of having a battle with the Mexicans—By 4 o'clock we were encamped in a fine cottonwood grove near Fray Crystobal, the very spot on which [the] Texan prisoners were encamped by Salasar 5 years ago—here we understood that there was no truth in the express sent us the previous evening.

Wednesday, 25th.

Remained in camp—Lt. Lee starts back to Headquarters—all the Traders ordered to one point—Fair weather—cold nights—in the vicinity of the White Mountain Apaches—River covered with running ice.

Thursday, 26th.

Remained in camp—visited the Traders' Corral—they are strongly fortified—they number 300 to 400 in all—they corralled upon this intelligence—2 spies taken were on their way from the Paso to the Valley of the Del Norte—they represented that 700 Mexicans were on their way to rob the Traders—2 other Spaniards were caught going down, having a great many letters in their possession from the Priests, Ricos & other men of influence, to the authorities of Chihuahua & Mexico, & accusing Armijo of arrant cowardice, &c.

Friday, 27th.

Yesterday the old shepherd we had employed took occasion to leave & take a good mule with him—other Spaniards left us & 17 government mules left with them—873 sheep were driven off either by the Spaniards employed to herd them or by the Navahoes—2 men, Robert Spears & James Stewart, followed the trail of the sheep & overtook them, but as they had no arms the villains fell upon them & killed them—one was pierced with 13 wounds, the other with 6 or 7 —the arrows were broken & the barbed heads left in the wounds— Their heads were mashed with rocks most brutally—Their clothes were stripped off them & only a part of them taken—They were both buried in the same grave, on the west bank of the Del Norte, under the bower of a small cottonwood tree—This grove is not far from Fray Crystobal & just below the crossing of the Del Norte above the Jornada.

Saturday, 28th.

Remained quiet in camp—Branum, Trader, announced to us that there [are] Englishmen, supposed to be spies, in their camp—the Captain went down to see them, & if they looked suspicious, to take them, but they returned without having seen them.

Sunday, 29th.

Rain—Lt. L. B. Sublett & 38 men that went in pursuit of the Indians returned without having seen anything of the villains—their mules gave out—they found no water—7 or 8 sheep were found in the chase—Roughest country perhaps in New Mexico—There are some fine groves of pine & oak in these deep valleys.

Monday, 30th.

Express sent Lt. Lee, commissary, at Albuquerque—The Del Norte is about 200 yards wide at this point—some signs of beaver—song & jokes go the rounds—Smoking & cigars—lounging, sleeping & reading—nothing of consequence occurred.

Tuesday, 1st December.

Remained in camp—A strong gale of wind blew constantly from the mountains—cold & disagreeable—calm at night.

Wednesday, 2d.

Fair & clear—Gentry & Cufford passed us with their train, 45 wagons. Most of the Mexican & English Traders have dismissed their American drivers, in conformity to the instructions of the Governor of Chihuahua, & procured Spanish ones in their places, so as to go in free of duty—The American Traders refused to do the same.

Thursday, 3d.

Fair & warm—Visited the Trading Caravan—I think all except the American Traders have concluded to go on & rely upon the statements of the British Agent. Traders impatient to get on—The same restless spirit manifested in our camp—12 Indians seen on the Del Norte.

Friday, 4th.

This morning Lt. T. H. Ogden with 24 men was dispatched to the Jornada with instructions not to permit the Trading Caravan to go on to El Paso, & also carrying a letter from the commandante of the camp forbidding either English, American, or Mexicans to drive their Teams any further.

Saturday 5th.

Being posted out as a sentinel last night, & while on guard I discovered by the glimmering moonlight 3 Mexicans making their way towards the American camp. I hailed them—they stopped and advanced to me—They proved to be friendly—They had met Gen. Kearny in the Apache country & he had pressed their mules (15) into the service & given them a check on Uncle Sam—they had a sealed package to Capt. Riche at Santa Fé—About 4 o'clock P. M. a personal rencounter took place between two young men of the same mess, Messrs. John D. Lard & Benj. W. Marsh, in which the latter shot the former with a pistol directly through the chest. Whether the wound will prove mortal remains yet to be seen—It is a most lamentable affair, having grown out of rough joking, &c.

Towards night a terrible gale of wind swept from the Sierra De Mimbres—cold—Rain, &c.

Sunday, 6th.

Calm but cloudy—peace & quiet in camp—prospect for Mr. Lard to recover—no news; Remained [in] camp.

Monday, 7th.

To-day we have been in the service 6 months. We have taken N. Mexico. The 1st Regiment is much scattered, & a good many have died—Snow & Rain—in camp still—no news from the Express—Provisions scarce—Sheep being stolen cuts short our rations—we will be under the necessity of pressing some 3 to 500 sheep in the course of 2 or 3 days—only 11 beeves on hand.

Tuesday, 8th.

The commandante sent 18 more men to assist Lt. Ogden in detaining the Caravan of Traders, a part of whom, the English & Mexicans, were disposed to resist his authority—cold in the morning & pleasant towards 12—Our Stock are driven every day to the mountains to graze, under a strong guard—The grass is good—Our Sutler not being present, many of the men procured supplies of clothing of some of the Traders—Arrival of Major Gilpin & 2 companies—death of Adjt. Butler at Cibolleta.

WEDNESDAY, 9TH.

Very sick with cholic—Capt. Reid arrived—Brought U. S. mail —we were much delighted to hear from the U. S.—no paper mail— Capt. Reid's Company Drew pay a few days since, not having received $42 at the Fort.

THURSDAY, 10TH.

Learned that H. H. Hughes' Brother had been very ill for 40 days in the Navajo country, & had been hauled as far as Socorro & left there—Although sick at the time & the inclemency of the weather being great, yet I saddled [my] mule & ventured to ride 30 miles to see him—met Col. Doniphan—informed that Major G. M. Butler, Adjt. to the 1st Regt., died on the 26th Nov.—Sent to St. Fé for 100 Artillerists, 10 pieces of cannon & Maj. Clark—Also 60 days' provision—& other troops, &c.—designs to take Chihuahua—General Rendezvous near the "Ruins of Valverde"—Sergeant Major Hinton Resigned, & was elected 1st Lt. of his company instead of Lt. DeCourcy appointed Adjt.

FRIDAY, 11TH.

Lt. Col. Jackson's command arrived in camp—The sick left in Soccorro, the last settlement of note before reaching El Paso, overlooked by a mountain 1900 feet in height—Settled by Renegades.

SATURDAY, 12TH.

Very unwell—lonely & desolate to a sick man—on the 26th Nov. Maj. G. M. Butler died in Cavaro—Wm. Sterne died 30th Sept. in the same place & not far distant. A Mr. C. T. Hopper died some time afterwards.

SUNDAY, 13TH.

Still in Soccorro—sick—Catholic Church—dreary times—nothing of interest occurred—moved camp further down the river for more convenience.

MONDAY, 14TH.

Fair weather—sick; on the mend—Lt. Col. Mitchell & Staff, & Capt. Hudson's company (new-raised) passed through Soccorro to-day.

TUESDAY, 15TH.

One hundred Mexicans went against the Navajoes, by order of Gen. Kearny—They returned with the loss of 9 men on the 14th—

Lt. Abert, Top. Engrs., passed here on his way to the States by way of the Canadian fork—Men came up from Cuvaro—Silas Eniara died in Cuvaro on the 7th.

WEDNESDAY, 16TH.

Fair & fine—nothing of interest—Col. Doniphan moved his camp below the Table Mountain—This is a triangular elevation of singular formation.

THURSDAY, 17TH.

Left Soccorro for the camp—all the Different Detachments ordered into camp. I rode 40 miles with Dr. T. M. Morton & 2 others.

FRIDAY, 18TH.

Moved off to the Jornada & made preparations for the difficult journey—Marched 10 miles & encamped in the Del Norte bottom—informed by Lt. Reed that Wm. Foster, Company A, died at Suna during the Navajo campaign—A man of Company E also died & they had not the means to bury him, & therefore covered his corpse with rocks—An Express sent back to hasten the provision Train & Artillery.

SATURDAY, 19TH.

Traders left & started across the "Great Sand Plain" last night—it is the custom of Travellers to commence this journey at night in order to reach water on the next day—Col. Doniphan starts over at about 11 o'clock—The camp is full of bustle & active preparations this morning—Col. D. has sent 500 men over under Lt. Col. Jackson & Maj. Gilpin & has about 400 with him, including Hudson's newly-raised company—A lofty ridge of Mountains lie parallel with the River, & this makes the Chihuahua Road cross the Desert Plain—Marched 18 miles & encamped on the Plain without wood or water—burnt the palmetta.

SUNDAY, 20TH.

By sunup we were on the march—10 miles we left the main road, & at right angles 6 miles off, pursuing the meanders of a ravine, we found plenty of water in a deep hole in a Rock—Returned to the Road—This is a noted watering place—Marched 15 miles further (37) encamped after night—no food—no fire—no sleep—very cold—An Express from Maj. Gilpin aroused the camp at 3 o'clock A. M.

MONDAY, 21ST.

By dawn we were on the march to relieve Gilpin—Severely cold —no fuel but the palmilla & the grease- or sage-bush—marched 15 miles without breakfast in order to get water, but there was none there—All hands are pushing on—we anticipate a battle at Doñana— We have marched 40 miles without food or water—After a tiresome march of 35 to 40 miles we angled to the right & found water in the River, 3 miles from camp. Here we overhauled a portion of the Traders.

TUESDAY, 22D.

Passed out of the Sand Plain about 3 o'clock & struck the River, much worn & fatigued by the march—we encamped on the Rio Grande in a grove of timber after a march of some 18 miles.

WEDNESDAY, 23D.

Marched 12 miles—passed through Doñana—obtained fruit & other luxuries—high mountains [to] the eastward—Capt. Waldo hurt by a fall from his horse—Spies returned, & brought no information of importance—joined Jackson & Gilpin—Capt. Reid commands the spy or scouting party—men feasted high since passing the Jornada.

THURSDAY, 24TH.

Moved off for the Pass—15 miles—encamped on the River— At this camp we found a dead Mexican, supposed to be the same that one of Capt. Reid's sentinels shot at night 2 days previous— Col. D. sent to the Traders to raise 100 or 150 men to join his Rgt. for the purpose of taking El Paso—very warm—Encamped on the River & the stock much scattered—At least 200 men were straggling along the road on the 25th in the morning.

FRIDAY, 25TH.

A brilliant sun lit up the Christmas morning—After a lively breakfast, in fine glee the troops set off for El Paso—Day warm & pleasant—18 miles, encamped on the bank of the River in open view— While the men were scattered everywhere in search of wood & grass, a cloud of dust was seen down the Road—in a moment the advance guard came running post-haste to the Col. [crying] "that the enemy were upon him"—the bugle sounded—the men were paraded—

cartridges distributed—in the confusion some could not find their flags & fought under any they could see—by this time the enemy had formed a line 2 miles long to flank us right and left—they numbered about 1100 men—2 pieces of artillery—300 Regulars—they were in part dressed in Red uniform, & made quite a cavalier appearance—our numbers were about 600 to 700 men. At the sound of the bugle the Mexicans made the charge. We reserved our fire & when they came in 60 yds we opened upon them a most galling fire—in about 30 minutes the Enemy began to retreat in confusion—the Mexicans lost 40 killed & perhaps twice as many wounded—21 prisoners—8 of the Regt. were slightly wounded—this was a Christmas frolic—we took a sound night's rest after the battle—the men & officers all behaved gallantly.

Saturday, 26th.

Buried the dead—Administered to the wounded—Marched in perfect order, the provision train in rear—A strong rear & advanced guard—flankers—15 miles—pitched camp at a salt lake near the Pass—2 false alarms—great excitement—men prompt—Col. sent Expresses to the Traders & Artillery.

Sunday, 27th.

To-day the troops made an imposing appearance—5 miles to the Pass; met a deputation with a white flag—tidings of peace—Rugged road 8 miles to the town—fine vineyards, orchards & fruits of all sorts—Ripe apples, Dried peaches, fresh pears—took peaceable & undisputed possession of the city—Encamped in Town—Warm & pleasant.

Monday, 28th.

Remained in camp—high winds—driven sands—citizens deserted the place—Governor Trias' Proclamation that the Americans were Infidels, heretics, Barbarians, &c. Released 3 men from prison—Pollard, Hutcherson & Hudson—who had been incarcerated five months, informed against by Graham, a Scotchman.

Tuesday, 29th.

Warm—Commenced a search for public arms—invoice of corn, wheat, &c—7 wagons taken by Lt. Sublett—An abundance of ammunition, arms, guns, spears, powder, cannons & canister shot—the search was made general—citizens treated kindly.

WEDNESDAY, 30TH.

Continued the search—2 wagon-loads ammunition discovered 4 miles below, a rich supply, indeed—Capt. Reid's cavalry sent to the Presidio—the arms & ammunition deposited in a public house, for the use of army.

THURSDAY, 31ST.

Cold & windy—Remained in camp—Sent a wagon after one additional load of ammunition. We now have an abundance of ammunition on hand—Major Gilpin & the 2 companies that went with him to the Presidio returned & report that from 2 to 400 Mexicans are within 75 miles of us—that they are fleeing from Gen. Wool. Took some ammunition & one cannon at the Presidio.

FRIDAY, JANUARY 1ST, 1847.

Troops in El Paso—cold & windy—Piquet Guard created an alarm. The companies drawn up in battle array—they displayed a dreadful front. Discovery of one more wagon-load of ammunition—the Colonel has now in his possession of the enemy's stores, 20,000 pounds of ammunition, 4 pieces of canon, 2 wall pieces, 500 stand of arms, 400 lances, & some of their colors—This is the Richest fruit valley in Mexico—Moved our quarters into town.

SATURDAY, 2D.

More pleasant—General Drill—Traders have all arrived & are making small sales—plaza publica fortified by wagons. The army feast highly upon the fine fruits of the place. The Colonel intends pushing on to Chihuahua as soon as his Artillery arrives at this City.

SUNDAY, 3D.

Windy & cool—Church & mass—Wrote to Missouri—Inhabitants not yet recovered from their fright—The Dragoons did not stop their precipitate retreat until they reached Chihuahua—As they passed here they levied upon all the mules & horses in the place—the Mexican Soldiers treated the El Pasenios worse than we, their conquerors—Col. sent an express for the Artillery & the Provision Train.

MONDAY, 4TH.

Thos. Caldwell, Interpreter & Guide for the Regiment, started for Santa Fé & Independence—Troops in fine condition—wounded recovering.

Tuesday, 5th.

Took an interesting ramble through town—fine fruits & wine—kind Treatment—the Mexicans recovering from their fright—Col. D. sent men up to the falls of the River to repair the Mexican's mills. The Army abundantly supplied. The Mexicans had a breastwork raised at the falls on the west side, supposing the Regiment would make its entrance through the Pass at that point—Strict Drill.

Wednesday, 6th.

Fine & fair weather—Capt. Stephenson & about 100 men, & the Commissary Train came up—Sick men, that had recovered in the Hospital, also arrived—the Square like a market place, & the scene of perpetual gambling, monte-dealing, chuck-luck &c—Spaniards & American soldiers block up the streets at monte-dealing.

Thursday & Friday, 7th & 8th.

Time passed without any remarkable incident—Weather fair & Pleasant—City Rambles—City full of bustle & trade—the merchant Traders busy &c—Pasanos well pleased with the conduct of the American Army. One prisoner taken by the guard states that there is a Mexican army at Caryzal—Col., suspecting that an express might be sent by the Paseneans to the Army at Caryzal, sent out a scout under two Lts. to intercept it; they returned & brought 3 prisoners, among whom was Ortiz the Cura or Chief priest of El Paso—Officers had a wine party.

Saturday, 9th.

Pleasant & fair—nothing of interest occurred except the officers had a rich Fandango.

Sunday, 10th.

Fair & warm. General drill on horse-back & inspection of arms. Charging with the Sabre—Church at the Catholic Meeting house—Traffic not stopped for Sunday. Capt. Hudson sent with 20 men down to the Presidio & further to reconnoitre the position of the enemy. Citizens of the town & families returning to their houses—some good looking women, &c—A Newmexican taken up by Capt. Reid; states that a Revolution is on foot in Santa Fé; that 3 others (officers) came down with him by the Rio Sacramento from San Migueil. Also 2 Soldiers from the Army of Chihuahua deserted &

came up to the Pass to see about their families—heard at Caryzal that the Americans had taken the Pass.

MONDAY, 11TH.

Fair & cold—Krenshaw appointed Sergeantmajor on the 9th, instead of John Palmer removed. Capt. Hudson failing to apprehend Manuel Pino, of New Mexico, the Col. Permitted 18 of us to go on foot, with side arms, & continue the search. We parted & 9 went in each squad. Many lively incidents took place—one in particular I will mention; about 12 o'clock P. M. the Squad which I accompanied espied a light at a distance, & heard the sound of music. Supposing there was a Fandango, we went towards the light, but a large saque interrupted our progress. We however effected a passage over the canal, & tapped at the door of the house—the door was opened:— we entered the family apartment peaceably as possible, but they were badly frightened at the appearance of 9 soldiers, armed "cap-a-pie," at such an unusual time of the night. There was one room still not opened, & observing that the old lady, & young man, posted themselves at the door, one of our number took a lighted candle & made as tho' he would enter—The old lady & son made the most strenuous opposition to it. As we could not speak the Spanish nor they the English language we were mutually confused. We were led either to believe that the Mexican, for whom we were searching, was concealed in that room. We insisted—they refused—at length they made us understand that the young ladies were in that room, & we, admiring the spirit of the young man in defending the chastity of his sisters, as no doubt he supposed, against midnight ruffians, peaceably withdrew. These things occurred at "Casa Grande" of Dr. Morales—We found nothing of the Mexican, Manuel Peno.

TUESDAY, 12TH.

Fair & pleasant—Continued our search until 12 o'clock—Drill & Sabre exercises—living & feasting highly. Francisco employed to interpret. Rubedeau, & Thos. Caldwell & Collins[1] were severally interpreters in the Regiment. No news.

NOTE 1.—Under date of November 27, 1906, Edward J. Glasgow writes me from Governor's Island, New York, about Collins as follows:

"James L. Collins was living in Chihuahua when I first went there. He came from Boonville, Mo. While the war was going on he was arrested as a spy

Wednesday, 13th.

Still pleasant & Fair—nothing of interest occurred—not many days ago the Col. borrowed money of Mr. Samuel Owen, for the use of the Quartermaster Department. It is said that one woman was killed in the battle of Brazito. She had followed her lover thither. Three men to be court-martialed for ravishing a Mexican woman. The three men belong to Hudson's Company.

Thursday, 14th.

Nothing of interest occurred—Courtmartial in session—Quartermaster continues to redeem the checks on the Government. This gives the Mexicans confidence in the Solvency of our Government.

Friday, 15th.

Wind exceedingly boisterous—The sport of gambling run so high that Col. Doniphan had to put a stop to it. Camp quiet—of nights the men institute mock-tryals by jury & fine those who have been guilty of the slightest misdemeanor—Certain Mexicans taken prisoner report that troops are flocking to Chihuahua to oppose us—Wool gone to Durango. Novel occurrences at a fandango—negroes took the shine & danced with the belle of El Paso.

Saturday, 16th.

Warm & pleasant as the Spring. Drill kept up daily—John Leland died in the hospital at El Paso of an inveterate attack of Typhoid Fever—he was buried in the Cemetery on Sunday the 17th with martial honors—the ground in the cemetery has been, no doubt, dug over at least a dozen times.

Sunday, 17th.

Arrival of the Sutler—news from the Artillery—men nearly naked & compelled to pay high prices for clothing—warm & sunny—Inspection of Arms on Sunday—Cavalry charges & sabre exercises—

---

at El Paso and brought to Chihuahua for trial. Mr. Pomeroy, of Lexington, Mo., employed a man to throw a rope over the prison-wall one dark night, by which Collins climbed over. He went to the livery stable, took out his mule and escaped, and met Sterling Price's force coming down for the last battle of the war, where General Trias was defeated at Santa Cruz, sixty miles south of Chihuahua. He was afterwards made depository of Government money at Santa Fé, and was found one morning dead from a pistol-shot in his office, with the safe door open."

Quiet prevails in camp—Algier & Gentry, two Traders, injudiciously moved their trains some 10 miles below out of the protection of the Army & thereby lost 280 head of their mules by the Apaches. They will pursue the villains into the mountains.

Monday, 18th.

Weather fine & fair—Spring is opening upon us—Capt. Hughes & 10 men who had been left sick at Socorro came into El Paso.

Tuesday, 19th & 20th (Wednesday).

Priests visits Col. Doniphan—the Colonel heard of his Artillery—fine weather—nothing of interest.

Wednesday, 20th.

On the evening of the 19th Lts. Hinton & Gordon, the latter acting quartermaster, arrived from Santa Fé. Gave us an account of the embarrassments & delays occasioned by the indecision of Col. Price, who countermanded the order of Col. Doniphan, & refused to send the cannon until he heard of the battle of the 25, on account of a rebellion set on foot by Gens. Otees, Salazar, & Surtuliti. Their object was to attack the different camps of the Americans on the 25th & thus recover the Department of New Mexico. the Secret was let out to Gov. Bent, by a woman of loose habits—Thus the conspiracy was detected & crushed. Col. Price has 15 of the ringleaders in prison. Cannon left Santa Fé on the 8th Jan. I received the following account from the hospital (viz)—

Wheeler,	Co. (D)	died October	18,	1846
Jett,	" E	" "	29	"
A. Cox,	" C	" Nov.	30	"
Maddox,	" H	" Dec.	13	"
Jones,	" B	" "	25	"

Col. Doniphan received a letter from Major Clark of the Artillery highly commending the gallantry & courage of the Vols. on the 25th in the battle of Brazito—The Colonel read the letter to the regiment assembled, & three cheers were given to Maj. Clark's patriotic & animating communication. He is a true-hearted native Missourian.

Thursday, 21st.

Spent last night with an old Castilian—fared well—has 100 gals. wine—Met Capt. Hudson's company & Lt. Col. Mitchel on their way to the Prasidio—Col. Doniphan sent mules back to Doniana to facilitate the progress of the Artillery, under Lt. Miller & 24 men—James Finley of Clay, a young man, aged 21 years, of unexceptionable morals, of most exemplary conduct in the Army, & of fine talent, died, & was buried in the Cemetery at El Paso. He fought gallantly at the battle of Brazito—his corpse was decently dressed & wound in the Flag of his country & buried with military honors—His effects are in the hands of his friends & the Captain—

> Peace to the shades of the virtuous brave,
> Who gallantly bore the perils of war;
> Who found an humble, yet honored grave,
> From kindred, home, & country far.

Lt. Lea arrived towards night-fall with 5 or 6 men & brought news of the battle of Monterey—Capt. Hudson's Company went to the Presidio.

FRIDAY, 22, 23, 24.

A Mr. Dyer of Co. (B) died in the hospital & was buried in the Cemetery—Capt. Hudson's Company returned from the Presidio—Wrote to Secretary of War.

MONDAY, 25TH.

Fine & fair weather. Capt. Hudson's man that pressed the soap into the Service. Spaniard whipped for stealing a handkerchief—Drill—Camp Jokes &c—Thos. Forsythe, Expressman, arrived from Santa Fé; just one month after the Battle of Bracito.

TUESDAY, 26TH.

Fair weather—Teams sent back to lighten the loads of the Commissary Teams. Jordan Hackley, a very fine young man from Howard, died in the hospital, & was burried on the morning of the 27th—An appropriate Service was read over the grave by Lt. Hinton on the morning of the 27th. James Rogers, a Yankee from Chihuahua, a cold & indifferent kind of man, suspected as being a spy in the employ of Gov. Trias, was taken up by the piquet Guard. Retained in custody.

WEDNESDAY, 27TH.

Fair & Pleasant. Nothing unusual brewing—The quartermaster Department of this little Army alone costs Uncle Sam 10 thousand Dollars every 30 days—Col. Doniphan by order put a stop to horse

& mule racing & Fandangoes. Two Mexican officers returned from Caryzal & brought before the Colonel; one of them had been wounded in the battle of Bracito.

Arrival of Major Clarke—news of the Artillery—expecting a battle—wiping guns, grinding Sabres & issuing 20 rounds of cartridges—Mexicans not well satisfied—Many malcontents.

Thursday, 28th.

Capts. Waldo & Kirker returned from their mountain excursion. Mail & a fuller account of the Battle of Monterey—quiet in camp. Nothing is talked of in camp but the anticipated battle of Chihuahua.

Friday, 29th & Saturday, 30th.

Pleasant—all is quiet—25 yoke of oxen stolen from the commissary teamsters near Donana; 20 yoke from the Mexican Algea.

Sunday, 31st.

General Drill—horses purchased for the use of the artillery. Usual amusements on hand.

Monday, 1st Feb.

Still quietly in camp—in the evening Lt. Hinton received a note from Capt. Waitman requesting him to send some provisions to meet his men, for they were worn down & hungry, as they had traveled day and night since they got the express in the Jornada that 4000 Mexicans were on their march to retake El Paso. Capt. J. C. Reid, Lt. Hinton & myself among others went out to meet & furnish them.

Tuesday, 2d.

Fair & fine—More Teams sent out to assist the Commissary's stores in—About 11 o'clock the cannon had crossed the River & fired a salute of 4 guns. In a few minutes the house-tops were covered with astonished Mexicans, eagerly endeavoring to get a sight of the long expected canones. Lt. Kribben fired a salute to them with the Brass piece taken in the battle of Bracito. (The cannon arrived on Monday.) Ten commissary wagons started off for Chihuahua. Nothing of interest on hand. The Quartermaster purchasing an outfit for the south—Preparations are busily making for the movement.

WEDNESDAY, 3D.

In Company with J. P. Campbell took a trip to the Trading Caravan & remained all night. To day Capt. Hudson's escort to Col. Mitchell passed on down to the presidio. 8 commissary wagons started for Chihuahua—Mitchels Teams on the Road. It is said a Mexican was killed by the Apaches in Socorro (on the island) & the population were entirely indifferent to it—Mezquit & Sage bush—Sandy soil—Warm.

THURSDAY, 4TH.

Made a visit to the Presidio & met with Mitchel's escort—on the North the outer walls are 216 yds, & on the inside 184. The west is 210 yds & the inner 176 yds—Thus:

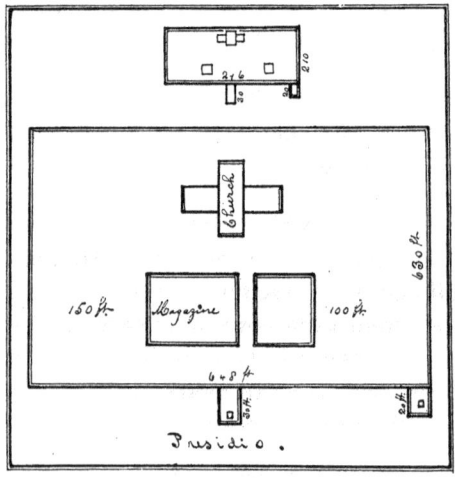

Mr. Chapin discharged in the Presidio on the departure of the Troops.

FRIDAY, 5TH.

Returned from the Prisidio to the town of Socorro & remained with Callisto Alguein. He showed me his private Sanctuary. Here I found the Savior nailed to the cross & the large inscription above *Inri*. The Virgin Mary large as life, a silver dagger in the breast, the images of Saints and household Gods & an infinite variety of Symbolical roses & other Artificial flowers &c—Returned to camp &c—Capt. Stephenson & Waldo with 30 men went to the Presidio to press some mules—The Govt. allows 40$ as the maximum for mules—on the 4th the commissary train got to El Paso. Today the Trains were to leave for Chihuahua—On the 3d Otees & Hacus were arrested & carried before the Col. for having received a courier from Chihuahua. Cufford & Gentry[2] left the Train & struck for Zacatacas.

SATURDAY, 6TH.

Capt. Stephenson obtained 65 yoke of cattle. A portion of them returned to their owners, & 20 to 50 kept. A great many prisoners taken on suspicion of sending information to Chihuahua. Among them Ramond Ortiz & Jaquez. In an affray Lt. Wells was stabbed by Lt. Barnett.[3] The officers mostly have been too Licentious in their conduct.

SUNDAY, 7TH.

Church as usual. Two Artillerists of Capt. Weightman's Company arrived, bringing news that Gov. Bent & all the Americans in Taos were assassinated. Boguin ordered to march against Taos. Information through Mexicans that Gen. Taylor is taken by Santa Anna's Gen. Urea & 2000 men with him. 6000 Americans killed & 10,000 Mexicans. The last of the baggage Train came in to-day. Order No. 80 to march at 8 o'clock on the 8th for Chihuahua. John Clark, of Company E, died in the hospital of Typhoid Fever. Capt. Kirker & Lt. Graves brought in 6 Mexicans as prisoners, hostages for the delivery of oxen.

MONDAY, 8TH.

The whole Army, Artillery, Escort, Volunteers, hospital Train, & commissary Train, a promiscuous host, set out under double colors, presenting a most martial sight. Major Clarke presented the Camps with a "Guidon" each—Curate & other Mexican prisoners—Camp above the Presidio. Water salt. Grass dry.

TUESDAY, 9TH.

The Army is to march in the following order—1. Artillery. 2. Ammunition wagons. 3. Volunteers. 4. Mitchell's Escort between the Battalions. 5. Prisoners Escort. 6. hospital Train. 7. Commissary Train. 8. Caravan—9. Rear Guard. An Advance Guard.

NOTE 2.—Should be Kerferd & Jenkin. See Report No. 458, 30th Congress—First Session, House of Representatives, to accompany Bill No. 388, p. 48.

NOTE 3.—See Meredith T. Moore's account of this affair, page 387.

All set in motion to-day—Encamped at Mitchell's camp just below the Presidio—To-night an express came from Santa Fé to Major Clarke to halt the Artillery. Battle in N. Mexico. 35 Mexicans killed, & 40 prisoners—3 Americans killed & Col. Price wounded.

Wednesday, 10th.

Bitter cold—Remained in Camp—Lt. Gordon purchased 85 yoke of oxen—Ortiz proposed to send a Mexican & an American to Chihuahua to negotiate an exchange of prisoners—Doniphan refused —Yesterday Capt. Kirker & 8 men sent out to espy—Ortiz & the Father disputed in council before the Battle of Brazito—The former for war, the latter for peace—The Father advised Col. D. to take with him to Chihuahua a certain suspicious character from the Presidio, otherwise he would excite the people to Rebellion—The Col. proposes organizing the Traders into Companies, to render their force efficient.

Thursday, 11th.

The whole Army & caravan moved off at an early hour—Commissary Teams very inefficient. Mr. Houke, Trader, Lost 85 to 90 oxen by the Apaches. Lt. Hinton, Mr. H., & 35 men went in pursuit of them. Towards evening they recovered all except 18 head— Lt. Hinton, Houke, F. Letcher & M. Jacks still pursued on & overhauled the savages and killed one of them, got 2 mules & the remainder of the cattle. They followed them 50 miles & rejoined the Army on the 12th. Bank of the Rio Grande—The army presented quite an interesting view.

Friday, 12th.

Warm & pleasant—All went on well—Lt. Hinton Returned & Brought An Apache Scalp—A company of Traders organized by order of Col. Doniphan & James Glasgow elected Captain on the 11— The bottom is heavily timbered with cottonwood—River deep and narrow.

Saturday, 13th.

Nights cold—days warm—making preparations to cross the Jornada; threw away all canister filled with copper slugs—the powder burnt & canister wasted—Mexican powder not good—Tried in the howitzer—Lt. Col. Mitchel, Capt. Reid & Lt. Choteau & 16 men sent back to bring up the Train of Mr. Harmony & Porus[4]—pretended that the Apaches had stolen their mules. Col. Mitchel made them produce them—had a long conversation with Ortiz in relation to Mr. Gizot's proposition to put the son of Louis Philip on the throne of Mexico. Rather be conquered by a sister Republic—found him intelligent & entertaining. Mr. Maxwell, Company F, & J. A. Wills Company C died & were interred on the morning of the 14th—Camp well regulated—Guard strong.

SUNDAY, 14TH.

Fair & bright—the whole Army moved off across the Jornada—This sand Plain is 60 miles over & we enter it 50 miles below El Paso—badly supplied with water—Some of the men filled their sabre scabbards with water—Grass fine—Traders are organized into two Companies, under command of Capts. Glasgow[5] & Skillman & Major Samuel Owens—Terrible work to get the trains of wagons along—Marched until 10 at night—Jolly songs & merry glee went the rounds—camped on a small drain.

MONDAY, 15TH.

Road sandy & heavy—Strong Guard out in Front & Rear. Mountains on both hands—no timber—immensity of prickly pears. A gentle shower last night refreshed us much—passed through a cañon or gorge in the mountains to the westward—Lt. Gordon & Mr. Collins, interpreter, with 12 men met Capt. Kirker with 8 men at the cañon & they all (23) proceeded to Caryzal & took possession of it in the name of our Govt. The Alcalde made a written article of sub-

---

NOTE 4.—The firm of Harmony was "P. Harmony, Nephews & Co." The Harmony train was in this instance in charge of Manuel X. Harmony. It was a Spanish firm doing business in New York city and trading to Mexico over the Santa Fé Trail. Manuel X. Harmony was a Spaniard. He filed a claim in Congress for damages on account of the action of Colonel Doniphan in relation to the Traders, and the whole matter is reviewed and set out in the Report referred to in the note giving the correct style of the firm of Kerferd & Jenkin—Report No. 458, 30th Congress—First Session, House of Representatives, to accompany Bill No. 388.

Porus, as it is in the text, should be J. Calistro Porras. See page 48 of the Report above referred to.

NOTE 5.—Edward J. Glasgow was a merchant long engaged in the trade with Mexico. He was born at Belleville, Illinois, in 1820, but in 1827 his father moved to St. Louis, which city has ever since been his home. In 1840 he went to Mazat-

mission to Lt. Gordon, throwing themselves upon the Generosity of the American Army—Received a large mail by one of the Artillery—numerous papers, etc. in the midst of the Jornada or sand-plain, 2 days from the Del Norte & no prospect of water for 36 hours—news refreshed us as much as a fountain.

lan, Mexico, and there engaged in business, his goods coming around Cape Horn in a vessel belonging to his firm. In 1843 he closed up his business at Mazatlan and went to Chihuahua, where he formed a partnership with Dr. Henry Connelly. (See the sketch of Dr. Connelly.) Mr. Glasgow has spent some time at Governor's Island, New York, from which place he has written me a number of

EDWARD J. GLASGOW.

Captain of the Traders' Battalion. Long a merchant in Chihuahua. Partner of Dr. Henry Connelly. Portrait made from a photograph in the possession of his great-niece, Miss Eleanor Glasgow Voorhis, of New York city.

letters in the year 1906 about matters connected with Doniphan's Expedition. These letters are very valuable and have been of much assistance in this work. The Traders' Battalion was honorably discharged at Chihuahua by Colonel Doniphan. The men who served in it were always wrongfully treated by the Government, no pensions being allowed them, the Department of War holding that Colonel Doniphan had no authority to muster into the service of the United States any additional men. But this battalion did noble service for the country, and the only man killed at the battle of Sacramento was its Major and commander.

TUESDAY, 16TH.

At break of day were on the march—dying for water—horse & man parched with thirst—At the first water horse, mule & man vied with each other in drinking out of the same puddles—5000 lbs flour thrown out of commissary Trains & a vast quantity of salt, 2 wagons &c—Teams much worn out—Army & Trains scattered for 20 miles —Arrived at Laguna Encampea—It is reported that 3 battles have been fought in New Mexico, at Bagas, La Canada, & Taos, in which 44 Americans were killed & upward of 250 Mexicans—Capt. Hendly killed & Col. Price wounded—Bent killed &c.—On arriving at the lake one of Capt. Hudson's men, Wm. Talley, just married, drank so exceedingly that he died during the night & was burried by the lake side on the 17th—Providential supply of water to the Army Train— favorable omen, &c.—Tall Rock 2000 feet high west of the lake— Ojo de los patos 2 miles south.

THURSDAY, 18TH.

Moved off to Caryzal, where Lt. Gordon had purchased corn for the animals—Road good—Snow—Stupendous Rock to the right. Caryzal contains about 400 inhabitants—Carrol Hughes resigned— Lost 27 yoke of oxen on the Desert—remained at Caryzal until the 20th.

SATURDAY, 20TH.

Fair & calm—took up the line of march—3 prisoners took last night at Cufford's Train—know nothing—dismissed—Maj. Owens has charge of the entire Train—Mr. Harrison charge of the commissary Train. Fine bold stream waters Caryzal—marched 6 miles—camped —Capt. Kirker, our Guide,[6] sent out with 16 men to Encineres & Sacramento to reconnoitre the enemy's position.

SUNDAY, 21ST.

Marched 4 miles & encamped at "Ojo Caliente" & made preparations for another "Jornada"—The stream is bold & about blood

---

NOTE 6.—Under date of November 27, 1906, Edward J. Glasgow, Esq., writing to the author from Governor's Island, New York, says:

"In regard to Mr. James Kirker: He was an Irishman by birth, a large, strong, athletic man, who had been with the fur company for some years among the Indians. He was employed by the State of Chihuahua to drive out the Apaches, and for that purpose employed a number of Delaware and Shawnee Indians. I was told that he received a stipulated sum, $40 each, I think, for the

warm—Lt. Col. Mitchell & Col. Doniphan went to the spring & bathed. Lt. Sublett & myself & others next succeeded—The basin of the spring is 40 yards long, 25 wide & has once been walled in by Puros who had at one time upon his Ranch 31,000 head of stock. Piquet Guard returning created a dust & the Army mistaking it for the Enemy soon formed a line of battle—The Artillery instantly rigged—12 miles—camped on the Desert.

MONDAY, 22D.

Continued the march on the Desert—passed the cañon with snow on either hand—mountains high—2000 ft. Tall—20 miles—encamped on a rocky bank where we found a little water—Cold without food we sank to rest.

TUESDAY, 23D.

Marched 10 miles to the Gyagus Springs. They issue out of the mountain sides in cooling, gushing streamlets—A drove of Antelope shot & all killed—Camped at the lower spring in a deep valley—fine water & Grass—Roads fine—Teams travel fine—mountain sides covered with spar & brilliant stalactites—Marion Robards of Howard died & was burried.

scalps of the men and half-price for those of the squaws and children, and succeeded in ridding the State of the Apache annoyance. He met Doniphan above El Paso and offered his services as scout and guide against the Mexicans. Doniphan accepted the services, but regarded him with suspicion, as he had been living with his family in Chihuahua and employed as above stated; and although he led the scouting parties in advance, men were watching him, ready to put a bullet in him in case of treachery. He proved faithful, however, to the end."

I find the following in *A Campaign in New Mexico with Colonel Doniphan.* By Frank S. Edwards, London, 1848, p. 62:

"The government of Chihuahua at one time set a price on every Apache scalp; it was, I believe, one hundred dollars for a man, fifty dollars for a squaw, and twenty-five dollars for a papoose. This plan was afterwards abandoned; and an Irishman, named James Kirker, was hired, at a high salary, to attempt the extermination of the tribe. This was rather an extensive operation, as they numbered about fifteen thousand. However, he, with a band of Americans and Mexicans, soon made the Apaches fear him. The Mexicans look upon him as almost superhuman; but I have heard from credible authority that his bravery is rather lukewarm, and that his victories have always been achieved through cunning. He has never risked a fight, unless when his own party has greatly outnumbered the Indians, or when he could catch them asleep,—and even then he himself prudently keeps in the background. He joined us the morning after the fight of Bracito, having given up hunting the Indians, in consequence of the Government having forgotten to pay him. He was very useful to us, serving as guide and interpreter during all the time we remained in the country."

WEDNESDAY, 24TH.

Paraded the cavalry companies—set out for the Laguna de Encineres. Road remarkably good—4 spies. Lt. Gordon, Bradford, C. F. Hughes & Henderson returned and reported the Enemy at the lake—14 miles—encamped without water.

THURSDAY, 25TH.

Early, marched to Laguna—high wind—fire in the prairie—dreadful conflagration—water salt—nooned & let fire get out—Escape of the Ammunition wagon—Cannon run into the lake to avoid fire—battle between the Regt. & fire—high wind—dreadful conflagration at night—awful scene—spies, Mr. Collins & Capt. Skillman report 1300 Mexicans, (3 pieces of Art.) on the retreat to Sacramento—Capt. Reid & 25 men went to Encineres & took possession—procured sheep, hogs & beef—men had been without meat 4 days.

FRIDAY, 26TH.

Tremendous high wind—driven sand distressing almost to suffocation—Fire run like a wild tornado—camped on a creek at a Fort, &c.

SATURDAY, 27TH.

Calm & fair—Moved in order, the caravan all in abreast—Capt. Skillman & others took a Spanish spy's horse—Lt. Col. Mitchell, Lt. Sprowls, Lt. Winston & myself & 2 other privates went up to the top of a high hill or mountain with good glasses to espy the Enemy's camp—had a plain view of it—Reported 2800 men—Camped on a lake—Day's march 8 miles.

SUNDAY, 28TH.

Being sanguine of a fight to day, all the arms were put in good condition. The day was fair & hot—200 Mexican horsemen were chased by the advanced Guard, Lt. Sublett—The Caravan marched 4 wagons abreast—The Artillery in the Center, 1st Battalion on the right between the wagons & the 2nd Bat. on the left in the same manner—Reid's select Mounted Company on the right in advance & Capt. Parsons' Mounted Company on the left in advance. The Staff in advance. At 12 the two armies were in plain view of each other—It was now evident the battle must be fought before we could rest—every heart beat with hope—every arm was nerved for the conflict

—Sheared off & crossed the Rio Sacramento above the enemy's camp—Conde with 1000 cavalry dashed down from the fortified heights to oppose us—Cannonading commenced at 900 yards—great destruction—50 minutes firing—Conde retreated behind the redoubts—our army moved on to the attack as follows (viz) Major Clarke's Artillery in the centre. 1st Battalion, Lts. Col. Mitchell & Jackson on the right, 2nd Battalion, Major Gilpin, on the extreme left, & the three select horse companies, Capts. Reid, Parsons, & Hudson, on the left of the artillery—Reid charged first—the improper halt'—carried the battery—all the mounted Comps. dashed into the charge—dismounted comps. followed in order—they routed the Mexicans from all the redoubts—the rout general—slaughter continued until night—300 Mexicans killed—500 wounded, 70 prisoners, 50,000 head sheep, 1500 head cattle, 100 mules, 25 wagons of provisions, 11 pieces of cannon, 6 wall pieces, 100 stands of arms, 100 stands colors &c.—Victory complete—camped on the battle field—lost Major S. Owens & Kirkpatrick—11 others wounded.

MARCH 1ST.

Collected up the spoils—Lt. Col. Mitchell & 150 men, (2 howitzers) took military possession of Chihuahua—camped in the Alamada by Hidalgo's monument. American residents intended to take the city that night if we had not come in—35 Mexicans died of their wounds on the night after the battle, among them Capt. Lopez of Durango—Sentence of death pronounced against all the American

NOTE 7.—This brings up the question of the confusion which resulted from the action of De Courcy in halting the charge. Mr. Edward J. Glasgow, in his letter of the 27th November, says:

"In reply to your other question, it was understood that Captain Reid, who had distinguished himself at the fight on the Christmas previous above El Paso, should lead the charge with one hundred picked men. They were well advanced when Adjutant De Courcy ordered a halt. Captain Reid and some others, not hearing the order, kept on alone, and finding his men had halted, rode back and asked the reason. Upon hearing that De Courcy had ordered them to stop, he exclaimed, 'Well, I order you to charge,' which was gallantly done.

"This circumstance is of course from hearsay, as I was bringing up the four columns of wagons, Major Owens having left me in charge and gone on with Reid. In this charge Major Owens was killed within twenty feet of the breastworks. I think Collins and Kirker were along, but I am not positive."

Mr. Glasgow drew for me a map of the movement of the American army to the right to gain the high ground to the west of the Mexican fortifications, the point from which the attack was made. This map is superior to all others I have examined in its illustration of this movement. It is of such value that I

THE HUGHES DIARY. 105

Residents if they were victorious—first cessation of cannonading victory was announced for the Mexicans—the populace excited—

have made a copy of it, from which it is here reproduced. It gives a clearer view of the battle and makes clearer the accounts found in the official reports than any other map of the battle.

Mr. Glasgow, in sending me the map, wrote as follows:

"The fortifications or earthworks thrown up by the Mexicans extended across the road leading from Santa Fé and El Paso to Chihuahua, and were on

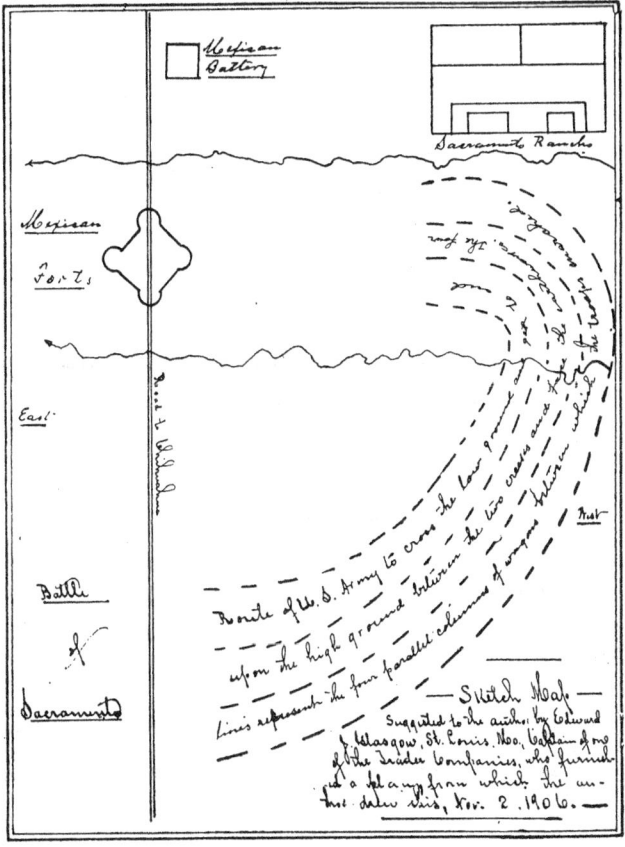

OUTLINE OF PRELIMINARY FORMATION AND MOVEMENT OF THE AMERICAN ARMY AT THE BATTLE OF SACRAMENTO.

knives and staves resorted to by the rabble—Second firing the prisoners revived with hope—at 7 P. M. news of victory reached the city by a courier on the 28th—Talked of mobbing us (150 men).

TUESDAY, 2D.

Lt. Col. Mitchel & Capt. Reid went into different public buildings—Traders came in to rent rooms—2 o'clock P. M. Col. Doniphan with his immense Train of captured cannon & baggage & fluttering colors entered in triumphal procession amidst the resounding cheers of soldiers & Resident Americans—No private property molested or taken for the use of the American Army.

WEDNESDAY, 3D.

Performed the funeral ceremony of Maj. Owens (who was a Catholic) with great pomp—Military honors—Search of public buildings continued—Camp on the hill.

THURSDAY, 4TH.

Search continued—resistance offered by Potts to Lt. Col. Mitchel —refused to give up the keys—Threatened us with his Government —Great excitement—2 howitzers brought to shoot open the door— submitted at length—Gen. Quitty taken prisoner by Col. Jackson & Capt. Hughes—A. A. Kirkpatrick died & was burried with Masonic & military honors—Capt. Weightman & Lt. Hinton with 70 men left for Peral on the night of the 3d—all quiet.

FRIDAY, 5TH.

Moved down into the City & quartered in the Treasury department—(2d Battalion)—1st Battalion remained to guard the cannon —Whipped a thief—Capt. Weightman & Capt. Kirker returned with Gen. Heredia's Rigging.

---

high ground between Sacramento creek and the bed of another dry creek. On arriving within a mile of them Col. Doniphan ordered all the wagons of the traders and army (about 160 in number) to be formed in four parallel columns, about thirty feet apart, and the army placed between them, when they turned off the road and crossed the dry creek nearly a mile to the west, coming up on higher ground, when they turned and faced the enemy. It looked as if the Mexicans thought Col. Doniphan was avoiding a battle and possibly seeking shelter in the buildings and walls of Sacramento Ranch, as they sent out a large body of cavalry to attack. When they came near, our artillery opened fire on them with solid shot and spherical case-shot, some of which burst among the cavalry, causing confusion and a rapid retreat to the main body. Doniphan's forces formed immediately and moved rapidly towards the earthworks under a fire of musketry

Saturday, 6th.

Whipped another thief—Colonel issued his proclamation to the citizens of Chihuahua to be quiet (see proclamation). Nothing of interest.

Sunday, 7th.

Drill 4 hours per day—Singular Idea. American Soldiers drilling in the Capital of the enemy's country. Men not so well off in a city as they are in a camp—Drunk.

Monday, 8th.

Capt. Hudson's Company converted into an Artillery Company. Dr. Connelly sent down to Peral or Parisal to redeem Magoffin & obtain an interview with Trias, &c. & To negotiate a treaty with Trias to allow our merchants to pursue their trade. Citizens excited against the Americans.

Tuesday, 9th.

Embargo laid on Maj. Campbell's operations—Governor Trias concentrating a force below here at Parisal or San Rosalia. Preparations making for departure—Col. Doniphan's official Report makes the Mexican strength as follows—1200 Durango cavalry, 300 Artillerists, 1200 infantry & 1420 Rancheros (4120) American force 924 men & some amateurs.

Sunday, 14th.

Maj. Campbell left for the United States. General Drill on horse back. News that Wool has been defeated by Gen. Santa Anna. Various Rumors.

Monday, 15th & Tuesday, 16th.

First number of the Anglo Saxon, a small paper printed [by] Lt. Kribben, issued. 4 men returned from Parrall who had been prisoners—They say the Mexicans heard that 300 American were marching upon them & they fled to Durango & these four men made their escape from prison. The camp continually excited by Rumors that the Mexicans are rallying to retake Chihuahua.

---

and artillery. On coming near, the Mexicans broke and fled in several directions, pursued by our men, and leaving their artillery and stores behind. The wagon columns kept their formation and moved as rapidly as possible and as near the army as possible, making a kind of moving fortification, as in case of a repulse our troops could have fallen back between the wagons, which could have been corralled into a fort."

Wednesday, 17th.

All is preparation to leave the city. Traders in a state of excitement—Their interest in jeopardy. Viewed the water-works by which the City is supplied with water. The "acequia" is supported by stupendous arches. The acqueduct leads out of the Rio Conchos some miles above the town. The city is entirely surrounded by high mountains.

Thursday, 18th.

Dr. Connelly Returned from Parrall & 3 commissioners with him to make a Treaty & Armstice—Report of the Battle of Augustura; 40 hours fighting—Santa Anna had 20,000 men & 50 pieces of cannon. Taylor 6,000 men & 26 pieces of Artillery. Taylor maintained his ground—Santa Anna lost 1000 men—no farther particulars.

Friday, 19th.

Council of the officers—Vote to go on carried (26 to 6)—the Commissioners as yet have made no proposition of interest.

Saturday, 20th.

Jas. L. Collins & 13 men started on Express to Saltillo & returned on the 23 of April. (See other book)—propositions of the Commissioners denyed or Refused by Col. Doniphan. A general order issued for the command to leave for the Conchos on the 5th April—Artillery & 2d Battalion left on the 6th & went as far as San Pablo & returned on the 9th in consequence of a Communication the Colonel received from Mr. Hicks stating that the Troops from Durango intended to make a descent upon Chihuahua—Apprehension that the expressmen were lost—Gen. order to leave on the 25th & leave the express—Nothing of interest occurred from 5th to the 25th April—Thieves &c.

Monday, 26th April.

Artillery Battalion left on the 25th & the first Battalion on the 26th—Ordered to await at San Pablo for the Rear.

Tuesday, 27th.

City in a tremendous bustle—Merchants in confusion—The Mexican prisoners delivered up to the citizens by order of the Colonel.

THE HUGHES DIARY.

WEDNESDAY, 28TH.

Col. Doniphan & all the Troops & Traders left this morning—Capt. Skillman & 20 men went back to Santa Fé—10 Merchants remained in Chihuahua. Dr. Connelly—Encamped at Rancho Bachimbo.

THURSDAY, 29TH.

Battalion left early—took the Santa Cruz Road—Crossed the Rio San Pedro & encamped at the mills—fine bathing in the Acequia—Rejuvinescing of facts—Pretty women—Rich place—American freighting goods to Chihuahua—Weather hot—1st Battalion left here this morning—Gov. Trias reported that we were killing, Robbing, ravishing, &c—Gordon purchased a fine lot of mules.

FRIDAY, 30TH.

Made an early march & encamped 2 miles from Soucillo on the Rio Conchos.

SATURDAY, 1ST MAY.

Marched early & overtook the 1st Battalion & the Battalion of Artillery at Santa Rosalia. hot—Train moved with great facility.

SUNDAY, 2D.

Lt. Col. Mitchel & a detachment of 27 men under Capt. Pike & 70 under Capt. John W. Reid left this morning for Parras—Regiment encamped 1 mile above Enramada—fine water & grass—Thompson & Henkle died in Chihuahua—Fortifications at Santa Rosalia against Wool.

MONDAY, 3D.

Made an early march—fine rain last night—Traveled briskly—The command encamped in the City of Guajuquilla—Supply of corn &c—population 4000.

TUESDAY, 4TH.

Moved up the River 6 miles to the Hacienda Dolores & remained until 4 P. M. & then started across the Jornada—Scenes and incidents of the march—Sullen clouds &c—Camped on the Desert.

WEDNESDAY, 5TH.

Left at an early hour—Dreadful Dust—dry march—Range mountains on the right—Dwarf mezquite & Governadora—The Guianita

—55 or 60 miles from Guajuquilla to the Ojo Santa Bernada—encamped at the Spring—fine grass & plenty of water—Cañon through the mountain at the Spring—the Alamos & willow—the Oasis.

Thursday, 6th & 7th.

Moved down the Rio Cero Gordo 10 miles—Water plenty—runs N. Easterly—30 miles to Pailaio—This is a small ranch & has a fort on a hill to defend against the Indians—At this place Mitchell expected to surround 50 soldiers—here a system of plunder was commenced upon private property, to which the Colonel put a stop by an order & collected the effects & restored to the owners—Lt. Choteau paid $5 to a lady for damages.

Saturday, 8th.

Left Pailaio early—Road runs South to the Caddenas 24 miles—Very hot—News of Scott's victory over Santa Anna at the Nation Bride [?]—Reported 9 to 11,000 Mexicans killed—Santa Anna retreated, with 6,000 men to the City of Mexico—Took 1 piece of Artillery, a 1 pounder.

Sunday, 9th.

Marched 22 miles to Mapimi—Remarkably hot & dusty—citizens of Mapimi fled—5 smelting furnaces. plenty of corn &c—papers confirming Scott's victory—Gov. Ochoa's proclamation exhorting the citizens to war—Lt. Jackson died & was burried with the honors due to his rank—the Priest and the boys with the white palises & candles & crucifix. the salute of 28 guns—the wreaths & green festoons upon the crosses at the road sides—Chaparral—the valley of the Nasas.

Monday, 10th.

Made a powerful march to San Sebastian of 35 miles—hot & dusty—Don Ignatius Jemenez fled to Durango—fish in the Rio Nasas—3 mouths into the 3 lakes Taguhhila, Lassabis & the Alamo—2 men King of Co. B & Ferguson of Co. D died on the march, of heat, fatigue & suffocation. Beautiful River—Rich soil—needs no rain.

Tuesday, 11th.

Marched from Sebastian 35 miles to San Lorenzo—Report of McGoffin being attacked by a Banditti—A. McClure of Co. E. died & burried in a Sand Bank—Description of a night spent in San Lorenzo

—Scene in the American camp—number of children &c.—American courier suspected as a spy taken up—A Mr. Mount [Thornton A. Mount] of Co. A missing—perhaps murdered by the Mexicans or Comanches.

WEDNESDAY, 12TH.

3 spies apprehended by the front Guard—15 miles to San Juan Baptisto on the Brazo—tall mezquite—No forage—plenty of Water—Lt. Gordon & 20 men sent to El Poso to have the vats and troughs filled with water.

THURSDAY, 13TH.

Lt. Gordon & his men arrived at the Poso at 9 o'clock—Here we found Capt. Reid & 13 men returned from Parras. They were in pursuit of a band of Comanches who had been on a war excursion to San Louis & the day previous had killed 5 Mexicans near Parras & driven off 200 horses & 300 mules & taken ten boys & 2 girls captives—We decoyed them to the coral & made a sortie upon them—they stood boldly—the battle lasted 2 hours—14 Comanches were killed & 20 wounded—Capt. Reid wounded—Very hot—men sick.

[By reference to page 118 it will be seen that these portraits were engraved from daguerreotypes, in 1847. They are photographic reproductions of the steel plates in the cloth-bound edition of the Work of Hughes.—W. E. C.]

REPRINT OF THE WORK OF JOHN T. HUGHES.

[The work of Colonel Hughes was printed almost sixty years ago. Within that time there has been great advancement in the art of printing. The following reprint is, as nearly as possible, an exact reproduction of the original, which has the capitalization, punctuation, orthography, etc., peculiar to its day. No change has been made except to correct manifest error, an instance of which is the form of the name of General Kearny; formerly it was erroneously written *Kearney*.---W. E. C.]

THE VOLUNTEER.

The above cut was originally drawn to represent J. W. PATTON, immediately after his first fire, at the battle of Brazito, but is here given as a sample of Colonel Doniphan's command.

[Photographic reproduction of the title-page to Hughes pamphlet.]

DONIPHAN'S EXPEDITION;

CONTAINING AN ACCOUNT OF THE

CONQUEST OF NEW MEXICO;

GENERAL KEARNEY'S OVERLAND EXPEDITION TO CALIFORNIA;
DONIPHAN'S CAMPAIGN AGAINST THE NAVAJOS; HIS
UNPARALLELED MARCH UPON CHIHUAHUA AND
DURANGO; AND THE OPERATIONS OF
GENERAL PRICE AT SANTA FE:

WITH

A SKETCH OF THE LIFE OF COL. DONIPHAN.

ILLUSTRATED WITH PLANS OF BATTLE-FIELDS AND FINE ENGRAVINGS.

BY JOHN T. HUGHES, A. B.,
OF THE FIRST REGIMENT OF MISSOURI CAVALRY.

"Cut the rope, or pull up the picket."

CINCINNATI:
U. P. JAMES, No. 167 WALNUT STREET,
BETWEEN FOURTH AND FIFTH.

ENTERED, according to Act of Congress, in the year 1847, by
J. A. & U. P. JAMES,
In the Clerk's Office of the District Court of Ohio.

PREFACE.

THE author is well apprised that any new publication, at this time, must either possess a high degree of literary merit, or treat of *events* in which all feel a lively interest, to recommend it to the favorable consideration of the reading public. For the success of this work he relies chiefly on the latter circumstance.

Mexico has recently been the theatre of many thrilling events. The presses of the country are teeming with books, written on Mexico, the Mexican war, and Mexican manners and customs. Descriptions of camps, marches, battles, capitulations, and victories, have almost sated the public mind. But these have all, or nearly all had reference to the central or southern wings of our army. Little has been said, or written, in regard to the "Army of the West." The object of the following pages is to supply this deficiency, and to do *justice* to the MEN, whose courage and conduct have accomplished the most wonderful military achievement of modern times. For, what can be more wonderful than the march, of a single regiment of undisciplined troops, through five populous States of the Mexican Republic—almost annihilating a powerful army—and finally returning home, after a march of near six thousand miles, graced with the trophies of victory.

To the kindness and courtesy of Cols. Doniphan and Price, Lieutenant-colonel Jackson and Major Gilpin, Captains Waldo and Reid, Montgomery P. Leintz, and Dudley H. Cooper, the author is indebted for much valuable information. He also desires to express the obligations under which he feels himself, to the late lamented Captain Johnston, aid-de-camp to Gen. Kearny, whose Notes were recently published, and to the Hon. Willard P. Hall, of Missouri, for an account of the march of Lieutenant-colonel Cooke to California, and of the subsequent operations of General Kearny in that country.

His acknowledgments are also due to his valued and] esteemed friend, L. A. Maclean, of the Missouri Horse Guards, who generously and gratuitously furnished most of the designs which embellish this work.* These sketches were engraved by H. C. Grosvenor, of Cincinnati. The steel engravings were executed from daguerreotype likenesses of Colonels Doniphan and Price, by C. A. Jewett, also of Cincinnati. The map illustrating the different Routes and Marches of the several sub-divisions of the Western Army was principally constructed from personal observation.

Except for the long-established custom of prefacing books, the reader would scarcely demand of the author an explanation of his motives, in attempting to publish to the world a full and faithful account of the WESTERN EXPEDITION: embracing the Conquest of New Mexico; the Treaty with the Navajo Indians; General Kearny's overland march to California; Colonel Doniphan's invasion and capture of Chihuahua; his triumphant march through the States of Durango and Coahuila; his junction with Generals Wool and Taylor; his return to New Orleans, by way of the Mexican Gulf, and his subsequent cordial reception, by the citizens of St. Louis, and Missouri generally;—together with the brilliant achievements of the army

---

*From a letter to me by Joseph F. Smith, of Lexington, Mo., dated January 1, 1907, I gather the following facts about L. A. MacLean, who made the illustrations as above stated:

Lachlan Allan MacLean.
[Courtesy of Lafayette County Historical Society, Lexington, Missouri.]

Lachlan Allan MacLean was born in Scotland; date not known. He came to Lafayette county, Mo., about the year 1846, and engaged in teaching school. He taught in both Lafayette and Saline counties, and was so engaged for some five or six years. He was elected County Surveyor of Lafayette county, and served four years. In 1849 he was married to Miss Eleanor N. Smith, of Lafayette county. In 1855 he was appointed to a position in the office of the Surveyor-General of Kansas, and took a prominent part in the border troubles. At the beginning of the Civil War he returned to Lafayette county, Mo., and joined the Confederate Army, and was made Adjutant to General Rains. When General Rains joined General Sterling Price, MacLean was made Adjutant to General Price. He was killed in Arkansas, in 1864, in a personal encounter with one of his own men.

MacLean was a member of Captain Reid's company (from Saline county), and was one of the engineers detailed at Santa Fé to locate, design and build Fort Marcy.—W. E. C.

under Colonel Price, at Santa Fé. These are subjects of great historical interest to every American citizen.

The author was an eye-witness of, and an actor in, many of the scenes which he essays to describe; having been present at the capture of Santa Fé, and in the battles of Brazito, Sacramento, and El Poso. The narrative has been prepared with a conscientious regard for TRUTH—the beauty of all history. He, therefore, trusts that his labors may meet with a favorable reception, by an enlightened and generous public. THE AUTHOR.

LIBERTY, MISSOURI, September 25, 1847.

CONTENTS.

	Page.
MEMOIR OF COL. W. A. DONIPHAN	123

CHAPTER I.

Origin of the War with Mexico—Hostilities begun—Act of Congress to raise troops—Plan of invasion—Causes which justify the war—Army of the West—Gov. Edwards' requisition—Troops rendezvous at Fort Leavenworth—Drill exercises—Election of field officers—Strength of the expedition—Ladies visit the fort—Presentation of flags—Two squadrons dispatched in pursuit of Speyres and Armijo—Departure of the expedition—March conducted by detachments—Scene at the Stranger—The Kansas—Shawnees—Bewilderment—Bluff hill—Santa Fé Trail—Fiery steeds—Description of troops composing the ARMY OF THE WEST..........................129

CHAPTER II.

View of the Army on the Prairies—Singular phenomenon—Attention to horses—Fourth of July—Council Grove—Its locale—Diamond Springs—Government trains—Interesting inquiry—Prairie fuel—Musquitoes and the black gnat—Express from Col. Doniphan—Altercation between officers—Chavez—his tragical end—The mirage—Sand-hills—The Big Arkansas — Buffalo — Pawnee Rock—Forces reunited at the Pawnee River—Difficult passage—The Infantry—Maj. Howard—Charge upon the Buffalo—Reptiles and insects—Flowers—Prairie dog villages—Death of Lesley—Attachment of men to their horses—Appearance of the Army—Fitzpatrick, the mountaineer — The report — Mexican spies taken—Army encamped in the Mexican territory....................154

CHAPTER III.

The Estampeda—Fort Bent—Lieut. De Courcy — Arapaho Chief — March resumed—The army passes the Desert— An adventure—Spanish peaks—Half Rations—Return of De Courcy—Doniphan's speech—Arrival at Las Bagas—Priest of San Miguel—Mexican Prisoners—The Pecos Ruins—Traditions and Legends—Anticipated Battle of the Cañon—Capture of Santa Fé—Gen. Kearny's speech—Camp rumors, &c..178

CHAPTER IV.

Grazing Detachment — American Residents at Santa Fé — Herkins — Gen. Kearny's Proclamation—New Mexico—Santa Fé—New Mexican Women—The Fandango—Lieut. Oldham—Deserters—The Express—A Pueblo Chief—Stamp Paper...........................207

CHAPTER V.

Excursion to San Tome—Supposed Rebellion—Departure for Albuquerque—Arrival at Del Gardo—Gen. Kearny and Capt. Reid—Rights of Volunteers—Error common to regular officers—Sham battle—The Rio del Norte—Irrigating canals—Algodones—Bernalillo—Albuquerque—Peralta—Reception of the troops at San Tome—Lieut. Col. Ruff—Grand celebration—Return to the capital 221

CHAPTER VI.

Territorial Laws—Mexican Printing Press—Appointments to office—Disease—Fort Marcy—Battle of Los Llanos—The Election—Detachments ordered to Abiquiu and Cebolleta—Gilpin's Return—Col. Doniphan and Hall—Gen. Kearny and the Apache Chief—Gen. Kearny's departure for California—Conduct of the Soldiers 238

CHAPTER VII.

Reinforcements — Organization of the Force—The march begun—The Mormon Battalion—Death of Capt. Allen—Another Estampeda—Col. Price's arrival

	Page.
at Santa Fé—Col. Daugherty's regiment—Disposition of the forces in New Mexico—Express from California—Preparations for the Chihuahua Expedition	256

CHAPTER VIII.

Doniphan ordered against the Navajoes—Plan of the March—Condition of the Troops—They take with them neither Baggage, Provision Wagons, nor Tents—Arrival at Albuquerque—A Squadron sent to Valverde—Death of Adjutant Butler—War Dance at Isleta—Express from the Merchants—Valverde........266

CHAPTER IX.

Col. Jackson's detachment—Don Chavez—Another War Dance—Cebolleta—Jackson's Mission—Capt. Reid's Expedition—Navajo dance — Narbona — Capt. Reid's Letter—Return of the Party—Habits of the Navajos—Their Wealth—Horses stolen by the Navajos—Their recovery............................284

CHAPTER X.

Major Gilpin and the Yutas—His march against the Navajos—His passage over the Cordilleras—Express to Col.Doniphan—The San Juan—Passage over the Tunicha mountains—Deep Snows—Maj Gilpin departs for the Ojo Oso—Col. Doniphan passes the Sierra Madre—Immense Snow Storm—Arrival at the Bear Spring—Doniphan's Speech to the Navajos—Their Chief's reply—Treaty concluded........................298

CHAPTER XI.

Return of the Troops to the Del Norte—Doniphan visits Zuni—Treaty between the Zunis and the Navajos—Description of Zuni and the Zunians—The Moquis—Ancient ruins—Remarks on the Navajo campaign—The Navajos—Their state and condition................309

CHAPTER XII.

Gen. Kearny's march to California—Passes the Del Norte at Albuquerque—Arrival at Socorro—The Alcalde—Kit Carson—The Express—Capt. Burgwin sent back—Lieut. Ingalls—Apaches—The Copper mines—Red Sleeve—Sierra del Buso—Difficulties — The Gilans — Lieut. Davidson—Hall of Montezuma—The Pimo villages....................317

CHAPTER XIII.

Barrebutt—Fable of the Pimos—Arrival at the Colorado—Mexican papers intercepted—The Jornada of ninety miles—Horse-flesh—The Mulada—Capt. Gillespie — Battle of San Pascual — Gen. Kearny's official report...............331

CHAPTER XIV.

Col. Stevenson—Com. Sloat and ¶ Lieut Col. Frémont — Gen. Castro — Com. Stockton—The Revolution in California — Mr. Talbot — The insurgents under Flores and Pico—Gen. Kearny marches upon Angeles—Battles of San Gabriel and the Mesa—Capital recovered—The Capitulation......................340

CHAPTER XV.

Gen. Kearny and W. P. Hall—Lieutenant Colonel Cooke—The Mormon Battalion—Lieut. Abert — San Bernadino destroyed by Apaches—The glazed plain—Arrival in Teuson—The honest Pimo chief—Arrival at San Diego—Com. Shubrick—Gen. Kearny proceeds to Monterey—Governor Frémont—Gen. Kearny and Governor Frémont — California — Its present state—Gen. Kearny's return to the United States............351

CHAPTER XVI.

Concentration of the forces at Valverde—Mitchell's Escort—Passage of the great "Jornada del Muerto" — Arrival at Donanna—Frank Smith and the Mexicans—Battle of Brazito—The Piratical Flag—Doniphan's order—Burial of the Dead—False Alarm—Surrender of El Paso—Release of American Prisoners..360

CHAPTER XVII.

The Commissioners—Assessment of property—Search for arms—Proclamation of. Gov. Trias—The American merchants—Strength of the Pass—Capt. Kirker—Kind treatment of the Pasenos—Resources of the valley of El Paso—Wolves—The Rebellion—Ramond Ortiz—The Apache Indians....................383

CHAPTER XVIII.

Departure from El Paso—Doniphan's position—Ramond Ortiz—Two Deserters—Battalion of Merchants—Passage of the Desert—The Ojo Caliente—Marksmanship — Lake of Encenillas — Dreadful Conflagration—Capt. Reid's adventure—The Reconnoissance—Plan of the March—Battle of Sacramento—Surrender of Chihuahua..................395

CHAPTER XIX.

Doniphan's proclamation—The American residents—The keys to the Mint—Mexican morals—Chihuahua—Its attractions—Express to Gen. Wool—The fourteen—Arrival at Saltillo—Visit to the battle-field of Buena Vista—Return of the Express 444

CHAPTER XX.

Departure of the army for Saltillo—Mexican girls—The Merchants—Arrival at Santa Rosalia—Mitchell's Advance—Guajuquilla—The Jornada—Palayo and Mapimi — Death of Lieut. Jackson—San Sebastian and San Lorenzo—Mrs. McGoffin — Battle of El Paso — Don Manuel Ybarro—Parras—Review of the Army by Gen. Wool—Reception by Gen. Taylor 464

CHAPTER XXI.

Departure for New Orleans—Execution of a Guerrilla Chief—Mier and Camargo—Death of Sergeant Swain—Arrival at Reynosa—Water Transportation—The Mouth—Brazos Santiago—The Troops sail for New Orleans — The Balize—Chivalry of the South—Reception in the Crescent City 487

CHAPTER XXII.

Discharge of the Troops—Their return to Missouri — Reception at St. Louis — Banquets and Honors — Doniphan crowned with a LAUREL WREATH—Conclusion 495

CHAPTER XXIII.

Col. Price — Disposition of the troops—The Conspiracy—Conspiracy detected—Second Conspiracy—Massacre of Gov. Bent and retinue—Battles of Canada, Embudo, Pueblo de Taos, and the Mora—Death of Capts. Burgwin and Hendley — Restoration of tranquillity....... 510

CHAPTER XXIV.

Increased vigilance of the troops—Suspicion—Battle of the Red river cañon—Murder of Lieut. Brown—Battle of Las Bagas—Six prisoners executed—Attack on the Cienega—Indian outrages—Robberies—Lieut. Love—Capt. Mann—The new levies........................ 519

MEMOIR

OF

COL. A. W. DONIPHAN.

ALEXANDER WILLIAM DONIPHAN, whose history is so thoroughly identified with that of Missouri, and who has acted so conspicuous a part in the recent war with Mexico, as the leader of the unexampled Expedition against Chihuahua, was born, of respectable parentage, on the 9th of July, 1808, in Mason county, Kentucky. He first breathed the air of that chivalrous State. There his tender years were spent, and his youthful mind received its first impressions. Amidst Kentucky's wild, romantic mountain scenery, his young faculties were first begun to be developed, unfolded, expanded. Here, also, from maternal lips,—the lips of a kind, patient, persevering, and intelligent mother,—he first learned sentiments of honor, honesty, and patriotism. His mind, from the very earliest age, was fired with an admiration of the ancient orators and sages. He no less admired the patriots of the revolution; ever regarding them as bright examples, and worthy of imitation. Possessed of a brilliant mind, he formed his life from the best models. Such is the influence which an affectionate and intelligent mother is capable of exerting over the destiny of her offspring.

His father, Joseph Doniphan, emigrated from Virginia to Kentucky amongst the earliest pioneers, having accompanied Daniel Boone, the great Adventurer, towards the far distant west, on one of his early visits to the "Dark and bloody Ground," then covered by unbroken forests and impervious canebrakes. Pleased with the country, he returned to Virginia, married, removed, and settled in Mason county. Here he established his fortunes; and, for many years, enjoyed uninterrupted peace and prosperity, except occasional disturbances with the Indians. At length, being seized by an indisposition, he died, devolving thereby the care of providing and educating his children upon his widow. The responsible duty was faithfully and cheerfully discharged.

Alexander's father dying when he was only six years of age, left him in charge of his mother. He was the object of her first and most especial regard. His education was, to her, a matter of the highest importance. Alexander being the youngest child, his mother discontinued the management of her farm, when he had attained an age to be sent to a better school than the vicinity in which they lived then afforded; having herself gone to live with a married daughter. Having attained his ninth year, he was placed under the guardianship of his elder brother, George Doniphan, of Augusta, Kentucky; to whose care and kind attention, Col. Doniphan acknowledges himself indebted for all his attainments, and whatever distinction he may have acquired in the world. The elder brother, therefore, enjoys the enviable satisfaction of knowing his efforts contributed to rear and give destiny to one of the GREAT MINDS of the age. Indeed, Colonel Doniphan's name and fame are familiar to every American citizen. Not only so,—the world regards him with admiration, and justly; for he towers amongst men as the stately oak amongst his compeers of the forest.

Five years after Alexander was removed to Augusta, the Conferences of Ohio and Kentucky determined to locate a college, at some point on the Ohio river convenient to the citizens of each State, to be under the control of the Methodist Episcopal Church. It was located at Augusta. At this institution Alexander graduated, with high honors, in 1827, in the 19th year of his age. He then read history, with great advantage, for six months, and in the spring of 1828 commenced the study of the law, under the supervision of that learned, profound, and able lawyer, Martin Marshall, of Augusta. He obtained a license to practise as an attorney, before the courts, in the fall of 1829; and, having spent the winter of that year in traveling over the south-western and western States, determined to locate himself at Lexington, Missouri. Here he remained, and enjoyed a lucrative practise for three years, during which he obtained considerable celebrity as an able and eloquent lawyer, and established his reputation as an intelligent and useful citizen. In 1833 he removed to Liberty, in Upper Missouri, more from its healthful situation and its salubrity, than from any other cause. He still resides in this romantic and pleasant village.*

From this period of his history, his success at the bar has been almost unexampled, in Missouri. Immediately upon his locating in Liberty, a heavy business flowed into his hands. The fame which he had previously acquired, as an able advocate and a sound lawyer, gave him advantages that but few can enjoy. Never did Pericles gain a more complete ascendant, over the minds of the Athenians, than Col. Doniphan, by his courteous conduct as a citizen, his capacity as a lawyer, his talent as a legislator, and his powers as an orator, has attained over the people of Upper Missouri. Although a majority of the people of Missouri are politically opposed to him, no one man enjoys more of their confidence and esteem, as a patriot and a citizen.

About this period of his life, he was united in marriage to the amiable and intelligent daughter of Colonel John Thornton, of Clay county. He has two little cherub boys, whose correct training, and proper education, appear to be matter of the highest concern and of first-rate importance with him. Therefore, instead of grasping after political preferment, for the purpose of satisfying a selfish and sordid ambition, we see him endeavoring to accomplish the noblest of earthly objects—*the proper training and instruction of his children.* To this end he is often seen in the district schools, as well as in the high school of the town, encouraging by his presence the young developing minds, and pointing them to the high rewards of industry and perseverance. The hero of Sacramento is now a trustee of the school in his own village!

He has long and honorably held the office of Brigadier-general, in the Militia of Missouri. In 1838, Gov. Boggs ordered a strong

---

* When any one inquires of Col. Doniphan, why he does not choose to live in a more considerable town than Liberty, he gives them Plutarch's reply: "If I should remove hence, the place would be of still less note than it now is."

Like Epaminondas, the great Bœotian, Col. Doniphan has mostly lived in a house neither splendidly furnished, nor painted, nor white-washed, but plain as the rest of his neighbors.

While commanding the army, Colonel Doniphan rarely wore any military dress; so he could not be distinguished, by a stranger, from one of the men whom he commanded. He fared as the soldiers, and often prepared his own meals. Any private man in his camp might approach him with the greatest freedom, and converse on whatever topics it pleased him; for he was always rejoiced to gain information from any one, though a common soldier. Whoever had business, might approach his tent and wake him, when asleep; for he neither had a body-guard, nor persons to transact his business for him.—HUGHES.

military force to proceed to Far West, the headquarters of the Mormon sect, and quell the disturbances and insurrectionary movements which had been excited by their Great Prophet, Jo Smith. This fanaticism and insubordination, threatened to embroil the whole country. In a short time, troops were in motion from all parts of the State. Military preparations were being actively pushed forward by the Prophet, to meet the emergency. A sanguinary slaughter was expected to ensue. Gen. Doniphan, with his brigade (belonging to the division of Major-general Lucas) rendered important service in overawing the insurgent forces, and quelling the disturbances without bloodshed. This was General Doniphan's first campaign.

In all the relations of social and private life, where a man's true character is best known, and where, lamentable to tell! most of our ostensibly great men are most sadly deficient, Col. Doniphan's conduct is most exemplary. Here his virtues shine brightest. As a husband, he is affectionate; as a father, he rules his household with reason and decision. A just and wise economy marks the administration of his family affairs. As a neighbor, he is sociable and pleasant; as a citizen, benevolent and extensively useful. In all his dealings with mankind, he is just and honorable. He is interesting and fluent in conversation. His manner and whole deportment are prepossessing; and one rarely makes his acquaintance, without forming a lasting attachment for him. As an orator, he possesses great and shining powers. His address is of the most agreeable nature; his air commanding; his language full and flowing; his gestures graceful; his enunciation distinct; his voice shrill and sonorous; his arguments convincing; his mind comprehensive and clear; his figures and illustrations happy and natural; his fancy not only brilliant, but dazzlingly vivid;—finally, when excited, the tide of his eloquence is almost irresistible. He is the very fullness of physical and intellectual vigor, and possesses, in an eminent degree, the original elements of greatness. His best speeches have always been delivered extemporaneously—much of the fire and pathos being lost, in the attempt to commit them to paper. He is not a member of any church, society, or fraternity; but, in his views, is tolerant of all, and is the devoted friend of UNIVERSAL EDUCATION. In stature, Col. Doniphan is upwards of six feet tall, well proportioned, altogether dignified in his appearance, and gentlemanly in his manners. His features are bold, his bright hazel eye dazzlingly keen and expressive, and his massive forehead is of the finest and most classic mould.

Unambitious of political advancement, he has never sought that unsubstantial, popular applause, which sometimes elevates men to stations far above their abilities and merits, and as often consigns them to useless obscurity, ever regarding fame as valuable and lasting only when based on virtue and substantial worth. For many years, having assiduously devoted his time and talent to his profession as a lawyer, he has acquired not only an enviable distinction amongst men, but has raised himself to ease and affluence. He commenced the world without fortune, and without the aid of powerful friends, to relieve him from those embarrassments which every man is destined to encounter who relies upon his own energy for success. But, by dint of perseverance, and a clear and well balanced judgment, he has arrived at both fame and fortune.

Never having been desirous of engaging permanently in political life, he has constantly refused to become a candidate for office, except on two occasions, notwithstanding he considers the public service to be the most honorable and exalted, and worthy to command the very best talent the country can afford. In 1836 he represented his county by an almost unanimous vote, although there was then a small majority in the county politically opposed to him. His success, in this election, was owing to his personal popularity and his great weight of character. In 1840, during that exciting political contest between Gen. Harrison and Mr. Van Buren, his political friends, in view of his great abilities as a stump-orator, almost forced him to take the field as a candidate once more—it being looked to as a test-race to decide the political complexion of the county. He was again elected by a large majority. While in the Legislature he distinguished himself for his boldness, independence, liberality of sentiment, and faithfulness as a representative. From this period he has pertinaciously refused to become a candidate for any office whatever, frequently declaring, in his public addresses, that he neither expects nor desires ever to be a candidate again.* He has made these declarations, not that he feels a contempt for the public service (for no one better

---

* In his speech at Independence, on the 29th of July, 1847, he declared he had not been a candidate for office for "SEVEN YEARS," and did not expect to be for the next "SEVENTY-SEVEN," to come.—HUGHES.

comprehends the value of liberty, or regards the prosperity of the country with more interest than Col. Doniphan,) but through a modest willingness to see the high functions of the government discharged by others, who have made these things the study of their whole lives.

In 1846, when hostilities were declared to exist between the United States and Mexico, and the executive proposed to send an invading army across the plains to the province of New Mexico, Gen. Doniphan actively interested himself in raising the requisite number of men to accompany the expedition. This expedition was to be under command of Colonel Kearny. To hasten the preparations for the departure of the expedition, General Doniphan visited many of the counties in Upper Missouri, harangued the people, and, in a very short space of time, the complement of men was raised. They assembled at Fort Leavenworth, and were there mustered into service. General Doniphan had volunteered as a private, in the company from his own county, commanded by his brother-in-law, Captain O. P. Moss. On the 18th of June, 1846, he was elected Colonel of the 1st Regiment of Missouri Cavalry, over his opponent, General J. W. Price, by a respectable majority. No fitter man could have been chosen; for his sagacity planned, his judgment conducted, and his energy, together with that of his officers and men, accomplished the most wonderful campaign of any age or country. This was done without an outfit, without money, and almost without ammunition, by the citizen-commander of citizen-soldiers. The history of this expedition will be Colonel Doniphan's most lasting monument. His deeds will ever live to praise him.

DONIPHAN'S EXPEDITION.

CHAPTER I.

Origin of the War with Mexico—Hostilities begun—Act of Congress to raise troops—Plan of invasion—Causes which justify the war—Army of the west—Gov. Edwards' requisition—Troops rendezvous at Fort Leavenworth—Drill exercises—Election of field officers—Strength of the expedition—Ladies visit the fort—Presentation of flags—Two squadrons dispatched in pursuit of Speyres and Armijo—Departure of the expedition—March conducted by detachments—Scene at the Stranger—The Kansas—Shawnees—Bewilderment—Bluff hill—Santa Fé Trail—Fiery Steeds—Description of troops composing the Army of the West.

The passage, by the American Congress, of the Resolutions of Annexation, by which the Republic of Texas was incorporated into the Union as one of the States, having merged her sovereignty into that of our own government, was the prime cause which led to the recent war with Mexico. However, the more immediate cause of the war may be traced to the occupation, by the American Army, of the strip of disputed territory lying between the Nueces and the Rio Grande. Bigoted and insulting Mexico, always prompt to manifest her hostility towards this government, sought the earliest plausible pretext for declaring war against the United States. This declaration of war by the Mexican Government (which bore date in April 1846), was quickly and spiritedly followed by a manifesto from our Congress at Washington, announcing that "a state of war exists between Mexico and the United States." Soon after this counter declaration, the Mexicans crossed the Rio Grande, in strong force, headed by the famous generals, Arista and Ampudia. This force as is well known, was defeated at Palo Alto on the 8th, and at Resaca de la Palma on the 9th of May, 1846, by the troops under command of Major-general Taylor, and repulsed with great slaughter. The whole Union was soon in a state of intense excitement. General Taylor's recent and glorious victories were the constant theme of universal admiration. The war had actually begun, and that, too, in a manner which demanded immediate and decisive action. The United States Congress passed an act, about the middle of April, 1846, authorizing the President to call into the field 50,000 volunteer troops, designed to operate against Mexico at three distinct points, namely: the southern wing or the "Army of Occupation," commanded by Major-general Taylor, to penetrate directly into the heart of the country; the column under Brigadier-general Wool, or the "Army of the Centre," to operate against the city of Chihuahua; and the expedition under the command of Colonel, now Brigadier-general Kearny, known as the "Army of the West," to direct its march upon the city of Santa Fé. This was the original plan of operation against Mexico. But subsequently the plan was changed; Maj. Gen. Scott, with a well appointed army, was sent to Vera Cruz; Gen. Wool effected a junction with Gen. Taylor at Saltillo, and Gen. Kearny divided his force into three separate commands; the first he led in person to the distant shores of the Pacific; a detachment of near 1000 Missouri volunteers, under command of Col. A. W. Doniphan, was ordered to make a descent upon the State of Chihuahua, expecting to join Gen. Wool's division at the Capital; while the greater part was left as a garrison at Santa Fé, under command of Col. Sterling Price. The greatest eagerness was manifested by the citizens of the United States to engage in the war; to redress our wrongs; to repel an insulting foe; and to vindicate our national honor, and the honor of our oft-insulted flag. The call of the President was promptly responded to; but of the 50,000 volunteers at first authorized to be raised, the services of only about 17,000 were required.

The cruel and inhuman butchery of Col. Fannin and his men, all Americans; the subsequent and indiscriminate murder of all Texans who unfortunately fell into Mexican hands; the repeated acts of cruelty and injustice perpetrated upon the persons and property of American citizens residing in the northern Mexican provinces; the imprisonment of American merchants without the semblance of a trial by jury, and the forcible seizure and confiscation of their goods; the robbing of American travelers and tourists in the Mexican country of their passports and other means of safety, whereby in certain instances they were for a time deprived of their liberty; the forcible detention of American citizens, sometimes in prison and at other times in free custody; the recent blockade of the Mexican ports against the United States' trade; the repeated insults offered our national flag; the contemptuous, ill-treatment of our ministers, some of whom were spurned with their credentials; the supercilious and menacing air uniformly manifested towards this government, which with characteristic forbearance and courtesy, has endeavored to maintain a friendly understanding; her hasty and unprovoked declaration of war against the United States; her army's unceremonious passage of the Rio Grande in strong force and with hostile intention; her refusal to pay indemnities; and a complication of less evils, all of which have been perpetrated by the Mexican authorities or by unauthorized Mexican citizens, in a manner which clearly evinced the determination on the part of Mexico to terminate the amicable relations hitherto existing between the two countries;— are the causes which justify the war. Are not these sufficient? Or should we have forborne until the catalogue of offences was still deeper dyed with infamous crimes, and until the blood of our brothers, friends, and consanguinity, like that of the murdered Abel, should cry to us from the ground? Who that has the spirit, the feelings, and the pride of an American, would willingly see his country submit to such a complication of injury and insult? In truth, the only cause of regret is, that the war was not prosecuted with more vigor, energy, and promptitude, from the commencement. This, perhaps, would have prevented the effusion of so much blood, and the expenditure of so much treasure.

It is the "Army of the West" that commands our immediate attention. About the middle of May, Gov. Edwards, of Missouri, made a requisition on the State for volunteers, to join the expedition to Santa Fé. This expedition was to be conducted by Col. Stephen W. Kearny, of the 1st Dragoons U. S. Army, a very able and skillful officer. The troops designed for this service, were required to rendezvous at Fort Leavenworth, situated on the right bank of the Missouri river, twenty-two miles above the mouth of the Kansas, which was the place of out-fit and departure for the western army.[13] The "Saint Louis Legion,"* commanded by Col. Easton, had already

* This corps was discharged at the expiration of six months.—HUGHES.

NOTE 13.—Fort Leavenworth was established September 19, 1827, and named by Colonel Henry H. Leavenworth for himself; he was Colonel of the Third United States Infantry Regiment, and as early as March, 1827, had been directed to se-

taken its departure for the Army of Occupation. Corps of mounted volunteers were speedily organized in various counties throughout the State in conformity to the Governor's requisition, and company officers elected. By the 5th of June, the companies began to arrive at the Fort, and were mustered into the service of the United States, and lettered in the order of their arrival.[14] The process of mustering the men into the United States service, and of valuing their horses, was entrusted to the late, lamented, Capt. Allen of the 1st Dragoons. Gen. Kearny had discretionary orders from the War Department as to the number of men which should compose his division, and what proportion of them should be cavalry and what infantry. Owing to the great distance across the plains, cavalry was deemed the better description of troops, and accordingly the whole western army, with the exception of one separate battalion, consisted of mounted men. For the space of twenty days, during which time portions of the volunteers remained at the fort, rigid drill twice per day, once before and after noon, was required to be performed by them,—in order to render their services the more efficient. These martial exercises, upon a small prairie adjacent to the fort, appropriately styled by the volunteers "Campus Martis," consisting of the march by sections of four, the sabre exercises, the charge, the rally, and other cavalry tactics, doubtless proved subsequently to be of the most essential service. It is due to the officers of the regular army, by whom the volunteer companies were principally carried through the drill exercises, to state that their instructions were always communicated in the kindest and most gentlemanly manner.

lect a site for a military post on the east bank of the Missouri river within twenty miles of the mouth of the Little Platte, either above or below. He found no suitable location on the east bank, and in July began the erection of barracks at the present location of the fort on the west bank of the Missouri, calling the place Cantonment Leavenworth, which name it bore until February 8, 1832, when all army posts were officially directed to be called forts. The Military Reservation contains about six thousand acres, with a frontage of about five miles on the Missouri river. Fort Leavenworth was established for the protection of the Santa Fé trade, and was always an important military post. After its establishment all western expeditions were outfitted there, and many of the great officers of the army were at some period of their service stationed there. The military roads from Fort Leavenworth to Forts Kearny and Laramie became the great highways to California and Oregon.

NOTE 14.—See rolls of the various companies published herein. Dates of leaving the counties in which they were enlisted are also given.

The election of field officers for the 1st Regiment Missouri Mounted Volunteers, was justly regarded as a matter of very great importance; as in the event of Gen. Kearny's death or disability, the Colonel of that regiment would be entitled to the command of the expedition. On the 18th of June, the full complement of companies having arrived, which were to compose the 1st Regiment, an election was holden, superintended by General Ward, of Platte, which resulted in the selection of ALEXANDER WILLIAM DONIPHAN, a private in the company from Clay county, an eminent lawyer,—a man who had distinguished himself as a Brigadier General in the campaign of 1838, against the Mormons at Far West, and who had honorably served his countrymen as a legislator,—for Colonel of the Regiment.[15] C. F. Ruff[16] was chosen Lt. Colonel, and Wm. Gilpin, Major.[17] Lt. Col. Ruff and Major Gilpin had both volunteered as privates, the former in the company from Clay, and the latter in that from Jackson county.

The 1st Regiment of Missouri mounted volunteers was composed of eight companies, A, B, C, D, E, F, G and H, respectively from the counties of Jackson, Lafayette, Clay, Saline, Franklin, Cole, Howard and Callaway, commanded by Capts. Waldo, Walton, Moss, Reid, Stephenson, Parsons, Jackson, and Rodgers, numbering 856 men.[18] The battalion of light artillery consisted of two companies from St. Louis under Captains Weightman and Fischer, numbering near 250

NOTE 15.—The opposing candidate was John W. Price, of Howard county.

NOTE 16.—Ruff was the candidate of the West-Pointers, and defeated Gilpin by but two votes. Ruff was afterwards in command of Fort Kearny, on the Platte, from which point he was sent to establish Fort Laramie, in July, 1849. (See Andreas, *History of Nebraska*, p. 1019.)

The *Army and Navy Register* has the following:

"Ruff, Chas. F. Born in Penn. Appointed from Penn. 2nd Lieut., 1st Dragoons, 1 July, 1838. Resigned 31 Dec., 1843. Lieut. Col. 1st Mo. Mounted Vols., 18 June, 1846. Resigned 17 Sept., 1846. Captain Mounted Rifles, 7 July, 1846. Brevet Major, Aug. 1, 1847, for gallant and meritorious conduct in the affair at San Juan de los Llanos, Mexico. Major Mounted Rifles, 30 Dec., 1856. Lieut. Col., 10 June, 1861. 3rd Cav. 3 Aug., 1861. Retired 30 March, 1864. Brevet Colonel and Brevet Brigadier Genl., 13 March, 1865, for faithful and meritorious service in recruiting the armies of the United States."

NOTE 17.—Gilpin was opposed by General Kearny. For an account of the election of these officers, see *Chronicles of the Builders of the Commonwealth*, by Hubert Howe Bancroft, p. 535.

NOTE 18.—*The Captains.*—David Waldo, Captain of Company A, was born April 30, 1802, at Clarksburg, Harrison county, Virginia (now West Virginia); died at Independence, Mo., May 20, 1878. His father was Jedediah and his mother

men, with Major Clark as its field officer. The battalion of Infantry from the counties of Cole and Platte, respectively commanded by Capts. Angney and Murphy, the former being the senior officer, numbered 145 men. The Laclede Rangers from Saint Louis, under command of Capt. Hudson, 107 in number, attached to the 1st Dragoons, whose strength was 300,—composed the entire force of Colonel Kearny. Thus it will appear that the advance of the Western Army under the immediate command of Colonel Kearny, consisted of 1,658 men, and sixteen pieces of ordnance, 12 six-pounders, and 4 twelve pound howitzers.

Polly (Porter) Waldo. In his youth he was engaged in rafting logs down the Ohio river. He moved to Missouri in 1826, (see *Early Western Travels*, Vol. 19, p. 164,) and cut pine timber on the Gasconade, which he floated to St. Louis, realizing from its sale enough money to carry him through the Medical Department of Transylvania University, Lexington, Ky. He returned to Missouri and lived for a time on the Gasconade, but moved to Osceola, St. Clair County, thence to Independence, Jackson county, where he practiced medicine. He relinquished his practice to engage in the Santa Fé trade. He became a merchant in Mexico, and in this trade he amassed a large fortune prior to the Mexican War. He was a man of great ability. Being familiar with the Spanish language, he often rendered valuable services in the translation of documents captured by the Americans. After his return from the Mexican War he married (March 27, 1849) at Independence, Eliza Jane, daughter of Edward and Margaret (Glasgow) Norris, of Culpeper, Va. He freighted and traded to Utah and the Platte river country after the Mexican War.

Captain William Parr Walton was born near Carthage, Smith county, Tennessee, in the year 1814. He was married to Miss Jane Tyree, of Gallatin, Sumner county, Tennessee, March 12, 1836. About 1838 he moved to Lafayette county, Missouri. He settled near Lexington, and engaged in farming. Was Captain of Company B, First Regiment Missouri Mounted Volunteers, and was a good officer. His company captured the celebrated cannon known as "Old Sacramento" at the battle of Sacramento, and the men brought it to Lexington with them on their return from the war. Captain Walton moved to Kansas City in 1860, but when the Civil War began he joined the Confederate army and served until the war closed. After his return from the war he resided two years in Lexington, then moved to Sweet Springs (then Brownsville), Saline county, Missouri where he died February 21, 1875.

Captain Walton had seven children, four sons and three daughters. Four of these survive. Of these I know of three,—J. R. Walton, Treasurer State Hospital, Nevada, Mo.; Mrs. Ella Walton Hall, Sweet Springs, Mo.; Mrs. R. S Kinney, San Antonio, Texas.

Captain Walton was eligible to membership in the Order of the Cincinnati though he never availed himself of his right.

Oliver Perry Moss, Captain of Company C, Clay county, was born at Maysville, Mason county, Kentucky, Sept. 26, 1813; died in Clay county, Mo., June 7,

When this column was on the eve of departure for the distant borders of New Mexico, the people of upper Missouri collected in crowds at the fort to bid their sons, brothers, and relatives, adieu, before they launched upon the boundless plains of the west. The ushering of an army upon the green bosom of the great prairies, with pennons gaily streaming in the breeze, is a sight no less interesting in its nature, and there can be no less solicitude felt for its safety, than is manifested at the departure of a fleet for some distant land, when, with spreading sails, the vessels launch upon the restless, heaving deep. Before the expedition set out, the patriotic ladies from the

---

1881. Married Caroline Marjery, daughter of John and Elizabeth Thornton, sister to the wife of Colonel Doniphan. He was thrice Sheriff of Clay county. He was a member of the Baptist Church for forty years, and did much to aid William and Jewell College. He was a good man, and his memory is honored by the citizens of Clay county. His sister was the beautiful widow Wilcox, who married General William Ashley, and, after his death, Senator John J. Crittenden, of Kentucky.

John W. Reid, Captain of Company D, Saline county, was born at Lynchburg, Va., June 14, 1820; died suddenly at Lee's Summit, Jackson county, Mo., but date of death is unknown to writer. Captain Reid came of patriotic families, and his ancestors fought in the Revolution; one of them founded Liberty Hall Academy, now Washington and Lee University, Virginia. He grew to manhood at La Porte, Indiana, where he was given a classical education. When but little more than twenty he moved to Missouri, and lived in Saline, Clay, Cass, and Jackson counties. He first taught school, then studied law and was admitted to the bar; he practiced with considerable success. His record as a soldier in the Mexican War is found in this volume. It was claimed that he was put forward on all occasions to enable him to make a great record; other captains claimed that he was too much favored; on this account he was not generally popular in the regiment. He was prominent in the border troubles between Missouri and Kansas prior to the Civil War, and commanded the Missouri forces that burned Osawatomie, Kansas Territory. In 1860 he was elected to Congress, but the coming of the war caused him to resign. He was appointed a commissioner to adjust claims against the Confederate Government, but seems to have done little work in that capacity. He spent a year in the Federal Military Prison at St. Louis, at the end of which time he was released on his parole and agreement to take no further part in the war. In 1865 he located in Kansas City and began the practice of law. He amassed a large estate. He did much for the growth of Kansas City. He was twice married: first, to a Mrs. Flournoy; second, to a Miss Magraw, daughter of M. F. Magraw, a pioneer Santa Fé trader, of Independence, Mo.

John Dunlap Stephenson (written also Stevenson) was born in Virginia, but date unknown to the writer; died June 22, 1897, in St. Louis. The survivors of the First Regiment, with whom I have talked, are almost unanimous in the statement that Stephenson was the ablest captain in it. His company was the best drilled, and was always under better discipline than any other. At the bat-

adjacent counties, on several occasions, came to the Fort, (on board the steamboats which were then almost daily arriving and departing,) to present their countrymen with Flags, wrought by their own hands,—at once the token of their regard, and the Star-lighted emblem of their country's liberty. On the presentation of these flags, the ladies usually delivered addresses, which seemed to inspire every heart with courage, and nerve every arm for the dangers of the campaign. On the 23d day of June, a large deputation of ladies from Clay [county], arrived at the Fort, on the Missouri Mail, with the finest flag, perhaps, of which the expedition could boast, and pre-

---

tle of Sacramento his company moved with greater military accuracy and precision, held together better, and fired with more deliberation than the others. The men of his company were completely under his control. *The Historical Register and Dictionary of the United States Army, 1789–1903*, contains the following record: "Stevenson, John Dunlap. Va. Mo. Capt. Mo. Mtd. vols. 27 June 1846 to 24 June 1847; col. 7 Mo. inf. 1 June 1861; brig. gen. vols. 29 Nov. 1862; resd. 22 April 1864; brig. gen. vols. 7 Aug. 1864 to rank from 29 Nov. 1862; bvt. maj. gen. vols. 13 Mch. 1865 for mer. ser. dur. the war; hon. must. out 15 Jan. 1866; col. 30 inf. 28 July 1866; unassd. 15 Mar. 1869; assd. to 25 inf. 15 Dec. 1870; bvt. brig. gen. 2 Mar. 1867 for gal. and mer. ser. at battle of Champion Hills Miss; hon. dischd. 31 Dec. 1870 at his own request."

Stephenson came to Missouri (Union, Franklin county), from Virginia, probably, but possibly from Maryland, about 1842. Was a lawyer; he and two other members of the bar rented a small log house and hired a negro to cook for them. One of them, W. N. V. Bray, was afterwards elected to Congress; the other, James Halligan, was elected to the State Senate and was a member of the Constitutional Convention. For service in the Mexican War Stephenson and the Sheriff, John D. Hamilton, each began to enlist a company, but as only one could be accepted the rolls were consolidated and Stephenson elected Captain by a large majority, Hamilton and some of his followers leaving the company and remaining at home. Clark Brown, publisher of the *Franklin County Tribune*, writes me as follows: "Stephenson is reported to have been absolutely fearless, and to have shot and instantly killed one of the most daring desperadoes who ever infested this part of Missouri, by the name of Bray, and who had joined the company. Upon the return of the company after the war a big picnic was given the boys in Union. It was attended by people from all over the country. The dinner was free, but the crowd was so big that a riot ensued in trying to get to the dinner-table. Stephenson remained in Union several years after the war, and accumulated some property. The large mansion which he built is still standing in good condition in a beautiful yard of several acres in the north part of Union. It is said he married Hannah Harmon, but when or where no one can tell."

Mosby Monroe Parsons, Captain of Company F, was born at Charlottesville, Virginia, May 21, 1822. In the spring of 1835 he moved with his father to Missouri, settling at Jefferson City. His education was completed at St. Charles, Mo., when he studied law, and was admitted to the bar in 1846. He raised the

sented it to Captain O. P. Moss, of their county, accompanied by the following patriotic address, delivered by Mrs. Cunningham:

"The ladies of Liberty and its vicinity have deputed me, as one of their number, to present this flag to the volunteers from Clay county, commanded by Capt. OLIVER PERRY MOSS, and I now, in their name, present it to you, as a token of their esteem for the manly and patriotic manner in which you have shown your willingness to sustain the honor of our common country, and to redress the indignities offered to its flag.

"In presenting to you this token of our regard and esteem, we wish you to remember that some of us have sons, some brothers, and all of us either friends or relatives among you, and that we would rather hear of your falling in honorable warfare, than to see you return sullied with crime, or disgraced by cowardice. We trust, then, that your conduct, in all circumstances, will be worthy the noble, intelligent and patriotic nation whose cause you have so generously volun-

---

Cole county company, and was elected its Captain. In the drawing at Fort Leavenworth he secured the senior captaincy, though he was the youngest officer in the regiment with that rank. This gained him the enmity and jealousy of some of the older captains, especially that of Reid, and it is said that this fact caused the others to combine to put Reid forward at all times and to prevent Captain Parsons from receiving the important assignments due his position. All agree that Parsons was a man of great ability and that his bravery was unquestioned. Next to Stephenson he was the best disciplinarian in the regiment. He was constantly on the lookout for the comfort of his men, and they were devoted to him. Upon his return to Jefferson City he resumed the practice of law. He was elected to the Legislature in 1856 and was made a State Senator in 1858. When the Civil War began he was appointed a Brigadier-General by Governor Jackson, and he made a brilliant record in the Confederate army. He was in nearly all the battles fought in Missouri and Arkansas, and was promoted to be a Major-General after the battle of Helena. When the war was over he and other Confederate officers determined to leave the United States and make homes for themselves and families in Brazil. In this party were Col. A. M. Standish, Col. A. H. Conron, Major S. C. Williams, and others. They left Shreveport, La., May 10, 1865, and went to Monterey, Mexico. There General Parsons determined to return to the United States, and with Col. Standish, Col. Conron, and Major Williams set out for home July 16. With them was "Dutch Bill," the servant of Col. Standish. On the same evening General Parsons, Col. Standish, Col. Conron, and "Dutch Bill" encamped near a small town called Chino, just beyond the San Juan river, leaving Major Williams back on the road to exchange his horse, which was lame. About nine o'clock that night General Parsons and his party were attacked by Mexican soldiers, and, after being overpowered, were murdered, and their bodies thrown into the river. On the following morning Major Williams made diligent search for them, but their bodies were never seen

teered to defend; your deportment will be such as will secure to you the highest praise and the warmest gratitude of the American people —in a word—let your motto be: 'DEATH BEFORE DISHONOR.' And to the gracious protection and guidance of HIM who rules the destinies of nations, we fervently commend you."

The captain modestly received the flag, in a brief and pathetic response. Its motto was, THE LOVE OF COUNTRY, IS THE LOVE OF GOD.

The above specimen is given as illustrative of the enthusiastic and uncalculating spirit of the western people, when the country calls them to vindicate her national honor. Without counting the cost, either of treasure or blood, they fly to arms, impelled by patriotism, and act upon the principle "we are for our country, right or wrong."

About this time, Captains Waldo and Reid, of the volunteers, and Capts. Moore and Burgwin, of the 1st Dragoons U. S. Army,

---

again. This fact made the families hope that they might have escaped, but this hope was finally abandoned. The facts in regard to the murder were not known until the families presented claims for indemnity against the Mexican Government, when the whole matter was made public. The claims were pending for ten years, but finally allowed, and paid in gold.

Colonel Austin M. Standish was born at Cahara House, County Limerick, Ireland, and came to the United States in 1851, locating in Missouri. He was an accomplished civil engineer, and was for years chief engineer of the Missouri Pacific Railroad. In 1857 he was married to Miss Mildred Parsons, sister to General Parsons, at Jefferson City. He was a splendid soldier. At Wilson Creek his horse was shot from under him, and his watch alone saved his life; at Pleasant Hill, La., he was painfully wounded. He was murdered with General Parsons and others by the Mexicans. The Mexicans afterwards displayed a case of engineering instruments which had belonged to him, also a watch taken from General Parsons.

Congreve Jackson, Captain of Company H, Howard county, succeeded Ruff as Lieutenant-Colonel of the regiment. I have made efforts to secure material for a sketch of his life, but without success; it may exist, but my letters to Howard county citizens failed to meet with any response. Jackson was in the Confederate army; at the siege of Lexington he was Colonel Commanding the Third Division, M. S. G.

Charles B. Rodgers, Captain of Company H, Callaway county, was a brave officer. He served under Col. Gentry in the Florida War, and was severely wounded at the battle of Okeechobee. Material for a sketch of his life could not be obtained. He has probably been dead many years, and his descendants, if any, could not be found.

were dispatched by Col. Kearny, with their respective companies, upon the route to Santa Fé, with orders to pursue with all possible vigor, and capture the trains of Messrs. Speyers and Armijo, of the trading caravan, who were far in advance of the other merchants, and who, it was understood, were furnished with British and Mexican passports, and were endeavoring to supply the enemy with munitions of war. The pursuit was vain, however, as the sequel will develop.[19]

The organization of the expedition was completed by the appointment to office of the following gentlemen, viz: Capt. Riche to be sutler to the dragoons; C. A. Perry to be sutler, G. M. Butler, adjutant, Dr. Geo. Penn, principal surgeon, and T. M. Morton and I. P. Vaughan, assistant surgeons, of the 1st Regiment.

About one hundred wagons, loaded with provisions for the army, having already been sent forward upon the road,[20] and other means

NOTE 19.—June 4, 1846, Col. Kearny wrote George T. Howard, then out some distance on the Santa Fé Trail: "I have just received yours of yesterday, stating that you were informed that 2 Cos. of Dragoons were marching from Santa Fé to escort a large quantity of Ammunition & Arms destined for that place & belonging to Armijo & Spiers. As you say you expect to overtake the Caravan this side of the Arkansas, I have to urge that you do so as soon as possible and that you cause the ammunition and arms alluded to, to be detained, till the 2 Cos. of my own Dragoons, which I will start tomorrow from here, come up with them. The escort of Dragoons which you have with you can be used for that purpose." In a letter dated June 6, to Captain B. D. Moore, commanding Companies C and G, sent out to aid in capturing the ammunition and arms, Col. Kearny says that Capt. Waldo informs him that Gov. Armijo has about $70,000 worth of goods near the head of the Cimarron that left Independence "about a fortnight since"; that Waldo was of the opinion, from his knowledge of the Governor's character, that "if we can secure that property, we hold the Governor our friend and ally." He directs that the force push on and overtake Armijo's caravan and hold it until he arrives. But this report must have been erroneous. Mr. Edward J. Glasgow, the partner of Dr. Henry Connelly, writes me under date of August 22, 1906, as follows: "I think there is some mistake in the items of your letter. Mr. Speyer had charge of his own train. Gov. Armijo had no train of goods that year. Some time after Speyer had gone, a report became current that he was carrying powder to the Mexicans, which report was afterwards shown to be erroneous. Col. Kearny, however, sent a company of dragoons from Fort Leavenworth, to stop Speyer, but the troops never caught up to him. They, however, stopped all other trains, ours included, until the army came up, and we followed in its rear."

NOTE 20.—General Odon Guitar, of Columbia, Mo., was in Company H, and was with this advance party, and he thus described it to me: "About ten days before the army marched from Fort Leavenworth, a train of wagons and eight hundred cattle was started over the Santa Fé Trail. This was a subsistence train

of transportation being furnished for whatever was thought necessary upon the expedition, by McKissack, quartermaster, on the 26th day of June, 1846, the main body of the western army commenced its march over the great Prairies or Plains, which extend from the western border of Missouri to the confines of New Mexico, a distance of near one thousand miles. The annual caravan or merchant train, of 414 wagons, heavily laden with dry goods for the markets of Santa Fé and Chihuahua, lined the road for miles. Independence was the point of departure for this army of merchants. Col. Kearny and the rear, consisting partly of volunteers and partly of the first dragoons, soon followed, having left the fort on the 29th of the same month.

The march of the "Army of the West," as it entered upon the great prairies, presented a scene of the most intense and thrilling interest. Such a scene was indeed worthy the pencil of the ablest artist, or the most graphic pen of the historian. The boundless plains, lying in ridges of wavy green not unlike the ocean, seemed to unite with the heavens in the distant horizon. As far as vision could penetrate, the long files of cavalry, the gay fluttering of banners, and the canvas-covered wagons of the merchant train glistening like

---

sent forward to be found by the army when it arrived on the Plains, that no time might be lost there on the march. No cattle were to be slaughtered by the detachment after the feeding-grounds of the buffalo had been reached and wild meat could be obtained. This detachment consisted of a detail of ten men from each company of the First Regiment, and Guitar was one of the men from his company. When the buffalo were found, a detail of hunters was made to kill them for the army. This company of hunters was under command of Thomas Forsythe, an old trapper and hunter. The hunters had a train of pack-mules to carry baggage, and with them were butchers to dress the carcasses of the buffalo and haul the meat to the site of the camp and have it ready for distribution when the army should arrive. The hunters and butchers were informed where the camp would be, and given a plan of it, that the meat might be placed in the most convenient place for distribution when rations were issued. The hunter train would leave camp about eleven P. M. and arrive at the site of the next camp by daylight. At Pawnee Rock Forsythe assembled the hunters and invited them to go to the summit of the Rock with him. The buffalo were so thick that the ground was covered as far as the eye could see, in every direction. Forsythe was asked how many buffalo could be seen there that morning. He replied that hunters had spent much time estimating the number of buffalo one could see on the Plains when packed as they then were. He said no agreement had been arrived at. It was his opinion that five hundred thousand buffalo were then in sight; other hunters, in whose judgment he had much confidence, believed that eight hundred thousand buffalo could be seen from the top of Pawnee Rock when as thickly packed as they were that morning."

banks of snow in the distance, might be seen winding their tortuous way over the undulating surface of the prairies. In thus witnessing the march of an army over the regions of uncultivated nature, which had hitherto been the pasture of the buffalo and the hunting ground of the wily savage, and where the eagle and the stars and stripes never before greeted the breeze, the heart could but swell with sentiments of honest pride, mingled with the most lively emotions.*

There are many obstacles which impede the progress of an army. There was no road, nor even a path leading from Fort Leavenworth into the regular Santa Fé trail. The army therefore steered its course south-westerly, with the view of intersecting the main Santa Fé trace, at or near the Narrows, sixty-five miles west of Independence. In accomplishing this, many deep ravines, and creeks with high and rugged banks, were to be encountered. The banks must be dug down, the asperities leveled, bridges built, and roads constructed, before the wagons could pass. All this required time and labor. The heat was often excessive; the grass was tall and rank; and the earth in many places so soft that the heavily loaded wagons would sink almost up to the axle upon the level prairie. The men were frequently compelled to dismount and drag them from the mire with their hands. The mules and other animals being mostly unused to the harness, often became refractory and balky. Numbers of wagons daily broke down. Time was required to make repairs. Hence the march was, of necessity, both slow and tedious.

On the 28th, the advanced battalion under command of Lieutenant-colonel Ruff, arrived upon the banks of Stranger creek, where it remained until the 30th.[21] Here also was presented a scene of some interest. Some of the men were reclining at ease in their tents, beguiling time with a novelette or a newspaper; some were engaged

* In a letter addressed by the author to the editor of the Tribune, a paper published in Liberty, about the time the expedition set forward, the following language was employed: "There is a novelty in this *anabasis* or invasion of Cols. Kearny and Doniphan. For the first time since the creation, the starred and striped banner of a free people is being borne over almost one thousand miles of trackless waste, and the principles of republicanism and civil liberty are about to be proclaimed to a nation fast sinking in slavery's arms; and fast closing her eyes upon the last expiring lights of religion, science and liberty."—HUGHES.

. NOTE 21.—Meredith T. Moore says that hundreds of snakes of all varieties common to the West infested the camp and its vicinity. They were even in the branches of the trees along the banks of the creek, as well as in the grass upon the ground. Rattlesnakes were the most common. Great numbers were killed by the soldiers, and not a man or animal was bitten.

in scouring and whetting their sabres, as if they already anticipated an attack from the Mexicans; others again were bathing their bodies in the limpid stream, or drawing the scaly fish to the shore. The Stranger is a branch of the Kansas, and drains one of the most fertile and picturesque districts of country over which the army passed.

About noon on the 30th, we arrived upon the banks of the Kansas river. This is a deep, rapid, yet beautiful stream, three hundred and fifty yards wide, and more than five hundred miles in length. It is no doubt navigable by steamboats of the smaller class, for a considerable distance above its mouth, without difficulty. We crossed the river in boats without loss or accident, and encamped for the night on the west bank, among the friendly Shawnees.[22] Some of the Shawnees have large farms, and as fine fields of corn as are to be met with in the States. They also have plenty of poultry, domestic animals, fine gardens, and many of the luxuries of civilized life. Here we obtained milk and butter; also peas, beans, potatoes, and other vegetables. The country between Fort Leavenworth and the Kansas, is very fine; the soil is exceedingly fertile,—vegetation is exuberant; and in many places the timber is tall and stately. Bold, fresh running springs gush from the ledges of limestone rock, and every river and creek is literally alive with the "finny tribe." It is destined perhaps at no distant day to sustain a dense and intelligent population. What a cheering reflection, that these beautiful ridges

NOTE 22.—The Kansas river was crossed at the mouth of the Wakarusa. The ferry was owned and operated by Paschal Fish, a Shawnee Indian, and a cousin to Tecumseh and the Prophet, and was known as "Fish's Ferry." Fish lived about a mile south of the river, on a road leading to Westport, and kept a tavern. The headquarters of the army remained at the ferry a day or two, and Col. Kearny wrote a letter to "His Excy. John E. Edwards, Gov. Missouri," dated as follows: "Head Qr. Army of the West, Camp at Fish's Ferry on Kansas River, July 2d,' 1846." In the "Notes of Lieutenant J. W. Abert" we find the following entry, on June 29th: "In the river we found two large flatboats or scows manned by Shawnee Indians, dressed in bright-colored shirts, with shawls around their heads. The current of the river was very rapid, so that it required the greatest exertions on the part of our ferrymen to prevent the boats from being swept far down the stream. We landed just at the mouth of Wakaroosa creek. . . . It was nearly 10 o'clock before all our company had crossed, and it was so dark that we could scarcely see to arrange camp. . . . The pure cold water of the Wakaroosa looked so inviting that some of us could not refrain from plunging beneath its crystal surface." In 1843 Odon Guitar crossed at the ferry. He was but a boy, and had run off to go to Santa Fé with Amos Marney, a freighter

and outstretched plains will ere long be dotted with the cities, villages, and habitations of civilized life!—that cultivated fields, surcharged with rich grains, will soon succeed to the seas of waving verdure which now luxuriously cover the earth! and that where now is heard the scream of the wild panther, and the startling yell of the savage, will soon become the busy scene of industry and domestic happiness!

On the first of July, the battalion continued its march in a southwesterly direction, to intersect the road leading from Independence to Santa Fé.[23] After a toilsome march of near fifteen miles, without a guide, through the tall prairie grass and matted pea-vines, over hill and dale, mound and mountain, in our bewilderment, sometimes directing our course to the southward, sometimes to the westward, we at length struck upon the old Santa Fé trace, and encamped for the night near the blackjack grove or the Narrows.* In our progress

*These points on the Santa Fé Trail were not identical, as the text seems to have them. Both were in what now is Douglas county, Kansas—Black Jack, a mile or two east of the present Baldwin, and the "Narrows" at Willow Springs, some eight or nine miles farther west, on the old trail. The army entered the trail near Black Jack.—W. E. C.

for Dr. Henry Connelly, and met with an accident which broke his thigh, at the point where Capt. Cooke was disarming the Texans, and was sent back to Fort Leavenworth by Cooke in an empty wagon returning there. He found the ferry operated for Fish by a man named Barnett. Guitar had suffered so much on the road that he could not eat. Barnett noticed that he looked thin and weak, and asked him if he could eat something. Guitar said he could eat roast chicken, cornbread, and fresh buttermilk. Barnett said he should have what he desired, but it was two hours before he returned with the food. He brought a fine roast chicken, some loaves of nicely browned corn-bread, and a large wooden bucket three-fourths full of fresh buttermilk. Guitar ate until he surprised even the Indian, and, fearing to eat more, quit before he was satisfied. He had not been able to sleep on the way, but after his meal he fell asleep immediately and slept soundly for two hours. When he awoke he was more hungry than at first, and at once devoured the remainder of the food brought by the Indian. No bad effects followed the enormous meal, and Guitar improved rapidly from the time he ate it.

NOTE 23.—For the identification of the Santa Fé Trail with the geography of the country as known to-day, see the Coues edition of *The Expeditions of Zebulon Montgomery Pike*, Francis P. Harper, New York, 1895, vol. II, pp. 517 to 522, note. For maps of the Santa Fé Trail, see *Notes of a Military Reconnoissance from Fort Leavenworth, in Missouri, to San Diego, California, made in 1846-7 with the Advance Guard of the "Army of the West,"* by W. H. Emory, Washington, 1848; this map gives the location of each camp made by the army between Fort

to-day, we encountered a formidable, precipitous and almost impassable hill or bluff, consisting of a solid ledge of limestone, which we were compelled to surmount, as it was impossible to avoid it by turning either to the right or the left. The ascent was steep, rugged, and at least two hundred feet in height, being the projecting spur of the high table land which divides the waters of the Kansas from those of the Osage. The wagons were principally drawn up this abrupt precipice by the power of hand, ropes being attached to them on both sides. More than one hundred men were often employed at once in drawing a heavily loaded government wagon to the summit of the hill. The heat was excessive.

It may be proper here to observe, that for the sake of convenience in procuring supplies of fuel and water, which can only be obtained at certain points, in crossing the Great Plains, Col. Kearny very prudently adopted the plan of conducting the march by separate detachments. These detachments (for convenience in traveling) generally consisted of a squadron of two or three companies, or of an entire battalion. The companies of volunteers were generally composed of 114 men each, including commissioned officers. Thus the march was chiefly conducted to the borders of New Mexico, or the boundary line which separates between Mexico and the United States.

Col. Doniphan and Maj. Gilpin,[24] with the second battalion, and Col. Kearny, with the battalion of artillery, the corps of field and topographical engineers, and a small squadron of volunteers and

---

Leavenworth and Santa Fé; *Memoir of a Tour to Northern Mexico Connected with Col. Doniphan's Expedition*, by A. Wislizenus, M. D., Washington, 1848; *Commerce of the Prairies*, by Josiah Gregg, New York, 1845; reprinted in *Early Western Travels*, vols. XIX, XX, the Arthur H. Clark Company, Cleveland, Ohio, 1905.

NOTE 24.—*William Gilpin.*—The ancestor of William Gilpin was one De Guylpyn, who came into Britain with William the Conqueror, and his descendants acted an honorable part in that country for centuries. One of them, Joseph Gilpin, a Quaker, in 1696 emigrated to America, and settled at the Birmingham meeting-house on the Brandywine, in what is now Delaware county, Pennsylvania. It is said that three States cornered in the Gilpin orchard when the lines were finally fixed between Pennsylvania, Maryland, and Delaware. Joseph Gilpin had a son Samuel, who had a son Thomas, who had a son Joshua, born in Philadelphia in 1765. William Gilpin was the eighth and youngest child of Joshua Gilpin. He was born at the old homestead on the Brandywine, Delaware county, Pennsylvania, October 4, 1822. Being Quakers of the straitest sort, the Gilpins took no part in the Revolution that required service in the army;

dragoons, followed closely in our rear; nothing of historical moment having occurred up to this time, since their departure from Fort

but they were true patriots, in full sympathy with their fellow-colonists, and the old home was the headquarters of General Lafayette at the battle of the Brandywine.

William Gilpin attended school in England, but returned to Philadelphia and graduated at the University of Pennsylvania. His tutor in preparation for the university was Nathaniel Hawthorne. President Jackson was on intimate terms with the Gilpin family, and appointed Henry Gilpin, brother of William,

WILLIAM GILPIN.

Explorer and statesman. Major First Regiment Missouri Volunteers. First Governor of Colorado.

(From steel engraving in "Chronicles of the Builders of the Commonwealth," by Hubert Howe Bancroft.)

Attorney-General for the United States. He also arranged for the attendance of William Gilpin at West Point, where his tutors were George G. Meade and Montgomery Blair. Upon his graduation from that institution Gilpin was appointed Second Lieutenant in the Second Dragoons and sent to Missouri to recruit troops for the Florida or Seminole War. His recruiting finished, he went to the front and saw considerable service in the field. At the end of the war he requested permission to lead an exploring expedition to the Columbia river, but this was not complied with. Thereupon he resigned from the army.

Leavenworth. Numerous trains of government wagons continued to be dispatched from the Fort upon the road to Santa Fé. Fort

Gilpin turned his face toward the setting sun. He saw that the greatness of the United States would result from the development of the West. At St. Louis he found work to do. He was editor of the *Missouri Argus* for a year, advocating the reëlection of Senators Lynn and Benton. The opposition had secured the presence of Daniel Webster in the campaign; he made a speech in St. Louis, in which he attacked Benton and advocated his defeat. But both Benton and Lynn were returned to the Senate. In this work there was formed a strong friendship between Benton and Gilpin, which endured through the lives of both. Gilpin was made Clerk of the Missouri House of Representatives in 1840. In 1841 he moved to Independence, Jackson county, Missouri, where he made his home for twenty years, though often absent, engaged in war or in the exploration of the West. Senator Benton owed much of his enthusiasm for the West to Gilpin. In this connection it is well to note the attitude of Daniel Webster toward the West; for it was the attitude of all New England, and had our development depended upon that section of the Union the western limits of the United States would never have passed the Mississippi. The entire West and its development as a part of the American Union resulted as a consequence of the political policy of the South. In opposing the establishment of a mail route from Independence, Missouri, to the mouth of the Columbia, Webster voiced the sentiment of New England, as follows:

"What do we want with this vast, worthless area? This region of savages and wild beasts, of deserts, of shifting sands and whirlwinds of dust, of cactus and prairie-dogs? To what use could we ever hope to put these great deserts, or those endless mountain ranges, impenetrable, and covered to their very base with eternal snow? What can we ever hope to do with the western coast, a coast of three thousand miles, rock-bound, cheerless, uninviting, and not a harbor on it? What use have we for such a country? Mr. President, I will never vote one cent from the public treasury to place the Pacific coast one inch nearer to Boston than it now is."

Gilpin purchased a large tract of land between the town of Independence and the Missouri river, and laid out Gilpintown. He had unbounded faith in the future of the country; and in the Kansas City Public Library there is preserved a map drawn by him showing the future city, under the name of Centropolis, extending from Independence to the Kansas river. He based his conclusions on observation of the physical conformation of the country. We have another map made by Gilpin, showing that a railroad from the western extremity of Lake Superior to Galveston, and one from Baltimore to the Pacific coast, would cross near the mouth of the Kansas river. Gilpin was, indeed, the prophet of Kansas City. The short period of sixty years has seen the accomplishment of all that he foretold. That great metropolis will not fail to duly honor William Gilpin in the years to come.

Gilpin was sent out with a party of ten men in 1843 to protect the New-Mexican traders, but they were too late to prevent the murder of Chavez by robbers, who carried away his money; but they were apprehended at Kansas City and taken to St. Louis, where four of them were hanged for the crime.

Upon his return from this expedition he sold his law library and some other personal effects to raise money with which to purchase an outfit suitable for an

Bent, on the Arkansas, nearly six hundred miles west of Independence, was, however, looked forward to as the first point of general expedition to the mouth of the Columbia river. Gilpin set out alone to make this journey, being accompanied as far as Lone Elm, on the Santa Fé Trail, by his friend David Waldo. There he fell in with the party of Frémont, as is said by his biographer, by accident; but Frémont says Gilpin had been invited to go out with the party. This meeting was on May 31, 1843, and is described by Bancroft (*Chronicles of the Builders of the Commonwealth*, p. 522) as follows:

"He went into camp the first evening, out about thirty miles, at a spot called the Lone Elm, David Waldo, the man who had loaned him the money, accompanying him thus far. He found encamped in this vicinity a few men whom he did not at first recognize, but to his surprise they proved to be the party of Frémont. This immortal pathfinder asked Gilpin where he was going, and was told. He expressed astonishment, and said: 'Why, even with my whole force I do not consider myself safe from massacre to-morrow; now if you are determined to go on, throw your pack into one of my *charettes*, turn your mule into my band, and let me have the reënforcement of your horse and rifle.' This arrangement was highly satisfactory to Gilpin, as it afforded him companionship and protection for a long distance."

The expedition arrived at Walla Walla about the middle of October. Gilpin went on to Vancouver, where he received a warm welcome from McLoughlin, factor of the Hudson Bay Company. There he remained for some time, learning all he could of the country and its resources. Some effort was made by the people in that region to form a provisional government, and Gilpin drew up a statement in favor of the movement. He submitted this document with his report March 2, 1846, at Washington, and it was ordered printed by the Senate. Another report was called for and furnished. These reports contained much information about Oregon entirely new to Congress.

Gilpin returned to Independence upon the declaration of war with Mexico. He desired to participate actively in this war. The manner of his enlistment is thus told by his biographer:

"After the declaration of war he had notified persons in Jackson county to raise a company, and they had saved a place for him, but this he did not want. From President Polk he had obtained permission to call out one regiment of Missouri cavalry, and to call it the Army of the West. Upon reaching Independence he found that a company of 105 men had been raised, and had proceeded to Fort Leavenworth to be mustered in.

"He at once proceeded to Fort Leavenworth, and there found six companies of the First Regiment Missouri Volunteers. Company A of this regiment was composed of his friends who were anxiously awaiting his arrival. Kearny was present, and as he did not feel kindly toward Gilpin he determined that he should have no command. Gilpin felt that he would be elected an officer if he could once gain admission to the company. He found in the company from Jackson county a boy, sixteen years old, whose widowed mother had claimed his discharge on account of his youth, and Gilpin paid this boy eighty-five dollars for his place in the ranks. Otherwise he could not have secured a place, as the company already numbered 105; but as they were strong, hardy, and desirable soldiers, they had been permitted to remain. Gilpin was a trained soldier from the school, and had also had experience on the field, and he drilled the companies up to the time of the election of officers. Among the men was an old classmate named Ruff. Some of the men were pleased to think they could prevent Gilpin from holding any office in the company, as he previously had worked his way up to a first-lieutenancy, and then, despising that rank, had resigned.

"Well, the election proceeded. A man named Doniphan was chosen colonel,

rendezvous for all the different detachments, and for the government trains. This post was subsequently converted into a provision depot for the United States' government.

The practicability of marching a large army over the waste, un-

and the election for lieutenant-colonel then came up. Doniphan desired Gilpin to have the place, but Ruff was the candidate of the West-Pointers. Ruff was elected by two votes. The office of major was still open. After the election had proceeded thus far, the regiment broke into confusion and declared that Gilpin should be major. Gilpin thereupon made them a speech of about twenty minutes' duration, after which he was informed that Kearny wished to see him in his office. He obeyed the summons, and Kearny said: 'I have received from the President an appointment for you as lieutenant-colonel of the Third Regiment, and I suppose this is followed by a life service if you choose. Had you not better withdraw now and avail yourself of this appointment?' Said Gilpin, 'I will not accept it.' He felt it was a measure which would turn him from the West. He returned to the parade-ground and was unanimously declared elected major, without the formality of balloting. In spite of his age, Gilpin had at that time had more frontier experience than any of the officers; his training had been thorough and varied, and he was virtually master of the situation. The army entered Santa Fé in triumph on the 14th of August, 1846. Kearny had become homesick, and desired to turn back."

The part borne by Gilpin in the war will develop in this work, and need not be reviewed here.

Gilpin returned from the Mexican War to Independence in wretched health. He took to his bed, and while prostrated there he was visited by Governor Edwards, who informed him that the Indians had been hostile along the Santa Fé Trail during the summer, murdering traders, freighters, teamsters and herders, stealing horses and cattle and burning trains. They threatened an invasion of the settlements, and this created excitement and uneasiness. The Governor told Gilpin that he came at the request of President Polk to induce him to raise a battalion of volunteers for the purpose of reopening and maintaining communications with New Mexico. Gilpin at first refused this service, but finally formulated conditions upon which he would accept it. These conditions were accepted, and Gilpin raised the battalion and marched it to Fort Leavenworth to be mustered into the service of the United States. There he had difficulty in securing supplies from Lieutenant-Colonel Clifton Wharton, though when the matter had reached the point where Gilpin had resolved to fight a duel with Wharton the supplies were forthcoming. They consisted of five hundred beef cattle, fifteen wagons of ammunition, and two hundred wagons of provisions. Gilpin left Fort Leavenworth with his army and train October 4, 1847. The first permanent camp was made on the Arkansas river, just below the present town of Pueblo. There the army spent the winter drilling and patrolling the Santa Fé Trail, and sometimes holding council with Indian tribes. In the spring active campaigning began. "Nine battles were fought from the middle of July to the end of August, and two hundred and fifty-three scalps of warriors were taken from first to last," is the record of the summer's fighting. So little has been known of this battalion of the Plains that some official data are here inserted concerning it.

GILPIN'S SANTA FÉ TRACE BATTALION.

Gilpin's Santa Fé Trace Battalion, Missouri Mounted Volunteers, Mexican War.

cultivated, uninhabited, prairie regions of the west, was universally regarded as problematical. But the matter has been tested. The experiment proved completely successful. Provisions, (chiefly bread-

---

This battalion was also known as "Gilpin's Battalion Missouri Mounted Volunteers," "Indian Battalion Missouri Volunteers," and "Battalion Missouri Voluntcers for the Plains."

The battalion consisted of Companies A, B, C, D, E. Company C was Captain William Pelzer's Artillery Company.

Mounted Companies ....A and B.
Artillery..C.
Not Mounted..D and E.

Roster of Company C shows 20 officers and 84 privates.
Roster of Company D shows 17 officers and 63 privates.
Roster of Company E shows 17 officers and 69 privates.
Rosters of Companies A and B not found in the office of the Adjutant-General, State of Missouri.

Field and Staff.

Field and Staff, Santa Fé Trace Battalion, Missouri Mounted Volunteers, Mexican War.

Muster Roll for September 18, 1847, to April 30, 1848, shows station at Fort Mann, Middle Arkansas [river; in what is now the State of Kansas.] This Roll bears date, June 25, for April 30—"*nunc pro tunc.*" Reason, "absence of myself and three Companies in the Comanche Country": W. Gilpin, Lt. Col. Commanding.

Roll signed: W. Gilpin, Lt. Col.

Muster Roll, April 30, to October 3, 1848, shows Company at Independence, Missouri. Roll signed: W. Gilpin, Lt. Col.

Field and Staff mustered for discharge at Independence, Missouri, October 3, 1848, and honorably discharged by E. A. Hitchcock, B. Col., U. S. A., Mustering Officer.

Roster of Field and Staff, Colonel W. Gilpin's Battalion of Missouri Volunteers, Mexican War.

Roster.

1. William Gilpin................................Lt. Col.
1. Henry L. Routt...............................Adjutant.
1. Ephraim P. January..........................Ass. Surgeon.
1. Ashley G. Gully..............................2nd Lieut.
2. Edward Colston..............................2nd Lieut.
1. Jacob T. Tindall.............................Sgt. Major.
1. Adam Krafft.................................Chief Bugler.
1. Benjamin S. Long............................Asst. Surgeon.
1. William Kuhlan..............................Q. M. Sgt.

Company A.

Captain John C. Griffith's Company A, Mounted Santa Fé Trace Battalion, Missouri Mounted Volunteers, Mexican War.

Muster-in Roll dated September 3, 1847, shows station of company at Fort Leavenworth.

Company arrived at Fort Leavenworth, Missouri, place of general rendezvous, September 1, 1847.

Company accepted into the service of the United States for term of "During the War with Mexico" from September 3, 1847, by C. Wharton, Lieut.-Colonel First Dragoons, Mustering Officer.

stuffs, salt, &c.,) were conveyed in wagons, and beef-cattle driven along for the use of the men. The animals subsisted entirely by grazing. To secure them from straying off at night, they were

Muster Roll, September 3, 1847, to April 30, 1848, shows station of company at Fort Mann, Middle Arkansas.
The company had been encamped and on the march in the Indian country since the middle of September, 1847, and during March, April and May, in the center of the Comanche country. This Muster Roll is therefore made at this date—"*nunc pro tunc.*" Roll dated June 24, 1848.
Roll signed: John C. Griffith, Captain.
Muster Roll, April 30, to September 28, 1848, shows station of company, Independence, Missouri.
Roll signed: John C. Griffith, Captain.
Company mustered for discharge at Independence, Missouri, September 28, 1848, and honorably discharged by E. A. Hitchcock, B. Col., U. S. A., Mustering Officer.

Company B.

Captain Thomas Jones's Company B, Mounted Santa Fé Trace Battalion, Missouri Volunteers, War with Mexico.
Muster-in Roll, dated September 11, 1847, shows station of company at Fort Leavenworth.
Company arrived at Fort Leavenworth, September 8, 1847.
[Other entries, similar to those made on the Rolls of Company A.]

Company C.

Captain William Pelzer's Company C, Artillery, Santa Fé Trace Battalion, Missouri Volunteers, Mexican War.
Muster-in Roll, dated September 10, 1847.
Company arrived at Fort Leavenworth, September 8, 1847.
Term of service same as Companies A and B.
Report from Fort Mann, Middle Arkansas, "*nunc pro tunc,*" owing to continued separation; difficulty of communication between detached portions of battalion; and absence of Paymaster.
Company discharged at Independence, Missouri, October 2, 1848.

Company D.

Captain Paul Holzscheiter's Company D, Santa Fé Trace Battalion, Missouri Volunteers, Mexican War.
Muster-in Roll, dated September 18, 1847.
Company at Fort Mann, Middle Arkansas, same dates and same reasons for "*nunc pro tunc*" reports as given by Companies A and B.
Company discharged at Independence, Mo., October 1, 1848.

Company E.

Captain Napoleon Koscialowski's Company E, Santa Fé Trace Battalion, Missouri Volunteers, Mexican War.
Muster Roll, September 18, 1847, to April 30, 1848, shows company at Fort Mann, Middle Arkansas. The above company being on the march through the center of the Comanche country during March, April and May, this Roll bears date in June—"*nunc pro tunc.*" W. Gilpin, Col. Comdg.
Roll signed: Napoleon Koscialowski, Captain.
Company Muster Roll, April 30 to September 30, 1848, shows company at Independence, Mo.
The company left Fort Leavenworth on the 4th day of October, 1847, and ascended the Arkansas to the foot of the Rocky Mountains at Bent's Fort. From thence with the cavalry companies under the Lieutenant-Colonel, crossed the Raton Mountains on the 10th of March, 1848, and descended the Canadian through the country of the Apache and Comanche Indians during March, April

either driven into corrals formed of the wagons, or tethered to an iron picket driven into the ground about fifteen inches.

At the outset of the expedition many laughable scenes took place. Our horses were generally wild, fiery, and ungovernable; wholly unused to military trappings and equipments. Amidst the fluttering of banners, the sounding of the bugles, the rattling of artillery,

---

and May, to the Antelope Buttes, being engaged in skirmishing warfare with the Comanche and Pawnee Indians on the Middle Arkansas and Kansas until the expiration of the term of service by the peace with Mexico.

The marches have exceeded 3000 miles in the aggregate, mostly being in the depth of winter.

Roll signed: Caleb S. Tuttle, Captain.

Company mustered for discharge at Independence, Mo., September 30, 1848, and honorably discharged (except Lieut. Colston) by E. A. Hitchcock, B. Col., U. S. A., Mustering Officer.

Fort Mann was situated about six miles west of the present Dodge City, three hundred and fifty-nine miles from Fort Leavenworth and four hundred and twenty-three miles from Santa Fé. It was established about 1845. The name was changed to that of Fort Mackay, in honor of Colonel A. Mackay, of the Quartermaster's Department; and later it was changed to Fort Atkinson. These changes of name led to confusion afterwards, writers locating each fort in a separate place, no record appearing that there was one fort with three different names.

Gilpin knew that the question of transportation was the question to be met and successfully solved if the development of the West was to be assured. He labored with tongue and pen in the interest of a railroad from the Missouri river to the Pacific ocean. In the early summer of 1849 he delivered an address on this subject to five thousand California emigrants assembled on the ground where Lawrence, Kansas, was afterward built. This address was repeated at a mass meeting at Independence, Missouri, November 5, 1849. It is a masterly production, and is published in his *Mission of the North American People*, Appendix II.

There was an effort made by the people living in the Indian country west of Missouri to secure the organization of a territory composed of what is now Kansas and Nebraska, and westward to the crest of the Rocky Mountains. Gilpin took an active interest in this movement. A meeting to forward this matter was held in the Council House of the Wyandots, in what is now Kansas City, Kansas, July 26, 1853, and a preamble and resolutions were adopted which served as a provisional constitution, and which indorsed the building of a railroad to the Pacific coast by what was termed the "Central Route" (up the Kansas Valley from the Missouri river). The document is the first State Paper of Kansas and Nebraska, and is published in *The Provisional Government of Nebraska Territory*, by the present author. As W. F. Dyer was Chairman of the Committee on Resolutions appointed by the meeting, I supposed that he of course wrote the preamble and resolutions; but since writing that book I have become familiar with the handwriting of William Gilpin, and know they were prepared and written by him.

Gilpin is said to have been the only man in Jackson county, Missouri, who voted for Abraham Lincoln for President in 1860. He was one of the company

the clattering of sabres, and cooking utensils, some of the horses took fright and scampered pell-mell, with rider and arms, over the wide prairie. Rider, arms and accoutrements, saddles, saddle-bags, tin-cups, and coffee-pots, were sometimes left far behind in the chase. No very serious or fatal accident, however, occurred from this cause. All was right again as soon as the affrighted animals were recovered.

The "Army of the West," was, perhaps, composed of as fine material as any other body of troops then in the field. The volunteer corps consisted almost entirely of the young men of the country; generally of the very first families of the State. All parties were united in one common cause for the vindication of the national honor. Every calling and profession contributed its share. There might be seen under arms, in the ranks, the lawyer, the doctor, the professor, the student, the legislator, the farmer, the mechanic, and artisans of every description, all united as a band of brothers to defend the

---

that attended President Lincoln from Springfield to Washington; and there he became one of the company of patriots that, under Senator James H. Lane of Kansas and Cassius M. Clay of Kentucky, guarded the capital for some time, sleeping at night in the White House.

President Lincoln appointed William Gilpin Governor of the Territory of Colorado, which position he filled for two years—1861–1863.

Gilpin was a ripe scholar. He wrote a number of works treating of the West and its development, among them *The Central Gold Region* (1860); *Mission of the North American People, Geographical, Social, and Political; Illustrated by six charts delineating the Physical Architecture and Thermal Laws of all the Continents* (1873). This is a most remarkable book. It predicted that a railroad would girdle the earth by way of Behring Strait. At the time it was written there was no railroad of importance in Asia. The prophecy is now fulfilled. The railroad is built through Alaska and across Siberia on the lines marked on Gilpin's chart.

The only biography of Gilpin worthy the name is found in *Chronicles of the Builders of the Commonwealth*, by Hubert Howe Bancroft, San Francisco, 1891. This sketch is drawn largely from that work.

William Gilpin was full six feet high, of spare form, and weighing about one hundred and sixty pounds. He had brown hair and dark hazel eyes. He married, February 12, 1874, Mrs. Julia Pratt Dickerson, of St. Louis, Mo. Three children were born of this marriage—William and Mary, twins, born May 12, 1875; and Louis, born July 10, 1877. Gilpin amassed a large fortune by prudent investments in land, mostly in Colorado.

William Gilpin was a clean, honorable, able, conscientious American citizen. He was one of the great men of his day. He stood among men who subdued the desert, watered the wastes, harnessed the mountains, utilized the rivers, and bound a girdle of steel across a continent. In this work he bore a noble part, and was the peer of any and of all.

He died in Denver, Colorado, January 19, 1894.

rights and honor of their country; to redress her wrongs and avenge her insults. This blooming host of young life, the elite of Missouri, was full of ardor, full of spirit, full of generous enthusiasm, burning for the battle field, and panting for the rewards of honorable victory. They were prompted to this gallant discharge of duty, and prepared to breast every storm of adversity, by the remembrance of the dear pledges of affection they left behind them; their mothers, their sisters, their young brides, their aged fathers, who, they knew would receive them with outstretched arms, if they returned triumphant from many a well contested field with the laurels of victory; but who, they were equally certain, would frown with indignation upon him who, in the hour of battle, would desert the flag of his country. Their chivalry failed them not.

CHAPTER II.

View of the Army on the Prairies—Singular phenomenon—Attention to horses—Fourth of July—Council Grove—Its locale—Diamond Springs—Government trains—Interesting inquiry—Prairie fuel—Musquitoes and the black gnat—Express from Col. Doniphan—Altercation between officers—Chavez—His tragical end—The mirage—Sand hills—The Big Arkansas—Buffalo—Pawnee Rock—Forces re-united at the Pawnee River—Difficult passage—The Infantry—Maj. Howard—Charge upon the Buffalo—Reptiles and insects—Flowers—Prairie dog villages—Death of Leslie—Attachment of men to their horses—appearance of the Army—Fitzpatrick, the mountaineer—The report—Mexican Spies taken—Army encamped in the Mexican territory.

All was now fairly upon the great Santa Fé road which led to the enemy's country. At break of day on the 2d of July, the reveillée was sounded. The army was on the march ere the first beams of the morning sun had kissed the glittering dew drops from the prairie grass, bearing aloft their streaming flags to the breeze, with their "broad stripes and bright stars," and "E Pluribus Unum." As the troops moved off majestically over the green prairie, they presented the most martial and animating sight. The long lines stretched over miles of level plain, or wound serpentinely over the beautifully undulating hills, with guns and sabres glittering in the sheen of the rising sun, while the American eagle seemed to spread his broad pinions, and westward bear the principles of republican government.

The following interesting phenomenon was related to the author by one who declares that he was an eye witness of the fact, and that twenty-eight others will testify to the truth of his declaration. "Early in the spring of 1846, before it was known, or even conjectured, that a state of war would be declared to exist between this government and Mexico, 29 traders, on their way from Santa Fé to Independence, beheld, just after a storm, and a little while before sunset, a perfectly distinct image of the "bird of liberty," the American eagle on the disc of the sun. When they beheld the interesting sight, they simultaneously, and almost involuntarily exclaimed that in less than twelve months the eagle of liberty would spread his broad pinions over the plains of the west, and that the flag of our country would wave over the cities of New Mexico and Chihuahua." The prediction has been literally and strikingly verified, although the story is, doubtless, more beautiful than true. Quite as much credit is due to it, however, as to the wonderful story about the chariots of fire, which the Romans are said to have seen in the heavens after the assassination of Cæsar by Brutus and Cassius in the Roman senate.

A march over the great plains is attended with a recurrence of pretty much the same scenes, from day to day. The same boundless green—the emerald prairies—seems to spread out before you; the same bright heavens are above; the same solid earth of uniform surface beneath; or if the monotony be at all broken, it is by the gradual change of the broad prairie into a succession of gently rolling hills, as when the unruffled bosom of the ocean is heaved into waves by the storm. Occasionally the dull scene is relieved by the appearance of a rill or brook, winding among the undulations of the prairie, skirted by clumps and groves of trees, or by the wild sunflower, pink, or rose, which seem to blossom only to cheer with their mellifluous odors the waste around them. Some witty remark, or lively song, will often create a hearty laugh; the feeling will perhaps be communicated from one end of the line to the other. In this way the greatest good humor and most cheerful flow of spirits are kept up continually on the march. An army is always cheerful and frolicsome.

On the plains our horses were the objects of our most especial attention. Whoever was so unfortunate as to lose his charger, was necessitated to continue the march on foot, or drive a wagon, both of which were unpleasant to the volunteer soldier, to say nothing of the chagrin of losing his place in his company as a cavalier. We therefore secured our horses with all possible care at night, to guard against escapes. Great prudence was also necessary in riding cautiously, and grazing carefully, to prevent the stock from failing on the road. Chasing deer, antelope and buffalo on the plain will ruin a horse, and speedily unfit him for military service. When a soldier by ill luck happened to lose his horse, he would purchase another at almost any cost, if there chanced to be a surplus one in camp. His situation enabled him fully to appreciate the force of the expression which Shakespeare puts into the mouth of King Richard, "*A kingdom for a horse!*" No wonder then that Alexander wept when Bucephalus died.

The 4th of July, independence day, seemed to inspire the troops with new life and cheerfulness;—although upon the wide prairies of the west, we could not forget to commemorate the annual return of the hallowed day that gave birth to our national liberty. Though on the march all day, and in the midst of a boundless solitude, with nothing for the eye to rest upon save the heaven above or the solid earth beneath, and none of the lovely objects of home around us, and none of the festivities spread before us, which usually greeted us on the anniversary of our liberty, yet our bosoms swelled with the same noble impulses and the same quenchless love of freedom, which animated the breast of our ancestors of '76, and caught inspiration from the memory of their achievements. Ever and anon the enthusiastic shout, the loud huzza, and the animating Yankee Doodle, were heard in honor of independence day. After a toilsome march of twenty-seven miles, upon the green, boundless plain, exposed to the heated rays of an almost vertical sun, we pitched our tents at sunset on the banks of Bluff creek, where we found plenty of cool spring water, and an abundant supply of grass and fuel. The greatest good humor prevailed in camp.

A march of twelve miles on the 5th, brought us to the famous Council Grove, a place remarkable in the history of the Santa Fé trade, and distinguished above all others as being the point of general rendezvous for traders, trappers, mountaineers, and others, of border life. Here, timbers for repairing wagons which may fail on the road across the great plains, are generally procured, this being the last grove where good timber can be obtained on the route. In this pleasant and romantic valley, the army detained two days for this purpose. The Council Grove is nothing more than a forest of timber, about one mile in width, skirting a beautiful, meandering stream, the head branch of the Neosho river, fed by innumerable rills and springs of the finest and most delicious water, although some writers have attempted to invest it with a sort of romantic interest and dignify it with a name calculated to induce the belief that the various wild tribes of the plains once met annually upon this consecrated spot "to smoke the calumet of peace." This grove, where the prairie traveler often takes a pleasant siesta, and where a few houses and a blacksmith shop have recently been erected for the use of the government, is situated about one hundred and fifty miles west of the western frontier of Missouri.[25]

NOTE 25.—Council Grove is now the county seat of Morris county, Kansas. It has a population of about twenty-five hundred. By Gregg's table of distances

Advancing about sixteen miles further, over high, rolling prairies, we encamped near the Diamond Springs. The heat was oppressive. The most enchanting spots ever depicted by the pen of the eastern romancer, possess not more charms for the youthful imagination, than do the groves and the fine, gushing, transparent Diamond Springs, for the thirsty, wayworn traveler on the plains. These crystal fountains derive their name from the limpidness of their waters. Travelers across the plains are compelled to stop at certain places for water, wood and rest. These places for convenience are mostly dignified with appropriate names, though in the midst of solitary wastes where there never existed, and perhaps never will exist, a human habitation, or the least vestige of civilization.

Our provisions becoming scant, on the 7th, Lieut. S. Jackson, of Howard, with four men, was sent forward seven or eight days march in advance of the command, with orders to halt a train of provisions wagons at the Pawnee Fork of the Arkansas. This order was promptly executed. It may not be improper in this connection, to observe, that the government trains, which were fitted up at Fort Leavenworth, were dispatched upon the road in companies of twenty-five or thirty wagons, irrespective of the marches of the different detachments of troops. It therefore often happened that some portions of the army, for short periods of time, were destitute of supplies upon the road. Each of these trains of wagons had a superintendent-general, or wagon-master, and the wagoners were well armed, so that there was no need of an escort or guard, as these brave and hardy teamsters were at all times prepared to fight their own battles against the Indians who beset the roads for plunder. Had the wagoners employed in Gen. Taylor's division of the army been equally well

---

on the Santa Fé Trail (see vol. II, p. 313, *Commerce of the Prairies*), it was 145 miles from Independence, Mo. It was one of the most important stations on the old trail. There the caravans assembled to form an organization for protection against the savages infesting the country to Santa Fé. In 1847 the Kansas Indians were placed on a reservation twenty miles square, which embraced Council Grove. In 1849, Waldo, Hall & Co. secured a contract to carry the United States mail from Independence to Santa Fé, and erected several buildings at Council Grove. For a history of Council Grove, see the Coues edition of *The Expeditions of Zebulon Montgomery Pike*, Gregg's *Commerce of the Prairies*, *Early Western Travels*, edited by R. G. Thwaites, 33 volumes, and *Cutler's History of Kansas*, commonly known as the "Kansas Herd-Book."

furnished with arms, perhaps so many of them would not have fallen a sacrifice to the Mexican guerillas.

After a progress of twenty-nine miles,* over a level, smooth surface, covered with tall, rank grass, waving in green ridges before the sporting breeze, we arrived upon the banks of the Cottonwood Fork[26] of the Neosho. On these elevated prairies, an interesting phenomenon is presented, worthy the consideration of the philosopher. A zigzag strip of grass, of more luxuriant growth than the rest, resembling the forky course of lightning, may often be distinctly traced by the eye. The proposition then arises, may not the lightning, in its course, thus have touched and marked the earth, communicating to the soil a degree of fertility, which manifests itself in the exuberant production alluded to? and may not barren countries and sterile lands be reclaimed, by conducting the electric fluid into the bosom of the earth by means of lightning-rods, or an iron forest? Surely these propositions are of some magnitude.

A march of fifteen miles brought us to Turkey creek, where we found a tolerable supply of grass and water, but not a stick of timber; not even a twig as large as a pipe-stem. This was the first time the men were necessitated to broil their meat and boil their coffee on a smouldering heap of the dried ordure of the buffalo, which lay scattered in great profusion upon the prairie. This "prairie fuel," as the volunteers termed it, is a tolerable substitute for wood, in dry, but is worse than useless in wet weather. It was our chief reliance, however, as we advanced further upon the great plains.

On the 9th, after a hurried march of twenty-five miles, we arrived upon the banks of the Little Arkansas,[27] about ten miles above its confluence with the main Arkansas river. Here the mosquitoes, and their allies, the black gnat, in swarms, attacked us in the most

* The distance of each day's march was generally reported by Captain Emory, of the Field and Topographical Engineers, and also the latitude and longitude of all places of importance on the route.—HUGHES.

NOTE 26.—The Cottonwood is one of the principal branches of the Neosho river, uniting with that stream about six miles below Emporia, Kansas. Its waters embrace Morris, Marion, Chase and Lyon counties. The Santa Fé Trail crossed its branches frequently, the first at or near Diamond Springs.

NOTE 27.—The Little Arkansas river has its sources in Ellsworth county, Kansas, and flows through Rice, McPherson, Reno, Harvey and Sedgwick counties, uniting with the Arkansas at Wichita. The Santa Fé Trail crossed it in Rice county.

heroic manner, and annoyed us as much, if not more than the Mexican lancers did at a subsequent period. While at this camp, an express arrived from the two detachments immediately under command of Cols. Doniphan and Kearny, representing them as being in a starving condition, and calling upon Lieutenant-colonel Ruff to furnish them with such portion of his provisions as could be spared. Lieutenant-colonel Ruff, being destitute himself, and having, as already noticed, sent an express to Pawnee Fork for supplies, directed the express men from Col. Kearny to proceed thither, and bring to a halt such a number of provision wagons as would be sufficient for the three detachments. One of these express men, A. E. Hughes, in attempting to swim the Pawnee river, at that time very much swollen by the recent freshets,[28] was drowned. His corpse was afterwards found floating in the stream, and was taken and buried with appropriate military honors.*

On the morning of the 10th, a heavy drenching rain was descending. Twenty or thirty men were sick, and comfortably sheltered by their tents from the driving storm. An order was given, however, to take up the line of march. Some of the captains, at first, refused to strike tents; not wishing to expose their sick men unnecessarily to the inclement weather. The order was regarded as ill-timed, and highly improper. An altercation took place between Captain Jackson and Lieutenant-colonel Ruff, commanding the detachment, the result of which, however, was less serious than was at first anticipated. At length, all struck their tents, and were ready for the march. We

* Mr. Innman, a merchant of Lexington, was drowned in the Missouri, at Fort Leavenworth, just before the expedition set forward. He was the first man lost. His interment took place at the fort.—HUGHES.

NOTE 28.—The army found this stream still high, and a rude bridge had to be constructed on the trunks of the cottonwoods cut on each bank to fall into the water, meeting in the middle of the river, for the passage of the troops and trains. The horses were made to swim. Meredith T. Moore drowned the horse of George L. Boone, his messmate. Boone was not well, and requested Moore to get his horse over for him. The horse would not swim, but turned back twice after reaching deep water. Moore mounted him and rode him into the stream again; he had heard that a horse could be made to swim by "ducking," and when the horse was forced beyond his depth Moore put his head under water. The horse sank like lead and was never seen again. Moore furnished Boone money with which to buy another horse. After the war Boone moved to Oregon, and in 1849 Moore went to California, hearing which, Boone bought a fine mule and outfit and sent it to Moore, but the Indians captured it.

left, at this camping place, for the detachment with Colonel Doniphan, the only provisions we had to spare, consisting of two barrels of flour, two of pork, and one of salt. This relieved the Colonel considerably, as he had with him only two companies, numbering about two hundred and twenty men. Colonel Kearny was still in the rear of Colonel Doniphan, about one day's march, with five companies, very scant of provisions, pushing forward with the utmost vigor. The two companies under Captains Reid and Waldo, were in our advance some three days' march, and still farther on was the detachment of dragoons, under Captains Moore, Burgwin, and Lieutenant Noble.

Col. Doniphan, having quickened his pace, overhauled the first battalion under command of Lieutenant-colonel Ruff, on the evening of the 11th, encamped on Cow creek.[29] This was the first time we had seen Col. Doniphan since leaving Fort Leavenworth, a distance of two hundred and fifty miles. Uniting the two detachments, his force was now swelled to near 700 men. It was on this creek that Don Antonio José Chavez, a New Mexican trader, was robbed and murdered, in the spring of 1843, by a marauding party of fifteen men, headed by Capt. John McDaniel, of Liberty, pretending to hold a commission under the government of Texas. This unfortunate Mexican had with him five servants, and about ten thousand dollars, principally in gold bullion. The perpetrators of this bloody deed were promptly arrested and brought to justice. The captain and one of his comrades being convicted of murder, before the United States' court at St. Louis, were executed according to law. The rest who were concerned in the robbery, were sentenced to fine and imprisonment. A few escaped.

Early on the morning of the 12th, the command left Cow creek, and after a march of twenty-six miles encamped for the night at Walnut creek,[30] near its junction with the Arkansas. The day was excessively hot. The thermometer, though exposed to the breeze, stood at ninety-five degrees Fahrenheit. The earth was literally

NOTE 29.—Cow creek rises near the south line of Russell county, and flows through Barton, Rice and Reno counties, and empties into the Arkansas near Hutchinson. It was crossed by the Santa Fé Trail in what is now Rice county.

NOTE 30.—Walnut creek takes its rise in Lane county, Kansas, and has a course of more than one hundred miles almost due east, and unites with the Arkansas a few miles below Great Bend. It flows through Lane, Ness and Barton counties. The Santa Fé Trail crossed it near the mouth, in Barton county.

parched to a crust, and the grass in many places crisped by the heat of the sun. In the distant horizon, upon the green plains, might be seen ephemeral rivers and lakes, inviting you to drink of their seemingly delicious waters. It is all, however, a tantalizing illusion; for as you approach the enchanting spot, the waters recede. This deceptive *mirage*, which so much resembles lakes and rivers of water, may perhaps be produced by the rays of the sun being reflected from the glossy green surface of the prairies, and also by their suffering some dispersion in their passage through the atmosphere, which, in that open and elevated country is in constant motion. These false ponds and rivers appear to be at the distance of about one mile from the spectator. In approaching the Arkansas, a landscape of the most imposing and picturesque nature makes its appearance—while the green, glossy undulations of the prairie to the right seem to spread out in infinite succession, like waves subsiding after a storm, covered with herds of gamboling buffalo; on the left towering to the height of seventy-five to one hundred feet, rise the yellow, golden, sun-gilt summits of the Sand Hills, among which winds the broad majestic river, "bespeckled with verdant islets thickly set with cottonwood timber." The Sand Hills in shape resemble heaps of driven snow.

The march had now been continued nearly all the day without water. The men and animals were growing faint with thirst; but the waters of the Big Arkansas, rolling silently and majestically through its own wide savannahs, suddenly appearing, re-invigorated them. Horse and man ran involuntarily into the river, and simultaneously slaked their burning thirst. The Arkansas here is a broad, sandy, shallow stream, with low banks, fordable at almost any point, and is skirted on either side by clumps of elm, oak, walnut, cottonwood, and other trees. The principal growth, however, is to be found on the islands, which chequer, with green spots, the broad course of the river. At Walnut creek, we overtook fifteen merchant wagons, belonging to the Santa Fé trade. Henceforward they continued with the army for the protection it afforded.

By the dawn of day on the 13th, we were on the march. Innumerable herds of buffalo presented themselves in all directions. The whole plain was literally alive with them as far as the eye could reach. These huge animals, whose flesh is esteemed the greatest delicacy on the plains, presents a sight of no ordinary interest to an army of hungry men, whose palates, more than their eyes or curiosity, need to be satisfied. Great numbers of them were killed, and the army feasted upon them most sumptuously. A march of fifteen miles brought us to the noted Pawnee Rock, of which Mr. Josiah Gregg,[31] in his "Commerce of the Prairies," thus speaks: this rock

NOTE 31.—*Dr. Josiah Gregg, Author of "Commerce of the Prairies."*—The founder of the Gregg family in America was William Gregg, an Ulster-Scot (Scotch-

DR. JOSIAH GREGG.

Author of *Commerce of the Prairies*. Trader to northern Mexico from Missouri over the Old Santa Fé Trail. In Mexican War was correspondent for American newspapers. Was an explorer of the Southwest. Was one of the Argonauts. Born in Overton County, Tennessee, July 19, 1806. Died in California in the winter of 1849-50, exact date unknown. One of the greatest Americans.

(Redrawn from photograph of old daguerreotype by Thompson, photographer, Kansas City, Mo.)

Irish) immigrant who arrived from North Ireland in the Province of Pennsylvania about 1682. He was of a Quaker family, and was among the earliest

"is situated at the projecting point of a ridge, and upon its surface are furrowed, in uncouth but legible characters, numerous dates, and the names of various travelers who have chanced to pass that way." A great battle, as the legend goes, was once fought near this rock, which appears conspicuous above the prairies at the distance of fifteen miles, between the Pawnees and their mortal enemies, the Cheyennes, whence the name. Digressing to the left, and proceeding from this point southwardly, four or five miles, for wood and water, we encamped on the east bank of the Arkansas. Here the men forded the river, and killed plenty of buffalo, elk, antelope and deer, and brought in quantities of grape, plum, ripe and of excellent

arrivals of the people of that faith in the colony established by William Penn. William Gregg had a son John, who was the father of William. William Gregg's son Jacob made more than one journey to the Quaker settlement at Cane Creek, North Carolina, to acquaint himself with that country. He finally settled near Cane Creek, where he lived until most of his children were grown up, when he moved to Arkansas, but to what particular locality is not certainly known, although there is some reason to believe that it was in the vicinity of Fort Smith and not far from the site of the present town of Van Buren.

Of the children of Jacob Gregg I know of but three—Harmon, William, and David.[1] It is said that the Greggs were at that time (removal to North Carolina) partly of German blood. Harmon Gregg married a Pennsylvania German— Miss Susannah Schmelzer, or Smelser, as it was written later. This marriage was in Pennsylvania.[2] Harmon Gregg settled on Elk river (or creek), in what is now Overton county, Tennessee, where he lived until the year 1809, when he moved to some point in Illinois. From Illinois he moved to the Territory of Missouri.

The date of the removal of Harmon Gregg from Illinois to Missouri is given as 1812. I am inclined to question the record in this instance, although it is supplemented by the family tradition as handed down at this time. In 1812 the three brothers, Harmon, William and David, were all inmates of Cooper's Fort, in what is now Howard county. William had married the daughter of

NOTE 1.—Campbell's Gazetteer of Missouri, published in St. Louis by R. A. Campbell, in 1884, page 247, under *Howard County*, shows as inhabitants or inmates of Cooper's Fort, Harmon Gregg, William Gregg, and David Gregg. They were undoubtedly brothers; their Christian names are yet common among the descendants of Harmon Gregg.

NOTE 2.—The funeral-card of Margaret Gregg Hardwicke, now in the possession of her granddaughter, Mrs. Dr. John H. Rothwell, of Liberty, Missouri, shown me June 29, 1906, is as follows:
"Her father was Harmon Gregg, of Pennsylvania, but of Scotch-Irish descent. Her mother was Susannah Smelser, also of Pennsylvania, but of German descent. She was born in Tennessee, July 31, 1804. She and her father's family were inmates of Cooper's Fort from 1812 to 1815. She was married to Philip Allan Hardwicke in Howard county, Missouri, Oct. 9, 1821. They moved to Clay county, Missouri, in 1824. She was received into the Cumberland Presbyterian Church, August 10, 1830, by Rev. Samuel King. Her funeral obsequies were attended by Elder Dan Carpenter of the same church. Died 29th of November, 1892."

☞ According to this card, Harmon Gregg was born in Pennsylvania, and his birth must have preceded the removal of his father to Cane Creek, North Carolina.

flavor. Here also fish were caught in abundance. The night was therefore consumed in feasting and merriment.

Early on the morning of the 14th, the army was put in motion, Capt. Congreve Jackson and his company being left to pay the last

---

Jesse Cox, a native of Madison county, Kentucky. Cox moved from Madison county to Illinois, and from thence to the Territory of Missouri, where he was a member of Benjamin Cooper's company of one hundred and fifty families who left Loutre Island, in the Missouri, below the mouth of the Gasconade, to settle in the Boone's Lick country. It would appear most probable that as Harmon Gregg had moved from Tennessee to Illinois in 1809, he had settled near his brother William; and it is reasonable to believe that he moved to Illinois because that brother, and possibly his brother David, were at the time living there. If this should prove true upon further investigation, then it is likely that the Greggs and Cox continued their further migrations together, which would make them all members of Colonel Cooper's company and give them a part in the establishment of Cooper's Fort.

William Gregg was killed by the Sac and Fox Indians in what is now Saline county, Missouri, the account of which is as follows:[3]

"In Christmas week, 1814, the little settlement was attacked one afternoon by a band of Sac and Fox Indians. . . . The Indians killed William Gregg, Cox's son-in-law, and destroyed the settlement. One account is that Gregg was shot down in his own dooryard and dragged into the house by the women, who barred the door against the savages, and held them at bay until relief came from Cooper's Fort. The other and more probable story is that Gregg had gone out from the house to drive in some calves, when he was shot and tomahawked by the Indians, who came on to the house, robbed it, and carried Miss Patsy Gregg, daughter of William Gregg, away with them as a prisoner; that Cox was also from the house at the time, but returned in a short time and sounded the alarm to the fort. A party was soon organized at the fort and hurried in pursuit of the savages. The latter crossed the Missouri, and the party from the fort overtook them on the Chariton river, in what is now Chariton county, and recaptured Miss Gregg.

"She was on horseback, seated behind an Indian warrior, to whom she was tied by one hand. The horse they were riding lagged behind all the rest of the party, by reason of its extra burthen. Miss Gregg was constantly looking back, hoping to see some friendly rescuing party. At last she discovered some horsemen, and with her freed hand motioning to them to be cautious and careful, she prepared to escape. She waited until the white men were within fifty yards of her, when with her unbound hand she suddenly seized the Indian's knife, drew it from its scabbard, cut the thongs which bound her other hand and sprang

---

NOTE 3.—*History of Saline County, Missouri*, published in St. Louis, by the Missouri Historical Company, 1881, pp. 145, 146. It is there said that—

"The settlers in Cox's bottom were mostly East Tennesseeans. It was said that every man in the bottom, when asked where he was from, would answer: 'Old Tennessee—Cocke county—Kit Boler's mill, on Big Pigeon, where there's better whisky and purtier gals than anywhar else in creation!' They were universally brave and warm-hearted, hospitable and jovial."

I give here a boast of the Tennesseean on his native hills, taken from the *History of Middle Tennessee*, by A. W. Putnam, Nashville, 1859:

"In boasting, many a backwoodsman gave in the inventory of his wealth as follows:
'The best shooting gun,
The fleetest nag,
The prettiest sister, and
The most fruitful wife.'"

honors to the remains of young N. Carson, who died suddenly the previous night. His burial took place near the Pawnee Rock, a decent grave being prepared to receive the corpse, wrapt in a blanket instead of a coffin and shroud. A tombstone was raised to mark the

from the horse's back to the ground and into the brush at the side of the trail— all this in almost an instant. As soon as Miss Gregg alighted, the pursuing whites fired at the savages, and the latter retreated with great precipitation. Miss Gregg was soon in the hands of friends, and speedily carried back to the fort, where she was joyously received by the inmates, who, while sorrowing over the tragic death of her father, were glad to know that his daughter had escaped from a fate worse than death."

I have not pursued the accounts of the family of William Gregg beyond the above incidents. I have made no effort to trace the family of David Gregg. The record of Harmon Gregg and his family is more complete and accessible. The family Bible of Harmon Gregg is now in the possession of Mrs. Mary Loughrey, wife of Andrew Loughrey, daughter of Philip Allan Hardwicke and his wife Margaret Gregg, four miles north of Harlem, in Clay county, Missouri.[4] The record in this Bible states the date of the birth of Harmon Gregg as February 21, 1774; he died August 10, 1844, in Jackson county, Missouri. Susannah Smelser was born September 17, 1774; died June 23, 1857, in Clay county. The record says she was born and was married in Pennsylvania. This Bible has the following record of the births of the children of Harmon Gregg and Susannah, his wife:

David Gregg, born October 28, 1797.[5]
John Gregg, born April 25, 1800.
Jacob Gregg, born April 9, 1802.
Margaret Gregg, born July 31, 1804. (Called Peggy in record.)
Josiah Gregg, born July 19, 1806.

NOTE 4.—In a recent letter to me Mrs. Loughrey says:

"You ask how the family Bible of the Greggs came to be in my possession. Grandmother Gregg came to live with her daughter, Mrs. Peggy Hardwicke, in 1850. When she died in 1857 she left the Bible to her, and as mother always lived with me after I was married she left the Bible to me at her death in 1892."

NOTE 5.—David Gregg was murdered by Colonel Charles R. Jennison in the public highway north of Parkville, Platte county, Missouri, September 15, 1864. For the date, see *Annals of Platte County, Missouri*, by W. M. Paxton, 1897, p. 379. The descendants of David Gregg are there given. Gregg was driving a yoke of cattle to a wagon, carrying some grain to the mill at Parkville. Jennison, at the head of his column, met him and questioned him upon his sympathies, and he frankly admitted that he favored the South, but on account of age had not taken any part in the war. Jennison drew his heavy holster-pistol and shot him dead. His grain was fed to the horses and one of his oxen was slaughtered and eaten. The action of Jennison was not approved by his soldiers. Gregg was old and harmless, and was known to be an upright citizen. One of Jennison's men said to him: "By God, that is the first time I ever knew a soldier to kill a dog that had no teeth," intimating that he protested against the killing of old men who took no part in the war. My informant, a responsible man holding a prominent position in a thriving city in Kansas, saw Jennison murder Gregg; he says that it would have taken little more to have caused the soldiers to make serious trouble for Colonel Jennison. In a letter to me dated July 24, 1906, Mrs. Loughrey says:

"Before Uncle David was murdered they went to his home and took the carriage and horses and everything else they could take. While they were ransacking the house there was one of the men (my aunt said he was just a boy) went to my aunt and said, 'Mother, I am very sorry for this, but I cannot hinder it.' She said to him, 'As you claim me I will own you; so, my son, how is it that I find you in such company?' Perhaps that was your friend, ———."

In the letter mentioned in the preceding note Mrs. Loughrey says:

"My grandfather, Harmon Gregg, was a wheelwright. I have a flax-wheel that he made for my mother in 1815."

spot where he reposes, with his name, age, and the date of his decease, engraved in large capitals. He slumbers in the wild Pawnee's land. This is but a sample of the interment of hundreds whose recent graves mark the march of the western army. A progress of fourteen miles brought us to the Pawnee Fork, where, to our great relief, we found Lieut. Jackson, who had been sent forward from the Diamond Springs, with twenty-five commissary wagons. To guard this provision train against the treacherous and wily Pawnees, who constantly beset the road for murder and plunder, Capt. Waldo had left Lieut. Reed with thirty-six men.

On the 15th, Col. Kearny, with the rear of the army, consisting of five companies, two of volunteer infantry, two of volunteer light artillery, one of mounted volunteers, and a small number of the 1st Dragoons, overhauled Col. Doniphan, forming a junction of their forces, at the Pawnee Fork. Mr. Riche, sutler to the 1st Dragoons, and post master on the expedition, brought up the mail to our encampment. This mail brought us the first, and only intelligence we had received from the States, since our departure from Fort Leavenworth,

Polly Gregg, born January 19, 1813.
Harmon Gregg, born December 20, 1815. (Harmon Gregg, Jun., in record.)
Susan Gregg, born December 13, 1818.

The following record appears in the Bible:

"*Marriages of the children of Harmon Gregg and Susannah Smelser.*"

"David Gregg was married to Nancy Adams, August 8, 1818.
"Peggy Gregg was married to Philip Allan Hardwick, October 9, 1821.
"Polly Gregg was married to James Lewis, November 6, 1827.
"Jacob Gregg was married to Nancy Lewis, March 14, 1828.
"John Gregg was married to Martha Eliza McClellan, November 25, 1835.
"Susan Gregg was married to John McClellan, August 15, 1838.
"Harmon Gregg, Jr., was married to Nancy Shortridge, March 10, 1842."
Josiah Gregg was never married.

Mrs. Loughrey says children were born between Josiah and Polly, and that they died in infancy. In this period Harmon Gregg was moving from Tennessee to Illinois and Missouri.

Harmon Gregg and his family were inmates of Cooper's Fort. If they did not arrive in Missouri until 1812, they were in the fort from that year until 1815. If it should develop that they came to the Boone's Lick country with Colonel Cooper's company, then they were inmates of the fort from the time of its erection until 1815. As said above, the family tradition is that they lived in Cooper's Fort from 1812 to 1815. Harmon Gregg remained in the country about the fort until 1825, in the fall of which year he moved with his family to what was known as the Blue river country, and settled four and one-half miles northeast of the present town of Independence, in Jackson county. Independence was not established until 1827. Harmon Gregg erected a house at the point mentioned,

although we had advanced upon the road three hundred miles. No one can so fully appreciate the value of a newspaper or a letter, as he who is cast abroad on the solitary plains, and cut off by intervening deserts, from all the enjoyments of society. Everything in the shape of news was devoured with the utmost eagerness. The river, swollen by recent showers, was impassable. Col. Kearny, however, with his accustomed energy, determined not to delay. He therefore caused trees to be felled across the deep, rapid current. This was the labor of a day. On the trunks of these trees the men passed over, carrying with them their sick, arms, accoutrements, tents and baggage. In this manner the principal loading of the wagons was also trans-

which is yet standing; he died there on date set out above.[6] That house was the home of Josiah Gregg.[7]

The object of this brief sketch is to identify Dr. Josiah Gregg. It is not designed to be a complete biography of him, nor is it intended to review his writings. Dr. Gregg has been a "lost author." It has been impossible from anything found in the publications of his time or any other period to identify him even as a resident of Missouri. It was not known but that he was some resident of another country who came into the West to regain his health and there embarked in the overland trade with northern Mexico. The only intimation to be found in his writings that he was an American is the statement that he had been cradled on the frontier. Authors and editors have endeavored time and again to trace him,

NOTE 6.—In a notice of Jacob Gregg in the *History of Jackson County, Missouri*, Kansas City, 1881, p. 316, there is some mention of his father, Harmon Gregg:

"Tennessee is his native State, where he lived till seven years of age, then came to the Territory of Illinois in the year 1809. In 1812 he came to Boone's Lick, in the Territory of Missouri, since Howard county. During his father's residence at Boone's Lick, after attaining his majority, he spent one year in Arkansas, then went on a trading expedition to New Mexico in the first wagon-train across the Plains, a distance of 800 miles. A short time after returning from Santa Fé he removed with his father to what was then known as the Blue River country, about four miles a little north of east from Independence. This was the fall of 1825, and only a few settlers then lived in what is now Jackson county. Jacob Gregg lived there with his father for about three years, and then, after living near the old homestead for about two years, removed to Independence, where he remained about two years. Then lived on two different farms east of Independence for several years, then came to Sni-a-bar township, in which he now lives. In the year 1826 he was appointed constable of Blue township by the authority of the county court of Lafayette county. In 1827, J. R. Walker was sheriff and Gregg his deputy, in which position he served for three years. During this time he was appointed county surveyor, and was surveyor till elected sheriff in the year 1832. He was sheriff till 1836, and in 1850 was elected to the General Assembly of Missouri, on the Whig ticket, and served one term. . . . Nine children, all of whom have grown to maturity, six sons and three daughters, constituted his family."

Jacob Gregg took the census to determine whether Jackson county had sufficient population to be organized. He accompanied the commissioners appointed to fix the location of the county seat. By law the county seat was to be located within two miles of the geographical center of the county. The commissioners sat upon a log to rest, where the court-house now stands in Independence. From their conversation Gregg believed they were about to select that place for the county seat. He called their attention to the requirement of the law. They replied that the place they were then at was about the geographical center of the *timbered* part of the county, and that it would be folly to consider the *prairie* part of the county, as it would never be settled upon in the world. And they agreed upon the place where they then were as the county seat, and it was approved, the town laid out, and named Independence.

NOTE 7.—The house is yet standing. It is a story-and-a-half log house, which was weatherboarded long after it was built.

ported. Our animals were forced to swim the stream. The wagons, the bodies being made fast to the running gear, were next floated across by means of ropes attached to them, and hauled up the hill by manual power. This immense labor having been accomplished without serious accident or loss, on the 17th, Col. Kearny put his whole column in motion. The sick were conveyed in the baggage wagons. This was a miserable arrangement. Spring carriages, for the use of the medical department, should have been fitted out by the government, to accompany the expedition. Had this been done, many valuable lives might have been saved.

The companies of infantry kept pace with the mounted men. Their feet were blistered by their long and almost incredible marches. The ground was often marked with blood in their foot-prints; yet with Roman fortitude they endured the toils of the campaign. Their courage could neither be abated by distance, nor their resolution relaxed by difficulties, nor their spirits subdued by privations, nor their ardor cooled by length of time. Diverging from the main Santa Fé road, we followed the Arkansas. Having performed a toilsome

but always without success.[8] Realizing the worth of the man and the great value of his book describing his commercial enterprises and giving a history of the most unique commerce ever developed on the continent, I set to work to gather from original sources, if anything existed and could be found, something of the life of this modest but virile pioneer of the American Southwest. I find that he was of the sixth generation of a pioneer family established by a hardy immigrant in the primeval forests of the Appalachians. This family kept steadily in the van of the westward movement of the American people to subdue and occupy the wilderness. And this developed in him that faith in himself, that reliance upon his own powers, that confidence in his own ability, that courage and hardihood of mind, that made him one of the greatest Americans. And his achievement is but another incident in that great movement from Missouri, by Missourians either native or adopted, to complete the girdle of civilization westward around the earth.

Nothing is known of the manner in which Josiah Gregg obtained an education. That he secured a classical education would seem probable from the

NOTE 8.—*Commerce of the Prairies* has been recently reprinted in the series of Early Western Travels, Vols. 19 and 20, edited by Dr. R. G. Thwaites, Secretary of the Wisconsin Historical Society, and published by the Arthur H. Clark Company, Cleveland, Ohio. I wrote Dr. Thwaites requesting that he furnish me with what he had been able to secure that was new about Gregg, as there was nothing of that nature in his introduction to the above-named work. He replied: "I spent a great deal of time looking up just such data regarding Gregg as you ask for, for the purpose of my own preface, and failed to get anything more than I gave." The search of Dr. Thwaites is always thorough, and his failure in this instance is not to be wondered at, for nothing accessible existed at the time. I was fortunate in living near the locality in which Harmon Gregg settled and where his descendants yet live. This circumstance enabled me to gather the information contained in this paper.

march of twenty-seven miles, over a level, sandy, bottom prairie, darkened by herds of lowing buffalo, and abounding with numerous insects and reptiles, we encamped for the night, and pitched our tents on the verge of that broad and beautiful stream. Our encampment, laid off in military order, resembled a small city, and seemed as though it had sprung up by enchantment. This river has some singular features: its banks are seldom elevated more than two feet above the surface of the water in the channel, which is remarkably broad and shallow. The current is swift. Consequently, under the agency of the wind and the heat of the sun, evaporation takes place rapidly. This is a wise provision of nature for furnishing moisture to the adjacent plains, which otherwise must have remained barren and parched, as but little rain falls during the year in this region. To-day Maj. Howard returned from Santa Fé, whither he had been dispatched by Col. Kearny, to ascertain the disposition of the New

numerous references to the classics to be found in his writings. It may be that with the scanty assistance he was able to secure in Missouri in pioneer days he educated himself. He was a mathematician, and had a knowledge of astronomy, for he made frequent astronomical observations with a view to determine locations in the country through which he traveled. He was a physician, but whether he attended at some medical institution or simply "read medicine" with some established practitioner, as was the custom in the West in his day, is not known.[9] As he began the life upon the Plains at the age of twenty-five, it is not likely that he ever practiced his profession to any great extent.

From the time when Dr. Gregg entered upon his life of a trader to northern Mexico we find an ample biography set down in the accounts of his various journeys and enterprises. This portion of his life will be passed over.

Dr. Gregg's book was published first in New York, in 1845. The full title is as follows: *Commerce of the Prairies, or the Journal of a Santa Fé Trader, During Eight Expeditions across the Great Western Prairies, and a Residence of Nearly Nine Years in Northern Mexico. By Josiah Gregg.* The great worth of the work was recognized at once. It became the authority on all subjects of which it treated, and it has not only retained the high place it immediately won, but its value has increased with a more extensive knowledge of its times. Much of the history of western Missouri, Kansas, New Mexico, northern Mexico, north Texas, and the entire territory embraced in the new State of Oklahoma, must finally rest upon the great work of Dr. Gregg. It embraces accounts of the Indian tribes inhabiting that vast country, and these accounts have stood the tests of the scientists of our own times. It contains acute delineations of the traits and

NOTE 9.—Mrs. Loughrey writes me that he came to her father's house when she was a little girl, and that while there he vaccinated the children. She concealed herself to avoid the operation, but he found her and induced her to submit along with the others by promising her a watch like the one he carried and which he allowed her to examine, the watch to be forthcoming when she became a young lady; and his untimely death alone prevented the fulfillment of his promise.

Mexicans in reference to submitting to the government of the United States. He failed, however, to accomplish fully the purpose of his mission; reporting that the common people, or plebeians, were inclined to favor the conditions of peace proposed by Colonel Kearny, to wit: that if they would lay down their arms and take the oath of allegiance to the government of the United States, they should, to all intents and purposes, become citizens of the same republic, receiving the protection and enjoying the liberties guaranteed to other American citizens; but that the patrician classes, who held the offices and ruled the country, were hostile, and were making warlike preparations. He added further, that 2,300 men were already armed for the defence of the capital, and that others were assembling at Taos. This report produced quite a sensation in our camp. It was now expected that Col. Kearny's entrance into Santa Fé would be obstinately disputed.

On the 20th, after a march of near thirty miles over a surface covered with friable, calcarious lime-stone, we arrived at the crossing of the Arkansas, where we found an abundant supply of grass, wood and water. During our progress to-day, we enjoyed a very

---

characteristics of the Mexican people. It gave the first accurate information of the geographical conformation of the country, the true course of its streams, the wild animals it contained, and its natural resources. The State of Oklahoma will need little better descriptions of its vast gypsum-beds than can be found on the burning pages of this book; and her salt deposits were carefully examined and adequately described. Dr. Gregg was the first to note the diminishing numbers of the buffalo, and he predicted their final extermination at no distant day. All this is beautifully told. His diction is masterful, and his style is simple, chaste, elegant, pleasing, and sometimes eloquent. His descriptions are complete and full, and never tedious. The whole work is dignified and scholarly. The map which he drew for his book was pronounced by Dr. Elliott Coues (the highest authority) the best of its time. Upon its publication the book was immediately recognized as a masterpiece, and that verdict will ever stand.

Dr. Gregg was a merchant, with his own money invested in competition with many others who were engaged in the same business. He sought new fields for his enterprises, he explored countries and laid out new routes over which to carry on his trade. He held his own against the Mexicans, who were bent on despoiling him, and when they sent troops to compel him to return to a town upon one occasion, he was confident of his ability to defeat them with only his servants. He chose to return, however, and he faced the authorities with such resolute bearing that he was suffered to depart with their apologies. His fearlessness is the prominent characteristic of all his intercourse with the Mexicans and Indians; and the accounts of his adventures with the latter, had he preserved them, would fill volumes. In his conflicts with them he never quailed, never gave an

fine view of a buffalo chase. Nothing except a charge upon the Mexicans could have animated the men more, or produced more thrilling sensations. The broad plain spread its green bosom before us; our bannered column extended for miles along its level surface. Suddenly a band of four hundred buffalo, emerging from the Arkansas, broke through our ranks, when our men charged upon them with guns, pistols, and drawn sabres. A scene of beautiful confusion ensued. Pell-mell they went scampering and thundering along the plain, exhibiting just such a tumult, as, perhaps, the solitudes never before witnessed. Several of those huge animals paid the forfeit of their lives for their temerity.

Early on the morning of the 21st, we continued our march, winding along the north margin of the river, leaving the main Santa Fé road by the Cimarron at the crossing. This part of the country abounds in serpents, chameleons, prairie lizards, horned frogs, dryland turtles, and the whole tribe of the entomologist. Grasshoppers are as numerous as were the locusts sent by the afflicting hand of

---

inch, but stood his ground determined and grim as death. His iron will is typical of that unconquerable spirit that carried American conquest to the Pacific Ocean.

After the publication of his book Dr. Gregg, for a time, made his home with his brother John, at Shreveport, Louisiana.[10] It is not known how long he re-

---

NOTE 10.—This fact is established by the following letter. It is the only one I ever saw which was written by Dr. Gregg; it belongs to Mrs. Loughrey. It was addressed to her father, Philip Allan Hardwicke:

SHREVEPORT, LA., Feb. 18, 1845.

DEAR PHILIP: I have already written you several letters, but have not heard a word from you or any of the kin since I left Missouri.
I arrived here a couple of weeks ago, safe and sound, and "right side up," and found John and family in like condition.
It is perfect spring with us here now—trees and flowers of the woods all beginning to bloom out—garden-stuff up, and many things, as lettuce, &c., fit to use—and many have their corn planted, which, in some cases, has been up and growing for some time. This is, in fact, a delightful climate, and will doubtless be a pleasant place to live, if one can enjoy health. And in this respect, it has been very fair thus far; for in all John's family, white and black—big and little—there has not been a case that could be called sickness, since he has been here, now nearly a year. In fact, the whole neighborhood was more healthy last summer than any part of Missouri I know of. Shreveport, however, and anywhere on the river and lakes, is obliged to be sickly; but the interior uplands will doubtless be reasonably healthy—particularly for persons acclimated to the South.
I have written to David and others of the boys, to send Noah and Dick to us, in case they should meet with anyone coming by this place (a safe and careful person), either mover or horse-drover. If you should hear of such an opportunity, I would be very glad you would let David know, and see that they are dispatched, as the boys would be of considerable use here. Should no person of full confidence be met with coming the whole way, they might almost any time be sent to Mr. Pickett, at Van Buren, as nearly all the drovers and movers to Texas from western Missouri pass by Van Buren. And then we could get them from there almost any time.
Do not fail to write me frequently. Give my love to Peggy and the children.
Your Brother, JOSIAH GREGG.

P. S.—John has moved on his new place, five miles from Shreveport—a very pretty and desirable situation, upon the whole—being on the main road leading west—a road more traveled, I believe, than any one road in western Missouri. Though the land looks poor to us Missourians, it produces cotton very well,—first rate, we may say,—the Red river bottoms only, being better.
John and Eliza send their affectionate remembrances to you, Peggy and the children.

Providence in swarms upon the land of Egypt. To cheer the solitude and break the monotony of the plains, in many places a rich variety of flowers blossom, and blush, and "waste their sweetness on the desert air." The prairie pink or *yamper*, is an exquisite flower of a rich purple color. The root of this plant is bulbous and esculent. When dried, the Indians use it for bread. The blue lily of the bottom prairie, the white poppy, and the mimic morning-glory, are interesting specimens of prairie flowers, and would do honor to the finest gardens in Missouri. After a progress of twenty-seven miles, we encamped on the river bank, in a rich bottom prairie. At this time, we had on the sick list, one hundred men.

Wednesday, 22d, we vigorously pushed forward, rarely ever losing sight of that broad, bright zone of water, the Arkansas, which was our only dependence for quenching thirst. In many places, scattering clumps of cottonwood trees border each of its banks, and, on every island (which is guarded by the stream from the sweeping, annual prairie conflagrations,) invite into their umbrageous bowers the sun-burnt, way-worn soldier. A few hours' rest refits him for the march. To-day, we passed Pawnee Fort, an old decayed stockade, and a few crumbling cabins, on an island where many years ago, as tradition says, a great battle was fought between the Pawnees and their besiegers, the Cheyennes. The face of the country is uniformly level. A great variety of pleasing and interesting flowers made their appearance;—prairie dog villages abound. These wide solitary domains

mained there; perhaps less than a year. When the Mexican War came on, his great knowledge of Mexico and her people caused his services in that country to be in demand. He went out with the American Army as a special correspondent for American newspapers. What particular papers he represented is not known, but the survivors of the Army of the West say one of them was the New Orleans *Picayune*.[11] It will be the work of some future biographer to ascertain the names

Note 11.—Dr. Gregg returned with the troops sent by General Taylor from Monterey to Colonel Doniphan at Chihuahua, and he accompanied Doniphan's forces in their march to join General Taylor. Meredith T. Moore (of the Cole County Company) told me the following incident of the march. The weather was extremely warm the day the army marched out of Chihuahua, and when the sand-wastes were reached it was scorching. Gregg was never physically a strong man, and at that time his health was poor. He raised a red-silk umbrella to protect himself from the intense heat. At that time he was near the rear of the line. The soldiers were always on the lookout for something to furnish them diversion and amusement. They all knew Dr. Gregg, and upon sight of his red umbrella they began to cheer and make such remarks as men in their situation always will. It was all good-naturedly meant, but he rode hurriedly down the line to escape it, which caused the efforts of the men to be redoubled. Gregg reached the position of Colonel Doniphan in no good-humor, believing that the men knew him well enough to realize that in even fair health he would rough it with any of them. He complained to Doniphan, but a few words from the Colonel restored his equanimity.

of the prairies, although they can never be occupied by civilized man, are nevertheless tenanted by very interesting little villagers. These little prairie dogs, or squirrels, which have attracted the attention of the traveler and the tourist, are queer creatures. They would sit perched on their domicils, and bark like a terrier at the whole army. A march of eighteen miles brought us to our camp on the river bank, where we obtained excellent water by sinking barrels two or three feet in the sand; the river water being rendered unpleasant by the excessive heat of the sun. The Arkansas is one of the finest streams in the world for bathing purposes. The water is generally two or three feet deep, swiftly rolling over a bed of yellow sand, no less beautiful than the golden sands of the fabled Pactolus. Of an evening I have witnessed more than five hundred men enjoying this reinvigorating luxury at one time, splashing and plunging about in the waves.

The march was continued on the 23d, without the occurrence of any event worthy of historical record. Mr. Augustus Leslie, an intelligent young man of the Cole company, died of a chronic affection on the 22d, and his corpse was decently interred to-day on the road side, in a desolate tract of country, four miles above Pawnee Fort; twelve rounds were fired over his grave, and a rude stone was placed to mark the spot where he rests. The army again becoming scant of

of these papers and collect his letters. Judging from his knowledge of the country and people and his ability as a writer, these letters should make a valuable contribution to the history of the Mexican War.

After the close of the war with Mexico Dr. Gregg probably returned to his home in Missouri, for in 1849 he went across the Plains and Mountains to California, as did every other Missourian who could possibly get there. The particulars of this journey over grassy stretches, up and over barren ranges, down rocky valleys, over plains above which whirled clouds of choking, blistering alkali, across the Sierras and down the golden streams to the Western Sea, are now known to none. Upon his arrival there he was employed in some capacity by the Government. He seems to have needed some ready money, which he obtained from a party named Jesse Sutton, who perhaps lived at San Francisco, but of whom I have learned nothing. He left all his papers and journals with Sutton, among these a manuscript entitled "Rovings Abroad," now lost, I fear, beyond recovery. For he never returned from the journey in the service of the Government.[12] He

NOTE 12.--The only knowledge the family ever had of the death of Dr. Gregg came in the following letters. They belong to Mrs. Loughrey, who permitted me to make copies of them. Mr. Hardwicke found it impossible to go to California in 1849, but he arranged with Dr. Gregg to meet him there the following year as soon as the trip across the Plains could be made. He arrived there in September, 1850. Mr. Hardwicke never reached home, but died on the ship in which he embarked to return, and was taken ashore and buried at some point on the

provisions, Lieut. Sublette with four men was sent in advance to bring to a halt a train of commissary wagons. This order was promptly put into execution by Lieut. Sublette, notwithstanding the wagons were much farther upon the road than was anticipated. Taking with him but two days' rations, and being out seven, he and his party were compelled to travel night and day to escape starvation.

On the 24th, we marched twelve miles, and nooned in a rich bottom prairie, where the grass was abundant and of good quality. The wild, spontaneous pumpkin vines made the prairie resemble the cultivated fields of Missouri. Limestone and sand-stone were here found promiscuously arranged, the latter predominating in the vicinity of the mountains. Eight miles further brought us to our camp on the river margin, densely covered with tall grass, pea-vines and rushes. Many of our horses had by this time failed, and had been abandoned to their fate on the great prairies. A man six hundred

---

died on the Trinity river in the winter of 1849-50—exact date unknown. At what place or upon what part of that river he died has not been determined. Where rests that which is mortal of the illustrious dead we may never know. He

---

west coast of Mexico, the location of which is not known. He wrote the following letter to his family:

SMITH'S TRADING HOUSE, CALIFORNIA,
Sept. 21, 1850.

DEAR WIFE AND CHILDREN: I have deferred writing to you for a short time after I arrived in Cal., that I might be better able to give you some information about Josiah and the prospect of the country.

I have heard nothing different from him, so think he must be dead,—others say he is not.

I saw one man who said that he saw him on Trinity river two or three hundred miles north of this, last winter, and that he was doing some business for the Government. I think that most likely. I shall continue to inquire till I learn something certain about him.

We had a long—very long and tedious trip. We got to Hangtown on the 2d day of September—four months and two days on the road.

John Gregg wrote the following letter to Mr. Hardwicke without knowledge of his departure from Missouri for California, or believing that it might reach him before he started. This it may have done, and the statement in his (Hardwicke's) letter—"I have heard nothing different from him, so think he must be dead"—may refer to the information contained in this letter, which he had before leaving Missouri:

SHREVEPORT, LA., May 16, 1850.

DEAR HARDWICKE: I have the melancholy news to convey to you of the death of Brother Josiah.

This news comes from a commercial house (Messrs. Robt. Smith & Co., unknown to me). They write simply that they had delivered to Jesse Sutton a manuscript work entitled "Rovings Abroad" by a request contained in a "letter to that Gentleman from your [my] brother, now deceased." There is not a word as to when, where or how he came to his death.

I am writing to Jesse Sutton and others in California to try and ascertain the particulars of his death.

The last letter I had from him was dated Trinity River, some 400 miles north of San Francisco. This river, I believe, empties into the ocean north of the Sacramento river.

We are well. Yet I am looking for sickness, as the spring is exceptionally wet and cold. Such weather has never been known here before.

Member us kindly to sister Peggy and The family, Yours truly, JOHN GREGG.

The following letter is addressed to "Peggy Hardwicke, Near Randolph, Mo.":

SHREVEPORT, LA., January 6-51.

MY DEAR SISTER: Your letter of the 25th Nov. has just been received. We are much gratified to hear from you, as also from mother. I had just written her and directed to Liberty

miles from the nearest civilized settlements, in a desert country, feels a kind of friendship and sympathy for his horse, when he abandons him on the plains to be devoured by wolves or captured by Comanches, that almost makes him shed tears. He feels as though he were abandoning his best friend to perish in a desolate land.

The march was continued with the utmost vigor on the 25th, 26th and 27th, following the course of the river, at an average of about twenty-seven miles per day, over a heavy, sandy road. Lieutenant-colonel Ruff, with the first battalion, being now some four or five miles in advance of the main army, halted and ordered drill until Col. Kearny should come up. This ill-timed order for drill, where Apollo's shafts fell thick and heavy, and where every breeze that swept across the parched and heated plain felt as withering as the breath of the Sahara, produced an excitement in his command which came near resulting in a total disregard of the order. In consequence of this and certain other strict orders subsequently issued, Lieutenant-colonel Ruff's popularity with his men began to wane. We were now passing beyond the region frequented by the buffalo, the most interesting and by far the most useful tenant of the plains, and entering upon the confines of a still more desolate tract. The earth was covered with a salinous incrustation, and the parched grass was

---

lies within the bounds of that great State which, more than all others, his Missouri fellow-citizens turned upside down to fill the world with gold. And of this honor to your care—having learned by letter from sister Susan that she expected to spend the winter at your house. This letter I will direct to Randolph, as I see yours was mailed there.

I have just received a letter from cousin Jacob Gregg, who gave me the first information I had of our good old Uncle Ayer's death. He says he did not see Mr. Hardwicke as they went on, but heard of him in the mines near HangTown. They were at Riley's, who lives at Napa City, near and north of the bay of San Francisco. His mother he said was in good health.

Just having written mother, I have but little to write you about ourselves, more than that we are in the enjoyment of reasonable health.

I have written many letters to California, trying to get some information in regard to brother Josiah's death, as well as his effects, but have been able to learn nothing. I lately wrote to Mr. Hardwicke. Cousin Jacob wrote me that Riley had been able to learn nothing; but supposed his effects, if any, were in the hands of Jesse Sutton. Sutton inclosed me brother Josiah's last letter to him, directing him to take charge of his effects and turn them over to me, in case he should be lost or never get back to San Francisco. He sent me his memoranda or Journal, and inclosed the letter I speak of above, but says nothing of anything else, but says he had written me before in regard to his death, &c. That letter I never got. Brother Josiah borrowed money from him on leaving San Francisco, and in the letter named above had directed him to pay himself out of his effects. It may be that it took everything to pay him. It may be that everything he had with him, when he died, was lost, as Sutton says his papers were lost.

I have not heard whether John McClellan has got back from El Paso, nor have I yet heard from Sister Susan since she got home. I wrote her a few days since.

We live on the most thronged highway in the Western Country; and the throng is now much increased by an extraordinary immigration to Texas. Shreveport is the receiving and shipping point for a large tract of country—extending far back into Texas. Its streets and sidewalks show the busy bustle of a large city.

I am in hopes you will write me often, and I am very anxious indeed to receive a letter with mother's name appended. To whom please remember me and Eliza kindly, as also to your children and the kin and friends generally.

And receive for yourself the kindest
wishes of Your Brother
JOHN.

stiffened by salt crystalizations. The pulverized earth resembled smouldering embers.

On the morning of the 28th, the whole army moved off, exhibiting a fine appearance, with streaming pennons and glittering arms, as they wound around the hills, or stretched along the level plain. The shrill notes of the clarion animated every heart. There are moments of pride in the history of every man's life; so there are crises of more than ordinary interest in the march of every army. This was one of them. Every bosom heaved with emotion; for we could now see, though we could not, like the ancient herald, hurl a spear into, the enemy's country. The earth was covered with pebbles washed by the rains, and worn by the winds as smooth as glass, and heated by the sun to such a degree that they would scorch the naked foot to a blister. The plain here is intersected by high ridges of hard sandstone, striped with blue and red, somewhat resembling the gaudy colors of the rainbow. This is a segment of the great American Sahara. Excepting in the Arkansas bottom, there is little or no vegetation. For many months in the year, neither dew nor rain falls upon the thirsty desert.

Continuing the march on the 29th, we met Fitzpatrick, the mountaineer, on express from Fort Bent to Col. Kearny, with the following information from Santa Fé: "That Governor Armijo had called

she has not known. His monument he builded with his own hands, but other pillars will be raised to his memory in many States by his grateful countrymen. And that erected by Old Missouri should overtop them all.[13]

NOTE 13.—The following was furnished me by Miss Mary Louise Dalton, Secretary of the Missouri Historical Society, St. Louis. It was furnished her by L. L. Gregg, Esq., of New York:

"Josiah Gregg was quite a genius as well as Santa Fé trader, traveler, author, and explorer. He explored many mountainous regions, discovered bays, etc., in California, he and his party being snowbound for several months, during which time they lived on bread made from acorns. Sometime in March, 1847, the party managed to extricate themselves from the snow-drifts and mountain fastnesses. Soon after they arrived at Clear Lake Valley, California, Mr. Gregg fell from his horse and expired, either from hardships and sufferings he had undergone, or heart trouble, as is now supposed by some of his relatives.

"On one of his many trips to Santa Fé he was employed by a priest to build a clock in the tower of his church, the contract-price for which was $1,000. Mr. Gregg, however, finished the work in much less time than was anticipated by the priest, and he refused to pay more than $700.

"When building the clock Mr. Gregg placed in it the image of a little negro, which, when the clock would strike, would come outside and dance. Some months after Mr. Gregg's return to the United States he received a letter from the priest stating that the little negro had ceased to perform his mission, and if he would return and repair it he would pay him the remainder of his money according to the original contract, $300. The following spring Mr. Gregg returned to Santa Fé and repaired the clock; and, on inquiry, he learned that the priest's flock had told him the reason the negro would not come out and dance as before, was because he had not paid the full price agreed upon. Mr. Gregg got his $300 and heard no more of the clock."

It will be observed that Mr. Gregg has an erroneous death-date. In the spring of 1847 Dr. Gregg was in Mexico, and later than the date given for his death he visited Colonel Doniphan at Chihuahua. He did not go to California until 1849, and the letters given here make it certain that he died in the winter of 1849–1850.

the chief men of counsel together to deliberate on the best means of defending the city of Santa Fé; that hostile preparations were rapidly going on in all parts of New Mexico; and that Col. Kearny's movements would be vigorously opposed." Three Mexicans were taken prisoners near Fort Bent, supposed to be spies, with blank letters upon their persons addressed to Col. Kearny. This piece of ingenuity was resorted to, no doubt to avoid detection by American residents and traders at Bent's Fort. These Mexicans were conducted, by order of Col. Kearny, through our camp and shown our artillery, then peaceably allowed to retire to Santa Fé, and report what they had seen.

The future was pregnant with consequences of the greatest moment. An uncertain destiny awaited us. Some anticipated victory; others apprehended disaster. Twenty-days were to determine our fate. We were already encamped in the enemy's territory. Were we to be defeated and completely overthrown? or were we to enter triumphantly into the capital and plant the flag of our country on its adobé walls? These were questions in the minds of all, which time alone could solve. The sequel, however, will develop the manner in which the principles of our republican government were established in that benighted and priest-governed land, without the anticipated effusion of blood.

CHAPTER III.

The Estampeda—Fort Bent—Lieut. De Courcy—Arapaho Chief—March resumed—The army passes the Desert—An adventure—Spanish peaks—Half Rations—Return of De Courcy—Doniphan's speech—Arrival at Las Bagas—Priest of San Miguel—Mexican Prisoners—The Pecos Ruins—Traditions and Legends—Anticipated Battle of the Cañon—Capture of Santa Fé—Gen. Kearny's Speech—Camp Rumors, &c.

Having on the 29th crossed the Arkansas and encamped in the Mexican territory, about eight miles below Bent's Fort, a greater degree of vigilance became necessary, to guard against the cunning of those Ishmaelites of the desert, the Comanches, whose country we had unceremoniously invaded, as well as to prevent surprise by the Mexicans themselves. Our encampment was therefore laid out with the most scrupulous regard to military exactness. A strong picket and also camp guard were detailed and posted. Our animals being much fatigued by long marches, it was deemed advisable to rest and recruit them some two or three days. They were, by order of the Colonel, turned loose upon the prairie to graze, under a strong guard, a few of them only being tethered. At first, a few of them took fright at an Indian, or perhaps a gang of prowling wolves, which by degrees was communicated to others, until the whole *caballada* took a general *estampeda*, and scampered over the plain in the most furious manner. This was a scene of the wildest and most terrible confusion. A thousand horses were dashing over the prairie without riders, enraged and driven to madness and desperation by the iron pickets and the lariats which goaded and lashed them at every step. After great labor, most of them were recovered, some of them thirty and some of them fifty miles from camp. About sixty-five of the best of them were irrecoverably lost.

Fort Bent is situated on the north bank of the Arkansas, six hundred and fifty miles west of Fort Leavenworth, in latitude 38° 02′ north, and longitude 103° 03′ west from Greenwich. The exterior walls of this fort, whose figure is that of an oblong square, are fifteen feet high and four feet thick. It is a hundred and eighty feet long, and one hundred thirty-five feet wide, and is divided into various compartments, the whole built of adobés, or sun-dried brick. It has been converted into a government depot. Here a great many of the government wagons were unloaded and sent back to Fort Leavenworth for additional supplies. Here also the caravans of traders awaited the arrival of the army, thenceforward to move under the wing of its protection.[32]

While in this encampment on the 30th, Capts. Reid and Waldo, of the volunteers, and Capts. Moore, and Burgwin, and Lieut. Noble of the 1st dragoons, with their respective commands, rejoined the army, having vainly pursued Speyers and Armijo, who, it was supposed were endeavoring to supply the enemy with ammunition and arms. About this time, Lieut. De Courcy was dispatched with twenty men with or-

NOTE 32.—*Bent's Fort.*—Silas Bent was born in Massachusetts, in 1744, and it is said that he was one of the party who threw the British tea into Boston harbor. He married Mary Carter, by whom he had seven children, the eldest being Silas. This son was born in 1768, and in 1788 he went to Ohio, where he practiced law and held various offices. In 1806 he was appointed by Albert Gallatin a deputy surveyor of Upper Louisiana, and moved to St. Louis. He held numerous offices there, and died in 1827. By his intermarriage with a Virginia lady, Martha Kerr, he had eleven children,—Charles, Julia Ann, John, Lucy, Dorcas, William, Mary, George, Robert, Edward, and Silas. Charles was appointed Governor of New Mexico by General Kearny. The Bent brothers were engaged in the fur trade, those best known in that connection being William and Charles. Associated with them was Ceran St. Vrain, of Canadian-French extraction; the firm was at one time known as Bent, St. Vrain & Co. They built a fort on the Arkansas river above the present city of Pueblo, at the mouth of Fountain creek, in 1826. This proved a poor location, and in 1828 they abandoned the place and went down the river, and in 1829 completed Fort William, so called for William Bent. This fort was long known as Bent's Fort, and in later years was spoken of as Bent's "old" fort. It was one of the most important posts in the West, being situated at the point of the Santa Fé Trail where the travel north and south from the Platte country to Santa Fé crossed it. The walls were of adobe, six feet thick at the base and four feet at the top; the floor was of clay, and the roofs of the covered portions were of clay and gravel supported on poles. At the northwest and southwest corners were round towers thirty feet high and ten feet clear on the inside, and loopholed for artillery and musketry. The entrance was on the east, and was closed by a heavy gate of wood. Inside the fort were two divisions—one for offices, living-rooms, and store-rooms; the other for yards for wagons, stock, etc. The dimensions of the fort were about as given by Hughes, though other authorities vary from these figures slightly. In 1852 William Bent destroyed the fort, burning the combustible portions and blowing up the walls with gunpowder. In 1853 he built Bent's "new" fort, about thirty-five miles lower down the Arkansas and on the same (north) side. It seems that he had long contemplated this removal, as the following quotation from the work of Emory will show:

"About 35 miles before reaching Bent's Fort is found what is called the 'big timber.' Here the valley of the river widens, and the banks on either side fall

ders to proceed directly through the mountains to the valley of Taos, and having ascertained the intentions and disposition of the people, to report to Col. Kearny on the road to Santa Fé as soon as practicable. Having received his instructions, this pacificator set forward on the 31st, prepared for either of the alternatives, peace or war.*

* The following interesting anecdote was related by the lieutenant who conducted this pioneer party:
"We took three pack-mules laden with provisions, and as we did not expect to be long absent, the men took no extra clothing.
"Three days after we left the column our mules fell down, and neither gentle means nor the points of sabres had the least effect in inducing them to rise. Their term of service with Uncle Sam was out. 'What's to be done?' said the sergeant. 'Dismount!' said I; '*Off with your shirts and drawers, men!*' tie up the sleeves and legs, and each man bag one-twentieth part of the flour!' Having done this, the bacon was distributed to the men and tied to the cruppers of their saddles. Thus loaded we pushed on without the slightest fear of our *provision train* being 'cut off.' "—HUGHES.

towards it in gentle slopes. The 'big timber' is a thinly scattered growth of large cottonwoods not more than three-quarters of a mile wide, and three or four miles long. It is here the Cheyennes, Arapahoes, and the Kioways sometimes winter, to avail themselves of the scanty supply of wood for fuel, and to let their animals browse on the twigs and bark of the cottonwood. The buffaloes are sometimes driven by the severity of the winter, which is here intense for the latitude, to the same place to feed upon the cottonwood. To this point, which has been indicated to the Government as a suitable one for a military post, Mr. Bent thinks of moving his establishment."

Bent transacted business at the new location until 1859, when the fort was leased to the Government. In the winter of 1859–60 Bent moved up to the mouth of the Purgatoire. The name of the fort was changed to Fort Wise in 1860, and in 1861 again changed, this time to Fort Lyon, in honor of General Nathaniel Lyon, the hero of Wilson Creek. Because of the encroachments of the river on its walls the fort was moved twenty miles lower down the river in 1866, but it served as a stage station for some years longer.

Lewis H. Garrard arrived at Bent's Fort November 1, 1846, and found lying in the court "a small brass cannon, burst in saluting General Kearny." (See *Wah-to-yah and the Taos Trail*, p. 42.)

Francis Parkman was at Bent's Fort shortly after the "Army of the West" had passed, and thus describes it:

"Bent's Fort stands on the river, about seventy-five miles below Pueblo. At noon of the third day we arrived within three or four miles of it, pitched our tent under a tree, hung our looking-glasses against its trunk, and having made our primitive toilet, rode towards the fort. We soon came in sight of it, for it is visible for a considerable distance, standing with its high clay walls in the midst of the scorching plains. It seemed as if a swarm of locusts had invaded the country. The grass for miles around was cropped close by the horses of General Kearny's soldiery. When we came to the fort we found that not only had the horses eaten up the grass, but their owners had made way with the stores of the little trading-post; so that we had great difficulty in procuring the few articles which we required for our homeward journey. The army was gone, the life and bustle passed away, and the fort was a scene of dull and lazy tranquillity. A few invalid officers and soldiers sauntered about the area, which was oppressively hot; for the glaring sun was reflected down upon it from the high white walls around."—*Oregon Trail*, pp. 306, 307.

William Bent was married to a Cheyenne woman. She is often mentioned in the work of Lewis H. Garrard, above quoted from.

Here it was that the Chief of the Arapaho tribe of Indians visited our camp to see the American commander, and look at his "big guns." With astonishment he expressed his admiration of the Americans, signifying that the New-Mexicans would not stand a moment before such terrible instruments of death, but would escape to the mountains with the utmost dispatch.

August 1st we moved up the river and encamped near Fort Bent. Here, by order of the colonel commanding, Dr. Vaughan of Howard, assistant surgeon, was left in charge of twenty-one sick men, who were unable to proceed further, and had been pronounced physically unfit for service. Of this number some died,* some were discharged and returned to Missouri, and others having recovered, came on and re-joined the army at Santa Fé.

The march upon Santa Fé was resumed August 2d, 1846, after a respite of three days in the neighborhood of Fort Bent.[33] As we passed the fort the American flag was raised, in compliment to our troops, and, in concert with our own, streamed most animatingly in the gale that swept from the desert, while the tops of the houses were crowded with Mexican girls, and Indian squaws, intently beholding the Amer-

* Wm. Duncan, and Fugitt, the former of Clay, and the latter of Jackson county, were among those who died. Four others died—names not known.
Besides these 21 volunteers, there was a number of dragoons and teamsters left sick, under the care of assistant surgeon Vaughan. The whole amounted to about sixty.—HUGHES.

NOTE 33.—July 31, Col. Kearny issued, at Fort Bent, the following proclamation:
"PROCLAMATION TO THE CITIZENS OF NEW MEXICO, BY COL. KEARNY, COMMANDING THE UNITED STATES FORCES.
The undersigned enters New Mexico with a large Military force, for the purpose of seeking Union with & ameliorating the conditions of its Inhabitants—this he does under instructions from his Government & with the assurance that he will be amply sustained in the accomplishment of this object—It is enjoined on the citizens of New Mexico to remain quietly at their homes & to pursue their avocations—So long as they continue in such pursuit, they will not be interfered with by the American Army, but will be respected & protected in their rights both civil & religious.
All who take up Arms or who encourage resistance against the Govt. of the U. S., will be regarded as enemies & will be treated accordingly.
Camp of Bents Fort on the Arkansas　　　S. W. KEARNY
　　July 31, 1846　　　　　　　　　　　　Col 1st Drags."
He also wrote to Governor Armijo as follows:
　　　　　　　　　　　　　　　Head Qr. Army of the West
　　　　　　　　　　　　　　　Camp on the Arkansas at Bents Fort
　　　　　　　　　　　　　　　　　Augt 1st 1846
SIR: By the annexation of Texas to the U. S., the Rio Grande from its mouth to its source forms at this time the Boundary between her & Mexico, & I come by orders of the Govt. to take possession of the Country, over a part of which you

ican army. After a march of twenty-four miles, following the course of the river, we pitched our tents on a perfectly bare sand beach, with scarcely a shrub or spear of grass for our almost famishing animals. The gale from the inhospitable desert, which extended southwardly to the Raton mountains, and south-eastwardly to the borders of Texas, and over which the next day we were to commence our march, furiously drove the sand, like pelting hail upon us. A few patches of the prickly pear, the wild sage, the spiral, or screw bush, and a mimic arbor vitæ, are the only green shrubs that can vegetate in this arid and parched waste.

After spending a comfortless night on the banks of the Arkansas, the water of which is very cool and refreshing, so near the mountains, on the morning of the 3d we struck off at right angles with the river from a point a few miles above the mouth of the Timpa, pursuing our course up that stream on account of water. The army was now upon the Great American Desert. The wind and driven sand continued to annoy both man and beast. The parched earth appeared as though it had not been refreshed by a shower since the days of Noah's flood. The wagons moved heavily, the wheels uniformly sinking over the felloes in the sand or pulverized earth. A toilsome march of twenty-five miles brought us to our camp, on a bare sand bank, totally destitute of green grass or other vegetation for our animals. The

---

are now presiding as Governor—I come as a friend & with the disposition & intention to consider all Mexicans & others as friends who will remain quietly & peaceably at their homes & attend to their own affairs—Such Persons shall not be disturbed by any one under my command either in their Persons, their Property or their Religion—I pledge myself for the fulfillment of this promise—I come to this part of the United States with a strong Military force & a yet stronger one is now following us as a reinforcement to us. We have many more troops than sufficient to put down any opposition that you can possibly bring against us, & I therefore for the sake of humanity call upon you to submit to fate, & to meet me with the same feelings of Peace & friendship which I now entertain for & offer to you & to all those over whom you are Governor—If you do so, it will be greatly to your own interest & to that of all your Countrymen & for which you will receive their blessing & their prayers—Should you however decide otherwise—determine upon resistance & oppose the troops, you can raise, against us, I then say, the blood which may follow—the sufferings & misery which may ensue will rest on your head, & instead of the blessing of your Countrymen, you will receive their curses, for I shall consider all whom you bring in Arms against us enemies & will treat them accordingly.

I send this communication by Capt Cooke of my own Regt, & recommend him & his small party of 12 Dragoons to your kindness & attention.

All Exmo Señor Gobernador   Very Resp-y Your ob. Servt.
    Don Manuel Armijo   S. W. KEARNY,
    Y Comdr Genl. Santa fe   Col 1st Drags.

Captain Cooke's account of this embassy is set out in *The Conquest of New*

water was scarce, muddy, bitter, filthy, and just such as Horace in his Brundusium letter pronounced "*vilissima rerum.*"

The American desert, is, perhaps, no less sterile, sandy, parched and destitute of water and every green herb and living thing, than the African Sahara. In the course of a long day's march we could scarcely find a pool of water to quench the thirst, a patch of grass to prevent our animals perishing, or an oasis to relieve the weary mind. Dreary, sultry, desolate, boundless solitude reigned as far as the eye could reach, and seemed to bound the distant horizon. We suffered much with the heat, and thirst, and the driven sand—which filled our eyes, and nostrils, and mouths, almost to suffocation. Many of our animals perished on the desert. A Mexican hare, or an antelope, skimming over the ground with the utmost velocity, was the only living creature seen upon this plain. The Roman army under Metellus, on its march through the deserts of Africa, never encountered more serious opposition from the elements than did our army in its passage over this American Sahara.

The march was continued on the 4th with little or no alteration. The wind still drove the sand furiously in our faces; the heat was oppressive; and the sand was deep and heavy. After a progress of twenty-seven miles we again encamped on the vile, filthy Timpa, the water of which was still bitter and nauseating. Our animals perished daily.

Vigorously pushing forward on the 5th, having made twenty-eight miles during the day, we passed out of the desert, crossed the river Purgatoire, and encamped on its southern bank. This lovely, clear, cool, rippling mountain stream was not less grateful to our army,

Mexico and California, by P. St. Geo. Cooke, New York, 1878. As to how he was impressed with the enterprise, he says (p. 6):

"*August 1st.*—About noon I was sent for, and the General greatly surprised me by a proposition that I should set out in advance, with a flag of truce, to Santa Fé, some three hundred miles. In our conversation, he assured me that he attached much importance to it—that he had *waited* for me; and otherwise would have sent his chief of staff; that if there should be fighting, I would undoubtedly return and meet him before it began. I go to-morrow, with twelve picked men of my troop. Mr. James Magoffin of Kentucky and Señor Gonzales of Chihuahua have permission to accompany me—both merchants of caravans, which, rather singularly, are now journeying to New Mexico and beyond."

Captain Cooke arrived at Santa Fé on the 12th. He was well received by Governor Armijo, but nothing came of the journey. Captain Cooke set out on his return on the 13th, accompanied by Dr. Henry Connelly, appointed a Commissioner by Governor Armijo to negotiate with General Kearny, but the nature

after four days' unparalleled marching on the desert, than was that stream to the Israelitish army, which gushed from the rock when struck by the rod of the prophet. The lofty Cimarron and Spanish peaks were distinctly visible to the south, and west, towering in awful grandeur far above the clouds, their summits capped with eternal snow.

After supper, W. P. Hall,* R. W. Fleming, M. Ringo, the author, and others whose names are not remembered, led by a spirit of adventure, as well as by a desire to recruit their horses, which had now been famishing for four days, determined to pass over the Purgatoire near to the base of the mountains towards the north-west, where there was plenty of good grass, and let them graze during the night. We went about two miles up the river before we ventured to cross. By this time it was dark. The valley for three miles in extent was covered with undergrowth, and matted together so thickly with vines that it was almost impervious. After hours of labor and bewilderment among the brush, we finally got into the stream. On the opposite side the black locusts and willows grew so densely that it was impossible to penetrate further. Our progress was thus impeded. There were only two alternatives, either to cut our way through, or return to camp. We chose the former. So we went to work with our

---

* Mr. W. P. Hall was chosen as a Representative to Congress while a private soldier in Col. Doniphan's regiment. He was an inmate of the same tent with the author.—HUGHES.

of his instructions and the result of his mission have not been ascertained. Captain Cooke records (p. 32) his conclusions:

"General Armijo, with little or no military experience, distrustful of the loyalty of the population he has habitually fleeced, and of their feeble ignorance which has been much impressed by our long commercial intercourse, is said to be in painful doubt and irresolution; halting between loyalty to his army commission, lately bestowed, and a desire to escape the dangers of war upon terms of personal advantage. . . . Undoubtedly he must go on to direct this current, but to some weak and disgraceful conclusion."

Col. Kearny was not sanguine of entering New Mexico without opposition. August 1 he wrote the War Department as follows, from Bent's Fort:

"I reached here with the Volunteers on the 29th Ulto, where I found Capt. Moore of my Regt with his command having the Santa fe traders with him & yesterday Capt Sumner with his squadron came up—The troops composing this Army (with the exception of some small Detachmts, as escorts for ammunition &c) are now concentrated, & will to-morrow move on towards Santa fe, which place I expect to have possession of by the 20th Inst—It is impossible for me to tell what opposition will be made to our entering New Mexico, but I at this time feel confident that our force is sufficient to over come any that may be offered—I have done all in my power to obtain possession of the Country quietly & peaceably & I hope to succeed in it."

bowieknives, chopping the brush in the dark and leading our horses in the space thus cleared. In this manner we made our way through that inexpressibly dismal brake which lines the margin of the Purgatoire. About midnight we got through into the open plain, close under the mountains, which towered high in the heavens, to the westward. Our horses fared well; but we, ourselves, returned the next morning entirely satisfied ever afterwards to remain in camp during the night.

On the 6th we advanced about seven miles, and encamped on a spring branch, issuing from the base of the Cimarron peak.* Here several of the men ascended to the summit of this lofty mountain, elevated many thousand feet above the plains and valleys below. The scene was truly grand and magnificent. The Spanish peaks, twin brothers in the midst of desolation, rose still above us to the westward, lifting high into the heavens their basaltic pillars and spurs, girt with clouds, and glistening with perennial snow: while towering still above these, rose the grander and loftier summits of the Cordilleras, like blue, amethystine clouds, in the distant south-western horizon. Thus surrounded by the grandest scenery the world can furnish, the author read with double enthusiasm the first canto of Campbell's Pleasures of Hope.

On the 7th, at an early hour, the advance was sounded. Our route led up a narrow defile through the mountains between the Cimarron and the Spanish peaks, called the Raton Pass. This day's march was extremely arduous and severe on our teams. Rough roads and rocky hills obstructed our progress. The wagons were often hauled up the abrupt and declivitous spurs of the mountains by means of ropes, and in the same manner let down on the opposite side. Progressing a distance of eighteen miles up this chasm, or pass, with mountains precipitously rising on both sides, we arrived at a point where they suddenly diverged on either hand, and several miles beyond, as suddenly contract, thus forming an amphitheatre on the grandest scale, sufficiently spacious to accommodate the whole human race in an area, so situated that one man might stand on the Cimarron peak and behold them all. The great amphitheatre of Statilius Taurus, with its seventy thousand seats rising in circular tiers one above an-

* The Cimarron peak is estimated to be thirteen thousand feet above the Gulf of Mexico —HUGHES.

other, would have been nought in the comparison. The knobs and peaks of basalt and granite, projecting into the region of the clouds, present a scene of true sublimity. This display of the Almighty's power, is sufficient to extort reverence from the lips of an infidel. Surely, the "undevout astronomer is mad." Near this romantic spot we encamped for the night. The grass was abundant and of excellent quality: the water cool and refreshing.

On the 8th,* the army vigorously set forward, and crossed the grand ridge which divides the waters of the Purgatoire, the Cimarron, and the Rio Colorado.† This elevated range of mountains is adorned by forests of pines and cedars. After an advance of eighteen miles, over the most difficult road, we encamped on the banks of the Colorado.

In consequence of the great fatigue in crossing the Cimarron ridge of mountains, the command was permitted a respite of one day, as there was here a fine supply of wood, water and grass, three things not only convenient, but almost essential to an army. This was the Sabbath, and the only Sabbath's rest we had enjoyed since our departure from Missouri. Here we shaved and dressed, not to attend church,—not to visit friends,—not in deference to the conventional rules of society,—but in remembrance of these privileges and requirements. Neither was this a day of feasting with us; for it was on this day that our rations, which had never been full, were cut down to *one-half*.‡ From this time on to Santa Fé, we were actually compelled to subsist on about *one-third rations*.[34] While the rays of the sun fell with unusual power in the valley, a heavy shower was refreshing the sides of the mountains; and as the cloud retreated, a brilliant rainbow "spanned with bright arch" their basaltic summits.

* This morning, Henry Moore, of Saline county, died, and was interred in the Raton Pass. Also, one of the infantry, belonging to Capt. Angney's company, was found in the road, in an almost lifeless state. The dragoons took care of him, and brought him up to camp. He afterwards died.—HUGHES.

† The Rio Colorado is the head branch of the Canadian fork of the Arkansas.—HUGHES.

‡ About one-third as much as the law contemplates as the *daily ration* of a soldier.—HUGHES.

NOTE 34.—Upon the subject of rations Captain Cooke had the following to say (pp. 39, 40), after the arrival at Santa Fé:

"The 'Army of the West' marched from Bent's Fort with only rations calculated to last, by uninterrupted and most rapid marches, until it should arrive at Santa Fé. Is this war? Tested by all the rules of science, this expedition is anomalous, not to say Quixotic. A colonel's command, called an army, marches eight hundred miles beyond its base, its communication liable to be cut off by

After several hours of drill out upon the level prairie, the volunteer regiment returned to camp to partake of their scanty allowance, not having eaten a bite that morning or the previous evening. But we were determined to make the best of a hard case, and trust Uncle Sam for his future good conduct. Therefore, all cheerfully submitted to the unavoidable privation. While encamped here, on the night of the 9th, Capt. Jackson's company lost about twenty horses in an estampeda, most of which, however, after an arduous search of one or two days in the mountains, were recovered.

After a forward movement of twenty-two miles on the 10th, with the gray tops of the mountains projecting above us on the right, and the gently sloping valley of the Colorado on the left, we pitched our tents on the green banks of the Bermejo, more seriously annoyed by the *half-ration* experiment than the dread of Mexican armies. It is but natural that those who have been reared in opulence, when they first experience hardships and privations, should look back with regret upon the luxuries and pleasures of life, which they have but recently exchanged for the toils of a long and arduous campaign. Our men, like good soldiers, however, bore the evils of the march with Roman fortitude, accommodating themselves to the actual circumstances which surrounded them. They never afterwards, during the campaign, had regular and ample supplies.

About noon on the 11th, we were rejoined by the detachment under Lieut. De Courcy, near the Poñi, returning from their excursion to Taos. They had with them fourteen Mexicans, prisoners, whom they had picked up in various places. These prisoners, in true Mexican style, reported "that the Pueblos, Yutas and other Indian tribes, to the number of 5,000, had combined with the New Mexicans to oppose our march, and that they would annoy our lines every day from San Miguel to Santa Fé." We soon learned how much credit was due to Mexican reports.* Having progressed seventeen miles, we

---

* *Punica fides* was the reproach of the ancient Carthaginians. *Fides Mexicana* is now a term of synonymous import, when applied to the Mexican people. Treachery is their national characteristic.—HUGHES.

---

the slightest effort of the enemy—mostly through a desert—the whole distance almost totally destitute of resources, to conquer a territory of 250,000 square miles, without a military chest; the people of this territory are declared citizens of the United States, and the invaders are thus debarred the rights of war to seize needful supplies; they arrive without food before the capital—a city two hundred and forty years old, habitually garrisoned by regular troops! I much doubt if any officer of rank but Stephen W. Kearny would have undertaken the enterprise; or, if induced to do so, would have accomplished it successfully."

encamped on the Reyado, a cool mountain stream, where there was neither grass nor fuel.

Early on the morning of the 12th, we passed the newly made grave of some unfortunate soldier,* who had died the previous day, and was buried, perhaps without ceremony, on the road side, Colonel Kearny being now some distance in advance of Colonel Doniphan, with near 500 men. Thus were our numbers diminished, not by the sword, but by disease. Almost every day some dragoon or volunteer, trader, teamster, or amateur, who had set out upon the expedition buoyant with life and flattered with hopes of future usefulness, actuated by a laudable desire to serve his country, found a grave on the solitary plains. To die in honorable warfare; to be struck down in the strife of battle; to perish on the field of honor; to sacrifice life for victory, is no hardship to the fallen brave; is no source of regret to surviving friends: for the remembrance of the noble deeds of the slain sweetens the cup of sorrow. But to see the gallant, the patriotic, the devoted soldier, sinking and wasting his energies under the slow, sure progress of disease, which finally freezes the current of life, fills the heart with melancholy. Such cases claim our sympathy and merit our remembrance.

A march of twenty miles, mostly through the gorges of the mountains, over a rocky, flinty road, brought us to the Ocaté, a limpid stream of fresh water, where we halted for the night. The nearest timber was two miles and a half distant. Of an evening when the army would halt for the purpose of selecting a camp ground, and the order was given to dismount, a busy scene ensued. Every man was his own servant. Some were scrambling after the scattering sticks of wood, or dry brush; some busy in pitching their tents and arranging them in order; some tethering the animals; and some bringing water for cooking purposes. At length, "all is set." The coffee is made, the meat broiled, and the bread prepared as it *may be,* when the several messes, gathering round their respective fires, seated upon the ground, with appetites sharpened by a long day's march, dispatch, in "double-quick time," their scanty fare. Supper over, the men next see after their horses, picket them on fresh grass, return to camp, spread their blankets upon the earth, wrap up in them,

---

* This was probably a dragoon. The initials E. M. were marked on the rude slab that designated his final resting place.—HUGHES.

and unceremoniously fall asleep,—leaving the spies and guard to take care of the enemy.

Here Col. Doniphan assembled his soldiers on the green, and briefly addressed them. He concluded by reproving them for their indiscretion in wasting their ammunition upon game, assuring them that there were only fifteen rounds of cartridge in camp; that there was every reason to apprehend an engagement with the enemy in a short time; that strict discipline and prompt obedience were essential to the safety of the expedition; that their own honor, and the reputation of their State, demanded the cheerful performance of duty; that to retreat or surrender was a proposition that could not be considered; and that we must conquer or die, for defeat was annihilation.

After a drive of nineteen miles, along a rugged road, through narrow defiles between the spurs of the mountains, we encamped on a ravine, bordered by a strip of fine grass, near the Santa Clara Spring, Col. Kearny having advanced six miles further, and taken his position on the river Mora.[35]

Having advanced, on the 14th, to the Mora, we rejoined Col. Kearny. We were now on the verge of the Mexican settlements. The country was becoming fit for cultivation. Droves of swine, herds of cattle, and flocks of sheep and goats, were feeding in the valleys and grassy glades. The hills and upland were adorned with comely groves of cedars and pines. Ranchos with their corn fields and gardens were making their appearance, and every thing began to wear the semblance of civilization. After a vigorous march of twenty-five miles, we encamped on the Gallinas creek, near the small town Las Bagas, the first Mexican village on the road. Strict orders were given the soldiers not to molest the inhabitants, and also to respect the lives and property of such Mexican citizens as remained peaceable and neutral.

At dawn of day on the morning of the 15th, the spies, Messrs. Bent and Estis, who had been sent out the previous evening to reconnoitre, and ascertain the position of the enemy, and learn if it

NOTE 35.—*Mora* means *mulberry*. The mulberry tree grew abundantly along this stream; hence the name. It is a considerable tributary of the Canadian, and it gave name to a New Mexico county. Its water is now almost entirely diverted for irrigation purposes. It was first settled in 1832. The town of Mora was burned by the Americans in 1847.

was his intention to make battle, returned and reported to Col. Kearny, that 2,000 Mexicans were encamped at a place about six miles from Las Bagas, called the Cañon or Pass, and that they intended there to give us battle. Major Swords had just arrived from Fort Leavenworth, with the United States' mail, bringing intelligence of the appointment by the President, of Colonel Kearny to be a Brigadier-general in the United States Army. Other important documents were received besides Colonel Kearny's commission as a Brigadier-general, but now there was no time for reading letters and newspapers.[36]

Gen. Kearny immediately formed the line of battle. The dragoons, with the St. Louis mounted volunteers were stationed in front; Major Clark, with the battalion of volunteer light artillery in the centre; and Col. Doniphan's regiment of mounted volunteers in the rear. The two companies of volunteer infantry were deployed on each side of the line of march, as flankers. The baggage and merchant trains were next in order, with Capt. Walton's mounted company (B) as a rear guard. There was also a strong advance guard. The cartridges were hastily distributed; the cannons swabbed and rigged; the port-fires burning; and every rifle charged. The advance was sounded by martial trumpet and horn. The banners streamed in every direction. The officers dashed along the lines—the high-toned chivalry of the American character beamed from every eye—in every countenance was expressed the settled determination to win—every heart was stout—every lip quivered with resolution, and every arm was nerved for the conflict.

In passing this little town, Las Bagas, the general halted the army, and on the top of a large flat-roofed building, assembled the Alcalde or magistrate and other men of distinction among the Mexicans, and there, on the holy cross, administered to them the oath of allegiance to the laws and the government of the United States.[37] This

---

NOTE 36.—W. H. Emory says, under date of August 15:

"Major Swords, of the quartermaster's department, Lieutenant Gilmer, of the engineers, and Captain Weightman joined us, from Fort Leavenworth, and presented Colonel Kearny with his commission as brigadier-general in the army of the United States. They had heard we were to have a battle, and rode sixty miles during the night to be in it."

NOTE 37.—Emory has preserved General Kearny's address to the Alcalde (p. 27), which is as follows:

"The general pointed to the top of one of their houses, which are built of one

done, the army hurried on to the Cañon in high spirits and hope, being confident of victory. When we arrived, however, at the place where we expected to engage with the enemy, to our great disappointment, the Mexicans had dispersed, and there was no one to oppose our march. It is perhaps better thus to have gained a bloodless victory by the terror of our arms, than to have purchased it with blood and loss of life.

---

story, and suggested to the alcalde that if he would go to that place, he and his staff would follow, and, from that point, where all could hear and see, he would speak to them; which he did, as follows:

"'Mr. Alcalde, and people of New Mexico: I have come amongst you by the orders of my Government, to take possession of your country, and extend over it the laws of the United States. We consider it, and have done so for some time, a part of the territory of the United States. We come amongst you as friends—not as enemies; as protectors—not as conquerors. We come among you for your benefit—not for your injury.

"'Henceforth I absolve you from all allegiance to the Mexican Government, and from all obedience to General Armijo. He is no longer your Governor; [great sensation]. I am your Governor. I shall not expect you to take up arms and follow me; but I now tell you, that those who remain peaceably at home, attending to their crops and their herds, shall be protected by me, in their property, their persons, and their religion; and not a pepper, not an onion, shall be disturbed or taken by my troops, without pay, or by the consent of the owner. But listen! he who promises to be quiet and is found in arms against me, I will hang!

"'From the Mexican Government you have never received protection. The Apaches and the Navajos come down from the mountains and carry off your sheep, and even your women, whenever they please. My Government will correct all this. It will keep off the Indians, protect you in your persons and property; and, I repeat again, will protect you in your religion. I know you are all great Catholics; that some of your priests have told you all sorts of stories—that we should ill-treat your women, and brand them on the cheek as you do your mules on the hip. It is all false. My Government respects your religion as much as the Protestant religion, and allows each man to worship his Creator as his heart tells him is best. Its laws protect the Catholic as well as the Protestant; the weak as well as the strong; the poor as well as the rich. I am not a Catholic myself—I was not brought up in that faith; but, at least one-third of my army are Catholics, and I respect a good Catholic as much as a good Protestant.

"'There goes my army—you see but a small portion of it; there are many more behind—resistance is useless.

"'Mr. Alcalde, and you two captains of militia, the laws of my country require that all men who hold office under [it] shall take the oath of allegiance. I do not wish, for the present, until affairs become more settled, to disturb your form of government. If you are prepared to take oaths of allegiance, I shall continue you in office, and support your authority.'

"This was a bitter pill; but it was swallowed by the discontented captain, with downcast eyes. The General remarked to him, in hearing of all the people: 'Captain, look me in the face, while you repeat the oath of office.' The hint was understood—the oath taken, and the alcalde and the two captains pronounced to be continued in office. The people were enjoined to obey the alcalde, &c. The citizens grinned, and exchanged looks of satisfaction, but seemed not to have the boldness to express what they evidently felt—that their burdens, if not relieved, were, at least, shifted to some ungalled part of the body.

"We descended the same rickety ladder by which we had climbed to the tops of the houses, mounted our horses, and rode briskly forward to encounter our 600 Mexicans in the gorge of the mountains, two miles distant."

About noon we passed the small village Tecolate, the inhabitants of which willingly received us, and cheerfully took the oath of allegiance to our government, administered to them by Gen. Kearny as at Las Bagas. Our men were covered with sweat and dust, from the exercise and excitement through which they had gone, so completely that it was impossible to tell one man from another. Having marched twenty miles, we encamped within about six miles of San Miguel, near a small rancho, where we found plenty of water, wood, and fine grass for our animals.

On the 16th, after a progress of six miles, we arrived at San Miguel, situated on the river Pecos, and famous as being the place near which the Texan army under command of Gen. McLeod, fell into the hands of Gen. Salezar and Gov. Armijo, in 1841.[38] Here again Gen. Kearny, assembling the citizens of the place, as usual, on the terraced roof of some spacious building, delivered to them a stern, sententious speech, absolving them from any further allegiance to the Mexican government. When the general was about to compel them to swear fealty to our government on the sacred cross, the Alcalde and Priest objected. The general inquired the grounds of their objection. They replied, that the oath he required them to take would virtually render them traitors to their country, a sin of which they disdained to be guilty. Gen. Kearny having promised protection to their persons and property, as to other citizens of the United States, and also having threatened to subvert the town unless they should submit, they were at length induced to take the oath.

The army having proceeded about ten miles farther, encamped on the Pecos, near San José. Here the water was excellent, but the grass was indifferent. Bold springs of delicious water gush from the rocks.

During the night of the 16th, while we were encamped at San José, the picket guard placed out by Col. Doniphan, took the son of the Mexican general, Salezar, prisoner. He was a spy, and was held in custody until our arrival at Santa Fé, where he was afterwards set at liberty. This prisoner's father, Gen. Salezar, is the same detestable wretch who captured the Texans near Anton Chico and San Miguel, and treated them with such wanton cruelty and inhumanity.

NOTE 38.—See *Narrative of the Texan Santa Fé Expedition*, by George Wilkins Kendall, 2 vols., New York, 1844.

It was by his order that G. Wilkins Kendall was robbed of his passports; it was his influence that procured the execution of the brave Howland, Rosenbury and Baker, all American citizens. Young Salezar was taken by James Chorn and Thomas McCarty, of the Clay company. Also, two other Mexican soldiers were made prisoners the same night.

On the morning of the 17th, these last mentioned prisoners were, by order of Gen. Kearny, conducted through our camps and shown our cannon. They were then suffered to depart, and tell their own people what they had seen. To color and exaggerate accounts is a truly Mexican characteristic. They therefore returned to their comrades in arms, representing our number at 5,000 men, and declaring we had so many pieces of cannon, that they could not count them. This highly colored account of our strength, no doubt spread dismay through their ranks, and increased the desertions from Armijo's standard, which were already going on to an extent well calculated to alarm him.

After a march of ten miles, we came to the Pecos village, now in ruins. This village was formerly the seat of a flourishing and powerful tribe, claiming to be the lineal descendants of the great Montezuma. "A tradition was prevalent among them," observes Mr. Gregg, "that Montezuma had kindled a holy fire, and enjoined their ancestors not to suffer it to be extinguished until he should return to deliver his people from the yoke of the Spaniards. In pursuance of these commands, a constant watch had been maintained for ages to prevent the fire from going out; and, as tradition further informed them, that Montezuma would appear with the sun, the deluded Indians were to be seen every clear morning upon the terraced roofs of their houses attentively watching for the appearance of the 'king of light,' in hopes of seeing him 'cheek by jowl,' with their immortal sovereign. Some say that they never lost hope in the final coming of Montezuma until, by some accident or other, or a lack of a sufficiency of warriors to watch it, the fire became extinguished; and that it was this catastrophe that induced them to abandon their villages."

The spacious temple, on whose altar the sacred Montezumian or vestal fire was kept alive for so many successive ages, was built of sun-dried bricks, as the tradition proceeds, more than three hundred years ago. This building appears to be of Mexican architecture, and is of the following dimensions:—its length is one hundred and ninety-one feet, breadth thirty-five feet, and fifty feet to the ceiling—the walls are six feet thick. The interior of the temple, the division into compartments, the subterranean cells, the decorations of the altar, and the stone cisterns and tanks, display some taste, although the edifice is but the wreck of what it has been, the turrets having tumbled to the ground. The entire village appears to have been originally surrounded by a stone wall eight feet in height and four in thickness.

Most of the Pueblos of New Mexico have similar traditions among them, respecting their great sovereign, Montezuma, and to this day look for him to come from the east to deliver his people from Mexican bondage. After our arrival in Santa Fé, an intelligent New Mexican declared to me, "that the Pueblo Indians could not be induced to unite their forces with the Mexicans in opposing the Americans, in consequence of an ancient and long cherished tradition among them, that at a certain period of time, succor would come from the east to deliver them from their Spanish oppressors, and to restore to them the kingdom of Montezuma; and that they hailed the American army as the long promised succor."

Gold is emphatically the god of the Mexicans. They have no motives but those of profit; no springs of action but those of self-love; no desires but those of gain; and no restraints but those of force. The eternal jingle of cash is music to their ears. Virtue, honesty, honor, piety, religion, patriotism, generosity, and reputation, are to them pompous and unmeaning terms; and he whose conduct is shaped by principles of fair dealing, is regarded as incomparably stupid. Vice, fraud, deceit, treachery, theft, plunder, murder and assassination, stalk abroad in open daylight, and set order, law and justice at defiance. The virtue of females is bought and sold. Such is the moral and social system in Mexico.

As our army passed by the villages and other settlements in New Mexico, the men, women, boys and girls, in great numbers would come out to the road, bringing with them vegetables, bread, milk, eggs, cheese, fruits, pepper, chickens, and other eatables, and with the utmost importunity, following along the lines, would seek a purchaser of their valuable stores. In this manner these traffickers drained most of the specie from the purses of the American soldiers.

Proceeding three miles beyond the Pecos Ruin, we encamped for the last time on the Pecos river, the water of which is exceedingly beautiful and transparent. The earth in many places is carpeted with fine grass, and adorned with shadowing pines and cedars.

When Gov. Don Manuel Armijo[39] learned more certainly that we were approaching Santa Fé, the capital of New Mexico and seat of his official residence, he assembled by proclamation, seven thousand troops, two thousand of whom were well armed, and the rest more indifferently armed, and marched them out to meet us at the Cañon or Pass of the Galisteo, about fifteen miles from Santa Fé, intending there to give us battle. He had written a note to Gen. Kearny the day previous, stating that he would meet him somewhere that day, or the day following. The letter was very politely dictated, and so ambiguous in its expressions, that it was impossible to know whether it was the Governor's intention to meet Gen. Kearny in council, or in

NOTE 39.—Kendall wrote in his work a biography of Armijo, a small portion of which is quoted here:

"Manuel Armijo was born of low and disreputable parents, at or near Albuquerque. From his earliest childhood his habits were bad. He commenced his career by petty pilfering, and as he advanced in years extended his operations until they grew into important larcenies. While yet a youth, he carried on an extensive business in sheep-stealing, admitted, I believe, to be the lowest species of robbery; yet so lucrative did the young Armijo find the business, that in his own neighborhood he gave it a tone of respectability. A wealthy *haciendero*, or large plantation-owner, in the vicinity of Albuquerque, named Francisco Chavez, suffered not a little from the exceedingly liberal system of helping himself adopted by the embryo governor. Chavez possessed his thousands and tens of thousands of sheep, large numbers of which he yearly drove to the southern cities of Mexico, and there disposed of for ready cash. At home, his business was to purchase at reduced prices all the sheep offered by his poorer neighbors, and so numerous were his flocks that he could not mark, much less recognize, one-tenth of what he possessed. Yet he always employed shepherds to watch his flocks, and used every precaution in his power to prevent his sheep from straying or being stolen. But to guard against a person of young Armijo's tact and perseverance was impossible. The scapegrace would enter his flocks while the shepherds were asleep, or suborn them if awake, and by much shrewd artifice contrived to levy a continual and profitable tax upon the substance of the elderly haciendero. The animals thus stolen, in good time would be sold for cash to their rightful but unsuspecting owner, and thus it sometimes happened that Armijo would re-steal and re-sell, time after time, the same identical sheep. Up to this day, when among his intimate friends, General Manuel Armijo boastingly relates the exploit of having sold to 'Old Chavez' the same ewe *fourteen different times*, and of having stolen her from him in even the first instance. By this means, and by having what is termed a good run of luck at dealing *monte*, he amassed no inconsiderable fortune. . . . When his majesty is in the street, each dutiful subject takes off whatever apology for a hat he may have on his head. Should the governor's wife, a gross, brazen-faced woman, issue from the building, the form is even more ridiculous, for then the cry of '*La gobernadora!*' or '*La commandante generala!*' resounds on every side. This woman is contaminated with every depraved habit known to human nature; and as her husband is a debauchee by 'special prerogative,' she does not scruple to act as his *alcahueta* in all his amours. In the meantime she is not without her own lovers—a worthy couple, truly!"

conflict. The general, however, hastened on, and arrived at the Cañon about noon on the 18th, with his whole army in battle array. Here, again, no enemy appeared to dispute our passage. The Mexicans had dispersed and fled to the mountains.* This Cañon is nothing more than a deep fissure or chasm, through the ridge of the mountains which divides the waters of the Pecos from those of the Rio Del Norte. Here the Mexicans had commenced fortifying against our approach by chopping away the timber, so their artillery could play to better advantage upon our lines, and throwing up temporary breast-works; but they lacked either courage or unanimity to defend a position apparently so well chosen.

It is stated upon good authority that Governor Armijo, Gen. Salezar, and other generals in the Mexican army, disputed for the supreme command, and that the common people being peaceably disposed towards the Americans, readily seized upon the dissention of their leaders as a pretext for abandoning the army.[39¼] Thus Gov.

* Gov. Armijo, with near two hundred dragoons made his escape in the direction of El Paso del Norte. He was subsequently heard of in Durango and Guadalajara.—HUGHES.

JAMES MAGOFFIN.
[From a portrait in possession of his son, Judge Joseph Magoffin, El Paso, Texas.]

NOTE 39½.—The secret history of the conquest of New Mexico is to be found in this biographical sketch of

JAMES MAGOFFIN.

The very important part played by James Magoffin in the Conquest of New Mexico, and the substantial aid he afforded Colonel Doniphan, require that we make some extended notice of his life. His son, Judge Joseph Magoffin, of El Paso, Texas, writes me as follows:

"In response to your favor requesting a sketch of my father, portrait or photograph, and his family history, I have to say that my father's parents were from County Down, Ireland. The name of his grandfather was Beriah Magoffin, whose wife was a Miss Wiley. Their son, Beriah Magoffin, married in Ireland Miss Jane McAfee. They came to this country prior to the year 1800, and settled in Harrodsburg, Mercer county, Kentucky. My father was born there in the year 1799, and was named James Wiley Magoffin. He had several brothers,—Samuel Magoffin, Ebenezer Magoffin, Beriah Magoffin, Governor of Kentucky, John, William, and Joseph; also three sisters, —Martha, Havena, and Sallie.

"My father married Mary Gertrude Valdez, of Chihuahua, about 1830. His

Armijo was left without soldiers to defend the Pass. However this may be, one thing is certain, that an army of near seven thousand Mexicans, with six pieces of cannon, and vastly the advantage of the ground, permitted Gen. Kearny, with less than two thousand Ameri-

brothers, Samuel and Beriah, married sisters, daughters of Isaac Shelby and granddaughters of Isaac Shelby, Sr., first Governor of Kentucky.

"I was born in Chihuahua, Mexico, in January, 1837, and settled in El Paso, Texas, in 1856. Was Major in the Confederate Army, with James P. Majors, of Missouri, and Chief Quartermaster and Commissary forces east to Mississippi river.

"My father engaged in merchandising in Chihuahua, Mexico, in the twenties, and was the first U. S. Consul of that State. Some years afterwards his brother Samuel entered into partnership with him. In 1844 my father and family and my Uncle Samuel, who was not then married, left Chihuahua for the States, and my father settled near Independence, Missouri. He bought a farm there, and my mother died there in January, 1845. Of course, our journey from Chihuahua to Independence was overland. After my mother's death my father took my brother Samuel and myself overland to St. Louis, thence to Louisville, Cincinnati, Pittsburg, Philadelphia, New York, and Washington. In Washington we met Hon. Thomas H. Benton. My father had purchased large quantities of goods on this trip. He placed us in school at Lexington, Kentucky, where we could see our relatives occasionally. We were under the charge of Uncle Beriah Magoffin. Two of my sisters, Josephine and Ursula, were placed in the Visitation Convent in St. Louis, under charge of James Harrison, my father's old-time friend. The balance of the family was left at Independence, under the care of three of my mother's sisters. About this time war was declared between the United States and Mexico. Doniphan's Expedition was organized. My father and Uncle Samuel had returned to Independence with their goods, when my father was sent for by the authorities at Washington, through Senator Benton. He was given a commission as secret agent of our Government and instructed to go with Doniphan; and on account of his extensive acquaintance with the people of New Mexico and the State of Chihuahua, to pave the way for the occupation of that country without bloodshed if possible. In this connection I refer you to Hon. Thomas H. Benton's *Thirty Years' View* and other works on the history of those times."

That James Magoffin, not General Kearny, secured New Mexico without the firing of a gun or the spilling of a drop of blood, is the testimony of Senator Thomas H. Benton. And as Senator Benton was responsible for the arrangements which produced that result, his statements cannot be questioned. They are given here at length as taken from his *Thirty Years' View*, Vol. II, pp. 682, 683, 684:

"General Kearny was directed to lead an expedition to New Mexico, setting out from the western frontier of Missouri, and mainly composed of volunteers from that State; and to conquer the province. He did so, without firing a gun, and the only inquiry is, how was it done?—how a province nine hundred miles distant, covered by a long range of mountains which could not well be turned, penetrable only by a defile which could not be forced, and defended by a numerous militia, could so easily be taken? This work does not write of military events, open to public history, but only of things less known, and to show how they were done: and in this point of view the easy and bloodless conquest of New Mexico, against such formidable obstacles, becomes an exception, and presents a proper problem for intimate historical solution. That solution is this: At the time of the fitting out that expedition there was a citizen of the United States, long resident in New Mexico, on a visit of business at Washington City—his name James Magoffin;—a man of mind, of will, of generous temper, patriotic, and rich. He knew every man in New Mexico and his character, and all the localities, and could

cans, to pass through the narrow defile and march right on to the capital of the State.*

Thus, on the 18th day of August, 1846, after a tiresome march of near nine hundred miles in less than fifty days, General Kearny with his whole command entered Santa Fé, the capital of the prov-

* The separate sovereignties which constitute the Mexican confederacy were formerly styled Departments. They are now called States.—HUGHES.

be of infinite service to the invading force. Mr. Benton proposed to him to go with it: he agreed. Mr. Benton took him to the President and Secretary at War, who gladly availed themselves of his agreement to go with General Kearny. He went: and approaching New Mexico, was sent ahead, with a staff officer— the officer charged with a mission, himself charged with his own plan: which was to operate upon Governor Armijo, and prevent his resistance to the entrance of the American troops. That was easily done. Armijo promised not to make a stand at the defile, after which the invaders would have no difficulty. But his second in command, Col. Archuletti, was determined to fight, and to defend that pass; and if he did, Armijo would have to do the same. It became indispensable to quiet Archuletti. He was of a different mould from the governor, and only accessible to a different class of considerations—those which addressed themselves to ambition. Magoffin knew the side on which to approach him. It so happened that General Kearny had set out to take the left bank of the Upper Del Norte— the eastern half of New Mexico—as part of Texas, leaving the western part untouched. Magoffin explained this to Archuletti, pointed to the western half of New Mexico as a derelict, not seized by the United States, and too far off to be protected by the central government: and recommended him to make a *pronunciamento*, and take that half to himself. The idea suited the temper of Archuletti. He agreed not to fight, and General Kearny was informed there would be no resistance at the defile: and there was none. Some thousands of militia collected there (and which could have stopped a large army), retired without firing a gun, and without knowing why. Armijo fled, and General Kearny occupied his capital: and the conquest was complete and bloodless: and this was the secret of that facile success—heralded in the newspapers as a masterpiece of generalship, but not so reported by the general.

"But there was an after-clap, to make blood flow for the recovery of a province which had been yielded without resistance. Mr. Magoffin was sincere and veracious in what he said to Col. Archuletti; but General Kearny soon (or before) had other orders, and took possession of the whole country! and Archuletti, deeming himself cheated, determined on a revolt. Events soon became favorable to him. General Kearny proceeded to California, leaving General Sterling Price in command, with some Missouri volunteers. Archuletti prepared his insurrection, and having got the upper country above Santa Fé ready, went below to prepare the lower part. While absent, the plot was detected and broke out, and led to bloody scenes in which there was severe fighting, and many deaths on both sides. It was in this insurrection that Governor Charles Bent, of New Mexico, and Captain Burgwin of the United States army, and many others, were killed. The insurgents fought with courage and desperation; but without their leader, without combination, without resources, they were soon suppressed; many being killed in action, and others hung for high treason—being tried by some sort of a court which had no jurisdiction of treason. All that were condemned were hanged except one, and he recommended to the President of the United States for pardon. Here was a dilemma for the administration. To pardon the man would be to admit the legality of the condemnation: not to pardon was to subject him to murder. A middle course was taken; the officers were directed to turn loose the condemned, and let him run. And this was the cause of the insurrection, and its upshot.

"Mr. Magoffin, having prepared the way for the entrance of General Kearny into Santa Fé, proceeded to the execution of the remaining part of his mission,

ince of New Mexico, and took peaceable and undisputed possession of the country, (without the loss of a single man, or the shedding of one drop of blood,) in the name of the government of the United States,

which was to do the same by Chihuahua for General Wool, then advancing upon that ancient capital of the Western Internal Provinces on a lower line. He arrived in that city—became suspected—was arrested—and confined. He was a social, generous-tempered man, a son of Erin: loved company, spoke Spanish fluently, entertained freely, and where it was some cost to entertain—claret $36.00 a dozen, champagne $50.00. He became a great favorite with the Mexican officers. One day the military judge advocate entered his quarters, and told him that Dr. Connelly, an American, coming from Santa Fé, had been captured near El Paso del Norte, his papers taken, and forwarded to Chihuahua, and placed in his hands, to see if there were any that needed government attention: and that he had found among the papers a letter addressed to him (Mr. Magoffin). He had the letter, unopened, and said he did not know what it might be; but being just ordered to join Santa Anna at San Luis Potosi, and being unwilling that any thing should happen after he was gone to a gentleman who had been so agreeable to him, he had brought it to him, that he might destroy it if there was any thing in it to commit him. Magoffin glanced his eye over the letter. It was an attestation from General Kearny of his services in New Mexico, recommending him to the acknowledgments of the American government in that invasion!—that is to say, it was his death warrant, if seen by the Mexican authorities. A look was exchanged: the letter went into the fire: and Magoffin escaped being shot.

"But he did not escape suspicion. He remained confined until the approach of Doniphan's expedition, and was then sent off to Durango, where he remained a prisoner to the end of the war. Returning to the United States after the peace, he came to Washington in the last days of Mr. Polk's administration, and expected remuneration. He had made no terms, asked nothing, and received nothing, and had expended his own money and that freely, for the public service. The administration had no money applicable to the object. Mr. Benton stated his case in secret session in the Senate, and obtained an appropriation, couched in general terms, of fifty thousand dollars for secret services rendered during the war. The appropriation, granted in the last night of the expiring administration, remained to be applied by the new one—to which the business was unknown, and had to be presented unsupported by a line of writing. Mr. Benton went with Magoffin to President Taylor, who, hearing what he had done, and what information he had gained for General Kearny, instantly expressed the wish that he had had some person to do the same for him,—observing that he got no information but what he obtained at the point of the bayonet. He gave orders to the Secretary at War to attend to the case as if there had been no change in the administration. The secretary (Mr. Crawford, of Georgia), higgled, required statements to be filed, almost in the nature of an account; and, finally, proposed thirty thousand dollars. It barely covered expenses and losses; but, having undertaken the service patriotically, Magoffin would not lower its character by standing out for more. The paper which he filed in the war office may furnish some material for history—some insight into the way of making conquests—if ever examined.

"This is the secret history of General Kearny's Expedition, and of the insurrection, given because it would not be found in the documents. The history of Doniphan's Expedition will be given for the same reason, and to show that a regiment of citizen volunteers, without a regular officer among them, almost without expense, and hardly with the knowledge of their government, performed actions as brilliant as any that illustrated the American arms in Mexico; and made a march in the enemy's country longer than that of the ten thousand under Xenophon."

For Senator Benton's account of Doniphan's Expedition, see his address of welcome delivered in St. Louis when the troops returned. It is given in full in this volume, *post*.

and planted the American flag in the public square, where the stars and stripes, and the eagle, still stream above the Palacio Grande, or stately residence of the ex-Governor Armijo.[40] When the American flag was raised, a national salute of twenty-eight guns was fired from the hill east of the town, by Maj. Clark's two batteries of six-pounders. At the same time the streets were filled with American cavalry, moving firmly and rapidly through the city, displaying their colors in the gayest and most gorgeous manner. This day we completed a march of twenty-nine miles, partly over a slippery road, (for a heavy rain had fallen the previous night,) and partly over a ragged, rocky way, through the mountain passes. After incredible exertions, and late at night, the baggage trains and the merchant wagons came into camp, a few of them having failed on the way, or fallen behind; so rapid was the march of our army during the whole day. General Kearny selected his camp-ground on the hill com-

NOTE 40.—The following is the first letter written by General Kearny after his occupation of Santa Fé which I have found. It will be observed that he says that he had issued a proclamation of even date with the letter, "claiming the whole Dept. with its original Bounderies for the United States & under the title of 'the Territory of New Mexico.'" A complete copy of this proclamation will be found in the following chapter. In his *History of the Pacific States*, Vol. XII, Hubert Howe Bancroft (pp. 417, 418) records the greater portion of the proclamation, with sneering comments interspersed:

            Head Qr. Army of the West
            Santa fe—New Mexico
            Augt 22, 1846

GENERAL: I have to inform you that on the 18th Instant without firing a gun or spilling a drop of blood, I took possession of this City the Capitol of the Dept of New Mexico & I have this day issued a Proclamation, claiming the whole Dept with its original Bounderies for the United States & under the title of "the Territory of New Mexico."

Everything here is quiet & peaceable—the People now understand the advantages they are to derive from the exchange of Government, & are much gratified with it—I have more troops (Missouri Vols.) following in my Rear—On their arrival there will be more than necessary for this Territory—I will send the surplus to you—Should you not want them, you can order them to Maj. Genl Taylor or to their homes as you may think the good of the public service requires—

I am destined for Upper California, & hope to start from here in the course of a few weeks—Success attend you

Brig. Genl J. E. Wool   Very Respectfully
 U. S. Army   Yr. ob. Servt
  Chihuahua   S. W. KEARNY
             Brig Genl. U. S. A.

General Kearny wrote the War Department on the 24th, as follows:

         Head Qr. Army of the West
         Santa fe New Mexico Augt 24, '46

SIR: I have to report that on the 18th Inst, the Army under my command marched into this city the capital of New Mexico, having met with no armed

manding the town from the east, a bare, gravelly spot of earth, where neither wood nor grass was to be obtained. So constant was the army kept in motion, that the men took no refreshments during the day, nor were the horses permitted to graze a moment. At night the men lay down to rest without eating or drinking, as they were almost overcome by fatigue. Our animals, for want of forage, were become feeble and incapable of further exertion. Without a blade of grass or other food, they stood tethered to their iron pickets, or sank to the earth of exhaustion. Many of them had performed their last noble day's service. Gen. Kearny had taken up his head-quarters in the Governor's palace, and caused the American colors to be raised above it. Thus the city of Santa Fé was bloodlessly possessed by the American forces.

On the morning of the 19th, General Kearny assembled the citizens of the town near the government building, and spoke to them in this manner, Robedou being the interpreter:

"New Mexicans! We have come amongst you to take possession of New Mexico, which we do in the name of the government of the United States. We have come with peaceable intentions and kind feelings towards you all. We come as friends, to better your condition and make you a part of the Republic of the United States. We mean not to murder you, or rob you of your property. Your families shall be free from molestation; your women secure from violence. My soldiers will take nothing from you but what they pay you for. In taking possession of New Mexico we do not mean to take away your religion from you. Religion and government have no connection in our country. There, all religions are equal; one has no preference over another; the Catholic and Protestant are esteemed alike.

"Every man has a right to serve God according to his heart.

---

resistance, the Mexican troops numbering about 4000 which had been collected on the Road under Govr. Armijo to oppose us having dispersed on our approaching them, & the Govr. himself having fled with a troop of his Dragoons towards Chihuahua—On the 22d I issued a proclamation claiming the whole of New Mexico with its then Boundaries as a Tery. of the U. S. of America, & taking it under our protection—I send herewith copies of all official Papers on the subject—The People of the Tery. are now perfectly tranquil & can easily be kept so—The intelligent portion know the advantages they are to derive from the change of Government & express their satisfaction at it.

In a few days I shall march down the Del Norte & visit some of the Principle cities below, for the purpose of seeing the People & explaining to them personally our intentions relating to the Territory. On my return (which will be in 2 or three weeks) a civil Government shall be organized & the officers appointed for it—After which I will be ready to start for Upper California which I hope may

When a man dies, he must render to his God an account of his acts here on earth, whether they be good or bad. In our government all men are equal. We esteem the most peaceable man, the best man. I advise you to attend to your domestic pursuits—cultivate industry—be peaceable and obedient to the laws. Do not resort to violent means, to correct abuses. I do hereby proclaim that, being in possession of Santa Fé, I am therefore virtually in possession of all New Mexico. Armijo is no longer your governor. His power is departed. But he will return and be as one of you. When he shall return you are not to molest him. You are no longer Mexican subjects: you are now become American citizens, subject only to the laws of the United States. A change of government has taken place in New Mexico, and you no longer owe allegiance to the Mexican government. I do hereby proclaim my intention to establish in this Department a civil government, on a republican basis, similar to those of our own States. It is my intention, also, to continue in office those by whom you have been governed, except the governor, and such other persons as I shall appoint to office by virtue of the authority vested in me. I am your governor,—henceforward look to me for protection."

The general next proceeded to inquire if they were willing to take the oath of allegiance to the United States' government, to which having given their consent, he then administered to the Governor, *ad interim*, the Secretary of State, the Prefecto, the Alcalde and other officers of State, the following oath: "Do you swear in good faith that under all circumstances you will bear allegiance to the laws and government of the United States, and that through good and evil you will demean yourselves as obedient and faithful citizens of the same, in the name of the Father, and of the Son, and of the Holy

---

be by the latter end of next Month & in such case I shall expect to have possession of that Dept by the close of November.

I have not heard from or of Col Price & his command which he was to raise & bring here & have received but vague rumors of Capt Allen & the Mormons—I suppose however they will all be here in a few weeks—Capt Allens command will accompany me to the Pacific, & the number of efficient Men he brings will determine the additional number I must take from here—After deciding upon that & upon the number which will be necessary to hold the Territory, I shall send the surplus to Chihuahua to report to Brig. Genl Wool—I enclose a copy of my communication to him of the 22d. Instant

On the 15th Inst, I recd. yours of July 2d. & 3d. the former enclosing a copy of a letter to Capt Tompkins 3d. Arty. from the Genl in chief the latter enclosing for me a Commission of Brig. Genl, which I hereby accept of, & for which I offer to the Presdt & Senate my acknowledgement & thanks for the honor they have conferred on me

Brig. Genl R. Jones　　　　　　　　Very Resp-y Yr. ob. Servt.
　Adj. Genl U. S. A　　　　　　　　　　S. W. Kearny
　　　W——n　　　　　　　　　　　　　　　Brig. Gen'l

Spirit. Amen." Here shouts and huzzas were raised by the Mexicans for Governor Kearny. A very aged Mexican embraced him and wept.[41]

Gen. Kearny having administered a similar oath to various delegations from the different Pueblos who came to offer submission, tranquillity and universal satisfaction seemed to prevail. Our commander next ordered a flag-staff, one hundred feet high, to be erected in the public square, from the top of which the American flag now streams over the capital.

Gen. Kearny's army was not well provisioned; nor was it furnished, in all its parts, with stout, able, and efficient teams, such as the difficult nature of the country over which it had to pass, required. The commissary and quartermaster departments were wretchedly managed. During much of the time, owing either to neglect or incom-

NOTE 41.—The authority under which General Kearny acted was stated to him in the following communication from the War Department:

[CONFIDENTIAL.]   WAR DEPARTMENT,
WASHINGTON, June 3, 1846.

SIR: I herewith send you a copy of my letter to the Governor of Missouri for an additional force of one thousand mounted men.

The object of thus adding to the force under your command is not, as you will perceive, fully set forth in that letter, for the reason that it is deemed prudent that it should not, at this time, become a matter of public notoriety; but to you it is proper and necessary that it should be stated.

It has been decided by the President to be of the greatest importance in the pending war with Mexico to take the earliest possession of Upper California. An expedition with that view is hereby ordered, and you are designated to command it. To enable you to be in sufficient force to conduct it successfully, this additional force of a thousand mounted men has been provided, to follow you in the direction of Santa Fé, to be under your orders or the officer you may leave in command at Santa Fé.

It cannot be determined how far this additional force will be behind that designated for the Santa Fé expedition, but it will not probably be more than a few weeks. When you arrive at Santa Fé with the force already called, and shall have taken possession of it, you may find yourself in a condition to garrison it with a small part of your command, (as the additional force will soon be at that place,) and with the remainder press forward to California. In that case you will make such arrangements as to being followed by the reinforcement before mentioned, as in your judgment may be deemed safe and prudent. I need not say to you that in case you conquer Santa Fé, (and with it will be included the Department or State of New Mexico,) it will be important to provide for retaining safe possession of it. Should you deem it prudent to have still more troops for the accomplishment of the objects herein designated, you will lose no time in communicating your opinion on that point, and all others connected with the enterprise, to this department. Indeed, you are hereby authorized to make a direct requisition for it upon the Governor of Missouri.

It is known that a large body of Mormon emigrants are *en route* to California for the purpose of settling in that country. You are desired to use all proper means to have a good understanding with them, to the end that the United States may have their coöperation in taking possession of and holding that country

petency of the heads of these departments, the general found it necessary to subsist his men on *half rations*. It repeatedly happened that the wagons, particularly of the volunteer corps, were left so far behind during a day's march that they did not come into camp before midnight. Thus the men had to *feast* or *famish* by turns, owing to the gross and culpable neglect of government agents. The volunteer troops were furnished with very sorry and indifferent wagons and teams, wholly inadequate for such an expedition, whilst the regulars were furnished in the very best manner. Owing to an unaccountable arrangement by the War Department, the volunteer regiment was not allowed a full staff of officers, and hence proceeded the ill-management of these affairs.

Rumor and exaggeration are two grand evils in an army. While

It has been suggested here that many of these Mormons would willingly enter into the service of the United States, and aid us in our expedition against California. You are hereby authorized to muster into service such as can be induced to volunteer; not, however, to a number exceeding one-third of your entire force. Should they enter the service they will be paid as other volunteers, and you can allow them to designate, so far as can be properly done, the persons to act as officers thereof. It is understood that a considerable number of American citizens are now settled on the Sacramento river, near *Sutter's* establishment, called "New Helvetia," who are well disposed towards the United States. Should you, on your arrival in that country, find this to be the true state of things there, you are authorized to organize and receive into the service of the United States such portion of these citizens as you may think useful to aid you to hold the possession of the country. You will in that case allow them, so far as you shall judge proper, to select their own officers. A large discretionary power is invested in you in regard to these matters, as well as to all others, in relation to the expeditions confided to your command.

The choice of routes by which you will enter California will be left to your better knowledge and ampler means of getting accurate information. We are assured that a southern route (called the caravan route, by which the wild horses are brought from that country into New Mexico) is practicable, and it is suggested as not improbable that it can be passed over in the winter months, or at least late in autumn. It is hoped that this information may prove to be correct.

In regard to the routes, the practicability of procuring needful supplies for men and animals, and transporting baggage, is a point to be well considered. Should the President be disappointed in his cherished hope that you will be able to reach the interior of Upper California before winter, you are then desired to make the best arrangement you can for sustaining your force during the winter, and for an early movement in the spring. Though it is very desirable that the expedition should reach California this season, (and the President does not doubt you will make every possible effort to accomplish this object,) yet if, in your judgment, it cannot be undertaken with a reasonable prospect of success, you will defer it, as above suggested, until spring. You are left unembarrassed by any specific directions in this matter.

It is expected that the naval forces of the United States which are now, or will soon be in the Pacific, will be in possession of all the towns on the seacoast, and will coöperate with you in the conquest of California. Arms, ordnance, munitions of war, and provisions to be used in that country, will be sent by sea to our squadron in the Pacific for the use of the land forces.

Should you conquer and take possession of New Mexico and Upper California,

on the march to New Mexico we were one day startled at the news that the Mexicans had driven all their cattle and sheep into the distant mountains, deserted their villages and ranchos, and burnt the grass* upon the road. Had this been the case our animals must inevitably have perished. On another, we were perhaps told that a body of eight or ten thousand Mexicans and Pueblo Indians combined, were advancing upon the road to meet us and give us battle. We were thus constantly kept in uncertainty, until experience brought the matter to a test. These pernicious rumors were generally spread through the camp by the Mexican prisoners that were daily picked up on the road. When we came to the Mexican ranchos or farm houses we found abundance of grass and thousands of horned cattle, and plenty of sheep and goats scattered upon the hills and mountains. These flocks had each of them its respective shepherd. We did not molest

* Owing to the dryness of the climate in New Mexico, the grass is parched and crisped at all seasons, and will almost as readily take fire in August as in November.—HUGHES.

or considerable places in either, you will establish temporary civil governments therein—abolishing all arbitrary restrictions that may exist, so far as it may be done with safety. In performing this duty, it would be wise and prudent to continue in their employment all such of the existing officers as are known to be friendly to the United States, and will take the oath of allegiance to them. The duties at the custom-house ought at once to be reduced to such a rate as may be barely sufficient to maintain the necessary officers, without yielding any revenue to the Government. You may assure the people of those provinces that it is the wish and design of the United States to provide for them a free government with the least possible delay, similar to that which exists in our Territories. They will then be called on to exercise the rights of freemen in electing their own representatives to the Territorial Legislature. It is foreseen that what relates to the civil government will be a difficult and unpleasant part of your duty, and much must necessarily be left to your own discretion. In your whole conduct you will act in such a manner as best to conciliate the inhabitants and render them friendly to the United States.

It is desirable that the usual trade between the citizens of the United States and the Mexican provinces should be continued, missing words practicable, under the changed condition of things between the two countries. In consequence? of tending to your expedition to California, it may be proper that you should increase your supply of goods to be distributed as presents to the Indians. The United States Superintendent of Indian Affairs at St. Louis will aid you in procuring these goods. You will be furnished with a proclamation in the Spanish language, to be issued by you and circulated among the Mexican people on your entering into or approaching their country. You will use your utmost endeavors to have the pledges and promises therein contained carried out to the utmost extent.

I am directed by the President to say that the rank of brevet brigadier-general will be conferred on you as soon as you commence your movement towards California, and sent round to you by sea or over the country, or to the care of the commandant of our squadron in the Pacific. In that way cannon, arms, ammunition, and supplies for the land forces will be sent to you.

Very respectfully, your obedient servant,
W. L. MARCY,
Secretary of War.

Colonel S. W. Kearny,
Fort Leavenworth, Missouri.

them. We took nothing, not even a melon, an ear of corn, a chicken, a goat or a sheep, from those poor people, for which we did not pay the money. This generous and Christian conduct on the part of the American army completely secured the good will and friendship of the Mexicans; for they supposed, and were even taught by their priests and rulers, to believe that they would be robbed, plundered, and murdered; and the whole country ravaged by the invading army. By this means the rulers hoped to stimulate the common people to oppose the Americans. Their appliances, however, failed of success. The kind treatment the Americans uniformly extended towards those people is worthy of the highest praise, and will doubtless, before the tribunal of a community of men who can justly appreciate the moral force of such an example, do the command more credit than the gaining of TEN VICTORIES.

BENT'S FORT.

CHAPTER IV.

Grazing Detachment—American Residents at Santa Fé—Herkins—Gen. Kearny's Proclamation—New Mexico—Santa Fé—New Mexican Women—The Fandango—Lieut. Oldham—Deserters—The Express—A Pueblo Chief—Stamp paper.

The next day after the capture of Santa Fé and its occupation by the American troops, a heavy detail was made from the different companies to conduct the horses and other animals belonging to the command, into the neighborhood of Galisteo, twenty-seven miles south-easterly from the capital, for the purpose of grazing them, forage being scarce and extremely difficult to be procured near town. This grazing party, to the command of which Lieutenant-colonel Ruff had been appointed, (the detachment from each company being under a lieutenant,) proceeded directly to the mountains and valleys of Galisteo creek, where, finding grass and water abundant and of good quality, they made their encampment. This encampment, however, was afterwards changed from one place to another, according as the pasturage demanded. This party of men was, at first, most scandalously neglected by the subsistence department at Santa Fé, supplies being sent them very sparingly, and irregularly. After much complaint, however, they were more liberally provisioned. The stock, which had been exhausted by want of forage and long marches, was soon in a thriving condition, and again fit for service; so fine and nutricious is the grass in the hill-country of New Mexico.

A few days previous to the Americans entering Santa Fé, the American merchants and other Americans, resident there, were under continual apprehensions of being robbed, mobbed and murdered by the enraged populace, whose supreme delight was best promoted by heaping reproaches on the "Texans" and "North American invaders," as they contemptuously styled us. The Americans, however, locked their store rooms, barred up their houses, and resolved, if an attack were made upon them, to occupy a strong building, and unitedly withstand a siege until relief could be sent them by Gen. Kearny. They were not, however, seriously molested, though frequently insulted.

On the morning of the 19th of August, a serious difficulty occurred between two volunteers, one of them, his name Herkins, being intoxicated. The affray took place in the plaza, under the eye of Gen. Kearny. Captain Turner, Major Swords and others, were immediately ordered to arrest the rioter. Herkins, with drawn sword, resisted. After giving and receiving several slight wounds, he was taken and confined. By the sentence of a court martial, his wages were withheld and he was "drummed out of the service" of the country.

Gen. Kearny's next official act, as the civil and military governor of the department of New Mexico, was the issuing of the following proclamation:

Proclamation to the inhabitants of New Mexico, by Brigadier-general S. W. KEARNY, commanding the army of the United States in the same.

As by the act of the Republic of Mexico, a state of war exists between that government and the United States, and as the undersigned, at the head of his troops, on the 18th instant, took possession of Santa Fé, the capital of the department of New Mexico, he now announces his intention to hold the department with its original boundaries (on both sides of the Del Norte) as a part of the United States, and under the name of the Territory of New Mexico.

The undersigned has come to New Mexico with a strong military force, and an equally strong one is following close in his rear. He has more troops than necessary to put down any opposition that can possibly be brought against him, and therefore it would be folly and madness for any dissatisfied or discontented persons to think of resisting him.

The undersigned has instructions from his government to respect the religious institutions of New Mexico, to protect the property of the church, to cause the worship of those belonging to it to be undisturbed, and their religious rights in the amplest manner preserved to them. Also to protect the person and property of all quiet and peaceable inhabitants within its boundaries, against their enemies, the Eutaws, Navajos, and others. And while he assures all that it will be his pleasure, as well as his duty, to comply with those instructions, he calls upon them to exert themselves in preserving order, in promoting concord, and in maintaining the authority and efficiency of the laws; and to require of those who have left their homes and taken up arms against the troops of the United States, to return forthwith to them, or else they will be considered as enemies and traitors, subjecting their persons to punishment, and their property to seizure and confiscation, for the benefit of the public treasury. It is the wish and intention of the United States to provide for New Mexico a free government, with the least possible delay, similar to those in the United States, and the people of New Mexico will then be called on to exercise the rights of freemen in electing their own representatives to the Territorial Legislature; but until this can be done, the laws hitherto in existence will be continued until changed or modified by competent authority, and those persons holding office will continue in the same for the present, provided, they will consider themselves good citizens, and willing to take the oath of allegiance to the United States.

The undersigned hereby absolves all persons residing within the boundary of New Mexico, from further allegiance to the republic of Mexico, and hereby claims them as citizens of the United States. Those who remain quiet and peaceable, will be considered as good citizens, and receive protection. Those who are found in arms, or instigating others against the United States, will be considered as traitors, and treated accordingly. Don Manuel Armijo, the late governor of this department, has fled from it. The undersigned has taken possession of it without firing a gun or shedding a drop of blood, in which he most truly rejoices, and for the present will be considered as governor of this territory.

Given at Santa Fé, the capital of the territory of New Mexico, this 22d day of August, 1846, and in the 71st year of the independence of the United States. By the governor:

S. W. KEARNY, *Brig. Gen.*

About this time, Gen. Kearny came in possession of six pieces of artillery, understood to be the same that Gov. Armijo had at the Galisteo pass on the 18th, which place he abandoned on our approach; and also a part of the ammunition carried out by Speyers and Armijo from Independence. These pieces of cannon were almost worthless, excepting one of them, a very fine Texan piece, inscribed with the name of General Lamar, President of Texas, which was taken in 1841 by General Salezar, from General McLeod, near San Miguel. These pieces were temporarily added to Major Clark's two batteries. The New Mexicans made use of copper slugs, instead of grape and canister shot. They also had copper balls.

New Mexico, whose climate is generally bland and salubrious, embraces within its ample territorial limits more than 200,000 square miles. Of this vast area, which includes a wilderness of bleak, desolate, unproductive snow-capped mountains, many of whose summits are 13,000 feet above the level of the sea, only the valleys which are susceptible of irrigation from constantly flowing streams, can be cultivated with any degree of success. It is traversed by numer-

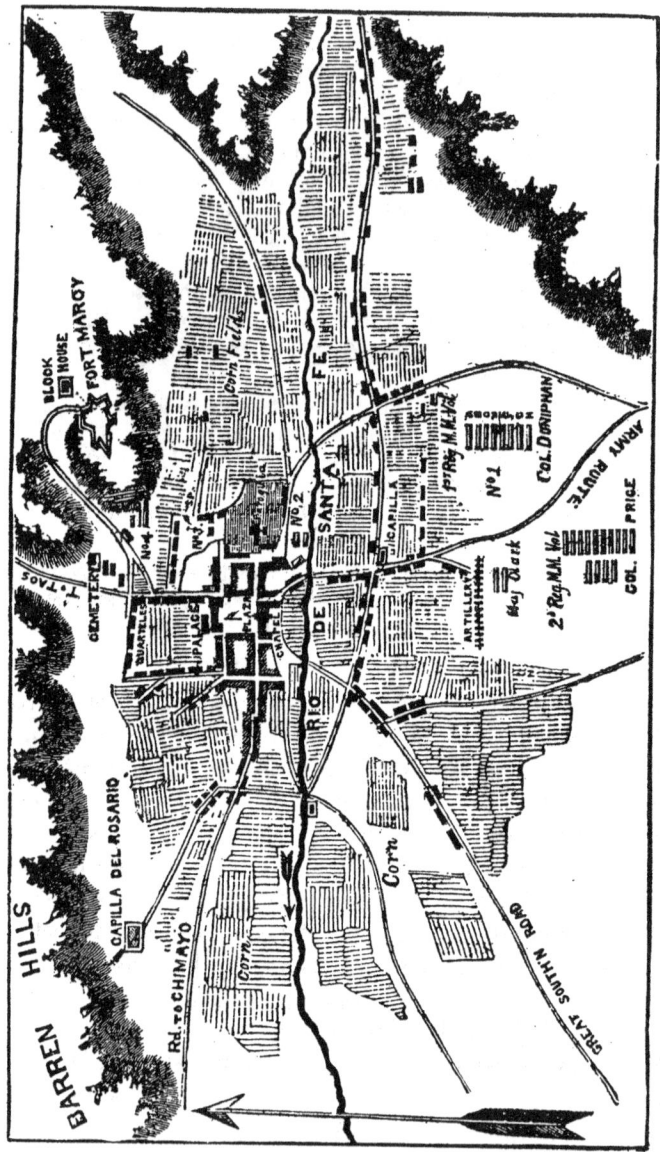

PLAN OF SANTA FÉ AND ITS ENVIRONS.

NOTE.—The Numbers, near the Encampments, show the regular order of the changes. No. 1 is the only instance in which the regiment was altogether; being afterwards broken up into detachments, and sent off into different parts of New Mexico. No. 2 shows the regiment decreased, &c. Distance, from salient angle of Fort Marcy, to the Flag-staff, in the center of the Plaza, six hundred and sixty-four yards.

The Flag-staff is one hundred feet high; it was made and erected by the volunteers. Fort Marcy mounts fourteen guns.— HUGHES.

ous elevated mountain-ranges, the principal of which are the Sierra Madre, or Cordilleras, and the Sierra Blanco. Between these spreads out the magnificent, basin-like valley of the Del Norte, coursed by a broad, bright zone of water, and dotted by towns, villages, ranchos, and farm houses. This valley contains the principal wealth of the state. Gardens richly blooming—orchards surcharged with ripened fruit—vineyards bending under the clustering grape—fields of wheat waving their golden harvests before the wind—shady groves of alamos, all irrigated by canals of clear, pure, rippling water, strongly contrast with the gigantic granite peaks, which, blue as amethyst, tower high into the heavens. These mountains, beyond doubt, contain inexhaustible stores of mineral wealth. Besides gold, silver, lead and copper, bituminous and anthracite coal, black oxides, brimstone in its pure state, salt, and vast quantities of gypsum, are known to abound. Corn, wheat, rye, beans, pulse, pepper and onions, are the staple productions of the country. Immense herds of cattle, droves of horses and mules, and innumerable flocks of sheep and goats feed upon the mountain pastures. The New Mexicans are emphatically a pastoral people. The bold unfailing mountain streams, with their foaming cascades and dashing cataracts, present fine facilities for manufacturing, and seem to invite enterprise.[42]

New Mexico contains, according to a census taken in 1844, a mixed population of 160,000; of which number one-third are Pueblo

NOTE 42.—*New Mexico.*—The origin of the name, New Mexico, lies in the mass of myth and romance which arose about the efforts of the Spaniards to penetrate the North. They were constantly seeking a new Mexico. The term was at first an appellation of indefinite import given to the country traversed by Coronado and other explorers. It can be traced back to about 1563. In later years it became the name of the country which still bears it and which should never be deprived of it.

It is stated in most works relating to the history of New Mexico that the first Europeans to enter its territory were Cabeza de Vaca (Alvar Nuñez), and his companions in misfortune, Andres Dorantes, Alonso del Castillo Maldonada, and a negro slave named Estevanico. They were the survivors of the unfortunate expedition of Pánfilo Narvaez to the Florida coasts of the Gulf of Mexico in 1528. After extensive wanderings and indescribable hardships they crossed the continent from some point in Texas to Sinaloa, arriving at San Miguel de Culican in April, 1536. While these men may have traversed the bounds of the present New Mexico, the evidence that they did so may be regarded as not conclusive. They may have, at most, but skirted its southern border westward from the vicinity of El Paso.

The accounts spread by these men upon their return to the Spanish settle-

Indians, the original proprietors of the soil, who submitted to the Spaniards in the early conquest of the country—profess the Romish

MEXICAN GROUP.

faith—have their churches and ecclesiastics, and yield an unforced obedience to the laws of the state, but live in villages, or Pueblos,

ments caused much excitement. Other countries like Peru and Mexico in wealth were supposed to exist. Coronado, Governor of New Galicia, sent Marcos de Niza, a monk of the order of St. Francis, to make a preliminary exploration of the country described by the returned castaways. This expedition was guided by Estevanico (Stephen). It reached the present Zuñi, at that time called Cibola. Stephen was killed there, and finding nothing of importance in that country, the party returned. To make amends for the lean list of substantial results which he should have submitted, the monk composed a report which was a marvelous production, mainly pure fiction. In 1540 Coronado himself undertook the discovery of the fabled cities in the North. His army consisted of 300 Spaniards and 800 Indians. He set out from Culican on Easter Monday. His route lay for the most part east of that taken by Niza, but the army reached and subdued Cibola. After the discovery that the reports of Niza were wholly unreliable, it was determined to continue the exploration or search for a rich country to plunder. The Indians, to be rid of their presence, no doubt, told them of rich countries to the east, to find which they departed. They entered New Mexico about the 10th of July, 1540 (7th to 10th, Bancroft says). The valley of the Rio Grande was explored in the vicinity of Santa Fé. This expedition passed eastward out into the great plains, and were the first Europeans to see and describe the buffalo. A good record of the route was preserved, but the absence of names

isolated from other New Mexican settlements, and enjoy a social system of their own, refusing, for the most part, to intermarry with their Mexican neighbors. They still retain a rancorous hatred towards their conquerors. More recently, however, New Mexico, owing to her remoteness from the central government, has been subject to the desolating incursions of the bordering tribes, and prostrated by

of streams that can be identified at this time, and other causes, render the location of this route and its extent extremely problematical.

The settlement of New Mexico began after the return of Coronado's company. This settlement was in the usual Spanish mode. Missions were established, often at great hazard, sometimes at the cost of life. Little real progress was made in the colonization of the country until 1595, when Oñate made what might be termed a conquest of the country now embraced in New Mexico. From this time the Spanish population increased rapidly. Mining gold and silver became the principal occupation of the people. The Indians were enslaved and forced to labor in the mines. In 1680 they rose in revolt against their Spanish masters. Their leader was Popé, who seems to have been a man of much native ability. He forced the Spanish Governor to evacuate Santa Fé and retire down the Rio Grande. The efforts to subdue the Indians were unsuccessful for thirteen years. In 1693 Diego de Vargas regained possession of the country and made peace with the Indians, stipulating that there should be no more Indian slavery in the mines. In fact, mining was not so extensively engaged in after the reoccupation of the country, the Indians having filled up the mines after the Spaniards had been driven out.

Occasional wars with the Indian tribes on the borders of the country occurred during the next century, but there is no event of importance to record. Captain Zebulon M. Pike was sent out to explore the country along the western limits of Louisiana in 1804. He erected a camp on the Mexican side of the line, was captured, and was sent as a prisoner to Chihuahua. He found an American living in Santa Fé. About this time Americans began to cross the plains, and, later, goods from the United States began to arrive overland at Santa Fé. This trade increased for a number of years, amounting at one time to considerable volume. In 1820 Mexico established her independence, and New Mexico was thenceforth governed by the Republic. The constitution of the country was changed, and what is known in the United States as a "carpet-bag" government was set up. The first alien sent to rule New Mexico was Albino Perez. The usual fate of such governments befel that of New Mexico. The oppression practiced produced a revolt which cost Perez his life. Other officials were killed. On August 10, 1837, a Taos Indian named José Gonzales was selected as Governor by the insurgents. He appears to have been a good man. General Manuel Armijo of Albuquerque raised a force for the suppression of the revolt; he defeated the rebels at Cañada, and captured and shot Gonzalez. He proclaimed himself Governor, in which office he was confirmed by the authorities of Mexico. Armijo retained the office of Governor, with but short intermissions, until the conquest of the country by the Americans in 1846, when he made no effort to defend his native land, and fled its borders.

The establishment of the authority of the United States will develop in this

feuds and intestine broils. Many bloody tragedies have been enacted there. Thus distracted and unsupported, she fell an easy prey to the victorious American arms.

Santa Fé, the capital of New Mexico, occupies the site of an ancient Pueblo, and contains an estimated population of six thousand. It is situated on Santa Fé creek, a beautiful, clear stream, issuing out of the mountains towards the east, having its source in a lake. From this creek various canals part, above the town, and lead through the fields, gardens, and orchards, for the purposes of irrigation.

work, making any extended notice of it here unnecessary. It was regularly organized as a Territory of the United States by Act of Congress September 9, 1850. The Civil War extended to this remote section. A Confederate army from Texas occupied Santa Fé March 10, 1862. This force was defeated at Glorieta March 28. April 8, it evacuated Santa Fé and left the country. The people were very loyal to the Government, and sent more than six thousand men into the Federal armies; there are no more patriotic people in the United States than the New-Mexicans.

The Atchison, Topeka and Santa Fé Railroad reached Las Vegas July 1, 1879; reached Santa Fé February 9, 1880; and Deming March 18, 1881. The first rail was laid in the Territory November 30, 1878.

The Territory contains 122,469 square miles, lying upon the southeastern portion of the Rocky Mountain plateau; only Texas, California and Montana are larger. It lies between parallels 31 and 37 north, and between meridians 103 and 109 west. In altitude it ranges from 2,900 feet to nearly 15,000 feet. The climate is dry and mild, and is considered to be extremely healthful. The Territory is called the Land of Sunshine. Twenty-five counties have been organized. In 1850 the population was 61,547; now it is more than 300,000, and less than half of Spanish, Mexican and Indian descent. Much of the country is pastoral and unfit for agriculture; but large areas are adapted to irrigation, and when water can be brought on the land it produces immense crops. The lands capable of irrigation lie in the valleys; and there are three large river systems,— the Colorado, the Rio Grande, and the Canadian. The Rio Grande flows across the Territory from north to south, dividing it into two nearly equal parts. It has many tributaries, the largest being the Pecos. The great system of irrigation canals projected, some of which are under construction, will reclaim millions of acres of as fertile land as there is to be found in the world. The principal crops are alfalfa, corn, wheat, potatoes, sugar beets, and a great variety of vegetables. It is becoming famous for its orchard crops and the products of its vineyards. More than a million cattle are on the ranges of the Territory, and the sheep number six millions. The annual wool-clip amounts to twenty-five million pounds. Horses are raised in great numbers, as are mules, asses, goats, and hogs; and poultry is produced in abundance.

In mineral wealth the Territory stands in the front rank, though development has not been as yet extensive. The coal-fields are large, and in quality the coal is very superior; anthracite coal exists in large quantities, fully as good as that produced in Pennsylvania. Zinc, copper, iron, gold, silver, lead, mica,

Families use the water of the canals. Their houses, generally flat-roofed, and one story high, are built of sun-dried bricks, called *adobes*, in the Spanish language. In the city there are six Catholic churches, but no public schools, the business of education being intrusted to ecclesiastics. The streets are crooked and narrow. The whole presents very much the appearance of an extensive brickyard. The public square is about ninety yards, from north to south, and one hundred from east to west. The governor's residence, or palace, is situated on the north side of the Plaza. The architecture is of the rudest order.[43]

For many years, Santa Fé has been the port of entry for American goods, and the great emporium where the merchants of central Mexico annually meet the American caravans, to purchase their stocks. It is a city of considerable trade.

The New Mexicans are generally under the medium size, and are of a swarthy, copper complexion; though every shade of color may sometimes be met with, from the fair Castilian to the darkest hue of the aborigines. They are hospitable, but ignorant and treacherous. The women, with few exceptions, are neither fair nor handsome, yet their dark, penetrating, lustrous, beaming eyes, peer out most cap-

---

sulphur, salt, alum, precious stones, petroleum, gypsum, cement-rock, lime-rock, clays, and commercial stone make up a part of the list of materials to be found. Ochres are also found, but are not yet utilized.

There are great forests of pine and spruce, and millions of feet of lumber are cut annually.

Mineral and hot springs are abundant.

The Territory is rich in prehistoric ruins, those of the cliff-dwellers being the most abundant.

There are 13,000 Indians in the Territory. Of these, 9,000 are Pueblos, 3,000 Navajos, and the remainder Apaches.

Taken all in all, the Territory is capable of wonderful development, and is destined to become one of the great commonwealths of the Union. It is in the process of assuming statehood, and it is expected that the remarkable resources of the new State will be rapidly developed.

And, so, the men who marched across the Plains in 1846 added an empire to our domain.

NOTE 43.—It is uncertain when Santa Fé was founded, but it is one of the oldest towns in the United States. Coronado visited the site in 1541. A settlement was made there by the Spaniards in 1598, and this is usually taken as the date of the founding of the city. It was made the first capital of New Mexico, and has always remained such. It was long the port of entry for American goods, and the overland commerce with the United States became known as the Santa Fé trade.

tivatingly from the folds of their rebozos,* and their black, glossy ringlets of hair, which, indeed, constitutes their greatest beauty. They seem to possess more intelligence than the men, and are infinitely their superiors in vivacity and gracefulness of demeanor.

The New Mexicans, both males and females, have a great fondness for jewelry, dress, and amusements. For amusement, the fandango appears to be the most fashionable place of resort, where every belle and beauty presents herself attired in the most costly manner, and displays her jewelry to the best advantage. To this place of recreation and pastime, which is generally a large, capacious saloon, or interior court, all descriptions of persons are allowed to come, free of charge, and without invitation. The fandango generally commences about nine o'clock, P. M.; and the tolling of the church bells is the signal for the ladies to make their appearance at the saloon; which they do almost simultaneously. The New Mexican ladies dress gaudily, but with little taste. They mostly wear dresses without bodies; having only the skirt, and a long, loose, flowing scarf or wrapper, dextrously thrown about the head and shoulders, so as to supersede both the use of dress bodies and bonnets. There is but little order kept at these fandangoes, and still less attention paid to the rules of etiquette.† A kind of swinging, gallopade waltz is their favorite dance—the cotillion is not much in vogue. Read Lord Byron's graphic description of the Dutch waltz, then stretch your imagination to its utmost tension, and you will perhaps have some faint conception of the Mexican fandango. Such familiarity of position would be repugnant to the refined rules of polite society, in our country; but among the New Mexicans, nothing is reckoned a greater accomplishment, than that of being able to pass handsomely through all the mazes of the waltz.

There is one republican feature about these fandangoes. It is here that all classes, rich and poor, meet and intermingle; as did the ancient Romans, at their Saturnalia, upon terms of equality. A sumptuous repast or collation is rarely ever prepared for the frolicsome coterie: but always an abundance of knicknacks, sweetmeats, and the exhilarating *vino*, or wine; and although it costs a man but

---

* The rebozo is a long scarf, or wrapper, used by the Mexican ladies to cover the head and shoulders.—HUGHES.

† The Author speaks of the fashions which prevailed in New Mexico during the continuance of the American army in that country.—HUGHES.

little to attend the fandango, and mingle in the gleeful throng, yet it very much resembles the descent of Æneas to the kingdom of Pluto —it is easy enough to get there, but to return—*hic est labor.*

Second Lieut. Jas. S. Oldham, of the company from Jackson county, was arrested on the 24th upon a charge of "disobedience to orders," by Lieutenant-colonel Ruff, and court-martialed on the 26th. He was deprived of his command and dismissed from the service "with a disability to serve in the armies of the United States for a period of twelve months." Not knowing all the circumstances of the case, and not having heard all the testimony before the court-martial, the author's opinion were better withheld than expressed. The head and front of his offending, however, was his persisting, contrary to order, in the determination to leave the grazing encampment, near Galisteo,[44] and proceed to Santa Fé, with the view of obtaining provisions for his men, who were then in pressing want. It has already been observed that this grazing party were supplied with the utmost parsimony.

About this time, when all was quiet in the camp, and in the capital, and universal satisfaction seemed to prevail, both among the conquerors and the conquered, six dragoons and two volunteers, without any apparent cause, deserted the army. The remembrance of the privations and hardships which they had suffered on the plains, and the thoughts of the still greater perils and sufferings yet to be encountered, perhaps determined them thus to sacrifice their honor and their usefulness, forgetting the duties which they owed to themselves, their friends and country. Whether they went over to the enemy, or returned to the States, was never certainly known. Arms, supposed to have been theirs, were subsequently found in the city of El Paso.

The whole of New Mexico being thus in quiet possession of the American troops, while deputations from the various Pueblos and villages were daily arriving at the capital, offering submission to the general, and cheerfully taking the oath of allegiance to the United States' government, an express, borne by five men, three regular

---

NOTE 44.—Galisteo was a mile and a half from the present town of that name. It was a pueblo of the Tanos Indians, and a mission was established there at a very early date. The inhabitants went to Santa Fé after the Spaniards were expelled in 1680, but they were driven away in 1 1Ω3.

dragoons and two volunteers, was sent, on the 25th, from Santa Fé to Fort Leavenworth, to be forwarded thence to Washington, containing a full account of Gen. Kearny's conquest of New Mexico, and asking for further instructions from the war department. The bearers of this express, having encountered the severest trials on the plains during the inclement winter season, returned to Santa Fé some time after Christmas.

Near this same time, the priest of San Filipé, and the curate of the churches in the valley of Taos, came to acknowledge the authority of the conqueror, receive his commands, and ask protection for the churches and church property. The general having assured them that their temples of worship would be respected, and their "religion in the amplest manner preserved to them," they returned home peaceably and favorably disposed towards the Americans, more subdued by kindness than by force of arms. They did not even forbear to speak in praise of the generous and magnanimous conduct of their conquerors.*

Also a young Pueblo chief, with a few of his warriors, came in to see the new governor. He said "he had heard of Gen. Kearny, and had come to see him; that he desired to know what his intentions were; whether he intended to protect the Pueblos, or murder them; that the priests had told him that the Americans would plunder and kill them, and take their wives and daughters away from them, and that such as they took prisoners they would brand on the face with a red-hot iron, and thus make them American citizens; that he now desired to know if such was the truth; that if it were so, he would go back to his people and encourage them to fight the Americans; that it was better to die honorably, in defence of his people and country, than to suffer these outrages." He also stated that "Gov. Armijo had visited Taos, and persuaded the Pueblos to join his army: but that the wise men of the Pueblos,—old, venerable men, who had great experience, and great knowledge,—told Armijo that it was useless to fight the Americans; that they were a numerous people; that if he whipped the Americans in one battle, or destroyed one army, others would keep on coming from the east, as long as the sun continued to shine; and that finally they would kill all the Mexicans, and then kill

* It was not long before the same faithless priests and leaders were detected in a conspiracy against the new government. — *fides Mexicana*.—HUGHES.

the Pueblos, their allies. Moreover, that Armijo would run when the fight came on, and leave the Pueblos to be slaughtered by the enraged Americans; that they first desired to have an interview with the American commander, to learn the truth of these things before they would go to war." Gen. Kearny then asked him what other rumors he had heard, to which he replied, that it was useless to tell a man of his information and knowledge about the tales that came like the wind, and had no responsible source; that "reports were for women and children to listen to, not men." Gen. Kearny, pleased with the boldness and magnanimity of the young chief, gave him some money and other presents, and dismissed him with the assurances of his friendship.

On the 29th, Gen. Kearny, having occasion to transfer some public property into the hands of a public functionary, took up a bit of blank paper and commenced writing, when the Alcalde, who happened to be present, remarked to the general that an instrument of writing was not legal, unless it were drawn up on paper stamped with the government seal or coat-of-arms, for the State of New Mexico. He then stepped and brought a few sheets of the government paper to Gen. Kearny, politely observing "that the government sold it at only eight dollars per sheet, a very moderate sum to pay for having an important document *strictly legal*." Without ceremony Gen. Kearny changed his purpose for the moment, and wrote, in substance, as follows: "The use of the 'stamp paper' by the government of New Mexico, is hereby abolished. Done by the Governor,

S. W. KEARNY, Brig. Gen.

"I will now," continued he, "take it at its real value, just as other paper." The Alcalde was astounded, for his prospects of further extortion were blasted. The common people, who had been compelled to pay the exorbitant sum of eight dollars for a sheet of paper, when an instrument of writing was wanted which required a seal, rejoiced that they were now relieved of a burdensome tax. It is thus, by acts of tyranny on the part of the government, that New Mexico has been the abode of misery and slavery, instead of happiness and liberty.[45]

NOTE 45.—The exact order made by General Kearny is as follows:

From this day so much of the law hitherto in force in New Mexico, which requires that Stamped Paper shall be used in certain transactions is disestablished
Santa Fe New Mexico   S. W. KEARNY
    Augt 29, 1846   Brig. Genl. U. S. A.

The orders previously made modifying the civil government are as follows:

The following sums will be collected in place of those established April 11th, 1844—

License for Dry Goods Store, per month		$2.00
" " Grocery, per month		4.00
" " Tavern, per month		5.00
" " Pub. Billiard Tables, per month		3.00
" " Monte Table, chura or game of chance, per night		1.50
" " Balls, where money is charged for attending		2.00

Licenses for the above must be obtained & paid for in advance If not, then five times the foregoing sums to be charged & the individuals confined until the amount is paid.

Waggons from the Arkansas or Chihuahua with goods belonging to Individuals & not Public ones, each	$4.00
Pleasure carriages from the above Places	2.00
Waggons or carriages belonging to Individuals entering the Public Plaza	.25

The above sums will be collected by the Collector of Santa fe, & turned over to the Treasurer of the city for the benefit thereof—The Treasurer & Collector keeping a correct account of all sums recd. & for which they will be held strictly responsible.

The Collector of Galisteo will collect the same amount for each Waggon or carriage as above, both to take effect from the 22d. Inst the day of New Mexico becoming a part of the United States. The above to continue in force until changed by proper authority.

Santa Fe New Mexico   S. W. KEARNY
    Augt 27, '46   Brig. Genl. U. S. A.

Henry S. Dodge is appointed Treasurer of Santa fe (New Mexico) in the place of Francisco Ortiz, who in consequence of sickness is unable to perform the duties—Mr. Ortiz will turn over to his successor any public funds, books or property pertaining to his office which he may have in his possession

Augt 28, 1846   S. W. KEARNY
                             Brig. Genl. U. S. A.

Tomas Rivera is appointed Collector of Santa fe Tery. of New Mexico in the place of José Garcia, who from deafness is unable to perform the duties—Mr. Garcia will turn over to his successor any public funds, books or property pertaining to his office which he may have in his possession

Santa Fe, New Mexico   S. W. KEARNY
    Augt 29, 1846   Brig. Genl. U. S. A.

CHAPTER V.

EXCURSION TO SAN TOME.

Supposed Rebellion—Departure for Albuquerque—Arrival at Del Gardo—Gen. Kearny and Capt. Reid—Rights of Volunteers—Error common to regular officers—Sham battle—The Rio del Norte—Irrigating canals—Algodones—Bernalillo—Albuquerque—Peralto—Reception of the troops at San Tome—Lieutenant-colonel Ruff—Grand celebration—Return to the capital.

In consequence of certain rumors which were almost daily brought to Gen. Kearny, that the malcontents, principally the friends and adherents of the deposed Governor Armijo, and some Pueblo Indians, were rallying and concentrating a large armed force somewhere in the vicinity of Albuquerque, with the view to make battle, and recover the capital from the hands of the Americans, he determined to silence these reports and disperse these "rebels" against his authority, by marching thither in person, and at the head of the following detachments of troops: One hundred artillerymen under Capts. Weightman and Fischer, forming an extra battalion, commanded by Maj. Clark,[46] manning eight pieces of cannon; forty-five dragoons, under Capt. Burgwin, and fifty-five of the St. Louis volunteers, (Laclede rangers,) under Capt. Hudson, being attached to the dragoons, forming a squadron of one hundred men, commanded by Burgwin, the oldest captain: and five hundred mounted volunteers under command of the following officers: The company from Jackson county furnished sixty-eight men under Lieut. Reed; the company from Lafayette, sixty, under Capt. Walton; the company from Clay, sixty-seven, under Lieut. Sublette[47]; the company from Saline, fifty-four, under Capt. Reid;

NOTE 46. Meriwether Lewis Clark was the eldest son of William Clark, of the Lewis and Clark expedition. He married first, Abigail Churchill. Their children were: William Hancock, who married Camilla Gaylord; Samuel Churchill; Mary Eliza; Meriwether Lewis, who married Mary Martin Anderson (their children being John Henry Churchill, Caroline Anderson, and Mary Barbaroux); John O'Fallon; George Rogers; Charles Jefferson, who married Lena Jacob (their children being Mary Susan, Evelyn Kennerly, and Margaret Vernon). The second wife of Major Clark was Julia Davidson.

NOTE 47.—Sublette was related to the famous Sublette brothers, early engaged in the fur business in the West. Before coming to Missouri he lived at Versailles, Ky., near which town lived a very rich and able lawyer named John U. Warren, a quarrelsome and dangerous man, who it was said had killed half a

the company from Franklin, sixty-eight, under Captain Stephenson; the company from Cole, sixty, under Capt. Parsons; the company from Howard, sixty, under Lieut. De Courcy; and that from Callaway, sixty-four, under Capt. Rodgers, with Lieut. Col. Ruff at the head of the regiment, Maj. Gilpin in command of the first battalion, and Walton, the senior captain, in command of the second. Gen. Kearny, with about twenty-five of his staff-officers and body-guard, and generally fifty or sixty fawning, sycophantic Mexicans, rode at the head of the column, which consisted of about seven hundred and twenty-five mounted men, exclusive of the general's *volunteer Mexican escort!* *

We left Santa Fé on the morning of the 2d of September, with all our banners gaily fluttering in the breeze, the men being in high spirits and possessing cheerful minds, as there was once again some faint prospect of an engagement with the enemy. Men, seeking that just and laudable praise which is the reward of the brave, encountering perils with resolution, enduring privations with fortitude, traversing plains and deserts with patience, and surmounting obstacles of every nature with courage, feel disappointed when the fleeing enemy bears with him those trophies which ought to belong to the victors, and which they would, should a battle ensue, take home with them as the evidence of their valor. It is the returning soldier, decorated with the spoils of the foe, and graced with the trophies of victory, more than he that has spent his strength in marches and pursuits, that receives the applause of his countrymen.

We took the main Chihuahua road leading directly south, with the view of striking the Rio Grande del Norte at the nearest point on account of water, as the country between Santa Fé and the Del Norte

---

* Quite too much consideration and kindness has been bestowed upon the treacherous Mexicans, by all the American generals. It was a common remark amongst the volunteers at Santa Fé, that General Kearny would *punish* a volunteer for an offence, for which a Mexican would be *excused*—in other words, that he "treated the Mexicans better than he did his own soldiers." The same remark applies to the conduct of Gen. Wool, while at Parras, and to that of Gen. Worth, while in command at La Puebla. However, the blame more justly rests on the War Department.—HUGHES.

dozen men in personal combat. He stabbed Sublette, who, from the wound, was at death's door a long time, but finally recovered. When strong enough to go about with his gun Sublette shot Warren, breaking his thigh and killing his horse. Afterward he shot Warren with a shotgun, and, supposing he had killed him, came to Missouri, leaving his family in charge of Smith Story. Story brought Sublette's family to Clay county, Mo., where both men made their homes.

(which is about thirty-five miles following the road) is remarkably dry and barren. The stream that waters the town of Santa Fé, and which furnishes abundant power for grist and saw mills, entirely disappears in the sand about five miles below the city. This day's march was over an undulating, sterile country, intersected by numerous deep, dry gullies, impassable by cavalry. The creeks were destitute of water; the surface of the earth was in some spots sandy and in others rocky, mostly covered with wild sage in the low-lands and with clumps of dwarf cedar on the sides of the hills and mountains. There were few flowers or other vegetable productions worthy of note, the earth being almost entirely bare. This part of New Mexico possesses considerable mineral wealth, which can and no doubt will be fully developed whenever the government becomes settled so as to afford security and protection to such scientific chemists as may desire to embark in a GOLDEN ENTERPRISE.

A progress of near twenty-five miles brought us to our encampment on the Galisteo creek, at Del Gardo, about fifteen miles from the gold mines in the Galisteo mountains, commonly known by the appellative, EL PLACER. Here there was water, in sufficient quantities for men and animals, but wood and grass could not be obtained without much labor.

On the morning of the 3d, the sun rose brightly and beautifully beaming over the lofty ridges of mountains to the eastward, and seemed to promise more than his usual quantum of heat during the day. There was no possibility of procuring any water between our encampment and the Rio del Norte, a distance of nearly fifteen miles. We prepared for an early start, put up our baggage, and filled our canteens with water. Much to the surprise and inconvenience of the volunteers, just as they were about moving off upon the march, General Kearny rode round among the troops, and seeing many of the men carelessly habited on account of the oppressive heat of the day, gave orders for "*every man to put on his coat, or he would dismiss him from the service of the country.*" This order came like a clap of thunder in a clear sky, as the heat was very great, and the reason and philosophy of the order did not so readily appear to the volunteers, who were accustomed to think for themselves, and consult their own convenience and comfort in matters of dress. However, after some hesitation they obeyed the order, sacrificing *their comfort* to the *general's taste,* upon the principle that they had better concede a portion of their liberty than assert their rights under the circumstances of the case, notwithstanding their opinions of law and propriety differed widely from the general's. The men thus reasoned one with another: "If we suffer this man to act the tyrant in things of small moment, where is the security that he will not tighten the reins of his authority over us until we shall finally become *his slaves* and no longer be the *servants of the public,* whose interest we believe we can promote as well, and whose cause we can serve as faithfully in one apparel as in another? is our service then to be less valued because we choose to appear on parade in *citizen's dress* in preference to the *soldier's uniform?* But on the contrary, if we contend one with another and our strength becomes divided, we shall presently fall a prey to the enemy, and instead of gaining the applause of our countrymen, after performing so many hard marches and suffering so many days with heat, and thirst, and hunger and sickness, we shall return home the most dishonored of men. Therefore let us make choice of the less of two evils." When the general came to where Capt. Reid had drawn up his men in wait for marching orders, observing *them* also attired carelessly, and feeling enraged that the captain had not enforced stricter discipline in regard to military dress, he said, "Captain, have your men no jackets?" to which the captain replied, "Some of them have, and some of them have not." The general continued, "Make your men, Captain Reid, put on their jackets, or I will dismiss them from the service—the government has paid them commutation for clothing, and expects every man to dress in a manner wholesome for military discipline." The captain rejoined, "My men, sir, came here, not to dress, but to fight the enemies of their country, and they are ever ready to be of service to you and the country in that way. As to the commutation which you say the government has paid my men for clothing, I must inform you that you misapprehend the truth. My men have never received *one dime* since they entered the service, and what money they brought from their homes with them they have already expended for bread while on half rations, owing to the neglect of your chief commissary. As to being dismissed from the service, sir, we do not fight for wages. If there is no place for us in the army, we will furnish ourselves and fight the enemy wherever we may find him. Acting thus we shall not lose the respect of our countrymen." Gen. Kearny bit his lips and rode off, giving orders for the march to commence.[48]

When volunteers, actuated by patriotic motives, leave their homes and friends—sacrifice pecuniary considerations—lay aside their peaceful pursuits and professions—throw down their implements of husbandry, and abandon their workshops, they have the right to "equip and clothe" themselves as to them shall seem fit and proper; and no officer can legally strip them of that right. When they obey all

---

NOTE 48.—Stephen Watts Kearny was born at Newark, N. J., in 1794; died at St. Louis, Mo., Oct. 31, 1848. He was a student at Princeton College at the commencement of the War of 1812, but secured a commission as First Lieutenant in the Thirteenth Infantry. His Captain was John E. Wool. He was captured at the battle of Queenstown Heights, but was exchanged and served through the

GENERAL S. W. KEARNY.
(From an old print.)

war, at the close of which he was made Captain and retained in the army. In 1823 he was made brevet Major and given command of four companies of the First Infantry at Bellefontaine, near St. Louis. With this force he accompanied General Atkinson on his exploring expedition to the Upper Missouri, going in keel-boats two thousand miles to the Yellowstone. Upon his return he was

reasonable orders from higher authority, in a prompt and cheerful manner, they perform their whole duty to the country, as citizen soldiers. There never was, perhaps, better material in an army, than that which composed the Army of the West. Never did a set of men—never did veteran soldiers more cheerfully and resolutely perform their duty, or show themselves more submissive to order and law. Would to God they had been governed, in every respect, in a manner more worthy of their obedience, their spirit, and their country. Many of the officers had performed their duty, up to this period, with signal ability; and it is a much more pleasing task to add, than detract from their just amount of praise—to bear testimony of their worth, than censure their conduct—to defend than despoil their reputation. General Kearny is a skillful, able, and sagacious officer, well fitted for the command of veteran troops; and his commission, as a brigadier-general commanding the ARMY OF THE WEST, was regarded with general satisfaction. An officer should not be condemned for a few faults only, unless they be of great magnitude. General Kearny's greatest error consisted in an effort to reduce the volunteers to the same discipline, and treat them with the same rigid austerity, and dissociability, which he was wont to exercise over the regular troops under his command. This is wrong; the former are bred to freedom, the latter trained to obedience;—patriotism makes those soldiers—these, the study of arms;—peace is the pursuit of the one—war the profession of the other. In battle, feeling, principle, honor, fire the one; science, experience, discipline, guide the other. They are equally brave.

---

made Major of the Third Regiment, and later was commissioned Lieutenant-Colonel of the First Dragoons, which he took in 1834 with Col. Dodge in his campaign against the Comanches in the Red River country. In 1835, with four companies of his command, he visited the Sioux on the Upper Missouri and settled the dispute between that people and the Sacs and Foxes. In 1836 he was commissioned Colonel of the First Dragoons and stationed at Fort Leavenworth. In 1842 he was given command of the Third Military Department, headquarters at St. Louis. With five companies he marched to the South Pass in 1845, returning by way of Fort Bent; in this campaign he held councils with various Indian tribes. He was designated in 1846 to command the expedition for the conquest of New Mexico and Upper California, which was successful. For undertaking this difficult mission he was made a Brigadier-General. He returned to St. Louis August 26, 1847, and went on to Washington. He saw no more active service, and lived little more than a year after that date. He was a faithful officer, devoted to his duty, and was always trusted by the Government.

This is an error very common to officers of the regular army, when commanding volunteer corps. It was a great error with Gen. Kearny, because three-fourths of his army consisted of volunteers—whose talent and good behavior entitled them to a respectful consideration, both at home and in the service of the country, and upon whose conduct and courage, mainly depended the success and safety of the expedition. Conciliation, not force, was therefore proper to be employed by the commander, to retain the affections and undivided services of his troops. To make make regulars of volunteers—to cramp their freedom, and move them as the magician moves his automata, is at once to extinguish that pride and spirit, that feeling of liberty, that chivalric patriotism, which renders them efficient troops, and which ought to make an officer of General Kearny's standing, proud to command them. The historian ever feels more inclined to extenuate than to magnify the faults of men high in power; yet, justice and impartiality, and the cause of truth, require that he should unsparingly chastise the vices, as well as extol the virtues of those whose acts he essays to record.

We pursued our way down the Galisteo, high spurs of mountains towering in wavy ridges towards the eastern bank of the Del Norte, and the huge masses of the Sierra de los Mimbres, lying imbedded in the blue mists to the westward. On leaving the Galisteo, by the left bank, and at the distance of four miles from it, the road forks. Here General Kearny and the dragoons took the right, which bears westward to the Indian town, Santo Domingo, a small Pueblo, having three hundred inhabitants, while the main body of the army followed on the direct road to San Felipé, on the Del Norte. The chief, or alcalde of Santo Domingo, at the head of about seventy dashing cavaliers, with a white flag, came out to escort the general into town, by way of winning favor, and also thereby intending him a compliment. They made a sham charge upon the general, and performed several evolutions about him, displaying consummate horsemanship, and brandishing their pointed lances, as if to show what they were capable of doing, had their intentions not been peaceable and friendly. The whole of their movements were plainly beheld by the volunteers, from an eminence two or three miles distant. At first, we were impressed with the belief that a skirmish was taking place between the forces of the alcalde and the general; but as we did not see the flash of their guns or hear the roar of the cannon, and after some time saw the Indians and the general's troops all move off together towards the village, we were satisfied of the sham, and concluded the general might drink his wine and puff his *cigaritos* without our aid; so we moved onward.[49]

We were now at no great distance from the Rio Grande del Norte, which all were very anxious to see, both on account of water, as we were very thirsty, and because we regarded it as the western limit of our present campaign. From the lofty bluffs on the eastern side, looking over the ledge of dry, rocky, treeless hills intervening, we could distinctly see the water in the channel of the river, three miles distant. We hastened forward, and were soon on the banks of the noted stream, at the foot of a conical shaped mound, resembling the frustum of a pyramid. San Felipé is situated on the western bank of the river,—contains a population of about 600, and has a Catholic church. The place submitted to the Americans without opposition. These people were friendly disposed, and sold our men such things as they desired to purchase. In a beautiful cottonwood grove, two miles below San Felipé, offering a delightful retreat, we encamped

---

NOTE 49.—General Kearny wrote the War Department Sept. 1, from Santa Fé, that he would "Leave here to-morrow taking about 700 Mounted Men to visit the lower country & to quiet the minds of the People." Emory (p. 37) gives the following account of meeting the Indians:

"When within a few miles of the town, we saw a cloud of dust rapidly advancing, and soon the air was rent with a terrible yell, resembling the Florida war-whoop. The first object that caught my eye through the column of dust was a fierce pair of buffalo-horns, overlapped with long shaggy hair. As they approached, the sturdy form of a naked Indian revealed itself beneath the horns, with shield and lance, dashing at full speed, on a white horse, which, like his own body, was painted all the colors of the rainbow; and then, one by one, his followers came on, painted to the eyes, their own heads and their horses' covered with all the strange equipments that the brute creation could afford in the way of horns, skulls, tails, feathers, and claws.

"As they passed us, one rank on each side, they fired a volley under our horses' bellies from the right and from the left. Our well-trained dragoons sat motionless on their horses, which went along without pricking an ear or showing any sign of excitement.

"Arrived in the rear, the Indians circled round, dropped into a walk on our flanks until their horses recovered breath, when off they went at full speed, passing to our front, and when there, the opposite files met, and each man selected his adversary and kept up a running fight, with muskets, lances, and bows and arrows. Sometimes a fellow would stoop almost to the earth to shoot under his horse's belly, at full speed, or to shield himself from an impending blow. So they continued to pass and repass us all the way to the steep cliff which overhangs the town. There they filed on each side of the road, which descends through a deep cañon, and halted on the peaks of the cliff. Their motionless forms, projected against the clear blue sky above, formed studies for an artist."

for the night, and enjoyed the luxury of washing, bathing and slaking our thirst in the celebrated Rio Bravo del Norte. The Mexicans brought into our camp great quantities of the Oporto grape, finely flavored and most luscious, matured in the most delightful climate. They were sold to the soldiers. The Mexicans transport these grapes when matured, to Santa Fé, and other markets, stored up in small square boxes made of wicker-work, and packed on mules and asses. The air in the river valley, is, at this season, extremely bland and balmy.

On the 4th we continued our march down the river on the eastern bank. The valley of this river is generally about six to ten miles wide, and is perhaps the best fruit country in the Department. The whole valley is finely irrigated by aqueducts which convey the water from the river above. It is done in this manner: a large canal leads the water out from the river generally along the base of the mountains or bluffs, encircling the entire area meant for tillage, while numerous smaller canals and ditches deriving their water from this, pass through all the lands, and irrigate the cornfields, gardens, vineyards, orchards and villages. This valley is hedged in by lofty mountains on both sides, consisting of sand and flint stone intermixed with basalt, forming a lane or strait; so were you to attempt to pass in any other direction than along the valley, your way would presently be barricaded, so steep and abrupt are the mountains. These people possess many rich vineyards, peach orchards, and groves of apricots, besides flocks of goats and sheep, which feed in the mountains and on the hills. Also melons, onions, pepper, salsify, garlic, and other vegetables abound. New Mexico, in places, is singularly destitute of timber. With the exception of a few clumps of dwarfish, wind-riven cedar on the overhanging bluffs, and the occasional cottonwood groves in the bottoms, the country is woodless, verdureless.

The Rio del Norte is more than two thousand miles in length, and from two hundred and fifty to three hundred yards wide at this point, and is so shallow that it may be forded almost anywhere. The water is cool, clear and palatable as it comes down from the mountains to the northward. This river is not navigable at this distance from the Gulf of Mexico.

After a march of eight miles from our last encampment we came to the city of Algodones, containing 1000 inhabitants. The place submitted willingly and received us kindly, and gratuitously offered us fruits, melons, and bread. This is one of the handsomest towns in New Mexico. The vineyards, yards, pleasure grounds, orchards and gardens are walled in neatly. The tops of the walls were bristling with cactus, to prevent theft and robbery. Here hundreds of Mexicans voluntarily fell in with the line of march, welcomed us, and would often exclaim, by way of complimenting us and testifying their respect and friendship, "Bueno Americano." They expressed themselves well pleased with the change of government and the new governor, and appeared to be proud of the idea of being considered citizens of the great American republic. In conversation with an intelligent Mexican, who spoke some broken words of English, inquiry was made what had become of the late governor, Armijo:—he laughingly replied: "*Armijo d—n—d rascal, gone to the d—l.*"

Twelve miles further we came to Bernalillo, a small town containing a population of about 500. After a farther advance of four miles we arrived at Sandia, of which the population is 300. These towns are inhabited by a mixed race of Mexicans and Pueblo Indians. They offered us no resistance. On both banks of the river, the towns, villages, and ranchos or farm houses cluster so thickly together that it presents the appearance of one continued village from Algodones to San Tomé, a distance of nearly sixty miles, resembling in some small degree that beautiful succession of stately mansions and farm houses which line the St. Lawrence from Kingston to Montreal, except that the Mexican houses are built of adobes or sun-dried bricks, having flat, parapetted roofs and small windows. This day's march was twenty-four miles. Our camps for the night were commonly placed near the river or an acequia* on account of water.

Albuquerque, the seat of the governor's private residence, his native town, and the place at which we had some anticipations of meeting him at the head of his troops, was reached after a march of eight miles. Early in the morning (September 5th) the advance was sounded by the bugles; the long files were soon moving down the river, followed by the artillery and baggage train. Our lines were arranged in order, each company in its proper place, officers and men at their respective posts, and our colors gallantly streaming above us as we entered the town. On our approach a salute of twenty guns (es-

* Acequia is the Mexican word for canal.—HUGHES.

copetas) was fired from the balustraded top of the Catholic church. This dispelled our apprehensions, or rather put an end to our hopes of an engagement with Col. Armijo.*

PLAZA AT ALBUQUERQUE.

These people received us with demonstrations of friendship, and submissively took the oath of allegiance to our government. Melons, grapes, apples, peaches, apricots and pears were brought out to us by the inhabitants, which the soldiers purchased liberally. This town, numbering about 800 inhabitants, takes its name from the apricot groves in its vicinity, this fruit being called by the Mexicans, *albuquerque*. Cranes, geese, ducks, brants, swans, and pelicans are found on the Del Norte. Very little dew or rain falls in this valley, although it rains or rather showers almost every day in the mountains.

The army, after a march of sixteen miles, encamped on the river, eight miles below Albuquerque.

* In addition to the various intrigues by which Col. Armijo crept into power in New Mexico, the following is confidently asserted to be true, by one who has resided thirteen years in that country. In his early life, Don Manuel Armijo was employed as a vaquero or herder of cattle in the mountains east of Albuquerque. About this time three wealthy citizens of New Mexico, Pino, Chavez, and one other, purchased 36,000 head of sheep, and started with them to the southern markets of Durango and Zacatecas. They spent one night in Albuquerque, during which Armijo came to them and engaged to drive sheep as one of their shepherds. He continued in this employment until they arrived in the Great Jornada or Desert intervening between El Paso and Laguna de los Patos, where he clandestinely took leave of them, disguising himself as an Apache chief, collecting twenty or thirty Apaches about him, and intercepted the flocks of his employers, killing some of the shepherds and driving the rest back to El Paso. Having divided the booty, Armijo and one Mexican accomplice, putting off their Indian disguise, drove their share of the flock to Durango, sold them, pocketed the change, and returned to their former employments in New Mexico. This trick and other similar intrigues furnished Armijo with means to ingratiate himself into public favor.—HUGHES.

This morning (6th) a deputation of some thirty well-dressed, intelligent-looking Mexicans, came up from Peralta, to offer submission to the general, whom they saluted as their new governor, assuring him that all was tranquil and orderly on the Rio Abajo, and that the people there desired to be our friends. They besought that their lives, families, and property, might be protected; of which being assured, they departed. The army having progressed eight miles, nooned at a beautiful cotton-wood grove, near the margin of the river, which from its regularity has the appearance of being artificial. Near the bluffs, on the east side of the river, are several large sand-drifts, or mounds of sand, as fine and white, almost, as the driven snow. These ephemeral sand-mountains continue to accumulate as long as the wind drives from the same point of the compass, but the current of the wind veering, they are swept away in less time than was required for their formation. At this place the grass was only moderate—wood scarce—blue pinks and other flowers were found. The flora of the Del Norte valley is rich, varied and interesting. Here we pitched our camps to spend the day, as it was the Sabbath, and as we were much in need of rest.*

While we were marching down the valley of the great River of the North, feasting upon the fruits and melons of that sunny climate, it was impossible not to contrast our condition, as a triumphant army, with that of the wretched, and ill-fated Texan prisoners, who were captured near San Miguel, and conducted in chains and under guard down the same road, over the same ground, emaciated with hunger and ill-usage, benumbed by the cold of winter, faint with sufferings, sinking under fatigues, and inhumanly butchered, by order

* The night we lay at this grove, the moon shone brightly. A small party of men having passed the sentry, went down to Peralta, where we expected to amuse ourselves a few hours at a Mexican fandango. In this, however, we were disappointed, for only the homeliest women, such as we cared not to dance with, made their appearance at the saloon, the young and fair *señoritas* being shy of men who wore side-arms. Returning in disgust soon after, we fell amongst the ditches and canals, and, having climbed several walls, at length fell into a vineyard, surcharged with clusters of the most delicious grapes. This was a fortunate mis-hap; for drawing our sabres. we cut off the large, ripe, enticing clusters, and carried an abundance of them to our companions in camp. These bunches were not, perhaps, as large as those the Hebrews hung upon a staff. and upon the shoulders of two men, brought down from Eschol, but they were, no doubt, as luscious. Of course the sentinels must have their share as we returned to camp.

Another party straggling about with similar motives met with more difficulty; for a part of them, carelessly scaling the walls of a vineyard in quest of grapes, jumped down on the inside, which was several feet lower than the ground on the outside. Having satisfied their appetites, they were unable to return. Their companions, who had remained without, were compelled to pull them over the walls by means of lariats.—HUGHES.

of that monster of cruelty, Gen. Salezar, when they became too feeble to endure the toils and hardships of the march. The remembrance of these outrages, practiced upon Texan and American citizens, so incensed the soldiers that they meditated wreaking their vengeance upon the heads of unoffending Mexicans. However, the more humane sentiment prevailed, that the innocent ought not to suffer for the guilty—that a magnanimous forbearance and forgiveness of injuries were more Christian and praise-worthy than the spirit of revenge. This reflection saved them.

Progressing on the 7th about three miles we passed the small town Peralto, the population of which is about three hundred. This town is the place of residence of the Chavez family, the brothers and relations of the Chavez who was murdered by Capt. McDaniel's band of marauders on Cow creek, a branch of the Little Arkansas. They are wealthy, and have chiefly educated their sons in the United States. They are friends to the Americans. The valley of the Del Norte heightens in interest, and in the richness and variety of its grain and fruit productions, as you descend towards the South; while the population gradually becomes more intelligent, and less mixed with the Pueblo Indian races, speaking a language more nearly resembling the Castilian, than the inhabitants in the more Northern districts. At the distance of about five miles below Peralta, we arrived at San Tomé, a small town containing eight hundred inhabitants. This place was named in honor of one of the Patron Saints of the country. Here the people were assembled from all the neighboring villages and ranchos, to the number of three thousand, for the purpose of celebrating the anniversary of the Holy Vision, or the Inception of the Virgin Mary. The occasion was rendered doubly grand when the inhabitants of the place were informed of the arrival of Gen. Kearny and his troops, as they were seemingly anxious both to testify their respect for the new governor, and also the more effectually to impress us with an idea of the pompous character of the church, to make a dazzling exhibition of its commemorative rites. They were ignorant of the fact, however, that we were plain republicans, and rather detested, than admired, their unmeaning pomp, and senseless mockery of religion. It should be observed here, that the doctrines of Catholicism, or of the Romish faith, are neither understood, nor practised in their purity, by the laity or clergy of New Mexico. Error has crept into the church. The worship has become encumbered by absurdities and the grossest ceremonies. The church is benighted. "Darkness has covered the earth and gross darkness the people." Hence their worship is little better than a caricature, on the more enlightened worship of the Catholic church in the United States, and other Christian countries.

The general and his staff took up their quarters in town, while the volunteers and regulars encamped in the suburbs. About 8 o'clock at night the town was most brilliantly illuminated by the pine faggots that blazed from all the walls of the city, and from the tops of the churches and the private houses. The general was saluted by the discharge of musketry and escopetas, as he entered the town. For four hours an incessant discharge of fire arms, and the throwing of sky-rockets and fire-balls were kept up. The elements were lurid with long, zig-zag streams of fire for three hundred feet high. The catherine-wheel made a circle of red light like a dizzy comet. These rockets would sometimes explode in the air, and sometimes fall among the throng and explode, producing great confusion and tremendous shouts of laughter.

At the same time that all this was going on, in another part of the public square, there were, perhaps, fifteen hundred persons, mostly women, boys and girls, sitting on the ground, listening to a comedy or some kind of theatrical exhibition, which was being performed by several ladies and gentlemen on a stage erected in a large piazza fronting the square. Everything was said in the Spanish language, so that the Americans who were present, (very few of whom could speak in that tongue,) were unable to appreciate the merits of the play, or say whether it was original, or whether it was from Shakespeare or the Bible. The women were promiscuously intermingled with the men, and the music of instruments with the discharge of rockets, fire arms, and the shouts of the throng. The whole made a horrid discord. The pageant would have been imposing had it been attended with order and solemnity. Was this "serving God in Spirit and in Truth"?

This strange performance attracted the attention of such of the men as were struck with its novelty. Some went, induced by curiosity, others that they might gain information of what was going on. When a goodly number of men had left camp and gone into town to witness what might be seen there, Lieutenant-colonel Ruff sent Lieut.

Sublette, the officer of the guard that night, with a file of men, who, proceeding into town, picked up such of the soldiers as had left camp without permission, and having collected seventy or eighty in this way, who offered no resistance, brought them to the Lieutenant-colonel's tent, who immediately ordered them to be detailed as an extra guard for the next day. Ruff, whose popularity had been constantly decreasing, was now become odious to the men. They held meetings in the camp. Some advised that he should no longer be allowed to hold the command; others, that they should baptize him in a filthy lake hard by; while others again thought the best means of treating him would be to tie two asses together with a lariat, and make one of them pass on one side of his tent and the other on a different side, and thus drag his tent down and roll him topsy-turvy in his sleep. "He would then rise," they said, "like Rip Van Winkle from forty years of slumber." All these expedients failing, it is said that the door of his tent was thrown full of the entrails of the sheep which had been slaughtered for the use of the army. His bedding was therefore blooded and his tent filled with the stench.

On the next day this celebration was renewed. The church was crowded to overflowing, though ample enough to contain two thousand persons. The altar was lighted up by twenty-four candles. Six priests officiated. Gen. Kearny and staff officers, and also some of the officers of the volunteer corps were present, and looked and no doubt *felt* supremely ridiculous, each one holding a long, greasy tallow candle in his hand, which was to be blown out and re-lighted at certain intervals during the ceremonies. But it is a good maxim perhaps, "when you are in Rome do as Rome does." Every Mexican that entered the church bowed and worshipped the Holy Virgin, then the infant Saviour in the manger, and then the crucified Saviour on the Cross. A very aged and decrepit lady came in much affected, bowed before the Saviour and worshipped him, and tremblingly wiped her falling tears on the robes with which the image was clad.

During the whole time, singing, instrumental music, and the firing of musketry were strangely commingled. The same airs were played in the church gallery on the violin, that were usually played at the Mexican fandangoes.

The PADRE walked about the Plaza, amongst the crowd, after the conclusion of the ceremonies, while four men suspended over his head a gilded canopy. He was also preceded by a file of men firing their escopetas, and followed by a number of altar boys throwing rockets, which kept up a continual racket, making the heavens dizzy with streams of fire.

As already observed, the Mexicans are remarkably fond of gaming, and other amusements. Accordingly, towards evening, horse-racing, dancing and gambling, occupied the attention of the throng. Great quantities of ripe fruit, grapes, melons, sweet-cakes, and various other commodities, were brought hither for sale by the market women, upon asses and sumpter horses.

San Tomé, which is about one hundred miles from the capital, was the southern terminus of our campaign. We returned to Santa Fé, arriving there on the 13th,[50] after an absence of twelve days; Major Gilpin being left, with a detachment of men to take care of the stock in the neighborhood of Del Gardo.

This campaign, which was effected without bloodshed, was attended by some beneficial results. General Kearny, in his procla-

NOTE 50.—General Kearny returned to Santa Fé with his troops on the 11th. He reported his campaign in the following letter:

HEAD QR. ARMY OF THE WEST
SANTA FÉ NEW MEXICO Sept 16, 1846

SIR: Since my communication to you of the 1st. Inst, I have marched with 700 Men about 100 miles down the Del Norte to the village of Tome—The Inhabitants of the Country were found to be highly satisfied & contented with the change of government, & apparently vied with each other to see who could show to us the greatest hospitality & kindness—There can no longer be apprehended any organized resistance in this Tery., to our troops, & the commander of them, whoever he may be will hereafter have nothing to attend to, but to secure the Inhabitants from further depredations from the Navajoe & Eutaw Indians and for this object Part 3 of Order No. 23 was this day issued, a copy of which is enclosed herewith.

As this Tery. is now perfectly quiet, I have determined (knowing the wishes of the Executive) to leave here for Upper California as soon as possible & have fixed upon the 25th, as the day of departure—As I am ignorant when to expect Capt Allen & his command, I have determined upon taking with me, Major Sumner & the efficient Men, (about 300) of the 1st Dragoons—Orders will be left for Capt Allen to follow on our trail.

From the most reliable information yet received as to the best route, we have determined upon marching about 200 miles down the Del Norte—then to the Gila—down that River near to its mouth, leaving which we cross the Colorado, & then keeping near the Pacific, up to Monterey—This route will carry us not far from & along the Southern boundary of New Mexico & Upper California & we hope to reach the Pacific by the end of November—No exertions will be wanting on the part of any one attached to this expedition in ensuring to it full & entire success—I have now to respectfully ask, that in the event of our getting possession of Upper California—of establishing a civil government there—securing Peace, Quiet & Order among the Inhabitants & Precluding the possibility of the Mexicans again having control there that I may be permitted to leave there next Summer with the 1st Dragoons & march them back to Fort Leavenworth on the Missouri—And I would respectfully request, that troops to remain in

mation of the 22d of August, had promised protection to such New Mexicans as should peaceably acquiesce in his government, both against the depredations of the Indians, and from acts of violence on the part of their conquerors. He had engaged to defend their persons from harm, and to preserve their rights and liberty in the amplest manner to them. He now visited the richest portion of the Department, that the people might see the conduct of his soldiers, and have confidence in the efficiency of the protection he had promised. The civil behavior of the troops toward the inhabitants, greatly conciliated those who were disaffected towards the American government.

California or Oregon should be raised expressly for the purpose—say for 3 years to be discharged at the expiration of that time, each Man from the Col to the Private receiving a number of acres of land in proportion to his rank—Regiments could easily be raised on such terms & when discharged, Military Colonies would thus be established by them—Surgn. De Camp will be left in charge of the Hospital at this Place & to superintend the Medical Dept in this Tery.—He is very desirous, as are the other officers of the Army now here, to leave next Summer. The Doctor wishes to return to Jeff'n Barr's, Saint Louis or to the Arsenal & I recommend that he be gratified—A large number of the troops are daily employed under the direction of Lieut Gilmer of the Eng's in erecting a Fort for the defense & protection of this city. And as this is the capital of the Tery. a new acquisition to the U. S., the Fort will be an important & a permanent one, & I have this day named it "Fort Marcy" & now ask for a confirmation of it—I have not heard of, or received a line from Col Price at any time, and know not if he or any part of his Regt, has ever left Fort Leavenworth.

I will write you again before leaving here & will then inform you of the arrangements made relating to the Civil Government for this Tery., which has been & continues a delicate & difficult task.

Brig. Genl R. Jones
   Adjt Genl U. S. A.
      W--------n

Very Resp-y Yr. ob. Servt.
    S. W. KEARNY
     Brig Genl U. S. A.

CHAPTER VI.

Territorial Laws—Mexican Printing Press—Appointments to office—Disease—Fort Marcy—Battle of Los Llanos—The Election—Detachments ordered to Abiquiu and Cebolletta—Gilpin's Return—Colonel Doniphan and Hall—Gen. Kearny and the Apache Chief—General Kearny's departure for California—Conduct of the Soldiers.

During General Kearny's absence on his excursion to San Tomé, nothing of very great moment transpired at Santa Fé. Colonel Doniphan remained in command of the troops which were left at the capital,—attended to the administration of the laws, as governor of the department—superintended the erection of Fort Marcy, on the hill overlooking Santa Fé to the northward, and completed, by the aid of Willard P. Hall,[51] the "ORGANIC LAWS AND CONSTITUTION" for the government of the new territory.

The American flag, liberty's emblem, continued to stream bravely from the top of the tall staff erected for the purpose, in the Plaza.

NOTE 51.—*Willard P. Hall.*—(Condensed from a paper read by John C. Gage before the Kansas City Bar Association, February 8, 1896.) Willard Preble Hall was born at Harper's Ferry, Virginia, May 9, 1820. He was of Puritan descent, his ancestors having emigrated to Massachusetts from England in 1634. In his ancestral lines, both paternal and maternal, were many of the eminent lawyers, judges and divines of New England. His father was a man of remarkable mechanical and scientific attainments, and a celebrated inventor. His preliminary education was had at Baltimore, Maryland, and he graduated from Yale College in the class of 1839—the same class in which were William M. Evarts and several other eminent men.

In 1840 he came to Missouri and studied law with his brother, Judge William A. Hall, of Randolph county. In 1841 he removed to Platte county, and settled at Sparta, then the county seat. A glimpse of him as he was then is given by an old citizen of Platte City, with whom he stopped overnight on his trip from Randolph county to Sparta. He described him as a pale, delicate youth, dressed in blue jeans, mounted on a pony, with a pair of leather saddlebags containing his wardrobe and library. In 1843 he removed to St. Joseph, which was his home during the remainder of his life.

He stepped into immediate prominence in his profession and in politics. In 1843 he was appointed circuit attorney, succeeding a very capable officer. General Doniphan, speaking of him at this period, says: "He succeeded at once. System and order and logical arrangement were natural with him. He had the criminal law, and especially the statutes of the State, at his fingers' ends, and could readily refer to them in a moment's time. Plain and simple in his manners as a child, naturally frank and easy with everyone, he soon became a favorite,

A civil government was established and put in motion. The constitution and laws for the government of the new territory, which had been drawn up with much haste, were chiefly derived from the laws of Missouri and Texas, and the Federal Constitution. The de-

and from his youthful appearance, even a pet, with his older friends. He was a very efficient and a very conscientious officer. He prevented grand juries from presenting anything that could not be sustained, and prosecuted with great energy those he believed guilty."

In 1844 he was one of the candidates on the Democratic electoral ticket, and canvassed western Missouri north of the Missouri river on behalf of Polk and Dallas, and the annexation of Texas. Doniphan was the Whig candidate for the same office, and was always his antagonist in this canvass. To those who know what northwest Missouri was in those old days, and what Doniphan was in his prime, it would be unnecessary,—to those who did not know them it would be impossible,—to explain what it meant for this stripling of twenty-four years to meet that matchless orator before a people who loved and honored him as Doniphan was loved and honored in northwest Missouri. How well he maintained himself in the contest is best shown by the fact that he won the unqualified praise and admiration of Doniphan, and as the result, was made the nominee of his party for Congress in 1846, over the heads of many able veterans of his party.

The great issue in the canvass of 1844 was the question of the annexation of Texas. In his canvass for Congress in the spring of 1846 Mr. Hall was taunted with the fact that the policy of annexation which he had advocated had plunged the country into war with Mexico. Possibly, in the heat of debate, he had made some pledges; but at any rate, he made proof of his good faith in his principles by volunteering as a private for service in the war. His company formed a part of Doniphan's command in his great expedition across the Plains and through New Mexico, conquering the country as he went, until he joined the army of General Scott in Old Mexico; a military feat which stands in history comparable alone with the retreat of the ten thousand Greeks recorded by Xenophon in the Anabasis. While the command was at Fort Leavenworth, preparing for its march, people from all parts of Hall's district came to the fort, bringing horses and mules and cattle, and other supplies for the army, and there they saw their young candidate clad in the garb and performing the menial services of a private soldier, unloading the stores from the boats and placing them in wagons. When they returned to their homes the story of his conduct was told all over the district, and the hearts of the people were touched to such an extent that, although he appeared no more in the canvass, when the election came on in August he was chosen to Congress by a majority of more than three thousand out of less than ten thousand votes.

After the conquest of New Mexico it became necessary to establish a government over that Territory, and for that purpose to frame a code of laws adapted to its condition. General Kearny, the commander, detailed Private Hall from the ranks to do this work in connection with Doniphan. Together they prepared the code which General Kearny afterwards proclaimed as the established military law of the Territory, and which was afterwards again adopted as the Territorial code, and remained for forty-five years the fundamental law of the Terri-

partment of New Mexico was styled "The Territory of New Mexico in the United States."

In the capital was found, upon the arrival of General Kearny at that place, a small printing-press, which was used for printing public laws, notices, proclamations, advertisements, manifestos, pronuncia-

tory. No one who knew Hall and Doniphan, and the capacity of the former and the disinclination of the latter for this kind of work, will doubt that much the greater part of the labor was done by Hall. And Doniphan often said that the work was mainly Hall's. It was certainly a most remarkable duty to which this private soldier was detailed, to write the laws that were to govern the conquered country. The code made a small volume, and on the 115 scanty pages is printed in both the English and Spanish languages this entire body of laws, and it would be impossible to find anywhere so complete and perfect a system of laws in many times the space covered here. Here we have a bill of rights announcing the great principles of civil and religious liberty which are repeated over in all our constitutions, and have passed through the hands of the greatest statesmen of England and America; but here we find them, amended and strengthened in expression, more complete and more beautiful than anywhere else. Examine this book and mark the evidences it contains of ripened and matured scholarship and statesmanship, and then,—remembering that it was prepared in a few days' time, amid the turmoil of the camp, by a youth of barely twenty-six years, whose short, active life had been passed on this far Western border, much of it in the saddle, in the midst of legal and political conflicts,—to thus determine with what equipment of native ability, of acquired scholarship and experience, this young man set out on his career.

Colonel Hughes, in his history of the Doniphan Expedition, tells us that one day as they were engaged in preparing this code in Santa Fé, General Doniphan entered the room and announced to Hall the fact of his election to Congress. This was in August, 1846. He was immediately relieved from further duty as a soldier, but voluntarily accompanied Colonel Philip St. George Cooke to California, returned to Missouri the next spring, and took his seat in Congress the following winter.

He was twice reëlected to Congress, and then declined further election. He acquired a high reputation in Congress as a working member.

His principal services were in securing the passage of the act donating some six hundred thousand acres of land to aid in the building of the Hannibal & St. Joseph Railroad, a donation which secured the construction of that road, and in greatly aiding the passage of the acts which gave to the State the school lands and the swamp lands.

At the end of his Congressional service he returned to St. Joseph and remained there in practice until 1861. In the winter of 1861 the Governor of Missouri and the Legislature, which was in session, were both strongly in favor of seceding and joining the Southern Confederacy, and for this purpose an act was passed calling an election to be held in February of that year to choose delegates to a State convention, the purpose of which, as stated in the act, was "To consider the then existing relations between the Government of the United States, the people and government of the different States, and the government and people

mentos, and other high-sounding Mexican documents, in the form of pamphlets and handbills. With this poor apology for a printing press, and such worn type, and indifferent ink, paper, and other materials as chanced to be about the establishment, the constitution and laws of the territory were published. As the Spanish language

of the State of Missouri, and to adopt such measures for vindicating the sovereignty of the State, and the protection of its institutions, as shall appear to them to be demanded."

Mr. Hall was elected to that convention as a Union man. In early life he had belonged to the extreme Southern wing of the Democratic party, but in 1861 his views had materially changed, and the great issue of that day found no stronger Union man in Missouri or elsewhere than Willard P. Hall. The convention met in due time, and instead of passing an ordinance of secession, as it was expected to do, resolved almost unanimously that Missouri had no just cause for secession.

Camp Jackson, Boonville, the flight of the State Government from Missouri, soon followed. On July 30th, the offices of Governor and Lieutenant-Governor were, by ordinance of the convention, declared vacant, and on July 31st Hamilton R. Gamble was chosen Provisional Governor and Willard P. Hall Lieutenant-Governor. It was then only intended that this government should be provisional and temporary until an election could be held, which was ordered for the following October. But the condition of affairs continued to be so disturbed that an election was impossible, or at least impracticable, and this provisional government remained in control during the entire war in Missouri. Governor Gamble was in feeble health much of the time, and often absent from the State for weeks and months, and died early in 1864. He was succeeded by Mr. Hall as Governor. The burdens of the administration, therefore, were thrown very heavily upon Hall's shoulders during the entire period.

The history of those four years of war, of that constitutional convention and that provisional government, is entirely unwritten and generally unknown to the people of Missouri. This government was the object of misrepresentation and abuse during its existence. No attempt has ever been made to rescue it from that reproach. The convention, by its action in refusing to secede, and the provisional government which was established in direct hostility to secession, provoked, naturally and immediately, the enmity and rage of all secessionists and their sympathizers in the State and elsewhere. It met with nothing but the bitterest opposition and war at their hands.

This provisional government was instituted to maintain law and order. All the criminal and disorderly elements of society, which became so numerous and so defiant in war, knew it for their enemy and fought it with a rage and hatred that was not exceeded by that of the secessionists. It stood for civil government and law, entitled and bound to maintain its rightful superiority over the military power, and thus it was a constant check and curb on the military officers who operated in the State, aroused their jealousy and met a very general opposition from them.

The question of the emancipation of slaves arose at an early period of its history, and the battle over it raged to the end. The provisional government

has no W, a difficulty presented itself in regard to the type, which was at length obviated by the substitution of two V's for one W. In this manner were the constitution and laws printed, both in the Spanish and English languages, in double column, placed in juxta-

occupied the conservative middle ground, and was equally obnoxious to the radical friends and foes of the measure. And so from first to last it was assailed by the combined forces of secession and radicalism, anti-emancipation and emancipation, and defied, thwarted and overridden by military power. It was almost destitute of financial resources. It had many active foes and few active friends, but those few were a host indeed, the ablest, truest and best men who ever lived in Missouri; and over and above all, it had the great weight of the countenance and confidence and support of Abraham Lincoln. It carried the flag of the State and of the Nation. It was the ark of public safety for Missouri. With Gamble and Hall as navigators, it found its way through the storms and tempests of those terrible years, and brought its priceless cargo safe to shore. But at the close, Gamble, worn out, lay dead in his grave, and Hall looked back on the weary waste he had passed over, the long succession of days and months and years of toil and vexation, wrong and abuse, and bitterness of soul, unrelieved by any evidence of gratitude or appreciation on the part of the great majority of the people.

In January, 1865, he was succeeded as Governor by Thomas C. Fletcher.

The statesmanship, fortitude and self-sacrificing devotion of Gamble and Hall during this period entitle their names to a record in letters of gold on the fairest page of the history of the State. He turned away from official life and from public affairs to devote his remaining life to the profession he loved so well and for which he was so eminently fitted. For nearly twenty years he followed it, practicing in all the State and Federal courts. Almost all the public improvements of the time in northwest Missouri, the construction of the railroads and bridges, were planned and carried out under his counsel and guidance. He was the adviser of Mr. James F. Joy in undertaking and completing his enterprises in that part of the State, such as the completion of the Cameron Branch Railroad, the bridge over the Missouri river, and the Fort Scott Railroad.

He was a remarkably fine and accurate general scholar, and he kept his classical learning, his Greek and Latin, so fresh that he was able in his later years to fit his son for Yale College. It was his habit for years to read some good case every day in the early morning when his mind was fresh and clear, and thoroughly digest all its facts and principles and reasoning.

He was always entirely respectful to the courts, no matter what might be his opinion of the capacity of the judge. In his arguments he was concise, clear, direct, logical, and entirely unostentatious. He displayed his case, not himself. The impression left from one of his arguments was of a statement of facts, clear and plain, of principles of law beyond question, and all applicable to the case, and of authorities exactly in point—rather than of any particular ability or skill in the lawyer. Tested by the maxim, *Ars est celare artem*, he was an incomparable artist. His manners were frank and simple, always precisely the same, whether greeting a supreme judge, a president, a cabinet minister, or one of his fellows at the bar. In this simplicity of demeanor and address there was recognized a dignity which was the more impressive the better he was known.

He died November 3, 1882.

position on each page. The arduous and difficult task of translating the laws into the Spanish, was assigned to Captain David Waldo, whose thorough acquaintance with the language and customs of the Mexicans, as well as accomplished general scholarship, not only qualified him for the undertaking, but rendered him eminently useful on several subsequent occasions during the campaign.

To the end that the machinery of this new government might be speedily put into operation, General Kearny, acting under authority from the President, made the following appointments to office, viz: Charles Bent to be governor of the Territory; Don Aduciano Vigil, secretary; Richard Dallan, marshal; Francis P. Blair, Jun., U. S. district attorney; Eugene Leitensdoffer, auditor of public accounts; Joab Houghton, Antonio José Otero, and Charles Baubien, judges of the Supreme Court. Some of these men were Americans, and others New Mexicans, the interests of both parties being consulted in the appointments. Thus was another star added to our constellation.[52]

NOTE 52.—The following copy of the original entries indicates the appointments made by General Kearny:

Francisco Saracino (of Pajarito) is hereby reappointed Prefect of the District of the South West, in place of Francisco Armijo y Ortiz this day removed

Miguel Romero is hereby appointed Alcalde at the Placaya in place of Julian Tenorio this day removed.
Santa Fe New Mexico   S. W. KEARNY
    Sept 22 1846   Brig. Genl U. S. A.

Being duly authorized by the Presdt. of the United States of America, I hereby make the following appointments for the Govt. of New Mexico a Territory of the U. States—The officers thus appointed will be obeyed & respected accordingly—
Charles Bent, to be .... Governor.
Donaiso Vigil, to be............................... Secy of Tery.
Richard Dallan, to be .... Marshal.
Francis P. Blair, to be............................ U. S. Dist Atty.
Charles Blummer, to be............................... Treasurer.
Eugene Leitrendorfer, to be............... Auditor of Pub. Accounts.
Joel Houghton—Antonio José Otero—Charles Beaubian to be judges of "the Superior Court"—
Given at Santa fe the Capital of the Tery. of New Mexico this 22d. day of Sept 1846, & in the 71st year of the independence of the United States.
                                    S. W. KEARNY
                                    Brig. Genl U. S. A.

And in relation to the code of laws prepared for the Territory General Kearny reports the following:
                        HEAD QR. ARMY OF THE WEST
                        SANTA FE N. MEXICO Sept 22, 1846
SIR: I enclose herewith a copy of the laws prepared for the Government of the Tery. of New Mexico & a list of appointments to the civil offices in the Tery., both of which I have this day signed & published. I take great pleasure in stating, that I am entirely indebted for these laws to Col A. W. Doniphan of the 1st

While the army lay inactive at Santa Fé the men did not quarter in houses, for this was impracticable, unless they first dispossessed Mexican families, which they did not think proper to do, but pitched their tents on the bare earth (which was covered with sand and gravel) where they both slept, and prepared and ate their food. Therefore by reason of exposure and the places of dissipation in the city, from which it was impossible to restrain them, very many of them took sick, many of them died, and others, lingering under a slow and wasting disease, soon became unfit for service and were discharged. Thus our numbers continually decreased, the hospitals being filled with invalids infected with various loathsome diseases.

On the 10th of September, Dr. Vaughan, assistant surgeon, who had been left at Fort Bent in charge of the sick, (about sixty in number,) arrived at Santa Fé in company with Lieut. Ingalls of the 1st Dragoons, commanding a small detachment, and Lieut. Albert of

---

Regt of Mo. Mounted Vols. who received much assistance from Privt. Willard P. Hall of his Regt These laws are taken part from the laws of Mexico retained as in the original—a part with such modifications as our laws & constitution made necessary—a part are from the laws of the Missouri Tery.—a part from the laws of Texas, & also of Texas & Cohuila—a part from the Statutes of Missouri & the remainder from Livingstons code—The Organic law is taken from the Organic Law of Missouri Territory see Act of Congress June 4th 1812.

The Adjt Genl	Very Resp-y Your ob. Servt.
U. S. Army	S. W. KEARNY
Washington	Brig Genl. U. S. A.

(The remainder of this note is the sketch of Francis P. Blair. There was no other place for it in the entire book.)

FRANCIS PRESTON BLAIR, JUNIOR.

Francis Preston Blair, Junior, was born at Lexington, Kentucky, February 19, 1821; died in St. Louis, Missouri, July 11, 1875. He was the son of Francis Preston Blair, Senior, who was the son of James Blair, who was the son of Rev. John Blair, who came from North Ireland to America about 1735. Rev. John Blair was an alumnus of the Log College, that famous pioneer institution established by the Presbyterians in America; and it was said of him, that "as a theologian he was not inferior to any man in the Presbyterian Church in his day." Upon his arrival in America he settled at Big Spring (now Newville), in the Cumberland Valley, in Pennsylvania, not far from Carlisle. From that place he was driven by the Indians. He had an older brother, Rev. Samuel Blair, who was principal of Fagg's Manor, another famous Presbyterian school; and upon his death Rev. John Blair was called to fill his place as principal, also as pastor of the church there. Later, this institution was succeeded by the New Jersey College (now Princeton), and Mr. Blair acted as its President until the arrival of Dr. Witherspoon. One of his sons was a minister at Richmond, Virginia, where a church was erected for him on Shockoe Hill.

James Blair, son of Rev. John Blair, married a Miss Smith in western Virginia. The sister of Miss Smith married Francis Preston, of Virginia, a noted

the topographical corps, and such of those who had been sick as survived and were able to pursue on and rejoin the army. Whether Dr. Vaughan treated the men with that attention and kindness which the condition of the sick requires, (especially on a campaign where few comforts can be administered to them at best,) was questioned by those who were under his direction. Their judgment, however, may have been the result of prejudice.

Fort Marcy, commanding the city from an eminence towards the north, was laid off by Lieut. Gilmer, of the topographical corps, and L. A. Maclean, a volunteer of Reid's company; and built by the volunteer troops, a certain number of men being detailed each day for the purpose. Those who labored ten days or more consecutively, received a compensation of eighteen cents per day in addition to their regular allowance. The figure of this fort is that of an irregular tridecagon, and is sufficiently ample to mount a great number of cannon

---

man in his day. For his brother-in-law, James Blair named a son Francis Preston Blair, the origin of the name Francis Preston in the Blair family. James Blair was a graduate of Princeton. He had the misfortune to lose a foot by accident in early life, and being of a sensitive nature, believed this made it necessary for him to become a lawyer rather than a minister, saying that his affliction might secure him a position which his ability might not deserve. After his admission to the bar in Virginia he moved to Kentucky, where he was elected Attorney-General of the Commonwealth. He rose to the first rank as a lawyer. His son, Francis Preston Blair (Senior), was the confidential friend and adviser of President Andrew Jackson and editor of the Washington *Globe*.

Francis Preston Blair, Junior, graduated at Princeton College in 1841. He "read law" in the office of Lewis Marshall, and, later, attended the Law Department of the Transylvania University, but did not graduate. His brother, Montgomery Blair, was in the practice of law at St. Louis, and in 1842 he and Francis P. became partners there. When Montgomery became Judge of the Court of Common Pleas, Francis P. opened an office for himself. His health was not good at the time, and in the hope of improving it he crossed the plains to New Mexico with Bent and St. Vrain in 1845. He went out again in 1846, this time with General Kearny, and was by him appointed Attorney-General of New Mexico upon the conquest of that country. He aided in the work of preparing a Code for the Territory. He served as Attorney-General until 1847. In that year he married Miss Appoline Alexander, of Woodford county, Kentucky, and settled permanently in St. Louis. He was one of the leading supporters of Senator Benton in his appeal from the Jackson Resolutions in 1849. He was a born leader of men, and, like his father, possessed a temperament that made it impossible for him to avoid active participation in politics. He was not originally an abolitionist, but was elected to the Missouri Legislature as a Free-Soiler in 1852, and reëlected in 1854. In 1856 he supported Frémont for President, as did his father, and was elected a member of Congress. In 1858 he was defeated

and accommodate 1000 soldiers. Its walls are massive, thick and strong, and are built of adobes two feet long, one foot broad, and six inches thick. It is a strong fortress, and perpetuates the name of the present Secretary of War.

By this time such Mexican families as had fled to the fastnesses of the mountains, upon the approach of the Americans, were returning to their homes and gradually gaining confidence in the new government. The administration of justice appeared to be conducted upon safer and broader principles than had hitherto been known in New Mexico. Industry, virtue, and honesty, and education, which is the parent of these, and which had been singularly neglected in that country, were encouraged and rewarded. Society seemed to be re-forming and re-establishing upon a new and republican basis. Thefts, robberies, riots, and murders, were punished with the utmost

---

for Congress, though he believed himself elected, and unsuccessfully contested the seat of his opponent. He was elected in 1860, and was made chairman of the Committee on Military Affairs. But it was not as a Member of Congress that he rendered the greatest service to his State and the country. He was the first man in public life in Missouri to realize the true import of the events transpiring in that State in 1860. He clearly saw that they meant war for the preservation of the Union, and he resolved that Missouri should not go with the South. And by prompt action and untiring energy he saved the State. Under his direction men were secretly drilled day and night that they might be ready to strike with powerful effect in the defense of St. Louis and the property of the Government. Lyon found an army ready made to his hand when he arrived in the city. With Lyon in command of this army, Blair effected the capture of Camp Jackson. That was the turning-point in Missouri. Blair did not stand on hair-splitting decisions of constitutional questions, but on the patriotic principle that the Union must be preserved. He believed that the severance of the Union was the destruction of the Constitution; and that it were far better to save the Union by a technical violation of the Constitution, if means for its preservation could be so construed, than to permit the total wreck of both Government and Constitution by secession. In his judgment, any government that could not or would not preserve its integrity and prevent its own dismemberment was unworthy to live. And he fully believed that the Constitution guaranteed its own existence.

In 1862 Blair was made a Major-General, and in the Vicksburg campaign he commanded the Second Division of Sherman's Corps. He was reëlected to Congress the same year. April 23, 1864, he was given command of the Seventeenth Army Corps, and went immediately to the front, taking part in the Georgia campaign and the march to the sea. In 1866 President Johnson appointed him Collector of Customs at St. Louis; but he failed of confirmation by the Senate, and was appointed Commissioner of the Pacific Railroad. In 1868 he was the Democratic candidate for Vice-President, the ticket being Seymour and Blair.

rigor. Thus law and order prevailed over anarchy and misrule—tranquillity was soon restored throughout the territory—and general satisfaction reigned.*

On the 17th of September, Lieutenant-colonel Ruff, of the 1st Regiment of Missouri mounted volunteers, in consequence of having received a captain's commission in the United States' army, and also feeling conscious that a large majority of the regiment were unwilling longer to suffer his government, and despised his efforts to extinguish in their bosoms that spirit of freedom and high-toned chivalry which make men proud of their country and of her service, resigned his command. The volunteers were ever ready to yield a will-

* At a later period the New Mexicans grew weary of their conquerors, and desired new rulers and a new government.—HUGHES.

He served in the United States Senate from 1871 to 1873, completing the term of Charles D. Drake, who resigned to accept the chairmanship of the Court of Claims.

In every relation of life Frank P. Blair was just, fair, magnanimous. With him, when peace was declared the war was over for good. He could not approve the injustice of the reconstruction plans of the radical element of his party. He opposed with all his power the test oaths and other forms of oppression imposed upon the South by irresponsible and disreputable carpet-bag governments established for the purposes of plunder and maintained by bayonets. He made the cause of the disfranchised Confederate soldiers his own; through his efforts they were restored to their civil rights. The dangers attending such a course can scarcely be realized now. The late Colonel W. F. Switzler, the historian of Missouri, has preserved (in the St. Louis *Globe-Democrat*, Feb. 19, 1899) two incidents illustrating the dangers which beset Blair in this struggle in Missouri. They are inserted here:

"On one occasion, soon after the war, the writer accompanied him to Mexico, Audrain county, where he had an appointment to address the people. Although his mission was one of peace and in the interest of a reconstructed Union and the restoration to a free ballot of all those who had been disfranchised by the Drake Constitution, there were present a small and boisterous coterie of ex-Union soldiers who threatened to take him from the stand. The crowd of citizens present was very great, and filled a large grove of forest trees in which the platform was erected. Attention was profound. Order was perfect, but just at the crisis of Blair's warming to his subject a large, stalwart man in the audience, dressed in the faded blue uniform of a soldier, in the midst of others similarly dressed, cried out: 'He's a d—n rebel! Let us take him down!' and moved toward the stand. The audience was panic-stricken, but Blair was unmoved. More than this—he was unawed. He waved his hand to the audience and said: 'Keep your seats; there's no danger.' At the same moment he laid two big revolvers on the stand in front of him and denounced the leader of the threatened mob as a coward, telling him to come on and take him down, and that he was ready for him. But he didn't come, and that was the end of it, except that Blair spoke for more than two hours amid demonstrations of great applause.

"He had similar experiences with similar results in St. Louis, Ironton, Marshall, Louisiana, and other places in the State. Only one other need be specially mentioned in this paper. The place was a sugar-tree grove in the suburbs of

ing and unforced obedience to his orders; for this was wholesome for discipline. But they were obstinate when driven. Col. Ruff, though ill qualified to govern volunteer troops, has some experience in military affairs, is well acquainted with tactics, and neither to "extenuate nor aught set down in malice," is certainly a brave man and a good soldier.

At a subsequent period Mr. Ruff, as captain of a mounted rifle company, rendered some very important service in Gen. Scott's division of the army. On the 29th of July, 1847, Capt. Ruff was dispatched by Gen. Smith with a squadron, composed of one company of the 2d dragoons under Lieut. Hawes and his own company of mounted riflemen, in all eighty-six men, to attack the town of San Juan de los Llaños. Capt. Ruff, finding about fifty cavalry drawn up in front of the town, who retired upon his approach, divided his command into three parts, and entered the town cautiously, towards

---

Louisiana, Pike county. Thousands of people were present, and the excitement was at fever heat. As soon as he was introduced to the audience, and before he had uttered a word, he unbuckled his belt and laid it, with two big navies, on the table. This he did in as perfunctory a way as if the pistols were campaign scrap-books. Then he commenced:

"'*Fellow-Citizens of Pike County:* I have an interesting item of news to tell you before I make my speech. I understand I am to be killed here to-day. As I have recently come out of four years of that business, I think the killing had better be attended to before the speaking begins.'

"Pausing, and no hostile demonstration being made, he proceeded with his speech. But a few minutes elapsed, however, before a big rough fellow in the audience arose, and, shouting that 'He's nothing but a rebel!' advanced toward the stand, crying aloud, 'Take him out, d—n him; take him out!' A panicky apprehension of danger seized the vast audience and it rose to its feet. But Blair stood in the stand as cool as a pillar of granite, and, crooking the index finger of his right hand at the author of the outcry, said, 'Well, you come on and take me out.' But the fellow, realizing that the next crook of that finger might be at the trigger of one of the navies, recoiled from the performance, for in very truth 'prudence is often the better part of valor' and 'practiced accents are throttled by fear.' Blair proceeded with his speech."

General William T. Sherman paid Blair the following compliment:

"I always had a most exalted regard for Frank Blair. I always regarded him as one of the truest patriots, most honest and honorable of men, and one of the most courageous soldiers this country ever produced. I never lost sight of the services he rendered the country in the outbreak of the war, and I fully concede and always have conceded that to his boldness, promptitude and firmness, more than to anything else, the country is indebted for the preservation of St. Louis as a strategic point, and for the salvation of Missouri from secession. He was a noble, generous, honest, brave, frank, sincere and unselfish man."

Blair died at St. Louis, of paralysis. He died a poor man. His wife, five sons, and three daughters survived him.

Missouri has placed a statue of Blair in the National Hall of Statuary at Washington.

The name of Francis Preston Blair, Junior, is imperishable so long as man shall love the right and strive for liberty.

the centre of which the stone houses and churches were filled with armed men. Lieut. Hawes first received the enemy's fire, whereupon dismounting and forming his men on foot, and being joined by Lieut. Walker of the mounted rifles, they very spiritedly returned the fire. The other party under Capt. Ruff advancing at the same time, they drove the enemy from house to house with great slaughter, until they reached the plaza. The fire of the riflemen was astonishingly destructive. Here two of the principal houses, one of them loop-holed, were defended with great obstinacy, but were finally carried. A party was now organized to assault the church, from the towers of which a continual fire had been kept up. But when the storming party began to advance, a white flag was hung out. Hereupon the firing ceased and the Mexicans capitulated. In this engagement the Mexicans lost forty-three killed and fifty-four wounded. Only one of the Americans was wounded—none killed.

It was this day that William Bray, a man belonging to Capt. Stephenson's company, became intoxicated and entirely incontrollable. After swearing and swaggering in a most unbecoming manner, resisting every effort which was made to pacify him, he seized his butcher-knife and made threats against the life of his captain. The captain for some time carefully avoided him, and endeavored to persuade him to his duty, but all in vain—he rushed furiously into the captain's tent with knife drawn, and made an attempt upon his life. The captain, in self-defence, drew a pistol and shot Bray through the heart, who fell dead in an instant with his knife clenched in his hand. This occurrence was the more lamentable, that Bray was sixty-three years of age, and had been one of Jackson's soldiers at the battle of New Orleans.[53] On the morning of the 18th, an election was ordered by Gen. Kearny to fill the vacancy occasioned by the resignation of Lieutenant-colonel Ruff,[54] which resulted in the choice

NOTE 53.—See sketch of Captain John D. Stephenson.

NOTE 54.—Ruff was a strict disciplinarian, and was not liked by the volunteers. It was by the greatest efforts of all the influence of the officers of the regular army at Fort Leavenworth that he was elected over Gilpin by two votes. The soldiers made it unpleasant for Ruff from the first. At night from one side of the camp some one would call out "Who is a scoundrel?" From a different quarter would come the answer "Ruff;· he is a d—d scoundrel!" And many other questions and answers were nightly asked and answered. Before any guard could arrive on the scene the questioners had disappeared and could not be apprehended.

of Capt. Congreve Jackson over Major William Gilpin, by a majority of one hundred and eighty-three votes.[55] Capt. Jackson's place was supplied by the election of H. H. Hughes to fill the vacancy; the same who commanded as Major in Gentry's Missouri Regiment of volunteers, at the battle of Okechubee in Florida in 1837. He was chosen from the ranks.

During this day a squadron of two companies, (Waldo's and Stephenson's) under command of Major Gilpin, was dispatched to the little town of Abiquiu, on the Rio de Chana, to keep the Indians in check in that part of the territory, and also a detachment of three companies, (Parsons', Reid's and Hughes',) under Lieutenant-colonel Jackson, was ordered to proceed to the town of Cebolleta, on the Rio Puerco, about one hundred and twenty miles south-westerly from the capital, for a like purpose.[56] These detachments were to remain at their respective posts until Col. Doniphan took up the line of march for Chihuahua, when they were to rejoin him in that expedition. This expedition was to commence its march against the State and city of Chihuahua, immediately upon the arrival of Col. Price's command at Santa Fé, in conformity to the following order, viz.:

"General Orders No. 30, Sec. 2.
"When all the companies of Col. Price's regiment shall have

NOTE 55.—Material for a sketch of the life of Congreve Jackson was not obtained. Perhaps it exists in Howard county, but my inquiries there were ignored. He was Colonel commanding the Third Division Missouri State Guards, under General Sterling Price, at the battle of Lexington, Mo.

NOTE 56.—Following is the official order:
HEAD QR. ARMY OF THE WEST
SANTA FE NEW MEXICO Sept 16, '46

SIR: I am instructed by the Gen'l Commg. to say, that on reaching the neighborhood of Cebolletta, you will dispose of the Troops under your command in such manner as to give greatest protection to the inhabitants of New Mexico on that frontier from the Navajoes ' other Indians—You will dispatch runners to the Navajoe country with instructions to invite 10 or 12 of their principal men to come to this city for the purpose of holding a Council with the Gen'l; and should they determine to do so, you will promise & give them protection while on the Route. Should you discover among the Navajoes any Property which may be recognized as having been stolen from the inhabitants of New Mexico, you will seize upon it, & cause it to be brought to this city, or turned over to the proper owners.

Lieut Col C. F. Ruff   I am Sir Very Resp. Yr. ob. Servt.
Mo. Mounted Vols.   H. S. TURNER
Present   Capt. A. A. A. Genl.

The order to Major Gilpin is a copy of the above, but he is ordered to the neighborhood of Abiqui with "2 Comps. of his Regt.," same date.

reached here, Col. Doniphan will proceed with his regiment to Chihuahua, and report to Brigadier-general Wool for duty. By order of Brig. Gen.   S. W. KEARNY.
[Signed,]   H. S. TURNER,
Capt. A. A. A. Gen."

It was not even doubted for a moment, by the most incredulous, that Gen. Wool's division would have taken possession of Chihuahua long before Col. Doniphan could possibly reach that place, and the latter did not at first so much as anticipate the honor of co-operating with the general in the reduction of THE STRONGHOLD OF THE NORTHERN PROVINCES, AND FORMERLY THE HEAD QUARTERS OF THE CAPTAINS-GENERAL OF THE VICE-REGAL GOVERNMENT OF NEW SPAIN. For it was well known throughout the United States, as well as in the "Army of the West," that Chihuahua was the unqualified destination of Gen. Wool's Army.

On the 20th, a deputation of Eutaws, or more properly Yutas, was brought in by Maj. Gilpin, to hold a council with the general, who made a speech to them through his interpreter, and gave them much good advice. On their part they promised to be peaceable, orderly, to respect the lives and property of the Mexicans, and to be obedient to the laws of the United States which were now extended to the territory of New Mexico. The general made them some trifling presents, which, however, were esteemed of great value among them, and they departed apparently well satisfied.

The same day an express arrived at the capital from Col. Price, informing the general that he was short of provisions, and asking fresh supplies. He was promptly furnished. This was the first, and only reliable information we had received of the colonel and his forces, since they left Fort Leavenworth. They were then at the Cimarron springs, nearly three hundred miles from Santa Fé, and were expected to arrive in fifteen or twenty days. By this express information was also brought, that W. P. Hall, a private, volunteer soldier, was elected to Congress, from one of the districts in Missouri, by a large majority. Hall, Lucas, and myself, were in one of the departments of the governor's house transcribing the new Constitution and laws of the territory, when Col. Doniphan entered bringing the intelligence. Hall was not moved or elated, but behaved very calmly. It is especially creditable to Col. Doniphan, that he should have been the first to announce to Mr. Hall the news of his success, when the latter and Col. Doniphan were strongly opposed in politics, and had often met each other on the stump or rostrum during a heated political contest. But such is the magnanimous character of Col. Doniphan.

September 23d, the chief of one branch of the Apaches, with about thirty of his tribe, came to hold a "grand council" with the Governor-general. The general made a long speech to them through an interpreter, encouraging them to industry, and peaceful pursuits, and particularly to the cultivation of the soil, as the surest and best mode of procuring an honorable subsistence; "that they must desist from all robberies, and the committing of all crimes against the laws of the territory; that if they did not he would send his soldiers amongst them and destroy them from the earth; but if they would be peaceable towards their white brethren he would protect and defend them as he would the New Mexicans, and make them all brothers to the white people, and citizens of the same republic, and children of the same father, the President, at Washington city."

To all these things the venerable Sachem replied in a spirit worthy his tribe, setting forth the wishes of his people in a strain of bold, commanding eloquence, which has ever characterized the aboriginal orator. He said: "Father, you give good advice for me and my people; but I am now old, and unable to work, and my tribe are unaccustomed to cultivating the soil for subsistence. The Apaches are poor; they have no clothes to protect them from the cold, and the game is fast disappearing from their hunting grounds. You must, therefore, if you wish us to be peaceable, speak a good word to the Comanches, the Yutas, the Navajos and the Arapahoes, our enemies, that they will allow us to kill buffalo on the great plains. You are rich—you have a great nation to feed and clothe you—I am poor, and have to crawl on my belly, like a cat, to shoot deer and buffalo for my people. I am not a bad man; I do not rob and steal; I speak truth. The Great Spirit gave me an honest heart, and a straight tongue. I have not two tongues that I should speak forked.

"My skin is red, my head sun-burnt, my eyes are dim with age, and I am a poor Indian, a *dog,* yet I am not guilty. There is no guilt there, (putting his hand on his breast,) no! I can look *you* in the face like a man. In the morning of my days my muscles were strong;

my arm was stout; my eye was bright; my mind was clear: but now I am weak, shriveled up with age, yet my heart is big, my tongue is straight. I will take your counsel because I am weak and you are strong."

The general then gave them some blankets, butcher-knives, beads, mirrors, and other presents for their squaws, and they departed under the promise that they would be *good and faithful citizens of the United States.*

On the 25th Gen. Kearny with a very inadequate force for such an enterprise, set out from the capital for the distant shores of the Pacific,[57] leaving Col. Doniphan in command of all the forces in New Mexico. The colonel was now actively employed in pushing forward preparations for his contemplated descent upon Chihuahua. Supplies were being procured for the men. Every soldier endeavored to mount himself upon a safe and durable animal, for the march was known to be long and perilous, passing through desert tracts of country. Wagons, for the transportation of baggage and provisions, were speedily being repaired. Harness and teams were put in readiness for the draught. It was the colonel's intention to begin his great march as soon as Col. Price should arrive at Santa Fé with his troops, and succeed him in the command at that place.

The author may perhaps be pardoned for adding, at the close of this chapter, a few brief remarks in commendation of the United

NOTE 57.—The final arrangements made by General Kearny before going on to California are described in the following letter:

HEAD QR. ARMY OF THE WEST
SANTA FE NEW MEXICO SEPT 24, '46

SIR: Having finished all my public business in this place having organized a civil government for the Tery. by appointing the officers & causing a set of laws to be prepared & published for it, & having made the necessary Military arrangements for maintaining the perfect order, peace & quiet, now so happily existing, I intend in compliance with the instructions from the War Dept to leave here to-morrow with Major Sumner & his 300 Dragoons for Upper California, as I informed you in my letter of the 16th Inst— I leave orders for Capt Allen & his (Infy.) command of Mormons to follow our trail, as soon as they reach here, & they will be accompanied from here by about 80 Mounted Vols. under Capt Hudson—I send to you copies of all orders which have been issued by my directions, which may explain some subjects omitted in my letters—On the 20th Inst I received a letter from Col Price dated the 10th & 12 miles West of the crossing of the Arkansas—He had with him 4 Cos. of his Regt 2 had proceeded up the Arkansas towards Bent's Fort, & the remaining 2 were several days march in his Rear. This is the only information Public or Private received by his express to me, & I was indebted for this to his being in want of Provisions, for which he asked, & which I ordered forthwith to be returned to him from a train coming from Bents Fort. We are very much behind the times in the way of information which causes some inconvenience here & may give more to others & to your office

States' troops, which will show the strong moral influence as well as the nationality of our republican institutions. He has observed his comrades in arms, after performing the severest toils during a long and fatiguing march of nine hundred miles, bearing with fortitude the burden and heat of the day, sometimes half faint of thirst and hunger, subsisting the greater part of the time upon half rations, refuse to pluck the ears of corn that grew thickly and invitingly around them. This exhibits a degree of moral firmness and a regard for the rights of property which is truly characteristic of the American people, is worthy of the highest praise, and is doubtless one of the happy results of our benign institutions. There was a *national* feeling in the army of the west. Every soldier felt that he was a *freeman;* that he was a citizen of the MODEL REPUBLIC; and that he ought to look upon the disgrace of the AMERICAN ARMS AS INDIVIDUAL DISHONOR. Hence their high moral sense and conscious superiority over the Mexican people. As the American soldier walked in the streets of the capital, and met a group of Mexican ladies and gentlemen going to the plaza with marketables, or in more gaudy attire passing up the walks to the Catholic churches, he paid them the same complimentary marks of courtesy and civility, with which he had been accustomed to greet his own *fairer* country-women and men in the streets

in Washington—We have not even received the Promotions & Appointments made in July, & know not who are the Field Officers of the 1st or 2d Dragoons—I leave directions for Col Price to remain in command of the Troops in this Tery.—He will have his own Regt of Mounted Vols.—a Battalion of 2 Cos. of Infy. under Capt Angney, & a Battn. of 2 Cos. of Horse Arty. & a part of Capt Hudsons Co of Laclede Rangers under Major Clark—These will be more than sufficient to preserve quiet thro'out the Tery. & to protect the inhabitants from the Navajo, Eutaw & Apache Indians, who have hitherto caused them so much trouble by killing their people & stealing their flocks & cattle—Deputations from the last two Nations have at my request been in to see me & promise good conduct in future—I hope to see in a few days a Deputation from the Navajoes—In my letter to you of the 1st Inst, I stated my intention of raising an Infy. Compy. from the Mexican Population—The Plan has been abandoned as unnecessary at this time—It may answer a good purpose next year—On the arrival of Col Prices Regt here, Col Doniphan with his Regt will proceed to Chihuahua & report to Brig Genl Wool (as will other troops, if any more should come here from Missouri) as I informed you in my letter of the 24th Ulto—Finding that horses cannot be of service in this Country & that they could not possibly travel to California, I have directed the Qr. Mr. to Mount the 1st Dragoons on Mules & to send the Dragoon horses back to Fort Leav-h, where they can be rendered serviceable—We will all use our exertions to reach Monterey as early as possible, from whence I hope to report to you by the 10th Decr. or before—I hope to hear from you at that place.

    Brig Genl R. Jones   Very Resp-y Yr. ob Servt.
       Adjt Genl. U. S. A.   S. W. KEARNY
          W——n   Brig Genl. U. S. A.

of St. Louis, Cincinnati, New York or Philadelphia. This honorable feeling* was never once forgotten or lost sight of by the CITIZEN SOLDIER.

* This remark is intended to apply to the conduct of the men generally. Individual instances of bad conduct may have been witnessed.—HUGHES.

CHAPTER VII.

Reinforcements—Organization of the Force—The march begun—Mormon Battalion—Death of Captain Allen—Another Estampeda—Col. Price's arrival at Santa Fé—Col. Daugherty's regiment—Disposition of the forces in New Mexico—Express from California—Preparations for the Chihuahua Expedition.

In the previous chapters it has been briefly related how the war between the United States and Mexico took its origin, and in what manner the President proposed to conduct the war, invading the latter country at several distinct points. It has also been shown how the Western Expedition was fitted out and dispatched across the great solitudes which intervene between Fort Leavenworth and Santa Fé; by what means the men were able to subsist themselves upon the plains; and how, for the greater convenience, the marches were conducted by separate companies, squadrons, and battalions. Finally, it has been related how the New Mexicans surrendered the capital into the hands of the Americans without resistance or bloodshed.

Lest the forces already dispatched under command of Gen. Kearny might not be able to accomplish the purposes of the expedition, or even to sustain themselves against the overwhelming numbers the enemy could bring into the field, it was deemed advisable by the President to send out a strong reinforcement. Sterling Price, a member of Congress from Missouri at the time, having resigned his membership early in the summer of 1846, and applied to President Polk, was appointed to the conduct of this new force. This reinforcement was to consist of one full mounted regiment, one mounted extra battalion, and one extra battalion of Mormon infantry, the whole to be filled up of volunteers.

After some delay the companies required rendezvoused at Fort Leavenworth, and were mustered into the service about the first of August. The companies from Boone, Benton, Carroll, Chariton, Linn, Livingston, Monroe, Randolph, St. Genevieve and St. Louis counties, respectively under command of Captains McMillan, Hollaway, Williams, Holley, Barbee, Slack, Giddings, H. Jackson, Horine, and Dent, composed the 2d Regiment. Notwithstanding the President had designated Sterling Price as a suitable man to command the 2d Regiment, the men thought he ought to be chosen by their free suffrages, or some other man in his stead. Accordingly they proceeded to hold an election that they might choose a commander. Sterling Price obtained the command. D. D. Mitchell was chosen lieutenant-colonel, and Capt. Edmondson, major. The appointment of R. Walker to be adjutant, and Stewart, sergeant-major, Dr. May, surgeon, and A. Wilson, sutler, completed the organization of the 2d regiment.

In the separate battalion, which was composed of the companies from the counties of Marion, Polk, Platte and Ray, respectively under command of Captains Smith, Robinson, Morin, and Hendley, Willock was chosen lieutenant-colonel. Thus the strength of Col. Price's command was about twelve hundred men. Besides this cavalry force, he had a considerable number of heavy pieces of artillery, and artillerymen to manage them, commanded by officers of the regular service, and a great number of baggage and provision wagons. These trains of wagons, used to transport the baggage and provisions of the men, generally set out in advance of the army, because, being heavily loaded, they could not travel as fast as the cavalry, and that, being wanted in the army, at any time it is easier for them to come to a halt, than to make a forced march, and each wagon having a driver well armed, and each train of thirty or more wagons a captain of the teamsters, they did not need to be protected by any other guard against the Indians, but went as fast as it pleased them, and when attacked by these barbarians, they presently converted the wagons into a *corral* or breastwork, so as to defend themselves from harm; except the baggage wagons, which traveled with the army when they could keep pace along with it. With this force, thus furnished, Col. Price set out for Santa Fé,* marching by separate detachments over the plains, as Gen. Kearny and Col. Doniphan had ordered their captains to do before, about the middle of August.[58]

Also about this period, Capt. Allen of the 1st Dragoons, acting

* It was the original intention of Col. Price to march his entire command to California by way of Santa Fé, if Gen. Kearny were in a condition not to need his services at the latter place. —HUGHES.

NOTE 58.—It will be seen from the following letter that it was originally the intention of Colonel Price to march to California by the way of South Pass, but the delays encountered at Fort Leavenworth caused him to march to Santa Fé.

under instructions from the War Department, proceeded to the Council Bluffs, where the Mormons had been collecting for several months with a view to make a settlement, and there raised a body of five hundred Mormons, all volunteer infantry. This body of troops also rendezvoused at Fort Leavenworth, and having been out-fitted, commenced its march, soon after the departure of Col. Price, for the shores of the Pacific, a distance of 1990 miles, where, having served to the expiration of one year, they were to be paid, discharged, and allowed to found settlements and bring their families. They were to proceed first to Santa Fé, and thence to California, following the route of Gen. Kearny.

This Mormon battalion consisted of five companies, lettered A, B, C, D, and E, respectively, under captains Hunt, Hunter, Brown, Higgins, and Davis, commanded by Lieut. Colonel Allen; Dykes being adjutant, and Glines being sergeant major. It was attended by 27 women, for laundresses, and was mustered into the service on the 16th of July. Lieutenant-colonel Allen, having delayed at the fort a short time after the companies began the march, to for-

---

General Kearny gave permission in this letter for Colonel Price to continue his march to California under certain conditions named:

HEAD QR. ARMY OF THE WEST
CAMP ON THE RIO DEL NORTE NEAR
JOYA—OCTOB 2D 1846

SIR: Your letter to the Gen'l Commg. dated the 29th of August [September] is received—You inform the General that you know it to be the desire of the President, that you should proceed to California & reach that Province before the commencement of cold weather. Also that had you been 20 days earlier with your command, you would, in accordance with a privilege granted you, have attempted forthwith to cross the Mountains by the South Pass—Under these circumstances I am instructed to say, that you are authorized to organize a force not to exceed 500 Men (Rank & File) out of your command, which force you are at liberty to conduct to California this fall, provided you shall be able to obtain a suitable outfit in provisions, transportation &c for it. And should you find it practicable to act upon the authority herein granted, Lieut Col Mitchell 2d Regt of M-o Mounted Vols. will be left in command of the Troops, to remain in this Tery. after the departure of Col Doniphan & yourself—& I am further instructed by the Genl to say, that the Gila rout to California was selected by him, from supposing it the most practicable, at this advanced state of the Season.

The Gen'l directs me to add, that had you complied with the last part of the Secy. of Wars letter to you of the 3d june & not observed an apparently studied silence, the public interest would have been advanced, & he would not have been subjected to embarrassment in relation to you & your command

Col Sterling Price I am Sir Very Resp-y Yr. ob Servt
  2d Regt M-o Md. Vols H. S. TURNER
    Santa fe N. Mexico Capt A. A. A. G.
copy of above furnished Adjt Genl & Col Doniphan Oct 3d.

ward some supplies, was suddenly taken ill, and expired shortly afterward, on the 22d of August.

Thus died Lieutenant-colonel Allen, of the 1st Dragoons, in the midst of a career of usefulness, under the favoring smiles of fortune, beloved while living, and regretted after death, by all who knew him, both among the volunteer and regular troops. The Mormons were then conducted to Santa Fé by Lieutenant Smith, of the 1st Dragoons.

The manner in which the advance of the Western Army immediately under Gen. Kearny and Col. Doniphan conducted its marches, and the great success which attended them, has been narrated in a previous chapter. Therefore, as this second force traveled over the same route, and was from the nature of the country necessitated to perform nearly the same daily marches, that it might obtain fuel, water and forage (or grass, which is the only forage the plains can supply), and also as the management which was necessary to be used for the rapid progress of the reinforcing army was similar to that which had been adopted by the preceding forces, and the scenes and incidents occurring on this campaign, as well as the leading features of the country passed over, being such as have already been described, it is not deemed necessary to recapitulate them.

They were not molested at any time, or put to any serious inconvenience by the Indians who dwell upon the plains. Many horses died or failed during the march. Those which failed, being abandoned by their owners, were soon killed and devoured by the gangs of wolves which daily followed the army.

These barbarous tribes of Indians seldom have the courage or daring to oppose the march of any considerable number of men, but attack with the greatest fury small parties of men who chance to fall in their way, and when they have captured them they never suffer them to escape, but uniformly torture and put them to death in the most cruel manner. Col. Price's forces feeling entirely secure against these hordes by reason of their number, placed out no picket guards as the other command had done, and sometimes had no sentinels about the camps at night. At a later period, however, the Indians infested the Santa Fé road with more boldness, and in several instances succeeded in killing Americans, and capturing provision wagons, and large droves of mules, oxen, and other stock belonging to the United States' government.

The troops composing this command, when they arrived at the crossing of the Arkansas, took the route by the Cimarron river, except two or three companies which proceeded, by way of Fort Bent and the Raton Pass to Santa Fé. The Cimarron route is perhaps one hundred miles the shorter way, but is not so well supplied with water or forage as the other. While the army lay encamped somewhere on the Arkansas, a general estampeda occurred among the horses. Wildly and madly they plunged over the plain, near a thousand head, stung and galled by the lariats and iron pickets which they dragged after them. After great labor the majority of them were recovered; the rest either went wild on the prairies, or were captured by the Comanches, who are excellent in horsemanship.

From the Cimarron Springs Col. Price sent forward an express to Santa Fé, representing to Gen. Kearny that his command was without supplies, and that his marches must of necessity be slow, unless he could furnish him. This express reached Santa Fé on the 20th of September, and provisions were forthwith dispatched upon the road to meet him. Meanwhile the colonel advanced upon the march as vigorously as the condition of his men and animals would permit. Thompson and Campbell, contractors to supply the army with beef, were on the road with fourteen hundred beef-cattle, but were too far behind to be of any service in the present exigency.

Col. Price, in a very feeble state of health, arrived at the capital in company with a few of his staff officers on the 28th of September, three days after Gen. Kearny's departure for California. The different detachments and companies of his command continued to come in almost daily. The greater part of them, however, together with the Mormon battalion, arrived on the 9th, 10th, 11th, and 12th days of October. They quartered out on the ground as Col. Doniphan's men were doing, there being no more houses in Santa Fé than barely enough to shelter the inhabitants from the inclement weather.

The capital was now literally alive with artillery, baggage wagons, commissary teams, beef-cattle and a promiscuous throng of American soldiers, traders, visitors, stragglers, trappers, amateurs, mountaineers, Mexicans, Pueblo Indians, women and children; numbering perhaps not less than fourteen thousand souls. The aggregate effective force of the American Army in New Mexico, at this time, was about three thousand, five hundred men.

Col. Price's command, during its long and toilsome march to Santa Fé, which was completed in about fifty-three days, in mid-summer, was attended with most singular good fortune; having lost only three soldiers on the way, one by accident, the other two by sickness.*

About the 10th of August another requisition was made upon the Governor of Missouri for one thousand additional volunteers, to join Gen. Kearny in New Mexico. This new force, the 3d Regiment of Missouri volunteers, was to consist entirely of infantry, and was to rendezvous also at Fort Leavenworth, where it was to be fitted out and be ready to march close in rear of Col. Price's command. In an incredibly short space of time, the requisite number of troops was raised and company officers chosen. Forthwith they repaired to the fort and reported for service. Major Daugherty, of Clay county, was elected to the command of this regiment, and while actively engaged in hastening preparations for the arduous march over the plains, he received orders from the President requiring him to desist from the enterprise and disband his force. This was accordingly done. The men, disappointed, returned to their homes. Thus those brave men, who had generously volunteered to serve the country on foot, in a cavalry expedition, were denied a share in the toils and honors of the campaign.

There being more troops in the capital, after the arrival of the recruits under the command of Col. Price, than were necessary to preserve order and tranquillity in the city, Col. Doniphan disposed of them in this manner:—The remaining three companies of the 1st Regiment were sent out to the grazing encampment, which, for better pasturage, had been moved from Galisteo to the mountains or dividing hills between the river Pecos and the Del Norte, about fifty miles from Santa Fé, and twenty from San Miguel. On this table-land the grass was very fine and nourishing, and there was a beautiful lake of fresh water near the camp-ground, abundantly sufficient for both men and horses. This glassy lake was situated in the edge of a glade several hundred yards wide, and skirted by the handsomest groves of pines and cedars, ever verdant; while the tall "*grama*," resembling a rich meadow, carpeted its margin, as well as covered

*These were Blount and Willhoit. They were both interred at Fort Marcy.—HUGHES.

the beautiful succession of hills and dales which lay spread out to view. In this truly romantic spot of country, the animals were soon refitted for service. A squadron of two companies under Major Edmondson was ordered to relieve Lieutenant-colonel Jackson at Cebolleta, and a detachment was sent to relieve Major Gilpin at Abiquiu; Jackson and Gilpin were severally to await at these places further orders. Also, one or two companies were sent back to forage or graze on the Mora, near the Santa Clara springs, to prevent the Mexicans and Indians driving off the mules and beef-cattle belonging to the army, that were grazing there. The remainder of the cavalry, together with all the artillery, was retained at Santa Fé.

Things being in this posture, on the 11th an express reached Santa Fé from California, by the hands of Fitzpatrick, the old mountaineer and pilot to Gen. Kearny. This express was from Commodore Stockton and Lieutenant-colonel Frémont. It met Gen. Kearny on his road to California, about one hundred and fifty miles from Santa Fé, by the hand of Lieut. Kit Carson,[59] one of Lieutenant-colonel Fré-

NOTE 59.—*Kit Carson.*—Christopher Carson was born in Madison county, Kentucky, December 24, 1809. His parents moved from Kentucky to Howard county, Missouri, in 1810, when he was not yet a year old. Carson grew up in the Boone's Lick country of Missouri, and it appears that Frémont entertained the erroneous belief that he was born there. No more suitable school existed in America for the training of men for great careers in the exploration of the Mountains and Plains than was Howard county, Missouri, from 1810 to 1820. The people were compelled to remain in forts the greater portion of the time. From these forts they issued forth in seasons of severe weather when the Indians could not prowl abroad, and cleared the rich bottoms and erected cabins. These clearings were made and cabins erected within calling distance of the forts, that all might rush to the assistance of any settler attacked by the savages. But all precautions could not completely protect the pioneers; alarms were frequent, and many a bold and hardy frontiersman lost his life about these outposts of American conquest. It was the history of Kentucky repeated.

In this school Carson was educated. His parents thought to confine him to the humdrum life of a village saddler, and put him out as an apprentice to learn that trade. But he developed no aptitude for work with clamp and awl, for beating dusty hair for saddle-pads, for headstalls and throatlatches and stirrup-leathers. His soul was in the forest, where roamed the shades of his pioneer ancestors. In 1826 he ran away from home and went with a caravan of traders over the old Santa Fé Trail. From the time when he first set foot on the Plains until his death, he was the most active and stirring pioneer that ever scaled a mountain or crossed a desert. Long before Frémont ever saw a prairie, Carson had been to Chihuahua, had explored the Upper Rockies, had obtained a correct knowledge of the geography of those countries through which flowed the Snake,

mont's men direct from Monterey. The express brought this intelligence: "The Pacific Squadron, Commodore Stockton, has taken possession of California, and the American Flag is now proudly streaming above the walls of Monterey, the capital of the country. Lieutenant-colonel Frémont was on the Rio Sacramento when the squadron arrived off the coast, and was not present when the capital surrendered. Five men-of-war were anchored in the bay when the express left Monterey. The inhabitants submitted without a struggle. Lieutenant-colonel Frémont had probably been appointed temporary governor of California." Kit Carson returned to California as pilot to Gen. Kearny, while Fitzpatrick, his former guide, was entrusted with the bearing of the dispatches to Fort Leavenworth, whence they were transmitted to Washington.

A great number of provision wagons was now daily coming in, and filling up the streets of the city. The commissary and quartermaster departments were extremely busy in receiving and storing provisions, and taking care of government stock. At the head of these departments were Major Swords and Captain McKissack.

---

the Columbia, and the Colorado, had fought Indians and trapped beaver all over the great wilderness, and had ridden over the old Spanish Trail to the Missions in the golden valleys of California. At some future time, it is to be hoped, the men who really explored the West will be given credit for it.

The accounts of Carson's journeys would alone fill a large volume, and an adequate biography of him would be a history of the discovery and exploration of a great portion of the West. He was guide to Frémont in 1842, and was with him in California in the Mexican War. Frémont desired to inform the Government of the course of events on the Pacific Coast, and required of Carson that he ride overland and appear at Washington inside of sixty days. He started September 15, 1846, the first man to attempt to carry dispatches overland across the continent. On the sixth of October he met General Kearny and was compelled to return and guide him to California, arriving there early in December. Kearny found himself hard pressed by the Mexicans, and sent Carson and Lieutenant Beale of the navy to San Diego. They got through, but the hardships endured made Beale insane for two years; such was the hardihood of Carson that he suffered no serious consequences.

In March, 1847, Carson was again put upon the journey overland to Washington with dispatches for the Government, and arrived there in June. He was given dispatches to carry back on his return. He made the trip of four thousand miles, and after hard fighting with savages arrived at Monterey. Early in 1848 he was sent again to Washington, and had to turn northward to the Platte to avoid the savages on the Arkansas. He completed this journey, and arrived, upon his return, at Santa Fé in October.

The endurance of man was never put to a more severe test than was that

There were also a great number of assistant commissaries and quartermasters,* and a tribe of clerks. Every exertion was now being used to provide a good outfit for Col. Doniphan's intended expedition against Chihuahua, which was looked upon as being both an arduous and a hazardous enterprise. The battalion of Mormons, to the future conduct of which Capt. Cooke[60] of the 1st Dragoons had been appointed, were waiting for a new outfit for transportation across the mountains to the Californias. Also Capt. Hudson, of St. Louis, having given up his command of the Laclede Rangers to his 1st lieutenant, Elliot, and acting under the permission of Gen. Kearny, had raised a new company of volunteers, one hundred strong, from the several corps at Santa Fé, designed for the California service.

* Lieutenants Pope Gordon and James Lea were appointed assistant commissary and quartermaster to the 1st regiment—both active, energetic men.—HUGHES.

of Carson in these long trips in quick succession across the continent. Only the West ever produced men of such iron constitution.

After the Mexican War Carson became a ranchman. But he was often called upon to fight Indians; and more than once he went out to roam over the boundless hunting-grounds of the Rocky Mountains to hunt, and to fight if it became necessary. He drove a large flock of sheep to California, and this proved a profitable venture and made him some money. In 1850 he went with a drove of horses to Fort Laramie. In 1851 he and Maxwell took a caravan across the Plains, and arrived at Santa Fé with the cargo intact after many adventures among the Indians. He was made Indian Agent for New Mexico, and in this capacity he insisted that the Indians be compelled to till the soil. His savage charge came to regard him as a father, and his administration was successful and satisfactory. In the Civil War Carson was made Colonel of a New-Mexican regiment, and, later, brevetted Brigadier-General.

Carson died at Fort Lyon, Colorado, May 23, 1869, from a hemorrhage caused by an aneurism of the aorta.

Carson was one of the "long-haired" men of the Mountains and Plains. He was hunter, trapper, explorer, guide, and trader. He was a brave soldier, and was one of those pioneers to whom we owe a debt of gratitude which all succeeding generations cannot pay. He was one of the great characters trained in the Missouri school of pioneer life to go forward in the work of completing the conquest of the Western wilderness. And, true to his race and his training, he failed in nothing. Great was Carson and great was his generation of Missourians.

NOTE 60.—Philip St. George Cooke was born in Virginia, in 1809. He graduated from West Point in 1827; was in the Black Hawk War, and at the battle of Bad Ax. In 1833 he was made a Lieutenant; saw much service on the Plains, principally in what is now Kansas, before the Mexican War; in this war he took a prominent part. During the fifties, in the border troubles in Kansas, he saw much service. In the Civil War he was for the Union. He was retired in 1873, having served continuously forty-six years. He died in 1895 (March 20).

This company, denominated the California Rangers,* must also be provided with means of transportation over the mountains. Besides this pressing current of business, large deputations of Indians, headed by their respective chiefs, were constantly coming in to hold a "Big Talk" or "Grand Council" with Col. Doniphan, who as yet was looked upon as commander of all the forces in New Mexico, and governor of the Department. Such then at this time was the posture of affairs in Santa Fé.

* This company was dissolved by Col. Doniphan as soon as he learned that California was in the hands of the Americans.—HUGHES.

CHAPTER VIII.

Doniphan ordered against the Navajos—Plan of the March—Condition of the Troops—They take with them neither Baggage, Provision Wagons, nor Tents—Arrival at Albuquerque—A Squadron sent to Valverde—Death of Adjutant Butler—War Dance at Isleta—Express from the Merchants—Valverde.

The express which reached Santa Fé on the 11th day of October, as already noticed, brought a communication from Gen. Kearny to Col. Doniphan, instructing him to delay for a time his contemplated movement upon Chihuahua, and desiring him to proceed with his regiment forthwith into the country inhabited by the Navajos, a large and powerful tribe of semi-civilized Indians, and chastise them for the depredations they have recently committed on the western frontiers of New Mexico, as also for having refused to come in to the capital, when sent for, to offer submission to the conqueror and acknowledge his government. This is a copy of the order:

HEADQUARTERS ARMY OF THE WEST,
Camp on the Rio del Norte near La Joya,
Oct. 2, 1846.

I. As the chiefs of the Navajos have been invited to Santa Fé by the commanding general, for the purpose of holding a council, and making a peace between them and the inhabitants of New Mexico, (now forming a part and under the protection of the United States,) and as they have promised to come, but have failed doing so, and instead thereof continue killing the people and committing depredations upon their property, it becomes necessary to send a military expedition into the country of these Indians, to secure a peace and better conduct from them in future.

II. For the reasons set forth in the foregoing paragraph, Col. Doniphan, of the 1st regiment Missouri mounted volunteers, previous to complying with paragraph II. of orders No. 30, dated September 23d, will march with his regiment into the Navajo country. He will cause all the prisoners, and all the property they hold, which may have been stolen from the inhabitants of the territory of New Mexico, to be given up—and he will require of them such security for their future good conduct, as he may think ample and sufficient, by taking hostages or otherwise.

III. After Col. Doniphan has fully complied with these instructions, he will proceed with his regiment to report to Brigadier-general Wool, as directed in order No. 30. By order of Brigadier-general.

S. W. KEARNY.

H. S. TURNER, Capt. A. A. A. Gen.

This order was founded upon the fact that the New Mexicans represented to Gen. Kearny as he passed near Socorro on his route to California, "that a party of Navajo Indians had recently crossed the mountains and made a sudden irruption into the settlements, (which Gen. Kearny had promised to protect,) killing seven or eight men, taking as many more women and children captives, and driving off ten thousand head of sheep, cattle and mules."

As the winter was now fast approaching, and the mountains would soon be impassable by reason of the great quantity of snow which falls in that elevated region early in the season, and also on account of the great difficulty of procuring forage for horses and mules at such a time, Col. Doniphan determined to execute the order with all possible expedition. Accordingly, having dispatched directions to Major Gilpin at Abiquiu, and Lieutenant-colonel Jackson at Cebolleta, thence to penetrate into the heart of the Navajo district by different routes through the mountains, chastising the Navajos wherever they appeared hostile, and taking their chiefs as hostages for their future good behavior wherever they were disposed to be peaceable, at last forming a junction of their forces at a noted place called the Ojo Oso or Bear Spring, he himself set out, taking with him the three companies he had called in from the Grazing Encampment near San Miguel, intending to take a medium course through the hills and sierras, having Gilpin on his right, and Jackson on his left, and thus to unite with them at the Bear Spring; Col. Price being left in command of the entire force at Santa Fé and the grazing grounds.

The three companies from the grazing grounds near San Miguel, having collected their stock together, commenced the march on the 26th of October, proceeded by way of Galisteo and Del Gardo to Santo Domingo,[61] where Col. Doniphan and staff, with his baggage and provision wagons, were in wait for them. Four months' pay was now due the soldiers, and many of them would soon be destitute of comfortable clothing, yet Col. Doniphan had neither a military chest, nor a paymaster, nor a dollar of government funds to silence the just complaints, or satisfy the reasonable wants, of his men. They looked

---

NOTE 61.—Santo Domingo pueblo was built by the Queres, but the exact site of the first town is not known. The town is on the left bank of the Rio Grande, immediately below the mouth of Galisteo creek, and has a population of some eight hundred.

upon it as a hardship, and with reason, that they were ordered against the Indians, without pay, and with little else than their summer clothing to protect them from the cold, in a country where they would be compelled to climb over the tallest mountains, and often encamp in the midst of snow, and ice, and rocks, and where it was impossible to procure either wood for fire, water to drink, or forage for horses and mules.

Now, besides these difficulties, the nature of the country is such, that it is impracticable for artillery, baggage or provision wagons, or even for the lightest carriages; so steep and abrupt are the rocks, hills, and mountains. Only pack mules and sumpter horses can be used with advantage. For this reason Major Gilpin sent all his baggage wagons back from Abiquiu[62] into the Del Norte valley; Lieutenant-colonel Jackson did the same thing from Cebolleta; and Colonel Doniphan the same. They also threw away their tents, that, being light armed and unembarrassed, they might make their marches with greater expedition amongst the rocks, ravines and steeps of the mountains. Moreover, the soldiers thought, as they had been previously ordered against Chihuahua, that some portion of the troops which were idle at Santa Fé, might have been sent on this service; that after having spent three or four months in pursuit of the Indians, amongst the gorges, and chasms, and fastnesses of the Cordilleras, they would then be marched off on the Chihuahua expedition, without being allowed one day to recuperate their wasted energies, or to rest their jaded animals; and that so much delay would give Gen. Wool time to anticipate them in his movement upon Chihuahua, thereby robbing them of their share of the honor; or, if it did not, that it would give the Mexicans ample time to learn of our intentions, and make preparations to defend themselves; and the city of Chihuahua to the best advantage, rendering it hazardous in the extreme for so small a force to venture thither, as Colonel Doniphan had at his command. This latter surmise proved true.

The detachment now, with Col. Doniphan, marched on the 30th of October down the country, keeping the river Del Norte on the right, and the mountains and craggy hills on the left, and arriving

---

NOTE 62.—Abiquiu is in the present Rio Arriba county, and is one of the oldest towns in New Mexico. It is in the valley of the Rio Chama, and was for years an outpost against the Apache and Ute Indians.

about sunset at the village Sandia, the men staid there during the night, encamping on the ground without much system, but wherever each soldier preferred to lie; for now there was no danger, and the men were tired of marching, and watching, and mounting guard. That night much rain fell, and the men endured it all; for by this time, few of them had any tents, and some of those who had, did not take pains to pitch them. It was here that a Mexican came into camp, and reported "that Gen. Wool had taken possession of Chihuahua with 6,000 men, and much heavy artillery, and that the Mexicans made but a feeble resistance." This did not prove true.

The next day the march was continued down the river, the men encamping on a "brazo," during the night. There was now plenty of provisions in the camp for the soldiers; but wood was so scarce that it was a difficult task for them to prepare anything to eat at supper. Some of them collected together a few little bunches of dry brush, while others as they could, picked up withered grass and weeds, and dry ordure from the cattle, and with these made a fire, and broiled their meat, and boiled their coffee. About this time an election was ordered in the companies, that they might each make choice of an additional second lieutenant, with the same rank and pay of the other lieutenants; so that there were now four commissioned officers to each company; one captain and three lieutenants. This order was made agreeably to an arrangement of the War Department, by which companies of one hundred men, or more, were entitled to four commissioned officers.

Early the next day the detachment arrived at the town of Albuquerque, where such of the men as were able, and desired it, purchased wine, and beer, and *mezcal*, which is made of the maguey, and of which the Mexicans are very fond; also bread, fresh meat, eggs and poultry. Lieutenant Noble, with about thirty of the 1st Dragoons, was at this place, recruiting the condition of his men and animals, some of the former being sick. Here the colonel crossed the river, his men following, and after them the provision and baggage trains. The river here is broad and shallow, not being above the hubs of the wagons; the bottom is so sandy, however, that if a wagon stops but a few minutes in the current, it will presently be buried in the water and sand. On this account, many of the teams coming to a halt that they might drink of the cold water, some of the wagons had to be drawn out by hand, the men wading into the water, rolling at the wheels, and pulling by ropes attached to the standards. This heavy work completed, the march was resumed, continuing down on the west bank of the river. That night the men encamped in a level bottom, where there was a moderate supply of forage, but no kind of fuel. Some of the men collected tufts of dry grass and weeds together, and setting fire to them, held their meat in the blaze until it was partially roasted. Thus they prepared their suppers.

It was here that the colonel received information from the caravan or merchant trains, which had advanced as far down the valley of the Del Norte as the ruins of Valverde, for the purpose of grazing their mules and other animals to better advantage, that they apprehended an attack from the Mexicans almost daily, who were said to be advancing, seven hundred strong, with the view of plundering the merchant wagons. In this perplexity, Col. Doniphan, that he might accomplish all his purposes, and fail in none, dispatched the three companies which he had with him, to protect the traders and their merchandise. Of this squadron Capt. Walton had the command, ranking the other two captains, Moss and Rodgers. Capt. Burgwin, (having been sent back by Gen. Kearny, with about two hundred men,) being previously apprized of the critical situation of the merchants, had already gone to afford them succor. Thus in a short time there were five hundred mounted men, besides three hundred merchants and teamsters at Valverde, ready to oppose any hostile movement the enemy might choose to make. The merchants had also corraled their wagons in such a manner as to receive troops within, and afford them shelter against an enemy, so that the besieged could fight with as much security as though they were in a fortress.

As to Col. Doniphan, he took his staff, (that part of it which happened to be with him) and attended by three or four other men, proceeded with great haste to Cuvarro, not far from the river Puerco,[63] making great marches and encamping on the ground wherever nightfall chanced to overtake him. This was on the 2d day of November.

NOTE 63.—The Puerco is a tributary of the Rio Grande, flowing in from the west and joining the mother stream just above Socorro. It has a length of near a hundred miles, but is shallow and drains a narrow valley. Its general course is southeastwardly.

At Cuvarro the colonel fell in with a few of Lieutenant-colonel Jackson's men, most of whom, being sick, were left behind, attended by their friends, that they might recover, and not be left without aid in that wild country. Of those who were sick a great number died, their diseases being such that the physicians could not relieve them. These diseases were typhoid fever, rheumatism, blumy, and other complaints produced by intense cold and great exposure. The patients became entirely helpless, and frequently lost the use of their legs. So they died. Others of them surviving for a time, were conveyed back to Socorro and Albuquerque, where some of them also died, and others recovered.

It was at Cuvarro that Adjutant G. W. Butler, of Col. Doniphan's staff, a brave and gallant man, beloved by all the regiment, was seized with a violent distemper, induced by cold, and died, much lamented, on the 26th of November. He was buried, (and also the rest of the dead, for others died near the same time,) with as much honor as could be shown to brave and gallant men in that destitute country; for it was not possible to procure coffins for the dead as in the United States, there being no timber there. Their bodies were wrapt in blankets, deposited in the grave, the vault being covered by broad rocks to prevent the wolves disturbing the dead, and then a certain number of rounds being fired over the grave, and the last one into it, the earth was heaved in and the "last resting place" completed in the usual manner. Thus were interred those who died in the service of their country.

Col. Doniphan advanced vigorously into the mountains, as we shall presently notice, attended by only a few men.

At the same time Col. Doniphan departed to the Navajo district, the detachment under command of Capt. Walton, with the baggage train, began the march towards Valverde, on the 2d day of November; passing through many ranchos on the river, and also the villages Pajaritto and Padillas, and the Pueblo of Isleta,[64] near which the soldiers encamped that night. The inhabitants of these places

NOTE 64.—The old pueblo of Isleta was built on an island in the Rio Grande. It was captured by Otermin in 1681, who carried many of the inhabitants to Texas, where they founded Isleta del Sur. Others of the inhabitants fled to the Mokis, but some of them returned in 1718 and rebuilt the pueblo near the old site, and it has been inhabited since that time. It has about one thousand inhabitants, Indians, who have a grant of land.

did not molest our men, nor manifest any hostility towards them, but sold them such things to eat as they could spare, and whatever commodities the soldiers desired to purchase. Now during the night there were a great shouting and yelling, and the firing of guns and ringing of bells, and also singing and dancing among the Pueblos of Isleta. Certain of the soldiers, thinking perhaps an attack was meditated by these people on our camp during the night, volunteered to go and learn what might be the occasion of so much noise and tumult. When they arrived there, they beheld various lights about the streets and squares, and groups of men and maidens, fantastically dressed and tattooed, dancing and singing with great merriment. On approaching a little nearer, they beheld on the tops of three tall lances or javelins, the scalps of three Navajo warriors, the long, straight, black hair sweeping in the wind. The Pueblos were celebrating a war dance. The men, inquiring how these scalps were obtained, received this account from the Pueblos:

"About three days ago a party of Navajos, between whom and us there are continual wars, descended from the mountains and seized one of our women, five of our children, and a great number of sheep and cattle, and mules, and having killed eight Mexicans and Pueblos, went off with their booty. These facts being reported to Capt. Burgwin, while on his way to Valverde, Lieut. Grier with about sixty men was detached to go in pursuit of this marauding party of Navajos, themselves numbering seventy. Lieut. Grier having pursued them about two days, (most of his men however having given over the pursuit on account of their horses failing,) came up with them in a cañon of the mountains, charged upon them, killing and scalping three of them, rescuing the captives, and recovering the stock." Lieut. Grier had one of his men slightly wounded, and an arrow lodged in his saddle near his thigh. However, he made good his retreat. It was thus the Pueblos of Isleta obtained the trophies which they were proudly displaying at the war-dance. This detachment now moving slowly down the river, completed in five days' march about thirty-five miles, passing through the villages Sineca, Lunaz, Chavez, and Jarrales. Encamping near the latter place, the inhabitants furnished wood for the soldiers and various articles of food, such as chickens, bread, cheese, molasses, melons, meal and flour, at a moderate price. That night some of the men witnessed the nuptial ceremonies of the Alcalde's daughter. She was married to a wealthy "ranchero" by the "cura" of the place.

From thence the march was continued through Belen and Sabinaz to the river Puerco, making only about twenty-five miles in three days. Here the detachment met Capt. Burgwin's command returning to Albuquerque, there being no danger of an attack on the merchant wagons. As it was now cold and disagreeable, the soldiers staid in camp three days. The next day they marched twelve miles over deep sand drifts and dry rocky creeks, and stopped for the night in a cottonwood grove, a pleasant retreat, where they staid three more days. From this place, on the 21st of November Capt. Rodgers' company returned to La Joya, on the east side of the river, to bury Lieut. Snell, one of their officers, who had died the previous day. This officer was much esteemed by his men. Captain Rodgers was also, at the same place, disabled by the kick of a horse. So the company was now commanded by Lieut. Harrison. From thence in one day's march they passed Socorro and Huertaz, making about twenty-two miles. These are the last Mexican settlements on the west bank of the river until you come to El Paso Del Norte. The next day (23d) they marched twelve miles, and encamped in a cottonwood forest, where there was grass, wood, and water, intending to spend one or two days at that place.

About tattoo the soldiers were suddenly aroused from their repose by the appearance in camp of a friendly Mexican, who had been dispatched thither by the merchants, with a letter addressed to the "commandante," requesting him to march with all possible haste to their relief; that they expected very soon to be attacked by a strong Mexican force. Two Americans came into camp next morning, and confirmed what the Mexican had said;—therefore the volunteers began to clean up their guns, adjust their flints, and see that their cartridge boxes were well supplied; for they now believed that an action would soon take place. A speedy march of fifteen miles was completed in less than half the day, which brought them to the Green valley, where the caravans had corralled for defence. They encamped in a large forest of cottonwood trees, on the west bank of the river, near the ruins of Valverde. The pasturage was excellent in the adjacent mountains. The exigency for succor, however, did not prove as great as was represented.

This being a favorable place from whence to afford protection to the caravan of traders, and also a convenient spot to procure pasturage for the animals, as well as a good position to shelter the men from the wind and violent snow storms, it was thought fit to make it a permanent encampment. It was also convenient to the water. Therefore this place became the headquarters of the commissary and quartermaster departments of the regiment, and the point from which Col. Doniphan, when he should collect his scattered forces together from the Navajo country, was to invade the state of Chihuahua. This was the 24th of November.

Lest it should be supposed that the three hundred men, who were detailed as a wagon guard to watch over and protect the interest of the merchant caravan, were less willing soldiers, or less desirous of serving the country, than those who went against the Navajos, let us consider the nature of the service which they were required to perform. There is no one so ignorant that he does not know it is more agreeable to be actively employed in marching, than confined in camps and placed on continual guards and watchings; just as the bears which run wild in the mountains enjoy more liberty than those which are kept in chains or in cages. Besides, this section of the army suffered much from cold, being stationed in an open valley on an exposed spot of earth, poorly supplied supplied with tents, almost destitute of comfortable clothing, and stinted in provisions. These were brave men and good soldiers. They were daily threatened by attacks from the Apaches on the east and west, and by the Mexicans on the south. Much vigilance was therefore necessary.

The traders had formed a corral for defence upon the intelligence obtained through two spies whom they had caught on their way from El Paso to Santa Fé, bearing communications to the principal men in the northern settlements. They represented "that seven hundred Mexicans were on their way from El Paso with the view to attack and rob the merchants, not knowing they were protected by the military." Two other Mexican spies or couriers were soon after caught by them, having in their possession a great many letters and other communications from the priests and leading characters of New Mexico, directed to the authorities of Chihuahua and Mexico, excusing themselves for permitting New Mexico to fall under the power of the *"Northern Yankees and Texans,"* and accusing Col. Armijo of the most arrant cowardice.

On the morning of the 27th the old Mexican shepherd who had been employed to take charge of the flock of sheep belonging to the detachment, was missing. None knew whither he had gone. After further inquiry, it was discovered that seventeen government mules were also missing. It was now plain how matters stood. He had driven them off the previous night and appropriated them to his own "use and benefit." Not long after it was ascertained that eight hundred and seventy-three head of sheep, the only dependence the detachment had for subsistence, had also been driven off, but in a different direction and by very different authors. Two men, James Stewart and Robert Speares, were detailed to follow the trail of the sheep, and discover the direction in which they had been driven. These two young men carelessly went out without their arms or any means of defence, not expecting to go far before returning to camp. Striking the trail, however, they pursued on with the view to drive the sheep back to camp at once. Proceeding about six miles towards the mountains westward they came up with the flock. Hereupon they were instantly attacked by a small party of renegade Navajos, and cruelly put to death. One of them was pierced by thirteen arrows and the other by nine; after which their heads were mashed and their bodies bruised with rocks in a most shocking manner. As these men did not return, it was not known by their companions in camp what had become of them. At length they were searched for, when their dead bodies were found, brought into camp, and decently buried. A detail of thirty-eight men, commanded by Lieut. Sublette, was sent in pursuit of the murderers. The pursuit having been prosecuted vigorously for sixty or seventy miles into the rocky recesses of the Sierra de los Mimbres, the animals beginning to fail and the number of the party thereby decreasing, and no water having been found by the way, the men were compelled to return without recovering the stock or chastising the authors of the bloody deed. In the deep valleys of this rugged range of mountains are extensive forests of pines, cedars and live-oaks.

When there was nothing important in camp to engage the attention of the soldiers, and the day was pleasant, they spent their time in contests of wrestling, running and jumping; also in jokes, songs and speaking; or else in smoking, lounging, sleeping, card-playing or reading, as the humor might prompt them. Strict guards were, however, kept about the camp day and night, and also a detail was daily made to drive the stock out into the mountains for the purpose of grazing them. These stock guards were always well armed, to prevent attacks by the Apaches and Navajos, who watch every opportunity of seizing upon whatever booty may chance to be in their power. The traders, who had a great number of mules and oxen, used the same method of subsisting them, sending a part of their own men out each day as a stock guard.

About this time an English officer, or rather embassador, made his appearance in the camp of the merchants, bringing proposals to them from the governor of Chihuahua to this effect: "That if they would first dismiss from their employ all their American teamsters, and employ in their stead, Mexicans, and then, upon their arrival at El Paso, where the customs for the State of Chihuahua are received, pay a duty of thirteen cents per pound on their importations, and such an internal or consumption tariff as should be fixed by law, they would be permitted to come into the city of Chihuahua and allowed the advantages of that market, free from molestation." So impatient to sell were some of the merchants who had embarked largely in the trade, and who were extremely anxious to have the advantage of the first market, that they were disposed to entertain these overtures with some degree of favor. Others, better acquainted with the Mexican character, looked upon it as a *ruse* or piece of management to get the merchants into their power, and then they could seize and confiscate their goods at pleasure.[65] The spoils could easily be divided afterwards. This indeed was their design.

Now while the great majority of the traders were Americans, there

---

NOTE 65.—*Dr. Henry Connelly.*—This was, perhaps, the opinion of Dr. Henry Connelly, one of the wealthy traders.

Dr. Henry Connelly was born in Nelson (now Spencer) county, Kentucky, in the year 1800, died at Santa Fé, New Mexico, in July, 1866, from the effects of an overdose of medicine, an opiate taken to induce sleep. He was descended from a patriotic family, founded and established in America by Thomas Connelly and his brother Edmund, who came from County Armagh, Ireland. They settled about the year 1689, at Albemarle Point, the settlement being moved later to become Charlestown, in the Colony of South Carolina; it is now the metropolis of the State of South Carolina, and the name is written Charleston. The genealogical records of the family are not complete, or, rather, have not been collected;

were also among them some English and Mexican merchants who could embrace the governor's terms with safety. These were anx-

but the foregoing is the well-defined family tradition, and it is undoubtedly correct. The descendants of Thomas are far more numerous than are those of Edmund. Dr. Henry Connelly was one of the descendants of Thomas.

These brothers were men of affairs. They obtained a large grant of land

DR. HENRY CONNELLY.

One of the first traders overland from Missouri to northern Mexico. An explorer in Mexico, New Mexico, Texas, and Oklahoma. Was long a merchant at Chihuahua. Appointed Governor of New Mexico by President Lincoln. Born in Nelson (now Spencer) County, Kentucky, in the year 1800. Died at Santa Fé, New Mexico, in July, 1866.

(From photograph in possession of his son, Peter Connelly, Kansas City, Mo.)

from the proprietors of the Colony, and this grant is said to have embraced a portion of the site of the city of Charleston. It is said, too, that they never parted with the title to this tract. They engaged in town-building and the purchase and sale of large tracts of land in the various colonies, but principally in

ious to reap the first fruits of the Chihuahua market. They therefore manifested symptoms of restlessness, and evinced a disposition and

Virginia and the Carolinas. They induced many Germans to move from Pennsylvania to the Carolinas, a colony of whom, so tradition says, they induced to settle on their lands near the present town of Camden, South Carolina. In this business their descendants were also engaged, and it became necessary for them to send members of the family to live in different parts of the country, especially in Pennsylvania and Virginia, to induce persons to migrate to their towns and colonies in the Carolinas. And they engaged largely in traffic and merchandising, trading extensively with the Indians, and being the proprietors of a number of vessels which plied between the different colonies, and some of them visited the West India Islands.

In the Revolution the Connellys fought in the patriot armies of Virginia, the Carolinas, and Pennsylvania. They served under Washington, Greene, Morgan, Gates, Howard (of Maryland), Lincoln, and Charles Cotesworth Pinckney. At the close of the Revolution many of them moved to the West, and the family became still more widely scattered. There is a belt of them extending across Indiana, Illinois, and to central Missouri. Some members of the family settled at a very early day in the wilderness of northwestern Pennsylvania, and many of their descendants are to be found there. Quite a number of them settled in Kentucky, in different parts of the State. Descendants of these pioneer brothers are to be found in Tennessee, Georgia, Alabama, Mississippi, Louisiana, and Texas. Indeed, there are descendants of this family in every Western State and Territory. They remain in large numbers in the Carolinas, Virginia, and Pennsylvania. They have been exceedingly prolific, very large families having been the rule from the first. Conservative estimates place the number of descendants of Captain Henry Connelly, who moved from North Carolina to Virginia and from thence to Kentucky after the Revolution, at certainly more than one thousand, and possibly nearly twice that number, counting living and dead. The writer once possessed a list of more than thirty Connelly families in eastern Kentucky, each having more than ten children. The name is now written in various forms, and there has been, of late years, a tendency to shorten to Conley, all the immediate relatives of this author so writing it. Some of the Illinois relatives write it Connelli, accenting the second syllable. Taken all together, the Connellys have been men of fair fortune. They have been men of influence in every community in which they have lived; and many of them have been possessed of fine literary taste, some of them with fair literary ability. They have been ever in the advance guard in the spread of civilization over the West, and in a number of States they have been pioneers. In the Civil War they were divided according to the locality in which they lived, but they fought on either one side or the other almost to a man. Constantine Conley, the father of this writer, was in the Union army, from eastern Kentucky (the Forty-fifth Regiment, Mounted Infantry). He carried a list of relatives serving in the Confederate army, for the family has been "clannish," and knowing it possible that he might find some of them prisoners or wounded on a battle-field, he hoped to assist them. And he knew that relatives in the Confederate army had lists, also, upon which his name appeared, and for a similar purpose.

John Donaldson Connelly and his twin brother, Sanford Ramey Connelly,

even a determination to go on in advance of the army which had guarded them thus far from the depredations of the Indians. This movement could not be tolerated. Lieut. Ogden with twenty-four men, (which number was afterwards increased to forty-two,) was

were born in Virginia (Fluvanna county, probably), in 1757. I have not succeeded in securing the records of the family, and cannot state positively which one of a number of brothers was their father. However, there is little doubt that it was Thomas, who, in his old age, visited Charleston, South Carolina, to look after some property or business connected with large tracts of land in South Carolina. While about this business the British threatened Charleston, and he enrolled himself in Captain Linning's company, and served under his friend and attorney, Charles Cotesworth Pinckney, in the defense of the city. Both John Donaldson Connelly and his brother, Sanford Ramey, in the Revolution, fought in the Virginia army, serving under Washington at the siege of Yorktown. Sanford Ramey Connelly married a Miss Edwards, of an old English family which came early to Virginia. Her brother Benjamin was a member of the State Convention of Maryland which ratified the National Constitution, and was a member of Congress. Another brother, John Edwards, was a member of the Virginia Convention, and afterwards Senator from Kentucky. Still another brother, Sanford Edwards, was a surgeon, and served under General Francis Marion. Miss Edwards was closely related to the families of Chief Justice Ninian Edwards, and the mother of Timothy Dwight, one of the presidents of Yale College.

John Donaldson Connelly married (in Virginia) Frances Brent, descended from Sir Robert de Brent of Cassington, Somerset, England, through William Brent, who came to Virginia, where he married the daughter of Rev. Hugh Innis. His home on the Potomac, near Acquia Creek, was burned by Lord Dunmore's troops in July, 1776. Charles Brent, son of William, married Ann Gunnell, and one of their daughters was Frances (born in 1769), who married John Donaldson Connelly. John Donaldson Connelly, his brother, Sanford Ramey, his two half-brothers, Jesse and James (Connelly), and his half-sister, Mary (Connelly), moved from Virginia to Nelson county, Kentucky, about the year 1789. Dr. Henry Connelly was among the younger of the nine children of John Donaldson Connelly and his wife Frances. He was sent to the schools of his native county, and was a good student. The education he obtained at school was completed under a teacher famous in that part of Kentucky, one James I. Dozier, a very scholarly man. Among his classmates were James Guthrie, Secretary of the Treasury under President Pierce and member of the United States Senate; and Joseph Holt, a member of President Lincoln's Cabinet; also, Dr. Ware May, who rose to the top in his profession and who married a sister of Peter H. Burnett, the first Governor of California. His brother, James Connelly, was also in his class.

Henry Connelly, his brother James, and Ware May seem to have gone directly from the school of James I. Dozier to attend at the Medical department of the Transylvania University, at Lexington, Kentucky, now the Kentucky University, and they were among the first to graduate from that department of the famous old institution. Dr. James Connelly did not leave Kentucky. Dr. Henry Connelly graduated in 1828, and he and Dr. Ware May set out for Missouri very soon after leaving school. Dr. Connelly opened an office at Liberty, Clay

dispatched to Fray Christobal, at the upper end of the Great Jornada del Muerto, with instructions from Capt. Walton, the commanding officer, to permit no portion of the caravan to pass that point until

county, but the blood of the pioneer coursed in his veins, and in the same year (1828) he joined a party under a man named Stephenson, bound for Chihuahua, Mexico.

Stephenson's party arrived at Chihuahua after many adventures with the Indians and much suffering from hunger and thirst. In that city Dr. Connelly engaged as a clerk in the store of a Mr. Powell. He was attentive to the business, mastered its details, and later bought the store from Powell. He continued in the business there for many years. He made numerous trips from Chihuahua to the Missouri river, first with pack-mules, later with wagon-trains, on which he carried back his goods. He was energetic and enterprising, and outfitted a train to go through north Texas to Fort Towson, on the Red river, in the Choctaw country. The expedition left Chihuahua April 3, 1839, and returned to that city August 27, 1840. The route passed for a considerable distance through north Texas, and in some parts of that country Dr. Connelly and his companions were the first white men known to have traversed it.

In 1843 Edward J. Glasgow, an American, closed up his business as a merchant at Mazatlan and went to Chihuahua. There he and Dr. Connelly formed a partnership to engage in the overland trade between that city and the United States, the American point being Independence, Missouri. In a letter to the author, dated Governor's Island, New York, August 13, 1906, Mr. Glasgow says:

"Dr. Connelly had already been in business several years in Chihuahua, was moderately well off and in good standing and credit as a merchant of ability, integrity and fair dealing, besides enjoying the personal friendship of many of the influential Mexicans and all of his own countrymen in that city. Our partnership continued until after the close of our war with Mexico in 1848.

"To keep up our supply of goods we made yearly expeditions across the Plains, transporting the goods in large wagons, and always at considerable risk of having our mules stampeded by thieving Indians at night.

"As I was much the younger partner, most of the traveling devolved on me, while Dr. Connelly kept the store in Chihuahua and managed the business there, and was residing there when the city was captured by Colonel Doniphan."

Prior to the formation of the partnership with Glasgow, Dr. Connelly lived for some time at Jesus Maria, a mining town near Chihuahua, where he also had an establishment. At that town he married a Spanish lady. Of that marriage three children were born: Joseph, August 23, 1838; Peter,[1] November 25, 1841;

NOTE 1.—Peter Connelly, son of Dr. Henry Connelly, late Governor of New Mexico, was born at the village of Jesus Maria, State of Chihuahua, Mexico, November 25, 1841. Was educated at the Masonic College, Lexington, Missouri (was at Lexington from 1853 to 1859). Returned to New Mexico, where he was Clerk of the Territorial Supreme Court. Married in 1868 to Miss Cornelia Davy, youngest child of Colonel Davy of Independence, Missouri. Of this marriage were born three children—Henry and Gertrude, now living, and Clarita, who died in infancy. Some years after the death of his first wife he married Miss Alice Doran, eldest child of Patrick Doran, of Wyandotte (Kansas City), Kansas, in 1877. Of the second marriage one child, Judith Wakefield, was born. He bought a large tract of land from Matthias Splitlog, a portion of which he platted into Connelly's Addition to Wyandotte. He engaged in the banking business, being connected with the Kansas City banking interests for many years. He engaged in many of the enterprises for the upbuilding of the great city at the mouth of the Kansas river. For many years last past he has lived in Kansas City, Mo.

Col. Doniphan should return from the Navajo country. This order was promptly put into execution by the lieutenant, notwithstand-

and Thomas, who died in infancy. In 1846 Dr. Connelly foresaw the war between the United States and Mexico. He took his two sons in that year and started with them to the United States. He fell in with other Americans getting out of Mexico. He met in this company an acquaintance, or at least with a gentleman, Adam Hill, of Jackson county, Missouri, in whom he placed much confidence, with whom he arranged for the care of his sons, returning himself to Chihuahua. His wife died a few years after his return. When war was declared, Dr. Connelly was at Chihuahua. He went to Santa Fé and was sent by the Governor with Captain Cooke to General Kearny, and his report as to the number and condition of the American army created a panic among the officials, and was the principal cause of the abandonment of New Mexico by Armijo. Mr. Glasgow was at that time at Independence, to bring out the annual cargo, which he did, going with Kearny and Doniphan, being made Captain of one of the two companies of traders organized by Colonel Doniphan, and entering Chihuahua with the American army. Dr. Connelly was arrested at El Paso early in December with James Magoffin while on the way to Chihuahua, but was released with the other Americans wrongfully held in confinement at Chihuahua by the Mexican authorities.

Both Dr. Connelly and Mr. Glasgow remained in Chihuahua until the close of the Mexican War. They went thence to New Mexico, where Dr. Connelly settled, and where he lived until his death. His permanent residence was at Peralta, Bernalillo (now Valencia) county. There he married Dolores Perea, widow of José Chavez, but not the man of that name who was murdered by McDaniel and his party at Chavez Creek, as some suppose, building thereon the romance of Dr. Connelly's subsequent courtship and the widow's acceptance out of gratitude for favors extended her in the troubles following the murder of her husband. The children of this marriage were Victoria, Henry, and Julian; exact dates of the birth not at hand, but they are approximately 1850, 1852, and 1854. They live in New Mexico. At the time of her marriage to Dr. Connelly, Mrs. Chavez had two children, José Francisco and Bonifacio. The last named died in the early sixties. José Francisco Chavez was a Colonel of Militia during the Civil War, and saw active service at the battle of Fort Craig and in the Canby Navajo expedition. He was Delegate in Congress from New Mexico one term, and was always active and influential in Territorial politics. He was assassinated at Las Vegas about 1904, the assassin shooting him through a window. The Perea family is one of the old, wealthy and influential families of New Mexico.

Dr. Connelly engaged in mercantile pursuits in New Mexico. He established houses at Peralta, Albuquerque, Santa Fé, and Las Vegas. These establishments, in all but his home town, were managed principally by partners. The business became the largest in New Mexico. The depression of 1857 and the general uncertainty and business demoralization immediately preceding the Civil War, in their effects, reached New Mexico. Moreover, Dr. Connelly was unfortunate in his business associates in this instance, for only two, an American at Las Vegas and a Mexican at Peralta, did not abuse the opportunity he gave to better their fortunes.

In the Civil War New Mexico was loyal to the Union, and this was due to the

ing the efforts of the English and Mexican merchants to elude his vigilance.

On the evening of the 5th, two soldiers, inmates of the same tent,

---

active influence of Dr. Connelly more than to that of all others. He saved the Territory. His long residence among the Mexican people made him familiar with their attitude towards all public matters. He knew how to appeal effectively to them. He was more widely known than any other resident of the Territory. His career had been honorable and upright, and his dealings with the people had been satisfactory in all respects. This confidence was mutual. He paid Mexican honesty this tribute: "In all my dealings with the Mexican people I lost less than five hundred dollars in bad debts." He had allied himself with the Spanish-speaking population by two marriages. He understood the people and they knew and trusted him as they did no other man. The Federal Territorial officers and the United States Army officers in the Territory had been appointed by President Buchanan. Under the influences which shaped his administration they were in open sympathy with the Southern Confederacy. They had little doubt of their ability to take the Territory over to the South. At the time of the first inauguration of President Lincoln (1861), two men practically controlled the situation in New Mexico,—Dr. Connelly and M. A. Otero, then Territorial Delegate in Congress. Otero could render his country far greater service at home than in Congress; for the same reason, Dr. Connelly did not desire the position of Delegate. President Lincoln appointed Dr. Connelly Governor and Otero Territorial Secretary. John S. Watts, a good man, and satisfactory to both Connelly and Mr. Otero, was elected Delegate to Congress. The administration of Governor Connelly was satisfactory to the people of New Mexico and to President Lincoln, and he was reappointed in 1864.

In 1862, Confederate troops from Texas invaded New Mexico. At first they were successful, the Union forces not being strong enough to resist successfully those of the enemy. Some troops were sent from Colorado to reinforce the New-Mexicans, and the Confederates were driven out, never to return.

Governor Connelly was succeeded by General R. B. Mitchell, of Kansas, soon after President Johnson's accession to office. His health had been failing for some years. He sought medical treatment in the States as early as 1863, securing relief which he believed permanent, but which proved only temporary. He died at Santa Fé in July, 1866, as hereinbefore stated.

Governor Connelly was a pioneer, the descendant of pioneers. He went out into the world to profit by the advantages offered a man of integrity and enterprise in a new country. He was to this commercial new world what Kit Carson, Frémont and others were in their spheres of action. Commerce, not the invader, is, after all, the conqueror. Governor Connelly was a gentleman of refinement and intelligence, honorable and upright in all the relations of life. He knew the people of New Mexico as no other American knew them, and largely through his influence they resigned themselves to their fate as a conquered people, and have become as patriotic American citizens as can be found in the Republic. His services to his country will at some time be more adequately treated in connection with the Kentuckians in the development of the West with special reference to New Mexico. The historian will have for his inspiration the brilliant deeds of Doniphan, Blair, Carson, Hughes, and many others, and as high as any name he finds will he write that of Henry Connelly.

their names J. D. Lard and B. W. Marsh, entered into a quarrel as they stood about their camp fires. At length the parties becoming somewhat excited, and mutually dealing upon each other an assortment of abusive epithets, the latter drew out his pistol and shot the former through the breast. Mr. Lard, after several days, was removed to Socorro, where he survived but a short time.[66]

This detachment, while it remained at the Valverde camp-grounds, lost seventeen mules, eight hundred and seventy-three sheep, a great number of horses and cattle, and six brave men, three of whom died of cold and through distress of their situation, and three in the manner above related. The various detachments which had been in the country of the Navajos arrived in camp at Valverde about the 12th of December.

NOTE 66.—Marsh was 4th Corporal of Company C, and Lard was a private in the same company. Lard was a man of domineering disposition, but a good citizen and an excellent soldier. He found Marsh standing about the camp-fire of some of the Lafayette company; both belonged to the same mess, and it being the turn of Marsh to cook dinner, Lard ordered him to go to his own camp and immediately cook the dinner. As Marsh did not seem disposed to obey at once, Lard kicked him and forced him to go. Marsh felt himself outraged, and, fearing another attack, buckled on his pistol. When Lard saw the pistol he asked Marsh what he expected to do with it. Marsh replied that he intended to defend himself if further molested. Lard was a man of great physical strength; he caught Marsh and demanded the pistol, saying, "Give me that pistol or I will put you in the fire." Marsh believed Lard would carry out his threat, and knowing that Lard was strong enough to put him in the fire, he drew his pistol and shot Lard. Lard lived two weeks, and acknowledged that he had been in the wrong; he requested that nothing be done with Marsh for the shooting.

CHAPTER IX.

Colonel Jackson's detachment—Don Chavez—Another war Dance—Cebolleta—Jackson's Mission—Capt. Reid's Expedition—Navajo Dance—Narbona—Capt. Reid's Letter—Return of the Party—Habits of the Navajos—Their Wealth—Horses stolen by the Navajos—Their recovery.

Lieutenant-colonel Jackson, with a detachment of three companies, under command of Capts. Reid, Parsons, and Hughes,* as already stated left Santa Fé on the 18th of September, and proceeded to Cebolleta, on the river Puerco, to keep the Indians in subordination in that part of the State, and there to await further orders. Their first march was from Santa Fé to Del Gardo, more than twenty miles, where they remained in camp two days, during which time they repaired their wagons, harness, saddle trappings, tents, clothes, collected their stock together, packed up their baggage, and did whatever else seemed to demand their attention.

From thence, on the next day, all things being made ready, and the soldiers having taken their breakfast, they commenced the march, and during this and four other days completed nearly one hundred miles, arriving at the Laguna fork of the river Puerco. This march led through Algodones, Bernalillo, Sandia, Albuquerque, where, crossing the river, it was continued through Pajarrito and other villages, thence striking off westerly to the Puerco. On the morning of the 27th, about fifty Pueblo Indians, with their arms in their hands, visited the camp, and informed Lieutenant-colonel Jackson that all the Pueblos from San Domingo to Isleta, many hundred in number, were on their way to Cebolleta to make war upon the Navajos in conjunction with him, insisting that Gen. Kearny had granted them permission to retake their stolen animals, and recover their people from captivity, great numbers of whom were in the hands of the Navajos. But as Col. Jackson was rather on a mission of peace than war, he accordingly ordered the Pueblos to return peaceably to their homes until their services should be required. To this they reluctantly consented.

On the hills and spurs of the mountains near the camp, were

* Hughes was chosen captain after the detachment arrived at Cebolleta, Lieut. De Courcy being in command for the present.—HUGHES.

large quantities of petrified timber. In some places entire trunks of trees, the remains of an extinct forest, were discovered, intermixed with the débris on the steep declivities and in the recesses of the craggy mountains. While at this camp, Don Chavez, a wealthy proprietor of the Laguna Pueblo, well disposed towards the Americans, came and made an offer of all his possessions, such as sheep, goats, cattle, and other stock to the commander, that his men might not be in want of provisions. The commander, however, accepted only so much of this generous tender as was sufficient to relieve his present necessities. Being requested, Don Chavez promised to use his endeavors to induce Sandoval, a chief of one branch or canton of the Navajo tribe, to bring his warriors into Cebolleta, and there conclude a treaty of friendship with the Americans. In this he partially succeeded.

After a short march on the 28th, this detachment encamped before Laguna, a rich pueblo, containing 2,000 inhabitants. Here the men procured such provisions as they were most in need of; the inhabitants supplying a market wherein they might purchase. Pigs, chickens, bread, cheese, molasses, and other things were brought to them. At this place the men witnessed another grand war dance around the scalps of four Navajo warriors, reared upon four lances, as at Isleta. It appeared that a party of Navajos, about the 24th, had made a sudden incursion from the mountains, plundering some of the houses in the suburbs of Laguna, and driving off large flocks of sheep from the neighboring plains and valleys. The Pueblos collected together and pursued them; finally overtaking them, killing four of the party and recovering a portion of the stock. This feast and war dance, which continued without intermission for fifteen hours, were meant to celebrate the achievement.

The next day the march was continued up the river, near the margin of which the soldiers encamped and spent the night. Here an amiable young man, by name Gwyn, died and was buried. On the 30th the detachment marched over and pitched camp near to Cebolleta. This place became the headquarters of the detachment, whence various smaller parties of men were sent to the hill-country and mountains, to put an end to the unjust exactions and contributions, (such as loss of life and property,) which the Navajos were perpetually levying upon the frontier Mexican and Pueblo villages.

The difficult nature of this enterprise, to the conduct of which Lieutenant-colonel Jackson was appointed, will more plainly appear when it is considered that his mission was of a two-fold character. He was first instructed by Gen. Kearny to negociate a triple league of peace between three powers, the Navajos, Mexicans and Pueblos, who dwell in New Mexico, and the Americans. The novel spectacle is here presented of the Navajo nation being required, first, to treat with the New Mexicans and Pueblos, their perpetual and implacable enemies; to bind themselves by articles of agreement to abstain from war; to bury their mutual hatred towards each other, and become friends for the future; and second, to treat with the Americans, of whom, perhaps, they had never before heard, and of whom they knew nothing, save that they were the conquerors of the New Mexicans, (for what causes they could not conceive) and might soon be their own conquerors, as they were now on the confines of the Navajo country, proposing terms of treaty with arms in their hands. The Navajos were willing to treat the Americans with friendship, and even to negotiate a permanent peace with them; but they were unable to comprehend the propriety and policy of entering into a league by which they would be compelled to surrender up the captives and property, which they had taken from the New Mexicans and Pueblos by valor in various wars, nor could they understand what right the Americans, "armed ministers of peace," had to impose upon them such conditions. Neither were they able to conceive why it was that the New Mexicans, since they were conquered, had been advanced to the condition of American citizens, so that an injury done to those people, should now be resented by the Americans, as though it were done them.

And secondly, if he could not effect these amicable arrangements with the Navajos, he was instructed to prosecute against them a hostile campaign. Hence, all the arts of diplomacy as well as those of war, were required to settle these questions involving the interests of three separate powers.

It was from this place that Sandoval, a noted chief of one of the Navajo[67] cantons, who had a friendly intercourse with the New Mexi-

---

Note 67.—The Navajo Indians belong to the Athabascan linguistic family of North-American Indians, and are closely related to the Apaches, of the same family. Since becoming known to the white man they have been more settled

cans on the frontier, was dispatched by Lieutenant-colonel Jackson, to see the principal men of his tribe, and ascertain if they were of a disposition to make an amicable arrangement of existing differences. Sandoval, after an absence of about two weeks, returned and reported "that he had seen all the head men of his nation, and that they were chiefly disposed for peace; but that they were unwilling to trust themselves among the New Mexicans, unless they should be furnished with an escort of "white men" whose protection would ensure their safety. And further, that before coming into the American camp, they wished to see some of the white men among them, that they might talk with them and learn what they desired. Sandoval further reported, "that the principal habitations or rather haunts of the Navajos, were two hundred miles west from Cebolleta, in the neighborhood of the great Tcheusca mountain, the grand dividing ridge between the Atlantic and Pacific waters, and upon the borders of the noted Laguna Colorado or Red Lake. This beautiful, romantic sheet of water, is near the western base of the Tcheusca ridge of the Cordilleras. It is fed by springs issuing from the base of the great mountain. In a lovely recess of this great mountain, and in sight of the fairy lake, is a spacious semicircular amphitheatre, sculptured by the hand of nature in the side of the solid masses of rock. It faces the south-westward. At each corner of this crescent temple of nature, and isolated from the main mountain, stands a mighty, colossal column of red sandstone, horizontally striped with violet and blue veins, towering to the height of three hundred feet. They are more than thirty feet in circumference, and as regular and smooth as if they had been polished by the chisel of some master sculptor.

Upon the representation of Sandoval, Capt. Reid applied to Lieutenant-colonel Jackson to permit him, with a small body of troops,

in their habits than the Apaches. Their country was between the Rio Grande and the Rio Colorado, perhaps not reaching either stream, but lying on the watershed and the valleys on each side. They became lovers of the domestic animals introduced by the Spaniards, especially the horse and the sheep, and accumulated large numbers of each. They were generally at war with the people of Mexico, often raiding their settlements and murdering the inhabitants; and they drove away many mules, horses and sheep every year. In their raids they rarely met with any resistance. They now live on the Navajo reservation, in the northwestern part of New Mexico, and number nearly two thousand.

to make an excursion into the country, and learn more certainly whether the Navajos were disposed for peace or war. In order to allay their suspicions and inspire them with confidence in the good intentions of the Americans, he thought it best to take only a few men. Accordingly, about the 20th of October, Capt. Reid with thirty men, who gallantly volunteered their services (ten from each of the companies present,) accompanied and aided by lieutenants DeCourcy and Wells, set out upon this hazardous enterprise, taking with him three mules packed with provisions, this being all that the scarcity of the camp would allow at that time, expecting to be gone about fifteen days. The New Mexicans were amazed at the temerity of Capt. Reid's proceeding. To enter the country of this powerful and warlike nation, which had for a series of years robbed and plundered their country with impunity, with less than an army, was considered by them as certain destruction. Sandoval, whose geographical knowledge of the country was extensive and minute, was taken as a guide; for no other could be procured. Some suspected that he would lead the party into an ambuscade, the more effectually to ingratiate himself into favor with his people. But he proved faithful. Besides, the New Mexicans have but a very limited knowledge of that mountain country, never departing far from their settlements, through fear of the Indians. Nor would a Mexican, though his knowledge of the country were ever so accurate, feel himself safe to accompany so small a number of men on so hazardous an enterprise. This party, in its march, surmounted difficulties of the most appalling nature. It passed over craggy mountains of stupendous height, winding its way up the steep and rugged acclivities, each man leading his horse among the slabs and fragments of great rocks which lay in confused masses along the sides of the mountains, having crumbled from some summit still above, obstructing the pass-way. Precipices and yawning chasms, fearful to behold, often left but a narrow passage, where a blunder either to the right or left would precipitate horse and man hundreds of feet below, among the jagged and pointed rocks. Indeed this party ascended and descended mountains, where, at first view, every attempt would seem fruitless and vain, and where the giddy heights and towering masses of granite seem to bid defiance to the puny efforts of man. Until SUCCESS showed what RESOLUTION could accomplish, these things were pronounced utterly impossible. But the energy of the Anglo-Saxons knows no bounds.

The ease with which these few hardy and adventurous men appeared to obviate the difficulties, and surmount the obstacles which impeded their progress, and which seemed, until essayed, incredible of performance, afforded convincing argument that, in the affairs of men, to RESOLVE IS TO CONQUER; and that *men*, at least AMERICANS, can accomplish whatever is within the scope of possibility. Having traveled five days with little or no intermission, through the gorges and fissures of the mountains, and over hills intersected by numerous ravines, with steep and almost impassable banks, they pitched camp near a moderate supply of wood, water and grass, in a narrow vale formed by projecting spurs of dark basalt and pudding stone, terminating in a succession of rocky ridges. Here they determined to remain a short time, that they might obtain a little rest and refreshment. Here also they met a few of Sandoval's people, who upon being assured that the Americans meant them no harm, returned with confidence to their several homes near camp. From thence having proceeded a short distance, they met with an advance party of about forty Navajo warriors, having with them a few women; an infallible sign of friendly intention. At first they were afraid. Hereupon Capt. Reid, leaving his men in the valley, and taking with him Sandoval, his interpreter and guide, rode to the top of the hill upon which they stood, stopped, and saluted them in a kind manner. After a few friendly signs and some conversation, Sandoval being interpreter, gaining confidence they approached the captain, rode down with him to the place where the men were pitching camp, and passed the night together, the utmost confidence seeming mutually to prevail. Presents were interchanged and conversation was commenced as they sat around their camp-fires. The night passed off most amicably.

The next morning, at the instance of the Indians, the party moved on again, having obtained from them this information: "That there was to be a grand collection of the young men and women of the Navajo tribe, at a place thirty miles further into the country, where some event was to be celebrated by much feasting and dancing." They expressed much solicitude that the captain and his men should be their guests on that occasion, adding, "that most of their people had never seen a WHITE MAN; but, having heard much of the power and wisdom of the Americans, and of the progress of the army in New Mexico, were very anxious to see and entertain them." This proposal according with the views of the captain and his brave comrades, whose object was to see as many of the tribes as possible, that whatever impression they made might be general, they agreed to attend. They set out.

When they arrived at the place designated, they found no less than five hundred men and women already congregated. Whether these Indians meant to deceive, and lead these few men into an ambuscade, and thereby treacherously entrap and put them to death, was uncertain. However, they resolved to proceed, and use the utmost vigilance, and if such an attempt should be made, also to use their *arms* to the best advantage. Seeing which, the Indians received them with the greatest professions of friendship, and kindly made them presents of some excellent sheep, and other meats, which were very acceptable, as the captain was now destitute. They pitched camp, which was no sooner done, than it was surrounded and filled by Indians, eagerly gratifying their curiosity. The "white men" were amongst them. To have kept these "sons of the forest" at a distance by guards, would have appeared but safe and prudent, yet it would have thwarted the purpose of the visit, which was to secure their friendship. To have showed any thing like suspicion, would have been insulting to their pride, and wounding to their feelings. It was therefore, perhaps, safer to risk the chances of treachery, than to use caution which would serve but to provoke. The feasting and dancing continued through the night, during which the captain and his men, at intervals, mixing in the crowd, participated in the festivities and amusements of the occasion, to the infinite satisfaction of their rude but hospitable entertainers. The scene was truly romantic. Contemplate five hundred dancers in the hollow recesses of the mountains, with the music of shells and timbrels, giving way to the most extravagant joy, and a band of thirty Americans, armed cap-a-pie with martial accoutrements, mingling in the throng! This was the 27th day of October.

The next morning, the captain proposed a "grand talk," but was told by the Indians "that none of the head chiefs or men of council were present; that there were *no* Navajos there;" (using the Mexican phrase, "*pocos, pocos,*" signifying very few,) but at the same time intimating, that by one day's march further into the country, they would see *muchos*, (very many,) and amongst them the old men of the nation, who, they said, had great knowledge and great experience.

Though this party was small, far from succor, scant of provisions, and in a country without supplies, except such as the Indians possessed, it was nevertheless voted to go on, and accomplish the original objects of the excursion. The captain suggested the condition of his commissary stores to his red friends, who assured him that there were numerous flocks of goats, sheep and cattle further in the mountains; and that, if he chose to accompany them he should be abundantly supplied. They started.

A march of thirty miles over the great dividing ridge of the Cordilleras, brought them to the waters of the Pacific, and into the very heart of the country occupied by the Navajos, the most powerful and civilized tribe in the west. This day's march led them through fissures, chasms, and cañons in the mountains, whose tops were capped with perpetual snow. Capt. Reid, in a letter to the author, thus describes the perils that surrounded him at this time:

"This was the most critical situation in which I ever found myself placed;—with only thirty men, in the very centre of a people the most savage and proverbially treacherous of any on the continent. Many of them were not very friendly. Being completely in their power, we, of course, had to play the game to the best advantage. As there was no pasturage near the camp, we had to send our horses out. Our numbers were too few to divide, or even all together to think of protecting the horses, if the Indians were disposed to take them. So I even made a virtue of necessity; and putting great confidence in the honesty of their intentions, I gave my horses in charge of one of the chiefs of these notorious horse stealers. He took them out some five miles to graze, and we, after taking supper, again joined in the dance, which was kept up until next morning. Our men happened to take the right course to please the Indians, participating in all their sports, and exchanging liveries with them. They seemed to be equally delighted to see themselves clothed in the vesture obtained from us, and to see our men adopting their costume. The emboldened confidence and freedom with which we mixed among them, seemed to win upon their feelings and make them disposed to grant whatever we asked. They taxed their powers of performance in all their games, to amuse us, and make the time pass agreeably, notwithstanding our imminently precarious situation.

"We had not arrived at the place of our camp before we were met by all the head men of the nation. The chief of all, NARBONA, being very sick, was nevertheless mounted on horseback, and brought in. He slept in my camp all night. Narbona, who was probably seventy years old, being held in great reverence by his tribe for the war-like exploits of his youth and manhood, was now a mere skeleton of a man, being completely prostrated by rheumatism, the only disease, though a very common one, in this country. Conformably to a custom of the chief men of his tribe, he wore his finger nails very long, probably one and a half inches—formidable weapons! He appeared to be a mild, amiable man, and though he had been a warrior himself, was very anxious before his death to secure for his people a peace with all their old enemies, as well as with us, the 'New Men,' as he called us.

"Upon the evening after our arrival we held a grand talk, in which all the old men participated. Most of them seemed disposed for peace, but some opposed it as being contrary to the honor of the Navajos, as well as their interest, to make peace with the Mexicans; though they were willing to do so with us. The peace party, however, prevailed, and by fair words and promises of protection, I succeeded in obtaining a promise from the principal men, that they would overtake me at the Agua Fria, a place some forty miles from Jackson's camp, from whence we would go together to Santa Fé and conclude the final treaty.* The night passed off in a variety of diversions, and in the morning, notwithstanding the most urgent desire on the part of our entertainers that we would stay, I thought it prudent to return, as we were running short of provision. Our horses were forthcoming without a single exception, and as soon as we caught them, we turned our faces towards camp.

"Although this expedition was one of much hazard, yet it turned out to be one of much pleasurable excitement, and attended with no loss or harm. The country through which we travelled is amongst the finest portions of Mexico;—decidedly the best for the growth of stock, and presenting more interest and variety in its features than any over which I travelled. It is, however, very destitute of water, so much so, as to make it dangerous for those who travel without a guide. On this account, more than by its mountain fastnesses, it is impregnable to invasion. The people who inhabit it, and who were the object of our visit, are in many respects singular and unlike any other of the aboriginal inhabitants of this continent.

---

* Capt. Reid at this time was not apprised of the fact that Col. Doniphan, who was invested with full powers to conclude a treaty of peace with the Navajos, had taken his departure from Santa Fé.—HUGHES.

Their habits are very similar to those of the Tartars. They are entirely a pastoral people, their flocks constituting their sole wealth. But little addicted to the chase, and never indulging in it, except when the game may be taken on horseback. Their weapons of war are the spear or lance, the bow, and the lazo, in the use of all which they are not excelled. They may be said literally to live on horseback. Of these animals they possess immense droves, and of a stock originally the same with the Mexican horse, yet wonderfully improved. They pay great attention to the breeding of their horses, and think scarcely less of them than do the Arabians. They also possess many mules, but these are generally the proceeds of their marauding expeditions against the Mexicans. Indeed the whole of New Mexico is subject to the devastating incursions of these lords of the mountains. Of this, however, you know as well as I."[68]

NOTE 68.—I have talked with Meredith T. Moore about this expedition. Moore was a member of it. I give here an account written from what Mr. Moore

NARBONA.

From "Reconnoissances of Routes from San Antonio to El Paso," etc.

has told me. The force of the expedition consisted of thirty men, ten from each of Companies F, D, and G. It was commanded by Captain Reid. Among the

The evening after the captain and his party left the grand camp of the Navajos, on their return to Cebolleta, as an evidence of the sincerity of their professions, they dispatched a runner to the Ameri-

men detailed from Moore's company were himself, Ab. Hughes, Joseph Yount, Nathan Walmsley, Berrymen Lack, and Lieut. R. A. Wells; Wells acted as First Lieutenant of the expedition. The commissary officer was Lieut. De Courcy, and the commissary train consisted of a few pack-mules. Sandoval, the guide, was a man of fine appearance. He was a "medicine man" as well as chief, and on the march would retire to a secluded place, where he performed his ceremonies, usually for an hour or more, to ascertain the locality of enemies that might be encountered, should any be abroad. He also made "smokes" and other signals to discover whether any of his own people were near, and if so, to invite them to camp. The expedition marched more than a week west from Cebolleta, and some of the men became suspicious of Sandoval, who assured the officers from day to day that they would reach the end of the journey "to-morrow." Sandoval said there were twelve tribes, bands, or clans of the Navajos. Moore thinks the expedition reached its objective point on the thirteenth day of the march. It was a great council-ground of the Navajos, in a valley on a high plateau. The councils were held near an immense cottonwood tree which grew in the valley, the only tree Moore saw in the vicinity. There was the bed of a stream on the plateau, but Moore saw no water in it. The plateau was covered with dead grass two feet high. Under the great cottonwood there was a spring of fine water, which furnished water sufficient for men and Indians and their horses without showing any diminution; a small stream ran from the spring, but was soon lost in the sandy soil. Thousand of sheep were in sight upon the plateau, some flocks black and others white, the Navajos keeping black sheep in separate flocks; Moore saw one flock of black sheep of more than five thousand animals. There were no buildings nor signs of permanent habitation on the plateau. Narbona claimed to be one hundred years old, but was not that by fifteen or twenty years, in Moore's judgment. He claimed to have been a great traveler, saying that he had seen salt water and ships, and this gave him prestige with his people. He was helpless from rheumatism, and was carried about on a litter made for the purpose, of willow boughs. His finger-nails were two or three inches in length. His wife was a little squaw fifty or sixty years of age, apparently, and dried and wrinkled, but very active and intelligent. Narbona had by this wife a son, an Indian of fine appearance and strong character, and next in power to his father. Hundreds of women came in on horseback, but Narbona's wife was the only woman permitted to be present at the council. Moore was told by the interpreter, a Mexican who had been a captive to the Navajos many years, that the wife of the head chief had a right to be present at any council, but all other women were prohibited from attending.

Upon the arrival of the expedition the Navajos took the horses of the Americans to a place where grass could be found, which was some distance away and unknown to the officers or men. Some of the men believed this was giving the Indians too great an advantage, for they did not see their horses again until the expedition was ready to return.

As soon as an interview could be had with Narbona he sent runners in every direction to summon the chiefs and warriors to council. These responded at

cans, to warn them to take care of their horses, for that some of their young men were ill disposed toward them, and might pursue them with the view of capturing their stock. They, however, effected once and began to assemble in large numbers, and by the third day thousands were on the plateau. They feasted on mutton, a liberal supply of which was given to the Americans. The council was held the third day after the arrival of the Americans. Narbona was borne to his place in the center of the assembly upon his mat, lying on the flat of his back. The chiefs and warriors arranged themselves about him in the order of their rank or importance in the nation. The guns of the Americans were stacked just outside the circle of councilors, and the men stood together near them. Captain Reid stated the desire of the Americans to hold a treaty with the Navajos, and requested that a general council for the purpose be convened at Zuñi to meet Col. Doniphan and other officers to enter into a general treaty. The council had been in session about an hour when the Captain concluded his address. At this point Narbona's wife arose and addressed the Navajos. She was agile, sprightly, and cunning. She opposed any council with the Americans. She proved herself an eloquent speaker, possessed of those oratorical qualities which convince and sway men. She said the white men were treacherous. She believed the Navajo chiefs and warriors who should attend the treaty would be slain. She cited in proof the murder of Jean José, chief of the Apaches, and his party, in 1837, by the Americans and Mexicans commanded by James Johnson. At this point in her address or harangue the warriors began to applaud. As she proceeded they raised a great outcry and ran to arms. A crisis was at hand. It looked as though the heroic little band of Americans would be massacred at once. Captain Reid did not move, but turning his head slightly he said to Moore, who was standing just behind him, "Tell the men to stand close to their guns." Moore delivered the order. No man expected to escape, but there was no excitement. They took their places about the stacked arms ready to grasp their guns at a moment's notice, determined to fight to the death. When the storm was about to break, Narbona tapped three times on the mat with his long nails. His son stooped to hear his commands. In a moment he rose up and spoke in a low voice to a chief at his side. Then they deliberately seized the squaw, one by each arm, and escorted her from the council-grounds; and she did not appear again. Instantly the clamor was hushed, the warriors silent. Moore says he never before witnessed a change so complete and sudden. The chiefs had shown no excitement; not a countenance changed in the whole group; the commands of Narbona and his son were given in voices so low that no one else knew what was said. The deliberations were resumed, and it was soon decided that the Navajos would meet the Americans at Zuñi to conclude a peace.

The Americans returned to Covero, or Cuvarro, as it was then written. Before starting on the expedition Moore had changed horses with T. W. Mahan. Moore's was much the better horse, but it had seen hard service and was worn down; Mahan had not been called upon for so much service, and his horse was in good condition. When the Navajos returned the horses of the Americans, that of Moore was thin and weak. At first Moore was at a loss to account for this, but he concluded that the Indians had been running his horse against their ponies, and had literally "run his horse to death." The horse broke down and

their return to Jackson's encampment without any serious molestation, or any considerable difficulty. The chiefs started according to promise, to overtake the captain at Agua Fria, but were induced to turn back by a miscreant Navajo, who assured them, that, if they

had to be abandoned two or three days before the detachment reached Covero, and the remainder of the way Moore "footed it." About the time Moore lost his horse a severe "norther" came on, and the men suffered much. William Stearns of Company G was so chilled that he could not ride, and on the afternoon of the day Covero was reached he was abandoned. When Joseph Yount discovered that Moore was not with the detachment he rode back in search of him, and Moore and Yount came upon Stearns; Stearns insisted that he could go no farther and must die. Moore urged him to make an effort to get to camp, but he would not do so, and wished Moore to take his mule, a very fine one, and go on and leave him to his fate. The men were starving, and while talking to Stearns they discovered smoke drifting above the trees at the foot of a mountain. Hoping to find food at the lodge of some Mexican or Indian, Moore and Yount went to where they had seen the smoke, and at the base of a range, in the mouth of a cañon, they found a cabin inhabited by an old Indian and his wife. They entered, and were given meat, which they ate after broiling it over the fire. This meat was taken from a bundle suspended from a pole of the wigwam, and while eating it Yount was closely scrutinizing the receptacle from which it had been taken, and finally he asked Moore if he knew what kind of meat they were eating. Moore replied that he did not know, but that to a starving man it tasted all right. "I know," said Yount. "What kind?" queried Moore as he fell to work on another slice just from the blaze. "Cogburn's old mare; I have just recognized her old sorrel hide hanging there with her flesh stored in it," said Yount. And sure enough, there hung her hide; but hunger allowed no squeamish freaks of appetite; though Moore ate little after the discovery, Yount only laughed, and continued to eat. Green B. Cogburn's mare had died from hard riding and starvation before the expedition left camp on the outward march, and these Indians had appropriated the carcass to take them through the winter. Moore and Yount took some of the meat with them, and broiled a piece for Stearns, but he could not eat. They put him on his mule and walked one on each side to support him; and in this way took him to Covero, where, in a day or two, he died and was buried.

Moore thinks the expedition made a wonderful trip, in which he is evidently correct. His recollections of it are vivid. They crossed mountains almost perpendicular, wound through cañons so deep and narrow that the sky could scarcely be seen from the bottom; made their way along narrow ridges of the snow-covered ranges, down precipitous steeps made treacherous by drifts of loose moving stones, and across valleys of shifting sand. Several parties of Indians, all Navajos, were encountered on the trip, with some of whom they danced and feasted. More than once they believed themselves lost, but never a cheek blanched nor a heart quailed. Sandoval proved a true friend, resourceful and of sound judgment. The full measure of the danger encountered was not realized by the men at the time, but the longer they reflected upon the trip the more wonderful did it become that any returned to tell the tale.

ventured to Santa Fé, they would all be killed. Having had so many evidences of the bad faith of the Mexicans, they were naturally suspicious, and therefore abandoned their purpose.

Thus terminated this most extraordinary adventure among the Navajos, which in point of excitement, interest, novelty and hazard, was equal, if not superior, to any enterprise connected with the Navajo expedition. Though this excursion was not productive of any immediate beneficial results, yet it was not without its more remote effects upon the people visited, in making up their estimate of the enterprise and good faith of the Americans. Both the captain and the men whom he led, were as gallant as ever drew steel. The party arrived safely at Cebolleta after an absence of twenty days.

Whilst Capt. Reid was on this excursion, a band of renegade Navajos came into the neighborhood of Cebolleta, and succeeded in driving off most of the stock, both mules and horses, belonging to the detachment under Lieutenant-colonel Jackson; for the recovery of which, Captain Parsons and Lieut. Jackson, with sixty men, were sent out in pursuit of them. After much difficulty, they finally succeeded in recovering a portion of them, and returned to camp about the same time with Capt. Reid. The remaining portion was recovered by Major Gilpin.

CHAPTER X.

Major Gilpin and the Yutas—His march against the Navajos—His passage over the Cordilleras—Express to Col. Doniphan—The San Juan—Passage over the Tunicha mountains—Deep Snows—Major Gilpin departs for the Ojo Oso—Col. Doniphan passes the Sierra Madre—Immense Snow Storm—Arrival at the Bear Spring—Doniphan's Speech to the Navajos—Their Chief's reply—Treaty concluded.

It has been related that, on the 18th of September, Major Gilpin, in command of two companies under Capts. Waldo and Stephenson, amounting in all to about one hundred and eighty men, left Santa Fé in obedience to an order from Gen. Kearny, and proceeded forthwith to the neighborhood of Abiquiu, on the Rio de Chama, to preserve order and quiet among the border tribes. It was not anticipated that this force would be required to penetrate further into the mountainous regions of the west, than its present encampment at Abiquiu, from whence it was expected that various small parties would make short excursions into the surrounding country, to clear it of marauders and depredators; the Navajo expedition being subsequently conceived and projected.

Most of the men composing this detachment, had not received their commutation for clothing, nor had any of them received any portion of the pay which had long been due them; they would therefore soon be in want of means of protecting themselves against the inclemency of the approaching winter. With troops thus poorly provided, a few baggage wagons, and a scanty supply of provisions, Major Gilpin arrived at the Chama about the 25th of the same month. Leaving the greater part of his men in this vicinity, he proceeded with a party of eighty-five men about one hundred miles above the valley of Taos, amongst the Yutas, a fierce and numerous tribe of Indians, with the view to conciliate them and dispose them to a friendly intercourse with the Americans. Having in an incredibly short space of time collected together about sixty of their principal men, he returned with them to Santa Fé, where they entered into treaty stipulations with Colonel Doniphan on the 13th of October.

After a short stay at the capital, Major Gilpin returned to his encampment at Abiquiu, where he remained in faithful discharge of the duties assigned him until he received orders to march against the Navajos. While in this quarter he preserved the utmost tranquillity amongst the Mexicans, Pueblos and Yutas, supplied his men with provisions from the adjacent country and villages, procured pack-mules, sumpter-horses for the Navajo campaign, and sent his provision and baggage wagons from Abiquiu to Santa Fé, that he might not be embarrassed by these things in his intended expedition across the mountains.

On the 22d of November, Major Gilpin, acting under instructions from Col. Doniphan, left his encampment on the Chama, and commenced his march against the Navajo Indians, completing in six days more than one hundred miles, having followed the Rio de Chama to its source in the snowy regions, transcending the elevated range of mountains which separate the waters of the two great oceans of the world, and descending into the valley of the San Juan, a branch of the western Colorado.[69]

Major Gilpin was accompanied by about sixty-five Mexican and Pueblo Indian allies, under command of a lieutenant.* The perils, hardships and sufferings of this march were almost incredible, yet they were encountered and endured by the men with Roman fortitude. The rugged ways, the precipitous mountains, the dangerous defiles, the narrow passes, the yawning chasms and fissures in vitreous, volcanic remains, and the giant fragments of rocks, which obstructed their passage, rendered the march arduous beyond the power of language to describe. The passage of the Carthaginian general over the Apennines, and his sudden descent upon the plains of Italy, attracted the admiration of all Europe. The march of Bonaparte and McDonough over the snow-capt peaks of the Alps, astonished the world. Major Gilpin's march over the grander and loftier summits

* This allied force consisted of twenty Taos Mexicans, commanded by Lieut. Vigil; twenty Pueblos under Tomas; and twenty-five *peones* in charge of the pack-mules. Santiago Conklin was Major Gilpin's Mexican, and Angel Chavez, his Navajo intrepreter. Ignacio Salezar, and Benezate Vilandi were his guides.—HUGHES.

NOTE 69.—It has been found impossible, so far, to identify the routes of Reid, Gilpin, and Doniphan, in their marches into the Indian country, with the modern geography of that region. So far, I know of no effort to do so by going over the routes and tracing them out. Until something of this nature is done, or the diaries (if any were kept) of soldiers on the marches can be found and published, no satisfactory identification can be made. The general routes are better described in the text than in any other account I have found.

of the Cordilleras, eternally crowned with snow, was certainly an achievement not less arduous or perilous.

On the evening of the 7th so much snow fell that it was with the utmost difficulty the men and animals could make their way among the mountain passes. In many places the snow had slid down from the peaks, as an avalanche, until it had accumulated many feet, and even fathoms, deep. This day some Indians were seen upon the eminences at a distance, watching the movements of our men. They were pursued, but without success. On the next day they appeared in like manner, but in greater numbers. They were again pursued hotly; but they were so active, and could escape with so much facility into their mountain fastnesses, that it was not possible to capture them. On the 9th the Indians appeared in considerable numbers, as before, upon the distant eminences. By the display of friendly signals they were induced to come into camp. They reported that they had seen some of the American forces and.formed a treaty with them. These were no doubt the same whom Capt. Reid had previously visited. Upon this information Major Gilpin sent one of them to bear an express to Colonel Doniphan, then on his way into the Navajo country, assuring them that no hostilities would be commenced until the messenger's return. Meanwhile the rest of the Indians remained quietly about camp, or followed the line of march.

The next two days the detachment traveled down the San Juan forty miles or more, meandering the stream, and encamping on its margin, for water and pasturage. This beautiful, fresh, mountain stream, whose limpid waters reveal the very pebbles and brilliant sands upon the bottom, and the fishes which sport in its waves, is about fifty yards wide, and was everywhere filled with Indians, watering their numerous herds of horses, sheep and other animals. From this cause the pasturage was greatly exhausted near the river, but was more abundant further out into the mountains. The three following days the march was continued towards the Tunicha mountains, whose bleak colossal summits tower magnificently above the clouds, and are plainly visible from the San Juan, a distance of seventy-five miles. This part of the march was over barren sandy plains and immense fields of gypsum, covered with pebbles worn smooth by attrition, which rendered the travel extremely laborious, the whole way being entirely destitute of either wood or grass, and only supplied with water which is both bitter to the taste and nauseating to the stomach.

On the 15th the march was commenced over the Tunicha ridge, the grandest of mountains, consisting of huge masses of granite piled on granite, until their summits penetrate far into the regions of clouds and perennial snows. The ascent was long and arduous. The men leading their horses and wading in the snow, were compelled to carry their arms, and thread their way amongst the huge slabs of granite and basalt which had crumbled from above, and lay in confused masses along the rugged ascent. Many animals were left and perished by the way. Some of them, by a misstep, tumbled headlong over the precipices, and fell hundreds of feet below. It was useless of course to look into the abysses whither they had fallen; for they were either dashed to pieces on the rocks, or buried in fathoms of accumulated snow. This day the Indian express-bearer returned to Major Gilpin, bringing orders from Col. Doniphan for him to be at Bear Spring on the 20th, stating that he would endeavor to meet him there, requesting him to bring into that place all the Navajo chiefs he could find.

The snow was now deep, and the weather excessively cold. The fierce winds whistled along the ragged granite hills and peaks. The prospect was horrid. Half of the animals had given out and were abandoned. Thus were these men situated—half of them on foot, carrying their arms, stinted in provisions, destitute of shoes and clothing, and their way barricaded by eternal rocks and snow. Sometimes when they lay down at night, wrapt in their blankets and the skins of wild beasts, before morning they would be completely enveloped in a new crop of snow, and they would rise at day-dawn with benumbed limbs and bristling icicles frozen to their hair and long whiskers. They persevered. This night's encampment was on the bare summit of the Tunicha mountain, where there was neither comfort for the men, nor food, nor water for the horses. The desolateness of the place was dreadful. The descent on the 16th was even more terrible than the ascent had been the previous day. The men had to walk, as it was impossible to ride down the precipitous crags and spurs of the mountain. The packs would sometimes slide forward on the mules, and tumble them down the rugged way. The crevices between the rocks were filled with driven snow, many fathoms deep, so that man and horse would often plunge into these through mistake, from whence it was difficult, without assistance, to extricate themselves. Having accomplished the descent at sunset, the men built their camp-fires (for they had no tents) on a brook issuing from a cleft in the mountain's side, where they found wood, water, and grass. Here they enjoyed the advantage of a little rest.

The next day the march was continued through lovely valleys and handsome upland, the snow falling excessively all day. The snow had now accumulated in such quantities that it was toilsome to advance at all. This night they staid at a place called *Cañon de Trigo*, where the Navajos cultivate considerable quantities of wheat, and other small grain. The next morning a great many Indians visited the camp, and signified their wish to be friendly with the Americans. This day they came to the Challé; and passed within a few miles of the celebrated strong-hold or presidio of the Navajos, called El Challé.

On the 19th Major Gilpin with about thirty men, starting at dawn, went on in advance so as to reach the Bear Spring on the 20th, leaving Capt. Waldo to bring up the main body of the detachment. He arrived there safely, and in anticipation of Col. Doniphan. Capt. Waldo brought up the rear in good order and time to the place appointed, where he effected a junction with Col. Doniphan's forces. Here they rested.

Let us now turn and consider the difficulties which Col. Doniphan and the men with him had to encounter in arriving at the same place. We have hitherto mentioned how Col. Doniphan left Santa Fé on the 26th of October, and with a body of three hundred men proceeded to Albuquerque; crossed the river; meditated a separate march into the Navajo district; was diverted from his purpose; compelled to send his troops to Valverde to protect the merchants; and how with a part of his staff, and four other men, he arrived at Cuvarro, on the 5th of November, where he found the detachment under Lieutenant-colonel Jackson, who had just moved his camp to that place from Cebolleta. Captains Parsons and Reid had just returned from their excursions into the Navajo country. Capt. Reid's company, in consideration of the duties it had performed, and that the men were almost destitute of comfortable clothing to defend themselves against the cold, was permitted to return to Albuquerque, to receive from the paymaster at that place their commutation for clothing, which had not yet been paid them. This sum was forty-two dollars to the private man and non-commissioned officer.

On the 12th of November Col. Doniphan, while at Cuvarro, received an express from Major Gilpin, then on the San Juan, which was brought into camp by a Navajo Indian. Major Gilpin represented that he had seen large numbers of Navajos, who pretended to have already entered into treaty stipulations with the United States' forces, no doubt alluding to the agreement which they had made with Capt. Reid, and failed to carry out. Col. Doniphan replied to Major Gilpin by the same Indian, that no such treaty had been made; that Capt. Reid had been sent out for the purpose by Lieutenant-colonel Jackson, and had visited many of the Navajo chiefs, but that no definite treaty had been ratified; and instructed him to bring all the Navajos he could find to the well known *Ojo Oso*, by the 20th of the month. This the major did.

It was now the 15th of November, when Colonel Doniphan and Lieutenant-colonel Jackson took up the line of march for the Bear Spring, with about one hundred and fifty men under Capt. Parsons and Lieut. De Courcy; Capt. Hughes and the other sick men being left at Cuvarro. This detachment was also scarce of provisions, and had neither tents, nor baggage wagons, but made use of pack-mules to transport provisions and cooking utensils.

For two days the march was conducted up through a rich valley country, in the direction of the sources of the Puerco. The grass was moderately good for grazing purposes, but wood was scarce, and the water muddy and filthy. This district of country was occupied by that canton of the Navajos, of whom Sandoval was the chief. On the evening of the latter day they encamped on a rivulet, whose waters came leaping down, in foaming cascades, from the mountain, and then disappeared in the sands of the valley. Having no tents, the soldiers quartered on the naked earth, in the open air; but so much snow fell that night, that at dawn it was not possible to distinguish where they lay, until they broke the snow which covered them, and came out as though they were rising from their graves; for in less than twelve hours the snow had fallen thirteen inches deep in the valleys, and thirty-six in the mountains.

On the 17th they marched north-westerly, leaving the heads of the Puerco to the right, and passing directly over the Sierra Madre. The march was difficult in the valleys; but when they came to ascend the steep spurs and bench lands, which lead up to the mountains, a horrid, dreary prospect opened above them. The men, and their commanders were almost up to their waists, toiling in the snow, breaking a way for the horses and mules to ascend. The lowest point, in the main mountain, rose to a sublime height; and to the right, still towering far above this, projected stupendous, colossal columns of ragged granite and iron colored basalt. In reaching the only point where the main ridge could be crossed, many smaller mountains, and intermediate, deep, narrow, rocky vales were to be passed. The snow in the gaps and narrow places among the rocks, was frequently a fathom in depth. After much toil they reached the summit. To accomplish the descent into the valleys on the west side, was a labor not much less difficult than that which the soldiers had just finished. They rested a moment, and then began the descent. After the most serious and arduous labor, they reached the base of the great mountain, late at night, and took up camp at a spring, the water of which flows towards the Pacific. The depth of the snow was less on the west, than in the mountains, or on the east side. Finding good grass, wood and water, the soldiers took their supper and recounted, as they sat around their camp-fires, the dangers and adventures of the day. At length their toils were forgotten in the slumbers of the night. The faithful sentinel, who after such a day's labor, stood wakeful all night in the snow, while his weary comrades slept, does he not, reader, deserve your gratitude? He has no other reward.

Having now passed the mountain, they traveled on the 18th, over a valley country, in a westerly direction;—gently rolling hills, then rocky bluffs, then bench-lands, then crags and bleak knobs, and then barren, naked, giant masses of gray granite and dark basalt rising on the right, and a heavy forest of pines and cedars, always verdant, spreading over the lowlands to the left. In many places these colossal granite peaks shoot almost perpendicularly out of the plain, more than six thousand feet high. The surface of the country continued uniform for the next two days' march, except in some places there were gently swelling hills, with grassy recesses between, on the one side, and a heavy, unbroken forest of evergreens on the other. Here the Navajos pasture their immense droves of horses and mules, and keep their numerous flocks of sheep and goats. The aspect of the country continued thus until they arrived at the Bear Spring, on the morning of the 21st; Major Gilpin, as already noticed, having got there on the day previous, with a number of the Navajo chiefs, who dwell in the country to the west and north-west of that place, commissioned to bind the nation.

There were now present at the Bear Spring, where the treaty was made, about one hundred and eighty Americans, and five hundred Navajo Indians, including all the head chiefs of each of the cantons, composing that powerful tribe of MOUNTAIN LORDS and SCOURGERS of New Mexico. The parties being all present, to whom power was delegated to conclude a lasting peace between three nations, the Navajos, Mexicans, and Americans, the treaty was commenced on the 21st; Col. Doniphan first stating explicitly, through an interpreter, T. Caldwell, the objects of his visit, and the designs and intentions of his government. One of their chiefs, Sarcilla Largo, a young man, very bold and intellectual, spoke for them: "He was gratified to learn the views of the Americans. He admired their spirit and enterprise, but detested the Mexicans." Their speeches were delivered alternately during the whole day. At sunset the parties adjourned to meet again the following morning.

Meanwhile they repaired to their respective camps, the Americans posting out sentinels, that they might not be surprised and massacred by the Navajos through treachery; and these that they might not come into the power of the Americans without their own consent.

On the 22d, Capt. Waldo having come in with one hundred and fifty men, swelling the aggregate number of the Americans present to three hundred and thirty, the treaty was recommenced. Col. Doniphan now explained to the chiefs, "that the United States had taken military possession of New Mexico; that her laws were now extended over that territory, that the New Mexicans would be protected against violence and invasion; and that their rights would be amply preserved to them; that the United States was also anxious to enter into a treaty of peace and lasting friendship with her red children, the Navajos; that the same protection would be given them against encroachments, and usurpation of their rights, as had been guaranteed the New Mexicans; that the United States claimed all the country by the right of conquest and both they and the New Mexicans were now become equally her children; that he had come with ample powers to negociate a permanent peace between the Navajos, the Americans, and New Mexicans; and that if they refused to treat on terms honorable to both parties, he was instructed to prosecute a war against them." He also admonished them, "to enter into no treaty stipulations unless they meant to observe them strictly, and in good faith; that the United States made no second treaty with the same people; that she first offered the olive branch, and if that were rejected, then powder, bullet, and the steel."

Then the same young chief, of great sagacity and boldness, stood up and replied to the American commander thus: "Americans! you have a strange cause of war against the Navajos. We have waged war against the New Mexicans for several years. We have plundered their villages and killed many of their people, and made many prisoners. We had just cause for all this. *You* have lately commenced a war against the same people. You are powerful. You have great guns and many brave soldiers. You have therefore conquered them, the very thing we have been attempting to do for so many years. You now turn upon us for attempting to do what you have done yourselves. We cannot see why you have cause of quarrel with us for fighting the New Mexicans on the west, while you do the same thing on the east. Look how matters stand. This is *our war*. We have more right to complain of you for interfering in our war, than you have to quarrel with us for continuing a war we had begun long before you got here. If you will act justly, you will allow us to settle our own differences."

Col. Doniphan then explained, "that the New Mexicans had surrendered; that they desired no more fighting; that it was a custom with the Americans when a people gave up, to treat them as friends thenceforward; that we now had full possession of New Mexico, and had attached it to our government; that the whole country and everything in it had become ours by conquest; and that when they *now* stole property from the New Mexicans, they were stealing from us; and when they killed them, they were killing our people, for they had now become ours; that this could not be suffered any longer; that it would be greatly to their advantage for the Americans to settle in New Mexico, and that they then could open a valuable trade with us, by which means they could obtain everything they needed to eat and wear in exchange for their furs and peltries."

Col. Doniphan then invited their young men to the United States to learn trades, as he discovered them to be very ingenious, that they might be serviceable to their people. This pleased them, and they desired very much to accompany him to the United States, but they did not wish to go through Chihuahua, for they feared the Mexicans would kill them. This induced them not to go.

Then the same chief said:—"If New Mexico be really in your possession, and it be the intention of your government to hold it, we will cease our depredations, and refrain from future wars upon that people; for we have no cause of quarrel with you, and do not desire to have any war with so powerful a nation. Let there be peace between us." This was the end of the speaking. After which the following articles of treaty were signed by both parties.

Memorandum of a treaty entered into between Col. A. W. Doniphan, commanding the United States' forces in the Navajo country, and the chiefs of the Navajo nation of Indians, viz.: Sarcilla Largo, Caballada de Mucho, Alexandro, Sandoval, Kiatanito José Largo, Narbona, Sagundo, Pedro José Manuelito, Tapio, and Archuletté, at the Ojo Oso, Navajo country, November 22d, 1846.

ART. 1. A firm and lasting peace and amity shall henceforth exist between the American people and the Navajo tribe of Indians.

ART. 2. The people of New Mexico and the Pueblo tribe of Indians are included in the term American people.

ART. 3. A mutual trade, as between people of the same nation, shall be carried on between these several parties; the Americans, Mexicans and Pueblos being free to visit all portions of the Navajo country, and the Navajos all portions of the American country without molestation, and full protection shall be *mutually* given.

ART. 4. There shall be a mutual restoration of all prisoners, the several parties being pledged to redeem by purchase such as may not be exchanged each for each.

ART. 5. All property taken by either party from the other, since the 18th day of August last, shall be restored.

The undersigned, fully empowered to represent and pledge to the above articles their respective nations, have accordingly hereunto signed their names and affixed their seals.
ALEXANDER W. DONIPHAN,
Col. commanding 1st Regt. Missouri Volunteers.
CONGREVE JACKSON,
Lieut. Col. commanding 1st Battalion.
WILLIAM GILPIN,
Major commanding 2d Battalion.

SIGNATURES OF THE NAVAJO CHIEFS.

Sarcilla Largo,	His X mark.		Sagundo,	His X mark.
Caballada de Mucho,	"		Pedro José,	"
Alexandro,	"		Manuelito,	"
Sandoval,	"		Tapio,	"
Kiatanito,	"		Archulette,	"
José Largo,	'		Juanico,	"
Narbona,	"		Savoietta Garcia,	"

The colonel then gave them some presents, which he had carried out from Santa Fé, for that purpose, explicitly stating that these presents were made, not by way of purchasing their friendship, for this the Americans were not accustomed to do, but were given as a testimony of his personal good will and friendship towards them, and as a sign that peace should exist between them.

In return, the chief presented Col. Doniphan with several fine Navajo blankets, the manufacture of which discovers great ingenuity, having been spun and woven without the advantage of wheels or looms, by a people living in the open air, without houses or tents. Of these the colors are exceedingly brilliant, and the designs and figurés in good taste. The fabric is not only so thick and compact as to turn rain, but to hold water as a vessel. They are used by the Navajos as a cloak in the day time, and converted into a pallet at night. Col. Doniphan designs sending those which he brought home with him to the war department at Washington, as specimens of Navajo manufacture.

Thus after almost unparalleled exertion a treaty of peace was concluded between the Navajos, New Mexicans, and Americans, in a manner honorable to all parties. This was a novel, highly important and interesting proceeding. The Navajos and New Mexicans had been at war from immemorial time. The frontier between them had been the scene of continual bloodshed and rapine. At this crisis the Americans, the enemies of the one, and strangers to the other, step in and accommodate their differences by a triple league, which secures peace between all three. This together with his previous service, and subsequent achievements, not only entitles Col. Doniphan to wear the laurel, but also the olive, for he has justly earned the distinguished titles of VICTOR and PACIFICATOR.

CHAPTER XI.

Return of the troops to the Del Norte—Doniphan visits Zuñi—Treaty between the Zuñis and the Navajos—Description of Zuñi and the Zuñians—The Moquis—Ancient ruins—Remarks on the Navajo campaign—The Navajos—Their state and condition.

On the morning of the 23d the Indians peaceably returned to their pastoral employments, and the Americans, in detached parties, for the sake of convenient traveling, returned to the valley of the Del Norte with the utmost expedition. The men were all in want of provisions, having none except what the friendly Navajos generously gave them, and the grizzly bears and black-tailed deer which they hunted in the mountains. This consideration quickened their marches.

Capt. Parsons and Lieut. De Courcy hastily returned to Cuvarro, with their respective commands, by the same route they had come to the Bear Spring. They arrived there without serious misfortune, having lost only a few horses and pack animals by the way. They found that some of their men, who were left sick at Cuvarro, had died, others were past recovery, and all in a destitute condition, having neither comfortable clothing nor a plentiful supply of provisions. All the sick who were able to bear moving, together with their attendants, were now conveyed down the river Puerco to its mouth, and thence to Socorro, where they were quartered. Amongst these were Capt. Hughes, and Lieut. Jackson. A few only, who were very ill, were left at Cuvarro. Of these some died,* and the survivors came on and rejoined their companies. This detachment arrived at the camp near Valverde, and formed a juncture with the three hundred, who remained as a guard to the traders, about the 12th of December, much worn by distressing marches. Here they rested.

The detachment under Major Gilpin, accompanied by Col. Doniphan, Lieutenant-colonel Jackson, and Lieut. Hinton, and the three Navajo chiefs, leaving the Ojo Oso on the same day, (23d of November) completed sixty miles in two days' march, and came to Zuñi,[70]

---
* Silas Inyard, C. T. Hopper, Wm. Sterne, and several others, died near Cuvarro.—HUGHES.

NOTE 70.—The Zuñi pueblo was one of the fabled seven cities of Cibola, and is in what is now McKinley county, New Mexico, though a part of the reservation runs over into Arizona. The reservation contains four hundred and twenty-

a city built after the manner of the ancient Aztecs; during which they passed over a high rolling country, well timbered with stately pines and cedars, presenting a beautiful contrast to the barren, bleak, rocky ridges of the Sierra Madre, and Sierra de los Mimbres, which now rose on the left.

This route lay over a ledge of gently swelling hills and high lands, dividing the head waters of the rivers Gila and Colorado. During this entire march there appeared numerous indications of the precious metals abounding. Blossoms of gold, silver, lead, and some specimens of copper were seen. This whole mountain region of country is unquestionably rich in mineral wealth. On arriving at Zuñi, Major Gilpin quartered his men, as usual, in the open air near town. Col. Doniphan and a few others, including the three Navajo chiefs, lodged themselves in a spacious adobé building in the city. Now, there was a continual war between the Navajos and the Zunians. On this account, these three Navajo chiefs durst not leave the colonel far at any time, because they feared that the Zunians would kill them. Col. Doniphan therefore appointed a guard for them, that they might not suffer any hurt. In the evening of the 25th, upwards of two hundred Zunians collected about the colonel's quarter. Having intimated that it was his intention on the next day to endeavor to bring them to a friendly understanding with the Navajos, their implacable enemies, the leading warriors of the Zunians drew near, (for they were friendly towards the Americans) and entered into a dispute with the Navajo chiefs. Fiery speeches were made by each of the parties. The Zunians thought to lay hold on them and detain them as prisoners of war; but they durst not do this through fear of the Americans, under whose protection the Navajo chiefs came in. One of the Navajo chiefs spoke for the rest. He said:

"The cause of your present dissatisfaction is just this. The war between us has been waged for plunder. You kill and drive off our flocks and herds, and subsist your people upon them, and use them for your own advantage. To resent this, we have plundered your vil-

---

seven square miles, and the population of the pueblo is something more than fifteen hundred. They raise wheat and vegetables, and some fruit. They irrigate the valleys of the branches of the Zuñi river. They are a strange and interesting people.

lages, taken your women and children captives, and made slaves of them. Lately you have been unsuccessful. We have *out stolen* you, and therefore you are mad and dissatisfied about it. But there is one thing you cannot accuse the Navajos of doing, and that is killing women and children. You know, not many years past, when our women and children went into the mountains to gather piñons, your warriors fell upon, and killed about forty of them. This cowardly act was perpetrated when there were no Navajo warriors to afford them succor."

A chief of the Zuñi tribe replied, indignantly repelling the charge, and threatening to hold the Navajo chiefs as hostages, until the Navajos should deliver up those of their people whom they held as captives. The Navajo rejoined:

"The Zunians may rest assured that we did not come over here relying on their generosity, magnanimity, or good faith: but, being invited by Col. Doniphan, we have come to see if we can make a peace with you, Zunians, which will be both honorable and advantageous to us. We rely alone on the integrity of the Americans, and their ability to protect us. We have not the slightest fear of any injury you may attempt to offer us, for we trust ourselves with a more honorable people.

Col. Doniphan here interposed, and advised them to meet the next morning and endeavor to form a treaty, stipulating entire friendship between the two nations; that it would be much better for both parties to live in peace; and that war was a great evil. He then appointed the American camp, near the town, as the place of meeting. They met accordingly, and, after much debate, consummated a treaty of peace and amity, on the 26th, just and honorable to both parties. This was the last treaty Col. Doniphan made with any tribe of Indians. His labors with the Indians were now finished.

Zuñi, one of the most extraordinary cities in the world, and perhaps the only one now known resembling those of the ancient Aztecs, is situated on the right bank of the river Piscao, a small branch of the Gila, or Colorado of California, near two hundred miles west of the Del Norte, and contains a singular and interesting population of upwards of six thousand, who derive their support almost exclusively from agriculture. They clothe themselves in blankets, and other fabrics of their own manufacture. The Zunians being friendly disposed towards the soldiers, these secured of them a supply of provisions, and also of various fruits in which the country abounds. The Zuñis, or Zunians, have long been celebrated not only for honesty and hospitality, but also for their intelligence and ingenuity in the manufacture of cotton and woolen fabrics.

The city of Zuñi was thus described by Col. Doniphan to Mr. T. B. Thorpe,* of New Orleans: "It is divided into four solid squares, having but two streets, crossing its centre at right angles. All the buildings are two stories high, composed of sun-dried brick. The first story presents a solid wall to the street, and is so constructed that each house joins, until one-fourth of the city may be said to be one building. The second stories rise from this vast, solid structure, so as to designate each house, leaving room to walk upon the roof of the first story between each building. The inhabitants of Zuñi enter the second story of their buildings by ladders, which they draw up at night, as a defense against any enemy that might be prowling about. In this city were seen some thirty Albino Indians, who have, no doubt, given rise to the story, that there is living in the Rocky Mountains a tribe of white aborigines. The discovery of this city of the Zunians will afford the most curious speculations among those who have so long searched in vain for a city of Indians, who possessed the manners and habits of the Aztecs. No doubt we have here a race living as did that people, when Cortez entered Mexico. It is a remarkable fact, that the Zunians have, since the Spaniards left the country, refused to have any intercourse with the modern Mexicans, looking upon them as an inferior people. They have also driven from among them [*not until recently, however*] the priests and other dignitaries, who formerly had power over them, and resumed habits and manners of their own; their great chief, or governor, being the civil and religious head. The country around the city of Zuñi is cultivated with a great deal of care, and affords food, not only for the inhabitants, but for large flocks of cattle and sheep."

The seven villages of the Môquis are situated about five leagues further to the westward, on the same small river. The Môquis are an inoffensive, peaceably disposed people, detesting war and rapine; yet they are both numerous and powerful. They manifest considerable skill in their manufactures, and subsist entirely by grazing and

---

* This account was written out by Mr. Thorpe, and first published in the New Orleans National, of which he is the editor.—HUGHES.

agriculture. Of these people Mr. Gregg thus speaks: "They formerly acknowledged the government and religion of the Spaniards, but have long since rejected both, and live in a state of independence and paganism. Their dwellings, however, like those of Zuñi, are similar to those of the interior Pueblos; and they are equally industrious and agricultural, and still more ingenious in their manufacturing. The language of the Môquis, or the Môquinos, is said to differ but little from that of the Navajos." The American army did not visit them, as they were at peace with all people, and stood aloof from the wars that continually raged around them.

The affairs of the Indians being thus settled, Major Gilpin's detachment, on the evening of the 26th, started for the valley of the Del Norte by way of Laguna on the Puerco. His first intention was, however, to proceed directly to Soccorro through the elevated range of mountains, called by the Mexicans, Sierra de los Mimbres, but was convinced of the impracticability of that route by the Zunians, who informed him of the great dearth of water which prevailed in that region, and induced him to change his purpose. He then marched hastily to Laguna by a more northern pass over the mountains, and fell in with Col. Doniphan at that place, one hundred miles from Zuñi, on the 2d of December.

It will be remembered that Col. Doniphan, Lieutenant-Colonel Jackson, and seven other men, separating from this detachment, left Zuñi on the 27th of November, and by a different manœuvre in the mountains, reached Cebolleta, and thence proceeded to Laguna, falling in with Major Gilpin, as above related. On the head waters of the Piscao, and high up in the mountains, Col. Doniphan relates that he came to the ruins of an ancient city. This city, according to the best information he could obtain, had been built more than two hundred years, entirely of stone, and had been deserted more than one hundred years, as is supposed, on account of the earthquakes in the vicinity. Near the ruins are immense beds of vitreous deposit, and blackened scoriæ, presenting the appearance of an extensive molten lake in the valleys, and other volcanic remains, with chasms and apertures opening down through this stratum of lava, to an unknown depth. The vitreous surface, with its sharp asperities, was exceedingly severe on the feet of the mules and horses, wearing them to the quick in a short time. The figure of the city was that of an exact square, set north and south, so that its four sides corresponded with the four cardinal points, being encircled by a double wall of stone, fourteen feet apart. These walls were three stories high; two entire stories being above ground, and the other partly above and partly below the surface. The space between these walls was divided into rooms of convenient size, (about fourteen feet square,) all opening into the interior. The remainder of the city, though much in ruins, appeared to have been built on streets running parallel to these walls. In the centre was a large square, or plaza, which, from its appearance, might have been used for military parade grounds, and for corralling stock in the night-time. In these rooms, large quantities of red cedar, which had been cut of convenient length for fire places, was discovered in a state of entire preservation, having been stored up for more than a century. Col. Doniphan and suite cooked their suppers, and made their camp-fires with some of it, and then traveled on. This is all that could be learned of that remarkable ruin.

Both of the routes traveled by Col. Doniphan and Major Gilpin, from Zuñi to Cebolleta and Laguna, and thence to the encampment at Valverde, were pronounced impracticable by the Mexicans. There were indeed long stretches, over sandy wastes, wherein no water could be obtained. These must be traversed. The soldiers and animals were therefore compelled to pass several consecutive days and nights, without eating or drinking. They effected their arrival at Valverde rendezvous, in parcels, between the 8th and 12th of December, Capt. Stephenson's company only being permitted to return to Albuquerque to receive the commutation for one year's clothing, which had long been due them.

The march of the squadron under command of Major Gilpin, ranks among the brightest achievements of the war. His passage over the Cordilleras, and Tunicha mountains, accomplished, as it was, in the depth of winter, when the elements and obstacles were ten times more dreadful than the foe, with men destitute of every thing but ARMS and RESOLUTION, meets not with a parallel in the annals of history. From the time of his leaving Santa Fé, including the diversion he made into the country of Yutas, north of Taos, his column marched at least seven hundred and fifty miles, before reaching Valverde, over the loftiest mountains, and most inaccessible regions, on the continent. By distress of marching he lost two brave men, Bryant and Foster, and one hundred and fifty head of stock. The success of the celebrated Navajo Treaty was not less owing to the gallantry and energy of this column in hunting up and bringing in the chiefs of that nation to the appointed place, than to the skill and diplomacy of Col. Doniphan, who brought the negotiations to so happy an issue. The marches of the other two columns, under Col. Doniphan and Lieutenant-colonel Jackson, and Capt. Reid, were scarcely less arduous or astonishing; nor was the country over which these passed less impracticable; for by reason of hardship and suffering, these lost a great number of animals and seven or eight brave soldiers.

Thus terminated this most arduous and difficult campaign against the Navajo Indians, of whom it may not be amiss to give a brief account, as touching their manners and habits of life.

The Navajos occupy a district of country scarcely less in extent than the State of Missouri. In their predatory excursions they roam from 33° to 38° of north latitude, and for the period of two hundred and fifty years, have with impunity, except in one or two instances, ravaged the whole Mexican frontier from Soccorro to the valley of Taos, plundering and destroying according as their caprices prompted them. Their strong places of retreat are in the Cordilleras, and that entire range of high lands which divides the waters of the Gila and the Colorado of the west from those of the Del Norte. They stretch from the borders of New Mexico on the east, to the settlements of California on the west. They are supreme lords of this mountain country; and, like the Asiatic Tartars, have no fixed abodes, but follow their flocks. Upon these, and the plunder they secure in their frequent incursions upon the New Mexican villages, they subsist themselves entirely. They are not addicted to the chase, except where the game may be taken on horseback. The bold and fearless character of the Navajos, together with the magnificent mountain scenery of the country which they inhabit, awakens in the mind reflections not unlike those which any one is apt to entertain of the Highlanders and highlands of Scotland, from reading the Scottish bards.

Mr. Thorpe, upon the authority of Col. Doniphan, thus alludes to the tribe of American Tartars: "The Navajo Indians are a warlike people; have no towns, houses, or lodges; they live in the open air, or on horseback, and are remarkably wealthy, having immense herds of horses, cattle, and sheep. They are celebrated for their intelligence and good order. They treat their women with great attention, consider them equals, and relieve them from the drudgery of menial work. They are handsome, well made, and in every respect a highly civilized people, being as a nation, of a higher order of beings than the mass of their neighbors, the Mexicans. About the time Col. Doniphan made his treaty, a division of his command was entirely out of provisions: the Navajos supplied its wants with liberality."

The art and skill which they possess in manufacturing woolen fabrics, (the texture of which is so dense and fine as to be impervious to water,) and apparently with such limited means, is really matter of astonishment. The Navajos can easily muster fifteen hundred warriors for battle; and their aggregate numbers cannot be less than twelve thousand. They are certainly the noblest of the American aborigines.

BLACK-TAILED DEER.

CHAPTER XII.

General Kearny's march to California—Passes the Del Norte at Albuquerque—Arrival at Soccorro—The Alcalde—Kit Carson—The Express—Capt. Burgwin sent back—Lieut. Ingalls—Apaches—The Copper mines—Red Sleeve—Sierra del Buso—Difficulties—The Gilans—Lieut. Davidson—Hall of Montezuma—The Pimo villages.

The manner in which Gen. Kearny settled the affairs, both civil and military, in New Mexico, and how the forces were disposed in different parts of that country for the preserving of good order, tranquillity, and subordination among the malcontents, has been related in the previous chapters. It now remains to speak of Gen. Kearny's stupendous march over the southern spurs of the Cordilleras to the settlements of California.

On the 25th of September, Gen. Kearny left Santa Fé and commenced his great march for the distant shores of the Pacific, taking with him his staff officers, three hundred of the 1st dragoons, baggage and provision wagons, and about sixty-five days' provisions.

The dragoons were commanded by captains (now Major) Sumner,* Cooke, Moore, Burgwin, and Lieut. Noble, in place of Capt. Allen. Their horses were now sent back to Fort Leavenworth, and mules substituted in their stead, as it was believed this animal possessed more endurance, and was better adapted to the travel through a dry, mountainous country, mostly destitute of water and grass, than the horse. The general left orders at Santa Fé for Capt. Hudson's California Rangers, and the battalion of Mormons under Lieutenant-Colonel Allen, to succeed him on the march as soon as the latter corps should arrive at that place.

The general proceeded this day no further than Major Sumner's grazing encampment on Santa Fé creek. Grass and good spring water were obtained in sufficient quantities for the night's use. The next morning the ox teams, and then the mule teams, as was the usual practice of the army, started on the way by daylight; for these necessarily travel slower than mounted men. The country during this day's march was thinly covered with grama grass and occasional

* Major Sumner subsequently rendered important service at the battles of Churubusco and Chapultepec.—HUGHES.

cedar shrubs, betokening the greatest sterility. Several mules being missing, and two wagons broken down, they encamped on the bank of the Del Norte, near San Filipé, where they spent the night, during which, some of their mules broke loose, and depredated upon the neighboring cornfields. The complaints of the Pueblos were silenced by the payment of damages.

This column now moved slowly down the valley of the Del Norte, passing through Algodones, Bernalillo, Sandia, Albuquerque, where crossing the river and proceeding about eight miles further, the general pitched his camp, on the 29th, near the village Pajarrito. Here owing to the scarcity of timber, the soldiers were compelled to buy fuel with which to cook their suppers. "A few days previous to this, and shortly after three companies of volunteers crossed the river on their way to Cebolleta," observes Capt. Johnston, "a party of Navajos crossed at this point, and killed eight Mexicans on the east bank of the Del Norte." Here, observes the same author, "the sand-drifts in various places had accumulated into hills. Drifting sand seems to adhere to its own kindred material. It is fortunate that it is so. This country would otherwise be impassable as well as uninhabitable. The inhabitable portion of New Mexico is confined to the immediate borders of the streams. The bottoms of the Del Norte are about one mile and a half wide on an average so far down, and are elevated but a few feet above the level of the running water. The Del Norte is rapid and regular, and its waters can be tapped at any point without a dam, so that irrigation is carried on successfully. It remains for greater improvements in this respect to develop the resources of the country. A large canal along the base of the hills might carry all the waters of the Del Norte, and be a means of transportation, while its surplus water could be employed in the winter for filling reservoirs, and during the summer to convey water directly upon the fields. In this way the country could be made to support ten times its present population. The rains of this country all fall upon the mountain-tops, and the valleys are thus dependent upon irrigation, as the water only reaches them in the big drains of nature. From our camp, during the night, we could see upon the distant hills the camp-fires of the shepherds who lead their flocks afar from their habitations."

From thence this column marched, in three days, about thirty-six miles, passing through Pajarrito, Padillas, Isleta, Sinecà, Lunas,

Belen, Sabinaz, and encamped opposite La Joya; during which some portions of the country were under a high state of cultivation, while in other places the earth was entirely bare, or covered by white efflorescences of soda. The river was occasionally skirted by clusters and groves of alamas. Here the soldiers took some fine turtle and cat-fish out of the Del Norte, upon which they feasted sumptuously during the night.

The next day, which was the 3d of October, the general lay in camp, awaiting the arrival of the Mexican *caretas* and the ox-teams which had fallen one day in the rear. "During the day, an express came in from Polvadera, twelve miles down the river, informing the general that the Navajos had attacked the village, and he had been sent by the Alcalde to bring the artillery, where they were still fighting when he left. Capt. Moore was sent with company (C) in defence of the Mexicans, and orders were sent to-day to Col. Doniphan [at Santa Fé] to make a campaign into the Navajo country."

The following day the general came to Polvadera, where he learned from Capt. Moore that about one hundred Navajos had visited the place and driven off into the mountains a great quantity of stock; but that no battle had taken place, as they appeared mutually to dread each other. "The general here gave permission to the people of New Mexico, living on the Rio Abarjo, to march against the Navajos in retaliation for the many outrages they had received at their hands." Thus it will appear, that the Pueblos who offered their services to Lieutenant-colonel Jackson before arriving at Cebolleta, and which were rejected, were not acting without instructions from the head of the government.[71]

NOTE 71.—The proclamation is as follows:

In consequence of the frequent & almost daily outrages committed by the Navajoes upon the Persons and Property of the Inhabitants of the Rio Abajo, by which several lives have been lost, & many horses, mules & cattle stolen from them. And in consequence of the many applications made by them to the Undersigned for permission to march into the country of these Indians. Now be it known to all, that I, Brig Genl S. W. Kearny Commg. the troops in the Tery. of New Mexico, hereby authorize all the inhabitants (Mexicans & Pueblos) living in the said district of country via Rio Abajo, to form War Parties to march into the country of their enemies, the Navajoes, to recover their Property, to make reprisals, & obtain redress for the many insults received from them. The old, the women & the children of the Navajoes must not be injured.

copy furnished Alcalde
Prefect Saracino—Adjt Genl
Gov. Bent—Col Doniphan

Given in Camp on the Del Norte near Socorro this 5th Octr. 1846
S. W. KEARNY
Brig Genl U. S. A.

Thence on the 5th, the march was continued through Limitar, Soccorro, and Huertus. It was at Soccorro the general took possession of certain mules, of which the Alcalde had deprived the legal owners in consequence of their carrying on contraband trade with the Apaches, and which he claimed as the rightful perquisites of his office. They now became the property of the American government, and were appropriated accordingly. The American army had not, hitherto, visited any of the settlements thus far south in the great Del Norte valley. The inhabitants therefore gazed with astonishment and admiration upon an army passing orderly, and silently through the country; abstaining from acts of violence and outrage, as though it were in the country of an ally.

Thence having progressed, on the 6th, about three miles, this column was met by Lieutenant Kit Carson with a party of fifteen men (among them, six Delaware Indians) direct, on express, from Monterey, with sealed dispatches for Washington. He represented California as being in quiet possession of the Americans. The general

MEXICAN CART.

then said—"Lieutenant! you have just passed over the country we intend to traverse, and you are well acquainted with it: we want you to go back with us as our guide, and pilot us through the mountains and deserts." Carson replied—"I have pledged myself to go to Washington, and I cannot think of neglecting to fulfil that promise." The general then said—"I will relieve you of all responsibility, and entrust the mail in the hands of a safe person, who will carry it on speedily." Carson finally consenting, "turned his face to the westward again, just as he was on the eve of entering the settlements after his arduous trip, and when he had set his hopes on seeing his family. It requires a brave man to give up his private feelings thus for the public good; Carson is one such."

Carson's party were not till then apprised of the conquest of New Mexico by the American troops, and therefore, although they had lost most of their animals, intended, if the New Mexicans should prove hostile, to make as speedy a transit across that country as possible, during which they counted on procuring such an outfit, and supply of provisions as would enable them to pass the plains, and reach the States. The column now moved on ten miles, encamping in a beautiful cottonwood grove, where the general issued orders, reducing his command to one hundred men. California being in quiet possession of the Americans, there appeared to be no advantage in carrying a strong force to that distant country. The rest of the command was now put under requisition to supply these with the best possible outfit for the long and arduous campaign. The new organization for the expedition stood thus: Gen. Kearny with his aids-de-camp, Captains Turner and Johnston; Major Swords, quartermaster; Griffin, assistant surgeon; Lieutenants Warner and Emory, topographical engineers; and two companies of the 1st dragoons, (fifty men each) commanded by Captain Moore and Lieutenant Hammond, including the section of mountain howitzers under Lieutenant Davidson, each company being furnished with three wagons, drawn by eight stout mules.[72]

This evening the Apaches brought unto the general four young men as guides. Their geographical knowledge was extensive and

---

NOTE 72.—Upon this occasion General Kearny wrote the following letter to the War Department:

HEAD QR. ARMY OF THE WEST
CAMP ON THE DEL NORTE, NEAR
SOCORRO—OCTOB 6TH 1846

SIR: I this morning met an express from Upper California to Washington city, sent by Lieut Col Frémont, reporting that the Americans have taken possession of that Department, in consequence of which I have reorganized the Party to accompany me to that country, as will be seen by orders N. 34 herewith enclosed. I take of the Staff Maj. Swords (Qr. Mr.) Asst Secy Griffin—Capt Turner (A. A. A. Genl) Johnston (A De Camp) Lieuts. Emory & Warner (Topo Engs.) And of the line Capt Moore in command of Cos. C & K (no total) 1st Dragoons, & leave Major Sumner here with Cos. B. G. I.—We are now 100 miles below Santa fe, & from this time expect less interruption from our Baggage train which has hitherto much retarded us—I have nothing more to report.

Brig Genl R. Jones Very Resp-y Yr. ob Servt
 Adjt Genl U. S. A. S. W. KEARNY
 W——n Brig Genl U. S. A.

accurate, yet they could not tell what route was practicable for wagons. Fitzpatrick was dispatched to Santa Fé, and thence to Fort Leavenworth, with the mail from California. The other three companies of the 1st dragoons, and the principal part of the baggage train were sent back under Major Sumner, to winter at Albuquerque.

From thence in three days' march they made fifty miles, crossed the river and encamped south-west of the Jornada mountain, which is a heap of volcanic cinders and igneous rocks; during which they passed much rough road, where the rocks, asperities and thickets of mezquite, rendered it necessary to send in advance a pioneer party with axes and picks to clear the way. The wagons progressed slowly; some of them were already broken, and many of the mules began to fail. The general determined to send from this place to Major Sumner for mules to haul the six wagons back to the valley of the Del Norte, and resolved to resort at once to pack-mules and sumpter-horses as a means of transporting his baggage and provisions, for he now foresaw the route would be impracticable to either light carriages or heavy wagons.

Accordingly Corporal Clapin and one Mexican, his name Zones, were dispatched for the purpose, after midnight, with orders to ride to Major Sumner's camp, sixty miles, without stopping. This they did. Meanwhile Captain Cooke was employed in opening a road for the howitzers and pack animals. The next four days they remained in camp, awaiting the arrival of the mules and pack-saddles.

At this point on the Del Norte were discovered signs of the otter, the catamount, the wild-cat, the racoon, the deer and the bear; also of the crane, the duck, the goose, the plover, and the California quail. This latter differs from the quail of the United States, the male having a dark bluish, and the female a reddish plumage. On the 13th Lieutenant Ingalls came up, bringing the pack-saddles and the United States' mail, containing general orders for General Kearny, and other letters and papers. These were answered, and all future communication with the States closed, for they had now passed beyond the reach of mail facilities.

On the 15th, this little army struck off from the Rio Del Norte in a southwesterly direction, ascending at once 200 feet to an elevated plain, intersected by numerous deep ravines, and dashing mountain streams, running through great chasms, and filled with the finest fish.

Having completed a progress of twenty-four miles, over a country where the hills were capped with iron-colored, basaltic rocks, and the valleys and margins of the streams beautified with a new caste of tropical walnut, oak, hackberry, birch and mezquite, the men encamped on a mountain rivulet, cooked their suppers and staid for the night.[73]

Marching the next two days they passed over a beautiful country, watered by fresh, leaping, mountain streams, issuing from the southern spurs of the Sierra de los Mimbres, bordered and shaded by a small growth of live-oak, walnut, acacia, grape-vines, canissa and

NOTE 73.—I find the following interesting item in the Kansas City *Star*, Aug. 19, 1906:

> Here lie the bones of Sancho Pedro, the only damn decent Greaser I ever knew.
>
> Killed by Apache Indians, 1846.
>
> Gen. S. W. K., U. S. A.

The letters had been burned into the pine slab with the corner of a branding-iron. The dry climate had kept the wood preserved, and there was no indication that it had stood for more than a few years, except from the date below the epitaph.

A few bullets, tributes of cowboys, who doubted that a greaser could be good even when dead, had splintered the sides of the slab.

It was an unusual epitaph. The fine slab stood in a sandhill far off from the Pecos river, up near the foothills in New Mexico. The epitaph was unusual because it spoke well of a Mexican half-breed. You might travel for days in New Mexico and Arizona and find neither on wood nor stone or the lips of a white man such flattery as that "a greaser was decent."

Sancho Pedro must have been an unusual half-breed to acquire the friendship of a general. The slab was found half buried in a sand-dune by a Mexican grading crew on the Santa Fé Railroad when they ran their line down the Pecos valley in the early '90s. Sancho's countrymen were disturbed by no niceties of sentiment when they ran onto the grave. They split the headpiece into paddles with which to clean their shovels and scrapers. They went down deeper and found the bones of a man and high-heeled Spanish boots. An iron crucifix and chain incrusted with rust were taken from around the neck by an Indian boy, who was carrying water for the men.

When he went back to Santa Fé he showed the crucifix to his grandfather, an old Navajo Indian, who had been with General Stephen W. Kearny. The old man in broken English and between many lapses of silence and puffs from a pipe, told of Sancho Pedro. He was a hostler for General Kearny, the old man said. He served the general for years, and was killed in a skirmish with Apache Indians down in the Pecos valley near the foothills in 1846. The general ordered him given decent burial, and burned the epitaph with his own hands on a pine slab with an old Spanish branding-iron.

The railroad desecrated Sancho's grave and threw his bones to whiten and waste away on the sands. His story would never have been known except for the crucifix the Indian boy took from his neck and kept. He liked to show it and repeat the story his grandfather had told to him of Sancho Pedro and the epitaph written by General Kearny.

Spanish bayonet, and also fringed by the richest growth of grama grass, and came to the river Minifres, about three miles beyond which they encamped on a small creek, in a cedar grove, near heaps of volcanic glass and igneous rocks, where they obtained a plentiful supply of fine grama grass for their stock. Here they rested for the night.

The next day the march was continued. Smoking fires were made on the tops of the hills near the way, as friendly signals to invite the Apaches into camp. At sunset they arrived at the celebrated copper mine in the northern part of the State of Chihuahua, which Capt. Johnston thus describes:

"The veins of sulphuret of copper run through a whitish, silicious rock, like the blue veins running through white marble; they vary in their knees, but traverse the whole substance. The rock breaks easily; and the pick appears to be the only tool used formerly. Occasional veins of pure copper, very yellow from the quantity of gold it contains, traverse the whole mass. I saw in the rollers lying over the mine masses of the blue limestone, supposed to be cretacious: the water had filled many of the abandoned chambers of the mine; in others, the flies had perched themselves in great numbers, to pass the winter. The fort, which was erected to defend the mines, was built in shape of an equilateral triangle, with round towers at the corners; it was built of adobe, with walls four feet thick. The fort was in tolerable preservation; some remains of the furnaces were left, and piles of cinders; but no idea could be formed of the manner of smelting the ore, except that charcoal, in quantities, was used. Several hundred dollars' worth of ore had been got ready for smelting, when the place was abandoned. McKnight, who was nine years a prisoner in Chihuahua, made a fortune here, and abandoned the mines in consequence of the Apache Indians cutting off his supplies. At one time they took eighty pack mules from him. The mine is very extensive, and doubtless immensely valuable. Water is abundant, and pasture fine, and many lands which will furnish breadstuffs by cultivation. Wood is very abundant, and particularly in the vicinity."

From thence, in one day's march, they completed thirty miles, passing the San Vicentia Spring, and the high rocky ridges that separate the waters of the Gulf of Mexico from the Gulf of California. Several mules failed on this march, and were abandoned amongst the rocks and crags.

The next morning, Red Sleeve,[74] an Apache chief, with twenty of his warriors and some squaws, visited the camp, and gave assurances of their friendly intentions and wishes. They were habited after the manner of the Mexicans, with wide drawers, moccasins turned up in front, and leggins to the knees, with a keen dagger-knife inserted in the folds of the leggin on the outside for convenient use in cases of sudden assault. Their hair was long and flowed loosely in the wind; they mostly had no head-dress. To turn the scorching rays of an almost vertical sun from their faces, and preserve their eyes, some of them used a fantastic kind of shield, made of raw-hide and dressed buckskin; while others of them employed a fan of twigs, or a buzzard's wing, for the same purpose. They were armed in part with Mexican fusils, partly with lances, and bows and arrows. The general gave Red Sleeve and two other chiefs, papers, showing that he had held a talk with them, and that they had promised perpetual friendship with the Americans.

Also another Apache chief came into camp, and harangued the general thus:—"You have taken Santa Fé; let us go on and take Chihuahua and Sonora; we will go with you. You fight for the *soul;* we fight for *plunder;* so we will agree perfectly; their people are bad Christians; let us chastise them as they deserve." The general of course rejected his proposal, and so they all went away. This day the march was down a deep valley of rich grama grass, watered by a cool rivulet, with high hills and piles of volcanic rock on either hand; and having completed five miles, they came to the famous river Gila, "a beautiful mountain stream about thirty feet wide, and a foot deep on the shallows, and hemmed in by mountains; the bottom being not more than a mile wide. The signs of beaver, bear, deer, and

NOTE 74.—Captain Cooke was notified of the appearance of Red Sleeve and his willingness to furnish guides:

HEAD QR. ARMY OF THE WEST
CAMP NEAR THE COPPER MINES—
NEW MEXICO—OCT 18, 1846.

CAPT: Red Sleeve the Apache chief has had an interview with the Gen'l today & has promised to send some of his Young Men to conduct you by a good Route to the Rio Gila, when they meet you, the Gen'l desires that you will treat them well & make use of them as Guides—They will take this note to you—As none of these Young Men will be able to speak the Spanish language, it is probable that Charbonneaux will understand and make himself understood by them by signs
    Capt P. S. G. Cooke
      1st Dragoons
        Commg. Battn. Mormons

I am Sir
Very Resp-y Yr. ob Servt
H. S. TURNER
Capt A. A. A. G

turkey, besides the tracks of herds of Indian horses, were plain to be seen, on the sand." Now turning south, they advanced about two miles and a half farther, and encamped at the base of a ledge of hills, with summits of dark, ragged, iron-colored rocks, where the river passes through a deep fissure or cañon, impassable by cavalry. Here the soldiers took some fish from the river, which were of delicate and excellent flavor. Therefore they feasted that night.

Thence, after eleven days, they came to the river San Francisco, emptying into the Gila by the left bank—during which they passed over rough mountains of dingy rock, and encountered the most serious opposition from the deep ravines, and chasms, and precipitous bluffs, which every where obstructed the way, and prevented the march.

From the summit of these mountains, near Sierra del Buso, a magnificent scene opens to view. The Gila,[75] winding its tortuous way through innumerable valleys and deep cañons; the dark, iron-colored peaks of the mountains limiting the horizon towards the south-westward; and the broad plain south of Del Buso, extending from the Del Norte to the Gila, richly carpeted with the grama, all exhibit a picture of a grand and sublime nature. The whole country appears to be a succession of valleys, hills, highlands, rocky ridges, mountains, and lofty peaks of granite, and black, igneous rocks, reaching far above the clouds. It was during their passage through one of these mountain ranges, that one of the howitzers and the draught mules, tumbled down a steep declivity in the night time, and entirely disappeared in a deep chasm or ravine, whence they were extricated by Lieutenant Davidson, after much labor, uninjured.

During this march they were necessitated, in consequence of the rocky and precipitous ranges of mountains which frequently traverse the river, and through which the water has forced its way in deep cañons and rocky passes, to cross and recross the Gila several times. On one occasion they were compelled to make a detour on the south side, of fourteen miles, to avoid one of those deep, rocky defiles, through which the river flows in dashing falls and foaming cascades, utterly impassable by man or horse. Also, in the valleys, near the

---

NOTE 75.—The Gilá was discovered by the Spaniards very soon after the conquest of Mexico, and by them called Rio del Nombre de Jesus, in 1604, which name it bore until 1697. It is a considerable stream, flowing from the watershed in New Mexico to the Colorado, into which it empties at Fort Yuma.

spurs and projecting points of the smaller class of mountain ranges, the diluvion is cut into immensely deep gutters and channels, which render the passage of an army almost impossible.

While encamped on the San Francisco, small groups of Gilans made their appearance on the tops of the distant hills and spurs of the mountains. They made friendly signals. Hereupon the Americans called them, and sent Captain Moore and Lieutenant Carson as messengers to them, bearing a white flag. The messengers shook them by the hand, and spoke to them kindly; but they could not be induced to come into camp. The reason of their extreme timidity towards the Americans, is said to be this:

"They have been harshly dealt with by Americans, in the employment of Chihuahua, who have hunted them, at fifty dollars a scalp, as we would hunt wolves; and one American decoyed a large number of their brethren in the rear of a wagon, to trade, and fired a field piece among them." This produced great havoc among them, and lasting dread of the Americans.

From thence they passed the Gila again, and having traveled eight miles, halted to refresh themselves, at the head of a cañon, preparatory to commencing the march over the Jornada, or sand plain, sixty miles in extent, without water. Here evidences of a former settlement were discovered, such as a profusion of red pottery scattered over the ground. They now, after a few hours rest, began their passage over a tall, rugged chain of mountains, leaving the river where it dashed, foaming through the gorge, skirted by clustering alamos. They ascended the mountains by an Indian trail, and, after traveling ten miles, halted near a spring, high up among the masses of rock. This day's march was arduous. Three mules used in drawing the artillery, failed, and one of the howitzers got broken. So rough and inaccessible were the ways, that Lieut. Davidson and party were obliged to abandon the howitzers, and come into camp for a guard to protect them from injury until the next morning. Accordingly a detail of six men was dispatched, long after dark, to watch over them until day-dawn, when they were conveyed into camp. This was near the mouth of the San Francisco.

A novel species of the cactus, which had made its appearance on the hill sides, and among the maguey and Spanish bayonet, deserves to be noticed. This species, called by the Mexicans *pateja*, is sometimes thirty feet high, two feet and a half in diameter, bears a fine fruit, and is notched with fifteen flutes, with an interior structure of wood, corresponding to each of the flutes.

The next morning the Apaches, in considerable numbers, perched on the distant hill tops and knobs, evinced, by friendly signals, a desire to hold council with the Americans. After some effort, one of them was induced to trust himself in camp, and given some presents; then came another, and another, each in turn gaining confidence that the Americans did not intend to capture or injure them. They promised to conduct the general to water, six miles further on the route, and expressed a desire to trade mules to the men. They then went away. Water was accordingly found.

"The wigwams of the Apaches," observes Captain Johnston, "scarce peep above the brushwood of the country, being not more than four feet high, slightly dug out in the centre, and the dirt thrown around the twigs, which are rudely woven into an oven-shape, as a canopy to the house. A tenement of a few hours' work is the home of a family for years, or a day."

After a march of four days, wandering and bewildered among the hills and rocks, and on the desert, they again reached the river below the cañon, where they rested and awaited the arrival of the howitzers one day. The next day they marched about eighteen miles, frequently crossing the Gila, and finally encamping on the right bank. Dark, rocky, projecting spurs of the mountains, approach near the river, covered with thickets of the mezquite, and the creosote plant. The valley was covered in places by the fragments of broken pottery. Some Apaches came to the tops of the mountain peaks, and hailed the column, displaying friendly signals. At length they were prevailed on by Capt. Moore to come into camp. They desired to conciliate the Americans. They staid one night, and having begged tobacco, went away.

The following day they marched down the Gila, crossing from one side to the other not less than a dozen times in fourteen miles, in consequence of the rough rocky points, which extend to the stream, rendering it impossible to pass altogether on either side. This river, during a greater part of its course, runs through immensely deep valleys, with lofty bluffs on either hand, or through great chasms where the mountains close into the water's edge. In these deep cañons where the bluffs stand perpendicularly, and rise to a frightful height, the water dashes along, foaming, and roaring, over the points of rocks, sometimes winding tortuously, and sometimes gliding volubly and rectilineally down the vent between the mountains. Pottery was still discovered and the ruins of several ancient buildings.

After a march of six miles on the 10th of November, passing over plains which had once sustained a dense population, they came to an extensive ruin, one building of which, called the "Hall of Montezuma," is still in a tolerable state of preservation. This building was fifty feet long, forty wide, and had been four stories high, but the floors and the roof had been burned out. The joists were made of round beams four feet in diameter. It had four entrances,—north, east, south and west. The walls were built of sun-dried brick, cemented with natural lime, which abounds in the adjacent country, and were four feet thick, having a curved inclination inwards towards the top, being smoothed outside and plastered inside. About one hundred and fifty yards from this building to the northward is a terrace one hundred yards long and seventy wide, elevated about five feet. Upon this is a pyramid, eight feet high and twenty-five yards square at the top. From the top of this, which has no doubt been used as a watchtower, the vast plains to the west and north-east for more than fifteen miles, lie in plain view. These lands had once been in cultivation, and the remains of a large acequia, or irrigating canal, could be distinctly traced along the range of dilapidated houses.

About the same day they came to the Pimo villages on the south side of the Gila. Captain Johnston observes: "Their answer to Carson when he went up and asked for provisions was, 'Bread to eat, not to sell—take what you want.' The general asked a Pimo who made the house I had seen. 'It is the Casa de Montezuma,' said he; 'It was built by the son of a most beautiful woman, who once dwelt in yon mountain. She was fair, and all the handsome men came to court her; but in vain. When they came they paid tribute, and out of this small store she fed all people in times of famine, and it did not diminish. At last as she lay asleep a drop of rain fell upon her navel, and she became pregnant, and brought forth a son, who was the builder of all these houses.'

"He appeared unwilling to discourse further about them, as though some melancholy fate had befallen the people who formerly inhabited them. These were his ancestors. At length, observing that there were a great many similar buildings in the north, south and west, he was silent. Some other Pimos Cocomiracopas[76] visited the camp. Messengers were now sent into their villages to purchase melons, fruits and provisions. These soon came, although the distance was several miles. They wanted white beads for what they had to sell, and knew the value of money. Seeing us eating, the interpreter told the general that he had tasted the liquor of Sonora and New Mexico, and would like to taste a sample of that of the United States. The dog had a liquorish tooth, and when given a drink of French brandy, pronounced it better than any he had ever tasted. The Mirocopa messenger came to ask the general what his business was, and where he was going? he said his people were at peace with all the world, except some of their neighbors, the Apaches,[77] and they did not desire any more enemies. He was of course told to say to his chief that our object was merely to pass peaceably through their country: that we had heard a great deal of the Pimos; and knew them to be a good people."

These Pimos approached the Americans with the greatest confidence and suavity of manners, possessing a natural grace of carriage, great good humor and unbounded loquacity. They are a virtuous, honest, and industrious race, and subsist entirely by agriculture and grazing, and clothe themselves with woolen and cotton fabrics of their own manufacture. The Pimos and Cocomiracopas at present live neighbors to each other, the latter having recently migrated from the mouth of the Gila, and the Colorado. They are distinct races, and speak different tongues. These together with the Miracopas, number more than four thousand souls.

NOTE 76.—The Coco-Maricopas belong to the Yuman linguistic family, and were formerly in confederacy with their kindred tribes, the Yumas and Cocopas. They lived along the Gila, principally on the south side of the stream. They now live on the Pima reservation, and number about three hundred.

NOTE 77.—The Apaches belong to the Athabascan linguistic stock, and were formerly very numerous, ranging over a vast extent of country. There are yet some six thousand of them, divided into various bands and kindred tribes. Their habitat extended from that of the Navajos far into the present Mexico. They were warlike and cruel. The Mexican authorities employed persons to hunt them down and kill them, paying so much for each scalp produced. After their removal to what is now Kansas, the Delaware and Shawnee Indians engaged in this work to some extent, and were very successful at it. White men who engaged in it usually employed members of these tribes to hunt the Apaches.

CHAPTER XIII.

Barrebutt—Fable of the Pimos—Arrival at the Colorado—Mexican papers intercepted—The Jornada of ninety miles—Horse-flesh—The Mulada—Capt. Gillespie—Battle of San Pascual—Gen. Kearny's official report.

"On the morning of the 12th," says Capt. Johnston, "we awoke to hear the crowing of the cock and the baying of the watch-dog, reminding us of civilization afar off in the green valleys of our country." Leaving some mules with the chief Barrebutt, they marched down through the settlements of the Pimos and Cocomiracopas, all of which are on the south side of the Gila, and having completed a distance of fifteen miles, encamped near the base of a mountain lying west of their villages. Both the houses and costume of these Indians are similar. Their winter lodges consists of a rib-work of poles, about fifteen feet in diameter, of convenient height, thatched with twigs and straw, and covered over with a layer of dirt, in the centre of which they build their fires. Their summer shelters are of a much more temporary nature, being constructed after the manner of a common arbor, covered with willow rods, to obstruct the rays of the vertical sun. "The fable of the Pimos is," says our author, "that their first parents were caught up to heaven, and from that time God lost sight of them, and they wandered to the west; that they came from the rising sun." The chief of the Pimos said to the general "that God had placed him over his people, and he endeavored to do the best for them. He gave them good advice, and they had fathers and grandfathers who gave them good advice also. They were told to take nothing but what belonged to them, and to ever speak the truth. They desired to be at peace with every one; therefore they would not join us or the Mexicans in our difficulties." He shook hands with us and bade us welcome, and hoped we might have good luck on our journey. He said we would find the chief of the Maricopas, a man like himself, and one who gave similar counsel to his people.

The entire plains adjacent are susceptible of irrigation, and have once sustained a numerous population, as is evidently shown by the ruins, and the remains of pottery scattered over the earth. These indications of the existence of a former race are still more numerous on the Salt and San Francisco rivers.

The next morning while they lay in camp, preparatory to commencing the march over the Tesotal Jornada, or journey of forty miles without water, the chiefs of the Cocomiracopas visited the general, and through an interpreter said: "You have seen our people. They do not steal. They are perhaps better some than others you have seen. All of our people have sold you provisions. It is good to do so when people have commodities to exchange. If you had come here hungry and poor, it would have afforded us pleasure to give you all you wanted without compensation. Our people desire to be friendly with the Americans."

From thence in ten days' march, following the course of the Gila, they came to the confluence of that stream with the Colorado, near which they encamped. Just before their arrival at this place, signs of a body of horsemen were discovered along the river, which excited some apprehension. It was at first conjectured that it might be Gen. Castro, on his way from Sonora, with a body of cavalry, to regain possession of California. Lieut. Emory with twenty men was sent out to reconnoitre, when presently he discovered it to be some Californians, with five hundred horses, on their way to Sonora. He brought a few of them to the general, one of whom said: "There is a party of eight hundred armed Californians in the Pueblo de los Angeles opposed to the Americans, and also a party of two hundred at San Diego, friendly to the United States." Another said: "The Mexicans at the Pueblo de los Angeles are quiet, and the Americans have quiet possession of the whole country." They both agreed that there were three ships-of-the-line at San Diego. The next morning a few of them were again brought into camp, one of whom was discovered by Lieut. Emory to have in his possession a package of letters. Some of these letters were directed to Gen. Castro. The seals were broken and the letters read by Gen. Kearny. One of the letters gave an account of an insurrection in California, and the placing of Don Flores at the head of the insurrectionists at Pueblo de los Angeles. This was addressed to Gen. Castro. In another letter to a different person, it was asserted that a body of eighty Mexican cavalry had vanquished four hundred Americans at the ravines between the Pueblo and San Pedro, and captured a cannon called Teazer. These letters were re-sealed by Capt. Turner, and returned to the Mexican, who was then dismissed with them. The General now supplied his men with fresh animals, as many of theirs by this time had failed, in crossing the deserts and mountains. They now rested two days before starting upon the desert, or jornada, of ninety miles without water, which lay on the route.

They passed the great Colorado of the west, below the mouth of the Gila, which was deep and rapid; yet all got over safely and began the march upon the desert, which was continued with little intermission for three days and nights, when they came to the Camisa, where they found a supply of water in a cañon of the mountains. Here they enjoyed the advantage of a little repose. Thence they marched over a rugged, rocky road, among hills and mountains, and after four days came to Warner's rancho, during which they lost many animals, and suffered much from hunger and fatigue, being compelled to subsist a part of the time on horse flesh. Here again they rested.

This rancho is sixty miles from San Diego, and eighty from the Pueblo de los Angeles. Learning that there was a herd of mules fifteen miles from this place belonging to Don Flores, the leader of the insurgents at the Pueblo, Lieut. Davidson with twenty-seven men was dispatched by Gen. Kearny at dark, with instructions to procure a sufficient number of horses and mules to remount the men. About this time, Mr. Stokes, an Englishman, came to Gen. Kearny, and informed him "that Commodore Stockton, with the greater part of his naval force, was at San Diego." The general immediately dispatched a letter to the commodore,[78] informing him of his arrival in the country, and expressing his intention to march directly to San Diego. The next day Lieut. Davidson and Carson returned, having

---

NOTE 78.—The letter is here set out:
          HEAD QR. ARMY OF THE WEST
          CAMP AT WARNERS DECR. 2, 1846]

SIR: I (this afternoon) reached here escorted by a part of the 1st Regt Dragoons—I came by orders from the Presdt of the U. S.—We left Santa fe on the 25th Sept having taken possession of New Mexico—annexed it to the U. S.—established a civil government in that Tery. & secured order, peace & quietness there—If you can send a party to open a communication with us on the Route to this Place & to inform me of the state of affairs in California, I wish you would do so, and as quickly as possible—The fear of this letter falling into Mexican hands prevents me from writing more—Your express by Mr. Canon was met on the Del Norte, & your mail must have reached Washington at least ten days since.
  Commr. R. F. Stockton   Very Resp-y Yr. ob. Servt
    U. S. Navy   S. W. KEARNY
Commg. Pacific Squadron—Diago   Brig Genl U. S. A.
  You might use the bearer of this (Mr. Stokes) as a guide to conduct your Party to this place.

in possession a large *mulada*. In a short time a party of French and Englishmen, and a Chilian, came to claim their stock, averring their intention to leave the country. The general restored them a portion of the animals, and put the remainder into service.

From thence on the 4th of December they advanced fifteen miles, and came to the old mission of Santa Isabella, *en route* to San Diego, where it was General Kearny's intention to communicate with the naval force under Commodore Stockton; and "on the 5th," observes Mr. Stanley, who accompanied Gen. Kearny on this expedition, "we met Capt. Gillespie and Lieut. Beall of the United States' navy with an escort of thirty-five men. After making a late camp, Gen. Kearny heard that an armed body of Californians was encamped about nine miles from us. Lieut. Hammond, with a small party, was sent out to reconnoitre. He returned about twelve o'clock, with intelligence that the camp was in the valley of San Pascual, but learned nothing of the extent of the force, although it was thought to be about one hundred and sixty. At two o'clock on the morning of the 6th the reveille sounded, and at three our force was formed in the order of battle and the march resumed. We arrived about daylight at the valley. The enemy were encamped about a mile from the declivity of the mountain over which we came, and as Lieut. Hammond had been discovered on the night previous, the Californians were waiting in their saddles for our approach.

"From a misapprehension of an order, the charge was not made by our whole force, or with as much precision as was desirable, but the Californians retreated on firing a single volley, to an open plain about half a mile distant. Capt. Johnston and one private were killed in this charge. The retreat of the enemy was followed with spirit by our troops, skirmishing the distance of half a mile. When they reached the plains, our force was somewhat scattered by the pursuit. The Californians, taking advantage of this disorganization, fought with desperation, making great havoc with their lances. It was a real hand-to-hand fight, and lasted half an hour. They were, however, driven from the field, with what loss we could not learn. Our loss was severe, seventeen being killed and fourteen wounded. Among the killed were Capt. Johnston, who led the charge of the advance guard, Capt. Benj. Moore and Lieut. Hammond. Gen.

Kearny, Capt. Gillespie and Lieut. Wm. H. Warner were slightly wounded. Several non-commissioned officers were killed.[79]

"We encamped on the field and collected the dead. At first, General Kearny thought to move on the same day. The dead were lashed on mules, and remained two hours, or more, in that posture. It was a sad and melancholy picture. We soon found, however, that our wounded were unable to travel. The mules were released of their packs, and the men engaged in fortifying the place for the night. During the day the enemy were in sight, curveting their horses, keeping our camp in constant excitement. Three of Capt. Gillespie's volunteers started with dispatches to Commodore Stockton. The dead were buried at night, and ambulances made for the wounded; and the next morning we started in face of the enemy's spies, being then about thirty-eight miles from San Diego. In our march we were constantly expecting an attack—spies could be seen on the top of every hill—but with a force of one hundred men, many of whom were occupied with the care of the wounded, we did not leave our trail.

"We had traveled about seven miles, when, just before sunset we were again attacked. The enemy came charging down a valley; about one hundred men well mounted. They were about dividing their force, probably with a view of attacking us in front and rear, when Gen. Kearny ordered his men to take possession of a hill on our left. The enemy seeing the movement, struck for the same point,

---

NOTE 79.—Captain Turner notified Commodore Stockton of this battle and its results in the following letter:

HEAD QUARTERS
CAMP NEAR SAN PASCHAL DEC. 6, '46

SIR: I have the honor to report to you, that at early dawn this morning, Gen'l Kearny with a Dett. of U. S. Dragoons & Capt Gillispies Co of Mounted Riflemen had an engagement with a very considerable Mexican force near this camp—We have about 18 killed, & 14 or 15 wounded, several so severely that it may be impracticable to move them for several days—I have to suggest to you the propriety of dispatching without delay a considerable force to meet us on the Route to San Diego, via the Solidad & San Bernado, or to find us at this place—also that you will send up carts or some other means of transporting our Wounded to San Diego. We are without provisions & in our present situation may not be able to obtain cattle from the Ranches in the vicinity—Gen'l Kearny is among the wounded but it is hoped not dangerously—Capt Moore & Johnston 1st Dragoons killed—Capt Gillespie badly, but not dangerously wounded Lieut Hammond 1st Dragoons dangerously wounded.

Commr R. F. Stockton   I am Sir Very Resp-y Yr ob. Servt
U. S. Navy   H. S. TURNER
Commg.   Capt 1st Drag
San Diego   Commg

reaching it before us, and as we ascended, they were pouring a very spirited fire upon us from behind the rocks. They were soon driven from the hill, only one or two being wounded on our side. Here, therefore, we were compelled to encamp, and also to destroy the most cumbersome of our camp equipage. A white flag was sent to Señor Pico, the Californian commandant, and an exchange of prisoners effected—our bearers of dispatches having been intercepted by the enemy. We were more fortunate in getting an express through to San Diego for a reinforcement, and at the expiration of four days, during which we lived on the meat of mules, horses and colts, without bread or other condiment, we were joined by a reinforcement of two hundred men, and on the 11th of December resumed our march. Not a Californian was to be seen, as we proceeded, and on the 12th we reached San Diego, and received from the officers a hearty welcome;" having completed a march of one thousand and ninety miles from Santa Fé.[80]

NOTE 80.—From San Diego General Kearny, in two letters, reported to the War Department the details of his march from Santa Fé. These letters are here given:

HEAD QR ARMY OF THE WEST
SAN DIEGO UPPER CALIFORNIA
DECR 12, 1846

SIR: As I have previously reported to you, I left Santa fe (New Mexico) for this country on the 25th Sept with 300 of the 1st Dragoons under Major Sumner—We crossed to the right bank of the Del Norte at Albuquerque (65 miles below Santa fe) continued down on that bank til the 6th Octob, when we met Mr. Kit Carson with a Party of 16 Men on his way to Washington city with a Mail & Papers—as express from Commr Stockton & Lieut Col Frémont—reporting that the Californians were already in possession of the Americans under their command that the American flag was flying from every important position in the Tery & that the country was forever free from Mexican control—the War ended & Peace & harmony re-established among the People. In consequence of this information, I directed that 200 Dragoons under Maj. Sumner should remain in New Mexico, & that the other 100 with 2 Mounted Howitzers under Capt Moore should accompany me as a guard to Upper California—With this guard we continued our march to the South on the right bank of the Del Norte, to the distance of 230 miles below Santa fe, when leaving that River on the 15th Octob in about the 33° of Lat, we marched Westward for the Copper Mines which we reached on the 18th & on the 20th reached the River Gila—proceeded down the Gila, crossing and recrossing it as often as obstructions in our front rendered necessary—on the 11th Nov. reached the Pimo Village about 80 miles from the settlements in Sonora—These Indians we found honest & living comfortably having made a good crop this year, & we remained with them 2 days to rest our Men—recruit our Animals & obtain Provisions—On the 22d Nov. reached the mouth of the Gila in lat about 32°:42′, our whole march on this River having been nearly 500 miles, & with but very little exception between the 32° & 33° of lat—This River (the Gila) more particularly the Northern side is bounded nearly the whole distance by a range of lofty Mountains, & if a tolerable Waggon Road to its mouth from the Del Norte is ever discovered, it must be on the South side, & therefore the Bound line between the U. States & Mexico

Another account makes the American loss twenty killed and fifteen wounded; among the former were Capts. Moore and Johnston, and Lieut. Hammond of the 1st dragoons; Sergeants Moore, Whitehurst, and Cox, and Corporals Clapin and West, and ten privates of the 1st dragoons; one private of the topographical engineers, and one volunteer. The wounded were Gen. Kearny; Lieut. Warner, of the topographical engineers; Capts. Gillespie and Gibson of the volunteers, and Mr. Robidou, interpreter, and ten privates of the 1st dragoons. Gen. Kearny's official account of this hard fought action is as follows:

"As the day dawned on the 6th of December, we approached the enemy, (one hundred and sixty,) at San Pascual, who was already in the saddle, when Captain Johnston made a furious charge upon them with his advance guard, and was in a short time after supported by the dragoons; soon after which the enemy gave way, having kept up, from the beginning, a continual fire upon us. Upon the retreat

should certainly not be North of the 32° of lat—The country is destitute of timber producing but few Cotton Wood & Mesquite trees, & tho' the soil on the Cotton [wood] lands is generally good, yet we found but very little grass, or vegetation in consequence of the dryness of the climate & the little rain which falls here—The Pimo Indians who make good crops of wheat, corn vegetables & irrigate the land by water from the Gila, as did the Astecs (the famous inhabitants of the country) the remains of whose Sequias or little canals were seen by us, as well as the position of many of their dwellings, and a large quantity of broken pottery & earthern ware used by them—
We crossed the Colorado about 10 miles below the mouth of the Gila, & marching near it about 30 miles further, turned off & crossed the "Desert" a distance of about 60 miles without water or grass—On the 2d December reached Warners Rancho (ana caliente) the frontier settlement in California on the Route leading to Sonora. On the 4th marched to Mr Stockes Ranch (San Isabella) & on the 5th was met by a small Party of Volunteers under Capt Gillespie sent out from San Diego by Commr Stockton to give us what information they possessed of the enemy, 6 or 700 of whom are now said to be in Arms & in the Field Thro' out the Tery, determined upon opposing the Americans & resisting their authority in the Country—Encamped that night near another Rancho (San Maria) of Mr Stokes about 40 miles from San Diego—The journals & maps kept & prepared by Capt Johnston 1st Dragoons (my Aide de Camp) & Lieut Emory, Topo Engs, which will accompany or follow this Report, will render anything further from me on this subject unnecessary—

Brig Genl. R. Jones	Very Resp-y Yr ob Servt
Adjt Genl U. S. A.	S. W. KEARNY
W——n.	Brig Genl U. S. A.

HEAD QR ARMY OF THE WEST
SAN DIEGO—UPPER CALIFORNIA
DECR 13, 1846

SIR: In my communication of yesterdays date, I brought the report of the movements of my Guard up to the evening of the 5th Inst in camp near a Rancho of Mr Stokes (San Maria) about 40 miles from San Diego—Having learned from Capt Gillespie of the Volunteers, that there was an armed Party of Californians with a number of extra horses at San Pasqual, three leagues distant—On a road

of the enemy, Captain Moore led off rapidly in pursuit, accompanied by the dragoons, mounted on horses, and was followed, though slowly, by the others on their tired mules: the enemy were mounted, and among the best horsemen in the world; after retreating about half a mile, and seeing an interval between Captain Moore with his advance, and the dragoons coming to his support, rallied their whole force, charged with their lancers, and on account of their greatly superior numbers, but few of us in front remained untouched; for five minutes they held the ground from us, when our men coming up, we again drove them, and they fled from the field, not to return to it, which we occupied and encamped upon.

"A most melancholy duty now remains for me:—it is to report the death of my aid-de-camp, Captain Johnston, who was shot dead at the commencement of the action; of Captain Moore, who was lanced just previous to the final retreat of the enemy; and of Lieutenant Hammond, also lanced, and who survived but a few hours. We had also killed, two sergeants, two corporals, and ten privates of the 1st dragoons, one private of the volunteers, and one man, an engage in the topographical department. Our howitzers were not brought into

---

leading to this place—I sent Lieut Hammond 1st Dragoons with a few Men to make a reconnoisance of them—He returned at 2 in the morning of the 6th Inst, reporting that he had found the Party in the place mentioned, & that he had been seen tho' not pursued by them—I then determined that I would march for & attack them by break of day—arrangements were accordingly made for the purpose—My Aide de Camp Capt Johnston 1st Drags was assigned to the command of the advanced Guards of 12 Dragoons mounted on the best horses we had—then followed about 50 Dragoons under Capt Moore, mounted with but few exceptions on the tired mules they had ridden from Santa fe (N. Mexico) 1050 miles—then about 20 Volunteers of Capt Gibsons Co under his command, & that of Capt Gillespie—then followed our 2 Mountain Howitzers with Dragoons to manage them & under the charge of Lieut Davidson of the Regt. the remainder of the Dragoons, Volunteers, & Citizens employed by the officers of the Staff &c were placed under the command of Major Swords (Qr Mr) with orders to follow on our trail with the baggage & to see to its safety—As the day (Decr 6) dawned, we approached the enemy at San Pasqual, who was already in the saddle when Capt Johnston made a furious charge upon them with his advanced Guard, & was in a short time after supported by the Dragoons, soon after which the enemy gave way, having kept up from the beginning a continuous fire upon us—Upon the retreat of the enemy, Capt Moore led off rapidly in pursuit, accompanied by the Dragoons Mounted on horses, & was followed, tho' slowly by the others on their tired Mules—The enemy well mounted & among the best horsemen in the world, after retreating about half a mile & seeing an interval between Capt Moore with his advance & the Dragoons coming to his support, rallied their whole force charged with their lances, & on account of their greatly superior numbers, but few of us in front remained untouched—for 5 minutes they held the ground from us, when our men coming up, we again drove them, & they fled from the field, not to return to it, which we occupied & encamped upon—A most melancholy duty now remains for me—It is to report the death of my Aide de Camp, Capt Johnston, who was shot dead at the commencement of the action—of Capt Moore who was lanced just previous to the final retreat of the enemy, & of Lieut Hammond also lanced & who survived but a few hours—We had also Killed 2 Sergts —2 Capts & 10 Privs of the 1st Dragoons—One Privt of the Vols & one man, an engagé in the Topo. Dept—Among the wounded are myself (in 2 places) Lieut

the action. The enemy proved to be a party of about one hundred and sixty Californians, under command of Andres Pico, brother of the late governor; the number of their dead and wounded must have been considerable, though I had no means of ascertaining how many, as just previous to their final retreat, they carried off all except six."

After the strife of the battle was over the surgeon came to General Kearny, who sat bleeding at three wounds, and offered to afford him all the relief that was in his power. "First go and dress the wounds of the soldiers," said he, "who require attention more than I do, and when you have done, then come to me." The surgeon proceeded to execute the order; but while busily employed, he looked around and saw the general fall backwards, exhausted by loss of blood. The surgeon immediately ran to his support, raised him from the ground, restored him, and dressed his wounds.

Warner, Topo Engs (in 3 places) Capts Gallespie & Gibson of the Vols (the former in three places) One Sergt one bugler & nine Privs of the Dragoons, many of these receiving from 2 to 10 lance wounds, most of them when unhorsed & incapable of resistance—Our Howitzers were not brought into the action, but coming to the front at the close of it, before they were turned so as to admit of being fired upon the retreating enemy, the 2 mules before one of them got alarmed & freeing themselves from their drivers ran off & among the enemy & was thus lost to us—The enemy proved to be a party of about 160 Californians under Andreas Pico, brother of the late Governor—The number of their dead & wounded must have been considerable, tho' I have no means of ascertaining how many, as just previous to their final retreat, they carried off all excepting six—The great number of our Killed & wounded proves that our officers & Men have fully sustained the high character & reputation of our troops, & the victory thus gained over more than double our force may assist in forming the wreath of our National glory—I have to return my thanks to many for their gallantry & good conduct on the field, & particularly to Capt Turner 1st Dragoons (A. A. A. G.) & to Lieut Emory (Topo Engs) who were active in performance of their duties, & in conveying orders from me to the command—

On the morning of the 7th having made ambulances for our wounded, & interred the dead, we proceeded on our march, when the enemy shewed himself occupying the hills in our front, but which they left as we approached 'till reaching San Bernado a party of them took possession of a hill near to it & maintained their position until attacked by our advance who quickly drove them from it, killing & wounding five of their number, with no loss on our part.

On account of our wounded Men & upon the report of the Surgeon that rest was necessary for them we remained at this place 'till the morning of the 11th when Lieut Gray of the Navy, in command of a Party of Sailors & Marines sent out from San Diego by Comr. Stockton joined us. We proceeded at 10 A. M., the enemy no longer showing himself, & on the 12th (yesterday) we reached this place; and I have now to offer my thanks to Com Stockton & all his gallant command for the very many kind attentions we have received & continue to receive from them.

Brig Genl R. Jones
Adjt Genl U. S. A.
W——n.

Very Resp-y Yr ob. Servt.
S. W. KEARNY
Brig Genl U. S. A.

CHAPTER XIV.

Col. Stevenson—Com. Sloat and Lieutenant-colonel Frémont—Gen. Castro—Com. Stockton—The Revolution in California—Mr. Talbot—The insurgents under Flores and Pico—Gen. Kearny marches upon Angeles—Battles of San Gabriel and the Mesa—Capital recovered—The Capitulation.

It is not proposed in this chapter, to give an historical account of the movements of the Pacific squadron, commanded by Commodores Sloat and Stockton, in taking possession of the coast of California; nor indeed of the land forces under Lieutenant-colonel Frémont, except so far as may serve to illustrate the operations of Gen. Kearny while in that country.

In the instructions furnished Gen. Kearny by the War Department on the 12th of September, 1846, he was assured that a regiment of volunteers had been raised in the State of New York, commanded by Col. J. D. Stevenson, whose term of service would not expire until the close of the war with Mexico, which would immediately sail for California, and would, when arrived there, constitute a portion of his command, to act as land forces. The Secretary of War, writing to General Kearny, under date of June 3d, 1846, further adds, "It is expected that the naval forces of the United States, which are now, or soon will be in the Pacific, will be in possession of all the towns on the sea-coast, and will coöperate with you in the conquest of California. Arms, ordnance, munitions of war, and provisions, to be used in that country, will be sent by sea to our squadron, in the Pacific, for the use of the land forces." A company of United States' artillery, commanded by Captain Tompkins, aided by Lieutenant Halleck, engineer, was also dispatched to the bay of Monterey, to coöperate with General Kearny and the marine forces in holding possession of California.

In the month of July, 1846, Commodore John D. Sloat, commanding the United States' Naval forces in the Pacific ocean, acting in anticipation of instructions from the Navy Department, and on his own responsibility and clear conception of duty as a naval officer, (having on the 7th heard of the existence of war between the United States and Mexico,) anchored in the bay of Monterey, with the Pacific squadron, and in less than twenty-four hours raised the American flag in the old capital of the country. The gallant marines led on on by the Commodore, proceeded on land, invested the city, and without bloodshed or strenuous opposition, took formal possession in the name of the government of the United States.

About the same period a corps of volunteers, consisting of American emigrants to California, commanded by General Ide and Captain Grigsby, raised the independent flag of the "*Bear and the Star,*" in the settlements on the Sacramento, and held that part of the province in quiet possession. Their intention was to establish an independent government of their own, in the event the United States' forces did not coöperate with them in wresting the country from the hands of the haughty Mexicans. These were styled the BEAR MEN.

Lieutenant-colonel Frémont[81] was, at this period, on the Bay of San Francisco, near the settlements of Sonoma, in command of the topographical corps, which had gone out from Missouri early in 1846, and a few California volunteers. Hearing of the capture of Monterey, he ventured to raise the standard of his country, that he might coöperate with the naval forces in the peaceable conquest of California. Thus was California bloodlessly and peaceably commenced to be revolutionized, and placed under the American flag, and American protection. The cities and settlements were soon occupied by the American arms, and the inhabitants, at first, treated with a clemency and consideration which very much conciliated and disposed them to desire a peace, and connection with the United States. They were

NOTE 81.—John Charles Frémont was born at Savannah, Georgia, January 21, 1813; died at New York, July 13, 1890. He made extensive explorations in the West, and was known as the "Pathfinder." But his services were not so much in discovering as in calling attention to routes through the Rocky Mountains, the routes having been known to hunters and trappers for years prior to the explorations of Frémont. He was at South Pass in 1842, and in 1843–44 he visited the Pacific slope. He was in California on an exploring expedition when the Mexican War came on in 1846, and he aided in the conquest of that country by the Americans. He was United States Senator from California two years— 1850–51. In 1856 he was the candidate of the Republican party for President of the United States, but was defeated at the polls. In 1861 he was Federal commander of the Western Department, with headquarters at St. Louis; and on August 31 of that year he issued a proclamation declaring that he would emancipate the slaves of persons in rebellion against the United States, but President Lincoln annulled it. He was Governor of Arizona four years, from 1878 to 1882. He married Jessie Benton, daughter of Senator Thomas H. Benton of Missouri.

accordingly protected in their persons and property in the amplest manner.

This brilliant and highly important service having been rendered the country in a manner that met the cordial approval of the Executive, Commodore Sloat, whose modesty is only equalled by his gallantry, returned to the United States, leaving Commodore R. F. Stockton commander-in-chief of the coast, and of the bays and harbors. Commodore Stockton, in his instructions from the Navy Department, was permitted to establish in California, a temporary, civil government, until the same should be abrogated or modified by competent authority. It may not be amiss in this connection to observe, that Commodore Sloat had been instructed by Mr. Bancroft, Secretary of the Navy, to blockade and hold possession of the bays and ports of San Francisco, Monterey, and San Diego; and, if he deemed it advisable, also to hold the ports of Guymas, Mazatlan and Acapulco in a state of vigorous blockade. These instructions descended to Commodore Stockton, his successor, in the command of the Pacific naval forces.

Commodore R. F. Stockton, and Lieutenant-colonel J. C. Frémont completed the conquest, which the gallant and modest Commodore John D. Sloat and his marines, had so gloriously and auspiciously begun. In a short time the whole of California was in the hands of the Americans, and the American flag waved from every important place in the country. The civil functions of the government were at an end, and the governor and his forces dispersed amongst the mountains and deserts. Gen. Castro, commander-in-chief, with a small body of men escaped to Sonora, having addressed the subjoined proclamation to the Californians.

"Fellow citizens:—I carry away my heart full of the heaviest weight in taking leave of you. I go out of the country in which I was born, but in the hope of returning to destroy the slavery in which I leave you. I will come the day in which our unfortunate country can chastise exemplarily an usurpation so rapacious and so unjust, and in the face of the world exact satisfactions for its wrongs. My friends, I confide in your loyalty and patriotism; and in proof of the confidence which you merit from me, I leave to you my wife and innocent children. They have no fortune, and are even without means of subsisting. I leave them to your favor and guidance, considering that I lose all to save national honor.

"I acknowledge the faithfulness that you have constantly manifested towards me. I believe it is right for me to exhort you again not to abandon the sentiments of fidelity for the mother country; preserve in your bosoms the holy fire of liberty, and the day of vengeance will come. Never deny the Mexican name. Fellow-citizens, adieu! In taking leave of you I feel my soul inundated with bitterness, considering I leave you as slaves; but the glorious day will come when you will break your chains and again be free and independent. God and Liberty."

Commodore Stockton next proceeded with a part of his force to San Pedro, where, disembarking them, he formed a junction with Lieutenant-colonel Frémont, in command of a small body of California volunteers, who had been recently enrolled for the service. With their united forces they now marched to the Pueblo de los Angeles, the new capital of the country. Upon their approach Gen. Castro and his troops fled without offering the slightest resistance. The Americans entered the city, and raised the flag of the "stars and stripes." Commodore Stockton, having issued a proclamation to the people of California, setting forth certain obnoxious ordinances and regulations, which subsequently proved the ground of the attempted revolution of Flores and Pico, and leaving Capt. Gillespie with nineteen volunteers to garrison the capital, returned to San Pedro. Not long afterwards the revolution breaking out, the insurgents compelled Capt. Gillespie to capitulate, and retire with his slender force to San Pedro. It is due to Capt. Gillespie, however, to state that the capitulation, under the circumstances, was highly honorable to him and his men. The forces of the enemy were overwhelming. The capital was now repossessed by the Californians.

Meanwhile Mr. Talbot, of the topographical corps, under Lieutenant-colonel Frémont, who had been stationed with sixteen men at Santa Barbara, was hotly besieged by an insurrectionary force, for a considerable time. Finally, however, he and his men, with much peril and difficulty, effected their escape to the mountains. After wandering among the rocks and fastnesses for several days, and suffering incredibly from fatigue, hunger, and other privations, they arrived at Monterey in the greatest destitution.

Not far from this period Commodore Stockton, leaving a sufficient garrison in Monterey, and a part of the fleet in the bay, sailed with three ships-of-war for the harbor of San Diego, with the view of marching thence against the insurgents, who were posted in considerable numbers at the Pueblo de los Angeles. At San Diego, on the 12th of December, he formed a junction of his marine and volunteer forces with the overland detachment of the 1st dragoons of the United States' army, under immediate command of General Kearny. The malcontents had concentrated at Angeles, and armed themselves, with the design of recovering the country from the hands of the Americans. They were six hundred strong, and were headed by Don Mariana Flores and Don Andres Pico, the latter of whom commanded the Californians on the 6th of December in the action at San Pascual. Having compelled the garrison, which was stationed at Angeles upon the conquest of the country, to capitulate; driven all the Americans from the interior to the seaboard; and come near defeating the marine expedition of Captain Mervine, the insurgents confidently hoped to reëstablish the former power and government of California.

On the 29th of December, General Kearny and Commodore Stockton, in joint command of five hundred men, consisting of marines, California volunteers, a detachment of the 1st dragoons of the United States' army, and a battery of artillery, left San Diego upon the march against the insurgent forces at the Pueblo de los Angeles, a distance of one hundred and forty-five miles. The entire force was on foot, with the exception of about sixty volunteer mounted riflemen, commanded by Captain Gillespie.

On the 8th of January the insurgents showed themselves, six hundred strong, with four pieces of artillery, occupying the heights, prepared to dispute the passage of the river San Gabriel. General Kearny now drew up his forces in order of battle, passed the river under a heavy fire from the enemy, charged the heights, drove him from his strong position, and gained a most signal victory. This action lasted one hour and a half. The next day, (the 9th,) continuing the march towards the capital, on the plains of the Mesa, the insurgents, having concealed their forces and cannon under the cover of a ravine, until the Americans were within gunshot, opened a galling fire upon their right flank, and at the same instant charged them in front and rear. In a short time, however, the insurgents were repulsed with considerable loss, and driven from the field. The loss of the Americans on both days was two killed and fifteen wounded;

that of the enemy was estimated in killed and wounded at no less than eighty-five. On the 10th the Americans repossessed the city without farther opposition, while the bayonets and lances of the

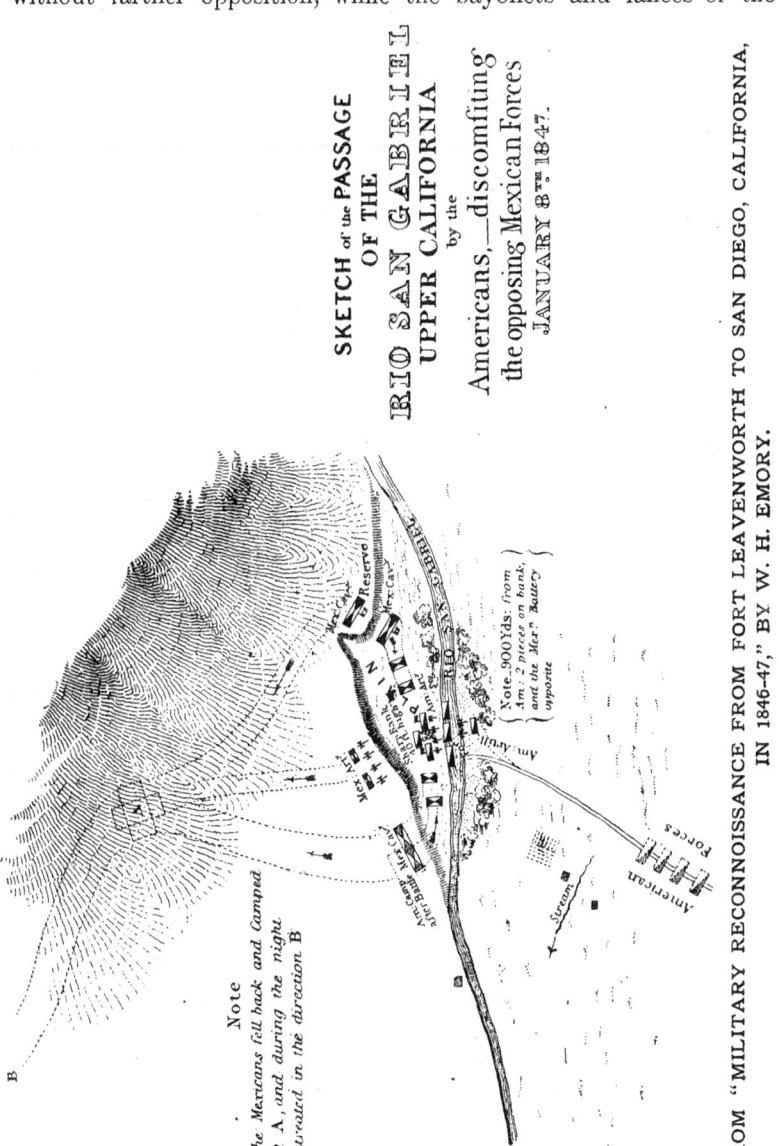

346   DONIPHAN'S EXPEDITION.

retreating insurgents glittered on the adjacent hills and mountains. Lieutenant-colonel Frémont, with his battalion of four hundred mounted California volunteers, whom he had recently enrolled for the service in the settlements of New Helvetia, Sonoma, and the north-

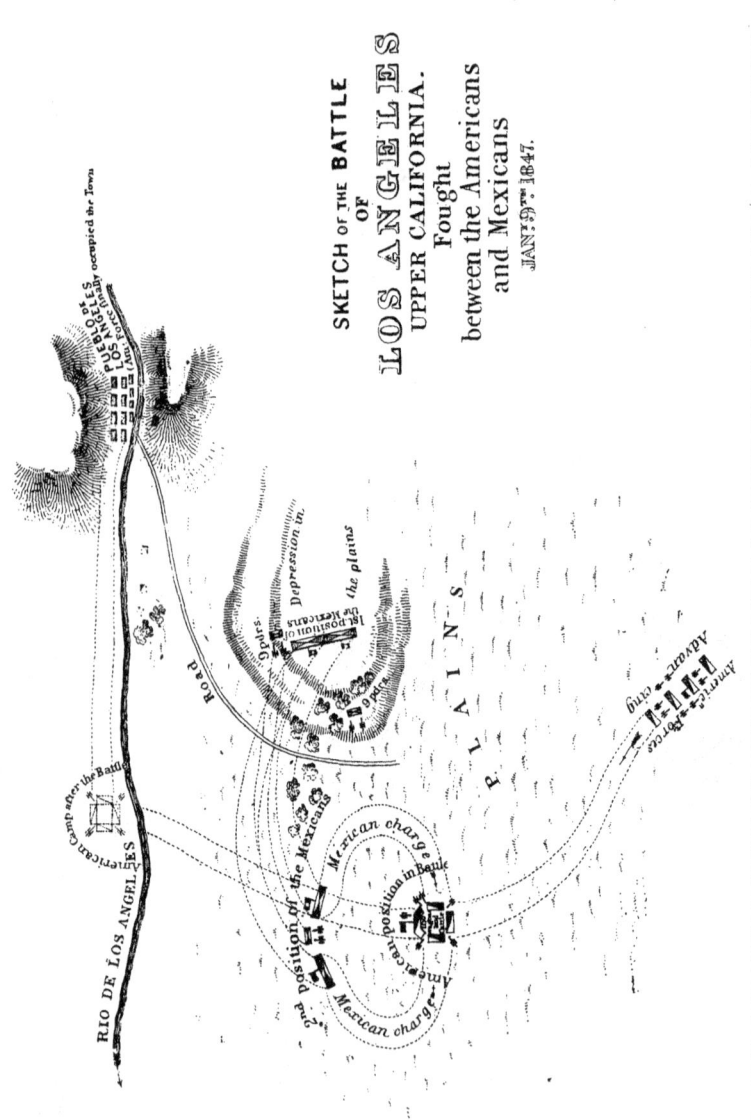

ern districts, had performed a march of one hundred and twenty miles, from Santa Barbara to San Fernando, while Gen. Kearny was marching from San Diego, in the hope that the former would be able to effect a junction with him in time to coöperate against the malcontents. In this expectation, however, the general was disappointed.

After the battle of the 9th, Andres Pico, the second in command of the insurgent forces, having, as some say, more than once forfeited his parole of honor, and expecting little clemency from Gen. Kearny, escaped with a few of his adherents, and on the 12th meeting Lieutenant-colonel Frémont on his way to Angeles, effected with that officer, (who as yet was not fully apprised of what had transpired) a stipulation, securing immunity for his crimes. This treaty was afterwards approved by the commander-in-chief, from motives of policy. The following is Commodore Stockton's account of the affair:

HEAD QUARTERS, CIUDAD DE LOS ANGELES,
January 11th, 1847.

SIR: I have the honor to inform you that it has pleased God to crown our poor efforts to put down the rebellion, and to retrieve the credit of our arms, with the most complete success. The insurgents determined, with their whole force, to meet us on our march from San Diego to this place, and to decide the fate of the territory by a general battle.

Having made the best preparation I could, in the face of a boasting and vigilant enemy, we left San Diego on the 29th day of December, (that portion of the insurgent army who had been watching and annoying us, having left to join the main body,) with about six hundred fighting men, composed of the detachment from the ships, aided by General Kearny with a detachment of sixty men on foot, from the first regiment of United States' dragoons, and by Capt. Gillespie, with sixty mounted riflemen.

We marched nearly one hundred and forty miles in ten days, and found the rebels, on the 8th day of January, in a strong position on the high bank of the river San Gabriel, with six hundred mounted men and four pieces of artillery, prepared to dispute our passage across the river.

We waded through the water, dragging our guns after us, against the galling fire of the enemy, without exchanging a shot until we reached the opposite shore, when the fight became general, and our troops having repelled a charge of the enemy, charged up the bank in a most gallant manner, and gained a complete victory over the insurgent army.

The next day, on our march across the plains of the Mesa to this place, the insurgents made another desperate effort to save the capital and their own necks. They were concealed with their artillery, in a ravine, until we came within gun-shot, when they opened a brisk fire from their field-pieces on our right flank, and at the same time charged on our front and rear. We soon silenced their guns and repelled the charge, when they fled, and permitted us the next morning to march into town without any further opposition.

We have rescued the country from the hands of the insurgents, but I fear the absence of Col. Frémont's battalion of mounted riflemen will enable most of the Mexican officers who have broken their parole, to escape to Sonora.

I am happy to say that our loss in killed and wounded, does not exceed twenty, whilst we are informed that the enemy has lost between seventy and eighty.

This dispatch must go immediately, and I will await another opportunity to furnish you with the details of these two battles, and the gallant conduct of the officers and men under my command, with their names.

Faithfully, your obedient servant,

R. F. STOCKTON, Com., &c.

To the Hon. George Bancroft, Secretary of the Navy, Washington, D. C.

HEAD QUARTERS, CIUDAD DE LOS ANGELES,
January 15th, 1847.

SIR: I have the honor to inform you of the arrival of Lieutenant-colonel Frémont at this place, with four hundred men—that some of the insurgents have made their escape to Sonora, and that the rest have surrendered to our arms.

Immediately after the battles on the 8th and 9th, they began to disperse; and I am sorry to say that their leader, José Ma. Flores, made his escape, and that the others have been pardoned by a capitulation agreed upon by Lieutenant-colonel Frémont.

José Ma. Flores, the commander of the insurgent forces, two or three days previous to the 8th, sent two commissioners with a flag of truce to my camp, to make "a treaty of peace." I informed the commissioners that I could not recognise José Ma. Flores, who had broken his parole, as an honorable man, or as one having any rightful authority, or worthy to be treated with—that he was a rebel in arms, and that if I caught him I would have him shot. It seems that not being able to negotiate with me, and having lost the battles of the 8th and 9th, they met Col. Frémont on the 12th instant, on his way here, who, not knowing what had occurred, entered into a capitulation with them, which I now send you; and, although I refused to do it myself, still I have thought it best to approve it.

The territory of California is again tranquil, and the civil government formed by me is again in operation in the places where it was interrupted by the insurgents.

Col. Frémont has four hundred men in his battalion, which will be quite sufficient to preserve the peace of the territory; and I will immediately withdraw my sailors and marines, and sail as soon as possible for the coast of Mexico, where I hope they will give a good account of themselves.

Faithfully, your obedient servant,

R. F. STOCKTON, Commodore, &c.

To the Hon. George Bancroft, Secretary of the Navy, Washington, D. C.

TO ALL TO WHOM THESE PRESENTS SHALL COME, GREETING:

Know ye, that in consequence of propositions of peace, or cessation of hostilities being submitted to me, as a commandant of the California battalion of United States' forces, which has so far been acceded to by me, as to cause me to appoint a board of commissioners, to confer with a similar board to be appointed by the Californians; and it requiring a little time to close the negotiations, it is agreed upon and ordered by me, that an entire cessation of hostilities shall take place until to-morrow afternoon, (January 13th,) and that the said Californians be permitted to bring in their wounded to the mission of San Fernandez, where also, if they choose, they can remove their camp, to facilitate said negotiations.

Given under my hand and seal, this 12th day of January, 1847.

J. C. FRÉMONT,

Lieut.-col. U.S. Army; and Military Commander of California.

The Commissioners appointed on the part of Lieutenant-colonel Frémont, to settle the terms of the capitulation, were Major P. B. Reading, L. McLane, and W. H. Russell, formerly of Missouri. Those selected by Andres Pico, were J. A. Carrillo, and A. Olvera. The first article of this capitulation required the insurgents to deliver up to Lieutenant-colonel Frémont their artillery and public arms, and peaceably return to their homes, yield obedience to the laws of the United States, and not again take up arms during the continuance of the war. They were also required to aid in preserving tranquillity throughout California. In the second article the American Commissioners guaranteed to the insurgents protection of life and property, whether on parole or otherwise, immediately upon their complying with the conditions of the first article. The remaining articles were unimportant.

The revolution of Flores was now crushed; the insurgents had taken refuge in the deserts and mountains, or dispersed to their several homes; the American flag was again hoisted in every part of the province; and general peace and quietude once more prevailed.

CHAPTER XV.

General Kearny and W. P. Hall—Lieutenant-colonel Cooke—The Mormon Battalion—Lieutenant Abert—San Bernardino destroyed by Apaches—The glazed plain—Arrival in Teuson—The honest Pimo chief—Arrival at San Diego—Commodore Shubrick—General Kearny proceeds to Monterey—Governor Frémont—General Kearny and Governor Frémont—California—Its present state—General Kearny's return to the United States.

Having settled the affairs of the government at Angeles, and restored the supremacy of the laws wherein they had been interrupted by the insurrectionists, General Kearny and Commodore Stockton hastily returned to San Diego, where they arrived about the 23d of the same month; the former marching his dismounted dragoons by land, and the latter conducting his marine forces to San Pedro, and sailing thence for the port of San Diego.

It was on this return march that General Kearny, dismounting, walked one hundred and forty-five miles with the common soldiers, covered with dust and sweat, having placed on his horse one of the sick men, whose feet were worn and blistered, and who, from exhaustion, was unable to proceed farther.

About this time the gallant WILLARD P. HALL, of the Missouri volunteers, Col. Doniphan's regiment, and member elect to Congress, came up, met General Kearny in the road, and reported to him the near approach to California of the Mormon battalion under command of Lieutenant-colonel Cooke. Hereupon Mr. Hall, seeing the general toiling in the dust with the common soldiers, generously offered him his charger, observing, "General! take my horse and ride; I am younger than you, and will walk." The general refused, saying, "No, I thank you; I am a soldier, and can walk better than you, as I am accustomed to it."

On the 15th of November, 1846, a small detachment of forty-five volunteers, commanded by Captains Burrows and Thompson, met and totally defeated two hundred Californians on the plain of Salinas, near Monterey, with considerable slaughter. The loss on the side of the Americans was four killed and two wounded: among the former were Captain Burrows and private Ames, of St. Louis, Missouri. About the 25th of January, 1847, and shortly after the return of the troops from Angeles to San Diego, Captain Emory, of the topographical corps, assistant acting adjutant general to the overland expedition, after the death of Captain Johnston, sailed as bearer of dispatches from General Kearny to Washington city, passing by the isthmus of Panama.

It will be remembered that the Mormons had not arrived at Santa Fé when General Kearny took his departure thence for California. Arriving shortly afterwards, however, Captain Cooke was dispatched from the Del Norte, below Soccorro, by General Kearny, to conduct them, as their lieutenant-colonel, to their destination on the Pacific coast, in the place of Captain Allen, who died at Fort Leavenworth. Their outfit being in readiness, they left Santa Fé and commenced their march on Sunday the 18th day of October, 1846, following the route of General Kearny down the Rio Del Norte to a point twenty-five miles below the Jornada mountain, where they struck off westerly over the southern spurs of the Sierra de los Mimbres. Lieutenant-colonel Cooke, perceiving that these spurs terminated abruptly, and that a broad plain spread out to the southward of them, very rightly conjectured that there might be found a pass from the Del Norte to the Gila, without encountering a single mountain. He, therefore, directed his course about sixty miles further south than that of General Kearny, thence striking out across the high plain, bordered by the precipitous points of the Sierras, out of which flowed cool streams of delicious water. These streams, issuing from the mountains, run down upon and fertilize the plain, and lose themselves in the sand, not far distant.

Before leaving the Del Norte valley, Lieutenant-colonel Cooke sent a part of his baggage train, and all the sick Mormons back to Fort Pueblo, on the Arkansas, above Fort Bent, at which place a large number of Mormon families were collecting, with the view of emigrating to California early in the spring of 1847. Accordingly, an emigration of not less than nine hundred Mormon families started from this, and other points, including the Council Bluffs, and are now on their way thither.

Also Lieutenant Abert, of the topographical corps, with a small party returned to the United States about the same time, passing the plains in the inclement season of winter. Being caught in a snow-storm about the 20th of February, which continued without intermission for thirty-six hours, some of his men froze to death, and the Pawnees robbed him of all his mules and other animals.

Lieutenant-colonel Cooke, with his troops, now prosecuted his march over the high plain, through an aperture in the great Cordilleras, finding generally water and pasturage, and meeting with no opposition on his way. He passed the deserted village, San Bernardino, which had once been very rich in cattle and other herds, but was now entirely abandoned on account of the frequent and desolating incursions of the Apaches. Thence he passed over to the San Pedro river, down which he continued his march for sixty miles. Thence striking off, he passed through Teuson, and arrived at the Gila, intersecting Gen. Kearny's route at the Pimo settlement.

On a certain occasion, the guides desired Lieutenant-colonel Cooke to march from the Ojo Vacca to Yanos in Chihuahua. This at first he assented to, but finding that the route urged by his guides led him too far south, he struck directly west, and found water after a march of twelve miles. The next day, he marched south-westerly, and encamped at night without water. At daybreak on the morning following, his command was again in motion, and after marching about twenty-five miles arrived at a plain destitute of grass or other vegetation, and as smooth and hard as polished marble; upon which, neither the nails of the shod animals, nor the iron tires of the loaded wagons, produced the slightest impression; extending forty or fifty miles from north to south, and two or three miles wide. Immediately after crossing this hard plain, (resembling the dry bed of a lake) in its narrowest direction, the party came upon springs furnishing an abundance of cool and delightful water. Here they all rejoiced and took rest.

On another occasion, when Lieutenant-colonel Cooke and his party were encamped within about six miles of the little town of Teuson, in the state of Sonora, where one hundred and fifty dragoons and two pieces of artillery had been stationed; the commandante having express orders from the governor not to permit their passage, three commissioners were sent into camp, to inquire into Col. Cooke's business and intentions, and to ask what terms he would exact of them in passing through the place. The commissioners also entreated him not to pass through the town, but to turn aside and march in some other direction, assuring him that he could do this with impunity, and without molestation. He, however, told them that he would require of the commandante one piece of artillery and certain small arms, and the submission of the place; the arms and cannon to be restored to them upon his departure. The commissioners then retired.

The next morning the Lieutenant-colonel, with his troops drawn up in order of battle, marched directly towards the town. Upon approaching it, he was met by a messenger who said: "Sir, your terms are hard, and such as the commandante never can and never will accede to." Whereupon the messenger returned. Col. Cooke now passed the order down the lines to "load." However, the men did not load their pieces, for very soon a great dust was seen to rise beyond the town, and a body of horsemen at a distance scampering off across the plain with the utmost expedition, leaving behind only such as were too old and helpless to effect their escape by flight. The men now entered the place, where they found an abundance of wheat for their animals, and some fruit and provisions to satisfy their keen appetites. Therefore all now fared well. Then they resumed the march.

Upon arriving at the Pimo villages or settlements, the chief of this honest and simple race of people delivered to Lieutenant-colonel Cooke, a letter and a bale of Indian goods, which Gen. Kearny had left in his charge for that purpose. He also delivered to him twenty-two mules, which, having failed, General Kearny had abandoned at different places. The Pimo Indians had collected these together, knowing that Cooke's forces were to pass that way. This is a remarkable instance of the honesty and good faith of the Pimos, a very peculiar and interesting race of people. "The Sonorans," said the honest chief, "have endeavored several times to prevail on me, both by promises and threats, to deliver this property up to them, but I would let no body have it except my friend Gen. Kearny, or some of his people." Lieutenant-colonel Cooke commended him for his strict honesty and integrity, and told him that in acting thus he would always enjoy the friendship and good opinion of the Americans. They then separated.

Now falling into Gen. Kearny's trail they marched down the Gila, crossed the Colorado below the confluence of the two rivers, proceeded through the Jornada of ninety miles in extent, and arrived at

San Diego, about the close of January, 1847, as already related. Meanwhile Commodore Shubrick arrived at Monterey on the 15th of January, on board the Independence, and superceded Commodore Stockton in command of the Pacific squadron, and the coast of California.

Gen. Kearny,* with Capt. Turner, and Lieut. Warner of the topographical corps, on the 2d of February went aboard the war vessel, Cyane, and proceeded directly to Monterey, leaving the Mormons at San Diego, and Lieutenant-colonel Frémont in command of the California battalion at the Pueblo de los Angeles, as temporary governor of the country, acting under appointment from Commodore Stockton; Angeles now being considered the capital, and seat of the new government.

Upon his arrival at Monterey, General Kearny waited upon Commodore Shubrick, then in command of the fleet in the bay, and let him know his instructions from the War Department, and the extent of his authority. Commodore Shubrick, and subsequently Commodore Biddle, most heartily and cordially coöperated with Gen. Kearny in carrying out his instructions. Thus harmony existed between the land and naval forces. Gen. Kearny,† for certain reasons, however, refused to organize for the people of California a civil government, similar to that which he had previously provided for the inhabitants of New Mexico, as his instructions permitted him.

On the first day of March 1847, Gen. Kearny assumed the reins of the civil government, (Com. Shubrick being in command of the naval forces) and on the same day issued the following proclamation to the inhabitants of California:

GENERAL KEARNY'S PROCLAMATION TO THE PEOPLE OF CALIFORNIA.

The President of the United States having devolved on the undersigned the civil government of California, he enters upon the discharge of his duties with an ardent desire to promote as far as possible the interests of the country and well being of its inhabitants.

The undersigned is instructed by the President to respect and

* About this time Major Swords quartermaster, was dispatched on board a public vessel to the Sandwich Islands, to purchase a supply of provisions for the army, there being no supplies in California.—HUGHES.

† These reason were, perhaps, the dissatisfaction that existed among the Americans who had emigrated to California; the acts of Commodore Stockton being partially in force; and the personal responsibility the work would involve.—HUGHES.

protect the religious institutions of California, to take care that the religious rights of its inhabitants are secured in the most ample manner, since the constitution of the United States allows to every individual the privilege of worshiping his Creator in whatever manner his conscience may dictate.

The undersigned is also instructed to protect the persons and property of the quiet and peaceable inhabitants of the country, against each and every enemy, whether foreign or domestic; and now assuring the Californians that his inclinations no less than his duty demand the fulfillment of these instructions, he invites them to use their best efforts to preserve order and tranquillity, to promote harmony and concord, and to maintain the authority and efficacy of the laws.

It is the desire and intention of the United States to procure for California as speedily as possible a free government like that of their own territories, and they will very soon invite the inhabitants to exercise the rights of free citizens in the choice of their own representatives, who may enact such laws as they deem best adapted to their interests and well being. But until this takes place, the laws actually in existence, which are not repugnant to the constitution of the United States, will continue in force until they are revoked by competent authority; and persons in the exercise of public employments will for the present remain in them, provided they swear to maintain the said constitution and faithfully to discharge their duties.

The undersigned, by these presents, absolves all the inhabitants of California of any further allegiance to the republic of Mexico, and regards them as citizens of the United States. Those who remain quiet and peaceable will be protected in their rights, but should any take up arms against the government of this territory, or join such as do so, or instigate others to do so—all these he will regard as enemies, and they will be treated as such.

When Mexico involved the United States in war, the latter had not time to invite the Californians to join their standard as friends, but found themselves compelled to take possession of the country to prevent its falling into the hands of some European power. In doing this there is no doubt that some excesses, some unauthorized acts, were committed by persons in the service of the United States, and that, in consequence, some of the inhabitants have sustained losses in their property. These losses shall be duly investigated, and those entitled to indemnification shall receive it.

For many years California has suffered great domestic convulsions; from civil wars, like poisoned fountains, have flowed calamity and pestilence over this beautiful region. These fountains are now dried up; the stars and stripes now float over California, and as long as the sun shall shed its light they will continue to wave over her, and over the natives of the country, and over those who shall seek a domicile in her bosom; and under the protection of this flag agriculture must advance, and the arts and sciences will flourish like seed in a rich and fertile soil.

Americans and Californians! from henceforth one people. Let us then indulge one desire, one hope; let that be for the peace and tranquillity of our country. Let us unite like brothers, and mutually strive for the improvement and advancement of this our beautiful country, which within a short period cannot fail to be not only beautiful but also prosperous and happy.

Given at Monterey, capital of California, this 1st day of March, in the year of our Lord, 1847, and of the Independence of the United States the seventy-first.

S. W. KEARNY,
Brig. Gen. U. S. A. and Governor of California.

Gen. Kearny now sent orders to Lieutenant-colonel Frémont at Angeles, requiring him to muster his men into the United States' service regularly, and agreeably to law, and repair with them to Monterey where they could be mustered for discharge and payment, and also to bring with him the archives of the State, and other documents and papers. At the same time he also sent an order to Lieutenant-colonel Cooke, to march with a part of his Mormon force from San Louis Rey to Angeles, and relieve Lieutenant-colonel Frémont. The California volunteers refused to be mustered into service as required, and therefore Lieutenant-colonel Frémont could not obey the orders of General Kearny. Towards the close of March, Lieutenant-colonel Frémont, unattended, left Angeles and repaired to Monterey. Here he had an interview with General Kearny; who in a short time, ordered him back to Angeles to transact certain business, important to be accomplished before their returning to the United States. Frémont being delayed in the execution of this work, General Kearny accompanied by Mr. Hall of Doniphan's regiment, started for the Pueblo, where they arrived on the 12th of May. The general, Mr. Hall, Lieutenant-colonel Frémont and others now returned to Monterey, arriving there near the close of the month.

General Kearny, THE LAWGIVER AND LAND-TRAVELER, having completed the work assigned him by his government, and being now on the eve of returning to the United States, disposed his forces in a manner to preserve entire submission and tranquillity in the country.

The Mormons, whose term of service would expire on the 16th of July, were stationed at San Diego, San Louis Rey, and Angeles. Colonel Stevenson with two companies of his regiment and one company of the 1st dragoons under Captain Smith, were also posted at Angeles. One company of Colonel Stevenson's regiment, and one of light artillery under Captain Tompkins, were retained as a garrison in Monterey.

Four companies of the New York regiment under Lieutenant-colonel Burton were garrisoning Santa Barbara; of which force, however, a squadron of two companies under command of Lieutenant-colonel Burton, were ordered to proceed by sea to Lower California, where they would disembark at La Paz, hoist the American flag, and take possession of the country. Of this regiment, also, one company under Captain Nagle would remain in the San Joaquin valley; a detachment of 30 men would stay at Sutter's settlement; and the remainder under Major Hardy would garrison the town of San Francisco.

Commodore Biddle having returned from China, on the 2d of March assumed the chief command of the naval forces on board the Columbus. Comm. Shubrick with the Independence, and Cyane, had been ordered to sail down the coast, and blockade the ports of Guymas and Mazatlan. Colonel R. B. Mason of the 1st dragoons, who was sent out by the government for the purpose, was left commander-in-chief of all the land forces, and *ex officio* governor of California. Therefore, on the 31st of May, General Kearny took his departure from Monterey, and, in company with Lieutenant-colonel Cooke, Major Swords, Captain Turner and Lieutenant Radford, of the navy; also Lieutenant-colonel Frémont, the Hon. Willard P. Hall, assistant surgeon Sanderson, and thirteen of the Mormon battalion, and nineteen of Lieutenant-colonel Frémont's topographical party, making an aggregate of forty men, returned to the United States by way of the Southern Pass, and arrived at Fort Leavenworth on the 22d *

* General Kearny arrested Col. Frémont on their arrival at Fort Leavenworth, August 22d. The trial is now in progress at Washington. Commodore Stockton and suite left the settlements of California on the 19th of July, and by the overland route, arrived at St. Joseph in October.—HUGHES.*

[*The charges preferred against Colonel Frémont by General Kearny were:
1. Mutiny;
2. Disobedience of the lawful command of a superior officer;
3. Conduct to the prejudice of good order and military discipline.
The trial began November 2, 1847, and was concluded January 31, 1848. Frémont was

of August following, having twice crossed the continent. On the 21st of June this party passed the main ridge of the Sierra Nevada, riding thirty-five miles chiefly over snow from five to twenty-five feet deep, under which water was running, and in many places in great torrents. Near the great Salt Lake, General Kearny and escort humanely gathered up and buried the bones of the emigrant party, who so miserably and wretchedly perished of cold and hunger during the winter of 1846. General Kearny immediately repaired to Washington, whence he will proceed to Southern Mexico and join General Scott's division of the army. Thus terminated the overland expedition to California, which scarcely meets with a parallel in the annals of history.

found guilty on each and every charge, and sentenced to be dismissed from the service. With the verdict was a recommendation that the President extend clemency to Frémont. The President refused to confirm the verdict as to the first charge, but approved it as to the other charges, which, however, he immediately remitted. Frémont could not bring himself to accept the clemency of the President, believing that to do so would be an admission of guilt, and resigned his position in the army. In the *Memoir of the Life and Public Services of John Charles Fremont*, by John Bigelow, New York, 1856, beginning at page 223 and ending at page 318, there is Frémont's "Defence." He could have been but technically guilty of any of the charges, as both Stockton and Kearny were his superior officers. As he had been subject to the orders of Stockton before the arrival of Kearny, he continued to obey him afterwards. It was not his duty to determine the relative ranks of his superior officers, and he suffered because of their quarrel over that point, each believing himself in the right. It was an unfortunate affair, and Frémont, who was much less to blame than the others, was the only one to suffer. This affair is discussed at length in H. H. Bancroft's *History of California*. It was a real dilemma for Bancroft, who always condemned the United States or any of its citizens, whatever the occasion. In this instance the parties were all citizens of the United States, and Bancroft condemned them all, then approved some portion of the doings of each.—W. E. C.]

CHAPTER XVI.

Concentration of the forces at Valverde—Mitchell's Escort—Passage of the great "Jornada del Muerto"—Arrival at Doñanna—Frank Smith and the Mexicans—Battle of Brazito—The Piratical Flag—Doniphan's order—Burial of the Dead—False Alarm—Surrender of El Paso—Release of American Prisoners.

Col. Doniphan, upon his return from the Navajo country,[82] dispatched Lieut. Hinton from Soccorro to Santa Fé, with orders to Col. Price, commanding the forces at the capital, to send him ten pieces of cannon, and one hundred and twenty-five artillery men. Col. Don-

---

NOTE 82.—Colonel Doniphan made no official report of the expeditions against the Indians until he arrived at Chihuahua. There he wrote and forwarded his official reports of these expeditions, the battle of Brazito, and the battle of Sacramento, his letter transmitting these being as follows:

HEADQUARTERS, DETACHMENT OF THE ARMY OF THE WEST,
CITY OF CHIHUAHUA, March 4, 1847.

SIR: Enclosed you will find three official reports—the two first have long since been due, but from my position it was impracticable to transmit them at an earlier date. We were ordered to report to General Wool at this place. On my arrival I found, from Mexico reports, that he was at Saltillo surrounded by General Santa Anna. Should he be defeated or driven back, I fear an immediate retreat will become necessary. We have been in the service nine months without receiving one dollar of pay.

Very respectfully, your obedient servant,
A. W. DONIPHAN,
Commanding 1st Missouri Mounted Volunteers.
Brig. Gen. R. Jones,
Adjutant General U. S. A.

The official report of the Indian expeditions is as follows:

HEADQUARTERS, DETACHMENT OF THE ARMY OF THE WEST.

I have the honor to report that, in obedience to the orders of Brigadier-General Kearny, — day of October, 1846, I left the town of Santa Fé on the 26th of October, and took up the line of march for the country inhabited by the Navajo Indians. This country lies west of the range of mountains bounding the valley of the Del Norte on the west, and extending down the tributaries of the Rio Colorado of the west, near the Pacific ocean. We invaded the country by three routes. Major Gilpin, with 200 men, marched by the northern route, leaving the valley of the Del Norte at the mouth of the Chamas; proceeded up the Chamas to the main dividing chain of mountains, separating the waters of the Del Norte and Colorado; thence down the San Juan, across the Techunica mountain, and by the Red Lake to the valley of the Little Colorado. The remaining portion of the regiment left the Del Norte at Albuquerque and passed up the valley of the Puevea of the west, almost to its source. Captain Reid marched with a detachment through the center of the country; Captain Parsons further south, and the remaining portion of the regiment further south. Every portion of their country was thus visited, and large numbers of them, perhaps three-fourths of their tribe, collected at the Ojo Oso, where we made a permanent treaty with them. We left the Del Norte the 2d of November, and returned to it near Socorro on the 12th of December, having traversed a country of moun-

iphan especially requested that he would send Capt. Weightman's[83] company of light artillery, leaving it discretionary with Major Clark

tains and valleys amid the intense cold winter. Our daily march was through snows, and over snow-capped mountains; but in a brief report I can give no sufficient description of a country and people abounding in interest. Major Gilpin and myself have full notes, from which the department shall be furnished with a more ample report after our return to Missouri.

We proceeded from Socorro to Valverde, where we found the large caravan of American merchants awaiting our arrival; and we proceeded to prepare our train to obey the order of General Kearny, requiring me to report to General Wool.

Very respectfully, your obedient servant,
A. W. DONIPHAN,
Commanding 1st Missouri Mounted Volunteers.

Brig. Gen. R. Jones,
Adjutant General U. S. A.

NOTE 83.—Richard Hanson Weightman was born in the District of Columbia, and was given a military education at West Point, and at the commencement

RICHARD HANSON WEIGHTMAN.
(From painting in Library of the Missouri Historical Society, St. Louis, Mo.)

of the Mexican War was a resident of St. Louis, but had never seen service (see *A Campaign in New Mexico with Colonel Doniphan*, by Frank S. Edwards, Lon-

whether he would remain at Santa Fé, or accompany the expedition against Chihuahua. He chose the latter.

don, 1848, p. 4). He was Captain of Artillery (see Roster of his company, published in this volume), and distinguished himself under Colonel Doniphan. He was appointed Paymaster in the United States Army May 10, 1848; discharged August 1, 1849. After the close of the Mexican War he returned to Santa Fé, where he conducted a small newspaper and practiced law, though both occupations were a failure with him. He entered politics in 1849, and with Captain Angney, who had also settled in Santa Fé, stirred up the public mind against Hugh N. Smith, who had been sent to Washington to look after the interests of the Territory; but Smith was later elected Delegate to Congress from New Mexico. In 1850 an abortive movement for statehood elected Weightman United States Senator. He was elected Delegate to Congress and served two years, 1851–52. During the publication of his paper in Santa Fé he killed F. X. Aubrey, the only account I have found of which, having any semblance of accuracy or probability, being that of William R. Bernard, published in the ninth volume of Kansas Historical Collections, and which I give:

"Mr. Bernard was well acquainted with F. X. Aubrey, and had many business transactions with him. He was an honest, simple-minded man, true to friends, but ever ready to resent any imputation against his honor. Aubrey was the first man to take a loaded train from the Missouri river to New Mexico in winter. He was the discoverer of a third route to Santa Fé, about 1849–'50. Before this there were but two, namely, that by way of the Cimarron, and the other by the way of the mountains, which was at a later date followed by the Santa Fé Railroad. Aubrey's route crossed the Arkansas river below the mouth of the Big Sandy, not far from Big Timbers. The greatest distance without water on this route was thirty miles, while on the Cimarron road the greatest distance without water was sixty miles; however, for various reasons the Aubrey road was not generally used. As has often been written and told, Aubrey was killed at Santa Fé, by Maj. Richard H. Weightman. Mr. Bernard's account of this tragedy was furnished by an eye-witness, and is as follows: Prior to Aubrey's trip to California, Captain Weightman had been conducting a small paper at Santa Fé, and through its columns had cast some doubt upon the discovery of the new pass through the mountains to California claimed by Aubrey. Some time thereafter Aubrey returned to Santa Fé, and meeting Captain Weightman the two adjourned to a neighboring saloon, in accordance with the custom of the time. Both men called for brandy. Aubrey raised his glass to his lips, and then putting it down said: 'What has become of your paper?' Weightman answered: 'Dead.' 'What killed it?' asked the other. 'Lack of support,' was the answer. 'The lie it told on me killed it,' said Aubrey. Without a word Weightman threw a glass of brandy into his opponent's face, and, while blinded by its effects, stabbed him to death.

"Mr. Bernard also knew Major Weightman, who, after the above tragedy, returned to Missouri. In speaking of the matter once, Major Weightman told Bernard that he saw that Aubrey was angry, and was drawing his pistol, and that one or the other must be killed, and that he only struck to save his own life. Mr. Bernard has no doubt that the reason given was both true and a good one."

The exact time of the return of Major Weightman to Missouri does not appear, nor have I been able to gather much concerning him from that time to the beginning of the Civil War. I find the following reference to him in the Missouri Historical Society publication entitled *A History of Battery "A" of St. Louis: With an Account of the Early Artillery Companies from which it is Descended*, by Valentine Mott Porter:

"Captain Richard Hanson Weightman, the West-Pointer who commanded

The camp at Valverde* was made the place of rendezvous, at which all the detachments and parcels of the regiment, were to re-unite. In fact the regiment was to be re-organized. Lt. DeCourcy[84] was appointed Adjutant, in the place of G. M. Butler, who died at Cuvarro;

* On the 17th day of December, at Valverde private W. P. Johnson, of Capt. Waldo's company, was honorably discharged from the service of the United States, and permitted to return home, to attend to the interests of his constituents, having been chosen a member of the Missouri legislature.—HUGHES.

Battery 'A' of St. Louis in the Mexican War, was a gallant, high-spirited daredevil such as one rarely encounters in real life. Once during the campaign a rumor reached him that he was being maligned by Lieut. Edmund ('Gessie') Chouteau. He sent for that gentleman and asked him what he meant by such talk. Chouteau said the Captain had not treated him fairly in some particular, and, enlarging upon his supposed grievance, grew angry and demanded a gentleman's satisfaction. Weightman readily assented to the proposal, but Chouteau, who was carrying a wounded right arm in a sling, asked that the meeting be postponed for a while, else he would be at some disadvantage. 'Oh, that's all right,' said Weightman; 'I'll hold my right hand behind me and we'll shoot with our left hands.' Fortunately, friends intervened in time to prevent the duel. After the Mexican War, Captain Weightman returned to Santa Fé, opened up a law office, and also ran a small newspaper. A man named Aubrey accused him of publishing a falsehood. In the quarrel that ensued, Weightman stabbed him dead.—One time in open court Weightman accused the judge of sitting in a case in which he was personally interested. The judge responded with a challenge. In the duel that followed soon afterwards Weightman alone fired at the command. The judge, who was deaf, ducked his head as the bullet whizzed by, and shouted, 'I didn't hear the command to fire.' 'All right,' called Weightman, holding up his hands; 'you have the right to shoot. Fire now.' The seconds rushed in and tried to induce Weightman to apologize and so stop the proceedings. 'I'll apologize,' said Weightman, 'as far as being sorry is concerned, but' (addressing his opponent) 'I can't take back what I said, Judge, for it was so.' The judge was willing to accept that as an apology, but he declared that if Weightman ever again insulted him on the bench he would shoot next time to kill."

Major Weightman was in General Price's army, and was killed at the battle of Wilson Creek. The following notice of him is taken from *Shelby and His Men*, by John N. Edwards, p. 36:

"The Confederates also lost many valuable officers, one of the noblest and the best being Colonel Richard Hanson Weightman—the hero of Carthage, the idol of his command, the peerless soldier, the chivalrous gentleman, and the costliest victim the South had yet offered upon the altar of her sacrifices. Amid the low growls of the subsiding battle, amid the slain of his heroic brigade, who had followed him three times to the crest of 'Bloody Hill,' and just as the shrill, impatient cheers of his victorious comrades rang out wildly on the battle-breeze, Weightman's devoted spirit passed away from earth, followed by the tears and heartfelt sorrow of the entire army."

NOTE 84.—Meredith T. Moore knew De Courcy well, and gave me something of his history. De Courcy was a Kentuckian—a lawyer, a bright man, but he drank to excess. He had a brother, or brothers, or other relatives engaged in the stage-coaching business in Kentucky. Moore visited Kentucky after the Mexican War, stopping some time at Georgetown, where he found De Courcy acting as manager of these stage lines. De Courcy was glad to see him, and gave him passes over the lines; but Moore did not ride on any of the lines and did not use the passes.

sergeant-major Hinton resigned, and was elected lieutenant in DeCourcy's stead; Palmer, a private, was appointed sergeant-major. Also, Surgeon Penn, and assistant surgeon Vaughan, having previously resigned and returned to Missouri, T. M. Morton now became principal surgeon, and J. F. Morton and Dr. Moore assistant surgeons.

With indefatigable labor and exertion, Lieuts. James Lea and Pope Gordon,[85] assistant quartermaster and commissary, had procured an outfit, and a supply of provisions for the expedition. These they had already at Valverde, or on the way thither, when the detachments returned from the campaign against the Navajos. The merchant trains had received permission to advance slowly down the country, until the army should take up the line of march, when they were to fall in rear with the baggage and provision trains, that they might be the more conveniently guarded.

NOTE 85.—G. Pope Gordon lived at Jefferson City; was Second Lieutenant of Company F. He married Mary Burch, sister of John C. Burch, a member of Congress from California in the fifties. Her father, —— Burch, and John C. Gordon were the first lessees of the Missouri penitentiary. John C. Gordon was from Virginia; he went to California in 1849, and settled at Santa Clara. Meredith T. Moore took Gordon's family across the Plains in 1852, also the family of his son-in-law, Thomas Wilburn, a tailor in Jefferson City with whom George L. Boone learned the trade of tailor. John C. Gordon had a son named Burns Gordon. Thomas Wilburn had a half-brother named Watt Cunningham, who crossed the Plains with Moore in 1852. When G. Pope Gordon was elected Second Lieutenant he was entitled to three horses, but had not the money with which to buy them. He was one of those honest, big-hearted, good fellows who never look out for to-morrow. Meredith T. Moore loaned him the money with which to buy the horses. Moore needed some money at Santa Fé to buy the necessary articles of food that the Government failed to furnish. He went to Gordon, but Gordon did not pay; he had money, and Moore saw him spending it, but could get none of it. He finally spoke to Dr. Winston, the Company Surgeon, about the matter. The doctor was greatly amused at Moore's story, laughed and haw-hawed. "The idea of Pope Gordon paying a debt!" said the merry physician. "He is one of the best fellows you ever saw, but he never paid a debt in the world and never will. But no one ever lost anything by loaning him money, for they always borrow it back. He will never pay you in the world, but he will lend you money as long as he has a cent. Borrow your money back from him." Moore thought the advice of the doctor good, and asked Gordon for a loan of ten dollars. It was handed over instantly. He borrowed from Gordon from time to time as he needed money, until but a small sum remained, and Gordon's clerk, Hamilton Fant, paid him that sum as the troops were embarking for New Orleans. Gordon's idea of debt-paying was only an eccentricity, and not caused by a desire to evade his obligations.

About the 1st of November, Dr. Connelly,[86] Doane, McManus, Valdez, and Jas. McGoffin, proceeded to El Paso, in advance of the army, and contrary to order, to ascertain upon what conditions their merchandise could be introduced through the custom house into the Chihuahua market. They were, immediately upon their arrival at El Paso, seized and conducted under an escort of twenty-six soldiers to the city of Chihuahua, where they remained in surveillance until liberated by the American army.

While Col. Doniphan was yet in the mountains, Lieutenant-colonel Mitchell of the 2d regiment, and Captain Thompson of the regular service, conceived the bold project of opening a communication between Santa Fé and Gen. Wool's army, at that time supposed to be advancing upon Chihuahua. For this purpose a volunteer company, consisting of one hundred and three men, raised from the different corps at Santa Fé, was organized under the name of the "Chihuahua Rangers,"[87] commanded by Captain Hudson, and Lieu-

NOTE 86.—See biographical sketch of Dr. Connelly, *ante*.

NOTE 87.—The organization of the "Chihuahua Rangers" is well described in the *Journal of William H. Richardson, a Private Soldier in the Campaign of New and Old Mexico*, New York, published by William H. Richardson, 1848, a pamphlet of ninety-six pages. This is one of the most reliable and valuable works on the conquest of New Mexico. Richardson left his home on West River, Anne Arundel county, Maryland, November 11, 1845, for a Southern tour, as he tells us. In the following spring he found himself permanently located in Carroll county, Missouri. July 4, 1846, he enlisted in the Carroll county company, under Captain Williams, and went immediately to Fort Leavenworth with the company, which was one of the Second Regiment Missouri Mounted Volunteers, commanded by Colonel Sterling Price. The Journal gives a daily record of the march of the regiment to Santa Fé, the only record I have found of the march. Hubert Howe Bancroft seems not to have known of this work, and laments the want of such a journal. (See his *History of New Mexico*.) The work contains the facsimile of a letter of indorsement written by Colonel Doniphan, in which the Colonel states that he well knew the man (Richardson), and he is certain that the work is accurate. The work is conservative and fair in statement, and taken altogether it is an invaluable record. The suffering of the troops for food is well told. Upon arrival at Santa Fé he was sent with others to a grazing-camp. There the men almost starved. Witness an entry: "Yesterday I traded off *two needles* to the Spanish girls for six ears of corn and some onions. A breakfast of coffee, some very poor beef soup, and onions sliced up with parched corn, made a better meal for us to-day than we have had for some days past." And this, under date of October 31: "Yesterday one of our beef cattle died from starvation. The Mexicans came down and took it off to their habitations. We might have made a speculation by selling it, but did not think of it." November 2 is the following

tenants Todd, Sproule, and Gibson. This force having advanced
entry: "Some Taos flour, coarsely ground in the little native mills on the Rio
Grande, badly baked in the ashes, and some coffee without sugar, now comprise our
only sustenance. Between meals, however, we parch some corn, which we now
and then procure of the natives in exchange for buttons [cut from their clothing],
needles, or any little matter we can spare." November 16: "This evening we are
without food, or nearly so. Martin Glaze, an old veteran, who has seen service,
and belongs to my mess, got a few ears of corn, and parched it in a pan, with a
small piece of pork, to make it greasy. When it was done, we all sat round the
fire and ate our supper of parched corn, greased with fat pork." November 17:
"A bull has just been killed, and the offals are being greedily devoured by our poor
fellows." The above indicates the fare the troops had from the time they left
Bent's Fort until they arrived at New Orleans, and it was borne without much
grumbling. Such men were heroes, and they proved it on the battle-field of Sacramento. They had their jokes and cut their capers, though starving. Richardson even falls into verse, as the following will show: "What a luxury, amid these
joys, to feel the delightful sensations produced by the gentle and graceful movements of a Spanish *louse*, as he journeys over one's body! The very thought of it
makes me poetic, and I cannot resist the temptation of dedicating a line to the
memory of moments so exquisite. How appropriate are the words of Moore to
such occasions of bliss!

>"Oft in the stilly night,
>   Ere slumber's chains have bound me,
>I felt the cursèd creatures bite,
>   As scores are crawling round me.

>"O not like one who treads alone,
>   The banquet halls deserted;—
>In crowds they crawl, despite the groan
>   Of him whose blood they started."

The first intimation that Richardson had of the organization of the Chihuahua
Rangers is given in the entry made on the 27th of November, as follows: "Last
night my messmate Phillips returned from Santa Fé, with a message from Col.
Price to the different captains, to send on ten men from each company, as an
escort for Col. Mitchell, who was about to start for Chihuahua. From thence he
is to proceed to open a communication with General Wool. To-day an express
arrived from Col. Mitchell for the same purpose. We were hastily paraded to
ascertain how many would volunteer to go, when I, with five others of my company, stepped out of the ranks, and had our names enrolled. We were satisfied
that we could not render our situation worse, and hoped any change might be
for the better."

The men went to Santa Fé, where they were organized and mustered, and
after looking over their accounts with the sutler they set out, under Lieutenant
Todd. At San Domingo they heard the firing of guns and an uproar, but investigation developed the fact that there was no battle in progress, but that an Indian chief
had died and the church people were trying by noise to keep his soul from sinking
into purgatory. As to food, on the 6th of December he says: "Everything has a
desolate and wintry appearance. There being no food for our horses, we chopped
down some limbs of the cottonwood tree for them to eat. Then went to a Mexican village to buy corn. Having no money, I took some tobacco and buttons to

down the valley of the Del Norte some distance below Valverde,[88] and hearing of a strong Mexican force near El Paso, durst not venture further, but returned and joined Col. Doniphan's column, which was then about being put in motion. All things were now ready for the march.

Accordingly, for the sake of convenience, in marching over the "Jornado del Muerto," or Great Desert, which extends from Fray Christobal[89] to Robledo, a distance of ninety miles, the Colonel dispatched Major Gilpin in the direction of El Paso on the 14th of December, in command of a division of three hundred men; on the 16th he started Lieut.-colonel Jackson with an additional force of two hundred; and on the 19th he marched in person with the remainder

trade for the corn. While here, I sold my greasy blanket for a Navajo one, with a meal for my horse in the bargain. The man with whom I traded was very kind; he set before me some corn-mush and sausage, but being seasoned with onions, I declined eating. He then brought in some cornstalk molasses, which I mixed with water and drank, thanking him for his hospitality." On his return to camp he found that Col. Mitchell had arrived, and on the 6th the march was resumed down the Rio Grande: "Our course is due south, keeping the river constantly on our right, and ranges of mountains on our left hand," he records. On the 8th he says: "I cut some buttons from a uniform jacket, and with them tried to purchase food for my horse, but I was refused everywhere." And on the 17th: "This morning we reached the *second crossing* of the Rio Grande. Four miles beyond the crossing we overtook Col. Doniphan's command, and encamped near them. Having to walk and lead my horse, I did not come up till all were fixed. I found our boys very angry at a circumstance which they related and made me write down, with a promise to publish it—which promise I now fulfill. While on the march to-day, the Captain ordered a halt, and told the soldiers that he had been requested by the lieutenants to beg them all to not come near their fires or tents, as it incommoded them greatly. He stated on his own behalf, as well as on behalf of the other officers, that it was quite a nuisance to have the privates lurking about their tents and fires. He said that something might be 'hooked,' and that the Lieutenant had already lost some saleratus, &c. This was a poser. Our poor fellows could hardly endure it. Some of them were much exasperated."

From the time that Colonel Doniphan's command was overtaken, the escort was a part of the command.

NOTE 88.—Valverde is on the east bank of the Rio Grande, just below the town of Socorro. It was formerly a town of importance, but now has a population of about three hundred.

NOTE 89.—Fray Cristobal was but a camping-place on the east bank of the Rio Grande, at the upper end of the Jornada del Muerto. It was not a town nor even a settlement.

of his command, including the provision and a part of the baggage trains.

In passing this dreadful desert, which is emphatically the "Journey of the Dead," the men suffered much; for the weather was now become extremely cold, and there was neither water to drink, nor wood for fire. Hence, it was not possible to prepare anything to eat. The

Colonel Doniphan's Army marching through the Jornada del Muerto, the "Journey of Death."
(Reproduced from the work of William H. Richardson.)

soldiers fatigued with marching, faint with hunger, and benumbed by the piercing winds, straggled along the road at night, (for there was not much halting for repose,) setting fire to the dry bunches of grass, and the stalks of the soap-plant, or *palmilla*, which would blaze up like a flash of powder, and as quickly extinguish, leaving the men shivering in the cold. For miles the road was most brilliantly illuminated by sudden flashes of light, which lasted but for a moment, and then again all was dark. At length towards midnight the front of the column would halt for a little repose. The straggling parties would continue to arrive at all hours of the night. The guards were posted out. The men without their suppers lay down upon the earth and rested. The teamsters were laboring incessantly night and day with their trains to keep pace with the march of the army. By daydawn the reveilée roused the tired soldier from his comfortless bed of gravel, and called him to resume the march, without taking breakfast, for this could not be provided on the desert. Such was the march for more than three days over the Jornado del Muerto.

On the 22d, Col. Doniphan overtook the detachments under Lieut.-colonel Jackson and Major Gilpin, near the little Mexican town Doñanna. Here the soldiers found plenty of grain and other forage for their animals, running streams of water, and abundance of dried fruit, corn-meal, and sheep and cattle. These they purchased; therefore they soon forgot the sufferings and privations which they had experienced on the desert. Here they feasted and reposed.

The army now encamped within the boundaries of the State of Chihuahua. The advanced detachments under Lieutenant-colonel Jackson and Major Gilpin, apprehending an attack from the Mexicans, about the 20th, had sent an express to Col. Doniphan, then on the desert, requesting him to quicken his march. Capt. Reid, with his company, had proceeded about 12 miles below Doñanna, for the purpose of making a reconnoissance, and of acting as a scout, or advanced guard. While encamped in the outskirts of a forest, on a point of hills which commanded the Chihuahua road, on the night of the 23d, one of the sentinels hailed to the Mexican spies, in the Spanish language. The spies mistaking the sentinel for a friend, advanced very near. At length, discovering their mistake, they wheeled to effect their escape by flight. The sentinel levelled his rifle-yager, and discharged the ball through the bodies of two of them. One of them tumbled from his horse, dead, after running a few hundred yards, and the other at a greater distance. Their dead bodies were afterwards discovered. This sentinel was FRANK SMITH, of Saline.

On the morning of the 24th, the whole command, including Lieut.-Col. Mitchell's escort, and the entire merchant, provision, and baggage trains, moved off in the direction of El Paso, and, after a progress of fifteen miles, encamped on the river for water. The forage was only moderately good; therefore the animals, which were not tethered, rambled and straggled far off into the adjacent bosquets and thickets during the night. The weather was pleasant.

On the morning of the 25th of December, a brilliant sun, rising above the Organic mountains to the eastward, burst forth upon the world in all his effulgence. The little army, at this time not exceeding eight hundred strong, was comfortably encamped on the east bank of the Del Norte. The men felt frolicksome indeed. They sang the cheering songs of Yankee Doodle, and Hail Columbia. Many guns were fired in honor of Christmas day. But there was no need of all this, had they known the sequel.

At an early hour the Colonel took up the line of march, with a strong front and rear guard. The rear guard under Capt. Moss, was delayed for a considerable part of the day in bringing up the trains, and the loose animals which had rambled off during the night. A great number of men were also straggling about in search of their lost stock. These were also delayed.

While on the march, the men most earnestly desired, that, if they had to encounter the enemy at all, they might meet him *this day*. They were gratified: for having proceeded about eighteen miles, the Colonel pitched his camp at a place called BRAZITO, or the LITTLE ARM, on the east bank of the river, in an open, level, bottom prairie, bordered next the mountains and river, on the east and south-east, by a mezquite and willow chaparral. Here the front guard had called a halt.

While the men were scattered everywhere in quest of wood and water, for cooking purposes, and fresh grass for their animals, and while the trains and straggling men were scattered along the road for miles in the rear, a cloud of dust, greater than usual, was observed in the direction of El Paso, and in less than fifteen minutes some one of the advance guard, coming at full speed, announced to the colonel, "that the enemy was advancing upon him."* The bugler was summoned. Assembly call was blown. The men, dashing down their loads of wood, and buckets of water, came running from all quarters, seized their arms, and fell into line under whatever flag was most convenient. As fast as those in the rear came up, they also fell into line under the nearest standards. The officers dashed from post to post,

---

* It is said that Col. Doniphan, and several of his officers and men, were at this moment engaged in playing a game of *three-trick loo*. At first he observed that the cloud of dust was perhaps produced by a gust of wind, and that they had as well play their *hands out*. In another moment the plumes and banners of the enemy were plainly in view. The colonel quickly sprang to his feet, threw down his cards, grasped his sabre, and observed, "Boys, I held an invincible hand, but I'll be d—mn'd if I don't have to play it out in steel now." Every man flew to his post.—HUGHES.

and in an incredibly short space of time the Missourians were marshaled on the field of fight.[90]

By this time the Mexican general had drawn up his forces in front, and on the right and left flanks of Colonel Doniphan's lines. Their strength was about thirteen hundred men, consisting of five hundred and fourteen regular dragoons, an old and well known corps from Vera Cruz and Zacatecas, and eight hundred volunteers, cavalry and infantry, from El Paso and Chihuahua, and four pieces of artillery. They exhibited a most gallant and imposing appearance; for the dragoons were dressed in a uniform of blue pantaloons, green coats

NOTE 90.—James Peacock, now Police Judge of Independence, Mo., was in the Jackson county company. He gave me a long statement of his services. He says the game of cards was to determine who should have a fine Mexican horse captured that day by the advance guard; "Doniphan and others were playing cards for this horse, when some one reported a big cloud of dust to the south. Doniphan ordered De Courcy to ride out and ascertain the cause. He returned and reported a Mexican army approaching. 'Then we must stop this game long enough to whip the Mexicans,' said Col. Doniphan; 'but remember that I am away ahead in the score and cannot be beaten, and we will play it out as soon as the battle is over.'" But in the confusion of the battle the horse was lost, and the game was never finished. General Wool's adjutant, who was with Doniphan, advised that the volunteers be placed down the river with a few regular troops along with the army in front of them, saying, "Raw troops rarely fight well; these may run when the firing begins." Col. Doniphan said he would not do so; that his men would fight; and that if it became necessary to run, all would run together. Peacock was standing by and heard the conversation. Doniphan told Peacock to get ready for battle. Peacock drove down the picket-pin which secured his horse and went to his company. The army fired about two volleys. A number of men fired several times. Peacock fired but once, as he "did not see anything to shoot at after the first volley." When the Mexican commander returned to El Paso after the battle, he was arrested for cowardice and taken to Chihuahua. There he was shown the fortifications at Sacramento erected for the reception of the Americans. He remarked, "Yes, these are all right; but those Americans will roll over them like hogs; they do not fight as we do." As to the cannon of the Mexicans, Peacock says: "Some one said when it was fired a time or two, 'What the hell you reckon that is?' 'A cannon, I believe,' said another. 'Let's go and get it,' cried a number; and a squad of the Howard county company ran into the Mexican lines and captured the cannon. Some of the Mexican artillerymen were so surprised that they did not escape, and were killed. When the cannon was captured a mule was seen running after the fleeing Mexicans. Some one said he believed the mule was carrying the ammunition for the cannon. 'Shoot it then,' was shouted. 'No, we will capture it and make it carry the ammunition for us,' said another." The mule was captured, though it ran among the retreating Mexicans before it was caught. But it was wounded, and died soon after being captured.

trimmed with scarlet, and tall caps plated in front with brass, on the tops of which fantastically waved a plume of horse-hair, or buffalo's tail. Their bright lances and swords glittered in the sheen of the sun. Thus marshaled they paused for a moment.

Meanwhile Col. Doniphan, and his field and company officers, appeared as calm and collected as when on drill; and, in the most spirited manner encouraged their men by the memory of their forefathers, by the past history of their country, by the recollection of the battle of Okeechobee which was fought on the same day in 1837, and by every consideration which renders life, liberty, and country valuable, to cherish no other thought than that of VICTORY.[91]

NOTE 91.—Richardson's account of the battle of Brazito is as follows:

"[Dec.] 25th.—In the union of our forces we were one thousand strong. Moved as early as usual from the position we have occupied the last three days, and after marching 12 miles, we came to Bracito, and encamped at 10 o'clock. We stripped our horses as usual, and picketed them out; went to hunt wood to cook our dinners. Some of the men had gone at least a mile from camp, when the alarm was given, 'To arms! to arms!' Looking in the direction pointed out, we saw a cloud of dust as if the whole of Mexico was coming down upon us. Unwilling to throw away our wood, we ran with our turns on our shoulders, when we heard an officer hallooing, 'Throw away your wood, and bring your horses into camp.' We obeyed the order as quickly as possible. We found our orderly at his post, directing the men to load their guns and get into line. Every man was at his proper place in a few minutes. By this time the Mexican army was in sight, and had formed in battle array at a distance of a mile from us. Presently an officer came out of their ranks, handsomely mounted, and bearing a black flag. Colonel Mitchell, accompanied with the interpreter, rode up to meet him on halfway ground, to inquire his business. He told them he had come to demand the surrender of our entire force; by submitting, he said, our lives would be spared; if we did not, every man would be put to death. Our interpreter cut short his harangue, by telling him to 'Go to hell and bring on his forces.' In the meantime our company (the Chihuahua Rangers) received orders from headquarters to right about face and march from the right, where we were somewhat protected by brush, weeds, and gopher-hills, to extreme left, in open ground, to withstand the charge of the Mexican cavalry; so off we marched in double-quick time, to our position on the left. Our Captain here told us to reserve our fire till the enemy was in fair rifle distance, and added that he hoped no man in his command would act the coward, but would all do their duty as volunteers and American soldiers. He had scarcely done speaking, when the enemy commenced firing at us, from three to four hundred yards distant. They advanced closer, and continued to advance, pouring in volley after volley, till the sound of bullets over our heads reminded me of a hail-storm.—We waited impatiently for the word of command. It was at length given, 'Fire!' One loud peal of thunder was heard from our Missouri rifles. Consternation and dismay was the result, for, thrown into confusion, the Mexicans commenced obliquing to our left. Another volley, well aimed, caused them to *retreat* towards our wagons. Here they were met by a round from the wagon company. In the meantime Captain Reid, at the head of eighteen men, well mounted, pushed after them, chasing them to the mountains. All their provisions, guns, sabres, camp furniture, &c., besides one 10-pound howitzer, fell into our hands. The Mexican loss was estimated at thirty or forty killed and wounded, while we had but two slightly wounded. The Mexicans left their dead on the field."

Before the battle commenced, and while the two armies stood marshaled front to front, the Mexican commander, General Poncé de Leon, dispatched a lieutenant to Col. Doniphan bearing a BLACK FLAG. This messenger coming with the speed of lightning, halted when within sixty yards of the American lines, and waved his ensign gracefully in salutation. Hereupon Col. Doniphan advancing towards him a little way, sent his interpreter, T. Caldwell, to know his demands. The ambassador said:—"The Mexican general summons your commander to appear before him." The interpreter replied: "If your general desires peace, let him come here." The other rejoined:—"Then we will break your ranks and take him there." "Come then and take him," retorted the interpreter. "Curses be upon you,—prepare then for a charge,—we neither ask nor give quarters," said the messenger; and waving his black flag over his head, galloped back to the Mexican lines.[92]

NOTE 92.—George R. Gibson was Second Lieutenant of the Platte county company, commanded by Captain William S. Murphy and later by Captain Jonas S. Woods. Gibson was one of the officers detailed in the escort of Col. Mitchell to go with Col. Doniphan. He wrote an account of the campaign. This account is contained in a large blank ledger, written in Gibson's hand, in the library of the Missouri Historical Society, St. Louis, Mo. He gives a long account of the battle of Brazito, from which I make some quotations here:

"The enemy made a handsome appearance from an Elevation $\frac{1}{2}$ a mile or $\frac{3}{4}$ distant where we first saw them and which they occupied to reconnoiter and where they formed in order of battle. They marched up in good order, but did not approach rapidly, as parts of the intermediate ground is a dense Chapporel low but thick on the ground and impeded their movements—Their Infantry met our right, the Howitzer was in their centre and the Cavalry on our Left—A Fiew muskeet bushes are along our Right wing and many between it and the River and in its Rear, with occasionally all over the field little hillocks of sand or rather irregularities in the ground—Capt. Reed had by this time collected about 14 mounted men who took post behind our centre and all the others were afoot. except Col. Donophan—Col. Mitchel—Capt. Thompson and the Adjt. and Guide—A Battle being unavoidable, we held ourselves ready and suffered them to fire 5 rounds and to approach within 150 yards, when the order was given to Let them have it. Our men standing previous to this with their guns cocked, and the officers telling them to hold on until they were close enough for our fire to have great effect—at the word No. 1 fired and then No. 2 our line being told off into files, and it was well done and had a fine effect their Cavalry reeling under it and whole line giveing. Before another could be fired the Cavalry passed around our Left and charged on the waggons, where they met a warm reception, having also held up their fire until every shot told as they were close—at this time Capt. Reed charged upon them and being unable to cut off our baggage and provisions they retreated in confusion, Capt. Reed and his squad giving a hot pursuit—Several lay dead upon this part of the field—when they charged our wagons our Right advanced and they were driven from every position, Their Howitzer being handsomely taken with a shout and put in charge of Lt. Kribben and the artillery in our Escort—our whole line now advanced until we reached the high ground where we first saw them, where a Halt was ordered as they were out of sight and Capt. Reed had gone in persuit. . . .

"Col. Mitchell wrode a white horse, which he valued highly and really was a

At the sound of the trumpet the Vera Cruz dragoons, who occupied the right of the enemy's line of battle, first made a bold charge upon the American left. When within a few rods the yagermen opened a most deadly fire upon them, producing great execution. At the same crisis Capt. Reid with a party of sixteen mounted men (for the rest were all on foot) charged upon them, broke through their ranks, hewed them to pieces with their sabres, and thereby contributed materially in throwing the enemy's right wing into confusion. A squad or section of dragoons, having flanked our left, now charged upon the commissary and baggage trains, but the gallant wagoners opened upon them a well directed fire, which threw them into disorder, and caused three of their number to pay the forfeit of their lives.

The Chihuahua infantry and cavalry were posted on their left, and consequently operated against our right wing. They advanced within gun-shot, and took shelter in the chaparral, discharging three full rounds upon our lines before we returned the fire. At this crisis Col. Doniphan ordered the men to *"lie down on their faces, and reserve their fire until the Mexicans came within sixty paces."* This was done. The Mexicans supposing they had wrought fearful execution in our ranks, as some were falling down while others stood up, began now to advance, and exultingly cry out *"bueno, bueno;"* whereupon our whole right wing, suddenly rising up, let fly such a galling volley of yager-balls into their ranks, that they wheeled about and fled in the utmost confusion.

---

fine one, and made a pretty appearance. He of course was a conspicuous object and most probably taken for our Commander as their fire was directed at him particularly—I once thought his Horse was shot seeing him flinch or give and the Col. told me in the evening he thought so, but could find no mark about him—Capt Hudson was in front of me and the Col. almost immediately in my rear at one time and this was probably the warmest place on the field on account of the white horse— . . .

"They always overshot us, both with their Howitzer and small arms. . . . Our men behaved like veterans and exhibited a coolness and obedience to orders worthy of any troops—Two old mountain men T. Forsythe and another dressed in their peculiar buckskin shirts made themselves conspicuous by advancing before the Line and firing with great deliberation, the sharp crack of their rifles announcing that some one had received a shot—Forsythe is an old and experienced Indian fighter and has already rendered great service, as a spy and to carry Expresses—when they fired our men gave a shout and advanced upon the Howitzer which they took, the Enemy flying in great precipitation. . . . It was late at night before all was quiet in Camp, being greatly exhilerated by our victory, without the loss of a man. . . . Col. Ponce De Leon commanded them and it is reported was wounded—supposed to have been shot by Forsythe."

By this time the Howard company, and others occupying the centre, had repulsed the enemy with considerable loss, and taken possession of one piece of his artillery, and the corresponding ammunition. This was a brass six-pound howitzer. Sergt. Calaway, and a few others of that company first gained possession of this piece of cannon, cut the dead animals loose from it, and were preparing to turn it upon the enemy, when Lieut. Kribben, with a file of artillerymen, was ordered to man it.*

The consternation now became general among the ranks of the Mexicans, and they commenced a precipitate retreat along the base of the mountains. Many of them took refuge in the craggy fastnesses. They were pursued by the Americans about one mile; Capt. Reid, and Capt. Walton, who by this time had mounted a few of his men, followed them still further. All now returned to camp, and congratulated one another on the achievement. The Mexican loss was seventy-one killed, five prisoners, and not less than one hundred and fifty wounded, among whom was their commanding officer, General PONCÉ DE LEON. Also, a considerable quantity of ammunition, baggage, wine, provisions, blankets, a great number of lances, some guns, and several stands of colors, were among the spoils. A number of horses were killed, and several were captured. The Americans had eight men wounded—none killed.

In this engagement, Col. Doniphan, his officers, and men, displayed the utmost courage, and determined resolution to conquer or perish in the conflict. Defeat would have been ruinous. Therefore all the companies vied with each other in endeavoring to render the country the most important service. The victory was complete on the part of the Americans. The battle continued about thirty minutes, and was fought about three o'clock P. M., on CHRISTMAS DAY, at Brazito, twenty-five miles from El Paso.[93]

* The other three pieces of artillery were not brought into the action.—HUGHES.

NOTE 93.—The black flag carried by the Mexicans was afterwards picked up on the battle-field of Sacramento. It came into the possession of Major Meriwether Lewis Clark, of the artillery, and was by him brought back to St. Louis. It now belongs to his nephew, Major William Clark Kennerly, who has lent it to the Missouri Historical Society, St. Louis, in the library of which institution it is carefully preserved. It is a small black flag, on one side of which, in white, are painted two skulls, with cross-bones below each. On the other side is the following inscription: *Libertad O Muerto.*

Not more than five hundred of Col. Doniphan's men were present when the battle commenced. The rest fell into line as they were enabled to reach the scene of action. Those who had been far in the

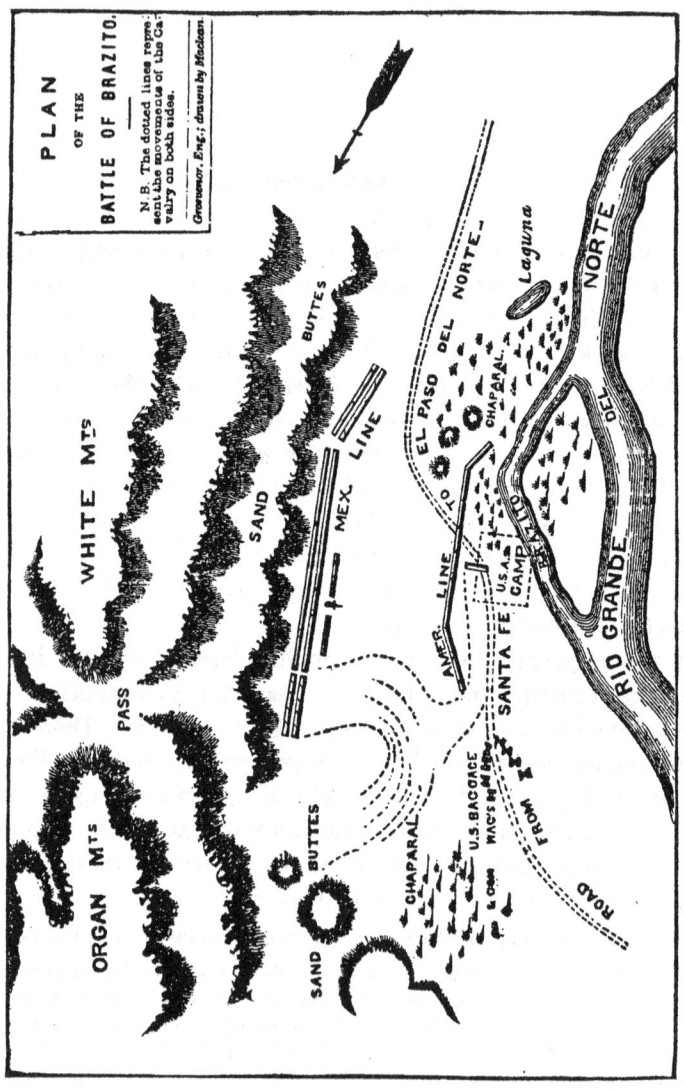

rear during the day, when they heard the firing, came running in great haste with their arms in their hands, to bring aid to their comrades, who were then engaged with the enemy. This created such a dust, that the enemy supposed a strong reinforcement was marching to our support. This circumstance, also, contributed to strike terror into the Mexican ranks.[94]

By this defeat the Mexican army was completely disorganized and dispersed. The volunteer troops returned with the utmost

NOTE 94.—Colonel Doniphan did not make his report of the battle of Brazito until after his arrival at Chihuahua, and it is dated at that city on the 4th of March, 1847, and is as follows:

HEADQUARTER, DETACHMENT OF THE ARMY OF THE WEST,
CITY OF CHIHUAHUA, March 4, 1847.

SIR: I have the honor to report that, in obedience to the order of Brigadier-General Kearny, requiring me to report my command to General Wool for duty, the advance of my command, consisting of 300 men under the command of Major Gilpin, took up the line of march from Valverde on the 14th of December, 1846, across the Jornada del Muerto, a plain of 90 miles, destitute of wood and water, and were directed to await the arrival of the main body at the village of Dona Anna. On the 16th, 200 men under the command of Lieutenant-Colonel Jackson, followed on the 18th, the remainder of my forces under my personal command, with an escort of 90 men accompanying Lieutenant-Colonel Mitchell, of the Second Regiment Missouri Mounted Volunteers. This escort had been sent by Colonel Price from Santa Fé during our campaign into the Navajo country to open communication between this city and Santa Fé, under the impression that General Wool had already marched upon this capital. Our whole force was 856 effective men, armed with rifles—no artillery. Before leaving Valverde, I had some information of a force having been sent to El Paso from this city, to prevent its conquest by our forces. I sent an order to Major Clarke, of the artillery, at Santa Fé, to join my forces at the earliest moment with 100 men and a battery of four six- and two 12-pound howitzers. On arriving at Dona Anna our whole force was consolidated, and we there received certain information that 700 men and six pieces of cannon had arrived at El Paso. Dona Anna is sixty miles from El Paso. On the 23d we commenced our march, and on the 25th our advance of 500 men had halted for the purpose of camping, about 3 o'clock. Our men were engaged in getting wood and water, when our advanced guard informed us the enemy was rapidly advancing at a short distance. The rear, under Lieutenant-Colonel Jackson, was several miles in the rear. The rally was immediately sounded, and our forces formed in open order on foot as skirmishers. The right wing was composed of Companies B, C and E; the center of D, H and G; the left of F, A, and Lieutenant-Colonel Mitchell's escort. The extreme points of the two wings were thrown towards the Del Norte so as to protect the flanks and baggage. The enemy halted at a half mile, and formed in line of battle,—the Vera Cruz dragoons on the left, the Actevo battalion of Chihuahua on the right, and their infantry, with the militia from El Paso, in the center. Before we had fully formed, they sent a lieutenant near our lines with a *black* flag, with the demand that the commander of our forces should go to their lines and confer with their commander; declaring, at the same time, unless it was complied with, they would charge *and take him, and neither ask nor give quarter.* The reply was more abrupt than decorous—to charge and be d——d. With my permission a hundred balls would have pierced the *pirate* flag; but I deemed it most proper for the honor of our country to restrain them. At the return of the *black* flag, the enemy commenced his charge and opened a fire on us from right to left at about 400 yards. Our forces were ordered to receive their fire, without returning it until it could prove effective. Three rounds were fired by the whole line, as also from the two-pound howitzer, before they had advanced within rifle-shot. Perceiving that they were attempting to file to the right and left and pass our wings, I ordered their fire to be returned, which was done from right to left along the whole line simultaneously, which completely checked their advance and threw them into great

expedition to their respective homes; while the regular troops continued their flight to Chihuahua, scarcely halting for refreshment in El Paso. On the retreat, many of the wounded died. Several were found dead by the road side, and the chaparral near the battle-field was stained with the blood of the retreating foe. The field was all trophied over with the spoils of the slain and the vanquished. Martial accoutrements, sacks and wallets of provisions, and gourds of the delicious wines of El Paso, were profusely scattered over miles of surface. These supplied our soldiers with a Christmas banquet. The whole affair resembled a Christmas frolic. This night the men encamped on the same spot where they were when attacked by the Mexicans. Having ate the bread and drank the wine which were taken in the engagement, they reposed on their arms, protected by a strong guard.[95]

On the following morning the dead were buried, and the wounded Mexican prisoners comfortably provided with means of conveyance

---

disorder. We had succeeded in mounting twenty men under the intrepid Captain Reed, and at this point he was ordered to charge the Vera Cruz dragoons, who seemed to be again rallying to charge on our left wing. The charge was gallantly made against a force thrice their own, and the fight was warmly contested for about twenty minutes on that wing. The enemy then fled to the mountains contiguous—one column having advanced about one mile during the battle. The force of the enemy was 1,220. Of this number 537 were cavalry, the remainder infantry. Half this force was from Chihuahua, the remainder militia, from El Paso, with one two-pound howitzer which was twice discharged, and was then charged and taken by Company G on foot. Our force was near 500, the rear under Lieutenant-Colonel Jackson not arriving until the battle was entirely ended. The loss of the enemy was 43 ascertained to be killed, about 150 reported at El Paso to have been wounded, of whom a large number died; one howitzer, a number of carbines, and some provisions, &c. Our loss was none killed—7 wounded, all since recovered. Thus ended the battle of Brazito.

I cannot speak too highly of the coolness and intrepid bravery of the officers and men under my command during this whole engagement: few of them had ever been in battle before. Lieutenant-Colonel Mitchell commanded the left wing and Major Gilpin the right wing. Captain Thompson of the First Dragoons acted as my aid and adviser, and was of the most essential service in forming the line and during the engagement. On the 27th we entered El Paso without opposition, and there learned that General Wool had not advanced upon the capital. We were therefore compelled to await the arrival of our artillery at that point until the first day of February, 1847, their baggage and provision train until the 5th. On the 8th we commenced our march for Chihuahua.

I have the honor to be, very respectfully, your obedient servant,

A. W. DONIPHAN.

Brig. Gen. R. Jones, Commanding 1st Reg't Missouri Mounted Vol.
   Adjutant General, U. S. A.

NOTE 95.—The deputation which met Colonel Doniphan to surrender El Paso gave some information as to how the Mexicans regarded the actions of the Americans in the battle of Brazito, which Gibson records as follows:

"It turned out to be a deputation from El Paso to surrender the place and to

to El Paso. Every needful attention was also given our own wounded by the surgeons. The column now, in perfect order, with the baggage, provision, hospital, ammunition, and merchant trains in the rear, and a strong rear and front guard, and a party of flankers on the right and left, moved cautiously in the direction of El Paso, apprehending another attack. After an advance of fifteen miles camp was selected near a small salt lake, where there was a moderate supply of natural forage such as grass and rushes. From this point Col. Doniphan sent back an express for the artillery to hasten forward, for he anticipated strenuous opposition at El Paso.[96]

While encamped here one of the picket guard, discovering a party of Mexicans passing along the base of the mountains toward the east, in which they had taken shelter during the day, endeavoring to make good their retreat to El Paso under cover of the night, fired upon them. This produced an ALARM in camp. The men were cooking their suppers; some of them had spread their beds for repose. Col. Doniphan ordered the fires to be extinguished. Whatever was in the vessels, on the fire, cooking, was now turned topsy-turvy in the effort to put out the light. For a moment all was confusion. Quickly, however, Col. Doniphan drew up his men in line of battle, and awaited the approach of the enemy. Lieutenant-colonel Jackson in the hurry to parade his men mounted his mule bare-back, with his sword and shot-gun. Many of the men were in ranks barefoot, and only half clad; for they had been roused from slumber. Finally, no enemy appearing, the soldiers were ordered to repair to their tents, and sleep

inform us that the Mexicans were totally defeated and never stopped, but continued on to Chihuahua in squads, dispersing in all directions. They also brought with them the mules and horses stolen from us, and which we supposed were lost, and said a large party of Apaches were on the mountains looking at the battle, and killed some of their men who fled to them. They told us the enemy were surprised we did not fire until they had several times, and began to think we intended to surrender. They asked what kind of people we are to stand up and be shot at and not return it. They say we killed and wounded a great many, and that one woman was killed at the howitzer—shot in the eye, and carried off; and that another—there being two on the field who would follow the troops—jumped on a mule and went under whip through El Paso to Chihuahua."

NOTE 96.—El Paso, or Paso del Norte, was on the south or west side of the Rio del Norte or Rio Grande. It was so called from the passage of the river through the mountains near by, and was at first but a camping-place for the caravans between the upper and the lower countries. About 1680 a settlement was founded there, from which date the founding of the town is now reckoned. El Paso, Texas, is on the north or east bank of the river, and was not in existence in the Mexican War.

on their arms. They ran, leaping, and hallooing, and cursing the FALSE ALARM. Before day another false alarm called them out in a similar manner. Therefore, this night the soldiers were much vexed.

The same order of march which had been adopted on the previous day was continued on the 27th, until the column reached El Paso.[97] On arriving at the Great Pass, or gorge in the mountains, through

NOTE 97.—Private Odon Guitar (now General Odon Guitar, Columbia, Mo.) had charge of a provision and ammunition train from Santa Fé to Colonel Doniphan at El Paso. Guitar had been sent to a grazing-camp from Santa Fé when the army first arrived there. With him was John Gray, who was discharged soon after their arrival at the camp, his mother, a widow, claiming that he was under age. When he left camp, Gray sold Guitar a very fine coat. This coat was too small for Guitar, rubbing one of his arms severely, and the injury became so serious that he was sent back to the hospital at Santa Fé, where he was when Colonel Doniphan marched to El Paso. In the hospital were a number of Guitar's friends, among them, Herman Habernicht, the son of a rich widow who lived at Göttingen, Germany; Habernicht had recently established himself as an artist at Fulton, Mo., and was a fine artist and painter. He enlisted in the Fulton county company. He died in California, in 1853. Other friends found by Guitar were Uriah Mattox and William ("Rocky") Brown. These and others, with Guitar, were discharged from the hospital soon after Colonel Doniphan left Valverde. A week later the train came in from Fort Leavenworth. It was understood between Doniphan and Price that Doniphan would send back an escort for the train, but this escort did not arrive at Santa Fé; seeing some Mexican soldiers at a ranch on the road, they were compelled to return. At Santa Fé the escort was daily expected, but as it did not arrive, Guitar requested that Colonel Price allow him to take charge of it until the escort should be met on the road. Colonel Price consented to this, believing the escort would be met very soon. All the First Regiment troops discharged from the hospital, some six or seven, were sent along, the remainder of the men with the train being teamsters, and Guitar was put in command. The train consisted of thirty wagons, drawn by oxen. In the afternoon of the day it reached Albuquerque the weather became suddenly damp and chilly, and at night a heavy black cloud rested on the mountains to the north. Old Mexicans said a severe "norther" was coming. In the night Guitar was aroused by Maddox and Brown and told to get out and kill some game for breakfast; they carried some geese, and told him the country was freezing down solid, the river being full of ice and the wild fowl huddled together helpless along the banks and islands. Guitar fired into the ducks, but found they would not fly, so killed enough for food for the following day with a club. It was more than forty years before another "norther" of like severity visited the country about Santa Fé. The oxen were thin and weak, and the cold affected them much.

Guitar called on Mr. Chavez, brother of Don Antonio José Chavez, who was robbed and murdered by McDaniel and his party. Chavez had brought out a merchant train of some thirty wagons in the trader caravan stopped by order of General Kearny. Guitar became acquainted with Chavez and his son, who

which the river appears to have forced its way, debouching into the valley below, over a system of rocky falls, in dashing cataracts, the colonel was met by a deputation of citizens from El Paso, bearing a white flag, proposing terms of peace, and offering to surrender the place into his hands, beseeching at the same time that he would use

was returning from some Eastern college. He was friendly to the Americans, and proposed to exchange strong oxen for the worn ones of Guitar's train, which was done; and this enabled Guitar to reach Colonel Doniphan. For, after the return of his escort, Colonel Doniphan supposed that Colonel Price would furnish an escort to bring on the train, and did not send up another. Guitar continued down the river, expecting daily to meet the escort. The army had left little forage in its wake, and the oxen toiled and starved. When the train emerged from the Jornada the cattle were reeling from exhaustion, and at a point eight miles north of Dona Anna they gave out entirely and were unable to proceed. Guitar found a small sheltered valley where a stream entered the Rio Grande, which could not be seen from the trail, and which contained a little grass. He concealed the wagons as best he could and turned the cattle out in the valley. Leaving the camp in charge of the teamsters, he took with him Maddox and Brown and set out for El Paso to secure assistance. Neither of them had ever been over the trail. At the point where the "Sandhill" route to Chihuahua left the Rio Grande the boys found also other roads branching off in various directions. Brown insisted that the Chihuahua trail was the route to El Paso; the others did not think so, but as none of them knew and Brown was positive, they crossed the river and followed the trail there found. It proved very difficult to travel, being through a loose, yielding sand, in which they sank above the ankles at every step. Maddox was a large fat fellow; in five miles he was exhausted. All decided that they were on the wrong trail, and they started to return. Maddox was soon unable to proceed, and had to be left in a little valley just off of the road. Guitar and Brown proceeded, and late that night arrived at El Paso. They aroused Colonel Doniphan, who was surprised at their story, but also much gratified that they had escaped capture on the trail. He had been expecting the arrival of the train every day under an escort sent by Colonel Price. He immediately sent out a guard with fresh teams to bring in the train. Directions for finding Maddox were given. He saw them approaching, and supposed them to be Mexicans. When they came up to him they found him asleep, or pretending that he was. One said in Spanish, "I think we will hang him." Another thought it best to shoot him. Maddox understood what was being said, and not doubting that they were Mexicans about to execute him on the spot, lost no time in getting on his legs to see what he might do to save his life, when he recognized some of the party. From that time he was known in the army as "the big possum." The train was found by the escort and taken in; except the oxen, it was in first-class condition. Most of the ammunition used by the army at the battle of Sacramento was carried in that train. How it escaped the banditti and Indians on the way down was a mystery Colonel Doniphan could solve only by saying that it was just blind luck of boys who had no comprehension of the danger they were in every hour.

his clemency towards them, in sparing their lives, and protecting their property. This the colonel was inclined to do. It was now about six miles to the city. All moved on, rejoicing in the prospect of rest, and something to appease the appetite.

Thus on the 27th the city of El Paso* was possessed by the American troops without further opposition, or greater effusion of blood. It was now night. Therefore the soldiers encamped and enjoyed the advantage of a little repose.

The men, at first, were encamped on a bare spot of earth, south of the Plaza, where the wind drove the sand furiously through the camp, dreadfully annoying both man and beast. In this comfortless situation, the soldiers remained for several days. At length, after great suffering from the driven sands, which filled the eyes, nostrils, and mouth to suffocation, the men were quartered in houses near the square.

One of the first acts of Col. Doniphan, after taking possession of El Paso, was the liberating of three American citizens who, without crime, had been immured in a dungeon for five months and one day. Thus have Americans been deprived of their liberty in Mexico. Col. Doniphan was their deliverer.

These three American citizens, Hudson, Pollard, and Hutchinson, had started from Van Buren in Arkansas, with the view of proceeding to Upper California, where they intended settling; and arriving safely at Santa Fé, they agreed to hire Graham, a Scotchman, to pilot them through the mountains to San Diego. Having purchased an outfit at Santa Fé, they were conducted by Graham down the Del Norte to El Paso, who told them the best route led from that place to Guadaloupe Calvo, and thence by San Bernardino, to the mouth of the Gila, whence they could easily arrive at San Diego. They followed their pilot. On reaching El Paso, however, Graham became intoxicated and informed against them, representing to the Prefecto of the place that they were Texan spies; whereupon they were apprehended and lodged in prison, where they lay until delivered by the American army.

* "When you learn," observes an intelligent volunteer, "that this place is the key by which you enter New Mexico, you will see at once the importance of the place. All communications, passing from Lower Mexico in the direction of Santa Fé, must necessarily pass through this place, or within a few miles of it. Is it not, therefore, most surprising that, with two thousand two hundred and forty fighting men in the town, besides the regular soldiers, five hundred and fourteen, who were stationed there, they should have surrendered the place so easily?"— HUGHES.

CHAPTER XVII.

The Commissioners—Assessment of property—Search for arms—Proclamation of Gov. Trias—The American merchants—Strength of the Pass—Capt. Kirker—Kind treatment of the Pasenos—Resources of the valley of El Paso—Wolves—The rebellion—Ramond Ortiz—The Apache Indians.

On the morning of the 28th, three commissioners, deputed by the citizens of El Paso, came into the American camp to negotiate more fully the terms of capitulation, and the nature of the peace which had been partially agreed upon the previous day. Col. Doniphan instructed them to say to the inhabitants of the settlement of El Paso "that he did not come to plunder and ravage, but to offer them liberty; that the lives and property of such as remained peaceable and neutral, during the existence of the war, would be fully and amply protected; but that such as neglected their industrial pursuits, and instigated other peaceable citizens to take up arms against the Americans, would be punished as their crimes deserved." He also encouraged them to industry, and the prosecution of their daily labor, advising them to prepare a market wherein his soldiers might purchase such things as they needed, excepting spirituous liquors, the sale of which he interdicted. He further assured them, "that his commissary and quartermaster would purchase of them such supplies of provisions and forage, as his men and animals might require, and that the beautiful settlement of El Paso should not be laid waste and destroyed by his soldiers." These things were done as Col. Doniphan promised.

On the same day an assessment was made of all the corn, wheat, and provender which could be found in the city, that the quartermaster might know whence to draw supplies, in case the proprietors refused to sell to the American army. When the estimate had been completed, it appeared that there were several hundred thousand fanegas of corn and wheat, and a vast quantity of fodder and other forage for horses and mules.* Also a search for public arms, ammuni-

---
* Col. Doniphan issued an order to the soldiers, forbidding them to take any property from the Mexicans, without paying its just equivalent to the owner. A waggish volunteer who was standing by observed, "Colonel! you don't care if we take *mice (maize)* do you?' The colonel, not suspecting his motive, replied in the negative. The volunteer went away, and in a short time returned to camp with great quantities of corn for his horse and those of his companions, for the Mexicans call *corn, mice,* (i. e.) *maize.* The colonel enjoyed the joke.
—Hughes.

tion, and stores was instituted, that if such things were found to abound, the army might not be in want of the means of defence, and also that the Mexicans, in case they attempted an insurrection, might not have in their power the means of prosecuting their designs with success, or of inflicting permanent injury upon our men. Therefore the field officers and captains, and lieutenants, with files of men went into all the houses, treating the families with respect, taking nothing save arms and other munitions of war; neither did they abuse any person.

When this search was completed, it was discovered that the colonel had come in possession of more than twenty thousand pounds of powder, lead, musket cartridge, cannon cartridge, and grape and canister shot; five hundred stands of small arms, four hundred lances, four pieces of cannon, several swivels and culverins, and several stands of colors.

On the 30th, a body of cavalry under Major Gilpin and Captain Reid was sent to the Presidio del Eclezario, twenty-two miles further down the river, for the purpose of making a reconnoissance. Here a strong body of Mexicans had been recently stationed, but abandoned the post, when Col. Doniphan entered El Paso. Several wagon-loads of ammunition, and one piece of cannon, were discovered *cached*, or buried in the sand.* These also were afterwards sent for by the commander. This body of cavalry having returned, reported a strong Mexican force on its march from Chihuahua to recover El Paso from the hands of the Americans. So the army was not yet free from apprehension.

The Americans now having complete possession of El Paso, and treating the inhabitants with great humanity, even those who fought against them under a *black, piratical flag* at Brazito, (for many of them were walking about town with bandages around their heads, and their arms in slings, and their other wounds bound up, which they had received in that action,) *they* in turn, generously and gratuitously supplied many of the soldiers with such things as they required to eat and drink, as though unwilling to be excelled in kindness. This is the character of the El Paseños. The soldiers spent much of their

* At this fort was also discovered a great number of bloody bandages; for the Mexicans who were wounded at Brazito had been conveyed thither to receive surgical attention.—HUGHES.

time pleasantly in feasting upon a variety of the best viands and finest fruits, such as fresh pears, quinces, apples, oranges; and dried pears, apples, peaches, and grapes which far excel the raisin for deliciousness of flavor. Besides these there was a great variety of sweet-meats in the market; and also *mezcal* and *pulque*, and beer, and the richest wines. The soldiers enjoyed all these luxuries, after so much privation.

Shortly after Col. Doniphan's arrival at El Paso, the proclamation of Angel Trias, governor of Chihuahua, to the Mexican troops before the battle of Brazito, fell into his hands; a copy of which, translated by Capt. David Waldo, here follows:—

SOLDIERS:—The sacrilegious invaders of Mexico are approaching the city of El Paso, an important part of the State, where the enemy intend establishing their winter quarters, and even pretend that they will advance further into our territory. It is entirely necessary that you go—you defenders of the honor and glory of the Republic, that you may give a lesson to these pirates.

The State calculated much upon the aid that would be given by the valiant and war-worn citizens of the Pass; but treason has sown there distrust, and the patriotic people, by a disgraceful mutiny, retreated at thirty leagues distance from a small force, under the command of Gen'l Kearny, when they might have taken him and his force prisoners at discretion. Subordination and discipline were wanting.

You go to reëstablish the character of those Mexicans, and to chastise the enemy if he should dare to touch the soil of the State; the State ennobled by the blood of the fathers of our Independence. I confide in your courage, and alone I recommend to you obedience to your commanders and the most perfect discipline.

All Chihuahua burn with the desire to go with you, because they are all Mexicans, possessed of the warmest enthusiasm and the purest patriotism. They will march to join you—at the first signal the circumstances of the war demand re-inforcements, they shall be forwarded, let it cost the State what it may. To the people of Chihuahua no sacrifice is reckoned when the honor of the republic is at stake.

The enthusiasm with which you march, and the sanctity of your noble cause, are sure evidences of victory. Yes, you are led by the God of battles and your brows shall be crowned with laurels. Thus trusts your friend and companion.

ANGEL TRIAS.

Chihuahua, Nov. 9, 1846.

On the morning of the 1st of January, 1847, a great cloud of dust was seen rising in the direction of Chihuahua, similar to that usually produced by the march of an army of cavalry. The picket guard came dashing in at full speed. Assembly was blown by the bugler. All apprehended an attack. The soldiers ran to their arms in great haste. The officers paraded their respective commands. The standards were displayed. The men were drawn up in order of battle. The Mexican pieces of artillery, recently taken, and the howitzer captured at Brazito, were put into an attitude of defence by a file of men under Lieutenant Kribben. The men who had straggled from camp into town, came running for their arms with the utmost expedition. Col. Doniphan, who now had his quarters in the town, also came running on foot with his holster-pistols swung across his left arm, having his drawn sword in his right hand. Lieutenant-colonel Mitchell, with a small body of cavalry, galloped off in the direction of the rising dust, and, having made a reconnoissance, reported that the dust proceeded from an atajo of pack mules and a train of Mexican caretas coming into town. This was another FALSE ALARM. The soldiers were now moved and quartered in houses, near the square, for better defence, both against the enemy and the high winds, which rage continually during the winter season, in that mountainous country.

The merchants and sutlers, upon arriving at El Paso, hired rooms and storehouses, where they exhibited their goods and commodities for sale. Many of them sold largely to the inhabitants, whereby they considerably lightened their burdens. Certain of the merchants advanced Col. Doniphan sums of money, for the use of the commissary and quartermaster departments of the army, taking, for these accommodations, checks on the United States' treasury. To a limited extent, also, they furnished some of the soldiers with clothing, and other necessaries.

About the 5th,[*] a lieutenant and a number of mechanics were sent up to the falls, to repair the grist-mills at that place. Large quantities of wheat were now ground, and the flour, unbolted, put up in sacks for the use of the army. For the present, therefore, the soldiers were bountifully supplied.

---

[*] Capts. Waldo, Kirker, Maclean, and a Mexican went on a hunting excursion up the Del Norte river. They were absent eight or ten days, during which they had much sport. They chased several small parties of Mexicans, and visited the house of the friendly Mexican, whose son had volunteered to serve under Gen. Poncé at Brazito, and was unfortunately shot, while endeavoring to come over to the American lines, in that action.—HUGHES

Near the mills the Mexican army, a short time previous to the battle at Brazito, had constructed a cordon or system of field works, extending from the mountains, and connecting with the river, on the west side, at the falls. Here, at first, it was proposed to give the "Northern Invaders" battle; than which it is difficult to conceive a stronger position for defence; but Gen. Cuilta, chief in command at that time, being seized with an indisposition, Gen. Poncé led the troops to Brazito, where he suffered a total defeat. The next day, Capt. Stephenson and about one hundred men, including some who had been left sick at Soccorro and Albuquerque, and had recovered, came up, escorting a large train of commissary wagons. This train had been ordered down from Santa Fé, when the troops came out of the Navajo country.

The soldiers, (such of them as were not on duty at any time,) now engaged in various pastimes and amusements with the Paseños; sometimes visiting and conversing with the fair Señoritas of the place, whose charms and unpurchased kindness almost induced some of the men to wish not to return home;—and at other times gleefully dancing at the fandango. When the weather was pleasant, the streets about the plaza were crowded with Mexicans, and American soldiers, engaged in betting at monté, chuck-luck, twenty-one, faro, or some other game at cards. This vice was carried to such an excess at one time, that Col. Doniphan was compelled to forbid *gambling* on the streets, in order to clear them of obstruction.[98]

NOTE 98.—A little Frenchman had a saloon on the southeast corner of the public square at El Paso. A number of soldiers got drunk there one night; among them, Robert Barnett of Company B, and Lieutenant R. A. Wells of Company F. They had a free-for-all-fight, in which Barnett stuck a bowie-knife through Wells's neck just below the ears. The knife went clear and clean through the neck, the point protruding more than an inch. Barnett jerked the knife out of the wound when he saw what he had done. Wells was brought to quarters, and the surgeon, Dr. Winston, examined the wound. He said no surgeon could put a knife through the neck at that point without causing death, and that none could withdraw a blade from such a wound without causing instant death. That Wells still lived, he said, was due to luck alone—such luck as will often attend a drunken man. Wells was full of whisky to the throat. The following morning Meredith T. Moore saw on the floor two trails from the mouth of Wells, one of blood from the wound, the other of whisky; they ran across the room side by side and would not mix. Wells was hauled in an ambulance to the sea, was brought home, and recovered. After his return to Missouri he studied medicine with Dr. Winston, and for many years they were partners in the practice in Jefferson City, under the firm-name of Winston & Wells. It is said that Wells was still living, in Montana, in August, 1906.

Capt. JAMES KIRKER, who has gained so much celebrity as an INDIAN FIGHTER, and who for many years past has been successfully employed by the State of Chihuahua against the Apaches, hearing that the American forces were advancing upon El Paso, left his family at Coralitus, and hastened to join his countrymen, that he might show his fidelity and patriotism. This conduct of Capt. Kirker was no less unexpected, than it was terrifying to the Chihuahuans. For he, who had so long been the TERROR of the Apaches, had now joined with his countrymen, to be henceforward equally the TERROR of the Chihuahuans. Captain Kirker, on account of his great knowledge of the country, and acquaintance with the language and customs of the Mexican people, became subsequently of the most essential service to Col. Doniphan as an interpreter and forage master. He returned with the army to the United States.[99]

NOTE 99.—Meredith T. Moore says that at the south end of the Jornada, above Brazito, a man appeared on the west bank of the Rio Grande and called over to the army. He was questioned by the officers, who finally ordered him to cross the river to the encampment, which he did, bringing with him some half-dozen Delaware Indians. He proved to be James Kirker. He was dressed as a frontiersman of his day—fringed buckskin hunting-shirt and breeches, heavy broad Mexican hat, and huge spurs, all embellished and ornamented with Mexican finery. He was mounted on a fine horse, which he regarded with great affection and to which he gave the most careful attention. In addition to a Hawkins rifle elegantly mounted and ornamented with silver inlaid on the stock, he was armed with a choice assortment of pistols and Mexican daggers. He said he had been living some years in Mexico in the service of the Governor, who contracted to pay him so much each for Apache scalps he might take. It hunting down these Indians he had employed a force of thirty or forty Delawares.. Some time before war was declared between the United States and Mexico the Governor of Chihuahua owed him $30,000 for Indian scalps, he said; and instead of paying him, had repudiated his claim and threatened to arrest him and his Delawares and throw them into prison. Most of the Indians had returned to their own country, but he, with those he could find, had set out for the American army. Some of the Delawares went on home by way of Santa Fé; others remained with the army and went home by way of New Orleans. James Peacock says the Delawares came with Kirker. Some of them had seen the fortifications at Sacramento, and one of them in conversation with Peacock drew in the sand with a stick a plan of all the works and a map of the locality in which they were situated. He told Peacock that the Mexicans reminded him of his first efforts to trap birds when he was a little boy; that they had constructed their fortifications on the theory that the Americans would walk into a trap set in plain view, when by deploying to the right the trap might be avoided; that the Mexicans expected the Americans would march along the road in the ravine upon which all their artillery was trained. Peacock took the Indian to Doniphan, for whom he drew designs of the Mexican

The universal kind treatment which the El Paseños received from the Americans, not only induced them to think well of the conduct of the army, but disposed them favorably towards the American government; for they began to consider how much more liberty and happiness they might enjoy, having connection with this republic, than in their present state. They saw also that the Americans were

fortifications, and gave a description of all the surrounding country. And the American army did at Sacramento exactly what the Delaware suggested to Peacock that it would do—turned to the right and avoided the Mexican artillery. The fact that it was the Delaware who had a knowledge of the Mexican fortifications would indicate that Kirker had not recently been at Chihuahua or Sacramento. Moore says Kirker was absolutely fearless; that he was a fine rider, well accomplished in the daring horsemanship affected by the old trappers and plainsmen of the time, such as leaning over from the saddle so far that his long hair would sweep the ground with the horse at full speed. He knew all the trails of northern Mexico, and where water could be found along them. He spoke the Spanish language well, also a number of Indian languages; he proved a valuable acquisition to the army. It will be observed that the text says Kirker came to the army directly from his home at Coralitus. In Vol. XX, *Early Western Travels* (reprint of Gregg's *Commerce of the Prairies*), p. 103, note by Dr. Thwaites, is the following:

"James Kirker, known to the Mexicans at Santiago Querque, was an American who led an adventurous life upon the plains. Like several others, he embarked in Apache warfare for the Government of Chihuahua; and was accused, probably unjustly, of cheating in the delivery of scalps. He retired in bad humor to his hacienda in Sonora; later removing to California, where he died about 1853."

In Kendall's *Texan Santa Fé Expedition*, Vol. II, p. 57, is the following:

"Some of the Mexicans also told us that a well-known American, named Kirker, had been engaged in the same business, and with a party of his countrymen had been very successful; but it being suspected that he was in the practice of bringing in counterfeit scalps—or in other words, that he did not scruple to kill any of the lower order of Mexicans he might meet with, where there was slight chance of being discovered, and pass off their topknots for those of true Apaches—a stop was put to the game, and afterwards, instead of paying him a certain sum for each scalp, he was allowed only one dollar a day for his services. This was the story I heard from the Mexicans, who added that Kirker immediately gave up the business and retired to Sonora, or the western part of Chihuahua, setting all attempts to arrest him at defiance. . . . I was extremely loath, at the time, to credit the Mexican accounts of Kirker and his doings, and have since been informed, by Americans who knew him well, that they are destitute of foundation. For many years Kirker led a wild border life, engaged in continual strife with the hostile Indians of the prairies and of Mexico, and in all his encounters with them came off victorious. He is now, or was a year since, quietly occupied in overlooking a hacienda not many days' travel from Chihuahua, ready to repel any attack his old enemies, the Apaches, may make upon him. His superior prowess and great daring may have first embittered the Mexicans against him, for no sooner has any foreigner signalized himself by deeds of noble daring in their cause, than he is looked upon with jealousy and distrust, and the first opportunity is embraced to oust him from the high estate his talents have destined him to fill. This spirit, in all probability, first engendered hostility against Kirker on the part of the Mexicans, and induced them to fabricate numerous stories of his cruelty and dishonesty."

not disposed to plunder; for being conquerors, they notwithstanding purchased of the conquered those things they wished to use, and forcibly took nothing. Nor would they permit the Apaches to kill and plunder the Mexican people. This pleased them, for they dread the Apaches. Besides, when a subaltern officer took provisions for his men, or forage for the animals, he gave the owner of the property an ORDER on the quartermaster. Such order was always accepted, and promptly redeemed. This, too, gave the Mexicans great confidence in the solvency and fairness of the American government.

Now, there are a great many wolves, which come down from the neighboring mountains, into the suburbs of El Paso, and kill the flocks when not penned in their folds, and also feed upon the offal about the shambles, and slaughter-pens. They kept up a dolorous serenade during the nights, and in many instances were so bold as almost to drive the sentinels from their posts. Oftentimes the sentinels were compelled to shoot them, in self-defence, as they would a prowling enemy. This would usually create a false alarm.

On one occasion several beeves had been slaughtered in a fold, or corral, for the use of the army. During the night the scent of the offal attracted the wolves. A considerable number of them coming down from their lairs among the rocks, leaped into the corral, and feasted sumptuously. The walls of the corral were many feet higher on the inside than on the outside, so, at day-dawn, when the wolves wished to retire, they could not repass the walls. The soldiers, therefore, in the morning, taking their sabres, went in amongst them, and, after much sport, killed them all. In such amusements did the soldiers delight.[100]

NOTE 100.—Many Mexican sheep were slaughtered for the troops at El Paso. These sheep were small, and often they were thin in flesh and made poor food. Upon one occasion the Quartermaster notified Company F to send up some one to draw its proportion of the carcasses of sheep to be issued that day. Joseph Yount was detailed to go. Yount was a powerful man, with extremely long arms. He was directed to receive the sheep and await a wagon which would follow him to bring back the meat. A short time after he departed some one saw a strange object entering the quarters of the company; the men came to look at what seemed a heap of dressed sheep moving into camp. At the commissary they were tumbled down and Yount emerged from the moving pile. He had carried in the full quota of the company—eleven sheep. When rallied upon the enormous load he had carried he picked up the lean carcass of a dressed sheep and said, "Look at that!" Then holding it between his eyes and the sun, exclaimed, "Why, I could read the Lord's Prayer through that sheep!"

On a certain occasion while the army remained here, two sentinels, Tungitt and Clarkin, were found sleeping on their posts, and their guns taken from them by the officer of the guard. This is a capital offence. They were brought before Col. Doniphan, under arrest, who thus addressed them:—"Gentlemen! you have committed a very high offence against the laws of the country, and propriety. By your neglect you have exposed the lives of all. You have laid the whole camp liable to be surprised by the enemy. Are you not sensible of the enormity of these offences?" To which they replied in the affirmative, "but we were tired and exhausted, and could not preserve our wakefulness—we will endeavor not to commit a similar offence in future." "Then go," says Col. Doniphan, "and hereafter be good soldiers and faithful sentinels—I will excuse you for the present." They departed, and were never known to be in default again.

About the 10th of January* we learned of the insurrection which had been set on foot in New Mexico by Gen. Archulette, Chavez, Ortiz, and others, and captured certain of their emissaries, endeavoring to instigate the inhabitants of El Paso to attempt the same there. This matter, being timely detected and exposed at El Paso by the vigilance of both officers and men, was crushed before the plan was matured. Also certain other Mexicans were detected, in secretly carrying on a correspondence with the troops at Chihuahua, whereby they were endeavoring to plot and work our destruction. Among these was Ramond Ortiz, the curate of El Paso, a very shrewd and intelligent man, and the same whom Kendall's graphic pen has immortalized. All of these were now held in custody under a strict guard.

The time was now occupied in procuring a supply of provisions, and a suitable outfit for the contemplated march upon Chihuahua. Preparatory to this, also, and for the more perfect organization and better discipline of the troops, the intermediate time was consumed in regimental and company drills:—in cavalry charges, and sword exercises. These wholesome military exercises gave greater efficiency to the corps, and it is due to the high-minded, honorable men, who composed this column, to bear testimony to the prompt and cheerful manner in which they performed every duty, and submitted to every

* About this time an American, his name Rodgers, escaped from Chihuahua, and reported to Col. Doniphan that Gen. Wool had abandoned his march upon that city, and that a formidable force was preparing to defend the place.—HUGHES.

burden, upon which they foresaw their safety, as an army, depended. Such was the spirit of the soldiers under the command of Col. Doniphan.*

On the 18th Capt. Hughes and Lieut. Jackson, with ten men, who had been left sick at Soccorro, and a few days afterwards Lieuts. Lea, Gordon and Hinton, who had been sent back to Santa Fé for provisions and the artillery, arrived at El Paso, and rejoined their companies. About this time also, five intelligent young men, who fought bravely at Brazito, died of typhoid fever, and were buried with the honors of war, in the El Paso cemetery.†

On the 25th the author made the subjoined statements of the resources of the rich valley of El Paso, to the War Department, after several weeks' careful observation, which was ordered to be printed.

For the consideration of the War Department, at Washington City.

The United States' forces under command of Col. Alexander W. Doniphan, took possession of the city of El Paso, in the Department of Chihuahua, on Sunday, the 27th December, 1846; two days after the battle of Brazito, the strength of his command being about nine hundred men.

My object, in this communication, is to give the War Department and the country at large some idea of the resources of the fruitful valley of El Paso, and of its importance to the United States. The settlement of the El Paso extends from the falls of the Rio Grande on the north, to the Presidio on the south, a distance of twenty-two miles, and is one continuous orchard and vineyard, embracing in its ample area an industrious and peaceable population of at least eight thousand. This spacious valley is about mid-way between Santa Fé and Chihuahua, and is isolated from all other Mexican settlements by the mountains that rise on the east and west, and close into the river on the north and south. The breadth of the valley is about ten miles. The falls of the river are two miles north of the "*plaza publica,*" or public square, and afford sufficient water-power for grist and saw-mills enough to supply the entire settlement with flour and lumber.

The most important production of the valley is the Grape, from which are annually manufactured not less than two hundred thousand gallons of perhaps the richest and best wine in the world. This

---

* On the 11th January, J. T. Crenshaw was appointed Sergeant-major, *vice* Palmer resigned.—HUGHES.

† These were James M. Finley, J. D. Leland, G. J. Hackley, J. Clark and a Mr. Dyer.
   Peace to the shades of the virtuous brave,
    Who gallantly bore the perils of war,
   Who found an humble, yet honored grave,
    From kindred, home, and country far.—HUGHES.

wine is worth two dollars per gallon, and constitutes the principal revenue of the city. Thus the wines of El Paso alone yield four hundred thousand dollars per annum. The El Paso wines are superior, in richness of flavor and pleasantness of taste, to anything of the kind I ever met with in the United States, and I doubt not that they are far superior to the best wines ever produced in the valley of the Rhine, or on the sunny hills of France. There is little or no rain in this elevated country, and hence the extraordinary sweetness and richness of the grape. Also, quantities of the grape of this valley are dried in clusters, and preserved for use during the winter months. In this state I regard them as far superior to the best raisins that are imported into the United States from the West India Islands and other tropical climates.

If this valley were cultivated by an energetic American population, it would yield, perhaps, ten times the quantity of wine and fruits at present produced. Were the wholesome influences and protection of our Republican Institutions extended to the Rio del Norte, an American population, possessing American feelings, and speaking the American language, would soon spring up here. To facilitate the peopling of this valley by the Anglo-American race, nothing would contribute so much as the opening of a communication between this rich valley and the western States of our union, by a turnpike, rail road, or some other thoroughfare which would afford a market for the fruits and wines of this river country. Perhaps the most feasible and economical, though not the most direct, plan of opening an outlet to the grape valley of the Rio Grande would be the construction of a Grand Canal from this place, following the meanderings of the river to its highest navigable point. If a communication, by either of these routes, were opened, this valley would soon become the seat of wealth, influence and refinement. It would become one of the richest and most fashionable parts of the continent. A communication between the valley of the Mississippi and that of the Rio del Norte, affording an easy method of exchanging the products of the one, for those of the other, will do more than any other cause to facilitate the westward march of civilization and republican government. It would be an act of charity to rid these people of their present governors and throw around them the shield of American protection.

That the idea of a canal following the course of the Del Norte, may not appear impracticable, it may not be amiss to state that no country in the world is better adapted for the construction of canals than this valley. As the earth is sandy, canals are easily constructed; but there is a kind of cement intermixed with the sand that renders the banks of canals as firm as a wall. There is already a grand canal, or "*acequia,*" leading out from the river above the falls, extending through the entire length of the valley of El Paso, irrigating every farm and vineyard, thence to the Presidio, where it rejoins the river.

Pears, peaches, apples, quinces and figs, are produced here in the greatest profusion. The climate of this country is most salubrious and healthful. The scenery is grand and picturesque beyond description. The inhabitants here suffer more from the depredations of the Apaches than from any other cause. They are frequently robbed of all they possess, in one night, by the incursions of these lawless plunderers. A few companies of American dragoons, would, however, soon drive them from their hiding places in the mountains, and put an end to their depredations.

Add to the fruits and wines of this rich valley, a vast quantity of corn, wheat and other small grain; and the surplus productions of the place will, under its present state of agriculture, amount to near *one million of dollars* per annum. What then would be the amount of the surplus under the advantages of American Agriculture? The entire valley of the Del Norte, from Albuquerque to Chihuahua, a distance of five hundred miles in length, is as well adapted to the cultivation of the grape, as the particular valley adjacent to El Paso.

I have thought proper to make these suggestion to the War Department, as there is no corps of Field and Topographical Engineers with this branch of the Western Army, whose duty it would have been to make such a report.

Very respectfully,
JOHN T. HUGHES.

His Excellency W. L. Marcy, Sec'y of War.
El Paso, January 25th, 1847.

The Apache Indians were continually making incursions from the mountains upon the settlements of El Paso, plundering and robbing whomsoever chanced to fall in their way, whether Mexican or American, and driving off large herds of mules and flocks of sheep. On one occasion they drove off two hundred and eighty mules belonging to Algea and Porus, Mexican merchants, traveling under the protection of the American army. They had previously driven off twenty yoke of oxen belonging to the commissary trains near the little town Donanna. And subsequently, when the army was encamped about thirty-five miles below El Paso, they stole a parcel of work oxen from Mr. Houke, an American trader, and made their escape to the mountains. The next morning information of the fact was given, when Mr. Houke, Lieut. Hinton and three other men pursued them, and after a toilsome march of about sixty miles, overtook the villains, killed one of their number, recovered the oxen, and returned to the army.

CHAPTER XVIII.

Departure from El Paso—Doniphan's position—Ramond Ortiz—Two Deserters—Battalion of Merchants—Passage of the desert—The Ojo Caliente—Marksmanship—Lake of Encenillas—Dreadful Conflagration—Capt. Reid's Adventure—The Reconnoissance—Plan of the March—Battle of Sacramento—Surrender of Chihuahua.

Colonel Doniphan delayed at El Paso forty-two days, awaiting the arrival of the artillery under Major Clark and Captain Weightman, which he had ordered Col. Price to forward him on the route to Chihuahua, immediately upon his return from the Indian campaign. Col. Price, having his mind turned on quelling the conspiracy which had been plotted by Gen. Archulette, and fearing, if he should send the artillery away, that it would too much weaken his force, and embolden the conspirators, hesitated several weeks before he would comply with the order. At length, however, he dispatched Major Clark with one hundred and seventeen men, and six pieces of cannon, four six pounders, and two twelve pound howitzers; which, after indefatigable exertion, and incessant toiling through the heavy snows, arrived at El Paso on the 1st of February.[101]

On the 8th the whole army, the merchant, baggage, commissary, hospital, sutler, and ammunition trains, and all the stragglers, amateurs, and gentlemen of leisure, under flying colors, presenting the most martial aspect, set out with buoyant hopes for the city of Chihuahua. There the soldiers expected to reap undying fame,—to

NOTE 101.—When the battery was entering El Paso the whole population of the town assembled to look on. People were on the tops of houses and barns, and standing on every object calculated to give them a view of the cannon. Some one suggested that the battery should be welcomed with a salute fired from the cannon captured at Brazito. Men hurried away to fire the salute. Haste was necessary, as the battery was entering the town when the suggestion was first made. The powder was poured into the cannon, but nothing could be found to put on top of it to make a blank shot. In this emergency one of the men pulled off his socks and rammed them down on the powder. In the hurry no attention was paid to the direction of the gun. When it was fired the socks hit a soldier in the face. He raised a great cry, which he kept up even when it was found he was not injured in the least. He was asked why he kept whining about the matter, and replied that he would rather have been shot with a solid ball than a pair of socks worn from Fort Leavenworth to El Paso, without change for eight months. He wanted the shooters punished.

gain a glorious victory—or perish on the field of honor. Nothing certain could be learned of the movements of Gen. Wool's column, which, at first, was destined to operate against Chihuahua. Col. Doniphan's orders were merely to *report* to Gen. Wool at that place,— not to *invade* the State. Vague and uncertain information had been obtained through the Mexicans, that Gen. Wool's advance had, at one time, reached Parras, but that the whole column had suddenly deflected to the left, for some cause to them and us equally unknown. Thus was Col. Doniphan circumstanced. With an army less than one thousand strong, he was on his march leading through inhospitable, sandy wastes, against a powerful city, which had been deemed of so much importance, by the government, that Gen. Wool, with three thousand five hundred men and a heavy park of artillery, had been directed thither to effect its subjugation. What then must have been the feelings of Col. Doniphan and his men, when they saw the states of Chihuahua and Durango in arms to receive them, not the remotest prospect of succor from Gen. Wool, and rocks and unpeopled deserts intervening, precluding the possibility of successful retreat? "*Victory or death*" were the two alternatives. Yet there was no faltering,— no pale faces,—no dismayed hearts. At this crisis, had Col. Doniphan inquired of his men what was to be done,[102] the response would have been unanimously given, LEAD US ON. But he needed not to make the inquiry, for he saw depicted in every countenance, the fixed resolve "TO DO OR DIE." Col. Doniphan's responsibility was therefore very great. The undertaking was stupendous. His success was brilliant and unparalleled. Who then will deny him the just meed of applause?

A deep gloom enshrouded the State of Missouri. Being apprised of Gen. Wool's movements, the people of the State were enabled to appreciate the full extent of the danger which threatened to overwhelm us. They saw our imminently perilous situation. They felt

---

NOTE 102.—The question of continuing the march towards Chihuahua was put to a vote of the troops, and there were but two or three dissenting votes. Samuel Maxwell, a blacksmith in Company F, was shoeing a horse when told of the result of the vote. It frightened him. He was opposed to going on. He dropped the foot of the horse upon which he was at work, and began to talk of the foolishness and danger of the march. He talked of nothing else and talked incessantly. It preyed on his mind and deranged his reason. In two weeks he had talked himself to death, and was buried at El Paso.

for the unsuccored army. The Executive himself was moved with sympathy, and fearful apprehension for its safety. But neither *he* nor the people could avert the coming storm, or convey timely warning to the commander of this *forlorn hope*. He had therefore to rely upon STEEL and the COURAGE of his men. The event is known.

The Colonel took with him Ramond Ortiz, Pino, and three other influential men of the malcontents, as hostages for the future good behavior of the inhabitants of El Paso. "By this means the safety of traders, and of all other persons passing up or down the country, was guarantied; for they were forewarned that if any depredations were committed upon citizens of the United States, at El Paso, they would be put to death."

Since that time no outrages have been perpetrated, at El Paso, upon any American citizen. It was at El Paso that two American soldiers conceived for two fair, young, Mexican girls, an affection so strong and ardent, that they did not choose to march any further with the army. Having marched with their companies one or two days, they deserted camp, at night, and returned to those they loved, and in a short time married them.

On the evening of the 12th, the column reached a point on the Del Norte,[103] about fifty miles below El Paso, where the road, turning to the right, strikes off at right angles with the river across the Jornada of sixty-five miles in extent, running through deep sand-drifts, nearly the whole way. On this desert-tract there is not one drop of water. Here, therefore, the command came to a halt, and tarried one day, that the men might prepare victuals, and such a supply of water, as they had means of conveying along with them, for the desert-journey.

Col. Doniphan now called upon the merchant caravan to meet, and organize themselves into companies, and elect officers to command them. This he did, that he might avail himself of their services, in

---

NOTE 103.—The Rio Grande, or Rio Del Norte as it was called by the Mexicans, takes its rise in Colorado, in the San Juan Mountains. It flows almost directly south, dividing New Mexico into two nearly equal parts. It breaks through the mountain-range at the northwest point of Texas, giving rise to "the pass," or El Paso, from which the Mexican and American towns of that name were so called. From El Paso to the Gulf it forms the boundary between Mexico and the United States. It is a shallow stream, and not navigable, though of great ength. It was crossed by Coronado, and had already been crossed by De Vaca.

the event that the troops, which he already had, should not prove sufficiently strong to cope with the enemy at Chihuahua. The merchants and the teamsters in their employ were quickly organized into two efficient companies, under Capts. Skillman and Glasgow, forming a battalion commanded by Samuel C. Owens, of Independence, whom they elected Major.[104]

This was a very effective corps, for both the merchants and the teamsters were well armed, and were very brave men. Besides, having a large capital invested in merchandise, they had the double incentive to fight bravely, first for their property, and then for their lives. These numbered about one hundred and fifty well armed men. Here, all the Mexican powder, and other munitions of war, which the colonel had taken at El Paso, and for which he had not the means of transportation, were destroyed. The powder was burnt, and the canister-shot and arms thrown into the river.

A few days previous to this, Cufford and Gentry, a strong firm, the former an Englishman, and the latter an American, both traveling with British passports, secretly and dishonorably abandoned the merchant caravan, and, contrary to their promise to Colonel Doniphan, slipped off at night with forty-five wagons, and hastened on to Chihuahua, and from thence on to Zacatecas.

Now, Harmony, a Spaniard, and Porus, a Mexican, fearing lest Doniphan might be defeated at Chihuahua, were loath to proceed

NOTE 104.—Edward J. Glasgow wrote me, August 13, 1906, as follows:

"On arriving at El Paso we learned that General Wool had joined his force with that of General Taylor at Monterey and Buena Vista. In consequence of this information, and that the Mexican force at Chihuahua far outnumbered ours, Colonel Doniphan issued an order that all American traders and their wagoners should form into two companies of infantry, elect their own officers, be mustered into the United States service, and accompany him,—which was done. The two companies numbered considerably over 200 men. Henry Skilman commanded one and I commanded the other, as captains, and the battalion was commanded by another trader, Samuel C. Owens, as major. On nearing the Sacramento Ranch, about sixteen miles from Chihuahua, it was found that the Mexicans had erected fortifications on the opposite side of the stream of that name, and on high ground awaited us. Our wagons were then formed in four parallel columns, about thirty feet apart, the army being inclosed inside, and turning off the road we crossed the stream nearly a mile distant and reached higher ground, when we turned toward the enemy and the fight began. A few rounds of grape and spherical case-shot soon drove back some cavalry which had come out from their works, when our whole force moved forward, with the result you know. The Traders' Battalion has been badly treated by the Government, for, although it participated in the battle and its Major, Samuel C. Owens, was killed in the engagement, none of us ever received any pay or pensions, the excuse given for refusal being that Colonel Doniphan had no legal authority to create any new companies of troops."

with their wagons any further, and desired to turn back to El Paso, and there make sale of their merchandize. This could not be permitted without endangering the safety of all; for the only safety was in union. Therefore Lieut. Col. Mitchell, Captain Reid, and Lieutenant Choteau, with sixteen men, went back several miles to compel these men to bring up their trains. At first they pretended that the Apaches had stolen all their mules, wherefore they could not move their wagons. But being threatened, they soon brought their animals from a place where they had purposely concealed them, that they might be permitted to remain. In a short time they were brought up, and forbidden to leave the army again.

While at this place the author held a conversation with Ortiz, the curate, in regard to the project of M. Guizot "*to preserve the balance of power*" by placing the son of Louis Philippe or some other monarch on the "throne of Mexico." The curate observed:—"Such an idea is too preposterous to deserve a serious consideration. The Mexicans, and especially those in the Northern States, would treat the proposition, if made to them seriously, with the indignation and contempt which it so richly merits. Mexicans, not less than Americans, love liberty. Mexico would rather be conquered by a sister Republic—rather lose her national existence, than submit to be governed by a foreign prince."

Having buried two brave men, Maxwell and Willis, on the 14th the army bade adieu to the Great River of the North, and commenced its march upon the dreadful desert. Some of the men having no canteens or other means of carrying water filled the sheaths of their sabres and swung the naked blades jingling at their sides. C. F. Hughes, quartermaster sergeant, had terrible work to force the trains along through the heavy sand-drifts. Oftentimes he was compelled to double his teams, and have a dozen or more men rolling at the wheels, to induce the wagons to move at all. The mules were weak, and sunk up to their knees in the sand, the wagons stood buried almost to the hubs. Thus were they embarrassed. The teams could not move them. The soldiers and teamsters would often leap down from their horses and mules and roll the wagons along with their hands until they got where the sand was lighter. Thus it was all through the desert. After an arduous march of twenty miles, the army encamped upon the plain without wood or water. On the next day, towards sunset, the army passed through a gap or cañon in a range of mountains which traverses the desert from north to south. This mountain shoots up abruptly from the plain into an innumerable set of knobs and rocky peaks consisting of dark, iron-colored, masses of basalt and puddingstone, and in some places of volcanic cinders. At this point, Lieutenant Gordon, and Collins, interpreter, with twelve other men, fell in company with Kirker's scouting party, which had been in advance several days. Kirker's party consisted of eight men. The whole now (being twenty-three in number) under Lieutenant Gordon, proceeded far in advance of the army by direction from the colonel, for the purpose of making a reconnoissance at Carrizal, where they had understood a body of Mexicans were posted. This place is on the other side of the desert. Before their arrival there, however, the Mexican soldiery abandoned the place. Therefore they entered it and took military possession in the name of the United States' government; the Alcalde, without offering the slightest resistance, giving a written certificate of submission, in which he claimed the colonel's clemency and threw himself on the generosity of the American army. He was not disappointed in receiving the amplest protection. By this time there was not a drop of water in the canteens, and all were suffering extremely with thirst. At this hour one of the artillerymen came up from Santa Fé having in possession the United States' mail; the only one of consequence which had been received for six months. Though at this crisis nothing could have been so refreshing to the BODY as cool water, yet newspapers and letters from home had a wonderfully cheering and talismanic influence on the MIND. Not a word however, could be learned of the movements of the army of Gen. Wool. After a toilsome march of twenty-four miles, about midnight the column halted to allow the men and animals a little rest. But they had no refreshment; for the men were again obliged to spend the night without their suppers and without water. The animals also were nearly perishing of thirst. It was now still twenty-one miles to water, over a heavy sandy road, and the teams had already become feeble and broken down. Ortiz, the benevolent curate, although a prisoner, and under a strict guard, generously gave many of the soldiers a draught of water, which he had provided to be brought from the Del Norte in a water vessel. For this and other instances of kindness towards the author, he now makes his grateful acknowledgments.

The next morning by day-dawn the army was on the march. The mules and horses were neighing and crying piteously for water. Some of them were too weak to proceed further. They were abandoned. Notwithstanding the eagerness of the men to get to water, a strong front and rear guard were detailed as usual, to prevent surprise by the enemy. Towards night, when the column had arrived within five miles of the Laguna de los Patos, the men could no longer be restrained in the lines, but in the greatest impatience hurried on in groups to quench their burning thirst. The commander seeing this, and knowing how his men suffered, (for he too suffered equally with them) did not attempt to prevent it, but taking his whole force hastened on to the lake as quick as possible, that all might be satisfied; having left an order for Capt. Parsons, who commanded the rear guard that day, to leave the trains, that his men might have water and rest. It was near sunset; meanwhile the quartermaster-sergeant, and the resolute and hardy teamsters, had the task of a Hercules before them in bringing up the trains through the deep, heavy sanddrifts. Having arrived within about ten miles of the Laguna, they found it impossible to advance further. The rear guard had left them with the view of getting water and then returning. They were sometimes compelled to quadruple the teams to move a wagon through the deep sand. The animals were dying of thirst and fatigue. Thirty-six yoke of oxen had been turned loose. Two wagons were abandoned amidst the sand hills. Eight thousand pounds of flour, and several barrels of salt had been thrown out upon the ground. Also some of the sutlers threw away their heavy commodities which they could not transport. The trains never could have proceeded ten miles farther. But the God who made the fountain leap from the rock to quench the thirst of the Israelitish army in the desert, now sent a cloud which hung upon the summits of the mountains to the right, and such a copious shower of rain descended that the mountain-torrents came rushing and foaming down from the rocks, and spread out upon the plains in such quantities that both the men and the animals were filled. Therefore, they staid all night at this place where the God-send had blessed them, and being much refreshed, next morning passed out of the desert. All were now at Laguna de los Patos, where they staid one day to recruit and gain strength. This is a beautiful lake of fresh water. It was here that W. Tolley, a volunteer, who, as it is said, left a charming young bride at home, drank so excessively of the cool, refreshing element, after so many days of toil on the desert, that he soon died. He was buried near the margin of the lake. Thus the army passed the desert sixty-five miles in extent.

On the morning of the 18th, the column and trains were again in motion. C. F. Hughes, in consideration of the service he had rendered in passing the desert, was now relieved from further duty by Mr. Harrison. To the right, at the distance of several miles from the Laguna, rises a stupendous, pyramidal rock, many thousand feet high. The existence of such abrupt, detached, masses of mountains, shows that the earth, by some wonderful agency, has been convulsed and upheaved. Who will say that the flood, which inundated the Old World, may not have been produced by the sudden upheavement, and emergement of the Western Continent, from the ocean, by some All-powerful Agency? A march of eighteen miles brought the Army to Carrizal, where there was much cool and delightful water, and where forage was obtained in abundance.

At meridian on Sunday the 21st, the command reached the celebrated "Ojo Caliente," or Warm Spring, where the men were again permitted to rest a few hours, and make preparations for crossing another desert forty-five miles wide without water. From this place Capt. Skillman, with twelve volunteers, was dispatched to the Laguna de Encenillas, to keep up a close espionage on the movements of the enemy; for it was now anticipated that he would give battle at that place. The Ojo Caliente is at the base of a ledge of rocky hills, and furnishes a vast volume of water, about blood-warm, which runs off in the direction of the Patos. The basin of the spring is about one hundred and twenty feet long and seventy-five wide, with an average depth of four feet. The bottom consists of sparkling, white sand, and the water is perfectly transparent. No effort, by disturbing the sand, was sufficient to becloud, or muddy the crystal water.* Col. Doniphan, and many of his officers and men, now enjoyed the most luxurious, and rejuvenescent bathing. Thus refreshed, the march was commenced upon the desert. Having advanced twelve miles, the men were encamped on the plain, without wood or water, indis-

* This ojo caliente was formerly the seat of a princely Hacienda, belonging to Porus, a Spanish nabob, who at one time, had grazing on his pastures more than thirty-six thousand head of cattle and sheep.—HUGHES.

pensable requisites for comfort in a military camp, after a hard day's march.

Continuing the march the next day, a cañon was passed in a high and craggy range of mountains, traversing the desert. These huge masses of basalt, which rise in many places two thousand feet almost perpendicularly, were capped with snow. Having completed twenty-two miles, the men halted for the night, on a rocky, flinty spot of earth, where there was neither wood, water, nor grass. Nor was it possible for the men to have the least comfort, as it was extremely cold. They tethered their animals, and wrapping themselves up in their blankets, lay down on the earth without taking supper.

The next day we marched twelve miles, and came to the Guyagas Springs. These issue in leaping, gushing, cool streamlets, out from the western base of a system of rocky bluffs, and refresh the neighboring plain. Here the men and animals slaked their burning thirst. Under the jutting rocks and archways of this mountain range, were seen dependent spar, crystal of quartz, and the most brilliant stalactites. Here a drove of twelve or thirteen antelopes, which had been feeding on the sides of the cliffs, seeing the men marching, and the banners and guidons fluttering, were affrighted at the unusual sight, and came bounding down from the rocks, as though they would break through the ranks; but as they neared the lines the men fired upon and killed them all, while bounding along. They were used for food. This evidence of MARKSMANSHIP struck the Mexican prisoners with astonishment, and caused them more than ever to dread the American rifles. Here in a narrow valley, with lofty, rocky ridges on either hand, the men were dismounted and allowed to rest for the night; during which M. Robards, a good soldier, died and was buried.

From thence, they marched the next day fifteen miles, and again encamped on the plain, without wood or water. Here part of the spies returned, and reported that there were seven hundred Mexicans at Encenillas, with artillery. Early the following morning, (which was the 25th,) Col. Doniphan drew up his forces in order of battle, and marched over to the north margin of the lake. Here he allowed his men a short respite, and some refreshment. This lake is about twenty miles long, and about three miles wide, and at the point where the army first encamped, there were near the margin white efflorescences of soda on the surface of the ground. Either this efflorescent soda, or the water of the lake, when put in flour, will quickly cause it to rise, or leaven. It was used instead of saleratus.

While nooning, the fire from one of the tents caught into the tall dry grass, and by a high wind was furiously driven over the plain, threatening destruction to every thing before it. In a short time the fire, which had broken out in a similar manner, from the camp near the Guyagas Springs, having almost kept pace with the army, came bursting and sweeping terribly over the summits of the mountains, and descending into the valley, united with the fire on the margin of the lake. The conflagration, now roaring and crackling. irresistibly swept along. The flame rose in dashing and bursting waves twenty feet high, and threatened to devour the whole train. The army was now put upon the march, and the trains endeavored to advance before the flames; but in vain. The wind blew steadily and powerfully in the direction the army was marching. The conflagration, gaining new strength from every puff of wind, came raging and sweeping like a wave. The column of flame, displaying a front of many miles, steadily advanced along the margin of the lake. This was a more terrible foe than an "army with banners." The fire now gained upon the trains. The ammunition wagons narrowly escaped. The artillery was run into the lake. Some of the wagons still passed onward.

The road runs parallel to the lake, and about two hundred yards from it. Colonel Doniphan and his men endeavored to trample down the grass from the road to the lake, in a narrow list, by frequently riding over the same ground. They also rode their horses into the water, and then quickly turned them upon the place where the grass was trodden down, that they might moisten it, and thereby stop the progress of the fire, between the road and the lake. But still the flames passed over, and heedlessly swept along. Capt. Reid with the "Horse Guards," adopting a different plan, upon the suggestion of a private, ordered his men to dismount about two miles in advance of the trains, and with their sabres hew and chop down the grass from the road to the lake, on a space thirty feet broad, and throw the cut grass out leeward. This was done. Fire was now set to the grass standing next to the wind, which burned slowly until it met the advancing conflagration. Thus the fire was checked on one side of the road.

On the other side, the volume of flame, increasing as the gale rose, rolled along the plain, and over the mountains, roaring and crackling, and careering in its resistless course, until the fuel which fed it was exhausted. The men spent the night on the bare and blackened earth, and the animals stood to their tethers without forage.

On the south-western side of this lake, and near its margin, stands the princely hacienda of Don Angel Trias, governor of Chihuahua. On this estate immense herds of cattle and flocks of sheep are produced. But the Mexican soldiers, seven hundred of whom on the morning of the 25th had been seen at the hacienda, had driven them all off, to prevent the Americans from subsisting on them. On the night of the 25th, and before it was known that the soldiery had evacuated the post, Capt. Reid, with twenty-five of the Horse Guards, volunteered to make a reconnoissance of the enemy, and report his position and strength. As, in the event the enemy was still occupying his position at the hacienda, strong guards would most probably be posted near the roads leading into the place from above and below the lake, the scouts, to prevent falling upon the guards, and to take the enemy by surprise, if it should be deemed advisable to attack him, crossed the lake, which was near three miles wide, and both deep and boggy, and hitherto considered impassable. Reaching the opposite shore, they saw no sentinel. Therefore they approached nearer. Still they saw no sentry. Cautiously, and with light footsteps, and in almost breathless silence, without a whisper or the jingling of a sabre, and under covering of the dark, they advanced a little. They heard the sound of music, and at intervals the trampling of horses. Perhaps it was the military patrol. None knew.

They now rode around the hacienda; but the high walls precluded the possibility of seeing within. No satisfactory reconnoissance could, therefore, be made. Not wishing to return to camp without effecting their object, the captain and his men, like McDonald and his mad-caps at Georgetown, made a sweeping dash, with drawn sabre and clattering arms, into the hacienda, to the infinite alarm of the inhabitants. They now had possession. The seven hundred soldiers had started, about an hour previous, to Sacramento. This was a bold and hazardous exploit. They then quartered in the place, which contains several hundred inhabitants, and were sumptuously entertained by the Administrador del Hacienda.* The next morning

---

* These fearless men were Captain Reid, C. Human, F. C. Hughes, W. Russell, J. Cooper, T. Bradford, Todd, I. Walker, L. A. Maclean, C. Clarkin, Long, T. Forysthe, Tungitt, Brown, W. McDaniel J. P. Campbell, T. Waugh, J. Vaughan, Boyce, Stewart, Antwine, and A. Henderson and J. Kirker, interpreters, and one or two others.—HUGHES.

they rejoined the army, then on the march, having with them several wild Mexican cattle. The whole force now moved on to a fort called Sanz, on a creek discharging into the Laguna de Encenillas. Here they encamped.

The next day the army and trains, including the merchant wagons, were drawn up in order of battle, ready to manœuvre expeditiously in the event of a sudden attack. The enemy was known to be at no great distance.* Thus the march was continued until night over a level, beautiful valley, with a high range of mountains running along on the left, and, at a greater distance, also on the right. A short time before sunset Lieutenant-colonel Mitchell, Lieutenants Winston and Sproule, Corporal Goodfellow, the author and one other volunteer, having proceeded about nine miles in advance of the column, and within five miles of the enemy's fortified position at Sacramento, ascended a high, rocky peak of the mountain, and, with good telescopes, enjoyed a fair view of the whole Mexican encampment. The enemy's whole line of field-works was distinctly viewed; the position of his batteries ascertained; and his probable numbers estimated. The result of this reconnoissance was duly reported to Colonel Doniphan, whereupon he immediately called a council of officers, and matured a plan for the conduct of the march on the following day. This night also the army encamped on a tributary of the lake of Encenillas.[105]

* Captain Skillman this day pursued one of the enemy's spies into the mountains so closely that he captured his horse, but the Mexican leaping off escaped on foot among the rocks.—HUGHES.

NOTE 105.—The night before the battle of Sacramento, Odon Guitar was detailed as one of the guards of Father Ortiz. As it was growing dark, Colonel Doniphan appeared and talked some time with the priest, saying, among other things, that it was uncertain where the carriage in which he was traveling would be placed during the battle. "I have not decided upon the location," said Colonel Doniphan; "what would you think should I place you in the front line of my army?" The priest knew that the Colonel was but jesting, and only laughed in reply. He assured Doniphan that he would go into the lines of the army of his country if he found opportunity to do so. Guitar did not hear Doniphan tell Ortiz where he would be placed during the battle; but he heard Ortiz tell Colonel Doniphan that the Mexicans would certainly defeat him. Doniphan replied that he did not fear defeat, and expressed confidence in his ability to defeat the Mexican army. This conversation occurred in the rear of the American camp, where Father Ortiz was under guard. He was sitting in his carriage, from which the horses were unharnessed, and Colonel Doniphan stood leaning on the carriage-door as he talked. When Colonel Doniphan went away, the guard was set. Gui-

On Sunday, the 28th of February, a bright and auspicious day, the American army, under Colonel Doniphan, arrived in sight of the Mexican encampment at Sacramento, which could be distinctly seen at the distance of four miles. His command consisted of the following corps and detachments of troops:

The 1st regiment, Col. Doniphan, numbering about eight hundred men; Lieutenant-colonel Mitchell's escort, ninety-seven men; artillery battalion, Major Clark and Captain Weightman, one hundred and seventeen men, with a light field battery of six pieces of cannon; and two companies of teamsters, under Captains Skillman and Glasgow, forming an extra battalion of about one hundred and fifty men, commanded by Major Owens, of Independence, making an aggregate force of one thousand one hundred and sixty-four men, all Missouri volunteers. The march of the day was conducted in the following order: the wagons, near four hundred in all, were thrown into four parallel files, with spaces of thirty feet between each. In the centre space marched the artillery battalion; in the space to the right, the 1st battalion, and in the space to the left, the 2d battalion. Masking these in front marched the three companies intended to act as cavalry, the Missouri horse guards, under Captain Reid, on the right, the Missouri dragoons under Captain Parsons on the left, and the Chihuahua rangers under Captain Hudson in the centre. Thus arranged, they approached the scene of action.*

The enemy had occupied the brow of a rocky eminence rising upon a plateau between the river Sacramento and the Arroya Seca, and near the Sacramento fort, eighteen miles from Chihuahua, and for-

* An eagle sometimes soaring aloft and sometimes swooping down amongst the fluttering banners, followed along the lines all day, and seemed to herald the news of victory. The men regarded the omen as good.—Hughes.

tar was placed on an upper seat, facing Father Ortiz, who talked with him until he was relieved. The priest said, "Young man, I perceive that you had in mind a good time when you enlisted in the army, and while you are not so intent on picking quarrels with the enemy, I have no doubt of your fighting well if you have to." A few years ago Guitar was in El Paso on business and made inquiry about Father Ortiz, finding that he lived some eighty miles away, though he was expected to officiate at one of the city churches the following Sunday. Guitar went to the church and saw the priest, who was then very old and almost blind. At first he did not recognize nor remember Guitar, but when the battle of Sacramento was mentioned he said: "Yes, I remember you now; you are the boy who sat in front of me the night before the battle and who was bent on having a good time at all hazards." He was much pleased to meet Guitar again.

tified its approaches by a line of field-works, consisting of twenty-eight strong redoubts and intrenchments. Here, in this apparently secure position, the Mexicans had determined to make a bold stand; for this pass was the key to the capital. So certain of victory were the Mexicans that they had prepared strings and hand-cuffs in which they meant to drive us, prisoners, to the city of Mexico, as they did the Texans in 1841. Thus fortified and intrenched, the Mexican army, consisting, according to a consolidated report of the adjutant-general which came into Col. Doniphan's possession after the battle, of four thousand two hundred and twenty men, commanded by Major-general José A. Heredia; aided by General Garcia Condé, former minister of war in Mexico, as commander of cavalry; General Mauricia Ugarté, commander of infantry; General Justiniani, commander of artillery, and Governor Angel Trias, brigadier-general, commanding the Chihuahua volunteers, awaited the approach of the Americans.[106]

When Col. Doniphan arrived within one mile and a half of the

NOTE 106.—At the battle of Sacramento Odon Guitar rode a Comanche mule which had its ears split from the points almost to its head, the mark of the Comanches. It had been captured at the battle of Brazito, loaded with two bags of ammunition. It was a splendid beast. Guitar was in the charge which swept the Mexicans from the field, and entered the fortifications with his battalion. Guitar was with the force directed to charge a battery across the Sacramento river which began to fire on the Americans after the main Mexican position had been carried. This battery was on the brow of a steep cliff, and almost inaccessible, but the Americans carried it without a halt. In scrambling up the steep hill Guitar had to dismount, and his mule broke away from him. But he captured at the battery a splendid Mexican horse richly furnished and caparisoned, and which proved to have belonged to the Mexican Adjutant. Attached to the saddle was a large portmanteau, in which Guitar found, incased in oiled silk, the rolls of the Mexican army. From these rolls was ascertained the exact number of troops the Mexicans had with which to oppose the Americans. It was dark when Guitar returned to camp from the pursuit of the routed Mexicans. On the following morning he carried the portmanteau to Colonel Doniphan, and was directed to turn over the rolls to De Courcy, the Adjutant. De Courcy demanded the portmanteau, but Guitar said that Colonel Doniphan had permitted him to return it. De Courcy was determined to have it, and the matter was referred to Colonel Doniphan, who not only directed that Guitar retain it, but reprimanded De Courcy. It was an elegant affair, and Guitar wished to bring it home with him; it was stolen, however, on board the vessel which conveyed the troops to New Orleans. Every man was searched or closely inspected as the troops disembarked, but the portmanteau was not found; it had evidently been thrown overboard by the thief, to escape detection.

enemy's fortifications, (a reconnoissance of his position having been made by Major Clark) leaving the main road which passed within the range of his batteries, he suddenly deflected to the right, crossed the rocky Arroya, expeditiously gained the plateau beyond, successfully deployed his men into line upon the highland, causing the enemy to change his first position, and made the assault from the west. This was the best point of attack that could possibly have been selected. The event of the day proves how well it was chosen.

In passing the Arroya the caravan and baggage trains followed close upon the rear of the army. Nothing could exceed in point of solemnity and grandeur the rumbling of the artillery, the firm moving of the caravan, the dashing to and fro of horsemen, and the waving of banners and gay fluttering guidons, as both armies advanced to the attack on the rocky plain; for at this crisis General Condé, with a select body of twelve hundred cavalry, dashed down from the fortified heights to commence the engagement. When within nine hundred and fifty yards of our alignment, Major Clark's battery of six pounders, and Weightman's section of howitzers opened upon them a well-directed and most destructive fire, producing fearful execution in their ranks. In some disorder they fell back a short distance, unmasking a battery of cannon, which immediately commenced its fire upon us. A brisk cannonading was now kept up on both sides for the space of fifty minutes, during which time the enemy suffered great loss, our battery discharging twenty-four rounds to the minute. The balls from the enemy's cannon whistled through our ranks in rapid succession. Many horses and other animals were killed, and the wagons much shattered. Sergeant A. Hughes, of the Missouri dragoons, had both his legs broken by a cannon-ball. In this action the enemy, who were drawn up in columns four deep, close order, lost about twenty-five killed, besides a great number of horses. The Americans, who stood dismounted, in two ranks, open order, suffered but slight injury.

General Condé with considerable disorder now fell back and rallied his men behind the intrenchments and redoubts. Col. Doniphan immediately ordered the buglers to sound the advance. Thereupon the American army moved forward in the following manner, to storm the enemy's breastworks:

The artillery battalion, Major Clark, in the center, firing occasionally on the advance; the 1st battalion, commanded by Lieutenant-colonels Jackson and Mitchell, composing the right wing; the two select companies of cavalry under Captains Reid and Parsons, and Captain Hudson's mounted company, immediately on the left of the artillery; and the 2d battalion on the extreme left commanded by Major Gilpin. The caravan and baggage trains, under command of Major Owens, followed close in the rear. Col. Doniphan and his aids, Capt. Thompson, U. S. Army, Adjutant De Courcy, and Sergeant-major Crenshaw acted between the battalions.

At this crisis a body of three hundred lancers, and *lazadors*, were discovered advancing upon our rear. These were exclusive of Heredia's main force, and were said to be criminals, turned loose from the Chihuahua prisons, that by some gallant exploit they might expurgate themselves of crime. To this end they were posted in the rear to cut off stragglers, prevent retreat, and capture and plunder the merchant wagons. The battalion of teamsters kept these at bay. Besides this force there were one thousand spectators, women, citizens, and rancheros, perched on the summits of the adjacent mountains and hills, watching the event of the day.

As we neared the enemy's redoubts, still inclining to the right, a heavy fire was opened upon us from his different batteries, consisting in all of sixteen pieces of cannon. But owing to the facility with which our movements were performed, and to the fact that the Mexicans were compelled to fire *plungingly* upon our lines, (their position being considerably elevated above the plateau, and particularly the battery placed on the brow of the Sacramento mountain with the design of enfilading our column,) we sustained but little damage.

When our column had approached within about four hundred yards of the enemy's line of field-works, the three cavalry companies, under Capts. Reid, Parsons, and Hudson, and Weightman's section of howitzers, were ordered to carry the main central battery, which had considerably annoyed our lines, and which was protected by a strong bastion. The charge was not made simultaneously as intended by the colonel; for this troop, having spurred forward a little way, was halted for a moment under a heavy cross-fire from the enemy, by the adjutant's misapprehending the order. However, Capt. Reid, either not hearing or disregarding the adjutant's order to halt, leading the way, waved his sword, and rising in his stirrups, exclaimed, "*will my men follow me?*" Hereupon Lieuts. Barnett, Hinton, and Moss, with about twenty-five men, bravely sprang forward, rose the hill with the captain, carried the battery and for a moment silenced the guns. But we were too weak to hold possession of it. By the overwhelming force of the enemy we were beaten back, and many of us wounded. Here Major SAMUEL C. OWENS, who had voluntarily charged upon the redoubt, received a cannon or musket shot which instantly killed both him and his horse. Capt. Reid's horse was shot under him, and a gallant young man of the same name immediately dismounted, and generously offered the captain his.

By this time the remainder of Captain Reid's company under Lieutenant Hicklin, and the section of howitzers under Capt. Weightman, and Lieuts. Choteau and Evans, rose the hill, and supported Capt. Reid. A deadly volley of grape and canister shot mingled with yager-balls, quickly cleared the intrenchments and the redoubt. The battery was re-taken and held. Almost at the same instant Capts. Parsons and Hudson, with the two remaining companies of cavalry, crossed the intrenchments to Reid's left, and successfully engaged with the enemy. They resolutely drove him back and held the ground.

All the companies were now pressing forward, and pouring over the intrenchments, and into the redoubts, eagerly vieing with each other in the noble struggle for victory. Each company, as well as each soldier, was ambitious to excel. Companies A, B, C, and a part of company D, composing the right wing, all dismounted, respectively under command of Capts. Waldo, Walton, Moss, and Lieut. Miller, led on by Lieut. Cols. Jackson and Mitchell, stormed a formidable line of redoubts on the enemy's left, defended by several pieces of cannon, and a great number of resolute and well-armed men. A part of this wing took possession of the strong battery on Sacramento hill, which had kept up a continued cross-firing upon our right during the whole engagement. Cols. Jackson and Mitchell, and their captains, lieutenants, non-commissioned officers, and men generally, behaved with commendable gallantry. Many instances of individual prowess were exhibited. But it is invidious to distinguish between men where all performed their duty so nobly.

Meanwhile the left wing also dismounted, commanded by Major

412   DONIPHAN'S EXPEDITION.

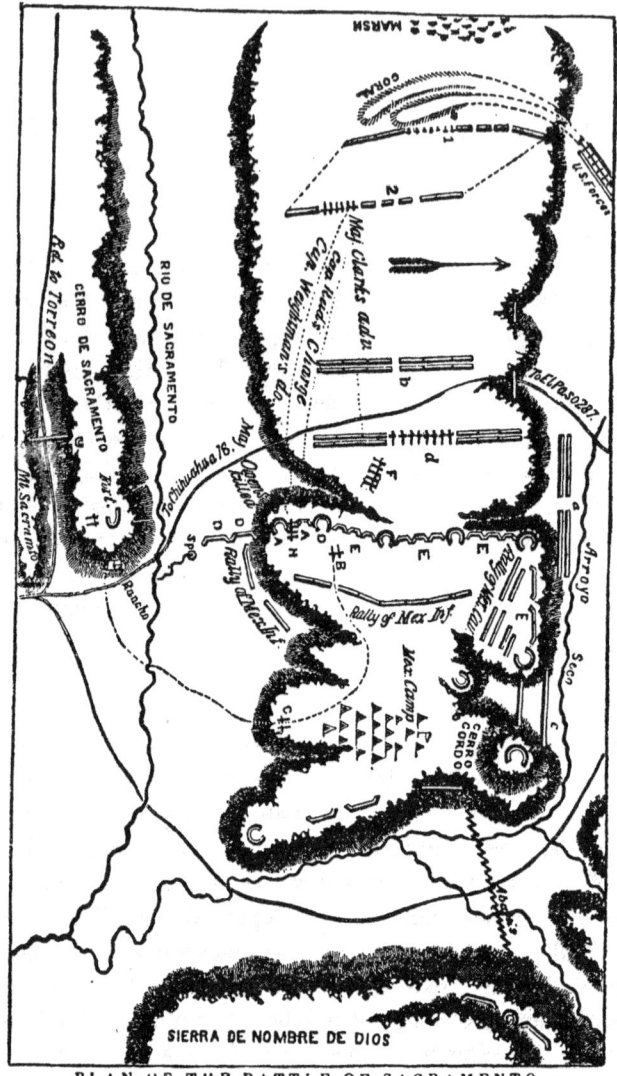

PLAN OF THE BATTLE OF SACRAMENTO.

Explanation.

⌣ Redoubts and intrenchments, filled with Mexican infantry.
1. First position U. S. forces. 2. Second do. *a*, First position Mexican cavalry. *b*. Second position Mexican do. *c*, First position Mexican infantry. *d*, Second position Mexican cavalry and infantry.

A A Red. and intrench. stormed by Capt. Reid's Horse Guards.
B First position of the howitzers on hill.
C Sec'd "   "   "   "
D D D Redoubts and intrenchments taken by the 1st batt.
E E E E Red. and Intrench. taken by 2d bat. and Mo. Drag.
F Major Clark's batt. dispersing the rally of Mexican cav.
H Fourth position Major Clark's batt., from which he silenced the fort on Sacramento hill.

List of Officers.

Col. A. W. Doniphan, *Comm. U. S. Forces.—Staff—*Capt. Tompson, U. S., D. A. de C—Lieut. De Courcy, Adjt. Surg., Morton; Asst. S., Moore & Morton.
Artillery; Maj. Clark, Adjt. Walker, Capt. Weightman, —Sect'n Howitz.; Lieuts. Chouteau and Evans.
Six lb'rs; Lts. Dorn, Kribben, Labeaume.
Cavalry; Missouri Horse Guards, Capt. Reid.—Lts., Hinton, Barnett, Moss and Hicklin.
Miss. Drag.; Capt. Parsons.—Lts., Winston & Harrison
Chihuahua Rang.; Capt. Hudson.—Lts. Sproule & Todd
Infantry; Lt. Cols., Mitchell and Jackson—Maj. Gilpin —Capts., Waldo, Walton, Moss, Stevensons, Hughes, and Rogers.—Lts., Reed Clayton, Childs, Lea Graves, Sublette, Ogden, Miller, Bush, M'Danald, Campbell, Gordon, Jackson, Wright, Duncan and Murray.

NOTE.—*Strength of the U. S. Forces:* Total, 924—6 pieces artillery.—Loss, 1 killed and 11 wounded (3 mortally) —*Mexican;* 4224—10 pieces artillery and 9 culvs.—Killed 320, wounded, 560, 72 prisoners.

Gilpin, a gallant and skillful officer, boldly scaled the heights, passed the intrenchments, cleared the redoubts, and with considerable slaughter forced the enemy to retreat from his position on the right.

CHARGE OF CAPTAIN REID, AT SACRAMENTO.

NOTE.—As Lieutenant-colonel Jackson, at the head of the first battalion, charged over the enemy's breastworks, with his long shot-gun in one hand and his drawn sabre in the other, almost the only order he gave, just at that time, was: "*Now, boys, every man for his turkey!*" And, it is said, almost every man singled out his "*yallow fellow*," as the colonel called the Mexicans, and brought the bead to bear upon him with as much certainty as if he were shooting at wild game in the forests of Missouri.

The next morning after the battle, Colonel Doniphan called on his battalion officers for a report of their respective commands. Majors Clark and Gilpin, each furnished a detailed account of the conduct of the troops under his immediate control. When he called on Lieutenant-colonel Jackson, for his report, he observed: "*Colonel! I am not a writing man—all I have to say is, that my men fought like h—ll, and wh pped everything before them!*"

The next day after the battle, Dr. Reese, who had been carried to Parral, as a prisoner, effected his escape. On his return to Chihuahua, he met many of the Mexicans, on the retreat towards Durango. The retreating host permitted him to pass on uninterrupted. At length he met a Mexican in full gallop, and almost frantic with despair. The Doctor hailed to him, and asked him whither he was going, in such haste. "*Corrajo! I am running from those d—n—d hairy Americans! They fight like devils incarnate!*"

One of the lieutenants of the Mexican artillery stood to his guns, until he was wounded and captured. Colonel Doniphan asked him if he did not know, before the action came on, that the Mexicans would be defeated. The lieutenant replied; "*I did not; and if they had stood to their posts, as I encouraged them to do, you never could have driven us from our strong position. I am now your prisoner; but I do not regret fighting for the liberty and honor of my country. I will still encourage my people to resist foreign invasion.*" Colonel Doniphan was so well pleased with the patriotic devotion of the young officer, that he immediately gave him his liberty.

Company G, under Capt. Hughes, and a part of company F, under Lieut. Gordon, stormed a battery of three brass four pounders strongly defended by embankments, and ditches filled by resolute and well-armed Mexican infantry. Some of the artillerists were made prisoners while endeavoring to touch off the cannon. Companies H and E, under Capts. Rodgers and Stephenson, and a part of Hudson's company under Lieut. Todd, on the extreme left, behaved nobly, and fought with great courage. They beat the Mexicans from their strong places, and chased them like blood-hounds. Major Gilpin was not behind his men in bravery—he encouraged them to fight by example.

Major Clark with his six pounders and Capt. Weightman with his howitzers, during the whole action rendered the most signal and essential service, and contributed much toward the success of the day. The gallant charge led by Capt. Reid and sustained by Capt. Weightman, in point of daring and brilliancy of execution, has not been excelled by any similar exploit during the war.

Gen. Heredia made several unsuccessful attempts to rally his retreating forces, to infuse into their minds new courage, and to close up the breaches already made in his lines. Gen. Condé, with his troop of horse, also vainly endeavored to check the advance of the MISSOURIANS. They were dislodged from their strong places, and forced from the hill in confusion.

The rout of the Mexican army now became general, and the slaughter continued until night put an end to the chase.[107] The battle lasted three hours and a half. The men returned to the battle-field

NOTE 107.—James Peacock (Independence, Mo.) has a clear recollection of the battle of Sacramento. He was very near Major Gilpin, and says that at the first order to charge Gilpin started with his men but was halted by De Courcy, and when the army was thrown into confusion Gilpin believed the Mexicans would discover it and take advantage of it. He urged Doniphan to order the charge. Peacock heard Gilpin say, "Are these men to be sacrificed? I will not stand it!" He then ordered his men to charge, and all started towards the Mexican works. Peacock does not remember that Colonel Doniphan gave the second order to charge before Major Gilpin gave the order to his men. While the army was advancing upon the Mexicans at Sacramento, before the battle, and came upon the high ground where the line was formed, a halt was called, to allow the army to close up, as only about 150 men were up to position. Captain Thompson thought the men might become demoralized standing inactive under the Mexican artillery fire, but Doniphan believed they would stand steady, which they did. The fire from the Mexican batteries was steady. Peacock's horse

after dark, completely worn out and exhausted with fatigue. The Mexicans lost 304 men, killed on the field, and a large number wounded, perhaps not less than 500, and 70 prisoners, among whom was Brig. Gen. Cuilta,* together with a vast quantity of provisions, six thousand dollars in specie, 50,000 head of sheep, 1,500 head of cattle, 100 mules, 20 wagons, 25 or 30 caretas, 25,000 pounds of ammunition,

* Gen. Cuilta was captured in Chihuahua, March 4th, by Lieut. Col. Jackson. and Capt Hughes.

would watch the cannon, and seemed to be able to tell whether the balls were coming in his direction; if he believed there was danger, he dodged at the right time, crowding the other horses and sometimes breaking the line. Jim Chandler, seeing how well the horse could dodge the balls, endeavored to keep directly behind him. The ground was covered with grass, and some of the horses, being very hungry, would attempt to graze; some of the men allowed their horses to eat the grass directly in front of them; this all tended to confusion. Finally, when all was ready, Colonel Doniphan directed Captain Thompson to order the charge, which he did. The charge was stopped by De Courcy, who, it was believed, was drunk at the time. Some of the soldiers believed there was a cabal in the army to push Captain Reid to the front on all occasions and give him the advantage in everything. De Courcy was supposed to be the head of this cabal, and it was believed by many that he intended all to stop in the charge but Captain Reid, who was to be given a good start ahead, and then the others were to be allowed to follow him. As it turned out, the whole line was thrown into confusion, and disaster might easily have followed. Peacock does not know anything positive about this cabal, and makes no statement about it. He is of the opinion that Major Samuel C. Owens was not killed by the wound which unhorsed him, nor was the horse killed. He saw Mexicans run from the redoubts with spears and pin horse and rider to the earth; these spears or lances were sticking through the bodies of both when the troops got up to the works; Peacock saw them. Holt, a very small fellow, a boy, was a soldier who had not marched two thousand miles from Missouri to hold horses, when he could do that at home. A big fellow, who proved a coward, named Hughes, said to him, "I will hold them for you, Holt." Holt went on up the hill, but Hughes did not hold the horses; he hid behind a boulder. The horses did not run off, though left loose. For a minute or two Peacock and some other Americans were in front of one of the redoubts. The Americans promptly shot every Mexican who showed his head above the embankment. The Mexicans began to poke their guns over the fortifications, extend their arms above their heads, point the guns down, and fire without showing themselves. No harm resulted from this form of firing; it lasted but a minute or two; then Major Gilpin and Captain Stephenson arrived, and their volley, followed immediately by grape from Captain Weightman's guns, completed the rout of the Mexicans. All the American troops went over the Mexican works and joined in the pursuit of the Mexicans. Peacock says it happened all at once; there was no halting of any company in front of the Mexican works. That charge swept everything before it and carried the men into the lines of the enemy. Peacock was in the pursuit of the Mexicans.

10 pieces of cannon of different calibres, varying from 4 to 9 pounders, 6 culverins or wall pieces, 100 stand of small arms, 100 stand of small colors, 7 fine carriages, the general's scrutoire, and many other things of less note. Our loss was Major Samuel C. Owens, killed, and 11 wounded,* three of whom have subsequently died.

Thus was the army of Central Mexico totally defeated, and completely disorganized, by a column of Missouri volunteers. The Mexicans retreated precipitately to Durango, and dispersed among the ranchos and villages. Their leaders were never able to rally them.[108]

* WOUNDED.—In Capt. Reid's mounted company: A. A. Kirkpatrick, mortally; J. L. MacGruder, mortally; J. Barnes, arm broken; L. A. MacLean, severely; J. Sullivan, slightly; J. T. Hughes, slightly. In Captain Parsons' mounted company:—W. Henkey, mortally; W. Gordon, severely; Serg't A. Hughes, both legs broken; J. B. Fleming, severely. In Hudson's mounted company:—J. Wolf, slightly.—HUGHES.

NOTE 108.—Meredith T. Moore, Cedar City, Mo., was a private in Company F. He is a man of great intelligence and undoubted veracity. His memory is marvelous and his power of expression splendid. He is President of the Mexican Veteran Association. I give in this note a description of the battle of Sacramento as he told it to me and as corrected by him. He ate some pork the day before the battle, and at night had a severe attack of cholera morbus. He was barely able to mount his horse, but would not be kept out of the battle. He became stronger during the day, the excitement of the battle stimulating him greatly. Position of the cavalry companies:
From left to right—
First, Company F, Captain Parsons.
Second, Company D, Captain Reid.
Third, Company E, Laclede Rangers, Captain Hudson.
Captain Weightman with battery.

Left wing, dismounted men, commanded by Major Gilpin. Gilpin was on the extreme right of his command and near Captain Parsons, who was at the left of his company. Moore was at the end of the cavalry column, very near Captain Parsons and Major Gilpin; he could hear distinctly what each one said. Colonel Doniphan was with Major Gilpin, usually just a little in advance of Gilpin, before the battle began, and in conversation with Gilpin and the officers of his staff. Kirker was with or near Colonel Doniphan, as was James L. Collins. Moore thinks Collins came to the army soon after it marched from El Paso. He had long been a trader to Mexico over the Santa Fé Trail, and Moore believes he lived at Boonville. He was a small man, gray-haired, about sixty, red-faced and plains-burned, vigorous, brave, reckless, possessed all the accomplishments of hunters and trappers, and was, like Kirker, a daredevil. At a sandy jornada passed by the army a short distance north of Sacramento the Americans met a trader, of whom the men obtained some whisky. Both Collins and Kirker became intoxicated, and, like all plainsmen under the influence of liquor, were quarrelsome. A difficulty between them arose over some trifling matter. In the bandy of words Collins called Kirker a coward. That meant a fight to the death, but Colonel Doniphan heard of the difficulty and prevented a duel. He told them the Mexican army would be encountered within a day or two, and

In this engagement Col. Doniphan was personally much exposed, and by reason of his stature was a conspicuous mark for the fire of the enemy's guns. He was all the while at the proper place, whether to dispense his orders, encourage his men, or to use his sabre in thin-

that their courage or cowardice could be tested on the field of battle—that nobody doubted the bravery of either—that he could not have his men killing one another in the very presence of the enemy. They agreed to postpone their meeting until after the battle with the Mexican army had been fought. It is necessary to a proper understanding of some things which occurred in the battle that the above statement of feeling between Kirker and Collins be made here.

Between the American line and the Mexican fortifications there was a deep ravine, but with sloping banks, thus:

The Mexican artillery had fired upon the Americans as they advanced to the position where the battle-line was formed, but had not done any damage. While the Americans were in battle-line and awaiting the final adjustment and completion of arrangements, the Mexicans continued this artillery fire. Montgomery P. Leintz and Robert Dunlap were very near Moore. A ball from a Mexican cannon came over and took off a part of Dunlap's cap, leaving his hair sticking out on that side; he said quietly: "I want to tell you they shoot mighty d—d close in this country!" He showed no appearance of excitement. Moore, Dunlap, Leintz, George L. Boone and Joseph Yount were together in the front line that day, facing the Mexican fortifications at Sacramento. Boone lives in Medford, Oregon; Dunlap is in a Home of some society in Rogue River Valley, Oregon; Leintz lives in Fulton, Mo.; Moore lives at Cedar City, Mo.; and Yount is blind and lives at San Bernardino, California.

As the formation of the American line was about completed, a command consisting of several hundred Mexican cavalry rode out in front of the fortifications and called for a parley. Colonel Doniphan ordered the interpreter to report what the Mexicans desired. The demand of the Mexicans was that the Americans surrender, threatening to charge if they did not do so. Doniphan told the interpreter to reply, "Charge and be d—d!" Captain Weightman was directed to fire, and discharged two blank shots straight up, and Colonel Doniphan ordered the charge.

Just as the charge was ordered a cannon-ball struck a few feet in front of Moore; he saw it coming and ducked his head just as his horse in excitement threw his head up, striking Moore on the nose and mashing it flat upon his face. The ball went between the front legs and between the hind legs of Moore's horse without doing any injury, and struck the left fore-leg of the horse of Ewing Van Bibber, who was in line exactly behind Moore. The ball stopped there, and Van Bibber picked it up and knocked the injured horse in the head with it. Major Gilpin asked Moore if he was hurt much, and Moore replied that he would report on the injury "to-morrow"—no time just then. He was soon covered with blood; he raised his nose with the thumb and forefinger of his right hand and went into battle without further thought about it. The injury healed without

ning the enemy's ranks.* His effective force actually engaged was about nine hundred and fifty men, including a considerable number of AMATEUR FIGHTERS, among whom James L. Collins, James Kirker, Messrs. Henderson and Anderson, interpreters, Major Campbell,

* His courage and gallant conduct were only equalled by his clear foresight, and great judgment.

leaving a mark of any kind. When the order to charge was given, Kirker immediately rode around the end of the infantry column to a point not more than fifty feet from Moore, and called out to Collins, "Let you and I see who can get into that Mexican battery first!" The battery referred to was in the second redoubt, and it was then firing on the Americans. Collins made no reply, but pulled his cap tightly down on his head, drew his sword, buried the rowels in the flanks of his horse and was away for the battery at full speed. And Kirker was at his side. This was before the order to charge was understood by the line, but no sooner had they gotten under way than they were followed full tilt by Captain Reid and Joseph Marshall of his company, Samuel C. Owens, and another man whose name Moore does not remember. The order to charge came after these men were under way, and the whole line leaped forward. From some cause never rightly understood, De Courcy rode down the line shouting, "Halt, Captain Parsons! halt, Captain Parsons! halt, Captain Parsons!" De Courcy was drunk, and should have been promptly shot. Moore believes his action arose from a dislike he bore Captain Parsons and a desire to hold his company back until that of Captain Reid had a good start. His action threw the whole line into confusion. The charge was stopped, some companies being considerably in advance of others, and the captains hesitated.

Meantime, Kirker, Collins, Captain Reid, Marshall, Owens, and the man whose name is forgotten by Moore, charged the redoubt designated by Kirker to Collins. Owens and his horse were killed almost at the redoubt, and the others turned to the left and ran along the Mexican front past several redoubts, drawing the fire of the entire Mexican line, finally returning to the American line unhurt. That action saved the lives of the Americans. Colonel Doniphan, seeing the confusion arising from De Courcy's action, galloped down the line shouting the order to charge. Many did not hear him because of the rattle of the Mexican fire drawn by Kirker and others, and several captains charged without knowing a second order directing them to do so had been given. One private, H. M. Bledsoe, of the Lafayette county company, gave an order to charge. Captain Parsons did not hear Colonel Doniphan's order, but Moore did hear it and called out, "Captain Parsons, Colonel Doniphan orders you to charge!" The men were enraged and impatient and they could not have been restrained a minute longer; they would have charged without orders. Major Gilpin said he would not see his men sacrificed. Captain Stephenson was holding his men with a strong hand, but they were straining at the leash. A storm of indignation and wrath was rising and would have broken in a minute; for the troops were not regular soldiers, disciplined to strict obedience. Each man thought for himself, knew what he was there for, and realized that his life depended upon the defeat of the Mexican army. But in a moment, as with a single movement, all were away with yells that startled the Mexicans, who had no time to reload their flint-locks just discharged at Kirker

and James Stewart, deserve to be favourably mentioned. They fought bravely. It was impossible for Captains Skillman and Glasgow to bring their companies of teamsters into the action. They deserve great honor for their gallantry in defending the trains. The

and others before the whole American line was over the redoubts. All the companies and battalions charged together when they finally got started—the cavalry of course going more rapidly than the infantry; rather, the mounted men more rapidly than the dismounted men. Of the mounted men Captain Reid's company was not in advance of any other, having been halted by De Courcy's insane action, being then just a little in advance of other companies.

Arrived at the redoubts, Moore saw a Mexican soldier shoot straight up in his excitement. Moore called to Yount, "Shoot that man, Joe." Yount fired, and Moore said, "You missed him, Joe; I saw the dirt fly when the ball struck the bank by his head." The Americans did not fire until they reached the Mexican works. Moore was one of the first to go through the Mexican lines; he and Yount went to the left around a redoubt about the center of the Mexican position. When they got on the inside the Mexicans were breaking and beginning to run, and Moore fired then for the first time.

The dismounted men almost kept pace with the cavalry in the charge. Moore saw Captain Stephenson running sidewise and backwards in front of his men, keeping them in perfect order and perfect step, and Moore believes a cannon-ball might have been fired between their legs down the line without injuring a man, so perfect was the step. He believes that Stephenson was the ablest captain in the First Regiment and one of the ablest men in the regiment; his company was the best drilled and best disciplined. The Mexicans were trying to rally and re-form back of their first line just as Captain Stephenson got his company inside the redoubts. There he ordered his men to fire for the first time, and the Mexicans fell like pigeons. Captain Weightman came up with the artillery with a rattle and crash almost on a line with the mounted men, and immediately after Captain Stephenson's company fired the artillery began the discharge of grape into the ranks of the enemy and kept it up as long as the Mexicans were in range; then he ordered the guns to advance after them. Major Gilpin, with the left wing, entered the redoubts at about the same instant that Captain Stephenson did, and seeing on his left a number of Mexican cavalry rallying, he gave them the benefit of his first round, and it scattered them for good.

These actions occurred rapidly, and Moore had not halted to observe them, being able to note them all by looking at the different parts of the field as he advanced upon the Mexicans with his company. After firing his first shot he charged to the left and got in advance of his company. He saw some Mexicans in a ravine back of the point where they had tried to make their last rally; they seemed to be consulting as to the best thing to do. Moore's horse was nervous and excited, and in order to take good aim he dismounted, and his shot created confusion in the crowd; but his horse broke away from him and ran into the Mexican lines. He began to reload his gun, but the ball stuck in the barrel. Three Americans—William Bolton, George W. Riggin, and William Gordon—came up at that instant, and one of them said, "There is a Mexican; shoot him and get his mule." Moore feared to shoot with the ball but half-way down his gun, but

soldiers encamped on the battle-field, within the enemy's intrenchments, and feasted sumptuously upon his viands, wines and poundcakes. There they rested.*

Col. Doniphan, not like Hannibal loitering on the plains of Italy,

---

*Previous to the commencement of the battle, the hostage, Ortiz, manifested considerable uneasiness, and showed an evident disposition not to be carried near the scene of strife, lest he too should suffer in the general slaughter, which he apprehended would take place among the Americans. He said to Col. Doniphan:—"Your force is too weak to contend against such a force as the Mexican army, and in so strong a position:—you will all be inevitably destroyed, or captured and put in chains. The Mexicans will whip you beyond a doubt. I beg that you will permit me to remain out of danger." Col. Doniphan good humoredly replied:—"If *I* should be victorious I will continue to treat you in a manner every way worthy your dignity. If your own people should be the conquerors, and you should fall into their hands, they will certainly do you no hurt. So, being safe in either event, you must have little cause of apprehension.". When the battle was over, Col. Doniphan observed to the curate:—"Well, Ortiz, what think you now about the Mexicans 'whipping' my boys?" The other replied:—"Ah! sir, they would have defeated you, if you had fought like men, but you fought like *devils*."

While the battle was raging, Captain Glasgow, of the merchant battalion, came up to the colonel, who was standing upon the hill from which the Mexicans had been repulsed, and asked him how the day was about to issue: "*Don't you see*," says the colonel, "*how my boys are knocking them down like nine-pins?*"

Just previous to the charge, the right and left wings were dismounted, and every seventh man detailed to hold horses. At this moment the volley of musketry, grape, and canister, from the enemy's lines was tremendous. As Col. Doniphan passed up the lines, a volunteer, who had seven horses in charge, called to him and said, "*See here, Colonel! am I compelled to stand here in this tempest of cannon and musket balls, and hold horses?*" "Yes," says the colonel, "*if you are detailed for the purpose.*" The volunteer quickly tying the several bridles together, dashed them down, seized his gun and sabre, and started off in the charge, exclaiming as he left the colonel, "*Hold hell in a fight! I didn't come here to hold horses—I can do that at home.*"

As the right wing scaled the breast-works, sergeant Tom Hinckle was one of the first who crossed the intrenchments, and got amongst the enemy. Having fired his yager and pistols, he was too hotly beleaguered to reload them. He laid them aside, and like Ajax Telamon, resolutely defended himself by throwing rocks.—HUGHES.

---

he brought up his gun as though he intended to shoot, and the Mexican dropped deftly off his mule and ran. Moore secured the mule, and taking up a stone, drove down the stuck ball by striking the ramrod. He mounted the mule, and at that instant discovered a Mexican crossing the battle-field in his direction. Moore brought his gun to firing position, seeing which, the Mexican dropped on his knees, praying and crossing himself. At this point John Rice, of Company F, came along; he was a German from Pennsylvania, living near Jefferson City, the best-natured, mildest-mannered man in the regiment; he had the sympathetic nature of a woman; always was sent to the hospital to care for the sick because of his tenderness of heart. But in battle Rice became a devil; his face changed, his eyes blazed with ferocity; his will hardened to iron, his sinews to steel; his presence became terrible, his action awful. In this battle he threw away his gun after the first fire and drew his sword. With this weapon banished aloft he was sweeping over the field, the impersonation of vengeance. He was riding towards the Mexican, then on his knees and crossing himself. Moore, seeing his intentions, shouted that the Mexican had surrendered. The victim also saw the approach of Rice, and a glance told him there was no mercy in him; he had a lance and rose to his feet. But Rice heeded nothing. Grim as death, inexorable as fate, as his horse descended from a bound he cleft the Mexican's head, splitting it to the neck, and was away without a check in his speed. And many a similar deed

after the battle of Cannæ, when he might have entered Rome in triumph, immediately followed up his success, and improved the advantage which his victory gave him. Early the next morning, (March 1st) he dispatched Lieutenant-colonel Mitchell, with one hundred and fifty men under command of Captains Reid and Weightman, and a section of artillery, to take formal possession of the capital, and occupy it in the name of his government. This detachment, before arriving in the city, was met by several American gentlemen escaping from confinement, who represented that the Mexican soldiery had left the place undefended, and fled with the utmost precipi-

---

did he perform that day. Moore heard a comrade drink this toast in after years: "Here's to John Rice, the only man who ever cut a Mexican in two twice with one sabre-stroke!"

After Rice had swept past like a Nemesis, Moore ran on in the direction of the retreating Mexicans. He discovered a Mexican officer passing in front of him from the right-oblique, and halted him. The officer surrendered, and Moore ordered him to advance; and as he was starting to Moore, Captain Reid came up at a gallop and turned in the direction of the officer. Moore called out that the officer had surrendered and was entitled to protection. Reid gave no heed to what Moore said, but galloped up to the officer with drawn sword. The officer saw he must fight. He was no coward. Drawing his sword he engaged with Reid, whose horse was carrying him beyond reach. He rode beside Captain Reid, who was turning to strike him, and the two fought with swords, their horses at full gallop and close together, and Moore saw the Mexican escape into his own lines, seemingly uninjured. Moore saw that he was having poor luck taking prisoners. As Captain Reid and the Mexican officer rode down the field with clashing swords, a splendid Mexican horse with fine trappings came by. Moore caught the horse and mounted him, abandoning the mule. As he rode in pursuit of the fleeing enemy some of Captain Reid's company fired on him by mistake and killed the horse. He ran after the enemy on foot, and below a small hill he found the pony of Lieutenant Benjamin Murray, of Company H. Supposing Murray dead, he mounted the pony and continued in the pursuit and fighting until after dark. When he stopped he found himself with one of Captain Weightman's artillerymen. They rode slowly in the direction of the American camp on the battle-field, where many fires shone brightly in the gloom of night. At a small stream Moore dismounted to get a drink of water. His previous illness and a day of great exertion without food, now that the reaction from the excitement of battle had come on, made him so weak that he had to be assisted on his horse. When he rode up to the camp-fire of his mess some one said, "Where did you get Lieutenant Murray's horse?" "Found it on the battle-field after mine was shot; I am afraid Lieutenant Murray has been killed," said Moore. Murray was in a tent near by and heard what Moore said. He replied, "I am not dead yet by a long shot; and you will have to give up my horse." The first thing Moore saw the following morning was his own horse standing near, tied to an artillery carriage.

tation to Durango. The Spanish consul, also, came out with the flag of his country, to salute and acknowledge the conqueror. This small body of troops entered and took military possession of Chihuahua, without the slightest resistance, and the following night occupied the Cuartel near Hidalgo's monument, which stands in the Alameda.

Meanwhile Col. Doniphan and his men collected the booty, tended the captured animals, refitted the trains, remounted those who had lost their steeds in the action, arranged the preliminaries of a procession, and having marched a few miles, encamped for the night. On the morning of the 2d day of March, Col. Doniphan, with all his military trains, the merchant caravan, gay, fluttering colors, and the whole SPOLIA OPIMA, triumphantly entered the city to the tunes of "Yankee Doodle" and "Hail Columbia," and fired in the public square a national salute of twenty-eight guns. This was a proud moment for the American troops. The battle of Sacramento gave them the capital, and now the stars and stripes, and serpent-eagle of the MODEL REPUBLIC, were streaming victoriously over the stronghold of Central Mexico.[109]

NOTE 109.—The battle of Sacramento is thus described by Richardson (*Journal of William H. Richardson*):

"*Sunday, 28th.*—At sunrise this morning we took up our line of march, having learned from our spies that the enemy in great numbers had fortified the pass of the river Sacramento, about fifteen miles off. Our trains, consisting of 315 traders' wagons and our commissary and company wagons, in all about 400, were formed into four columns, so as to shorten our lines. The whole command marched in right order between the columns, thus concealing our force from the enemy. When we arrived within three miles of their entrenchments, Col. Doniphan made a reconnoissance of their position, and examined the arrangements of their forces. This was easily done, as our road led through an open prairie valley between the high mountains. The pass of the Sacramento is formed by a point of the mountains on our right, their left extending into the valley, so as to narrow the valley about one and a half miles. On our left was a deep, dry channel of a creek, and between these points the plain rises abruptly about fifty or sixty feet. The road passes down the center of the valley, and in the distance we had a full view of the Mexican army. On the point of the mountains they had a battery of four guns, so elevated as to sweep the plain. On the left there was another battery commanding the road, with six-pounders and rampart pieces, mounted on carriages. Their cavalry was drawn up in front of their redoubts, in the interval of four deep. When we had arrived near their entrenchments, our columns suddenly diverged to the right, so as to gain the elevation, which the enemy endeavored to prevent by moving forward with four pieces of cannon and 1000 cavalry. But our movements were so rapid that we not only gained the eminence, but were formed in order for their reception. Our company (Capt. Hudson's) now dismounted, and every eighth man was detailed to hold horses and mules. It fell to my lot to hold eight mules. The action now by a brisk fire from our cannons, doing considerable execution at the distance of twelve hundred yards, killing fifteen of the enemy, and disabling one of their guns. Our fire was briskly returned from fourteen pieces of artillery, sending ragged balls, and heavy copper ore. But being badly aimed they struck in the

Col. Doniphan's official account of the memorable battle of the 28th of February is here subjoined:

Head Quarters of the Army; Chihuahua,
City of Chihuahua, March 4th, 1847.

I have the honor to report to you the movements of the army under my command since my last official report.

On the evening of the 8th of February 1847, we left the town of El Paso del Norte, escorting the merchant train or caravan of about three hundred and fifteen wagons, for the city of Chihuahua. Our force consisted of nine hundred and twenty four effective men;

---

ground about forty or fifty yards before us, and, rebounding, passed over our heads without harm, except slightly wounding two men and killing several horses and mules in the rear. Our guns were so well aimed as to compel the enemy to fall behind the breastworks. We resumed our march in our former order, diverging as much as possible to the right, to avoid a heavy battery, and their strongest redoubts, which were on our left, near the common road. After marching as far as we thought it prudent, without coming in range of their heavy battery, Capt. Weightman of the artillery was ordered to charge it with two twelve-pound howitzers, to be supported by the cavalry under Captains Reid, Parsons, and Hudson. We then remounted and charged the battery from right to left; with a brisk and deadly fire from our rifles. We then advanced to the very brink of their redoubts, and drove them out with our sabres. The enemy now fell back on their center battery, where they made a desperate rally, and gave us a shower of balls and copper ore, which whizzed over our heads without doing us any injury except wounding several men and killing a few mules and horses. Major Clarke was ordered to commence a heavy fire upon this battery, which, being well directed, together with the rapid advance of our columns, put them to flight over the mountains in utter confusion, leaving all their cannons, and the ground strewed with their dead and wounded. Thus ended the battle of Sacramento, which commenced about three o'clock and ended about sunset. The enemy numbered 4220 rank and file, and lost 300 killed, 500 wounded, besides 40 prisoners. The American force consisted of 924 effective men, 1 killed, 11 wounded. Our success is to be attributed entirely to the superior skill of our commander. Had he not taken advantage of position, in keeping out of range of redoubts and batteries, we should all have shared a common fate, as the black piratical flag was captured, together with a wagon-load of that formidable weapon, the lariat, which was intended to tie us all to our saddles in case of a defeat. The Mexicans lost ten pieces of artillery, varying from five to ten pounds, and seven one-pound culverines. One of the cannon is very valuable, being composed of silver and brass melted together. They also lost all their baggage, ammunition, &c., and provisions enough to last us three months were found in their wagons, together with $4000 in specie. It was gratifying to see the soldiers shaking hands with their officers after the engagement, and tendering their congratulations to their commander for his skill and bravery displayed on this memorable occasion. The surgeons are now busily engaged in administering relief to the wounded Mexicans, and it is a sight to see the pile of legs and arms that have been amputated. The cries and groans of the poor fellows are distressing in the extreme. It is a fact worthy of note, that the atmosphere here in this mountainous region is so perfectly pure and clear that a cannon-shot can be seen coming when it is a considerable distance off, by leaving a blue streak in the air. Many a soldier saved his life in the battle by dodging the balls as they came forward. When a flash would be seen from the enemy's battery, you could hear the soldiers cry out: "Watch the ball, boys!—here comes a ball, boys"; and they invariably avoided them, or the slaughter must have been very great. I saw a ball coming in the direction where I was, when, immediately falling off my mule, it passed just over my

one hundred and seventeen officers and privates of the artillery; ninety three of Lieutenant-colonel Mitchell's escort, and the remainder, the first regiment Missouri mounted volunteers. We progressed in the direction of this place until the 25th, when we were informed by our spies that the enemy, to the number of one thousand five hundred men, were at Encinillas, the country seat of governor Trias, about twenty five miles in advance.

When we arrived on the evening of the 26th, near that point, we found that the force had retreated in the direction of this city. On the evening of the 27th we arrived at Sans, and learned from our spies that the enemy, in great force had fortified the pass of the Sac-

saddle without injury. Our rapid movements seemed to astonish the enemy. Our four pieces of flying artillery, discharging five times in a minute, volleys of grape and canister, with chain-shot, would rake the enemy's redoubts and cut roads through their lines, while our twelve-pound howitzers, throwing a constant shower of bombs into the middle of their entrenchments, and the unerring aim of our Mississippi rifles, acting in concert, cast terror and dismay among the cowardly and unprincipled foe. Our men acted nobly, and in the hand-to-hand fight in the redoubts they fought to desperation. Lieutenant Sprawl, our Second Lieutenant, a man over six feet high, with bared arms, and without his hat, his long hair and beard streaming in the wind, with sword in hand, was charging the enemy at every point, when a ball struck his splendid charger, and he fell. But, seizing his carbine, he kept up with us on foot. Another of our men, being unhorsed, and fighting near me, was attacked by a Mexican, who was about to lance him, and the poor fellow's gun being discharged, he picked up a rock, and throwing it, struck his enemy on the head, which felled him to the earth, when he knocked his brains out with the butt of his gun. These were but common occurrences in that hard-contested fight, where we had to contend with nearly five to one."

The following account of the battle of Sacramento is taken from *A Campaign in New Mexico with Colonel Doniphan*, by Frank S. Edwards, London, 1848. Edwards belonged to Captain Weightman's artillery company:

"Although I was very unwell and almost unable to ride, I had gone forward with three others to reconnoiter; and getting upon some rising ground, with the aid of a telescope I obtained a fine view of the whole of the Mexican force; and I do not hesitate to say that, as I turned from viewing that dense mass of soldiery to look at our little band as it came slowly but steadily on, my heart felt a little faint. I could see the numerous entrenchments and batteries of the Mexicans; and I observed to myself that there was but one way by which we could possibly fight them on at all even ground,—and this was, by crossing a deep gully, when we should get upon a grassy plain, extending with a slight ascent up to their position. On all other sides the high bluff-bank forbade all attempt.

"I rejoined our company, and found that Colonel Doniphan had resolved to attack; following exactly the route I have mentioned. And now, spades and pickaxes are put in requisition, and numerous willing hands soon fill up the gully.

"As our troops cross it, the trumpets sound the *trot*. All move out from the cover of the wagons and take up a position about nine hundred yards from the most advanced of the enemy, and, from the sloping ground, rather below them. Nothing can exceed the enthusiasm of the men—one would suppose they are rather thinking of getting up a fandango, than of going into such an unequal fight. That overwhelming force in their front had no other effect than to raise their spirits still higher.

"But slowly and majestically above our heads sails America's bird, a large bald eagle. 'An omen! an omen!' runs through our ranks, and all eyes glance at him for a moment.

ramento, about fifteen miles in advance, and about the same distance from this city. We were also informed that there was no water between the point we were at and that occupied by the enemy; we therefore determined to halt until morning. At sunrise on the 28th, the last day of February, we took up the line of march and formed the whole train, consisting of three hundred and fifteen heavy traders' wagons, and our commissary and company wagons, into four columns, thus shortening our line so as to make it more easily protected. We placed the artillery and all the command except two hundred cavalry proper, in the intervals between the columns of wagons. We thus fully concealed our force and its position by masking our force with

"Our little battery occupies the center of our position. On the right and left of it are two companies of cavalry, one of them Col. Mitchell's escort, and, behind them, dismounted and acting as infantry, impatiently stand the rest of Doniphan's regiment.

"As we form, the enemy's artillery opens upon us, and at that instant Weightman's clear voice is heard: 'Form battery, action front, load and fire at will,' and our pieces ring out the death-knell of the enemy. Now comes the friendly struggle between our gunners, who shall pour in the deadliest and quickest fire, and beautifully are those pieces served, mowing lane after lane through the solid columns of the Mexicans. In the center of the battery, their horses bounding at every discharge, stand Clark and his officers; as the balls fly through the opposite ranks and the shells tear their columns, shout after shout is heard from our men.

"Further to our right sits Colonel Doniphan on his beautiful chestnut charger, with his leg crossed over the saddle, steadily whittling a piece of wood, but with his eye glancing proudly over the ranks of his little band. As the cannonading becomes hotter, he quietly says: 'Well! they're giving us —— now, boys!' and passes coolly to the left of our position, untouched by the copper hail that pours around him.

"And here *we* are (at a distance too great for anything but cannon), sitting on our horses dodging Mexican balls as they come humming through our ranks, first striking the ground about midway, and so becoming visible. It was surprising the skill which we soon obtained in this employment. After a few shots, we could tell to a foot where the copper messengers would alight. Although, a few minutes before, joke after joke was passing among us, the silence was now almost unbroken, for nothing acts so well, by way of safety-valve to a man's courage, as having to sit on horseback half an hour and dodge cannon-balls. As yet we know of no injuries amongst us; but suddenly a German close by blurts out, 'I'se kilt!' and, tumbling off his horse, rolls up his trowsers, showing a severe contusion on his leg, caused by a stone thrown up by the ricochet of a cannon-ball; round the limb goes a handkerchief, and up mounts the man again. At that moment a groan bursts from the line to my left, and a man is borne dying from the ranks, while off goes the head of Lieutenant Dorn's horse. Hot work on all sides!

"So confident are the Mexicans, that some of the richest citizens of Chihuahua have come out as spectators; but now, judging wisely, off they fly at full speed to the city, giving notice of the probable result, but are so little believed that, like true prophets before them, they are actually stoned in the streets.

"A shell explodes directly in the ranks of the enemy—they draw back behind their entrenchments, and we immediately advance until within four hundred yards; again the deadly shower opens from our ranks, fiercely returned. The order to charge rings through our lines—Colonel Mitchell, on his favorite white charger Roderick, waves his saber as he leads us on; rumbling and crashing behind us comes Weightman with his howitzers, leaving the rest of the battery in position to cover our advance. Dashing past us goes Major Owens, waving his hand in an exulting manner, and shouting out, 'Give it to them, boys! They

the cavalry. When we arrived within three miles of the enemy, we made a reconnoissance of his position and the arrangement of his forces. This we could easily do, the road leading through an open prairie valley between two sterile mountains. The pass of the Sacramento is formed by a point of the mountains on our right, their left extending into the valley or plain so as to narrow the valley to about one and a half miles. On our left was a deep, dry sandy channel of a creek, and between these points the plain rises to sixty feet abruptly. This rise is in the form of a crescent, the convex part being to the north of our forces. On the right, from the point of mountains, a narrow part of the plain extends north one and a half miles

can't withstand us'—and away he goes:" falling, in two minutes, a corpse, struck in the forehead by a grape-shot while storming the redoubts, and being so close to the gun that the fire actually burned his clothes. Rapidly is our charge made; but just fairly under way, it is about to be ruined! A countermanding order, as if from Doniphan, is given by a drunken officer whose rank (alone) requires respect. In surprise we suddenly halt within a few yards of the redoubts, and are fully exposed to the whole enemy's fire. 'For God's sake, advance!' roars out Sutler Pomeroy, who was fighting in the ranks. Our hesitation vanishes, and away we instantly dash forward, gallantly led by Mitchell and Gilpin, while Weightman fires his howitzers loaded with canister, with great effect, and again advancing, wheels them to the right and left, throwing in another charge of grape and canister, and raking the whole line of the enemy's position. To our left is a battalion of brave cavalry from Durango, who have arrived on the field only half an hour before—'tis their last fight—they are terribly cut to pieces, and are forced to retreat. A piece of their artillery, being dismounted, they attempt to 'snake,' by fastening their lassos to it, and drag it along the ground, but they are overtaken and made prisoners, and the gun is ours. Our men, pouring over the embankments, actually push the Mexicans out. Now comes the rout; the Mexicans give way; and *sauve-qui-peut* is their only object. We are in possession of their main position. The rest of our battery comes galloping up to occupy it. A body of their lancers re-forms and prepares to renew the attack—but—they are soon sent after their flying companions. We are about congratulating ourselves on a victory, when—bang goes a cannon, and a ball bounds amongst us, knocking the saddle-blanket off the mule of one of our company, from which he has this instant dismounted. A cloud of white smoke curls gracefully upward from a hitherto masked battery to the right upon yon high mountain, as shot after shot falls amongst us. Two of our six-pounders are at once placed in one of the deserted entrenchments and commence a well-directed fire, which soon dismounts one of the enemy's pieces. Up charges Mitchell at the head of his company, and takes the position; yet down, with headlong speed, dashes an officer, waving a Mexican flag—one of our gunners points his cannon at him—a moment and he would have been no more, but his horse is recognized, 'tis Colonel Mitchell's Roderick, while the Colonel himself is the standard-bearer.

"Numerous skirmishes occur as pursuit takes the place of resistance. Weightman dashes on with the cavalry towards the city. Looking over his shoulder, he sees his howitzers halted on the hillside instead of following him, and galloping back, he shouts 'On with that battery! If I knew who had halted you I'd cut him down.' The officer who had done so said not a word.

• "But the battle is won. And gradually we assemble on the battle-field. The enemy are fast disappearing in the distance, baffling pursuit.

"And what has, all this time, been the conduct of the priest Ortiz and the three other Spaniards we brought down to see the fight? At the commencement of the struggle they stand up in their light carriages, to which two mules are attached, and which still remains in the center of our wagon columns. Seeing the dense mass of their countrymen, they cannot contain their joy. The first few

further than on the left. The main road passes down the centre of the valley and across the crescent, near the left or dry branch.

The Sacramento rises in the mountains on the right, and the road falls onto it about one mile below the battle-field or intrenchment of the enemy. We ascertained that the enemy had one battery of four guns, two nine and two six pounders on the point of the mountain on our right (their left) at a good elevation to sweep the plain, and at the point where the mountains extended furthest into the plain. On our left (their right) they had another battery on an elevation commanding the road, and three intrenchments of two six pounders, and on the brow of the crescent near the center,

shots are exchanged. Ortiz and his three companions are still standing in the vehicle with outstretched necks and eager eyes. But see—the Mexican columns waver, and rank after rank bites the dust. At last, they fly—the countenances of the priest and his companions fall, their bright visions vanish, and, jumping out, they run behind that very large wagon-wheel. Good men, they are praying and telling their beads with unusual rapidity, with trembling voices and shaking hands. A sad task was the priest's that night, and many a poor Mexican soldier died murmuring his confession into his ear. . . .

"A detachment was at once sent on to the city, to secure it, and to send the alcalde to bury the dead, which he did, by having them thrown into the trenches and tumbling the embankments upon them. Little did those now under them think, when throwing up the redoubts, that they were digging their own graves.

"I have understood that, as we started on the charge, Colonel Doniphan covered his face with his hands, and almost groaned out, 'My God! they're gone! the boys will all be killed!' Then instantly raising his head, he stuck his spurs into his horse's sides and came dashing after us."

Colonel Doniphan forwarded the reports of his officers to the War Department, the date of his letter of transmission being March 4, 1847. These reports are set out here:

HEADQUARTERS ARMY IN CHIHUAHUA,
March 4, 1847.

SIR: Enclosed you will find the reports of my field officers of the battle of the 28th. I regret their great length—except Lieutenant-Colonel's Mitchell's; also a plan of the field by Major Clark.

Very respectfully, your obedient servant,
A. W. DONIPHAN,
Colonel 1st Reg't Missouri Mounted Volunteers.
Brigadier-General R. Jones,
Adjutant General, U. S. Army.

MITCHELL'S REPORT.

CHIHUAHUA, March 5, 1847.

SIR: In compliance with your request, I submit the following report "in relation to the Battle of Sacramento."

Immediately after gaining the table-land on the enemy's left, I took command of the right wing of the army, in obedience to your orders, and at the same time gave the necessary instructions to the traders and teamsters in our rear, so as to form a field-work with the wagons to fall back upon, in the event of our being too hardly pressed by overwhelming numbers. After the artillery firing (on both sides) ceased for a few moments, I ordered the right wing, consisting of about 450 mounted riflemen, to advance in a gallop towards the enemy's intrenchments on their left.

During this movement a battery of five pieces of artillery on the point of a hill, 600 yards to our right, opened an enfilade fire on the left of our column, which did no execution. By a rapid advance we reached a deep ravine within 150

another of two, six and two four, and six culverins, or rampart pieces, mounted on carriages; and on the crest of the hill or ascent between the batteries, on the right and left they had twenty-seven redoubts dug and thrown up, extending at short intervals across the whole ground. In these their infantry were placed and were entirely protected. Their cavalry was drawn up in front of the redoubts in the intervals four deep, and in front of the redoubts two deep, so as to mask them as far as practicable. When we had arrived within one and a half miles of their intrenchments along the main road, we advanced the cavalry still farther, and suddenly diverged with the columns to the right so as to gain the narrow parts of the ascent on our paces in the front of the enemy's field-works; here I ordered troops to dismount and charge as skirmishers. The Mexican troops maintained their position with much gallantry until we advanced within 25 or 30 paces of their entrenchments; at this distance the fire of our men was unerring, and any Mexican who raised his head above the breastworks fell. They soon after broke and fled in the utmost confusion and in every direction towards the surrounding mountains. I immediately ordered the men to remount and charge the battery on our right. This was done in gallant style, we being supported by two field howitzers under the command of Captain Weightman, of Major Clark's battalion. When we reached the top of the hill we found that the Mexicans had fled, leaving the whole of their cannon, ammunition, wagons, etc. I saw them retreating in every direction on foot; as cavalry we could have followed them and cut off great numbers, but the victory was complete, and I wished to spare the useless effusion of blood.

In justice to the officers and men under my command, I have only to say that they did their duty as citizen-soldiers, and their conduct would have reflected credit upon the best troops in the world.

The morning after the battle I entered the city of Chihuahua, at the head of two companies of mounted men and two field or mountain howitzers from Major Clark's battalion. In obedience to your orders, I examined all the public buildings and public property; this will form the subject of a separate report.

Very respectfully, your obedient servant,
D. D. MITCHELL,
Lieutenant-Colonel 2nd Regiment, etc.
Col. A. W. Doniphan, Commanding.

GILPIN'S REPORT.

CHIHUAHUA, MEXICO, March 2, 1847.

SIR: On the evening of the 22d of February, the American army, under Colonel Doniphan, being encamped at the Little Laguna of Lous, it was ascertained from the reports of the scouts and from actual reconnoissance that the Mexican army, 4200 strong, occupied a fortified position in the pass of the Sacramento, in advance of that stream. From Lous to the Sacramento the distance is eighteen miles, the road following an open valley of grass, perfectly level and incased on either side in mountains. There is neither wood nor water in this distance, to obtain which the Americans were obliged to force the Mexican position and reach the Sacramento. The Colonel commanding having made his dispositions, the army moved from its encampment after daylight on the morning of the 28th.

The wagons, 300 in number, being arranged in columns of four parallel lines, with intervals of 50 yards, the artillery marched in the intervals of the center, the first battalion in the interval on the right and the second in the interval on the left. In advance of the whole were the cavalry companies of the first and second battalions and the Chihuahua Rangers. By this arrangement, giving compactness to our force and effectually concealing our numbers, the whole army could be deployed in battle order to the front, rear, or on either flank, the wagons at the same time forming a corral sufficiently large, if necessary, to envelop and protect

right which the enemy discovering, endeavored to prevent by moving forward with one thousand cavalry and four pieces of cannon in their rear masked by them. Our movements were so rapid that we gained the elevation with our forces and the advance of our wagons in time to form before they arrived within reach of our guns. The enemy halted, and we advanced the head of our columns within 1200 yards of them, so as to let our wagons attain the high lands and form as before.

We now commenced the action by a brisk fire from our battery, and the enemy unmasked and commenced also; our fires proved effective at this distance, killing fifteen men, wounding a number, and

---

it. The army pursuing their march in this order, reached about noon the rising ground seven miles from the Sacramento, from which point the country slopes gently down to that stream.

From hence the forces of the enemy, deployed behind their fortified lines, were distinctly in view. A broad sandy arroya passed athwart the valley (here about four miles wide), itself running nearly parallel with the Sacramento, crosses the main road two miles north of the ford, and running out to the foot of the mountains on the left, binds all the right and joins the river seven and a half miles below the ford. The road after crossing this arroya runs in a perfectly straight line due south to the ford of the Sacramento, where, upon the other bank, is also the daubie house, known as the hacienda of the Sacramento. Before reaching the arroya, two other roads branch off—one, leading to the right, crosses the Sacramento at the hacienda of Tession [?], three miles above the ford, passes then by ravines behind the point of the mountain, which rises abruptly above the house at the ford, and rejoins the main road six miles below. The other road branches off to the left, following the ravine of the arroya along its left bank to its junction with the Sacramento.

The large peninsula thus contained between the two streams and the distant mountains on the right is traversed nearly centrally by a main road, the half upon the right hand passing to the mountains in a plane of unbroken level. But the left half rises in a second bench some fifty feet high, along the base of which the road runs. The second bench slopes upwards from every side, towards the northeast corner, where it culminates in a rocky knoll three hundred feet in height. This whole mass of elevated ground, in shape an irregular square of one and a half miles on each side, was encased with field-works and fortifications admirably planned to sweep both roads leading to the Sacramento, and to destroy any force attempting to pass along either.

In the center of all, passing out by the southeast corner towards the Sacramento, is a broad, smooth hollow, in which was the Mexican camp, which served to conceal their numbers and curtain the movements of their troops and batteries. Upon the northern face of this square, which rises all along in a high, rocky bluff from the arroya, and which itself rises towards the northeastern knoll, were four large redoubts for cannon, having externally a circular ditch three feet deep, within this a stone wall four feet high, crowned with broken rocks and surrounded by fascines of brush. The first of these forts, located on the northwestern angle, commanded the main road as it crosses the arroya and rises upon the lower bench. The fourth fort was upon the high knoll at the northeast corner. The second and third forts intermediate, forming a connected range for cannon and successively more elevated, each commanding the one on the left in case it should be taken by assault. Smooth roads led from one to the other, to enable the cannon to change position at a gallop. Across the main road and filling up the intervals between the forts were redoubts for infantry, trenches three feet deep, fronted with breastworks of stone. Such was the line of the enemy which presented itself to our front, swept throughout by the range of their cannon, manned all along with infantry, commanding the left-hand road running along its front for two miles, and also the

disabling one of the enemy's guns. We had two men slightly wounded and several horses and mules killed. The enemy then slowly retreated behind their works in some confusion, and we resumed our march in our former order, still diverging more to the right to avoid their battery on our left, (their right,) and their strongest redoubts, which were on the left, near where the road passes. After marching as far as we safely could, without coming within range of their heavy batteries on our right, Captain Weightman, of the artillery, was ordered to charge with the two 12-pound howitzers, to be supported by the cavalry, under Capts. Reid, Parsons, and Hudson. The howitzers charged at speed, and were gallantly sustained by Capt. Reid; but,

---

main road where it crosses the arroya and rises upon the lower plain. Upon this formidable line of defenses was deployed the Mexican army. On their extreme left, and in front of the redoubt of the main road, was 1000 cavalry, drawn up in four masses, two on the right hand and two on the left of the road. In the redoubt was infantry. In the first fort immediately on the right, two ten-pound, two six-pound pieces of artillery and six musquetoons, mounted upon carriages. In the second fort, two six-pounders; in the third fort, two four-pounders; and in the fort upon the knoll, two six-pounders and three musquetoons. These pieces of artillery are all of brass, drawn by eight mules each, served by three hundred artillerymen, and supplied from ten large wagons and many pack-mules loaded with ammunition. Along the trenches in the intervals of the forts were 2100 infantry; in their rear and in the camp, 800 rancheros, mounted infantry, and many hundred spectators, assembled from the surrounding country. As the American columns, enveloped in their wagon-trains, approached this formidable line, the colonel commanding (having ascertained by reconnoissance its strength and the practicability of turning and rendering it useless by a flank movement), when within two miles of the enemy turned off suddenly to the right, crossed the arroya one and a half miles above the enemy's left, and, having successfully debouched upon the lower plain, formed in battle order fronting the enemy, who had assumed a new position. The American line was parallel with the main road, about 1200 yards to the north and 100 yards in front of the wagons. In the meantime the enemy, embarrassed by the change of direction in the American column, and finding their position useless, withdrawing from every point, formed upon their second line. This line consisted of thirteen redoubts of infantry, forming a continuous chain along the crest of the bench flanking the main road, and terminating in a fifth redoubt for the cannon at the southwest corner of the highland, where it commands the ford of the Sacramento. To mask the movements of the artillery and infantry and their deployment upon the second line, the whole Mexican cavalry descending upon the lower plain, formed in battle order, remaining halted in front of the American line. At this moment our battery opened a fire of round shot and shells, which, taking effect upon the cavalry, and being replied to by the enemy's guns stationed upon the bench and firing above their own cavalry, the latter retreated in disorder along the Chihuahua road. The cannonade between our battery and the Mexican continued at very long range for half an hour, during which the Mexican cavalry, passing down the ravine of the Sacramento and up the hollow, rallied in the rear of the Mexican battery. At this time the train [?] from the Mexican batteries having ceased (one of their six-pounders being struck and dismounted by a ball from our battery), and our wagons having closed up, the American line, followed closely by the wagons, commenced advancing obliquely to the front and right without any change of form, except the second battalion marching in column with its front resting upon the main line.

In this form we reached the southern edge of the plain beneath which the Sacramento runs, and advanced within 500 yards of the Mexican army, posted in the round battery and the trenches, extending along the crest of the bench to the right, and in three trenches strengthened by a large stone corral, and trees filling

by some misunderstanding, my order was not given to the other companies. Capt. Hudson, anticipated my order, charged in time to give ample support to the howitzers. Capt. Parsons, at the same moment, came to me, and asked permission for his company to charge the redoubts immediately to the left of Capt. Weightman, which he did very gallantly. The remainder of the two battalions of the first regiment were dismounted during the cavalry charge, and followed rapidly on foot, and Major Clark advancing as fast as practicable with the remainder of our battery; we charged their redoubts from right to left, with a brisk and deadly fire of riflemen, while Major Clark opened a rapid and well-directed fire on a column of cavalry,

up the connection with the ford and the house of the Sacramento on the left. Between the two armies and beneath the Mexican works in our front ran a deep gully, impassable for our cannon and strengthening their position.

During these movements the Mexican artillery, escorted by their cavalry, by a movement to their rear had crossed the Sacramento, and passing behind the house, established itself in a third position of great strength. The mountain on the fourth bank rises abruptly for 350 feet behind the house and above the stream; forming here an extensive bench, it again rises behind in a lofty peak of rocks.

On the edge of this bench was a strong fort which the Mexican battery occupied, supported by the cavalry. The balls and grape-shot from this position raked with a plunging fire the American line, the whole ravine of the Sacramento down which the road passes to the ford, also sweeping the gully and ground between us and the Mexican entrenchment in our front.

At this moment the battle was divided by a series of brilliant charges, made simultaneously by our artillery, cavalry, and the battalions dismounted. The onset was commenced by a charge at full gallop of Captain Reid's cavalry, accompanied by the howitzers of our battery, upon the round fort in front. These coming upon the gully beneath the Mexican works, the howitzers turned off to the left, and passing around the head of the gully, unlimbered close under the Mexican muskets and commenced firing shells and grape. The horsemen, some leaping over and others riding around the gully, charged up the slope, supporting the howitzers, but being few in number and coming suddenly upon the dense masses of the enemy thronged up in their breastworks and assailing them with a thick hail of bullets, they obliqued to the left along the slope under the trenches, seeking intervals between the redoubts through which to charge and firing their carbines into the redoubts as they passed in front of them. This having been seen by the second battalion, which had advanced in a trot up to the brink of the gully, that battalion deployed to the front at a gallop, leaped from their horses, running at full speed up the hill, and carrying with them the howitzers and cavalry, the whole by one simultaneous charge cleared the works of the enemy and sent them whirling in headlong flight, pursuing them with immense slaughter through their camp and completely across the plains. During this charge, the cavalry of the second battalion, followed by our main battery, passing by the extreme left, dispersed a body of the enemy's horse, which menaced our left flank, and continuing the pursuit of the enemy, with great slaughter, to the mountains and along their base, effectually completed their total rout. Whilst the battle thus raged upon the left, immediately under my own eye, the line of redoubts and strong corral extending from the stone fort across the ravine of the Sacramento, were similarly carried by the first battalion and the Chihuahua Rangers. The first cannonade had commenced at twenty minutes before three o'clock, and now at five the enemy were completely driven from all their positions in advance of the Sacramento, with the loss of two brass six-pounders, all their infantry, their camp, ammunition and provisions. The American wagons had arrived, corralled upon the battle-ground, and the battalions rallied from the pursuit, leaving that to the cavalry.

The Mexicans still occupied their third position upon the mountain bench

attempting to pass to our left so as to attack the wagons, and our rear. The fire was so well-directed as to force them to fall back; and our riflemen, with the cavalry and howitzers, cleared the redoubts after an obstinate resistance. Our forces advanced to the very brink of their redoubts, and attacked them with their sabres. When the redoubts were cleared, and the batteries in the center and our left were silenced, the main battery on our right still continued to pour in a constant and heavy fire, as it had done during the heat of the engagement; but as the whole fate of the battle depended upon the carrying

beyond the Sacramento, with six of their heaviest and best guns, supported by 800 cavalry, having also a fourth fortified position two miles in their rear, where the road from the lower Ternon [Tession?] descends by a gorge to join the Chihuahua road in the plain of the lower Sacramento. The colonel commanding having directed this position to be taken by a combined attack, our battery of six-pounders formed upon the edge of the battle-ground, fronting the Mexican battery and firing into it across the ravine of the Sacramento. The Chihuahua Rangers, the howitzers and a portion of the first battalion (mounted) charged by the main road, leading across the ford round the house, and ascending into the rear of the position. The second battalion marched on foot to cross the Sacramento higher up, scale the mountain above the position and attack it in the rear. The first two shots from our battery across the ravine having dismounted one of the Mexican guns, and a third shot having cut in two one of their ammunition wagons, and our horsemen appearing at full gallop ascending the road leading to their position, the Mexicans fled headlong, leaving their guns, ammunition and colors on the ground. They fled wildly at full gallop through their fourth position, where they abandoned their last gun, a six-pounder, choked with a ball. So that the sun having set and our parties returned to the battle-field, the first shadows cast by the moon found the American army camped upon the battle-field, after having, in a contest of four hours, annihilated a force six times their number and driven the enemy from four positions of great natural strength, fortified by thirty-six forts and redoubts, taken four times their strength in artillery, the whole transportation, food and ammunition of the Mexicans, and performed a march of twenty miles without water.

Such was the battle of Sacramento, as I saw it, faithfully but imperfectly described. Of the bravery and discipline of our men I know not how to speak, for it appeared to me equal with them all, and preëminently brilliant. When deployed on the first line of battle, and receiving at a halt the long cannonade of the enemy, the gaiety of the men burst out in jokes and laughter at their ineffectual shots. Sergeant Hughes, of F company, was shot through both ankles, and being taken to the wagons, his companions closed up. A cannon-ball knocked from under him the horse of private Trimble of H Company; he continued for some time in the ranks on foot, but soon after caught a horse and fought upon it through the battle. The charge of the enemy's redoubts, under a hail of bullets, was done with such fiery courage and rapidity that it seemed to have lasted but a minute.

My battalion was all present throughout the fight, and to do justice to the merits I should specify them all.

First Lieutenant Hinton, of G Company, and a portion of his men, were amongst the leading files of Capt. Reid's command, heading the first charge upon the enemy. Captain Parsons, of F Company, commanded the cavalry of the second battalion, with Third Lieutenant Winston, of the same, and Third Lieutenant Harrison, of H Company, privates Gordon and Feuke of F Company, Fleming of H, and Hughes of G, were severely wounded whilst charging impetuously upon the enemy in the rout.

Under my own immediate command the companies of my battalion charged,— Company E upon the extreme left, under Capt. Stevenson and Lieuts. McDonald, Richardson and Campbell; Company F upon the right, under Second Lieutenant

the redoubts and center battery, this one on the right remained unattacked, and the enemy had rallied there, five hundred strong.

Major Clark was directed to commence a heavy fire upon it, while Lieutenants-Colonel Mitchell and Jackson, commanding the 1st battalion, were ordered to remount and charge the battery on the left, while Major Gilpin was directed to pass the 2d battalion on foot up the rough ascent of the mountain on the opposite side. The fire of our battery was so effective as to completely silence theirs, and the rapid advance of our column put them to flight over the mountains in great confusion.

Captain Thompson, of the 1st dragoons, acted as my aid and

Gordon; Companies G and H in the center, the latter under the veteran Capt. Rodgers (a first lieutenant of Missouri volunteers in the battle of Ochechobee and there severely wounded), Lieuts. Duncan and Murray.

I must also add to the above my praise of the coolness and precision manifested by the drivers of the wagon-train and their officers, who were within my eye during the day of the battle. They contributed largely to the victory.

Should you design to place the achievements of our officers and soldiers under the eye of the President, allow me to recommend them as having conquered for themselves at Bracito and Sacramento a glory equal to those who fought at Palo Alto, Resaca de la Palma, and Monterey.

Yours, respectfully,
W. GILPIN,
Major 1st Regiment of Mounted Missouri Volunteers.
To Col. A. W. Doniphan,
Commanding the Army of Chihuahua.

MAJOR CLARK'S REPORT.

HEADQUARTERS, BATTALION MISSOURI LIGHT ARTILLERY,
CAMP NEAR CHIHUAHUA, MEXICO, March 2d, 1847.

SIR: I have the honor to report that, agreeable to your instructions, I left the camp near Sauz on the morning of the 28th ultimo, accompanied by my adjutant, Lieutenant L. D. Walker, and non-commissioned staff, and proceeded in advance to a position commanding a full view of the enemy's camp and entrenchments, situated about four miles distant from this point; the enemy was discovered to be in force awaiting our approach, having occupied the ridge and neighboring heights about Sacramento. Upon examination it was ascertained that his intrenchments and redoubts occupied the brow of an elevation extending across the ridge between the Arroya Seco and that of the Sacramento, both of which, at this point, cross the valley from the elevated ridge of mountains in the rear of the village of Torreen, known by the name of Sierra de Victorino, to that of Nombrero de Dios, on the east, and through which runs the Rio del Nombrero de Dios. This valley is about four miles in width, and entrenched by the enemy entirely across from mountain to mountain, the road to the city of Chihuahua running directly through its center, and, of necessity, passing near to and crossing the Rio Sacramento at the rancho Sacramento, a strongly built and fortified house with adjoining corrals and other enclosures, belonging to Angel Trias, the governor of Chihuahua. From observation it was ascertained that the enemy had occupied the site between these hills, and that the batteries upon them were supported by infantry, his cavalry being in advanced positions, formed into three columns, between the Arroya Seco and our advance; during these observations, the enemy's advance guard, discovering my party, approached rapidly with the evident intention of intercepting it, but being met by that of our troops, which I had sent forward, it as rapidly retreated; at this time, also, the three columns of the enemy's cavalry recrossed the Arroya Seco and retired behind their entrenchments. I then approached within 600 yards of the most advanced redoubt, from which point the enemy's formation was plainly discernible; the entrenchments consisted

adviser on the field during the whole engagement, and was of the most essential service to me. Also, Lieut. Wooster, of the United States army, who acted very cool and gallantly. Major Campbell, of Springfield, Missouri, also acted as a volunteer aid during part of the time, but left me and joined Capt. Reid in his gallant charge. Thus ended the battle of Sacramento. The force of the enemy was 1,200 cavalry from Durango and Chihuahua, with the Vera Cruz dragoons, 1,200 infantry from Chihuahua, 300 artillerists, and 1,420 rancheros, badly armed with lassos, lances, and machetos, or corn knives, ten pieces of artillery, 2 nine, 2 eight, four 6, and 2 four-pounders, and six culverines, or rampart pieces. Their forces were commanded by Major-

---

of a line with intervals composed of circular redoubts, from three to five hundred yards interval, with entrenchments between each, covering batteries partly masked by cavalry; the redoubt nearest to my position contained two pieces of cannon, supported by several hundred infantry. The enemy's right and left were strong positions, the Cerro Frijoles, on his right, having high precipitous sides, with a redoubt commanding the surrounding country and the pass leading towards Chihuahua through the Arroya Seco. The Cerro Sacramento on his left, consisting of a pile of immense volcanic rocks, surmounted by a battery, commanded the main road to Chihuahua, leading directly in front of the enemy's entrenchments, crossing the Rio Sacramento at the rancho directly under its fire, and also commanding the road from Terreon immediately in its rear. The crossing of the main road over the Arroya Seco, at the point from which my reconnoissance was made, laid directly under the fire of the batteries on the enemy's right, which rendered it necessary to ascertain the practicability of a route more distant from the enemy's entrenchments; the passage was found to be practicable with some little labor, and a point selected as the best for the passage of the artillery and wagons and merchant trains. The whole front of the enemy's line of entrenchments appeared to be about two miles, and his force 3000 men. The artillery being masked, the number and caliber of the cannon could not be estimated. Further, I have the honor to report that the battalion of artillery, under my command, composed of 110 men and 7 officers, with a battery of 6 pieces of artillery, were, on the morning of the battle, directed to form, under the direction of Captain Weightman, between the two columns of merchant and provision wagons, being thus masked from the view of the enemy; in this column my troops continued to march to within about 1500 yards of the enemy's most advanced position; our direction was then changed to the right, and the column, having crossed the Arroya Seco without reach of the enemy's force, rapidly advanced towards the table-land between the Seco and Sacramento. At this time the enemy was perceived advancing from his entrenchments to prevent our seizing upon these heights, but, by a rapid movement of the battery, it was quickly drawn from its mask, and, seizing upon a favorable position, protected in the rear by a marsh 'from the attack of a large body of the enemy's cavalry ascertained to be hanging on our rear, it was formed, and at once opened its fire upon the enemy's cavalry rapidly advancing upon us; at this moment his charging column was about 900 yards distant, and the effect of our strap-shot and shells was such as to break his ranks and throw his cavalry into confusion.

The enemy now rapidly deployed into line, bringing up his artillery from the entrenchments. During this time our line was preparing for a charge; my artillery advanced by hand and firing. The enemy now opened a heavy fire of cannon upon our line, mainly directed upon the battery, but with little effect. Lieutenant Done had his horse shot under him by a nine-pound ball at this stage of the action; and several mules and oxen in the merchant wagons in our rear were wounded or killed, which, however, was the only damage done. The fire of our cannon at this time had such good effect as to dismount one of the enemy's pieces, and completely to disperse his cavalry and drive him from his position,

General Heredia, general of Durango, Chihuahua, Sonora, and New Mexico; Brigadier-General Justiniani, Brigadier-General Garcia Condé, former minister of war for the republic of Mexico, who is a scientific man, and planned their whole field of defence; General Uguarte, and Governor Trias, who acted as brigadier-general on the field, and colonels and other officers without number.

Our force was nine hundred and twenty-four effective men, at least one hundred of whom were engaged in holding horses and driving teams.

The loss of the enemy was his entire artillery, 20 wagons, masses of beans and pinola, and other Mexican provisions, about three hun-

forcing him to again retire behind his entrenchments. In a short time the firing on either side now ceased, and the enemy appeared to be moving his cannon and wounded, whilst our line prepared to a change of position more towards the right, for the purpose of occupying a more advantageous ground. Our object being soon gained, the order to advance was given; and, immediately after, I was directed to send the section of howitzers to support a charge on the enemy's left. I immediately ordered Captain R. H. Weightman to detach the section composed of two twelve-pound mountain howitzers, mounted upon carriages constructed especially for field prairie service, and drawn by two horses each. These were commanded by Lieutenants E. F. Chouteau and H. D. Evans, and manned by some twenty men, whose conduct in this action cannot be too much commended. Captain Weightman charged at full gallop upon the enemy's left, preceded by Captain Reid and his company of horse; and, after crossing a ravine some 150 yards from the enemy, he unlimbered the guns within fifty yards of the entrenchment, and opened a destructive fire of canister into his ranks, which was warmly returned, but without effect. Captain Weightman again advanced upon the entrenchments, pressing through them in the face of the enemy, and within a few feet of the ditches, and in the midst of a cross-fire from three directions, again opened his fire to the right and left with such effect that, with the formidable charge of the cavalry and dismounted men of your own regiment and Lieutenant-Colonel Mitchell's escort, the enemy were driven from the breastworks on our right in great confusion. As this time, under a heavy cross-fire from the battery on Cerro Sacramento, I was advancing with our battery of four six-pounders under Lieuts. Done, Kribbin and Labeaume, upon the enemy's right, supported by Major Gilpin on the left, and the wagon-train, escorted by two companies of infantry, under Captains E. J. Glasgow and Skillman, in the rear, when Major Gilpin charged upon the enemy's center and forced him from his entrenchments, under a heavy fire of artillery and small-arms; at the same time the fire of our battery was upon the enemy's extreme right, from which a continued fire had been kept up on our line and the wagon-train. Two of the enemy's guns were now soon dismounted on their right, that battery silenced, and the enemy dislodged from the redoubts on the Cerro Frijoles. Perceiving a body of lancers forming for the purpose of outflanking our left and attacking the merchants' wagons under Captain Glasgow, I again opened upon them a very destructive fire of grape and spherical case-shot, which soon cleared the left of our line. The enemy vacating his entrenchments and deserting his guns, was hotly pursued towards the mountains beyond Cerro Frijoles and down the Arroya Seco to Sacramento by both wings of the army, under Lieut.-Colonel Mitchell, Lieut.-Colonel Jackson and Major Gilpin, and by Captain Weightman with the section of howitzers. During this pursuit, my officers repeatedly opened their fire upon the enemy with great effect. To cover this flight of the enemy's forces from the entrenched camp, the heaviest of his cannon had been taken from the entrenchments to the Cerro Sacramento, and a heavy fire opened upon our pursuing forces and wagons following in the rear. To silence this battery, I had the honor to anticipate your order to that effect by at once occupying the nearest of the enemy's entrenchments, 1225

dred killed and the same number wounded, many of whom have since died, and forty prisoners.

The field was literally covered with the dead and wounded from our artillery and the unerring fire of our riflemen. Night put a stop to the carnage, the battle having commenced about three o'clock. Our loss was one killed, one mortally wounded, and seven so wounded as to recover without any loss of limbs. I cannot speak too highly of the coolness, gallantry, and bravery of the officers and men under my command.

I was ably sustained by the field officers, Lieutenant-Colonels Mitchell and Jackson, of the first battalion and Major Gilpin, of the

---

yards distant; and notwithstanding the elevated position of the Mexican battery, giving him a plunging fire into his entrenchment, which was not defiladed, and the greater range of his long nine-pounders, the first fire of our guns dismounted one of his largest pieces, and the fire was kept up with such briskness and precision of aim that this battery was soon silenced and the enemy seen precipitately retreating. The fire was then continued upon the rancho Sacramento and the enemy's ammunition and baggage train retreating upon the road to Chihuahua. By this fire the house and several wagons were rendered untenable and useless. By this time Lieut.-Colonel Mitchell had scaled the hill, followed by the section of howitzers under Capt. Weightman, and the last position of the Mexicans taken possession of by our troops, thus leaving the American forces masters of the field. Having silenced the fire from Cerro Sacramento, one battery was removed into the plain at the rancho, where we gained the road, and were in pursuit of the enemy when I received your order to return and encamp within the enemy's entrenchments for the night. From the time of first opening my fire upon the Mexican cavalry to the cessation of the firing on the rancho and battery of Sacramento was about three hours; and during the whole time of the action, I take the utmost pleasure in stating that every officer and man of my command did his duty with cheerfulness, coolness and precision, which is sufficiently shown by the admirable effects produced by their fire, the great accuracy of their aim, their expediency and ingenuity in supplying deficiencies in the field during the action, and the prompt management of their pieces, rendered still more remarkable by the fact that I had during the fight less than two-thirds the number of cannoniers generally required for the service of light artillery, and but four of the twelve artillery carriages belonging to my battery harnessed with horses, the remaining eight carriages being harnessed to mules of the country.

During the day my staff were of the greatest service,—Adjutant L. D. Walker having been sent with the howitzers and the non-commissioned officers remaining with me to assist in the service of the battery. In this action, the troops in your command have captured from the enemy one nine-pounder, mounted on a check-rail carriage, one nine-pound, one six-pound and seven four-pound guns, all mounted on new stock-trail carriages. These pieces were all manufactured at Chihuahua except the six-pounder, which is an old Spanish piece; three of the four-pounders were made at the mint in Chihuahua; seven of the ten pieces were spiked, but have been unspiked since their capture; four of them were rendered unserviceable in the action,—one entirely dismounted and seized by my adjutant whilst in the act of being dragged from the field by the retreating enemy. There were also taken two pieces of artillery, mounting three wall-pieces of one and a half inch calibre each, and these are formidable weapons upon a charging force; with these twelve pieces of artillery was taken a due proportion of ammunition, implements, harness, mules, etc., and they may be rendered serviceable by being properly prepared and manned, and for which purpose I would ask for further reinforcements of my command.

It is with feelings of gratitude to the Ruler of all battles that I have now the honor to report, that not a man of my command has been hurt, nor any animals

2d battalion; and Major Clark and his artillery acted nobly and did the most effective service in every part of the field. It is abundantly shown, in the charge made by Captain Weightman with the section of howitzers, that they can be used in any charge of cavalry with great effect. Much has been said, and justly, of the gallantry of our artillery, unlimbering within two hundred and fifty yards of the enemy at Palo Alto; but how much more daring was the charge of Capt. Weightman, when he unlimbered within fifty yards of the redoubts of the enemy.

On the first day of March we took formal possession of the capital of Chihuahua in the name of our government. We were ordered by

with the exception of one horse, killed under Lieut. Done, chief of the first section of six-pounder guns, and of one mule belonging to the United States, shot under one of the cannoniers. Neither has a gun or other carriage of my battery been touched, except in one instance, when a nine-pound ball struck the tire of a wheel, without producing injury. This is a fact worthy of notice, that so little damage was done to a command greatly exposed to the enemy's fire and of itself made a point of attack by the enemy, if I may so judge by the showers of cannon and other shot constantly poured into us as long as the enemy continued to occupy his positions. 1 might call your attention to the individual instances of personal courage and good conduct of the men of my command, as well as of the intrepid bravery and cool and determined courage of many of your own regiment and Lieut.-Colonel Mitchell's escort, who charged with us upon the enemy's works, were it not impossible in any reasonable space to name so many equally worthy of distinction, and did I not presume other field officers on the occasion would report the proceedings of their own commands and of the praiseworthy conduct of their own officers and men.

With great respect, I am, sir, yours, most obedient,
M. LEWIS CLARK,
Major commanding Battalion Missouri Light Artillery.
To Colonel A. W. Doniphan,
Commanding American forces in the State of Chihuahua.

I have enclosed a topographical sketch of the battle-ground and the movements of the troops on both sides, made from a survey after the battle.
M. L. CLARK, Major, &c.

EXTRACT FROM THE REPORT OF HON. W. L. MARCY, SECRETARY OF WAR, DECEMBER 2, 1847.

"As early as August, 1846, General Kearny informed the Department, in a letter from Santa Fé, that he should have a disposable force at that place beyond that which would be required to hold it and to accompany him to California, and he proposed to send a detachment to Chihuahua, to join General Wool, who was advancing upon that place. On the 23d of September he ordered Colonel Doniphan, with the First Regiment of Missouri Volunteers, on that service. After being detained some time for the reduction of the Navajo Indians—a restless and predatory tribe inhabiting the regions of New Mexico west of the range of mountains bordering the valley of the Rio Grande—Colonel Doniphan proceeded on this expedition, attended with a large company of American merchants. On the 25th of December the advance of the command was met by the enemy in considerable force near Brazito, when an engagement took place, which resulted in the total defeat of the Mexicans, with a loss on their part of nearly two hundred in killed and wounded, and on ours of only seven wounded. The force engaged in this affair, on our side, was less than five hundred, and on that of the enemy one thousand two hundred and twenty, of which over five hundred were cavalry. Pursuing its march, the command entered El Paso without further opposition. Here it was ascertained that the column under General Wool had been diverted from its original destination. It therefore became necessary for the detachment

General Kearny to report to General Wool at this place: since our arrival we hear he is at Saltillo, surrounded by the enemy. Our present purpose is either to force our way to him, or to return by Bexar, as our term of service expires on the last day of May next.

I have the honor to be your obedient servant,

A. W. DONIPHAN,
Colonel 1st Reg't Missouri Mounted Volunteers.

Brig. R. JONES, Adjutant-General U. S. Army.

On the morning after the engagement Major Clark, in reporting to Col. Doniphan the conduct of the troops under his command, holds the following language:

"Capt. Weightman charged at full gallop upon the enemy's left,

to remain at El Paso until reinforced by artillery, which had been previously ordered from Santa Fé. This accession of force did not join the command until early in February, and then it moved forward towards Chihuahua. On its arrival at the Pass of the Sacramento, about fifteen miles from the capital of the State, on the 28th of February, the enemy was there discovered in great force, strongly posted on the commanding heights, fortified by entrenchments, and well supplied with artillery. Arrangements were promptly made for an attack and a fire at once opened from our batteries. The action soon became general, and lasted from three o'clock in the afternoon until near dark. All of the enemy's redoubts were carried, and he was driven with great slaughter from the field, and completely dispersed. His artillery, consisting of ten pieces and some culverines, was captured, and his loss in killed and wounded was about 600, while ours did not exceed 9 men. The numerical strength of the enemy in this engagement was over 4000—1200 infantry, 1200 cavalry, 300 artillery, and over 1400 rancheros—under the command of several officers of high rank and distinction. Our entire force in the action was less than 900. On the succeeding day our victorious troops entered the capital of Chihuahua, and, after remaining there some weeks, proceeded to join the army under Major-General Taylor, at Monterey.

"This adventurous march by Colonel Doniphan and his small and gallant command, of more than 1000 miles through a hostile country, in the course of which two battles were fought against vastly superior numbers, and decisive victories won, with great loss on the part of the enemy and almost bloodless on ours, is an achievement to which it would be difficult to find a parallel in the history of military operations."

WILLIAM CULLEN BRYANT'S TRIBUTE.

"XENOPHON AND DONIPHAN.—These are the names of two military commanders who have made the most extraordinary marches known in the annals of warfare of their times. Col. Xenophon, as in modern phrase he has justly a right to be called, lived about one hundred years earlier than the Christian era. Born in Greece, and educated under Socrates as a favorite pupil, he, at the age of nearly forty years, joined a regiment of Greeks, who had enlisted under Cyrus the younger for a campaign, as it was pretended, against the Pisidians, but, in reality, against Persia, as the Greeks soon discovered after their march had begun. The object of Cyrus, as our readers well know, was to dethrone his brother, the King of Persia. After a long march through Asia Minor, Syria, and the sandy tract east of the Euphrates, the two brothers met at Cunaxa, not far from Babylon. Cyrus fell in the almost bloodless battle that ensued, his barbarian troops were discouraged and dispersed, and the Greeks were left alone in the center of the Persian empire. The Greek officers were soon massacred by the treachery of the Persians. Xenophon stepped forward, and soon became one of the most active leaders; and, under his judicious guidance, the Greeks effected their retreat northward

preceded by Capt. Reid and his company of horse, and after crossing a ravine some hundred and fifty yards from the enemy, he unlimbered the guns within fifty yards of the intrenchment, and opened a destructive fire of canister into his ranks, which was warmly returned, but without effect. Capt. Weightman again advanced upon the intrenchment, passing through it in the face of the enemy, and within a few feet of the ditches, and in the midst of cross-fires from three directions, again opened his fire to the right and left with such effect, that with the formidable charge of the cavalry and dismounted men of your own regiment and Lieutenant-Colonel Mitchell's escort, the enemy were driven from their breastworks on our right in great confusion.

across the high lands of Armenia, and arrived at Trebisond, on the southeast coast of the Black Sea.

"From thence they proceeded to Chrysopolis, opposite Constantinople. Both Colonel Xenophon and the regiment, consisting of about five hundred men, were greatly distressed, having lost almost everything excepting their lives and their arms. The length of the entire march of the Greek force, as nearly as we can now estimate it, was three thousand four hundred and sixty-five English miles. It was accomplished in fifteen months, and a large part of it through an unknown, mountainous, and hostile country, and in an inclement season. The history of this march has survived the ravages of two thousand years; and, as one of the best productions of a Greek scholar, is now used as a text-book in our schools.

"Turning now to the wonderful march of Colonel Doniphan, we find the First Regiment of Missouri Mounted Volunteers mustered into the service of the United States at Fort Leavenworth, on the 6th of June last year, and on the 22d of the same month they commenced their march across the Plains of Mexico. After a march of fifty-seven days' duration they entered Santa Fé. On the 16th of the present month we find this regiment at New Orleans, about to be discharged, as their enlistment for a year was nearly expired. In the mean time this body of men has fought three battles, viz.: Bracito, Sacramento, and El Paso. That of Bracito was on Christmas day, and opened an entrance into El Paso Del Norte. The Mexicans had twelve hundred and fifty men and one piece of artillery; the Americans four hundred and twenty-five infantry—the piece of cannon was captured, and the Mexican army entirely destroyed. That of Sacramento was fought on the 28th of February. This battle—one of the most remarkable in the war—is familiar through the reports of Col. Doniphan and other field officers. The battle of El Paso was fought about the 13th of May, by the advanced guard under Capt. Reid—the Americans had twenty-five men and the Comanches sixty-five. The Indians were routed, and left seventeen bodies on the field. Three hundred and fifty head of cattle, twenty-five Mexican prisoners, and, a great deal of Mexican plunder, were captured.

"The battle of Sacramento lasted three hours and a half; and the slaughter of the Mexican army continued until night put an end to the chase. The men returned to the battle-field after dark, completely worn out and exhausted with fatigue. The Mexicans lost 300 men killed on the field, and a large number of wounded, perhaps 400 or 500, and 60 or 70 prisoners, together with a vast quantity of provisions, several thousand dollars in money, 50,000 head of sheep, 1500 head of cattle, 100 mules, 20 wagons, 25 or 30 carts, 25,000 lbs. ammunition, 11 pieces of cannon, mostly brass six-pounders, 6 wall-pieces, 100 stand of arms, 100 stand of colors, and many other things of less note.

"This body of men conquered the States of New Mexico and Chihuahua, and traversed Durango and New Leon. In this march they traveled more than six thousand miles, consuming twelve months. During all this time not one word of information reached them from the Government, nor any order whatsoever; they neither received any supplies of any kind nor one cent of pay. They lived exclusively on the country through which they passed; and supplied themselves

At this time under a heavy cross-fire from the battery of four six-pounders, under Lieuts. Dorn, Kribbin, and Labeaume, upon the enemy's right, supported by Major Gilpin on the left, and the wagon train escorted by two companies of infantry under Captains E. F. Glasgow and Skillman in the rear, Major Gilpin charged upon the enemy's center and forced him from his intrenchments under a heavy fire of artillery and small arms. At the same time the fire of our own battery was opened upon the enemy's extreme right, from which a continued fire had been kept up upon our line and the wagon train. Two of the enemy's guns were now soon dismounted on their right, that battery silenced and the enemy dislodged from the redoubt on the

with powder and ball by capturing them from the enemy. From Chihuahua to Matamoras, a distance of nine hundred miles, they marched in forty-five days, bringing with them seventeen pieces of heavy artillery as trophies.

"It must be confessed, that in many very important particulars these two expeditions differ from each other. One was the march of a conqueror, the other was the retreat of an inferior force. One was made on horseback, and the other on foot at an inclement season of the year. One was made at an early age of the world, when military science was undeveloped, the other was made with all the advantage of modern improvements. But our object is not so much to draw comparisons between these two expeditions as to notice the circumstances that these two men, whose names are in sound so similar, have each performed the most wonderful in the annals of warfare. If Col. Doniphan will now imitate the example of Col. Xenophon, and give to the world as charming and as perfect a history of his expedition as the latter has done, mankind, two thousand years hence, will admire and honor him."

LIEUTENANT GIBSON'S DESCRIPTION OF THE BATTLE OF SACRAMENTO.

"The battle we were about to have not only gave increased reputation to our arms, but was one of the most important which occurred during the war in its results and effects. It was the means of keeping down the disturbances which had broken out in New Mexico a short time previous, and secured peace in our newly acquired possessions in that quarter. It made the Indian tribes look upon us as a race far superior to the Mexican, and overawed them. It prevented a large amount of property in the hands of the traders from falling into their hands; property which was sufficient to have supported the whole Mexican army for several months, and at that particular time would have been of the utmost value to Santa Anna and the Government.

"It was an evidence to the northern part of Mexico, where no resistance had been made, of what they might expect if they undertook to resist again, and will be the means of securing to our fellow-citizens in future better treatment in their trade and intercourse with them. These are all positive advantages acquired over and above the fruits of victory which we obtained on the field and in the city. Our troops were all well aware of its importance, and felt themselves called on for the utmost energy and activity which they could display; besides, the black flag at Brazito and the known character of the enemy gave us no room to expect even decent treatment in case of defeat, and every man seemed to feel himself called on to have victory or death. All these things had been duly considered beforehand, which, with the disparity in numbers, made us regard it as no ordinary action. The battle-field itself was as well selected and as pretty a place for such a scene as I ever saw, and has to be seen, fully to comprehend their and our positions, as it is different from all others. Their redoubts lined the road, and to put ourselves on an equal footing we left it, and took to the right to reach the high ground they occupied between the Sacramento and an arroya which we found very bad to cross with the wagons, one at least having to be left until after night. Just as we reached the arroya a column of about 1000 mounted

Cerro Frigolis. Perceiving a body of lancers forming, for the purpose of outflanking our left, and attacking the merchant train under Capts. Glasgow and Skillman, I again opened upon them a very destructive fire of grape and spherical case shot, which soon cleared the left of our line. The enemy vacating his intrenchments and deserting his guns, was hotly pursued towards the mountains beyond Cerro Frigolis, and down Arroya Seco la Sacramento by both wings of the army under Lieut. colonel Mitchell, Lieut. colonel Jackson and Major Gilpin, and by Capt. Weightman, with the section of howitzers. During this pursuit my officers repeatedly opened their fires upon the re-

---

men came out in front of their position, intending, no doubt, to charge on our rear and the wagons whilst in confusion crossing. But the drivers and men urged the animals through, and it proved to be only a demonstration which in the end turned to our advantage.

"As soon as we reached the high ground with the long train of wagons, Capt. Waitman opened a fire upon the body of mounted troops that came out; and so well directed was it that a few shot served to drive them back upon the fortifications and produced a panic from which they never recovered. When we opened our fire they returned it, their balls being well directed and killing several of our animals and striking the wagons. Just about this time also Capt. Skilman's horse was shot under him, and Lt. Dorris when we were about 1000 yards from the redoubts. The wagons, troops and all continued to march up as speedily as possible, it being intended to use the wagons for defense if any disaster occurred to us, and we all kept together. The two mounted companies, Captains Reed and Parsons, and about half of the escort who had good horses, charged boldly up to their works, and the remainder as speedily as possible—all pushing forward with the utmost speed. There was but one order 'To charge'—and each man fought as he best could, some riding and dismounting to fire and again remounting and continuing the pursuit. They really made no stand at any place, being driven from every position as fast as we could come up. Maj. Owens was shot at the first redoubt, and expired instantly. He had been with me but a few minutes before, in the finest spirits and sure of a victory, and never stopped when he left my side until both him and his horse fell. He was a great loss, for we could perhaps have spared any other man better, his influence being great and his judgment sound. We should have obtained much more in the city with him in the lead. Sergt. Kirkpatrick was also shot early in the action, and suffered a great deal of pain on the field, though he lived several days. The enemy fled in all directions, and for miles around, horses, mules, oxen and men could be seen either wounded or dead. Our troops as we came up looked small compared with the crowds of them which covered the hills, and had they only fought coolly and directed their musketry well, we must have suffered heavy loss. But they kept themselves concealed behind the breastworks and in the ditches, and held their guns out so as to shoot without aim, and hardly ever in our direction. The whole field was strewed with lances, arms, provisions, dead men, &c., and our men raised a shout which almost made the dead awaken when they carefully examined and saw how strong a place they had taken with such odds on their side. Some of their best officers and most distinguished men were present—Conde, Heredia, Trias, Ugarti, Cordero, Olivares, and many others—with about 4000 men, and we had about 1000 to their 40,000. Twenty-two hundred were regulars, well drilled in all things except the use of arms and the conduct becoming a soldier. Hardly a man of ours came in without bringing something—some trophy or memento— flags—clothing—money. Provisions of various kinds, and articles which they threw away in their fright, filled our camp, with relations of occurrences in different places. They tried to get their artillery on the hill on the west side of the Sacramento, and had nearly succeeded when a few shots from our eight-pounders and Col. Jackson charging up at the same time put them all to flight, one piece

treating enemy with great effect. To cover this flight of the enemy's forces from the intrenched camp, the heaviest of his cannon had been taken from the intrenchment to Cerro Sacramento, and a heavy fire opened upon our pursuing forces and the wagons following in the rear. To silence this battery I had the honor to anticipate your order to that effect, by at once occupying the nearest of the enemy's intrenchments, 1225 yards distant, and notwithstanding the elevated position of the Mexican battery, giving him a plunging fire into my intrenchment, which was not defiladed, and the greater range of his long nine-pounders, the first fire of our guns dismounted one of his largest pieces, and the fire was kept up with such briskness and pre-

being dismounted by our first shot. The ten pieces of artillery which we took, the wagons of ammunition and provisions were all brought into camp, and there was but little sleep that night, the very fact that we had lost but two men and several badly wounded in achieving the victory being alone sufficient to create a hilarity which but seldom exists. Our transportation is greatly added to, and it takes all the extra animals we have as well as the captured ones to get the wagons and artillery to the city. Every man is loaded down with spoil, and the greatest difficulty is to get along with the plunder of all kinds.

"Many of the prisoners died, and the spectacle next morning was such that no man could help but feel that war was an evil of the worst kind, and one which should if possible be avoided. Had politicians who spent so [much time] carefully in these matters been able to look upon it, they would have used more precaution in their acts, and many a private and public calamity would have been averted which they brought on. Some were awfully mangled by our artillery; one very decent and respectable officer had both legs shot off, and the little care which the wounded must receive from necessity blunts and hardens men's feelings until they become perfectly indifferent. One of their surgeons was brought into camp a prisoner, taken in the mountains, and immediately released and sent to administer to our wounded enemies, so that they perhaps fared better than usual; but the few accommodations which belong to an army always make a bed of sickness one of great suffering, and of course more generally fatal than a man who has his friends and home around him.

"A large quantity of powder fell into our hands, and cartridges of all kinds. I had one ten-mule team of the latter for artillery, which I took to the city and there turned over to Major Clark. We also captured the black flag which cut such a conspicuous figure at Brazito, but the bearer of it made his escape,—and it was well he did, for our men would have made mince-meat of him. We found in a trunk $3000 in copper coin, which appeared to be their military chest, but the men made large acquisitions of silver, and one I understand got 100 doubloons. They however never turned them over, and took good care to say but little about it. We also found the next day a great many cattle, mules and horses between the battle-field and city, all of which were driven up as legal spoils, and came very seasonably to supply the quartermaster and commissary departments, besides furnishing the men who were afoot and had lost their animals either on the road or in the battle.

"It was dark before the men all got into camp, having pursued them several miles into the mountains, and captured some artillery which they tried to get off. The next day we only marched about six miles, except a part of the artillery and Col. Mitchell, who took possession of the city to secure the public property, the army being incumbered with the spoils taken on the field. The weather was delightful, and nothing was talked about in camp but the fight, and the hairbreadth escapes, and the consternation of the enemy, and a thousand little incidents; each one having something to tell, some incident to relate in which he was a party.

"We never got close enough to the main body for our small-arms to have effect,

cision of aim, that the battery was soon silenced and the enemy seen precipitately retreating. The fire was then continued upon the Rancho Sacramento, and the enemy's ammunition and wagon train retreating upon the road to Chihuahua. By their fire the house and several wagons were rendered untenable and useless. By this time Lieut. colonel Mitchell had scaled the hill, followed by the section of howitzers under Capt. Weightman, and the last position of the Mexican forces was taken possession of by our troops; thus leaving the American forces master of the field."

and consequently we neither killed in proportion to the numbers nor took many prisoners, their animals being fresh and ours jaded by the long march.

"All the foreigners friendly to us came out and met us the next day, and were greatly relieved at our victory. Had we been whipped they would all have been murdered, making a narrow escape as it was, and having to lock themselves up to keep off a mob which raised. So confident were they of success, that they had made arrangements to dispose of all the goods of the traders, and we were to be tied and led captives into the city.

"We found every now and then on the road dead or wounded horses, one just outside of the city, which had carried its rider that far and fallen dead. The French and Spanish Consul came out with his flag to meet Col. Mitchell, and treated us throughout as well as he could.

"It appeared miraculous that we all escaped as we did, the balls passing either over us, under us, or just between us, and all admitted that Providence seemed to have some agency in our preservation. Many escaped by dismounting from their horses as a cannon-ball came bounding along; some stepped to one side, let them pass, and again pushed forward; and as much, perhaps, was owing to the watchfulness of our men, who kept an eye to their safety as well as manifested a courage and resolution which none except the best of troops could withstand."

CHAPTER XIX.

Doniphan's proclamation—The American residents—The keys to the Mint—Mexican morals—Chihuahua—Its attractions—Express to Gen. Wool—The fourteen—Arrival at Saltillo—Visit to the battle field of Buena Vista—Return of the Express.

Colonel Doniphan, now having actual possession of the city of Chihuahua,[110] and virtual possession of the State; having quartered his soldiers in the public buildings near the Plaza, and other houses vacated by the families who fled at his approach; having stationed his artillery in a manner to command the streets and other avenues leading into the square, for the perfect defence of the capital; having sent the Prefecto of the city to the battle-field with a number of Mexicans to bury their dead; and having set the curate, Ortiz, and the other hostages at liberty, issued the following proclamation to the inhabitants of Chihuahua:

"The commander of the North American forces in Chihuahua, informs the citizens of this State, that he has taken military possession of this capital, and has the satisfaction to assure them that complete tranquillity exists therein.

"He invites all the citizens to return to their houses and continue their ordinary occupations, under the security that their persons, religion and property shall be respected.

"He declares, likewise, in the name of his government, that having taken possession of the capital, after conquering the forces of the State, he has equally taken possession of the State.

"He invites the citizens of all the towns and *ranchos* to continue their traffic, to come to this capital to buy and sell as formerly before the late occurrences, under the assurance they shall in no manner be molested or troubled, and as already said, their property shall be respected; for if the troops under his command shall stand in need of anything, a fair price shall be given for the value thereof with the utmost punctuality.

"He likewise declares, that the American troops will punish with promptitude any excess that may be committed, whether it be by the barbarous Indians or by any other individual.

NOTE 110.—Chihuahua was founded in 1690 or 1691. It was one of the principal cities of Mexico under Spanish rule, and is in the center of a rich mining district. For extensive descriptions of the city and adjacent country, see the writings of Gregg and Kendall.

Lastly, we assure all good citizens, that we carry on war against the armies alone, and not against individual citizens who are unarmed.

"We, therefore, only exact, not that any Mexican shall assist us against his country, but that in the present war he remain neutral; for it cannot be expected, in a contrary event, that we shall respect the rights of those who take up arms against our lives."

Preceding the battle of Sacramento, the American residents and merchants in Chihuahua, of whom there were about 30, received ill-treatment from the Mexican populace. Indignities and insults were offered them. They were mostly kept in custody, and not permitted to pass without the limits of the city. They were tauntingly told that when Col. Doniphan and his handful of men arrived there, they would be handcuffed and delivered over to the populace, to be dealt with as their caprices should suggest, and their humor prompt them. They even exulted in the anticipation of the tortures and cruelties they meant to inflict upon the "*presumptuous, northern invaders.*" To this they often added the epithets, "*Texans, yankees, heretics and pirates.*" When the action commenced the cannonading was distinctly heard in Chihuahua. The tide of battle was known to be raging, but the event was doubtful. When the first cannonading ceased it was announced that the Americans were defeated—that victory had perched on the Mexican flag. The resident Americans now lost all hope. The rabble triumphed, and exulted over them. In a fit of immoderate excitement, the *greasers* seized staves, knives, stones, and whatever else chance had thrown in their way, and threatened to kill them without distinction. But hark! the thunders of the battle are renewed. The merchants' hearts began to revive. The cannon's roar, the vollies of musketry, and the sharp-shooting yagers, are heard until darkness envelopes the earth. At length a courier, "frantic with despair," arrives in the city and exclaims, "*Perdemos! Perdemos!*" we are lost, defeated, ruined. Then the generals, the governor, and the retreating host came, and in hot haste passed on to Parral, and thence to Durango, scarcely halting in the city to take a little refreshment. The star of the northern republic was in the ascendant, and in the pride of their hearts the Americans resident shouted "victory and triumph." Only one American, James Magoffin, a Kentuckian and a naturalized Mexican, was retained a prisoner, and sent to Durango. The rest were liberated.

On the 3d of March, the funeral ceremonies of Major Owens were performed in the Catholic church in Chihuahua, with great pomp. The Mexican priests officiated on the occasion. His corpse was thence conveyed to the cemetery, and interred with masonic and martial honors. On the following day sergeant Kirkpatrick died, and was buried with similar honors. "*Dulce et decorum est pro patria mori.*"

The same day Lieutenant-colonel Mitchell, accompanied by several officers and a file of men, went into the public buildings to take possession of such public property as might be found in the city, for the benefit of the United States' treasury. When he called on Mr. Potts, who claimed to be acting English consul at Chihuahua, he refused to give him the keys of the mint, alleging "that he had a private claim upon the mint, and did not intend to permit the Americans to go into it." Hereupon great excitement prevailed among the soldiers; for upon the consul's refusing admittance into so spacious a building, it was conjectured that the Governor and a body of troops might be concealed therein. About five hundred soldiers ran to their arms and made ready for the emergency. Captain Weightman sent for his section of howitzers to be used as *keys* in entering the building. When their muzzles were turned upon the doors, and the port-fires lighted, the consul, seeing no other alternative, delivered up the keys.

It has been said, with much justice, that the Mexicans both in central and northern Mexico, have an unconquerable propensity for amusements and gambling. Their thieving propensities are equally irrepressible. This remark is more especially intended to apply to the lower classes, among whom there is but little of either modesty, truth, virtue, intelligence, honor, or honesty. They were frequently detected in stealing mules, horses, and other property from the American camp while in Chihuahua, and from Jackson's camp at the Bull-pen* in the suburbs of the city. No argument less potent

* The Bull-pen ranks among the public buildings of Chihuahua, is situated in the suburbs of the city, is built after the manner of an amphitheatre, and is spacious enough to contain five thousand people. It is circular and is furnished with tiers of seats rising one above the other, the top of the structure being flat and sufficiently large to accommodate a vast number of spectators. Here Mexican lancers and gladiators engage in combat with the fiercest wild bulls, goaded to madness and rendered frantic by repeated thrusts of the lance, for the amusement of the people. In such sport do the Mexican people, of both sexes, delight. This institution is a monstrous type of the moral sentiment of the Mexican nation. If, indeed, the morals of the Mexicans generally are ascribable to the established religion of the country, it is then much to be regretted that such a system ever swayed the minds of any people.—HUGHES.

than a teamster's wagon-whip was sufficient to restrain them. They were therefore often scourged for their offences, and that sometimes publicly. This was necessary even to the preserving of tolerable order amongst them.

The people of central Mexico, however, are upon an average much more enlightened, and possess a higher degree of moral honesty than the inhabitants of the more northern provinces, yet their complexion and language are very much the same. The Mexicans generally, both men and women, are exceedingly vivacious; showy and facile, and at the same time shallow in conversation; extremely fond of dress and toys; hospitable when the humor prompts them; yet indolent and addicted to every extreme of vicious indulgence; cowardly, and at the same time cruel; serving rather their appetites, than following the admonitions of conscience; and possessing elastic and accommodating moral principles. Modest, chaste, virtuous, intelligent females are rarely to be met with, yet, notwithstanding they are few, there are some such. Many of the females of that country, are gifted with sprightly minds, possess rare personal beauty, and most gentle and winning grace of manners. Their lustrous, dark, sparkling eyes, and tresses of glossy, black hair, constitutes a fair share of their charms.

Bathing is regarded, in Mexico, as one of the choicest luxurise of fashionable life; to which practice both sexes are much addicted. In Chihuahua there are many bath-houses, and pools of beautiful water, conveniently arranged for public accommodation. These are constantly filled by the young and gay of both sexes, promiscuously splashing and swimming about, with their long black hair spread out on the water, without one thought of modesty.

The city of Chihuahua, and the capital of the State, was built during the Spanish viceroyalty by the Spanish capitalists and nabobs, who were allured thither from the south, by the rich mines of gold and silver in the neighboring mountains. At present it contains twenty-five thousand inhabitants. The streets about the plaza are neatly paved and curbed.

The exterior of the plaza, next the streets, is paved beautifully with white porphyry, in such manner as to form a promenade, furnished with numerous seats carved out of solid masses of the same material, having backs to rest against as a sofa. This promenade was constructed for evening gossip and recreation.

In the center of the plaza mayor stands a square structure of hewn marble, about ten feet high, having four jets supplied by a subterranean aqueduct, which discharges an abundance of cool and delightful water into an octagonal basin, about thirty feet in diameter, and three in depth, constructed also of hewn stone, laid in cement, and bound firmly together by a joint-work of lead, rendering the whole perfectly impervious to water.

The houses in Chihuahua are chiefly constructed of the adobé, cornered and fronted with hewn stone, having flat roofs, and being two stories high. Many of them are in good taste and furnished in a costly manner. The catholic cathedral, a magnificent structure, and other public works in the city, are thus alluded to by Mr. Gregg, upon whose descriptions it were needless to attempt an improvement:

"The most splendid edifice in Chihuahua is the principal church, which is said to equal in architectural grandeur anything of the sort in the republic. The steeples, of which there is one at each front corner, rise over one hundred feet above the azotea. They are composed of very fancifully-carved columns; and in appropriate niches of the frontispiece, which is also an elaborate piece of sculpture, are to be seen a number of statues, as large as life, the whole forming a complete representation of Christ and the twelve apostles. This church was built about a century ago, by contributions levied upon the mines of Santa Eulalia, fifteen miles from the city, which paid over a per centage on all the metal extracted therefrom; a *medio* being levied upon each *marco* of eight ounces. In this way about one million of dollars was raised and expended in some thirty years, the time employed in the construction of the building.

"A little below the *Plaza Mayor* stand the ruins of San Francisco— the mere skeleton of another great church of hewn stone, which was commenced by the Jesuits previous to their expulsion in 1767, but never finished. By the outlines still traceable amid the desolation which reigns around, it would appear that the plan of this edifice was conceived in a spirit of still greater magnificence than the Parroquia which I have been describing. The abounding architectural treasures that are mouldering and ready to tumble to the ground, bear sufficient evidence that the mind that had directed its progress, was at once bold, vigorous, and comprehensive.

"This dilapitated building has since been converted into a sort of state prison, particularly for the incarceration of distinguished prisoners. It was here that the principals of the famous Texan Santa Fé expedition were confined, when they passed through the place, on their way to the city of Mexico. This edifice has also acquired considerable celebrity as having received within its gloomy embraces several of the most distinguished patriots who were taken prisoners during the first infant struggles for Mexican independence. Among these was the illustrious ecclesiastic, Don Miguel Hidalgo, who made the first declaration at the village of Dolores, September 16, 1810. He was taken prisoner in March, 1811, some time after his total defeat at Guadalaxara; and being brought to Chihuahua, he was shot on the 30th of July following, in a little square back of the prison, where a plain white monument of hewn stone has been erected to his memory. It consists of an octagon base of about twenty-five feet in diameter, upon which rises a square unornamented pyramid, to the height of about thirty feet. The monument indeed, is not an unapt emblem of the purity and simplicity of the curate's character.

"Among the few remarkable objects which attract the attention of the traveler, is a row of columns supporting a large number of stupendous arches, which may be seen from the heights, long before approaching the city from the north. This is an aqueduct of considerable magnitude, which conveys water from the little river of Chihuahua, to an eminence above the town, whence it is passed through a succession of pipes to the main public square, where it empties itself into a large stone cistern, and by this method the city is supplied with water. This, and other public works to be met with in Chihuahua, and in the southern cities, are glorious remnants of the prosperous times of the Spanish empire."

The city is supplied with wood and charcoal, brought in from the distant mountains on mules and asses. The wood is lashed on

Mexican Woodman.

the backs of these docile animals by means of raw-hide thongs, while the charcoal is put into sacks, and secured in like manner.

One of these Mexican arrieros, or wood-men, will often enter the city with an atajo of several hundred of these beasts, each burdened with its cargo of fuel.

On the 7th, Colonel Doniphan addressed the following letter to Major Ryland, of Lexington, Missouri:

"DEAR MAJOR:—How often have I again and again determined to send you my hearty curses of every thing Mexican? But, then I knew that you had seen the sterile and miserable country, and its description would be, of course, no novelty to you. To give you, however, a brief outline of our movements, I have to say, that we have marched to Santa Fé, by Bent's Fort; thence through the country of the Navajo Indians to the waters of the Pacific ocean; down the St. Juan river, the Rio Colorado and the Gila, back again to the Rio del Norte; across the Jornada del Muerto to Brazito, where we fought the battle of which you have doubtless seen the account; thence to the town of El Paso del Norte, which was taken by us; thence across two other Jornadas, and fought the battle of the Sacramento, and have sent you herewith, a copy of my official report of the same. We are now in the beautiful city of Chihuahua, and myself in the palace of Governor TRIAS.

"My orders are to report to Gen. Wool; but I now learn, that instead of taking the city of Chihuahua, he is shut up at Saltillo, by Santa Anna. Our position will be ticklish, if Santa Anna should compel Taylor and Wool even to fall back. All Durango, Zacatecas and Chihuahua will be down upon my little army. We are out of the reach of help, and it would be as unsafe to go backward as forward. High spirits and a bold front, is perhaps the best and the safest policy. My men are rough, ragged, and ready, having one more of the R's than General Taylor himself. We have been in service nine months, and my men, after marching two thousand miles, over mountains and deserts, have not received one dollar of their pay, yet they stand it without murmuring. Half rations, hard marches, and no clothes! but they are still game to the last, and curse and praise their country by turns, but fight for her all the time.

"No troops could have behaved more gallantly than ours in the battle of the Sacramento. When we approached the enemy, their numbers and position would have deterred any troops, less brave and determined, from the attack; but as I rode from rank to rank, I could see nothing but the stern resolve to conquer or die—there was no trepidation, and no pale faces. I cannot discriminate between companies or individuals; all have done their duty, and done it nobly."

On the 8th, Dr. Connelly, an American merchant resident in

Chihuahua, was sent by Col. Doniphan to Parral, to hold an interview with Governor Trias, to offer him conditions of peace, and invite him back to the capital. The governor, however, refused to return; but appointed three commissioners to confer with Col. Doniphan, or with such commissioners as he might designate, in regard to concluding an honorable peace. Col. Doniphan's desire was to enter into treaty stipulations with the authorities of Chihuahua, whereby the American merchants, after the payment of legal duties, might be suffered to remain in security, and sell their merchandize, and the State be bound to remain neutral during the continuance of the war. After much delay, all negotiation was suspended between the parties, without coming to any definite agreement on the subject.

On the 14th, Major Campbell,[111] and Forsythe, with thirty-eight

NOTE 111.—Major John P. Campbell was the founder of Springfield, Missouri. He was a man of enterprise and public spirit, and his selection of the site of Springfield to be one of the principal cities of Missouri shows him to have been a man of sound judgment and great foresight.

Mrs. Rush Campbell Owen, the only surviving child of Major Campbell, writes me:

"My father, John Polk Campbell, was born in Mecklenburg county, North Carolina, in 1804. He was the third son of John Campbell, whose ancestors moved to North Carolina from the Wyoming Valley in Pennsylvania, and Matilda Golden Polk, daughter of Ezekiel Polk, that delightful old optimist known as 'Old Zeke Polk, the Tory,' who was brother to old Tam Polk, who declared independence long before anybody else did. Ezekiel Polk was a great-grandson of Robert Pollock (the original form of the name), who abandoned his estate in the barony of Ross, County Donegal, Ireland, and settled on the Eastern Shore in Maryland and gave to America one of its most distinguished families. Ezekiel Polk was captured at the battle of Guilford Court House, and confined on board a prison-ship in Charleston harbor. After many months he, with many others, was given the choice of transportation or taking the oath of allegiance. He took the oath and never violated it. He was the grandfather of James Knox Polk, eleventh President of the United States, whose administration made more history than that of any other President except those of Washington, Lincoln, and McKinley.

"John Campbell, father of John Polk Campbell, was lost during the War of 1812, and his fate remains a mystery to his descendants. His wife was left with ten children, a farm on Carter's creek, Maury county, Tennessee, several slaves, and a debt of one hundred and seventy-six dollars. She often described herself as wild with grief, but the duties of every-day life pressed too heavily upon her to allow inactivity. After long months of uncertainty she called the children together and said: 'This debt must be paid if we have to live on yellow cornmeal mush and buttermilk.' Wages then were twenty-five cents a day, and usually paid in produce. In after years her children laughingly declared they did so live; it has encouraged many of her descendants, in times of sadness and depression, to renewed efforts and ultimate success.

"In the autumn of 1828 John Polk Campbell and his elder brother, E. M. Campbell, visited their grandfather Polk in the Western District of Tennessee, and their Uncle William Polk, of Walnut Bend, Arkansas, father of Olivia Polk, who was the wife of D. D. Berry, one of the first merchants of Springfield, Mo. On this trip to the West they visited Van Buren, Arkansas, and southwestern

men, left Chihuahua, with the view of returning to the United States by way of the Presidio del Rio Grande, and thence across the plains to fort Towson[112] on Red River. Without meeting with any very serious opposition from the Indians, or other cause, this party reached the frontiers of Arkansas in safety, where, separating, they returned to their respective homes.

On the 18th the American troops at Chihuahua received intelligence, through the Mexican papers and by Mexican rumor, of the

---

Missouri, camping on the fine prairie where John P. Campbell afterwards located the town of Springfield. Upon their return home they made immediate preparations to move to the Ozark country of Missouri. The first party consisted of John P. Campbell, his wife, baby daughter, and several slaves, and his friends Joseph Roundtree and Joseph Miller, with their families. They were followed by many families, and John P. Campbell built and vacated successively thirteen log cabins in one year to accommodate his friends. He founded the city of Springfield, giving for a town-site fifty-three acres of land. He engaged in the trade with northern Mexico and with Texas. He spent much of his time on the Plains, which he crossed and recrossed many times. He was employed to lay out a road from the Texas settlements to Chihuahua, and was to receive a grant of land for this service, but it was never given him, although the road was completed. He aided Colonel Doniphan and fought in the battle of Sacramento. He brought home with him several Mexican flags and two beautiful blankets; also a solid silver bell which was given him by a Mexican officer, who was seriously wounded and whom my father saved from being trampled to death on the field of Sacramento. Father reached the Texas frontier in a starving condition after leaving Colonel Doniphan, having been continually pursued and harassed by hostile Indians. He was finally rescued by a Kickapoo Indian whom he had many years before, saved from freezing to death, but who had killed a Delaware Indian and fled to the wild Western tribes. He recognized my father instantly, furnished him and his party with food, and guided them safely to the Texas frontier settlements. In the hardships of this trip he contracted scurvy, from which he never recovered, and from the effects of which he died May 28, 1851.

"My father was a man of enterprise and great self-reliance. At the age of

NOTE 112.—Fort Towson was built on Gates creek, near the northeast corner of the present township six, south, range nineteen, east, in the Choctaw country. It was five or six miles north of Red river, though it was usually spoken of as being on that stream. It was built in 1826, by Colonel Cummings, and named in honor of General Towson. It was established to protect the settlements of Arkansas, Louisiana, and east Texas from the Comanches, Caddoes, and other wild tribes; and it is said they succeeded in burning the fort before 1830, for in that year it was either rebuilt or enlarged by Colonel Derusey. Still further additions were made in 1842. It was constructed of squared pine logs. The names of the officers who commanded there are Colonel Cummings, Colonel Derusey, Colonel Vose, Colonel Veal, Major Andrews, Lieutenant Bacon, for two years; Lieutenant Foot, who was in command at the close of the Mexican War; Captain Marcy, with two companies of infantry; Colonel Abercrombie; Captain Marcy, again; Major Whiting. The fort was abandoned in June, 1854. Dr. Henry Connelly and other merchants of Chihuahua spent the winter of 1839–40 at Fort Towson, and in the spring of 1840 they took a large caravan of wagons loaded with goods from that point to Chihuahua, passing through north Texas. See Gregg's *Commerce of the Prairies*, Vol. II, p. 163.

great battle of Buena Vista or Angostura. The Mexicans represented the issue of the battle as being entirely favorable to themselves, but taking it for granted the American arms were victorious, Col. Doniphan ordered a salute to be fired in honor of Generals Taylor and Wool, and the brave troops under their command.

Col. Doniphan had been ordered by General Kearny to report to Brigadier-general Wool at Chihuahua. Instead of finding General Wool in possession of that capital as anticipated, he now had information that both he and General Taylor were shut up at Saltillo, and hotly beleaguered by Santa Anna, with an overwhelming force. Notwithstanding this *strait of affairs*, Col. Doniphan felt it his duty to report to Gen. Wool, wherever he might be found, and afford him whatever succor might be in his power. Therefore on the 20th he dispatched an express to Saltillo bearing communications to Gen. Wool. Besides a copy of his official report of the battle of Sacramento, was the following dispatch:

---

thirteen he walked from Maury county, Tennessee, to Mecklenburg county, North Carolina, that he might attend school and get some education. He lived some years in the family of General Nathaniel Greene, and attended school. He was a great admirer of General Greene, and caused Greene county, Missouri, to be named in his honor. He was a student as long as he lived. In Missouri in his day, books were scarce and high-priced, but he gathered a quite large library, which was free to his neighbors and which gave many of the citizens of Springfield their first opportunity for general reading in their younger days. After the battle of Wilson Creek most of his books were scattered and lost.

"My father was six feet two inches in height, fair, with light-brown hair that curled, and eyes that were keen and piercing when he was aroused, but usually open and mirthful. He and his brother William were sweet singers, with that remarkable timbre heard rarely in the Cumberland and Ozark mountains, but nowhere else on earth. To hear it once, even, is a joy forever. I have heard them sing—heard the music of their voices drifting over the moonlit prairies—have stood between them with my arms about each as they sang, breathless with ecstacy. My Uncle William's favorite author was Thomas Moore, but my father preferred the writings of Robert Burns to all others.

"John Polk Campbell was married August 28, 1827, near Spring Hill, Maury county, Tennessee, to Louisa Terrell Cheairs, the daughter of a French Huguenot. The Civil War scattered his family. Four sons entered the Confederate army— L. A. Campbell, Colonel Third Missouri; John N. Campbell, Captain in the Thirtieth Mississippi, and Thomas Polk and Samuel in the Third Missouri. I was left a widow at the age of twenty-four, with four children, the eldest six years of age, the youngest a few days old, five hundred miles from my beloved Ozark mountains, all my possessions being twenty dollars in Confederate money. For many months I lived in a lonely farm-house between the Federal and Confederate lines, always treated with courtesy and kindness by both armies. In August, 1864, I returned to Springfield, leaving my children with a kind relative. And right here I want to say that during these dark days I realized to the fullest extent the benefits derived from being kin to all the prominent families south of Mason and Dixon's line. Later, my brother, Colonel L. A. Campbell, joined me. I brought my children home, and we began to pick up the ends of our broken fortune. We went to the old home of my father, the last of many he built in Springfield, consecrated by his presence and by his long, fatal illness."

Head Quarters of the Army in Chihuahua,
City of Chihuahua, March 20, 1847.

SIR: The forces under my command are a portion of the Missouri volunteers, called into service for the purpose of invading New Mexico, under the command of Brigadier-general (then colonel) Kearny. After the conquest of New Mexico, and before General Kearny's departure for California, information was received that another regiment and an extra battalion of Missouri volunteers would follow us to Santa Fé. The services of so large a force being wholly unnecessary in that State, I prevailed on General Kearny to order my regiment to report to you at this city. The order was given on the 23d of September, 1846, but after the general had arrived at La Joya, in the southern part of the State, he issued an order requiring my regiment to make a campaign into the country inhabited by the Navajo Indians, lying between the waters of the Rio del Norte, and the Rio Colorado of the west. This campaign detained me until the 14th of December, before our return to the Del Norte. We immediately commenced our march for El Paso del Norte with about eight hundred riflemen. All communication between Chihuahua and New Mexico was entirely prevented. On the 25th of December, 1846, my van-guard was attacked at Brazito by the Mexican force from this State; our force was about four hundred and fifty, and the force of the enemy, eleven hundred; the engagement lasted about forty minutes, when the enemy fled, leaving sixty-three killed and since dead, one hundred and fifty wounded, and one howitzer, the only piece of artillery in the engagement on either side. On the 27th we entered El Paso without further opposition; from the prisoners and others I learned that you had not marched upon this State. I then determined to order a battery and one hundred artillerists from New Mexico. They arrived in El Paso about the 5th of February, when we took up the line of march for this place. A copy of my official report of the battle of Sacramento, enclosed to you, will show you all our subsequent movements up to our taking military possession of this capital. The day of my arrival, I had determined to send an express to you forthwith; but the whole intermediate country was in the hands of the enemy, and we were cut off, and had been for many months, from all information respecting the American Army. Mexican reports are never to be fully credited; yet, from all we could learn, we did not doubt that you would be forced by overwhelming numbers to abandon Saltillo, and of course we would send no express under such circumstances. On yesterday we received the first even tolerably reliable information, that a battle had been fought near Saltillo between the American and Mexican forces, and that Santa Anna had probably fallen back on San Louis de Potosi.

My position here is exceedingly embarrassing. In the first place, most of the men under my command have been in service since the 1st of June, have never received one cent of pay. Their marches have been hard, especially in the Navajo country, and no forage; so that they are literally without horses, clothes, or money, having nothing but arms and a disposition to use them. They are all volunteers, officers and men, and although ready for any hardships or danger, are wholly unfit to garrison a town or city. "It is confusion worse confounded." Having performed a march of more than two thousand miles, and their term of service rapidly expiring, they are restless to join the army under your command. Still we cannot leave this point safely for some days—the American merchants here oppose it violently, and have several hundred thousand dollars at stake. They have sent me a memorial, and my determination has been made known to them. A copy of both they will send you. Of one thing it is necessary to inform you: the merchants admit that their goods could not be sold here in five years; if they go south they will be as near the markets of Durango and Zacatecas as they now are. I am anxious and willing to protect the merchants as far as practicable; but I protest against remaining here as a mere wagon-guard, to garrison a city with troops wholly unfitted for it, and who will soon be wholly ruined by improper indulgences. Having been originally ordered to this point, you know the wishes of the Government in relation to it, and of course your orders will be promptly and cheerfully obeyed. I fear there is ample use for us with you, and we would greatly prefer joining you before our term of service expires.

All information relative to my previous operations, present condition, &c., will be given you by Mr. J. Collins, the bearer of dispatches. He is a highly honorable gentleman, and was an amateur soldier at Sacramento.

Very respectfully, your obedient servant,

A. W. DONIPHAN,
Colonel 1st Regiment Missouri Cavalry.
Brigadier-General Wool, U. S. Army.

The following letters, written by the author, to a friend in Missouri, will show the progress and adventures of the express-party, from the time of their leaving Chihuahua, on the 20th of March, until their return, on the 23d of April:

HEAD QUARTERS, ARMY OF OCCUPATION,
Saltillo, April 4th, 1847.

MR. MILLER: It has been just one month since I wrote you from the city of Chihuahua. I am now in Saltillo, the capital of the State of Coahuila—the camp of Generals Taylor and Wool, six hundred and seventy-five miles from Col. Doniphan's Army. Briefly and without embellishment, I will relate the story of our adventures before arriving here. The important work of opening a communication between the Army of the West, now in Chihuahua, and the Army of Occupation in and near Saltillo, was entrusted to the hands of the following fourteen men, viz.: J. L. Collins, interpreter and bearer of dispatches, T. Bradford, T. H. Massie, T. Harrison, J. Sanderson, I. Walker, R. D. Walker, S. Asbury, J. Andrews, G. Brown, J. Lewis, J. Moutray, R. W. Fleming, and myself, escort. There never was a more dangerous and arduous undertaking accomplished with better success by the same number of men. Every foot of the route led through the enemy's country and was attended with imminent peril. We left Chihuahua on the 20th of March, and having performed almost the entire march by night, over stupendous mountains clad with horrible *cactus* and the *maguey*, and through vallies of mezquite, we arrived here safely on the 2d of April. We may very properly be styled the NIGHT RIDERS OF MEXICO. We traveled about fifty miles per day by the following route, from Chihuahua to the rancho Bachimbo, thence to San Pablo, thence to Soucillo on the main branch of the river Conchos; here we attempted to diverge to the left, and cross the arid plains by a *traversia* (by-path,) leading to the city of Monclova, but having traveled two days and nights in the deserts and mountains, without one drop of water, and having used our utmost exertions to find the noted watering places, "*Coutero*" and "Agua Chele" unsuccessfully, we were compelled to return to the river Conchos at Soucillo, to avoid perishing of thirst, on the arid plains. Just before returning to the Conchos we thought we would make one more effort to discover water. Messrs. Collins, Massie, Bradford, and myself, ascended a high mountain, and as we thought, beheld a lake of water some five or six miles distant. We were confident we could see the banks of the lake and the green verdure circling the water's edge as well as the waves rolling before the gentle wind. With revived hearts we set out for the refreshing element. We traveled and traveled, but the lake receded. At length we came upon a glassy sand beach, (the bed of a dry lake,) and the water, or mirage appeared behind and around us; we were pursuing a phantom. We were perishing with internal heat and thirst. It was growing dark, and there was no prospect of obtaining water without returning to the river Conchos. Accordingly we turned about and started for the river, and having rode hard all night and until sunrise next morning we arrived at the transparent, cool, refreshing stream. Great God! what a blessing to man hast thou made this one element, and how poorly does he appreciate it until he is cast off upon the desert!

We passed from Soucillo to La Cruz, thence to Santa Rosalia on the Rio Florida. This town contains about five thousand inhabitants. We passed rancho Enramida, rancho Blanco, and Guajuquilla. Three commissioners were sent out to inquire into our business; but having told them we intended to pass peaceably through the country, they permitted us to pass unmolested. This region of the country is majestically barren—there is a grandeur in the very desolation around you. The eternal mountains with the cactus bristling on their sides shut out the horizon, the rising and setting sun, and lift their bald rocky summits high in the azure of heaven. Becoming satisfied that every effort would be made to rob us of our papers and send us as prisoners to Durango, we halted near a gorge in the mountains, and examined and burnt all the letters of our friends and every other paper and letter of introduction, which we had, except Col. Doniphan's official communications to Gen. Wool, and these we sewed up in the pad of one of our saddles. This we did, that nothing might be found in our possession that would betray us as express men, in the event we should fall into the hands of the enemy, which we had great reason to apprehend. We passed the city of Malpimi, in Durango, about midnight. On the 29th we beheld a cloud of dust before us, and saw various companies of animals, which looked very much like companies of cavalry. We at first supposed it was Gen. Martinez, of Durango, returning to Malpimi after the battle of Saltillo. Of course we felt the necessity of avoiding them, and accordingly directed our course towards the mountains. At length we were able to discover that, instead of being cavalry, it was several large atajos of pack-mules on their way from Monterey to Chihuahua, with peloncillo (cake sugar) for sale. About sundown we arrived at San Sebastian, on the Rio Nazas, where we stopped to prepare a little coffee. Don Ignacio Jirmenez, a wealthy and influential citizen of the place, collected about one hundred men together, and notified us that he had orders from the authorities of Durango to stop us and make us prisoners. Collins says "well, what are you going to do about it?" Jirmenez replies "I shall put the order into execution." Collins—"I am going, and you can use your pleasure about stopping us." Jirmenez—"Have you and your men passports." Collins—"Yes, sir, we have." Jirmenez—"Let me see them." Collins, holding his rifle in one hand and revolver in the other—"These are our passports, sir, and we think they are sufficient." This ended the parley. We buckled on our pistols and bowie-knives, shouldered our rifles, and left *sans ceremonie*. We traveled all night and all next day until sunset, and having arrived near the base of a high mountain in the State of Coahuila, we stopped again to take some refreshment, and graze our animals a moment. While taking our coffee this same Ignacio Jirmenez surrounded us, with a band of seventy-five well armed men, and no doubt with the view of first murdering and then plundering us. We quickly formed a line of battle, heavily charged our holsters, revolvers and rifles, and through our interpreter gave him the Spartan reply: "*Here we are, if you want us come and take us!*" After curveting and manœuvering around us near an hour, during which time we gained the base of the mountain, he concluded that we were a stubborn set to deal with, and accordingly took the prudent plan of withdrawing his forces. There was but one sentiment in our little band, and that was to fight until the last man expired. About midnight we arrived at El Pozo, where we purchased corn for our animals and took a little rest, as we had traveled night and day since we left Chihuahua.

Without further difficulty, except the failure of some of our animals, we arrived at the large and beautiful hacienda of Don Manuel Ybarro, near the city of Parras. Manuel was educated in Bardstown, Kentucky, is a friend to the Americans, and received us kindly. He gave us all the information we desired about the American troops and the battle of Buena Vista. After showing us his fine houses, gardens with roses richly blooming, and premises generally, he gave us comfortable quarters during the night, a fresh supply of mules, and a guide through the mountains, in order to expedite our march to Gen. Wool's camp. Ybarro speaks good English, is a full American in feeling, and merits our highest approbation for his disinterested, kind treatment. Without any occurrence of any very remarkable incident we passed, by a very rocky, rugged, mountainous traversia, the haciendas, Castanuella and the Florida, and arrived in Saltillo at sunset on the 2d of April. Our dispatches were forthwith delivered to Gen. Wool, but as Gen. Taylor, who has just gone to Monterey, is in command of this branch of the army, the dispatches were sent to him, early on the morning of the 3d April. Respectfully,

JOHN T. HUGHES.

SALTILLO, April 5th, 1847.

MR. MILLER: This day Mr. Collins and myself, accompanied by Gen. Wool's chief engineer, rode over the great battle-field of BUENA VISTA, where Gen. Taylor with five thousand men, mostly volunteers, measured his strength with Gen. Santa Anna at the head of twenty-two thousand of the best troops Mexico ever sent into the field. Gen. Taylor, for having defeated and almost annihilated the flower of the Mexican army with so slender a force, deserves the gratitude of the American people. Nor do the brave men who fought with him, deserve less.

An awful melancholy creeps over the soul, and deeply stirs the feelings, and opens the fountains of sympathy, as you pass over the ground covered with the mutilated dead, and dyed with the blood of friend and foe. As Santa Anna says in his official report, "The ground is" truly "strewed with the dead, and the blood has flowed in torrents." We stood one moment on the spot where Col. Yell of Arkansas yielded up his life for his country, and then admiringly turned to view the ground still crimsoned by the blood of Col. Hardin of Illinois, and Cols. McKee and Clay of Kentucky. The blood of the gallant dead was still red on the rocks around us. Here the last prayer, and the last throbbings of many a noble heart were hushed in death forever.

The engineer pointed us to the place where the Mexican general had marshaled his hosts with a bristling forest of glittering steel. The costly trappings of the officers and the bright bayonets of the men, glistened in the sheen of the sun. He then showed us where Washington's, Bragg's, Sherman's, and O'Brien's batteries, with thundering roar, mowed down the enemy's advancing columns; and where the chivalrous Kentuckians, the gallant Mississippians, the indomitable Illinoisans, the much abused Indianians, and other equally courageous volunteer troops, dashed into the Mexican lines, opening wide breaches and spreading fearful havoc amongst their successively advancing squadrons. The half-wasted frames of the Mexican soldiers, yet lay profusely scattered over the plateau where the armies of the two republics disputed for supremacy.

Sadly we returned to Gen. Wool's tent from the field of his glorious strife. He conversed freely, and pleasantly communicated to us important information respecting his great battle. He read to us his official account of the action; after which he made this flattering statement in relation to the conduct of the "Army of the West:"— "Missouri has acquitted herself most gloriously. Col. Doniphan has fought the most fortunate battle, and gained the most brilliant victory, which has been achieved during the war. I have every confidence in the bravery and gallantry of the troops under his command. Would to God I had them and their artillery here! Santa Anna might then return to Buena Vista and welcome." Respectfully,

JOHN T. HUGHES.

CHIHUAHUA, April 25th, 1847.

MR. MILLER: On the 9th of April Gen. Taylor's dispatches to Colonel Doniphan, arrived at Saltillo by the hands of Major Howard. Col. Doniphan is ordered to march with his column forthwith to Saltillo, and return to the United States by way of Matamoras and the Gulf. For the safe conveyance of the orders, and the protection of the express-men, Gen. Wool sent Capt. Pike of the Arkansas cavalry with twenty-six men to act as an escort or convoy. We were also accompanied by Mr. Gregg, author of "Commerce on the Prairies," having along a set of astronomical instruments, for taking the latitude and longitude of places. Our party now being increased to forty-two men, and provided with a fresh supply of animals, we left Saltillo on the 9th, and on the same day arrived at Florida, a small town, about forty miles distant. From thence we passed thirty-five miles to Castanuella, where we met with a very hospitable Irish lady who had married a Mexican. Here also we saw a man singularly deformed. His head and body were of the ordinary size for a man; but his arms and legs were about eighteen inches long. His appearance, when he made an attempt to walk, was very singular, for he could scarcely get along, except where the ground was quite level. When mounted on horseback his appearance was still more strange. This man had a wife and children. From thence, passing through the mountains, we came to the princely estate of Don Manuel Ybarro, and again enjoyed his kind hospitalities, and received numerous instances of his disinterested, marked friendship, for which our cordial thanks and grateful acknowledgments are due. Thence in three days we traveled about one hundred and ten miles, and came to Alimeto, having passed El Pozo, San Nicolas, and San Lorenzo. Here we encamped in the plaza, and took possession of two small cannon. This place contains about fifteen hundred inhabitants, and is situated in the valley of the Rio Nazas. The next day we traveled about forty miles, and came to the cañon in the mountains of Mapimi, where we staid for the night. This day it rained copiously. While at this place commissioners came out from Mapimi to inquire if our intentions were pacific; that otherwise we could not be permitted to pass. Captain Pike replied to them:—"We intend to molest nothing. It is the custom of the Americans to respect life and the rights of property. At all hazards, however, we intend to pass on our way." The next morning as we approached Mapimi, two of the deputies came out and entreated Capt. Pike not to pass through the town. Not knowing what forces might be concealed in the place, (for troops had recently been stationed there,) he took their counsel. We therefore proceeded on our way, and that night arrived at Jarilito, a deserted town, after a march of thirty-seven miles. We were now scant of provisions. The following morning we proceeded about nine miles to the Salt Spring, where finding a drove of wild Mexican cattle, we pounced in amongst them with our rifles, and soon had enough of beef to supply a small army. After a few hours rest and a little refreshment we started for the Rio Cerro Gordo, a distance of thirty miles, where we arrived at sunset.

On the morning of the 18th, after a progress of ten miles we came to the Green Springs, near a cañon in the mountains, which the Mexicans dignify with the title of Santa Bernada. Near this stands a deserted rancho. Having nooned and regaled ourselves a little under the shade of the Alamos, we launched out upon the desert or Jornada, seventy-five miles without water. This desert extends to Guajuquilla from Santa Bernada. Having completed about forty-five miles this day, we encamped for the night on the plain, without wood or water. The next day, having traveled about twenty-five miles, and by this time being very thirsty, we overhauled a train of wagons belonging to one Minos, a Mexican, some of which contained oranges and peloncillo from Zacatecas, designed for the markets of Parral and Chihuahua. Eagerly we purchased a supply of of oranges, and sucked the luscious juice from that delicious fruit. Now revived and reinvigorated, we pressed forward to Guajuquilla, a town on the Rio Florida, containing four thousand inhabitants, where we quartered in a spacious corral, well adapted for defence, and stationed out a night guard. These people were not friendly, but they durst not attack us through fear. Here we found several Americans, who had met with a singularly hard fate. They gave me this recital of their misfortunes:—"Twenty-one of us were in the employ of Speyers and Amijo, who traveled under British passports.[113] They promised us protection, but upon our arrival at Chi-

---

NOTE 113.—The following is from *Ruxton's Adventures in Mexico*, pp. 118, 119:

"*October 12, 1846.*—At daybreak this morning I descried three figures, evidently armed and mounted men, descending and advancing towards me. As in this country to meet a living soul on the road is perhaps to meet an enemy thirsting for your property or your life, I stopped my animals, and, uncovering my rifle, rode on to reconnoiter. The strangers also halted on seeing me, and, again moving on when they saw me alone, we advanced, cautiously and prepared, toward each other. As they drew near I at once saw by the heavy rifle which each carried across his saddle-bow that they were from New Mexico, and that one was a white man. He proved to be a German named Spiers, who was on his way to the fair of San Juan with a caravan of nearly forty wagons loaded with merchandise from the United States. He had left the frontier of Missouri in May, crossing the grand prairies to Santa Fé; and, learning that his American teamsters would not be permitted to enter Durango, he had ridden on in advance to obtain permission for their admittance. His wagons had been already nearly six months on the road, traveling the whole time, and were now a few miles behind them. He gave a dismal account of the state of the country through which, I was about to pass. The Comanches were everywhere, and two days before had killed two of his men; and not a soul ventured out of his house in that part of the country. He likewise said it was impossible that I could reach Chihuahua alone, and urged me strongly to return. The runaway Governor of New Mexico, General Armijo, was traveling in company with his caravan, on his way to Mexico, to give an account of his shameful cowardice in surrendering Santa Fé to the Americans without out a show of resistance.

"A little farther on I saw the long line of wagons, like ships at sea, crossing a plain before me. They were all drawn by teams of eight fine mules, and under the charge and escort of some thirty strapping young Missourians, each with a long, heavy rifle across his saddle. I stopped and had a long chat with Armijo, who, a mountain of fat, rolled out of his American dearborn, and inquired the price of cotton goods in Durango, he having some seven wagon-loads with him; and also what they said in Mexico of the doings in Santa Fé, alluding to its capture by the Americans without any resistance. I told him that there was but one opinion respecting it expressed all over the country—that General Armijo and the New-Mexicans were a pack of arrant cowards; to which he answered, 'Adois! They

huahua we were all made prisoners, and under strict guards conducted in the direction of the city of Mexico. On arriving at the little town of Zarcas we effected our escape by night, and attempted to penetrate into Texas by way of Mapimi, Laguna del Tagualila, and thence to the Rio Grande. Having traveled for fourteen days in the arid deserts between Mapimi and the Rio Grande, mostly without water or provision, eleven of our number perished miserably of thirst and fatigue, and the other ten, changing their course and subsisting upon the flesh of the only remaining horse we had, finally succeeded in reaching Guajuquilla." We took one of the survivors to Chihuahua; the others remained, having no means of traveling.

Thence passing Enramada, Santa Rosalia, and San Pablo, we arrived at Bachimbo, thirty-six miles from Chihuahua, on the 22d, and making an early start the next morning, we hastened forward to rejoin our companions in the capital. When we had approached within about five miles of the city, we beheld at a distance a great cloud of dust rising in front of us. We could not at first conceive the purport of all this. In a few moments, however, a body of horsemen were seen in the distance, making towards us with great haste. We were now impressed with the belief that it was either a body of Mexican guerrilleros endeavoring to cut us off from any communication with the army, or Colonel Doniphan's picket guard, who, mistaking us for a party of Mexicans, had dashed out in the hopes of a skirmish. At first Captain Pike halted the little column to make an observation. But we were soon very pleasantly undeceived; for, the body of horsemen turned out to be a company of our friends, who hearing of our approach, had come to greet us and offer us a new relay of horses. Colonel Doniphan had thrice been solemnly assured that the express party were all either killed or made prisoners and sent to Durango to undergo the most cruel tortures, and had accordingly issued orders to his troops to evacuate the capital on the 25th, and return to the United States by way of the Presidio del Rio Grande and San Antonio in Texas. We now

don't know that I had but seventy-five men to fight three thousand. What could I do?' Twenty-one of the teamsters belonging to this caravan had left it a few days previously, with the intention of returning to the United States, by way of Texas."

The twenty-one teamsters mentioned by Ruxton were those met by this detachment returning with that of Colonel Doniphan to Chihuahua. It would seem that Spiers and Armijo must have had a common interest in the cargo taken from Independence by Spiers in the spring of 1846, and which General Kearny tried to overhaul. The goods in the wagons met by Ruxton were a portion of those so carried out. Dr. Wislizenus was with Spiers much of the way from Independence to Chihuahua, and his work has much mention of him. Spiers lived in Denver, Colorado, for a time after the Civil War.

entered Chihuahua amidst the deafening peals of the great church bells, the firing of artillery, and the cordial welcomes and heartfelt congratulations of friends, who pressed around to shake us by the hands and inquire what were the ORDERS from Generals Taylor and Wool. Colonel Doniphan, having unsealed the dispatches, announced to his soldiers that he was required TO MARCH FORTHWITH TO SALTILLO, where he would receive further orders.

Respectfully,

JOHN T. HUGHES.

CHAPTER XX.

Departure of the Army for Saltillo—Mexican girls—The Merchants—Arrival at Santa Rosalia—Mitchell's Advance—Guajuquilla—The Jornada—Palayo and Mapimi—Death of Lieutenant Jackson—San Sebastian and San Lorenzo—Mrs. Magoffin—Battle of El Pozo—Don Manuel Ybarro—Parras—Review of the Army by Gen. Wool—Reception by Gen. Taylor.

It was Col. Doniphan's intention, when he dispatched the express to Saltillo, to move his forces to San Pablo, in the valley of the Conchos, or to Santa Rosalia, according as he might find forage, leaving only such a garrison in Chihuahua as would be sufficient to afford protection to the American merchants.

Conformably to this design, on the 5th of April, the 2d battalion, under Major Gilpin, and the battalion of artillery, under Major Clark, (which now consisted of two companies commanded by Weightman and Hudson, the latter having charge of the Mexican pieces,) were ordered to proceed to San Pablo. The 1st battalion, under Lieutenant-colonel Jackson, was soon to succeed them. On the 9th, however, Col. Doniphan, while at San Pablo, received a communication from Hicks, an American at Parral, advising him that a strong Mexican force was on the march from Durango to Chihuahua, to recover the capital, and sieze the goods of the American merchants. Col. Doniphan, not suspecting but such a project was in contemplation, from the rumors and statements which had come to him, determined to return and hold possession of the capital, until he should hear from Gen. Wool. Jackson's battalion did not leave the city.[114]

NOTE 114.—This matter is described by Hubert Howe Bancroft in his *Chronicles of the Builders of the Commonwealth*, p. 537, as follows:

"The average age of the army was 22 years, and there was a difference of sentiment among the men, the younger ones wishing to push on into the Mexican country, and the others desiring to return. Gilpin's idea was this: That as they had possession of that magnificent city, and as the mint contained about $800,000, they should confiscate that money, as they had a right to do, as spoils of war. Up to this time the army had not received any pay or recognition of their valor from home. Finally Doniphan agreed to call a court-martial and submit the question as to whether the army should retrace its steps, or push on to conquer the whole Mexican country. Thus far, besides doing their own work, they had done that which had been allotted to General Wool. Doniphan picked the members of the court-martial, such as would favor his views, as nearly as he was able; but Gilpin had all the young men on his side. The question was put, and it was decided to push on to the city of Mexico. They then made a three days' march in that direction, Doniphan accompanying them, although protesting at every step,

Meanwhile the American merchants had established themselves on the most active and busy streets of the city, and were using every exertion to effect sales of their immense merchandize; for, as yet, it was uncertain what the orders of Gen. Wool to Col. Doniphan would be, and to what extent their interests might be affected. Many of them had embarked largely in the trade, and it was essential to dispose of their goods mainly before the army, (which had for months acted as a guard and convoy to their trains,) should receive orders to evacuate the place. Business soon became moderately

and offering to resign his command to Gilpin and return home. The third day they halted at San Felipe. Doniphan had left two companies at Chihuahua to guard the city; also a number of the merchants who wished to sell out their goods. At San Felipe, on the following morning, when they were expecting to pursue their way, and while Gilpin was waiting for the order of march from Doniphan, to his surprise no such order came. What still more astonished him was to see Doniphan and several of his friends mount and take the back trail to Chihuahua. One of Doniphan's men came up presently and said that the orders were that the whole army should return to Chihuahua; that the country was full of hostile bands, and that the soldiers left at Chihuahua would be massacred, and that he would not expose them in such a manner; so the whole army turned back. Arriving at Chihuahua there was another discussion as to whether the army should return home or not, and Gilpin succeeded in preventing this. Doniphan finally agreed to compromise the matter, the Gilpin party agreeing not to resume the march to Mexico, and Doniphan not to return to Missouri."

See *Memoir of a Tour to Northern Mexico*, by A. Wislizenus, M. D., p. 61, for a discussion of this matter, the following quotations being made therefrom:

"Having conquered Chihuahua, and not finding General Wool there, an express was sent from here to his camp near Saltillo to ask further orders. John Collins, Esq., of Boonville, Missouri, a trader, who had volunteered in the battle of Sacramento, undertook the dangerous excursion with only 12 men. The regiment was stationed in the meanwhile in Chihuahua, and indulged in the luxuries of the town. Towards the end of March the first news of the battle of Buena Vista was received. Although Santa Anna claimed, in his official report that reached Chihuahua, a victory on his part, the Americans were too well versed in translation of Mexican reports not to consider themselves privileged to fire a salute on the plaza in honor of *our* victory.

"Most men of the regiment got at last tired of the inactive life in Chihuahua, and in a council of war an expedition to the southern part of the State was agreed upon. Some negotiations with the old Mexican authorities of Chihuahua, who had fled in this direction, failed to produce any result; they kept up, on the contrary, a shadow of Mexican government in the south of the State, at Parral. A march of the American troops there would have broken up that government at once, and being nearer to the seat of war, the regiment might, according to circumstances, have either thrown itself upon the State of Durango·or marched towards Saltillo.

"On April 5, 1847, 600 men, with 14 cannon, left Chihuahua for that purpose, while about 300 men, with some pieces of artillery, were left behind for the safekeeping of the city. As there was at that time a want of surgeons in the regiment, an appointment to that effect was offered to me, which I accepted. I left Chihuahua with the troops, moving towards the south.

"Passing through Mapula and Bachimba, we reached within three days San Pablo, 50 miles southeast of Chihuahua. Here we were met by an express, sent from Americans below, and reporting that a large Mexican force was approaching from the south to reconquer Chihuahua, that the Mexican govern-

brisk, and the majority of them were successful in disposing of their heavy stocks. The aggregate amount of the importation for the year, could not have been less than ONE MILLION AND A HALF OF DOLLARS, at the Chihuahua prices.

"For fifty-nine days," observes an intelligent volunteer, "we held full and undisturbed possession of the city, keeping up strict discipline with a constant guard, consisting of a camp and picket guard and a patrol during the whole night, visiting every part of the city. Various rumors were afloat of the intended march of the ment had fled at the first news of our march, and that General Taylor had lef- Saltillo, etc. Upon these reports Colonel Doniphan resolved to return to Chihuahua, and defend that place at all hazards. With some reluctance the troops returned; the chivalric sons of Missouri relied so much upon their own bravery and good fortune, that they disliked every retrograde movement, although policy might command it. Two days afterwards we entered Chihuahua again, to the astonishment of friend and foe. Many Mexican families that had stayed in town left it now, from fear of a new battle. But, for two weeks we waited in vain for the large army from the south, till we became convinced at last that it was but a hoax—invented, in Chihuahua, by some persons whose interest it was to keep the troops there as long as possible. As the prospects of a battle diminished, the regiment, whose term of service came near expiring, and which during the campaign had received glory enough, but neither pay nor clothes, became every day more anxious to return to the United States, and a day was at last fixed for the final departure of the whole regiment, if the express sent to General Wool should not return up to that time. Our route in that case would have been by Presidio del Norte and the Red river, to Fort Towson. But in due time Mr. Collins made his appearance. In about thirty days he had traveled, with a mere handful of men, about 1000 miles through a hostile country, with no other passports but their rifles. In going out, his party consisted of but 12 men; on his return it was increased to about 40. The gallant Squire was received in Chihuahua with enthusiastic joy. He brought us definite orders from General Wool to march at once, and on the most direct road to Saltillo. Within two days our troops were on the march. Colonel Doniphan, before he left, called on the Mexican authorities of the place and made them promise to treat the American residents of Chihuahua in a decent manner, and threatened them, in case of disorder, with a return of the American troops and a severe chastisement. The Mexicans promised everything. Many American and other foreign residents, however, had so little confidence in Mexican faith that they preferred to accompany the army."

Edwards, in his *A Campaign in New Mexico with Colonel Doniphan*, p. 90, has an account of this matter, as follows:

"While we were in this city, a council of war was called. We had expected to have here met and joined General Wool; however, we had done our work without him; but what course were we now to take?—for there was danger at all points! A few of the officers proposed staying in Chihuahua, others were for trying to join General Taylor, and some suggested a retrograde march to Santa Fé; most, however, were in favor of pressing home by way of Monterey. No ultimate decision was at that time had; but a short time afterwards another council was held, and at this time most of the officers were for remaining in quarters. Doniphan heard them for some time, but with impatience, and at last, bringing his heavy fist down on the table, he gave the board to understand that they might possibly have found *fair* reasons for staying, 'but, gentlemen,' added the Colonel, '*I'm for going home to Sarah and the children.*' The reader may be assured that we caught up these words, and often afterwards spoke of 'going home to Sarah and the children.'"

enemy, to attack us, and sometimes report said, that several thousand were on the road; but it is certain, that if we had remained in the place until this day, they never would have approached it, with any force, less than eight or ten thousand; and, having the advantage of the houses and walls, a less number never could have driven us from the city. The rights of the citizens there, as in every other place, were duly respected; and their conduct since our departure up to the latest accounts shows, that this treatment was not lost upon them; for several traders who remained there, have been well treated and their rights duly regarded."

Every preparation having been completed by the indefatigable exertions of the quartermaster, and officers of subsistence, which was necessary for the long and arduous march to Saltillo, a distance of 675 miles through an arid and desolate country, the battalion of artillery commenced the march on the 25th of April, and was succeeded on the following day by the first battalion. These were to await the rear, and the merchant and baggage trains, at Santa Rosalia, one hundred and twenty miles from Chihuahua.

On the morning of the 28th, a scene of the most busy and animating nature ensued. The Americans were actively engaged in hastening preparations for their departure. 'The Mexicans, with their serapes thrown around them, were standing at the corners of the streets in groups, speculating as to the future. The long trains of baggage and provision wagons were stretching out towards the south. Part of the merchant trains were moving off in the direction of New Mexico, taking with them little, however, except their specie, or bullion. The 2nd battalion, with colors thrown to the breeze, was anxiously awaiting the order to march.

Certain of the fair Mexican girls, who had conceived an unconquerable attachment for some favorite paramour of the Anglo-Saxon race, with "blue eyes and fair hair," dressed in the habit of Mexican youths, were gaily dashing through the streets on their curvetting steeds. They accompanied their lovers on the march to Saltillo, and bivouacked with them on the deserts.[115]

NOTE 115.—Human nature is ever the same. At El Paso there were a number of instances of this kind; and it was said that the attachment was so strong that three or four men returned there after their discharge, and remained permanently The females who followed the army from Chihuahua wore male attire. Colonel

About ten o'clock, Col. Doniphan, having delivered over to the city authorities the Mexican prisoners, captured at Sacramento, to be disposed of by them as deemed advisable for the public good, quietly evacuated the capital, leaving the government in the hands of its former rulers. About ten American merchants remained, and trusted their lives to the "magnanimous Mexican people." These were chiefly such men as had great knowledge of the Mexican customs and language, and had taken the oath of allegiance to that government. The magnificent, architectural beauty of the city was left wholly unimpaired, and the property of the citizens uninjured.

Two days after Col. Doniphan's departure from Chihuahua, the American merchants, who remained, entered into a treaty stipulation with the city authorities, whereby they agreed to pay the legal rates of duty upon their entire importation of goods, both sold and unsold. They were to be amply protected in their rights and liberty. The conditions of this treaty have been fully complied with by the Mexicans, except in one single instance. On the 23d of June, a band of ruffians violently entered the store-room of JAMES AULL,[116] of Lexington, (Mo.), and having brutally assassinated him, plundered the house of five thousand dollars. The assassins were subsequently apprehended, and thrown into prison, but we have not learned that they received the punishment due to their crimes. The other company of merchants returned to Santa Fé by way of Coralitus, and Ojo Vacca, leaving El Paso to the east. Thence they returned to Independence, where they arrived in the month of July.

Col. Doniphan, by unparalleled marches, overtook the advance at Santa Rosalia, on the 1st of May, having in four days passed Bachimbo, Santa Cruz, Soucillo, and completed one hundred and twenty miles. Santa Rosalia contains about five thousand inhabitants, and is situated at the junction of the Conchos and Florida rivers. Here

---

Doniphan sent them back when his attention was called to their presence. One, named Ramona, followed Lieutenant Gordon several days. It was to these numerous attachments that Colonel Doniphan referred in the council when he said some of the officers might have found "fair" reasons for wishing to remain at Chihuahua.

NOTE 116.—James Aull was the partner of Major Samuel C. Owens, killed at the battle of Sacramento. The style of the firm was Owens & Aull. See p. 48, Report No. 458, to accompany bill H. R. No. 388, House of Representatives, Thirtieth Congress.

the Mexican forces under General Heridia had thrown up a line of fortifications, entirely surrounding the city, except where the rivers and the bluffs were impassable, strengthened by an almost impregnable fortress. On the outside of the embankments were intrenchments, impassable by cavalry. These embankments were also strengthened by numerous bastions, in which cannon were to be employed.

Some assert that these fortifications were thrown up to defend the place against the approach of Gen. Wool, who was expected to pass that way on his march upon Chihuahua. Others aver that it was the intention of the Mexicans, if defeated at Sacramento, to remove the public archives, and all their munitions of war, into this strong hold, and there make a desperate stand; but that losing all their cannon and means of defence in the action of the 28th, they abandoned their purpose. It is true, however, that extensive preparations had been made to defend the city against an invading army.

On the 2nd Lieutenant-colonel Mitchell, a detachment of twenty-six men, under Capt. Pike, of the Arkansas cavalry, and seventy men, under Capt. Reid, left the main body of the army, and proceeded in advance to Parras, a distance of near five hundred miles. The movements of the main column, however, were so rapid that the pioneer party, in case of any sudden emergency, could have fallen back upon it for support. The object of the reconnoitering party was to obtain the earliest information of either a covert or open enemy, who might meditate an attack upon the trains, or seize upon some favorable moment to surprise the army; and also to procure at Parras such supplies as might be necessary for the use of the men and animals.

After a hasty march of sixty miles in two days we came to Guajuquilla, on the Rio Florida, containing an industrious and agricultural population, where we obtained an abundance of forage. Here, also, the soldiers purchased chickens, pigs, cheese, eggs, bread, wine, and a variety of vegetables.

At this place there are a great number of beautiful canals, which convey the most lovely and delightful streams of water through the whole town and neighboring fields and gardens. This valley, if properly cultivated, would yield a support for a dense population. The soil is fertile, and the nature of the ground is such that it is susceptible of complete irrigation.

Early the next day the commander moved his forces up the river about six miles, to the Hacienda Dolores. Here he allowed them a short respite, ordered them to prepare provisions, and fill their canteens with water, before commencing the march over the desert, upon which they were now to enter. This desert is seventy-five miles over, extending to the Santa Bernada spring, and the road is terrible by reason of the dust. The troops having taken a few hours rest, and a little refreshment, launched out in long files upon the jornada, followed by all the baggage, provision, and merchant trains, a great cloud of dust hanging heavily and gloomily along the line of march.[117]

After sunset a sullen, lowering cloud arose in the south-west, heavily charged with electric fluid, and with frequent flashes of lightning, and hoarse, distant thunder, swept majestically over the rocky summits of the detached mountains, which everywhere traverse the elevated plains of Mexico. Heavy, gloomy, pitchy darkness enveloped the earth. The road could only be seen, when revealed by a sudden flash of lightning. The pennons continued to stream and flutter in the wild gales of the desert. These, together with the rising column of dust, served as guides to the soldiers in the rear. The artillery rumbled over the rocks, and the fire sparkled beneath the wheels. At length heavy sleep and fatigue oppressed many; but the NIGHT MARCH ON THE DESERT was still continued. It were folly to halt, for no water could be obtained. The soldiers were greatly wearied; some of them almost fell from their horses. Some dropped their arms, and were necessitated to search after them, while the rest marched by, wagged their heads, and made sport and laughter. Some straggled off and lay down upon the desert, overpowered by sleep. Some, gifted with a richer fund of wit, a finer flow of spirits, a nobler store of mental treasure, and more physical endurance, sang Yankee Doodle, love songs, and related stories to the groups that gathered round, as it were, to extract one spark of life to aid them on the march. About midnight a halt was ordered. The tired and sleepy soldiers tethered their animals, and lay down in the dark pro-

NOTE 117.—The route of the march from Chihuahua to the Rio Grande is laid down on one of the maps accompanying the work of Dr. Wislizenus, hereinbefore referred to, which contains also a journal of the march. Journals of the march may be found also in the works of Richardson and Edwards, both quoted from in this work.

miscuously, on the desert, wherever they chanced to find a smooth spot of earth. They took no supper that night.

There are a great many lizards in Chihuahua and Durango, and it appeared as if this desert was their headquarters; for they crept into the men's blankets, and bedding, and annoyed them greatly while sleeping. Suddenly aroused from slumber by these slimy companions, the soldiers would sometimes shake their blankets, toss the scorpions and lizards, and alacrans, upon their sleeping neighbors, exclaiming angrily, "d—n the scorpion family." The others, half overpowered by sleep, would sullenly articulate, "don't throw your d—n-d lizards here." Thus they lay, more anxious to obtain a little slumber than to escape a swarm of these repulsive reptiles.

The march was commenced early the next morning. The dust was absolutely intolerable. The soldiers could not march in lines. They were now already become thirsty, and it was yet forty miles to water. The dust filled their mouths, and nostrils, and eyes, and covered them completely. They were much distressed during the whole day. Many of them became faint, and their tongues swollen. The horses, and often the stubborn, refractory mules, would fail in the sand, and neither the spur nor the point of the sabre were sufficient to stimulate them. Sometimes the volunteer, boiling with ire, would dismount and attempt to drag the sullen mule along by the lariat. How

"D—mn a mule, any how."

The soldier pulling the mule is Judge James Peacock, of Independence, Missouri. The incident occurred on the march from Chihuahua to Saltillo. Judge Peacock was a private in Company B, First Missouri Mounted Volunteers Mexican War. Born in Madison County, Kentucky, August 5, 1824. Crossed the Plains to California in 1850. Has been Judge in Independence, Missouri, for many years.

earnestly he then desired once more to be in the land of gushing fountains, verdant groves, rail roads, steam boats and telegraphic wires!

The teamsters, and those with the artillery, and the animals, suffered extremely. But they endured it all with patience. After suffering every hardship, privation and distress by marching, which men must necessarily experience in passing such a desert, they arrived at the spring, Santa Bernada, at sunset. Here there is a grove of willows and alamos. These afforded a pleasant shade. There is also at this place a copious, gushing spring, which furnished an abundance of water for the men and the animals. This spot, with its groves and springs, disrobed of all poetry, proved in reality to be an oasis, a smiling, inviting retreat in a desert, desolate, treeless waste of sand, rocks and naked mountains. Here the soldiers took rest and repose.[118]

On the 6th of May the army advanced into the State of Durango, to the Cerro Gordo. This river terminates in Laguna de Xacco. The following day we arrived at the out post, Palayo, where our advance had the previous day taken some horses and a few Mexican soldiers. This small military station is about one league from the town of Jarilito, which is now entirely deserted on account of the depredations and incursions of the Comanches. Since 1835 the Indians have encroached upon the frontiers of Mexico and laid waste many flourishing settlements, waging a predatory warfare, and leading women and children into captivity. In fact the whole of Mexico is a FRONTIER. An elevated Table Plain extends from the gulf of Mexico to the foot of the Cordilleras, intersected by innumerable ranges of mountains, and clustering, isolated and conical-shaped peaks, invariably infested by bands of savages, and still fiercer Mexican banditti. No effort of the Mexican government has been able to suppress and oust these ruthless invaders of the country.

NOTE 118.—It was at this camp that the incident occurred which was made the subject of the illustration, " D—n a mule, anyhow." Hughes was walking about camp the next morning, and saw the incident. James Peacock, of Company A, had picketed his mule on a small island in the lagoon made by the spring, where the grass was high and fine. He was on the island to get his mule to prepare for the march, when Hughes strolled by. The mule was not ready to quit so good a pasture so soon after his long fast on the deserts. As Peacock jumped to clear the channel the mule set back with all feet braced forward, and, as Peacock had hold of the halter and had not noticed the action of the mule, his leap was interfered with, and he landed in water and mud up to his knees. Then, as he strained on the halter to pull the mule off the island, he gave expression to his feelings in the language put below the picture.

At Palayo some of the men killed a few beeves, pigs and chickens belonging to the Mexicans, and feasted upon them at night. There was much to palliate this offence. The regiment had been marched at the rate of 35 or 40 miles per day, over a dusty, desert country, almost entirely destitute of water. Most of the men had not had a pound of meat for the last three days. Besides the exigency of the case, the State of Durango was at that very moment in arms against us. Would the most scrupulously moral man in Missouri denounce his son as a thief and a robber, because, after traveling more than 3,000 miles by land, and háving spent the last cent of his slender resources for bread, coldly neglected by his government, he found it necessary to kill an ox or a pig to satisfy hunger, or should think proper to mount himself on a Mexican horse, in a country which the prowess of his own arm had been instrumental in subduing? It is one thing for the philosopher to sit in his studio and spin out his finely drawn metaphysical doctrines, and another, and entirely different thing, to put them in practice under every adverse circumstance. What is most beautiful in THEORY is not always WISEST IN PRACTICE.

On the 8th the command reached the Hacienda Cadenas, 24 miles from Palayo. Here we obtained the first information of Gen. Scott's great victory at Cerro Gordo. At such welcome tidings a thrilling sensation of joy pervaded our camp. Here we took possession of another piece of cannon, which, although well mounted, Col. Doniphan restored to the inhabitants. On the 9th, a march of 22 miles brought us to the city of Mapimi, which had steadily manifested the greatest hostility to the Americans. This is a mining town. It has five furnaces for smelting silver ore, and one for smelting lead ore. It is one of the richest towns in the State, excepting the capital. The Mexican forces, 3,000 strong, fled from Mapimi and Durango upon our approach, and left the state completely in our power, had Gen. Wool but permitted us to visit the capital. Gen. Heredia, and Governor Ochoa of Durango, wrote to Santa Anna to send them 20 pieces of cannon and 5,000 regular troops, or the State of Durango would immediately fall into the hands of Col. Doniphan's regiment, if he saw proper to direct his march against it. Upon our arrival at Mapimi we obtained more certain intelligence of the victory of the American forces over the Mexicans at Cerro Gordo, in honor of which a national salute of 28 guns was fired by Weightman's battery. Here also a copy of Gov. Ochoa's proclamation was found, in which he earnestly exhorted the inhabitants of Durango never to cease warring until they had repelled the "North American invaders" from the soil of Mexico.

This day's march had been excessively hot and suffocating, and extremely severe upon the sick. Just before reaching Mapimi, 2d Lieutenant Stephen Jackson, of Howard, died of an inveterate attack of typhoid fever. Lieutenant Jackson was taken ill in the Navajo country, and had never entirely recovered. He was not at the battle of Brazito, being at that time sick in Soccorro; but he afterwards fought with great bravery in the more important action at Sacramento. His corpse was interred (on Sunday the 9th) with appropriate military honors. Also, the priest of Mapimi in his robes, with the Bible in his hands, and three boys dressed in white pelisses, two of them bearing torches, and the third in the centre with a crucifix reared upon a staff, preceded the bier first to the catholic church and then to the grave, at both of which places the catholic ceremonies were performed.

On the 10th we made a powerful march of near forty miles to San Sebastian on the Rio Nazas. The heat and dust were almost insufferable. Don Ignacio Jermanez, who attempted to capture the Express-men, fled to the city of Durango. The army foraged upon him for the night, with the promise to pay him in powder and ball at sight. The Rio Nazas is a beautiful stream, full of fish, and empties into the three lakes, Tagualila, Las Abas, and Del Alamo. During this fatiguing march, two men, King and Ferguson, died of sickness, heat and suffocation. They were buried at San Sebastian.

On the 11th the command marched to San Lorenzo, a distance of thirty-five miles, along a heavy, dusty road, hedged in by an immense and almost impervious chaparral. The heat was absolutely oppressive—water scarce. In this thick chaparral, Canales, with a band of about four hundred robbers, had concealed himself with the view of cutting off stragglers from our army and committing depredations upon our merchant and provision trains. But our method of marching with the artillery and one battalion in front, and the other battalion in rear of the trains and droves of mules, anticipated his pre-meditated attack. After our arrival in San Lorenzo, a Mexican courier came to the colonel with news that Canales had made an attack upon Magoffin's train of wagons, and that Magoffin and his lady were likely to fall into his hands. A detachment of sixty men under Lieut. Gordon was quickly sent to his relief. They anticipated Canales' movement. This little village, San Lorenzo, has an over portion of inhabitants. Every house and hut was crowded with men, boys, women and children. Almost every woman, old and young, had a child in her arms, and some of them more than one. Whether this superabundance of population is the legitimate effect of the salubrious climate, or is produced by some other circumstances, is left for the reader to consider. The march to-day was distressingly hot and dusty. A Mr. Mount, of the company from Jackson county, straggled off in the chaparral, and has never since been heard of:—he was doubtless murdered and then robbed by lurking Mexicans.

On the 12th, early in the morning, the front guard charged upon and took three Mexicans prisoners; they were armed and lurking in the mezquite chaparral near the road, and were doubtless spies sent out by Canales to obtain information of our movements, but no positive proof appearing against them they were released. As our animals were much worn down by the previous day's march, and it being impossible to procure forage for them, we only marched fifteen miles to-day to the little rancho, San Juan, on a BRAZO or arm of the Rio Nazas. Here both man and horse fared badly. As our next day's march was to be over a desert region of near forty miles without a drop of water, or even a mouthful of food for our famishing animals; and also as the water had to be raised from a well into pools and vats at El Pozo where the army was to encamp on the night of the 13th, Lieut. Pope Gordon and fifteen or twenty men were sent at midnight, in advance to draw water for the use of the army. The author went along as their guide, having traveled the same route on express to Saltillo. At 9 A. M. Lieut. Gordon and his advance arrived at El Pozo, where we found Captain Reid, with fourteen men. Captain Reid, as elsewhere observed, had accompanied Lieutenant-colonel Mitchell on his way to Saltillo, with a detachment of seventy or eighty men. Upon their arrival at Parras (a city where Gen. Wool had taken up his headquarters before he formed a junction with Gen. Taylor, and which had been very friendly to the Americans, in the way of furnishing supplies and taking care of Gen. Wool's sick men) they found the inhabitants in much distress. A band of Comanches had just made a descent from the mountains upon the city, and killed eight or ten of the citizens, carried off nineteen girls and boys into captivity, and driven off three hundred mules and two hundred horses. Besides this, they had robbed houses of money, blankets, and the sacred household gods. They besought Capt. Reid to interfere in their behalf; that although they were considered enemies to the Americans, it did not become the magnanimity of the Americans soldiers to see them robbed and murdered by a lawless band of savages, the avowed enemies both of the Mexicans and Americans. Captain Reid undertook to recover the innocent captives and chastise the brutal savages. This is the occasion of Capt. Reid's being at El Pozo on the morning of the 13th. Just as Lieutenant Gordon and Capt. Reid joined their forces, the Indians, about sixty-five in number, made their appearance, advancing upon the hacienda from a CAÑON or pass in the mountains towards the south. They had all their spoils and captives with them. Their intention was to water their stock at El Poso, and augment the number of their prisoners and animals. Thus boldly do the Indians invade this country. Captain Reid concealed his men (about thirty-five in number) in the hacienda, and sent out Don Manuel Ybarro, a Mexican, and three or four of his servants, to decoy the Indians to the hacienda. The feint succeeded. When the Indians came within half a mile the order was given to charge upon them, which was gallantly and promptly done. Capt. Reid, Lieuts. Gordon, Winston and Sproule, were the officers present in this engagement, all of whom behaved very gallantly. The Indians fought with desperation for their rich spoils. Many instances of individual prowess and daring were exhibited by Capt. Reid and his men, too numerous, indeed, to recount in detail; the captain himself, in a daring charge upon the savages, received two severe wounds, one in the face and the other in the shoulder. These wounds were both produced by steel pointed arrows. The engagement lasted not less than two hours, and was kept up hotly until the Indians made good their retreat to the mountains. In this skirmish we lost none. The Indians lost seventeen killed on the field, and not less than twenty-five badly wounded, among the former was the Chief or Sachem. We recovered in this battle, all the animals and spoils which the

Indians had taken from the Mexicans, and restored the captive boys and girls to their friends and relatives.[119]

Let those whose moral scruples induce them to doubt the propriety of Captain Reid's brilliant sortie upon the Indians, consider, that the Comanches have rarely failed to murder and torture in the most cruel manner, without discrimination, all Americans who have unfortunately fallen into their hands. The Comanches are our uncompromising enemies. Read the brutal treatment Mrs. Horn and others received from them, and you can but justify Capt. Reid's conduct. In truth he deserves the gratitude of both Mexicans and Americans, for the chastisement he visited upon the heads of these barbarous wretches. The people of Parras expressed their gratitude

NOTE 119.—Manuel X. Harmony was a native of Spain, living and doing business in New York city at the time of the declaration of war between the United States and Mexico. He was engaged in the trade with northern Mexico over the Santa Fé Trail, and in the spring of 1846 he left Independence, Mo., with the other traders, and was stopped at Pawnee Fork by Captain Moore. He had goods to the amount of $38,739 and an outfit valued at $10,000. By direction of General Kearny and Colonel Doniphan he was detained with the other traders, and entered the city of Chihuahua with the American army. He was one of the traders who believed it unsafe to remain at Chihuahua after the army should depart, and so went with the Americans to join General Taylor. He believed himself damaged by the action of the American officers, and filed a claim in Congress for these damages. The whole matter is set out in a document of 66 pages as Report No. 458, to accompany Bill H. R. No. 388, House of Representatives, Thirtieth Congress. Harmony was given an escort of American troops and allowed to travel as he wished, but under orders to keep in communication with the army. To avoid the heat, he traveled mostly at night and camped in the day. He provided himself with all the refreshments to be obtained in Chihuahua, and had them carried along. He traveled in a large carriage drawn by several mules. In the escort was private Odon Guitar, of the Boone county company, now General Odon Guitar, of Columbia, Mo. The escort consisted of twenty-five soldiers. While the fight of Captain Reid with the Indians at El Pozo was in progress, Harmony and his escort came in sight on a hill overlooking the rancho. They could see that the attacking party was Captain Reid, but the great number of horses in sight caused them to believe that he was surrounded by a Mexican army. The escort broke into a gallop, and with yells and shouts attacked the Comanches (as they supposed the Indians to be when it was discovered they were Indians), who then for the first time realized that they were not fighting the ranch force. They raised the cry "Tejanos! Tejanos! [Texans! Texans!]", believing the new troops to be a body of Texans. When the Harmony escort charged the Comanches, Captain Reid emerged the fourth time from the corrals, and the combined force soon put the Indians to flight, with a loss of seventeen killed, including their "medicine-man," and all their prisoners and booty. There was a considerable sum of gold coin captured that could not be identified, and it

to Capt. Reid and his men in the following handsome and complimentary terms:

Letter of thanks from the people of Parras to Captain John W. Reid and his men after the battle of the Poso, translated by Captain David Waldo.

POLITICAL HEAD OF THE DEPARTMENT OF PARRAS.

At the first notice that the Indians, after having murdered many of our citizens and taken others captives, were returning to their homes through this vicinity, you, most generously and gallantly, offered, with fifteen of your countrymen, to combat them at the Pozo, which you most bravely executed with celerity, skill, and heroism, and worthy of all encomium, meriting your brilliant success, which we shall ever commemorate. You re-took many animals, and other property which had been captured, and liberated eighteen captives, who by your gallantry and good conduct have been restored to their families and homes, giving you the most hearty and cordial thanks, ever feeling grateful to you as their liberator from a life of

was divided among the American force that won the victory; Guitar was paid his proportion. After the battle the vaqueros went out and collected the dead Indians. They dragged them up to the ranch-gate with lassos attached to the horns of their saddles, and deposited them side by side. Guitar noted that they were fine-looking fellows, muscular, and well-formed. They resembled bronze statues thrown upon the ground.

Meredith T. Moore did not see this battle. He arrived just in time to see the dead Indians dragged up to the gate; the soldiers who had been in the engagement told him all the particulars of the fight. Moore says the Indians were a branch of the Comanches or Apaches called Lipans. They believed at first that they were fighting the ranch force. They carried bull-hide shields, which turned the balls of the American rifles. Seeing this, Dr. Winston shouted to a comrade to shoot a warrior's horse, saying that he would take care of the Indian. The Indian was thus killed, and that manner of fighting was adopted by the Americans in the last sally. That, and the orders to the soldiers given in English, convinced the Indians that they were in error as to the identity of their opponents, and they began to cry "Tejanos! Tejanos!" The battle ended quickly after this cry was raised. The force of Captain Reid had been driven inside the corral three times before Harmony's escort arrived. Dr. Winston shot the Indian he directed to be dismounted, but did not seriously wound him. The warrior put an arrow to his bowstring and began to draw it back to the head and relax it, then to draw it again, walking all the time towards Winston, who was reloading his gun and whose horse was prancing from excitement. He got near Winston and was drawing the shaft to the barb for the last time, when he was shot by an American who happened to see his comrade's danger. Captain Reid was wounded twice in this fight, each time with an arrow armed with a steel point. The first was on the back of the neck. The second arrow struck him a glancing blow in the mouth, breaking two or three teeth. Neither wound was of consequence. Don Manuel Ybarro fought with the Americans, and fought as valiantly as any

ignominy and thraldom, with the deep gratitude the whole population of this place entertain in ever living thanks. One half of the Indians being killed in the combat, and many flying badly wounded, does not quiet the pain that all of us feel for the wound that you received in rescuing Christian beings from the cruelty of the most inhuman of savages.

All of us ardently hope that you may soon recover of your wound, and though they know that the noblest reward of the gallant soul is to have done well for his country, yet they cannot forego this expression of their gratitude.

I consider it a high honor to be the organ of their will in conveying to you the general feeling of the people of the place; and I pray you to accept the assurance of my high respect. God and Liberty.

DON IGNACIO ARRABE.

Parras, 18 May, 1847.

On the evening of the 14th of May the army reached the delightful city of Parras, handsomely situated at the northern base of a lofty range of them. Among the captives recovered from the Indians was a beautiful young woman. She was found very ill, and was taken into the house, where Dr. Winston was called to attend her. She said every Indian in the band had violated her, some of them repeatedly. Dr. Winston said she could not recover.

Dr. Wislizenus, in his work before referred to, has an account of this battle, which he fixes on the 13th of May:

" I had been riding ahead this morning, and reached Pozo early, though not in time to take part in a skirmish between our vanguard and a party of Indians. When I arrived, some Mexicans were engaged in lassoing several dead bodies of Indians and dragging them into a heap together. The skirmish had taken place under the following circumstances: Two days before, a party of Lipan Indians, upon one of their predatory excursions, had stolen from a hacienda near Parras several hundred mules and horses, and killed several men. The proprietor of the hacienda, Don Manuel de Ibarra, applied to Captain Reid, of our regiment (who was then ahead of us with Lieut. Colonel Mitchell's party), for aid against these Indians. The captain, one of our most gallant officers, took but eight men along, and, accompanied by the Don himself, went back to El Pozo, where the Indians, on their march to the mountains, had to pass, being the only watering-place in that neighborhood. There they hid themselves in a corral, to wait for the arrival of the Indians. Quite unexpected, about 20 men of our vanguard came very early this morning to El Pozo, and increased their party to 30 men. Soon afterwards the Indians appeared— from 40 to 50 warriors. When our men rushed on horseback out of the corral to attack them, the Indians (probably supposing them to be Mexicans) received them with sneering and very contemptuous provocations, and their confidence in their bows and arrows was increased when the Americans, firing their rifles from horseback, killed none at the first charge. But as soon as our men alighted and took good aim with their rifles, the Indians fell on all sides. Nevertheless, they fought most desperately, and did not retire till half of them were either dead or wounded. But at last they had to run for their lives, and to leave all their dead and their booty behind. Besides the stolen stock, thirteen prisoners, Mexican women and children, whom they had carried along, were retaken and released from the brutality of their savage masters. Fifteen Indians were lying dead on the field, On our side, Captain Reid was wounded by some arrows, but not dangerously.

of mountains running east and west, after having performed a fatiguing march of thirty-six miles, without one drop of water, and almost without seeing one sprig of green vegetation, save the pointed maguey, and the bristling cactus. At Parras we found a plentiful supply of good water and forage for our perishing animals. We found Parras in reality to possess whatever of charm the imagination has thrown around one of the most beautiful of oases. We found a lovely alameda to screen us from the scorching rays of an almost vertical sun; besides a variety of fruits to satisfy the eager appetite. Parras is famous for its pretty women, and for the intelligence of its population generally, many of the citizens having received an English education in the United States. The people here are much inclined to favor the institutions and government of our country. Don Manuel Ybarro, the proprietor of a large hacienda near Parras, was educated at Bardstown, Ky., and has acted a very friendly part towards the American troops. For his numerous acts of kindness

Most of the dead Indians had fine blankets; some even carried gold; all were armed with bows and arrows, and a few with elegant shields of leather; and the 'medicine-man,' who was foremost in the action, and fought most bravely, wore a head-dress of feathers and horns. Our men, of course, took of these curiosities whatever they liked, and the Mexicans stripped them of the rest, and dragged their bodies together. The fallen Indians were all of medium size, but well proportioned and very muscular; their skulls and faces bore all the characteristics of the Indian race, but their skin looked whiter than I have ever seen it in Indians. The dead were lying there all day; neither Americans nor Mexicans seemed to care about them, and their burial was no doubt left to the wolves. I saw, therefore, no impropriety in taking another curiosity along for scientific purposes—to wit, the skull of the medicine-man, which I have, since my return, presented to that distinguished craniologist, Professor Samuel G. Morton, of Philadelphia. In relation to the tribe of Lipans, I could only ascertain from the Mexicans that they live in the mountains of the Bolson, extend their stealing and robbing excursions very far south, and have the reputation of being a most brutal and cruel set of Indians, though brave in battle."

Both Richardson and Edwards, in their works mentioned herein, give accounts of this battle. Richardson says it was the chief who was killed, not the medicine-man. Edwards says that the mess to which Dr. Wislizenus belonged complained of the smell of the skull he says he cut from the Indian.

The Lipan Indians have been called Gipans, Lapans, Lapana, Lapane, Lee Pani, Lee Pawnee, Lipan, Lipau, Lipaw, Seepan, Sinapan, Sipan, and other similar-sounding names. Coues (*On the Trail of a Spanish Explorer*, Vol. II, p. 460, *note*) says their name is *Ipa-nde*. In his edition of *The Expedition of Zebulon M. Pike*, Vol. II, p. 764, note, he says they were a sort of Apaches who scoured the plains of Texas from Red river to the Rio Grande, and that they were sometimes called Lipan Apaches, and ranged as far south as Durango. Coues mentions this fight at El Pozo, and also the fact that Dr. Wislizenus carried away the skull of the chief.

towards the author and his companions in arms, he desires to return his grateful acknowledgments.

Upon Col. Doniphan's reaching Parras, he received a communication from Gen. Wool, by the hands of Ybarro, in which he was authorized to purchase, on the credit of the United States, such provisions and forage, as his men and animals required; he was also instructed to allow his men such respite as their condition, after so much toil, and so many distressing marches, seemed to demand, and to extend to the intelligent and hospitable citizens of Parras kind treatment in reciprocation for their numerous acts of benevolence towards the sick Americans, whom he had been forced to leave at that place, upon his forming a junction with Gen. Taylor, at Saltillo.

Though the Missourians manifested the utmost civility towards the inhabitants of Parras, one incident occurred to mar the general harmony and good feeling which had prevailed. A few disaffected Mexicans fell upon a man, Lickenlighter, in the employ of the artillery, and with staves, and stones, bruised him so that he subsequently died in Monterey. This aggravated instance of cruelty, commenced by the Mexicans, excited the artillery-men, and all the Missourians, to such a degree that they fell upon whatever Mexicans exhibited the least insolence, and beat them severely. Some say that two of them were killed, but of this nothing certain is known. Nor were the officers able to restrain the men. Capt. Pike and a portion of the advance under Lieutenant-colonel Mitchell, having halted at this place, now rejoined the army.

On the morning of the 17th, the whole force moved off in the direction of Saltillo, and in less than five days, having completed more than one hundred miles, the Missourians pitched their camps with the Arkansas cavalry, at Encantada, near the battle-field of Buena Vista, where there is an abundant supply of cool and delightful water.

During this march they passed through a rugged, mountainous country, almost entirely destitute of vegetation, producing only mezquite chaparral, clusters of dwarfish acacia, Spanish bayonet, maguey, and palmilla. This last often grows thirty feet in height, and three feet in diameter, the body of which is sometimes used as timber for the construction of bridges. On the tops of the mountain peaks, and sometimes by the way side, might be seen the cross, the symbol of the national faith, and object of universal reverence, constructed in the rudest and most primitive manner, with a small heap of stones at its foot, and fancifully and reverentially entwined with festoons of wild flowers. This march passed by the Haciendas Ybarro, Cienega Grande, Castanuella, the princely Hacienda de Patos, and the ruins of San Juan, where there is much water. This last place had been destroyed by the Americans.

CROSS BY THE WAYSIDE.

On the 22d of May, the regiment was reviewed by Gen. Wool in person, accompanied by his staff, and the following complimentary order made, viz.:[120] HEADQUARTERS, BUENA VISTA, May 22d, 1847.

The general commanding takes great pleasure in expressing the

---

NOTE 120.—James Peacock relates the following incidents which occurred while the army was at the camp of General Wool. There the Missourians received full rations for the first time during their service. They drew so much that they could not take care of it; every skillet, kettle and bag was filled. And still a portion was left; and the soldiers left among other articles all the soap issued to them. The commissary officer called their attention to it: "Here, you fellows, you are leaving your soap; come back and get it." Some soldier replied, "Soap! hell—what do we want with soap? We have no clothes to wash!"

General Doniphan got his men in line as well as he could for the purpose of having General Wool review them. The General was about an hour making his appearance, and the men became impatient, and straggled; when the General did finally appear in his gorgeous trappings of war, accompanied by his well-dressed and well-mounted staff, the line was very irregular. The soldiers had never seen anything so fine as General Wool and staff, and they crowded about to get a full view. One man was reproved for getting out of line, but justified himself by saying that he could not see otherwise, so he "stood out" and "looked at the show." General Wool went down the front of the line and returned up the rear. As he turned around the line many of the Missourians turned also, and those who did not craned their necks to look over their shoulders. It was said that General Wool was not pleased with this review, but the ridiculous features of it afterwards appealed to him, and he related an account of it at many a banquet in after life.

gratification he has received this afternoon in meeting the Missouri volunteers. They are about to close their present term of military service, after having rendered, in the course of the arduous duties they have been called on to perform, a series of highly important services, crowned by decisive and glorious victories.

No troops can point to a more brilliant career than those commanded by Col. Doniphan, and no one will ever hear of the battles of Brazito or Sacramento without a feeling of admiration for the men who gained them.

The State of Missouri has just cause to be proud of the achievements of the men who have represented her in the army against Mexico, and she will without doubt, receive them on their return with all the joy and satisfaction to which a due appreciation of their merits and services so justly entitle them.[121]

In bidding them adieu, the general wishes to Col. Doniphan, his officers and men, a happy return to their families.

By command of Brig. Gen. WOOL:

IRVIN MCDOWELL, A. A. A. Gen.

On the 23d the Missourians marched to Gen. Wool's* camp, where Capt. Weightman delivered up his battery to Captain Washington. The Mexican cannon which were captured in the action at Sacramento, they were permitted to retain as the trophies of their victory. These were subsequently presented by Colonel Doniphan to the State of Missouri, to be the evidences through all time to come, of the valor, chivalry and good conduct of the troops under his command.[122]

The Missouri column, now passing Saltillo, the Grand cañon of the Rinconada, Santa Catarina, and the city of Monterey, arrived in the American camp at the Walnut Springs, on the 26th, having in three days performed a march of seventy miles, during which two brave

* To those readers who desire to peruse a full and faithful account of the operations of Generals Wool, Taylor. Patterson, Quitman and Scott, the author would recommend the "Twelve Months' Volunteer," a new and interesting history by G. C. Furber, of the Tennessee cavalry, recently published by J. A. & U. P. James, Cincinnati.—HUGHES.

NOTE 121.—General Wool made an effort to induce the Missourians to enlist in his army, but without success. Both Edwards and Richardson mention this fact. Under date of May 22, Richardson says: "After spending an hour or two in camp, I returned to our boys, whom I found assembled in a congregation, and Captain Reid holding forth in a speech, trying all his might to get some of our men to volunteer again, their term being nearly expired."

NOTE 122.—James Bates was a prominent Kentuckian who lived just outside the city of Louisville. Meredith T. Moore had gone to school with his children, and was regarded as a very intimate friend of the family. After the war Moore

soldiers, Smith and Smart, died, and were buried with becoming military honors. Major-General Taylor,[123] having reviewed the Missouri troops on the morning of the 27th, issued the following order:

HEADQUARTERS, ARMY OF OCCUPATION,
Camp near Monterey, May 27, 1847.

Col. Doniphan's command of Missouri volunteers will proceed, *via* Camargo, to the mouth of the river, or Brazos island, where it will take water transportation to New Orleans.

On reaching New Orleans, Col. Doniphan will report to Gen. Brooke, commanding the Western Division, and also to Col. Churchill,

---

made a tour of Kentucky to visit relatives and friends, and he called, of course, at the Bates home. Bates had been a guest at the banquet given by Louisville to General Wool, after his return from Mexico. At the banquet General Wool related the following incident in his speech:

When Colonel Doniphan's regiment came to him from Chihuahua, General Wool announced that as many of the Missourians as desired to have him point out the important places on the battle-field of Buena Vista and go over the principal events of the great battle might assemble on a hill overlooking the field. General Wool sat in a camp-chair and pointed out the interesting features and explained the battle. He came down to the last day of the battle, and told of the supreme effort of Santa Anna to overwhelm the Americans; how the Mexicans killed the American officers; how the effort failed, and how at night the Mexicans retired and never returned, and the victory remained with the Americans. "And," continued the General, "while I had been telling them this, a brawny young Missourian, almost naked, dirty, bearded like a pirate, hair unkempt and falling over his shoulders, but of fine appearance and manly countenance, was squatting beside me, completely absorbed in the story. When I concluded he slapped me on the thigh and said: 'Right there is where you made a mistake, General! When they retreated you ought to have pressed them and charged them like we did at Sacramento! If you had done that you would have destroyed them, as we did! Yes, sir, there is where you made a d—d bad mistake!'"

General Wool did not learn the name of his critic. Moore had heard of the incident when it occurred; and the Missourian who believed that General Wool had failed to do his whole duty was Robert D. Walker, a private in Company G, brother of John Walker, who was afterwards Auditor of State for the State of Missouri.

NOTE 123.—James Peacock relates an incident that came under his notice while the Missourians were at General Taylor's camp. General Taylor was not a stickler for dress as was General Wool. He came among the troops wearing a short brown coat and a straw hat—no part of a uniform. Lem White, of Jackson county, saw General Taylor, and supposed him to be some hanger-on or camp-follower; and going up to the General, inquired where he could get some good whisky. The General pointed out the sutler's quarters and said it could be had there, and added: "But you had better not let General Taylor know you get any whisky, for he might make trouble for you." White soon returned to

inspector general, who will muster the command for discharge and payment.

At Camargo Col. Doniphan will detach a sufficient number of men from each company to conduct the horses and other animals of the command by land to Missouri. The men so detached will leave the necessary papers to enable their pay to be drawn when their companies are discharged at New Orleans.

The Quartermaster Department will furnish the necessary transportation to carry out the above orders.

The trophies captured at the battle of Sacramento will be conveyed by Col. Doniphan to Missouri, and there turned over to the Governor, subject to the final disposition of the War Department.

In thus announcing the arrangements which close the arduous and honorable service of the Missouri volunteers, the commanding general extends to them his earnest wishes for their prosperity and happiness, and for a safe return to their families and homes.

By command of Maj. Gen. TAYLOR:

W. W. BLISS, A. A. A. G.

When Gen. Taylor received authentic information of the fall of Vera Cruz, the capitulation of the castle of San Juan d' Ullua, and the capture of Chihuahua, he published the following order to the troops under his command:

HEADQUARTERS, ARMY OF OCCUPATION,
Camp near Monterey, April 14, 1847.

The commanding general has the satisfaction to announce to the troops under his command, that authentic information has been received of the fall of Vera Cruz, and of San Juan de Ullua, which capitulated on the 27th to the forces of Maj. Gen. Scott. This highly important victory reflects new lustre on the reputation of our arms.

---

camp with the whisky and asked of some of his comrades: "Where is that fat old fellow that was around here awhile ago and told me where to get some good whisky? I got the whisky, and I want to treat him." No one could tell him. Then he wanted to treat Colonel Doniphan, and was told that he had gone to General Taylor's headquarters. White followed him there, hoping to slyly give his beloved commander a drink while General Taylor was looking the other way. He was bulging into General Taylor's tent when halted by a guard. He thought it an outrage that he was not allowed to see his Colonel, as it was the first time he had ever failed to see him whenever he pleased. But he would not tell the sentry why he wished to see the Colonel. He stooped, and peeped into the tent, hoping to catch the eye of his commander and motion him out, but was disappointed. But finally he saw General Taylor. "Who is that fat old fellow sitting in there?" he asked of the guard. "That," the sentry replied, "is General Taylor." "The hell you say!" exclaimed White in alarm. "Why, that's the very old rascal that told me where to get this whisky!" And he left in a hurry.

The commanding general would, at the same time, announce another signal success, won by the gallantry of our troops on the 28th of February, near the city of Chihuahua. A column of Missouri volunteers, less than one thousand strong, under command of Col. Doniphan, with a light field battery, attacked a Mexican force many times superior, in an intrenched position, captured its artillery and baggage, and defeated it with heavy loss.

In publishing to the troops the grateful tidings, the general is sure that they will learn, with joy and pride, the triumphs of their comrades on distant fields.

By order of Maj. Gen. TAYLOR:

W. W. BLISS, A. A. A. G.

CHAPTER XXI.

Departure for New Orleans—Execution of a Guerrilla Chief—Mier and Camargo—Death of Sergeant Swain—Arrival at Reynosa—Water Transportation—The Mouth—Brazos Santiago—The Troops sail for New Orleans—The Balize—Chivalry of the South—Reception in the Crescent City.

Having left our sick men at Monterey, after a hasty march of thirty miles on the 26th of May, during which we passed the rivers Agua Fria and Salinas de Parras, we encamped in the small town, Marin, where there was but little forage, and not the semblance of either green or dry grass. The next day, passing through a country covered with an almost impervious mezquite chaparral, and over the ground where Gen. Urea's band captured Gen. Taylor's provision train, and barbarously and inhumanly murdered the unarmed teamsters, whose skeletons and half-devoured frames still lay scattered promiscuously along the road, over which vultures, dogs, and wolves, were yet holding carnival, and having progressed thirty-five miles, we encamped at a fine, bold running spring, not far from Cerralvo.

The next day, advancing about seven miles, to Cerralvo, we halted to take some refreshment. Here we witnessed the execution, by the Texan Rangers, of a Mexican guerrilla chief, one of Urea's men, who had been captured the previous night. His captors promised to spare his life, upon condition that he would reveal to them, where his comrades might be found. He refused to betray them, averring that he had killed many Americans, and he would kill many more if it were in his power. He added:—"My life is now in the hands of my enemies; I am prepared to yield it up: only I ask that I may not be tied, and that I may be allowed to face my executioners." Having lighted his *cigarrito*, with the utmost nonchalance, he faced his executioners, (a file of six Texan Rangers,) who were detailed for the purpose. They were ordered to fire. Five balls penetrated the skull of the guerrilla chief. He instantly expired.[124]

NOTE 124.—This matter came near making trouble, I am informed by General Guitar, who writes me as follows, under date of June 14, 1906:

"The incident was one of the most outrageous events of the Mexican War, and came nigh resulting in a mutiny in our regiment. A majority of us were in favor of rescuing him [the guerrilla chief], and it would have been done but for the personal influence of Colonel Doniphan and our other officers had over us.

On the 30th, we encamped in Mier, situated on the small river Alcantro, and famous for having been the place where the Texans capitulated to Gen. Ampudia. The next day we reached Camargo, on the San Juan, where we obtained an abundant supply of provisions, for this place had been converted into a government depot. This river admits of steamboat navigation. While here one of our companions, Tharp, who had performed much hard service, died of sickness. He was buried with the honors due to a brave soldier.

On the 1st of June, Major Gilpin, with a small detachment of men, started in advance of the column, with the intention of proceeding to Reynosa, to engage transportation for the army, by steamboats, thence to the mouth of the Rio Grande. After proceeding a few miles, one of his party, Sergeant Swain, a good soldier, having imprudently straggled on ahead, by himself, was shot by Mexicans lurking in the chaparral. To avenge his death the party charged, as soon as practicable, upon the Mexicans, who were adroitly making their escape, and killed one of them. Four others were, a short time afterwards, captured by Capt. Walton, with a small detachment of men, at a neighboring rancho, and carried to camp at Upper Reynosa, at which place we found Col. Webb, of the 16th regiment, U. S. Army. The prisoners were delivered over to him; but finding no *positive* evidence that they were the same, who had committed the bloody deed, although one of them had blood on his clothes, they were discharged, and conducted out of camp by a guard. But the company to which Swain belonged, were so much enraged that, as it is said, they went out from camp, and killed part of them as soon as dismissed by the guard. Of the truth of this, we are not certainly informed; for those who knew, would not divulge the truth, lest they should be

I have always insisted that he was the *coolest and bravest* soldier that ever died for his country. A circumstantial recital of the facts attending the execution of the Mexican officer would bring tears to the eyes of every brave and generous-hearted man who might read it, as it did to my eyes, in after days, when I recalled them. I am still determined, if I can, to have the authorities of Mexico erect a monument to his memory at the City of Mexico. This incident alone, with appropriate comment, would furnish matter for a volume."

Under date of May 29, Richardson gives the following account. And his work contains an illustration of the execution, which is reproduced herein:

"While we were at Seralvo, a Mexican was caught, who belonged to the gang that murdered the teamsters, and burned up 150 wagons, which were on their way to the army. At three o'clock he was brought out in the plaza, and placed against the wall. A file of six men (Texan Rangers) stood some ten yards

censured by those in command; but the fire of their guns was distinctly heard.

off. The prisoner was told by the Colonel that his time was at hand. He was then ordered to turn his back. This he not only refused to do, but struck fire

Texan Rangers shooting a Mexican guerrilla in the presence of Colonel Doniphan's Army, near the Rio Grande.
(Reproduced from the work of William H. Richardson.)

and lighted his cigar. The word was given—all fired—and he fell dead. Three balls entered his breast, and three his head. A Texan, whose brother had been

After resting a few hours, and burying the dead, the march was continued down the river, through the chaparral all day, and all the following night. At sunrise the advance of the column arrived at Reynosa, where we were greeted by the sight of steam vessels ready to transport us to the Gulf.[125]

Colonel Doniphan, now taking the sick men on board the first transport that could be obtained, proceeded to the mouth of the river, to engage shipping, as early as practicable, for New Orleans, leaving Lieutenant-colonel Jackson, Major Gilpin, and Major Clark, to pro-

murdered in the wagon-train, gave a five-dollar gold-piece to take the place of one who was chosen to do this melancholy business."

Under date of May 29, Dr. Wislizenus says:

"Some troops of North Carolina and a company of Texan Rangers were stationed here [Cerralbo]. The latter had captured this morning a well-known chief of a guerrilla band, who was said to have committed many cruelties against Americans. He was sentenced to be shot, but refused to make any confessions. He boasted of having killed many men, and that he did not expect any better fate for himself. The execution took place on the plaza. When led there, and placed against the wall of a house, he requested not to be blindfolded, or shot in the back, according to Mexican custom, which was granted. After a short conversation with a priest, he prepared and lit a cigarito with a steady hand, and had not quite finished smoking it when some well-aimed balls pierced his heart and head. He died instantly. His name was Nicholas Garcia; and whether guilty or innocent, he died like a brave man. Some rumor was afterwards started that he was the brother of General Canales, but in Cerralbo I understood that he was well known there; that his mother lived there yet, and that he had no other connection with Canales than having belonged to his bands."

Edwards, in *A Campaign in New Mexico with Colonel Doniphan*, p. 110, gives the following account:

"While we rested at Ceralvo I witnessed the execution of a Mexican supposed to be one of Urrea's lawless band. The Texans pretended to consider him as such; but there was no doubt that this was only used as a cloak to cover their insatiable desire to destroy those they so bitterly hate. A furlough was found upon this Mexican, from his army, to visit his family, ending as our furloughs do, that should he overstay his leave of absence he would be considered a deserter. This time he had considerably overstayed; and he himself stated that he had never intended to return, being in favor of the Americans. But the Rangers tried him by court-martial, and adjudged him to be shot that very day. As the hour struck, he was led into the public plaza; and five Rangers took their post a few feet off, as executioners. The condemned coolly pulled out his flint and steel, and little paper cigarito, and, striking a light, commenced smoking as calmly as can possible be imagined, and—in two minutes—fell a corpse, with the still smoking cigarito yet between his lips. I did not see a muscle of his face quiver when the rifles were leveled at him, but he looked coolly at his executioners, pressing a small cross which hung to his neck, firmly against his breast. I turned from the scene, sickened at heart."

NOTE 125.—On the transports down the Rio Grande the captain of the vessel said to James Peacock: "I took up some New-Yorkers not long since; they scratched themselves in a leisurely sort of way. But you fellows scratch with great earnestness—scratch yourselves all over—scratch rapidly—violently—

vide the means of transporting their respective battalions down the river. Certain of the soldiers, impatient at the delay, and anxious to get home, censured Col. Doniphan for leaving them at Reynosa, without providing them with immediate transportation; but they did not consider how important it was that he should go in advance to Brazos Island, and have ships ready engaged to convey them without delay to New Orleans. Without such precaution on the part of the commander, the whole column might have been obliged to lie many days on the beach, waiting for vessels in which to cross the Gulf. This, therefore, eventuated most opportunely, for ships were made ready in the harbor, before the men arrived at the Brazos.

Meanwhile the troops at Reynosa were obliged to lie one or two days on the river bank in a comfortless and miserable plight, (for it rained incessantly, and the men had no place to lie, nor tents to shelter them, but stood as cattle in the mud both day and night,) before they could secure transports.

On the fourth and fifth, the men having burned their saddles, and other horse rigging, and sent their animals by land to Missouri, went aboard steam-vessels, and on the seventh the whole force arrived safely at the mouth of the river, where they disembarked, and bivouacked upon the margin of the stream until the morning of the ninth, the intermediate time being spent by the soldiers in the most refreshing and pleasant bathings in the River and the Gulf.

Lieutenant James Lea, quartermaster, proceeded with his trains from Reynosa to Matamoras, and turned over to the quartermaster at that place all his wagons, mules, and commissary stores.

General Taylor's order requiring a "sufficient number of men" to be detailed at Camargo for the purpose of conducting "the horses and other animals of the command by land to Missouri," was not complied with; for the volunteers did not choose to obey the order, regarding the stock of but little value. However, Sergeant Van Bibber, and about thirty-five other men, voluntarily agreed to drive the stock, (of such as would allow them a compensation of ten dollars per

---

scratch all the time. What's the matter with you? Got fleas?" To which Peacock replied with indignation: "Fleas! Do you think we are dogs, to go about infested with fleas?" Then with pride he continued: "These are lice! We work harder than the New-Yorkers because we have more to do. Our lice are big handsome fellows, and we have plenty of them—got them in Mexico!"

head for their pains) through Texas to Missouri, and deliver them in the county where the owner resided. Accordingly this party, with about seven hundred head of stock, leaving Reynosa on the 4th, proceeded to Camargo, and thence into the United States, arriving in Missouri, with the loss of near half the animals, about the 15th of August.

On the 9th we walked over to the harbor at the north end of Brazos Island, whence we were to take shipping for New Orleans, and on the following day the artillery and about two hundred and fifty men embarked on the schooner MURILLO, and Col. Doniphan with seven hundred men embarked on the stately sail-ship REPUBLIC, and under a favoring gale arrived safely in New Orleans on the 15th, having, in twelve months, performed a grand detour through the Mexican Republic, of near four thousand miles by land and water.

This most extraordinay march, conducted by Colonel Doniphan, the Xenophon of the age, with great good fortune, meets not with a parallel in the annals of the world.

Our passage across the gulf was speedy and prosperous. One of our number, only, was committed to a watery grave. This was Christopher Smith, than whom none was a better soldier. Ridge, also a brave soldier, died, and was conveyed to New Orleans for interment.

We had now been in the service twelve months, had traversed the plains and solitudes of the west, waded through the snows in the mountains of New Mexico, had traveled over the great deserts of Chihuahua, Durango, Coahuila, Nueva Leon, and Tamaulipas, half naked, and but poorly supplied with provisions, and were weary of camp service, and packing up baggage. Therefore we were anxious to return to our homes and our families. When the men came within sight of the Balize—when they could but just discover, through the mist, low in the horizon, the distant, green, looming shores of their native country, they shouted aloud in the pride of their hearts, and, Columbus-like, gave thanks to the beneficent Author of all good, not only for the prosperous voyage over the Gulf, but the unparalleled success of the Great Expedition.

The chivalry of the South is unsurpassed; the generosity of the southern people unequalled. Their feelings are alive to every noble and magnanimous impulse. Their breasts are swayed by sentiments of true honor. Who will deny that the population of the Crescent city inspires patriotism from very proximity to the field immortalized by Jackson's victory? New Orleans, for months previous to the arrival of Col. Doniphan, had been wound up to the highest degree of military excitement, and had, in truth, been the great thoroughfare for the departure and return of perhaps more than ten thousand volunteers, destined for the war, and returning from their various fields of glory; yet, the Missourians, rough clad, were received with unabated enthusiasm, and a cordiality for which they will ever gratefully remember their friends of the south. As they passed up the Mississippi, the streaming of flags from the tops of the houses, and the waving of white handkerchiefs by the ladies, as a token of approval, from the windows and balconies of the stately mansions which every where beautify the green banks of the "Inland Sea," announced to them that their return was hailed with universal joy; that their arduous services were duly appreciated; and that Louisianians are not only generous and brave, but nobly patriotic. Such a reception was worth the toil of an hundred battle-fields.

Isolated from every other branch of the army, barred by intervening deserts from all communication with the government, thrown entirely upon its own resources, compelled to draw supplies from a hostile country, and in the absence of instructions or succors, Col. Doniphan's command was left to cut its way through the country of a subtle and treacherous enemy. Destitute of clothing, and the means of procuring it—not having received a dime since the day of enlistment, and none then, save forty-two dollars commutation for clothing—the men almost grew as did Nebuchadnezzar, being indeed, rough samples of Rocky Mountain life. Their long-grown beards flowed in the wind similar to those of the rude Cossacks of Northern Europe, while their garments were worn to shreds, bivouacking on the rocks and sands of Mexico.[126] Their dishevelled hair, their long-

NOTE 126.—In 1845 George L. Boone made a trip from Jefferson City to Taos, New Mexico. He was a tailor. While at Taos he made two complete suits of buckskin. One suit was highly ornamented, the other plain. Upon his return he presented the plain suit to Meredith T. Moore; the ornamented one he wore himself. The young men donned these suits when they enlisted, and they wore them continuously until they arrived at New Orleans. There they were cast off—and none too soon, either. Many of the soldiers were almost naked when they arrived at New Orleans. One man marched off the ship with only a pair of thin drawers on, and they were quite ragged.

grown whiskers, their buck-skin apparel, their stern and uncouth appearance, their determined and resolved looks, and their careless and nonchalant air, attracted the gaze, and won the admiration of all people. Though they were somewhat undisciplined, yet they were hardy, unshrinking, resolute, independent, chivalrous, honorable and intelligent men, such as, indeed, "would not flatter Neptune for his trident, nor Jove for his power to thunder."

CHAPTER XXII.

Discharge of the Troops—Their Return to Missouri—Reception at St. Louis—Banquets and Honors—Doniphan crowned with a LAUREL WREATH—Conclusion.

We have hitherto considered in what manner the troops under Col. Doniphan were conducted over the great solitudes to Santa Fé; how they invaded the snow-capped mountains in pursuit of the fearless Navajos; how General Kearny with a small force crossed the continent, and held California in quiet possession; how Col. Price succeeded to the command of the troops in New Mexico; how Col. Doniphan invaded and conquered the states of Chihuahua and Durango; thence traversing extensive deserts, treeless, barren and waterless; oftentimes subsisting his army on half rations and less; and how, after infinite suffering and toil, he arrived at the Gulf, and sailed for New Orleans.

The Missourians were now permitted to turn over to the ordnance master, at New Orleans, the arms they had used on the expedition, and with which they had achieved signal victories. They were forthwith mustered for discharge and payment by Col. Churchill, which process was completed between the 22d and the 28th of June. Having received payment, and an honorable discharge from the service, they departed to their respective homes in detached parties, each one now traveling according to his own convenience, and being no longer subject to command. They generally arrived in Missouri about the 1st of July, having been absent thirteen months.

Anticipating the arrival of the returning volunteers, the generous citizens of St. Louis had made ample preparations to give them a hearty, welcome, cordial reception, and testify to them the esteem in which their services were held by their fellow citizens. But as the volunteer soldiers, who were now become citizens, returned in detached parties, and were very anxious to visit their families and friends from whom they had so long been separated, they could not all be induced to remain and partake of the proffered hospitality. However, the company under Capt. Hudson, having in charge the captured Mexican cannon, and near three hundred officers and privates of different companies, being in the city on the 2d of July, it was agreed that the formalities of the reception should be gone through with. Accordingly the various military, and fire companies, of the city, were paraded in full uniform; the people collected in great crowds; the Mexican cannon, the trophies of victory, were dragged along the streets, crowned with garlands: and an immense procession was formed, conducted by T. Grimsley, chief marshal, which, after a brief, animating speech from the Hon. J. B. Bowlin, and a still briefer response from Lieutenant-colonel Mitchell, proceeded to Camp Lucas, where the Hon. T. H. Benton delivered to the returned volunteers, and a concourse of more than seven thousand people, a most thrilling and eloquent address,* recounting, with astonishing accuracy, and extraordinary minuteness, the events of the great campaign.[127]

* See Benton's and Doniphan's speeches, Missouri Republican, July 3d, 1847.—HUGHES.

NOTE 127.—The following description of the reception tendered the First Regiment at St. Louis is taken from *History of Saint Louis City and County*, by J. Thomas Scharf, Vol. I, beginning at page 379:

Anticipating the arrival of the returning volunteers, the generous and patriotic citizens of St. Louis determined to give them a hearty welcome. Accordingly the Mayor and City Council called a meeting of the citizens in the rotunda of the court-house on June 23, 1847, to make arrangements "to welcome home the returning Missouri and Illinois volunteers, and also to pay suitable honors to the remains of Col. J. J. Hardin and others, who fell gloriously in the Mexican War." On motion of Maj. Wetmore, Bryan Mullanphy, Mayor of the city, was called to preside, and on motion of Dr. George Wilson, Louis V. Bogy and Thomas Harney were appointed secretaries. The chairman then explained the object of the meeting. On motion of R. S. Blennerhassett, a committee of five persons was appointed to prepare suitable resolutions expressive of the sense of the meeting; whereupon the chair appointed R. S. Blennerhassett, Wm. M. Campbell, S. Treat, Chas. Keemle, and A. B. Chambers. During the absence of the committee the meeting was addressed by Messrs. Blennerhassett, Hadges, Bowlin, Wright, and Eager. The committee soon returned, and reported a series of resolutions, which were adopted, recommending that the hospitalities of the city be tendered to the returning volunteers under the command of Col. Doniphan, and that the men be invited to accept suitable testimonials of the citizens' gratitude and respect for their patriotic services. A committee of arrangements, composed of Benjamin Soulard, David Chambers, Cornelius Campbell, Dr. J. Sykes, A. B. Chambers, J. Prentis Moss, Michael Suter, Thornton Grimsley, Geo. Wilson, Geo. K. McGunnegle, Samuel Willi, Napoleon Koscialowski, Wm. Christy, Theron Barnum, C. D. Walton, D. A. Magehan, Patrick Gorman, T. O. Duncan, John W. Scott, Wm. Clark, and B. F. Jennings, was appointed, with full power to make all necessary preparations for the reception of and demonstration of respect to the volunteers. The City Council also appointed a committee of eight, to act in connection with the citizens' committee, and they met

When the honorable Senator concluded, Col. Doniphan was loudly and enthusiastically called to the stand; whereupon he rose and responded in a very chaste, and modest, yet graphic address, in which he ascribed the great success and good fortune, which continually attended him on his expedition, rather to the bravery and conduct of his soldiers, than to his own generalship.

For months succeeding the return, to the State, of the Missouri volunteers, sumptuous dinners, banquets, and balls, tables loaded with delicate viands, and the richest wines, were everywhere spread to do them honor, as if thereby to compensate, in some measure, for past hardships, and the immensity of toil and peril, which they had experienced in climbing over rugged, snow-capped mountains; in contending with the overwhelming forces of the enemy; in enduring bitter cold, pinching hunger, burning thirst, incredible fatigue, and

---

at the Planters' House on the following day to make the necessary arrangements. The joint committee was organized, with George K. McGunnegle as chairman and A. B. Chambers as secretary. The committee adopted the following order of proceedings for the reception and entertainment of the Missouri volunteers:

"The procession will be formed on Fourth street, the right resting on Market, as follows:

Band of Music.
Mayor and City Council.
Committee of Arrangements.
Officers of the Army and Navy of the United States.
United States Troops.
Military escort of Infantry, the Volunteer Corps of the city.
The Missouri Volunteers, under Col. A. W. Doniphan, returning from the campaign in Mexico.
Volunteer Cavalry.
The several societies, institutions, fire companies, and public bodies of the city will be assigned stations as they arrive upon the ground.
Citizens on foot.
Citizens in carriages.
Citizens on horse.

"On the approach of the volunteers to the city, thirteen guns will be fired from Camp Lucas (west of the city), and the bells of the churches and fire companies rung.

"Upon this signal the military companies will immediately form on Fourth street, in front of the court-house, and await further orders.

"The several societies, institutions, fire companies, public bodies, and others will form on Fourth street, or the cross-streets leading into it, and report to the chief marshal.

"The steamboats and other public places will display their flags at topmast.

"The aids and assistant marshals will report themselves to the chief marshal *at the earliest possible moment*, at the east front of the court-house.

"A national salute of thirty-one guns will be fired when the vessels containing the volunteers arrive in front of the city.

"From the uncertainty of the hour of their arrival, the line of march is not designated.

"At Camp Lucas, after the delivery of the oration and response of the volunteers, the civic part of the procession will be dismissed, and the returning volunteers, under the escort prescribed in the programme of the Committee of Arrangements, will be conducted to the St. Louis Park, to partake of a collation."

sleepless nights of watching, and in bivouacking upon the waterless, arid deserts of Mexico. But their past dangers, both from the foe and the elements, were now soon forgotten amidst the kind caresses of friends, and the cordial reception with which their fellow-citizens continually greeted them. The maxim which has descended from former ages, and which has met the sanction of all nations, that REPUBLICS ARE UNGRATEFUL, has not in this instance proved true; for there was now a *campaign* of feasting and honors.

On the 29th of July a public dinner was given by the citizens of Independence, (Mo.,) in honor of Colonel Doniphan, his officers, and men, on which occasion the ladies, being anxious to testify their respect to the hero of Sacramento, and those who followed where he dared to lead, had prepared the LAUREL WREATH, in all ages the "gift of beauty to valor," for the VICTOR's brow. After the welcoming

---

The following committees were also appointed to carry out the objects of the meeting:

"To meet the volunteers and apprise them of the purposes of the citizens, Messrs. J. Sykes, J. B. Bowlin, and George W. Olney.

"To select the orators of the day, and make all necessary arrangements pertaining thereto, Messrs. Blennerhassett, Schaumburg, and Campbell.

"To prepare the catafalque, and all other necessary preparations pertaining thereto, Messrs. Koscialowski, Magehan, and Ladew.

"To provide the collations, and all pertaining thereto, Messrs. Barnum, Wilson, and Walton.

"To receive and audit accounts, and report the same to the City Council, Messrs. McGunnegle, Blennerhassett, and Thomas."

The orators of the day were Hon. Thomas H. Benton and Hon. James B. Bowlin. Col. Thornton Grimsley was selected as chief marshal, with the following aids and assistant marshal: Aids, Davis Chambers and Frederick Kretschmar; assistant marshals, T. B. Targee, George Gannet, David Tatum, Wm. C. Wright, Gregory Byrne, John Hanson, Samuel Willi, N. Koscialowski, Wm. G. Clarke, A. H. Glasby, C. D. Walton, James A. Rogers, N. Aldrich.

The City Council appropriated sufficient money to defray the expenses of the reception of the volunteers; but the bill was vetoed by Mayor Mullanphy, and the veto was sustained by the Board of Aldermen. This proceeding of the Mayor caused much indignation among the citizens, and at a large public meeting it was resolved "that his presence in welcoming the volunteers as chairman of the committee on reception has been dispensed with."

The course pursued by the Mayor compelled the committee of arrangements to apply to the citizens for subscriptions to defray the expenses of receiving and entertaining the volunteers, the Mayor himself being a large contributor. The following gentlemen from each ward of the city were appointed to wait on the citizens for donations:

First Ward.—Messrs. R. S. Blennerhassett, N. Koscialowski, and John Dunn.
Second Ward.—Messrs. John Kern, G. R. Taylor, and J. P. Thomas.

speech, by S. H. Woodson, and a thrilling and stirring response by Col. Doniphan, Mrs. Buchanan, in behalf of the ladies, delivered from the stand, in the presence of five thousand people, the subjoined eloquent address:

"*Respected Friends:*—Long had the world echoed to the voice of Fame when her brazen trumpet spoke of the glories of Greece and Rome. The sun looked proudly down upon Thermopylæ when Leonidas had won a name bright and glorious as his own golden beams. The soft air of the Italian clime glowed, as the splendor of a Roman triumph flashed through the eternal city. But the mantle of desolation now wraps the mouldering pillars of Athens and of Rome, and fame deserting her ancient haunts, now fills our own fair land with the matchless deeds of her heroic sons. Like the diamond in the recesses of the mine, lay for centuries the land of Columbia. Like that diamond when art's transforming fingers have

---

Third Ward.—Messrs. David Chambers, T. B. Targee, A. L. Mills, and J. Jacoby.
Fourth Ward.—Messrs. J. B. Brant, Edw. Walsh, and Richard J. Lockwood.
Fifth Ward.—Messrs. A. H. Glasby, Hugh Rose, and Dr. R. Knox.
Sixth Ward.—Messrs. Gregory Byrne, J. R. Hammond, and P. G. Camden.

On Sunday, June 27th, there arrived from New Orleans, on the steamer "Hard Times," forty privates of Company B, belonging to Col. Doniphan's command, from Lafayette county; on the "Memphis," about thirty volunteers belonging to various companies; and on the "J. M. White," sixty-eight members of Company G, from Howard county, and twenty-one members of other companies. But few of the officers arrived on these boats. On Monday, the 28th, a meeting of the citizens was held in the rotunda of the court-house to receive and welcome the Missouri volunteers who had arrived from New Orleans the day before, and to prevail on them to remain until the rest of their command should reach the city. Addresses were made by Col. Thornton Grimsley, G. K. McGunnegle, Judge Bowlin, and Dr. Sykes, on behalf of the committee of arrangements to welcome the volunteers, and Captain Reid responded in an eloquent manner, and accepted for the volunteers then in the city the invitation to remain and partake of the proffered hospitalities. On the 30th of June the steamer "Old Hickory" arrived from New Orleans, having on board as passengers Lieut.-Col. Morrison, of the Illinois volunteers, who had been at New Orleans awaiting the arrival of his regiment, but had returned home in consequence of ill-health; Col. Doniphan, Maj. Gilpin, Adjt. De Courcy, Lieut. Lee, quartermaster; Capt. Rogers, Company H, Callaway county; Capt. Parsons, Company F, Cole county; Capt. Moss, Company C, Clay county; Lieuts. Duncan and Murray, Company H, Callaway county; Lieuts. Gordon, Wells, and Winston, Company F, Cole county; Lieut. Graves, Company B, Lafayette county; Surgeons Thomas and James Morton. There was also a large number of privates on board. The "Harry of the West" and "Di Vernon" also brought considerable bodies of volunteers.

The uncertainty which attended the arrival of the volunteers, the limited number arriving in each boat, and the very great desire of many of them to re-

polished its peerless lustre, it now shines the most resplendent gem in the coronal of nations.

"The records of the Revolution, that dazzling picture in the Temple of History, presents us with the astonishing sight of men whose feet had never trodden the strict paths of military discipline, defying, conquering the trained ranks of the British army; whose trade is war. Nor did their patriotism, their energy, die with the Fathers of the Revolution—their spirit lives in their sons.

"The star which represents Missouri, shone not on the banner that shadowed the venerated head of Washington. But the unrivaled deeds of the Missouri Volunteers have added such brilliancy to its beams, that even *he* whose hand laid the corner-stone of the temple of American liberty, and placed on its finished shrines the rescued flag of his country, would feel proud to give the star of Missouri a place amidst the time-honored, the far-famed 'old thirteen.' The Spartan, the Athenian, the Roman, who offered on the altar of Mars

turn to their homes and friends, all conspired to create solicitude on the part of those who were anxious that everything should go off well at their reception. This was the case up to Friday morning, July 2d, when, at an early hour, the "Clarksville" came into port, having on board Maj. M. L. Clark, Capt. Weightman, Lieuts. Dorn and Chouteau, and other officers, and some of the privates of the battalion of light artillery. Their arrival determined the committee of arrangements to proceed with the ceremonies, and under their instruction the chief marshal issued orders to that effect. Thousands of citizens, leaving their usual vocations, turned out to honor the guests of the city, and long before the time appointed for the reception, in front of the Planters' House and in the streets leading to it a dense multitude of people collected. Flags were displayed in every direction, and the bells of the churches and of the various engine-houses rang a merry peal. Just as everything was ready for the orator appointed to welcome the volunteers to proceed with his address, it was announced by the chief marshal that the "Pride of the West," having on board Capt. Hudson and several other officers of the command, and also the artillery captured from the Mexicans at the battle of Sacramento, was in sight, and by common consent further proceedings were postponed until they could arrive and be participants in them. New spirit seemed to be infused into the multitude by this fortunate coincidence. The committee of arrangements at once repaired to the boat, and through Mr. Blennerhassett tendered the soldiers the hospitalities of the city and an invitation to partake in the festival. This invitation was responded to by Capt. Hudson, and in a very short time the volunteers and the train of artillery were on their way to Fourth street, where, in front of the Planters' House, it was arranged that the addresses welcoming the volunteers to the city should be made. Judge Bowlin, who had been selected for the purpose, then delivered an eloquent and patriotic address. In addressing Col. Doniphan and the officers and soldiers of the Missouri volunteers, he said:

"In the name and on the behalf of the people of St. Louis, I bid you a warm and cordial welcome back to the land of your cherished homes, and tender you the hospitalities of their city,—a city proud of her identity with your gallant

the most brilliant sacrifices, were trained even from their infancy, in all the arts of war. The service of the bloody god was to them the business of life, aye, even its pastime; their very dreams were full of the tumult of battle, but they who hewed asunder, with their good swords, the chains of a British tyrant, and they who have rendered the names of BRAZITO and SACRAMENTO watch words to rouse the valor of succeeding ages, hurried from the quiet labors of the field, the peaceful halls of justice, the cell of the student, and the familiar hearth of home, to swell the ranks of the defenders of their native land.

"*Volunteers of Missouri:*—In the history of your country, no brighter page can be found than that which records your own bright deeds. Many of you had never welcomed the morning light without the sunshine of a mother's smile to make it brighter; many of you had known the cares and hardships of life only in name; still you left the home of your childhood, and encountered perils and sufferings achievements. In doing this it becomes me to assure you, gentlemen, we are performing no idle ceremonial in which the heart has no participation, but it is the spontaneous homage which we, as your fellow-countrymen, feel proud to award your patriotism, your valor, your self-sacrificing devotion to country. Indeed, we hail your return to your homes with no ordinary emotions, as long anxiety for your safety, a consciousness of the perils that everywhere environed you, a dubiousness of your fate, spread a gloom over the community which your security has dispelled, and awakened in lieu of it mingled feelings of gratitude for your deliverance and admiration for the heroic deeds that won it. Besides, we feel proud, as your countrymen, in sharing that halo of glory which your gallant deeds have thrown around the name of the 'Missouri volunteer.' You have baptized that glorious title with your blood and laureled it with brilliant victories, the memory of which can only perish with the language in which they are recorded. Your deeds have encircled around that hallowed name a wreath of imperishable renown, never to fade or decay,—

'For the true laurel wreath which glory weaves
Is from that tree no bolt of thunder cleaves.'"

After alluding to the condition of the country, and noticing some details of the heroic achievements of the volunteers, he closed his address as follows:

"In conclusion, I again bid you welcome to the shores of our own Missouri; welcome to her proud and favored city; welcome to the hospitality of her people; welcome to all that a generous and chivalrous heart casts at the shrine of valor; welcome to the homage due to the brave; welcome to our hearths and our hearts."

To this address Lieut.-Col. Mitchell responded in a brief but appropriate speech.

Under the escort of the volunteer companies of the city, Col. Kennett commanding, the procession was then formed and marched to Camp Lucas. As the returning veterans, roughly clad, and with their long beards and torn battle-flags flowing in the wind, marched through the streets of the city, they were received with unabated enthusiasm. Along the route the display of flags from the houses and the waving of handkerchiefs by the ladies from windows and balconies announced to them that their return was hailed with universal joy, and that their arduous services were duly appreciated by their fellow-citizens of St. Louis.

Among the organizations which formed the escort were the Grays, Capt.

that would make the cheek of a Roman soldier turn pale; and encountered them so gallantly that time in his vast calendar of centuries can show none more bravely, more freely borne.

"We welcome you back to your home. The triumph which hailed the return of the Cæsars, to whose war-chariot was chained the known world, is not ours to give; nor do you need it. A prouder triumph than Rome could bestow is yours, in the undying fame of your proud achievements. But if the welcome of hearts filled with warm love and well merited admiration; *hearts best known and longest tried*, be a triumph, it is yours in the fullest extent.

"The torrent of eloquence to which you have just listened, the rich feast that awaits you, are the tributes of your own sex: but we, the fairer part of creation, must offer ours also.

"*Colonel Doniphan:*—In the name of the ladies who surround me, I bestow on you this laurel wreath—in every age and every clime, the gift of *beauty to valor*. In placing it on the brow of him who now

West; the Montgomery Guards, Capt. Watson; the Jaegers, Capt. Resick; the Missouri Dragoons, Capt. Steitz; and a company of mounted men. Several of the engine companies in full uniform were also in the procession. At Camp Lucas an immense crowd of people had assembled, and very soon the chief marshal introduced in fitting terms the Hon. Thomas H. Benton, who had been selected to deliver the reception speech.

Senator Benton addressed the returned volunteers as follows:

"COL. DONIPHAN, AND OFFICERS AND MEN: I have been appointed to an honorable and pleasant duty—that of making you the congratulations of your fellow-citizens of St. Louis on your happy return from your long and almost fabulous expedition. You have indeed marched far, and done much, and suffered much, and well entitled yourselves to the applause of your fellow-citizens, as well as the rewards and thanks of your Government. A year ago you left home. Going out from the western border of your State, you reënter it on the east, having made a circuit equal to the fourth of the circumference of the globe, providing for yourselves as you went, and returning with trophies taken from fields the names of which were unknown to yourselves and your country until revealed by your enterprise, illustrated by your valor, and immortalized by your deeds. History has but few such expeditions to record; and when they occur, it is as honorable and useful as it is just and wise to celebrate and commemorate the events which entitle them to renown.

"Your march and exploits have been among the most wonderful of the age. At the call of your country you marched a thousand miles to the conquest of New Mexico, as part of the force under General Kearny, and achieved that conquest without the loss of a man or the firing of a gun. That work finished, and New Mexico, itself so distant and so lately the *ultima thule*,—the outside boundary of speculation and enterprise,—so lately a distant point to be attained, becomes itself a point of departure, a beginning-point for new and far more extended expeditions. You look across the long and lofty chain—the Cordilleras of North America—which divide the Atlantic from the Pacific waters, and you see beyond that ridge a savage tribe which had been long in the habit of depredating upon the province which had just become an American conquest. You, a part only of the subsequent Chihuahua column under Jackson and Gilpin, march upon them, bring them to terms, and they sign a treaty with Col. Doniphan, in which they bind themselves to cease their depredations on the Mexicans, and to become the friends of the United States. A novel treaty that, signed on the western con-

kneels to receive it, I place it on the brows of ALL who followed where, so brave, so dauntless a commander led. It is true that around the laurel wreath is twined every association of genius, glory and valor, but I feel assured that it was never placed on a brow more worthy to receive it than his on which it now rests—THE HERO OF SACRAMENTO."

It does not become the author to extol in unmeasured terms the gallant officers who led with such marvelous success, nor the brave men who bore with Roman fortitude and patience, the fatigues of the WESTERN EXPEDITION, beyond what every candid and generous mind will readily concede. Equally the conduct of both is worthy of encomium. They performed all, and more than all, the government expected at their hands. After the conquest of New Mexico, Gen. Kearny with one hundred men, completed an astonishing overland

fines of New Mexico, between parties who had hardly ever heard each others' names before, and to give peace and protection to Mexicans who were hostile to both. This was the meeting and this the parting of the Missouri volunteers with the numerous and savage tribe of the Navajo Indians, living on the waters of the Gulf of California, and so long the terror and scourge of Sonora, Sinaloa, and New Mexico.

"This object accomplished, and impatient of inactivity, and without orders (Gen. Kearny having departed for California), you cast about to carve out some new work for yourselves. Chihuahua, a rich and populous city of nearly thirty thousand souls, the seat of government of the State of that name, and formerly the residence of the Captains-General of the internal provinces under the viceregal government of New Spain, was the captivating object which fixed your attention. It was a far-distant city, about as far from St. Louis as Moscow is from Paris, and towns and enemies, and a large river, and defiles and mountains, and the desert, whose ominous name portended death to travelers—*el jornada do los muertos* (the journey of the dead)—all lay between you. It was a perilous enterprise, and a discouraging one for a thousand men, badly equipped, to contemplate. No matter. Danger and hardship lent it a charm, and the adventurous march was resolved on, and the execution commenced. First, the ominous desert was passed, its character vindicating its title to its mournful appellation,—an arid plain of ninety miles, strewed with bones of animals perished of hunger and thirst; little hillocks of stone and the solitary cross, erected by pious hands, marking the spot where some Christian had fallen, victim of the savage, of the robber, or of the desert itself,—no water, no animal life, no sign of habitation. There the Texan prisoners, driven by the cruel Salazar, had met their direst sufferings, unrelieved, as in other parts of their march in the settled portions of the country, by the compassionate ministrations (for where is it that *woman* is not compassionate?) of the pitying women. The desert was passed, and the place for crossing the river approached. A little arm of the river, Bracito (in Spanish), made out from its side. There the enemy in superior numbers, and confident in cavalry and artillery, undertook to bar the way. Vain pretension. Their discovery, attack, and rout were about simultaneous operations. A few minutes did the work. And in this way our Missouri volunteers of the Chihuahua column spent their Christmas-day of the year 1846.

"The victory of the Bracito opened the way to the crossing of the river Del Norte, and to admission into the beautiful little town of the Paso del Norte, where a neat cultivation, a comfortable people, and vineyards, and a hospitable reception offered the rest and refreshment which toils and dangers and victory had won.

expedition to the shores of the Pacific, one thousand and ninety miles distant from Santa Fé. This great march was conducted over stony mountains, barren plains, and inhospitable deserts.

Colonel Doniphan and his men scaled the granite heights of the Cordilleras, amidst fathoms of accumulated, eternal snows, in the depth of winter, when the wide waste of rocks and the horrid, driving snow-storms were their most relentless enemies. Having spent three months, and performed a campaign of 750 miles in the most rugged and inhospitable regions on the continent, they return to the valley of the Del Norte. Here they refresh themselves, and recruit two days; after which they commence the grand march upon Chihuahua, and gain immortal renown on the trophied fields of Brazito and Sacramento. The Capital and the State, with two hundred thousand inhabitants, become a conquest to less than a thousand Missourians.

You rested there till artillery was brought down from Santa Fé, but the pretty town of the Paso del Norte, with all its enjoyments, and they were many, and the greater for the place in which they were found, was not a Capua to the men of Missouri. You moved forward in February, and the battle of the Sacramento, one of the military marvels of the age, cleared the road to Chihuahua, which was entered without further resistance. It had been entered once before by a detachment of American troops, but under circumstances how different. In the year 1807, Lieut. Pike and his thirty brave men, taken prisoners on the head of the Rio del Norte, had been marched captives into Chihuahua; in the year 1847, Doniphan and his men enter it as conquerors. The paltry triumph of a Captain-General over a Lieutenant was effaced in the triumphal entrance of a thousand Missourians into the grand and ancient capital of all the internal provinces, and old men, still alive, could remark the grandeur of the American spirit under both events,— the proud and lofty bearing of the captive thirty, the mildness and moderation of the conquering thousand.

"Chihuahua was taken, and responsible duties more delicate than those of arms were to be performed. Many American citizens were there engaged in trade; much American property was there. All this was to be protected, both lives and property, and by peaceful arrangement, for the command was too small to admit of division and of leaving a garrison. Conciliation and negotiation were resorted to, and successfully. Every American interest was provided for and placed under the safeguard, first, of good-will, and next, of guarantees not to be violated with impunity.

"Chihuahua gained, it became, like Santa Fé, not the terminating-point of a long expedition, but the beginning-point of a new one. Gen. Taylor was somewhere, no one knew exactly where, but some seven or eight hundred miles towards the other side of Mexico. You had heard that he had been defeated, that Buena Vista had not been a good prospect to him. Like good Americans, you did not believe a word of it, but, like good soldiers, you thought it best to go and see. A volunteer party of fourteen, headed by Collins of Boonville, undertake to penetrate to Saltillo, and bring you information of his condition. They set out. Amidst innumerable dangers they accomplish their purpose and return. You march. A vanguard of one hundred men, led by Lieut.-Col. Mitchell, led the way. Then came the main body (if the name is not a burlesque on such a handful), commanded by Col. Doniphan himself.

"The whole table-land of Mexico, in all its breadth from west to east, was to be traversed. A numerous and hostile population in towns, treacherous Coman-

This march was near six hundred miles through barren and waterless regions.

The nation almost trembled for the safety of Gen. Wool's column thirty-five hundred strong with heavy artillery, when he set out from San Antonio on his intended expedition against Chihuahua. Many apprehended his complete overthrow, and argued that it would result in a prodigal waste of means, and a useless and wanton sacrifice of human life for so small a force to march against so powerful and populous a state. But the strong hold of Central Mexico is in possession of the hero of Sacramento, with nine hundred and twenty-four Missourians, and the American flag floats in triumph over its walls.

Leaving Chihuahua for more extended operations, and a new theatre of action, they move off through the states of Durango and Coahuila, traversing parched, arid, waterless wastes, for more than

ches in the mountains, were to be passed. Everything was to be self-provided,—provisions, transportation, fresh horses for remounts, and even the means of victory,—and all without a military chest, or even an empty box, in which Government gold had ever reposed. All was accomplished. Mexican towns were passed in order and quiet, plundering Comanches were punished, means were obtained from traders to liquidate indispensable contributions, and the wants that could not be supplied were endured like soldiers of veteran service.

"I say the Comanches were punished. And here presents itself an episode of novel, extraordinary, and romantic kind,—Americans chasing savages for plundering people whom they themselves came to conquer, and forcing the restitution of captives and of plundered property. A strange story this to tell in Europe, where backwoods character—Western character—is not yet completely known. But to the facts. In the mesquite forest of the *Bolson de Mapima*, and in the sierras around the beautiful town and fertile district of Parras, and in all the open country for hundreds of miles round about, the savage Comanches have held dominion ever since the usurper Santa Anna disarmed the people, and sally forth from their fastnesses to slaughter men, plunder cattle, and carry off women and children. An exploit of this kind had just been performed on the line of the Missourians' march, not far from Parras, and an advanced party chanced to be in that town at the time the news of the depredation arrived there. It was only fifteen strong. Moved by gratitude for the kind attentions of the people, especially the women, to the sick of Gen. Wool's command, necessarily left in Parras, and unwilling to be outdone by enemies in generosity, the heroic fifteen, upon the spot, volunteered to go back, hunt out the depredators, and punish them, without regard to numbers. A grateful Mexican became their guide. On their way they fell in with fifteen more of their comrades, and in a short time seventeen Comanches killed out of sixty-five, eighteen captives restored to their families, and three hundred and fifty head of cattle recovered for their owners, was the fruit of this sudden and romantic episode.

"Such noble conduct was not without its effect on the minds of the astonished Mexicans. An official document from the prefect of the place to Capt. Reid, leader of this detachment, attests the verity of the fact and the gratitude of the Mexicans, and constitutes a trophy of a new kind in the annals of war. Here it is in the original Spanish, and I will read it off in English. It is officially dated from the prefecture of the Department of Parras, signed by the prefect, José Ignacio Arrabe, and addressed to Capt. Reid, the 18th of May, and says:

"'At the first notice that the barbarians, after killing many and taking captives, were returning to their haunts, you generously and bravely offered, with

six hundred miles, ready to succor General Taylor, if beleaguered in Saltillo, or to accompany him over the Cedral Desert in his contemplated descent upon San Louis de Potosi, having previously sent fourteen express-men on a most perilous enterprise to learn the General's wishes.

Their services being now no longer required, the commander-in-chief dispatches them to the United States, by way of Matamoras and the Mexican Gulf. They sail for New Orleans, where they are discharged. They return to Missouri from the eastward graced with the trophies of the vanquished foe, having in twelve months, performed a magnificent circuit of more than 3500 miles by land, and 2500 by water, with the loss of less than one hundred of their original number.

The expedition of Cyrus against his brother, Artaxerxes, and the retreat of the ten thousand Greeks, famous through all time, con-

---

fifteen of your subordinates, to fight them on their crossing by the Pozo, executing this enterprise with celerity, address, and bravery worthy of all eulogy, and worthy of the brilliant issue which all celebrate. You recovered many animals and much plundered property, and eighteen captives were restored to liberty and to social enjoyments, their souls overflowing with a lively sentiment of joy and gratitude, which all the inhabitants of this town equally breathe, in favor of their generous deliverers and their valiant chief. The half of the Indians killed in the combat and those which fly wounded, do not calm the pain which all feel for the wound which your Excellency received defending Christians and civilized beings against the rage and brutality of savages. All desire the speedy reëstablishment of your health, and although they know that your own noble soul will be found the best reward of your conduct, they desire also to address you the expression of their gratitude and high esteem. I am honored in being the organ of the public sentiment, and pray you to accept it, with the assurance of my most distinguished esteem. God and Liberty.'

"This is a trophy of a new kind in war, won by thirty Missourians, and worthy to be held up to the admiration of Christendom.

"The long march from Chihuahua to Monterey was made more in the character of protection and deliverance than of conquest and invasion. Armed enemies were not met, and peaceful people were not disturbed. You arrived in the month of May in Gen. Taylor's camp, and about in a condition to vindicate, each of you for himself, your lawful title to the double *sobriquet* of the general, with the addition to it, which the Colonel of the expedition has supplied, 'ragged, as well as rough and ready.' No doubt you all showed title at that time to that third *sobriquet;* but to see you now, so gayly attired, so sprucely equipped, one might suppose that you had never for an instant been a stranger to the virtues of soap and water, or the magic ministrations of the *blanchisseuse* and the elegant transformations of the fashionable tailor. Thanks, perhaps, to the difference between pay in the lump at the end of service and the driblets along in the course of it.

"You arrived in General Taylor's camp ragged and rough, as we can well conceive, and ready, as I can quickly show. You reported for duty! You asked for service!—such as a march upon San Luis de Potosi, Zacatecas, or the 'Halls of the Montezumas,' or anything in that way that the General should have a mind to. If he was going upon any excursion of that kind, all right. No matter about fatigues that were past, or expirations of service that might accrue: you came to go, and only asked the privilege. That is what I call ready. Unhappily, the

ducted by Xenophon and Cherisopus, forms the only parallel to Col. Doniphan's expedition, recorded in history. In fifteen months Cyrus and Xenophon conduct this expedition about 3450 English miles, with the loss of several thousand brave men, and finally return to Greece, possessing nothing save their lives and their arms. In thirteen months Col. Doniphan and his Missourians, accomplish a similar expedition, (except as to its objects) of more than 5500 miles, returning decorated with the spoils of war, and meeting with the hearty approval of their countrymen.

The distance over which Gen. Kearny marched, was perhaps greater than that over which Col. Doniphan passed; but the former conducted an army only to California, returning privately; while the latter commanded and provided for his men, and that too without funds, until they were disbanded at New Orleans.

conqueror of Palo Alto, Resaca de la Palma, Monterey, and Buena Vista was not exactly in the condition that the Lieutenant-General might have intended him to be. He was not at the head of twenty thousand men; he was not at the head of any thousand that would enable him to march, and had to decline the proffered service. Thus the long-marched and well-fought volunteers—the rough, the ready, and the ragged—had to turn their faces towards home, still more than two thousand miles distant. But this being mostly by water, you hardly count it in the recital of your march. But this is an unjust omission, and against the precedents as well as unjust. 'The Ten Thousand' counted the voyage on the Black Sea as well as the march from Babylon, and twenty centuries admit the validity of the count. The present age and posterity will include in 'the going out and coming in' of the Missouri volunteers the water voyage as well as the land march, and then the expedition of the One Thousand will exceed that of the Ten by some two thousand miles.

"The last nine hundred miles of your land march, from Chihuahua to Matamoras, you made in forty-five days, bringing seventeen pieces of artillery, eleven of which were taken from the Sacramento and Bracito. Your horses, traveling the whole distance without United States provender, were astonished to find themselves regaled, on their arrival on the Rio Grande frontier, with hay, corn, and oats from the States. You marched farther than the farthest, fought as well as the best, left order and quiet in your train, and cost less money than any.

"You arrive here to-day, absent one year, marching and fighting all the time, bringing trophies of cannon and standards from fields whose names were unknown to you before you set out, and only grieving that you could not have gone farther. Ten pieces of cannon, rolled out of Chihuahua to arrest your march, now roll through the streets of St. Louis to grace your triumphal return. Many standards, all pierced with bullets while waving over the heads of the enemy at the Sacramento, now wave at the head of your column. The black flag, brought to the Bracito to indicate the refusal of that quarter which its bearers so soon needed and received, now takes its place among your trophies, and hangs drooping in their nobler presence. To crown the whole, to make public and private happiness go together, to spare the cypress where the laurel hangs in clusters, this long and perilous march, with all its accidents of field and camp, presents an incredibly small list of comrades lost. Almost all return! and the joy of families resounds intermingled with the applauses of the State.

"I have said that you made your long expedition without Government orders; and so indeed you did. You received no orders from your Government, but, without knowing it, you were fulfilling its orders, orders which never reached

But where are the permanent, the beneficial results of this wonderful, this almost fabulous Expedition of Col. Doniphan?—the utilitarian will inquire. The facts, that the Chihuahua market, which the war had closed, was re-opened for the admittance of several hundred thousand dollars worth of American goods, which otherwise would have been sacrificed, to the ruin of the merchants, if not indemnified by the Government; that new and more desirable commercial relations will henceforward assuredly spring up between Chihuahua and the western States, and on a safer and more equitable basis; that the insults and wrongs which had been repeatedly heaped on American citizens, and the decimation of the Mier prisoners, were now completely avenged by the defeat of a haughty and supercilious foe; that great light has been thrown on the political condition and geographical position of central Mexico, which had hitherto been but little

---

you. Happy the soldier who executes the command of his Government; happier still he who anticipates command and does what is wanted before he is bid. This is your case. You did the right thing at the right time, and what the Government intended you to do, and without knowing its intentions. The facts are these: Early in the month of November last the President asked my opinion on the manner of conducting the war. I submitted a plan to him which, in addition to other things, required all the disposable troops in New Mexico, and all the Americans in that quarter who could be engaged for a dashing expedition, to move down through Chihuahua and the State of Durango, and if necessary to Zacatecas, and get into communication with Gen. Taylor's right as early as possible in the month of March. In fact, the disposable Missourians in New Mexico were to be one of three columns destined for a combined movement on the City of Mexico, all to be on the table-land and ready for the movement in the month of March. The President approved the plan, and the Missourians being most distant, orders were dispatched to New Mexico to put them in motion. Mr. Solomon Sublette carried the order, and delivered it to the commanding officer at Santa Fé, Col. Price, on the 23d day of February, just five days before you fought the marvelous battle of Sacramento.

"I well remember what passed between the President and myself at the time he resolved to give this order. It awakened his solicitude for your safety. It was to send a small body of men a great distance, into the heart of a hostile country, and upon the contingency of uniting in a combined movement, the means for which had not yet been obtained from Congress. The President made it a question, and very properly, whether it was safe or prudent to start the small Missouri column before the movement of the left and center was assured. I answered that my own rule in public affairs was to do what I thought was right, and leave it with others to do what they thought was right, and that I believed it the proper course for him to follow on the present occasion. On this view he acted. He gave the order to go, without waiting to see whether Congress would furnish the means of executing the combined plan; and, for his consolation, I undertook to guarantee your safety. Let the worst come to the worst, I promised him that you would take care of yourselves. Though the other parts of the plan should fail, though you should become far involved in the advance, and deeply compromised in the enemy's country, and without support, still I relied on your courage, skill and enterprise to extricate yourselves from every danger, to make daylight through all the Mexicans that should stand before you, cut your way out, and make good your retreat to Taylor's camp. This is what I promised the President in November last, and what you have so manfully fulfilled. And here is a little manuscript volume (the duplicate of it in the hands of the President), from which

explored by Americans; that the Mexican people have now been taught something of the strength of their northern neighbors; that they have acquired some knowledge of the effects of free institutions, liberty, and general education upon mankind; and that all central Mexico was thereby neutralized during the war,—will sufficiently answer the important inquiry.

Thus terminated the most extraordinary and wonderful Expedition of the age, attended throughout by the most singular good fortune, conducted under the auspices of Col. Doniphan, who has been very justly styled the GREAT MILITARY PEDESTRIAN, THE VICTOR AND DIPLOMATIST.

I will read you a page to show you that you are the happy soldiers who have done the will of the Government without knowing its will:

"'THE RIGHT WING.—To be composed of all the disposable troops in New Mexico, to advance rapidly through the States of Chihuahua and Durango, and towards Zacatecas, and to attain a position about on a line with Gen. Taylor in the month of March, and be ready to push on the capital. This column to move light, to have no rear, to keep itself mounted from horse in the country, and to join the center column, or cut its way out if the main object fails.'

"This is what was proposed for you in the month of November last, and what I pledged myself to the President that you would perform, and nobly have you redeemed the pledge.

"But this was not the first or the only time that I pledged myself for you. As far back as June, 1846, when a separate expedition to Chihuahua was first projected, I told the President that it was unnecessary; that the Missouri troops under Gen. Kearny would take that place, in addition to the conquest of New Mexico, and that he might order the column under Gen. Wool to deflect to the left and join Gen. Taylor as soon as he pleased. Again, when I received a letter from Lieut.-Col. Mitchell, dated in November last, and informing me that he was leaving Santa Fé with one hundred men to open a communication with Gen. Wool, I read the letter to the President and told him that they would do it. And, again, when we heard that Col. Doniphan, with a thousand men, after curbing the Navajos, was turning down towards the south, and threatening the ancient capital of the Captains-General of the internal provinces, I told him they would take it. In short, my confidence in Missouri enterprise, courage, and skill was boundless. My promises were boundless. Your performance has been boundless. And now let boundless honor and joy salute, as it does, your return to the soil of your State, and to the bosoms of your families."

When Senator Benton had concluded, Col. Doniphan was loudly and enthusiastically called to the stand, whereupon he rose and responded in a chaste and modest yet graphic address, in which he ascribed the great success and good fortune which continually attended him on his expedition rather to the bravery and conduct of his soldiers than to his own generalship.

As soon as Col. Doniphan's speech was concluded Capt. Hudson was called for, but upon his suggestion that a very agreeable part of the entertainment, the collation, remained to be discussed, the company adjourned to the St. Louis Park, and did full justice to the ample cheer provided for them.

Speeches and toasts followed the dinner. In answer to calls of the company, Col. Mitchell, Maj. Clark, Capt. Weightman, Capt. Hudson, Col. Benton, Col. Grimsley, Capt. Reid, and others made speeches.

Soon after, the crowd dispersed, and Col. Doniphan and a large number of volunteers took passage on the "Little Missouri" for home.

CHAPTER XXIII.

Col. Price—Disposition of the troops—The Conspiracy—Conspiracy detected—Second Conspiracy—Massacre of Gov. Bent and retinue—Battles of Canada, Embudo, Pueblo de Taos, and the Mora—Death of Capts. Burgwin and Hendley—Restoration of tranquillity.

It will be remembered that on the 26th of October, 1846, Col. Doniphan took his departure from Santa Fé, on an excursion against the Navajo Indians, and was rejoined at Santo Domingo by three hundred of his own regiment, who had been previously stationed at the grazing encampment near San Miguel, but were now ordered to proceed into the mountains, on a most serious and trying campaign. Col. Doniphan returned no more to Santa Fé.

The command of the troops in New Mexico thenceforward, devolved on Colonel, now Brigadier-General STERLING PRICE. For the preservation of health and activity among his troops—which consisted of the 2d regiment under his own immediate command, an extra battalion under Lieut.-Col. Willock, a battalion of infantry under Captains Angney and Murphy, one company of light artillery under Captain Fischer, the Laclede Rangers under Lieut. Elliott, two hundred of the 1st dragoons under Capt. Burgwin, (Major Sumner having returned to the United States on the 18th of October), and some additional artillery and miscellaneous troops under Lieuts. Dyer and Wilson of the U. S. Army, making an aggregate force of near 2,000 men—and also for the preservation of good order, quiet, and entire submission on the part of the malcontent New Mexicans and Pueblo Indians, Col. Price at first thus disposed of his forces:

Capt. Burgwin, with the 1st dragoons, was stationed at Albuquerque to maintain tranquillity on the Rio Abajo; a squadron of two hundred men, under Major Edmondson, was scouring about Cebolleta; a small force under Capt. Hendley was ordered to the valley of the Mora, with the view of finding forage for the stock, and of preserving peace and subordination in that quarter, as well as also to check the predatory incursions of the border Indians, who were becoming quite troublesome and deserving of chastisement; the remaining forces were retained at the capital as a garrison.

On the 28th of October, two days after the departure of Col. Doniphan from Santa Fé, Col. Price issued an order requiring the troops under his command to appear on parade, for drill and discipline, twice each day. The officers were required to perform an extra drill, that they might be better qualified to instruct the men. This discipline was rigidly adhered to. Every one, the least acquainted with military affairs, is aware how difficult a matter it is to preserve good order and wholesome discipline in a garrison composed entirely of volunteers. The unrestrained, independent life to which the citizen soldier has been accustomed, unfits him for garrison service. He becomes impatient of discipline, and desires active, useful, honorable employment. For this reason regular troops are much better for garrisons than volunteers; but none are their superiors in an arduous and daring campaign.

About the 1st of December, the most distinguished of the malcontents began to hold secret cabals and consultations, and to plot the overthrow of the actual, existing government. Oftentimes the conspirators, like Catiline and his accomplices in guilt, would withdraw into some retired room in the capital, or on the flat top of some unfrequented building, and there at the silent hour of midnight machinate a scheme for the massacre of all the Americans, the establishment of a new government, and installation of new governors. The leaders of this dark and desperate conspiracy were Don Tomas Ortiz, who aspired to be governor of the province; Don Diego Archulette, who had been nominated as commanding general; and Seniores Nicholas Pino, Miguel Pino, Santiago Armijo, Manuel Chavez, Domingo Baca, Pablo Dominguez, Juan Lopez, and many others, all men of great and restless ambition, and expectants of office if the conspiracy should have a favorable issue.

The 19th of December, at midnight, was the time at first appointed for the revolt to commence, which was to be simultaneous all over the department. In the meantime each one of the conspirators had a particular part of the state assigned him, to the end that they might gain over the whole people of the province. The profoundest secrecy was to be preserved, and the most influential men, whose ambition induced them to seek preferment, were alone to be made acquainted with the plot. No woman was to be privy to these things, lest they should be divulged.

Each having pledged himself to the others on the cross that he would be faithful and vigilant in consummating their designs, as speedily and successfully as possible, departed, some into one place and some into another. For his part Tomas Ortiz, who had been second in command to Armijo, the late governor, went to El Bado, that he might stir up the people there; Diego Archulette hastened to the valley of Taos, to make known his plans and solicit aid in that quarter; Domingo Baca departed to the Rio Abajo to excite the inhabitants, and procure assistance there; Pablo Dominguez and Miguel Pino proceeded to the settlements on the river Tesuca, to enlist them in the enterprise; and the priest Leyba would propose the same to the people at San Miguel and Las Bagas.

For the more certain success of the revolution, the conspirators assembled in secret conclave in the capital, on the night of the 15th of December, to consult, mature their plans, and arrange the method of attack. Don Sanchez, when apprehended and brought before the tribunal, testified that Don Diego Archulette commenced the discourse:—"I make the motion that there be an act to nominate a governor and a commander-general, and I would nominate Tomas Ortiz for the first office, and Diego Archulette for the second." This was unanimously carried, and the act signed by every individual present. After this was concluded, they commenced a discourse relative to the method of surprising the government at Santa Fé, and taking possession of the place. They decided upon the following plan: "On Saturday evening, the 19th of December, all were to assemble with their men at the parish church. Having divided themselves into several parties, they were to sally forth, some to seize the pieces of artillery, others to go to the quarters of the colonel, and others to the palace of the Governor, (if he should be there,) and if not, to send an order to Taos to seize him, because he would give the most trouble. This act was also agreed on by all. The sound of the church bell was to be the signal for the assault by the forces concealed in the church, and those which Don Diego Archulette should have brought near the city—midnight was the time agreed on, when all were to enter the "plaza" at the same moment, seize the pieces of artillery and point them into the streets. The meeting now dissolved."

Owing to a want of complete organization and concert, and that the conspiracy was not yet fully matured, it was concluded to suspend the attack for a time, and fix on Christmas-eve night for the assault, when the soldiers and garrison would be indulging in wine and feasting, and scattered about through the city at the fandangos, not having their arms in their hands. All the Americans, without distinction, throughout the state, and such New Mexicans as had favored the American government, and accepted office by appointment of Gen. Kearny, were to be massacred or driven from the country, and the conspirators were to seize upon and occupy the government. This enterprise, however, failed of success, being detected, exposed and crushed by the vigilance of Col. Price, his officers and men.

The conspiracy was detected in the following manner: a mulatto girl, residing in Santa Fé, had married one of the conspirators, and had by degrees obtained a knowledge of their movements and secret meetings. To prevent the effusion of blood which would inevitably be the result of a revolution, she communicated to Col. Price, all the facts of which she was in possession, and warned him to use the utmost vigilance. The rebellion was immediately suppressed.

But the restless and unsatisfied ambition of the leaders of the conspiracy did not long permit them to remain inactive. The rebellion had been detected and smothered, but not completely crushed. A second and still more dangerous conspiracy was plotted. The most powerful and influential men in the State favored the design. An organized plan of operations was adopted. The profoundest secrecy was preserved. While all appeared to be quiet and secure, the machinations of the conspirators were maturing, and gaining strength. Even the officers of State, and the priests, gave their aid and counsel. The people every where, in the towns, villages, and settlements, were exhorted to arm and equip themselves, to strike for their faith, their religion, and their altars, and drive the "heretics," the "unjust invaders of the country," from their soil, and with fire and sword pursue them to annihilation. On the 19th of January, this rebellion broke out in every part of the State simultaneously.

On the 14th of January, Governor Charles Bent, attended by an escort of five persons, among whom were the sheriff, circuit attorney, and the prefecto, left Santa Fé and proceeded to Taos. Upon his arrival there he was applied to by the Pueblo Indians, to release from prison, two of their number, who, for some misdemeanor, had been incarcerated by the authorities. The governor told them they must await the ordinary process of the laws.

On the 19th of the same month the governor and his retinue were murdered in the most cruel and inhuman manner, by the Pueblos and Mexicans at the village San Fernando. On the same day seven other Americans, after standing a siege of two days, were overpowered, taken and butchered in cold blood at the Arroyo Hondo; also four at the town Mora, and two on the Colorado.*

The insurgents had assembled in strong force at La Cañada, under command of Gens. Ortiz, Lafoya, Chavez, and Montoya, with the view of making a descent upon Santa Fé. Col. Price having ordered Major Edmondson and Captain Burgwin, with their respective commands from the Rio Abajo, on the morning of the 23d, at the head of 353 men,† which number was afterwards augmented to four hundred and eighty, and four mountain howitzers, marched against the insurgents, leaving Lieut. colonel Willock, with a strong garrison, in command of the capital. The weather was extremely inclement, and the earth covered with snow.

"On the evening of the 24th, Colonel Price encountered the enemy at Cañada, numbering about 2,000 men, under the command of Gens. Tofaya, Chavez, and Montoya. The enemy were posted on the hills commanding each side of the road. About two o'clock P. M. a brisk fire from the artillery under the command of Lieuts. Dyer (of the regular army) and Harsentiver, was opened upon them, but from their being so much scattered, it had but little effect.

The artillery were within such short distance as to be exposed to a hot fire, which either wounded or penetrated the clothes of 19 or 20 men who served the guns. Col. Price seeing the slight effect which the artillery had upon them, ordered Capt. Angney[128] with

---

* The following persons fell victims to the conspiracy. At Taos, C. Bent, governor; S. Lee, sheriff; J. W. Leal, circuit attorney; C. Vigil, (Mexican,) prefecto; N. Baubien, son of Judge Baubein; and Jirmia, a Mexican. At the Arroya Hondo, twelve miles from Taos—S. Turley, A. Cooper, W. Harfield, L. Folque, P. Roberts, J. Marshall, and W. Austin. At the Rio Colorado—M. Head, and W. Harwood. At the Mora—L. Waldo, R. Culver, Noyes, and two others.—HUGHES.

† See Col. Price's official dispatch, February 15th, 1847.—HUGHES.

NOTE 128.—W. Z. Angney came to Jefferson City, Mo., about the year 1843. I am indebted to Dr. W. A. Curry, of Kansas City, for all my information about Angney. Dr. Curry believes that Angney was a native of Pennsylvania. He was a lawyer, and opened an office for the practice of his profession upon his

his battalion to charge the hill, which was gallantly done, being supported by Capt. St. Vrain, of the citizens, and Lieut. White, of the Carroll companies. The charge lasted until sundown. Our loss was two killed and seven wounded. The Mexicans acknowledge a loss of 36 killed, and 45 taken prisoners. The enemy retreated towards Taos, their stronghold. Colonel Price on the 27th took up his line of march for Taos, and again encountered them at El Embudo on the 29th. They were discovered in the thick brush on each side of the road, at the entrance of a defile, by a party of spies, who immediately fired upon them. Capt. Burgwin, who had that morning joined Colonel Price with his company of dragoons, hearing the firing, came up, together with Captain St. Vrain's, and Lieutenant White's companies. A charge was made by the three companies, resulting in the total rout of the Mexicans and Indians. The battle lasted about half an hour; but the pursuit was kept up for two hours.

The march was resumed on the next day, and met with no opposition until the evening of the 3d of February, at which time they arrived at the Pueblo de Taos, where they found the Mexicans and Indians strongly fortified. A few rounds were fired by the artillery that evening, but it was deemed advisable not to make a general attack then, but wait until morning. The attack was commenced in the morning by two batteries under the command of Lieuts. Dyer and

---

arrival at Jefferson City. He was an able man and a good lawyer, and soon obtained a remunerative practice. He was a Democrat, and took an active part in politics. Under the first call for troops he raised a company at Jefferson City and went with it to St. Louis, but was turned back, as were companies from other counties. He returned to Jefferson City to find that Captain Parsons had raised another company under the second call and had marched to Fort Leavenworth. Angney and his company followed, and there found the First Regiment already organized. He found the Platte county company under Captain Murray in the same predicament that he was. They managed in some way to prevail upon the authorities to accept their companies as infantry, and they were accordingly so mustered into the service of the United States. They were a part of the Army of the West, but did not go beyond New Mexico. Detachments from each company went with Doniphan and participated in all the achievements of that immortal band. Those who remained in New Mexico were, like all Missouri volunteers, excellent soldiers, and saw much service. They returned with General Price, and were mustered out at Fort Leavenworth. The roster of each of these companies is published herein. Captain Angney located in Santa Fé, and engaged in the practice of law, upon his discharge from the service; he was also active politically. He moved from New Mexico to California before the Civil War.

Wilson, of the regular army, and Lieut. Harsentiver of the light artillery, by throwing shells into the town. About meridian, a charge was ordered and gallantly executed by Capt. Burgwin's company, supported by Capt. McMillan's company and Capt. Angney's battalion of infantry, supported by Capt. Burbee's company. The church, which had been used as a part of the fortifications, was taken by this charge. The fight was hotly contested until night, when two white flags were hoisted, but were immediately shot down. In the morning the Fort was surrounded. The old men, the priest and the matrons, bringing their children and their sacred household gods in their hands, besought the clemency and mercy of their conquerors. Pardon was granted. In this battle fell Capt. Burgwin, than whom a braver soldier, or better man, never poured out his blood in his country's cause.

The total loss of the Mexicans in the three engagements, is estimated at two hundred and eighty-two killed; the number of their wounded is unknown. Our total loss was fifteen killed,* and forty-seven wounded.

Learning of the insurrectionary movements on the 20th of January, Capt. Hendley, who was in command of the grazing detachment on the Pecos, immediately took possession of Las Bagas, where the insurgents were beginning to concentrate their forces. He now ordered the different grazing parties to unite with him, and prepare for offensive and defensive warfare. In a short time he was joined by various detachments, increasing his numbers to two hundred and twenty-five men.

Lieut. Hawkins, with thirty-five men, was dispatched on the 22d to escort a train of wagons into Las Bagas, the Mexicans having sent out a party to plunder them. He soon met Capt. Murphy, with a train of wagons, convoyed by a detachment of Capt. Jackson's company, having in his possession about three hundred thousand dollars in specie. The convoy returned about one day's march to guard the provision train, while the specie train moved on, escorted by Lieut. Hawkins.

Capt. Hendley, leaving the greater part of his force at Las Bagas, on the 22d, with eighty men started for the Mora, where he had learned

* Killed—Capt. Burgwin, Lieut. Van Valkenburg, Sergts. Caldwell, Ross and Hart, and privates Graham, Smith Papin, Bower. Brooks, Levicy. Hansuker, Truax, Austin and Bebee.—Hughes.

the Mexicans were embodied, two hundred strong. He arrived before the place on the 24th, "found a body of Mexicans under arms, prepared to defend the town, and while forming his men in a line for attack, a small party of insurgents were seen running from the hills. A detachment was ordered to cut them off, which was attacked by the main body of the enemy. A general engagement immediately ensued, the Mexicans retreating, and firing from the windows and loop-holes in their houses. Capt. Hendley and his men closely pursued them, rushing into their houses with them, shooting some, and running others through with bayonets. A large body of the insurgents had taken possession of an old fort, and commenced a fire from the loop-holes upon the Americans. Capt. Hendley with a small party had taken possession of an apartment in the fort, and while preparing to fire it, he was struck by a ball from an adjoining room. He fell, and died in a few minutes. Our men having no artillery, and the fort being impregnable without it, retired to Las Bagas. The enemy had twenty-five killed, and seventeen taken prisoners. Our loss was one killed, and three wounded.

"Thus fell the brave Captain Hendley, almost in the very moment of victory; and while we lament his loss, it is some consolation to know that he died like a soldier. His body was taken to Santa Fé, where he was buried with all the honors of war."*

On the 1st of February, the death of Capt. Hendley, as well as that of Messrs. Waldo, Noyes, Culver and others, was avenged by Capt. Morin and his men, in the complete demolition of the village Mora. The insurgents fled to the mountains. The dead bodies of the Americans who had been assassinated, were conveyed to Las Bagas for interment.

The battles of La Cañada, Embudo, Pueblo de Taos, and the Mora, in all of which the insurgents were vanquished with heavy loss, suppressed the insurrection, and once more restored quiet, law and order throughout the territory. On the 6th of February, Montoya, one of the leaders of the conspiracy, who had styled himself the Santa Anna of the North, was court-martialed and sentenced to

* The remains of Capts. Hendley and Burgwin, several Lieutenants, and sutler Albert Wilson, were exhumed at Santa Fé, and brought to Fort Leavenworth, where they were interred on the 22d of September, 1847: except those of Capt. Hendley, which were conveyed to Richmond, and buried on the 23d.—HUGHES.

be hung. He was executed on the 7th,* in the presence of the army. Fourteen others who were concerned in the murder of Gov. Bent, were tried, convicted, and executed in a similar manner, in the neighborhood of Taos.

Leaving a detachment of infantry in the valley of Taos, under the command of Capt. Angney, Colonel Price returned to Santa Fé, where he continued to discharge the highest civil and military functions of the territory. At a subsequent period, however, Capt. Angney was relieved by Lieut.-colonel Willock's battalion of cavalry.

The leading instigators of the revolution having fallen in battle, been executed upon a charge of treason, or escaped the punishment merited by their offences, by flight to the mountains, the country once more enjoyed a short repose. The insurgent armies were dispersed. The people returned from the hills and mountains, whither many of them had fled for refuge during the excitement, to their respective homes, and resumed their daily avocations. Peace and harmony once more reigned throughout the province.

* The court-martial consisted of six officers, Capts. Angney, Barbee, and Slack; Lieuts. Ingalls, White and Eastin; the latter being Judge Advocate of the court.—HUGHES.

CHAPTER XXIV.

Increased vigilance of the troops—Suspicion—Battle of the Red river cañon—Murder of Lieut. Brown—Battle of Las Bagas—Six prisoners executed—Attack on the Cienega—Indian outrages—Robberies—Lieut. Love—Capt. Mann—The new levies.

After the suppression of the rebellion in New Mexico, the troops were posted in almost every part of the country. A greater degree of vigilance was observed, and stricter discipline enforced. The conduct of the Mexicans was watched with the utmost scrutiny. No house was permitted to retain arms, or other munitions of war; nor was any Mexican cavalier suffered, as had hitherto been the case, to ride with impunity about the country, and through the American camps, displaying his weapons and warlike trappings, making estimates of the American forces, and keeping a strict espionage upon their movements. The American soldiers, roused to indignation by the brutal massacres and frequent assassinations which had already blackened the annals of the campaign, and thrown a dark shade over the conquest of the country, scarcely spared the innocent and unoffending. However, no acts of violence were perpetrated.

The soldiers slept upon their arms. They never left their quarters, or rode out of the city, or visited the villages, or passed through the country, without their arms in their hands. They were always prepared, both night and day, for any sudden emergency that might arise; with such suspicion and animosity did the Americans and New Mexicans now regard each other. A suspicious quietude reigned throughout the territory, but it was only that the rebellion might break out afresh on the first favorable opportunity.

On the 26th of May, 1847, Maj. Edmondson, with a detachment of two hundred men under Capts. Hollaway & Robinson, and Lieuts. Elliott and Hughes, was vigorously attacked by a large body of Mexicans, Apache, Comanche, and Kiawa Indians combined, at the "Red river cañon," about one hundred and twenty miles from Santa Fé. The enemy were supposed to number about five hundred. The action commenced about sunset, and continued until dark. The defile was narrow, and on either hand the spurs of the mountains were rugged and inaccessible to cavalry. The pass led through a morass or quagmire, so difficult of passage that many of the horses stuck fast in the mud. The cavalry could not act to any advantage. Major Edmondson therefore dismounted the men, and cautiously advanced against the enemy, under the heavy fire. The enemy was repulsed; but gaining fresh courage, he renewed the attack with more vigor than ever. The Americans now slowly retired in good order a few hundred paces, and occupied a more favorable position for defence. The retreat was covered by Lieut. Elliott, with the Laclede rangers. It was now dark. The next morning Major Edmondson led his force through the cañon to renew the attack; but the enemy had retreated. In this engagement the Americans lost one man killed, and had several slightly injured. The Mexicans and Indians suffered a loss of seventeen killed, and no doubt many more wounded.

On the 26th of June, the horses belonging to Capt. Horine's company of mounted men, stationed under Major Edmondson, near Las Bagas, were stolen by the Mexicans, and driven into the neighboring mountains. On the 28th Lieut. Brown and privates McClanahan and Quisenbury, together with one Mexican as a guide, were dispatched in pursuit of them. Not returning on the following day as they intended, their companions rightly conjectured that they had been murdered. On the 5th of July a Mexican lady came into Las Bagas and stated that three Americans and one Mexican had recently been slain, and their dead bodies consumed to ashes.

Major Edmondson, immediately after receiving this information, posted out a strong picket guard, with instructions to permit no one to enter the camp, without first being brought before him. On the same day, private William Cox, of Capt. Hollaway's company, while hunting in the mountains, discovered three suspicious looking Mexicans, endeavoring to shun him, whereupon he captured and brought them into camp. They were separately examined by Major Edmondson, but not being able to extort from them a satisfactory answer, one of them was hanged by the neck several times, and until he had almost expired. When let down the third time, he stated that three Americans and one Mexican had been recently murdered, and their dead bodies burnt, near Las Bagas. When this confession was extorted, Major Edmondson quickly ordered the detachment, which consisted of twenty-nine cavalry, thirty-three infantry, and one twelve-pound mountain howitzer, to prepare for the march, expecting to reach town before daylight the next morning.

Major Edmondson, ascertaining that he would not be able to reach Las Bagas as soon as he desired, hurried on with the cavalry, leaving orders for the infantry and artillery to follow in his rear with all possible haste. On reaching the place, he divided his men into two parties, under command of Capts. Hollaway and Horine. They were now ordered to charge at full speed on the right and left at the same moment, and gain possession of the town. The charge was gallantly made. The Mexicans commenced a precipitate retreat towards the mountains. A part of the Americans fired upon them, while the others entered the town. In less than fifteen minutes ten Mexicans were slain, the fugitives were captured, and the town, with fifty prisoners, taken. The Americans sustained no loss. In this engagement Capt. Jackson and Lieut. Oxley fought as privates. The dead body of Lieut. Brown, having the cross suspended from the neck, was not burned, but secreted among the rocks. Such reverence is paid to the cross by the most cruel men. The clothes, guns, sabres, holsters, pistols, bowie-knives and trinkets of these unfortunate men were discovered, secreted in various houses. Their ashes were also found. The greater part of the town was reduced to ashes, only a sufficient number of houses being left to shelter the women and children. Also the mills, a few miles from Las Bagas, which belonged to the alcalde, who was known to have participated in the murder of Lt. Brown's party, were consumed.

The prisoners, by order of Col. Price, were conveyed to Santa Fé, where they were tried before a drum-head court-martial, and six of them sentenced to death. This sentence was, accordingly, put into execution in Santa Fé, on the 3d of August, in the presence of the army.

On the 9th of July, a detachment of thirty-one men, belonging to Capt. Morin's company, stationed on the Cienega, eighteen miles from Taos, was furiously attacked, two hours before daylight, by two hundred Mexicans and Pueblo Indians combined. Five of our men were killed,* and nine wounded. The remainder of the party retired under the banks of the Cienega, which position they gallantly held until Capt. Shepherd arrived with his company, and assisted them in vanquishing the enemy.

* The killed were Lieut. Larkin, W. Owens, J. A. Wright, W. S. Mason, and —— Wilkinson. The loss of the enemy was not ascertained.—HUGHES.

In the spring of 1847 the Indians, principally the Pawnees and Comanches, infested the Santa Fé road, committed repeated depredations on the government trains, fearlessly attacked the escorts, killed and drove off great numbers of horses, mules and oxen, belonging to the government, and in several instances, overpowered, and slew, or captured many of our people. They openly declared that they would cut off all communication between the Western States and New Mexico, and capture and enslave every American, who might venture to pass the plains.

In pursuance of these views, a large body of Indians, on the 22d of June, attacked a returning government train near the grand Arkansas, drove off eighty yoke of oxen, and in sight of the teamsters, whose force was too weak to offer effectual resistance, wantonly and cruelly slaughtered them for amusement, and for the gratification of their savage propensities.

On the 26th Lieut. Love's convoy, with 300,000 dollars in specie encamped near the Arkansas. He was furiously assailed by a body of 500 savages, who had taken their position in the road, and lain in wait to surprise him at dawn. They succeeded in frightening the stock. One hundred and fifty yoke of oxen, in an estampeda, wildly campered off, and crossed the river, followed by the Indians, yelling and firing amongst the herd. Twenty of Lieutenant Love's men pursued to recover the cattle, while the rest remained to protect the train. They charged the Indians about one mile, who retired; but this was a *ruse* to lead them into an ambuscade. At this moment more than 100 Indians sallied forth from an ambush, intercepted their retreat, and fiercely attacked them. They were now completely surrounded by the savages. The engagement became close and severe. At length the Americans charged through the enemy's ranks, and made good their retreat. The loss of the Indians in this action was 25 killed, and perhaps double that number wounded. The Americans, in killed and wounded lost eleven. The savages were mounted on horses, and armed with guns, pistols, lances, shields, and bows and arrows.

On the 27th of October, 1846, Capt. Mann's train of twenty-four government wagons was encamped, thirty miles below the crossing of the Arkansas. The next morning two of the best mules were missing. The captain and Yates started in search of them.

They had not proceeded far when they saw signs of Indians. They returned to camp—geared up—and started off, leaving Woodson and Stricklin a short distance in the rear, with one wagon.

At this crisis several hundred Indians came charging and yelling furiously from the hills, and some attacked the train, while others surrounded the two men with the wagon. The trains were halted and the wagons corraled. Woodson and Stricklin were rescued, but the wagon which contained the captain's scrutoire and three years' outfit of clothing was taken, rifled and burned. The American loss was one killed, and four wounded—loss of the Indians not ascertained.

The Indians now surrounded the corral;—night approaching, Capt. Mann and his men determined to gear up, take the wounded, and decamp. Accordingly a white flag was hoisted, and the train moved off. In a short time they were overtaken by the savages, who told them they desired to be friendly. A halt was ordered and the wagons again corraled. About ten o'clock at night the Indians came rushing and yelling, like a legion of devils, and drove off two hundred and eighty mules, leaving only twelve behind. The party now decamped, left the trains, and traveled on foot thirty miles, carrying the wounded, where they overtook Capt. McIlvaine, who sent back for the wagons. Here they fortified, four miles below the crossing, and sent the wounded to Fort Bent.

About the 1st of July, 1847, a regiment of volunteer infantry, raised in Illinois, and commanded by Cols. Newby and Boyakin, were outfitted at Fort Leavenworth, and dispatched across the plains, to relieve the troops under Col. Price, at Santa Fé, whose term of service would soon expire. This is the 6th Illinois regiment.

Also between the 5th and 20th of August a battalion of infantry under command of Lieutenant-colonel Easton, and a full regiment of cavalry, commanded by Cols. Ralls and Jones, and Major Reynolds, all Missouri volunteers, departed from Fort Leavenworth, destined for Santa Fé. This is the 4th regiment, and the fourth separate battalion of volunteers, Missouri has furnished for the war with Mexico.

About the 27th of September, the fifth separate battalion of Missouri volunteers, under Lieutenant-colonel Powell, left Fort Leavenworth for its destination, on the Oregon route. This is denominated the Oregon battalion, and it will be employed in constructing a cordon of military posts from Western Missouri to the Oregon territory. It is a cavalry corps.

Between the 1st and 15th of August, Gen. Price, and the troops under his command, returned to Missouri, where they arrived about the 25th of September, having lost more than four hundred men, in battle and by disease. A garrison of five companies, three of volunteers and two of regulars, was left in Santa Fé, under Lieutenant-colonel Walker. Gen. Price has returned to Santa Fé. His force is now about three thousand men.

In consequence of the recent, repeated aggressions of the Indians on the Santa Fé road, the Executive determined to send against them a body of troops. Accordingly on the 24th of July a requisition was made on the State of Missouri for five companies of volunteers, two of cavalry, two of infantry, and one of artillery. This corps, the sixth separate battalion of Missouri volunteers, commanded by Lieutenant-colonel Gilpin, was outfitted at Fort Leavenworth, and took its departure thence for the plains, on the 6th of October, where it will be employed in quelling and overawing the savages, who beset the Santa Fé road for booty. This is called the Indian Battalion.

These new levies are now in their various fields of operation. Little else remains for them to accomplish, but to secure and maintain the conquests which have already been made. If, however, their subsequent achievements should be deemed worthy of historic record, they may be embraced in a future edition of this work.

The author has now finished his labors, and if he has afforded entertainment for the curious, truth for the inquisitive, novelty for the lover of romance, instruction for the student of history, or information for the general reader, he feels himself amply rewarded for his pains. Should any one, however, think that the narrative herein given of the expedition, is unfaithful, or incomplete, let him consider how difficult it is to write history; how impossible it is to feast every appetite; and how diverse are the sentiments of mankind.

OFFICIAL ROSTERS.

COLONEL ALEXANDER W. DONIPHAN.
(From painting in the Library of the Missouri Historical Society, St. Louis, Mo.)

OFFICIAL ROSTERS

Various Bodies Army of the West,
including

FIRST REGIMENT MISSOURI MOUNTED VOLUNTEERS.

The original rolls of the various bodies of troops composing the Army of the West are in the files of the War Department at Washington. Copies of certain portions of these rolls are to be found in the office of the Adjutant-General of Missouri. These copies are no more than rosters of the different companies and other military organizations. They do not show the age of any soldier, his native State, description of him, whether he was sick or wounded during his service, nor any of the various things we should like to know beyond the mere name. These copies seem to have been made by the War Department. Nothing was found to show any detachment service, which is a serious defect, for without rolls of the detachments it is impossible to determine the names of all the men who served under Colonel Doniphan in his invasion of northern Mexico. The rolls of the Traders' Battalion are not in the Missouri State archives. A detachment of Company A, Battalion Missouri Light Artillery, Captain Weightman, was in Santa Fé at the time the company was discharged at New Orleans, but there is nothing on file giving either the number or the names of the troops in this detachment. Other instances of this character could be cited.

The copies of the rolls to be found in the office of the Adjutant-General are accompanied by cards, made also by the War Department, giving a few facts relating to each company. While these facts are very meager, they contain valuable information, and I have copied them entire and put them at the head of the rosters of the respective companies. They contain the extent of service, the dates of muster and discharge, and in some instances a record of events. That preceding the roster of the Battalion Missouri Light Artillery will be found particularly valuable. I have included rosters of some companies that did not serve under Colonel Doniphan, for the reason that detachments which served under him included some of their troops.

The copying and recopying of these rolls before they came to the files of the office of the Adjutant-General of Missouri has undoubtedly caused many names to be misspelled. I give the names as they appear in the archives of Missouri. In going over the roster of the Clay county company with D. C. Allen, Esq., of Liberty, a number of errors were discovered. And Meredith T. Moore, Esq., of Cedar City, pointed out errors in the roster of the Cole county company. I obtained from the above-named gentlemen, John Smith Story, of Liberty, and J. Hale, Esq., of Lexington, Mo., material for notes of identification for some members of the companies with the names of which they were familiar. It is to be regretted that such identification could not be made more complete, and that material of this nature cannot be had for all the troops.

Missouri is a great State, and rich and prosperous. Taxes in Missouri are lower than in any other State with the affairs of which I am familiar. Her people are brave, and she has furnished many soldiers to the various wars that have been waged since she was organized as a Territory, and these soldiers have been among the bravest and best in the world. She should obtain from the War Department complete rolls of all her soldiers from the very first. Then a report should be provided for, to be made by the Adjutant-General, which should include every Missouri soldier that ever served in any capacity on any side. This report should be published, and a copy of it placed in every library in the State; and a large number should be provided for general distribution. Nearly all the soldiers of the Mexican War went to California in 1849, and those who could not get there in 1849 went as soon as they could afterwards. Many of them never returned, and their descendants live in that country to this day. They look back to Missouri for their genealogical records. The same is in large degree true of soldiers of the Civil War, with the exception that they went to every Western State and Territory. In Linn county, Oregon, I was told that Price's army had settled there, and many of his soldiers undoubtedly did go there to begin life anew in the world. They look back to Missouri with affection and regard her as their mother. No greater or better work can be done by the State than to print the rolls bearing the names of these men. Such a report as I suggest will bear the names of the men who have made the glory and honor of Missouri and spread her fame abroad in all the earth.

W. E. C.

REGIMENTAL FIELD AND STAFF.

[The statements preceding the Rosters are verbatim copies of the official records in the office of the Adjutant-General of the State of Missouri, and are not in the language of the author.]

Field and Staff, First Regiment Missouri Mounted Volunteers, Mexican War. Muster Roll, June 18, 1846, to June 24, 1847, shows station at New Orleans, La. No Record of Events given.

Roll signed: A. W. Doniphan, Col.

Field and Staff mustered for discharge at New Orleans, La., June 24, 1847, and honorably discharged by S. Churchill, Insp. Gen., Mustering officer, except Th. M. Morton, retained in service.

NON-COMMISSIONED STAFF.

Muster Roll, June 7 to August 31, 1846, shows station at Santa Fé, N. M.

Private John Hinton was appointed Sergt. Major, July 28, 1846.

Francis C. Hughes, private in Company C, was appointed Q. M. Sergt., July 15, 1846.

Nicholas Snyder, Bugler in Company F, was appointed Chief Bugler, July 15, 1846.

Roll signed: A. W. Doniphan, Col.

ROSTER.

1. Alexander W. Doniphan, Colonel.
1. Congreve Jackson, L. Colonel.
2. Charles F. Ruff, L. Colonel.
1. William Gilpin, Major.
1. James A. De Courcy, Adjutant.
2. G. M. Butler, Adjutant.
1. Thomas M. Morton, Acting Surgeon.
2. George Penn, Surgeon.
1. B. W. D. Moore, Assistant Surgeon.
2. I. F. Morton, Assistant Surgeon.

3. I. P. Vaughan, Assistant Surgeon.
1. James Lea, 1st Lieut. & Actg. A. Q. M.
1. Geo. P. Gordon, 2nd Lieut. & Actg. A. C. S.
1. John T. Crenshaw, Sgt. Major.
2. John Hinton, Sgt. Major.
1. F. C. Hughes, Q. M. Sgt.
1. Nicholas Snyder, Cf. Bugler.

COMPANY A.
[JACKSON COUNTY.]

Roster showing Names and Rank of Captain David Waldo's Company A, in the First Regiment, Missouri Mounted Volunteers, Mexican War.

Endorsed: Doniphan's Regt.

David Waldo, Capt.

Memo.: Roll signed, David Waldo, Captain.

Company accepted into the service of the U. S. for term of twelve months from June 6, 1846, by J. Allen, Captain First Dragoons, Insp. and Mustering Officer.

The following certificate appears on the roll:

CAMP, PEAK OF PERDENAL, October 22, 1846.—I certify on honor that this is a correct copy of the original Muster Roll, with the exception of Private James E. Lacey, who deserted the 18th day of June, 1846, and private Ezekiel Carlton, in the place of R. B. Bowers, who was mustered into the service of the United States the 28th of June, 1846, by order of Col. S. W. Kearny, and John S. Webb, who was mustered into the service of the United States on the 19th day of September, 1846, all of which cases have arisen between the 6th of June, 1846, and the present time.

I also certify on honor, that all the names which affect the rights of the non-commissioned officers and men to one year's allowance of clothing have been put on this Muster Roll.

JOHN REID,
1st Lieutenant Co. A, 1st Regt. Missouri Mounted Rifles.

Memo.: Capt. David Waldo's Co. A, 1st Regt. Missouri Mounted Vols., Mexican War. Company Muster Roll for June 6, 1846, to June 22, 1847, shows station of company, New Orleans, La.

Record of Events:

The company was organized at Independence, Jackson county,

OFFICIAL ROSTERS AND RECORDS. 531

Mo., and marched from Independence on the 4th of June to Fort Leavenworth and arrived the 6th day of June.

Extract from Order No. 59 of Maj. Gen. Taylor, dated Camp near Monterey, Mexico, May 26, 1847. [This applies to all companies, and is set down in the cards of all, but will be omitted from records of companies following.—W. E. C.]

At Camargo, Col. Doniphan will detach a sufficient number of men from each company to conduct the horses and other animals of the command by land to Mo. The men so detached will leave the necessary papers to enable their pay to be drawn when their companies are discharged at New Orleans, La. By order Maj. Gen. Taylor.

(Signed) W. W. BLISS, A. A. A. G.

Roll signed: David Waldo, Captain.

Company was mustered for discharge at New Orleans, La., June 22, 1847, and honorably discharged by, S. Churchill, Insp. Gen., Mustering Officer.

ROSTER.

1. David Waldo..................................Captain.
1. John Reid....................................1st Lieut.
1. David I. Clayton.............................2nd Lieut.
2. Henry I. Chiles..............................2nd Lieut.
1. John S. Webb.................................1st Sergt.
2. Richard B. Buckner...........................Sergt.
3. Samuel S. White..............................Sergt.
4. Richard Simpson..............................Sergt.
1. James Mundy..................................Corpl.
2. Thos. Moore..................................Corpl.
3. Jesse Frierson...............................Corpl.
4. William E. Bush..............................Corpl.
1. Lemuel Jepson................................Bugler.
2. Chas. Miller.................................Bugler.
1. Joseph W. Hamilton...........................Farrier.

    1. Aud, Francis L...........................Private.
    2. Asbury, Squire...........................Private.
    3. Bean, Samuel.............................Private.
    4. Boswell, William.........................Private.
    5. Bush, William D..........................Private.
    6. Burton, William T........................Private.
    7. Burton, Beverly I........................Private.
    8. Bowland, James...........................Private.
    9. Clift, James H...........................Private.

10. Cogswell, William.........................Private.
11. Copeland, William L......................Private.
12. Copeland, Anthony N.....................Private.
13. Carlton, Ezekiel...........................Private.
14. Cannon, William N.......................Private.
15. Campbell, John E.........................Private.
16. Clayton, James R.........................Private.
17. Capell, Britton............................Private.
18. Capell, John I.............................Private.
19. Chiles, Elijah J...........................Private.
20. Crenshaw, John T........................Private.
21. Ells, Nathan...............................Private.
22. Forrest, Lorenzo D.......................Private.
23. Flournoy, Matthew I.....................Private.
24. Franklin, John R..........................Private.
25. Gilpin, William............................Private.
26. Gibson, John R............................Private.
27. Greenwood, Fontleroy D.................Private.
28. Hamilton, Christopher C.................Private.
29. Haines, Michael D........................Private.
30. Hildebrand, Levi..........................Private.
31. Jones, David A............................Private.
32. Jenks, Christopher........................Private.
33. Killbuck, Washington.....................Private.
34. Knighton, Perry...........................Private.
35. Lucas, John T..............................Private.
36. Lucas, James A............................Private.
37. Latz, Benjamin............................Private.
38. Lindsay, Alfred O.........................Private.
39. Lillard, Morgan............................Private.
40. Lemmons, Benjamin......................Private.
41. Lemmons, Washington...................Private.
42. Lewis, Richard.............................Private.
43. Moody, Andrew J.........................Private.
44. Meek, Robert G...........................Private.
45. Maim, Christopher........................Private.
46. Maim, Elson...............................Private.
47. McMurray, John H........................Private.
48. Massie, Thomas H........................Private.
49. McElrath, James..........................Private.
50. McKeller, John............................Private.
51. Nichols, Daniel............................Private.
52. Noland, Jesse..............................Private.
53. Overton, William R.......................Private.

54. Owens, James W..........................Private.
55. Patton, John W. H......................Private.
56. Pringle, George A.......................Private.
57. Palmer, Jonathan R....................Private.
58. Parish, Sidney G.........................Private.
59. Phelps, Richard S.......................Private.
60. Patterson, Andrew J...................Private.
61. Patrick, Dudley..........................Private.
62. Pool, James M...........................Private.
63. Powell, David I..........................Private.
64. Pollard, Samuel A......................Private.
65. Ryan, Henry M..........................Private.
66. Rennick, Chatham E...................Private.
67. Riggs, Henry C..........................Private.
68. Riggs, William A........................Private.
69. Smith, Hugh N..........................Private.
70. Sprague, Davis...........................Private.
71. Sharpe, George..........................Private.
72. Sharp, Leonard B.......................Private.
73. Sears, Peter A...........................Private.
74. Speed, James............................Private.
75. Triplett, Zela.............................Private.
76. Tyler, Perry I............................Private.
77. Vigus, John K............................Private.
78. White, Wafer S..........................Private.
79. Wear, John...............................Private.
80. Wear, James A..........................Private.
81. Wear, Abraham W......................Private.
82. Wear, Samuel C.........................Private.
83. Watts, John S............................Private.
84. Wilson, John C...........................Private.
85. Waller, Shelby............................Private.
86. Webb, George B.........................Private.
87. Walker, Collins...........................Private.
88. Woodland, John L.......................Private.
89. Wallace, James W.......................Private.
90. Young, William M.......................Private.
91. Zellers, Henry............................Private.
92. King, Walter..............................Private.
93. Cox, James................................Private.
94. Douglas, Oliver T........................Private.
95. Fugate, Francis..........................Private.
96. Mount, Thornton A.....................Private.
97. Riggs, Green B...........................Private.

98. Crabtree, Isaac......................Private.
99. Johnson, Waldo P....................Private.
100. Oldham, Simeon.....................2nd Lieut.
101. Foster, William....................Private.
102. Lacy, I. E.........................Private.

COMPANY B.
[LAFAYETTE COUNTY.]

Captain William P. Walton's Company B, First Regiment Missouri Mounted Volunteers, Mexican War.

Company Muster-in Roll, dated June 7, 1846, shows station of company, Fort Leavenworth.

Record of Events: None given.

Roll not signed.

The following certificate appears on the Roll:

I certify that the above is a true copy of the Muster Roll of this Company, except the three last named privates (James Mitchum, O. H. P. Lucas, James C. Beatie) as mustered by Captain Allen, First Dragoons, on the 7th of June, 1846.

(Signed) Wm. P. WALTON,
Capt. Commanding Co. B, Mo. Mounted Vols.

Company was mustered for discharge at New Orleans, La., June 18, 1847, and honorably discharged, by S. Churchill, Insp. Gen'l, Mustering Officer.

Col. Doniphan's command reached Monterey, 26 May, 1847.

ROSTER.

1. William P. Walton....................Captain.
1. James Lea............................1st Lieut.
1. Robert I. Barnett....................2nd Lieut.
2. D. B. Graves........................2nd Lieut.
1. Thomas Hinkley......................1st Sgt.
2. William Allen.......................Sgt.
3. Joseph Pearson......................Sgt.
4. William P. Tyree....................Sgt.
1. James H. Mallory....................Corp.
2. William A. Ardinger.................Corp.
3. William Hale.......................Corp.
4. George C. Spears....................Corp.
1. B. F. Gordon........................Bugler.
1. John G. Ridge.......................Farrier.

OFFICIAL ROSTERS AND RECORDS.

1. Ashford, William H....................Private.
2. Bays, Charles C.......................Private.
3. Bradford, Thomas H...................Private.
4. Bledsoe, H. M., Jr....................Private.
5. Bear, Jeremiah........................Private.
6. Brown, Gabriel F......................Private.
7. Byrum, William F......................Private.
8. Braden, Isaac.........................Private.
9. Boykin, John..........................Private.
10. Browder, John........................Private.
11. Burton, Robert.......................Private.
12. Beattie, James.......................Private.
13. Chinn, Joseph G......................Private.
14. Chinn, William F.....................Private.
15. Cook, William F......................Private.
16. Chanster, William A..................Private.
17. Curry, Joseph........................Private.
18. Comstock, Marshall H.................Private.
19. Cromwell, William V..................Private.
20. Defreese, James......................Private.
21. Davis, Thomas E......................Private.
22. Elliott, Samuel......................Private.
23. Ewing, Theodore......................Private.
24. Erwin, Green.........................Private.
25. Erwin, William H.....................Private.
26. Evans, Thomas........................Private.
27. Ferguson, William J..................Private.
28. Fandree, S. W........................Private.
29. Gibbons, William.....................Private.
30. Gatlin, Ephraim......................Private.
31. Graham, Ewing........................Private.
32. George, Isaac........................Private.
33. Handley, William.....................Private.
34. Hayes, Andrew J......................Private.
35. Houston, Quincy......................Private.
36. Hardy, B. W..........................Private.
37. Hickland, John.......................Private.
38. Horn, Daniel.........................Private.
39. Hewes, Thomas........................Private.
40. Hall, Palestine......................Private.
41. Hall, Benjamin R.....................Private.
42. Irick, Frederick.....................Private.
43. Jones, James.........................Private.
44. Johnson, James T.....................Private.

45. Kirby, Alexander.........................Private.
46. Kirby, John...............................Private.
47. Kesterson, John..........................Private.
48. Kavanaugh, C. B.........................Private.
49. Kingcaid, J. C............................Private.
50. Landon, Samuel L.......................Private.
51. Letton, Reuben P........................Private.
52. Lucas, O. H. P...........................Private.
53. Lorrell, Philip............................Private.
54. Mitchum, James.........................Private.
55. Musick, John.............................Private.
56. Mason, Eli................................Private.
57. McRoney, Hugh..........................Private.
58. McDougall, John.........................Private.
59. McIlvrain, H. J...........................Private.
60. Mosby, John S...........................Private.
61. MacGruder, John S......................Private.
62. Nelson, William..........................Private.
63. Osborne, William.........................Private.
64. O'Brian, Francis..........................Private.
65. Peacock, James..........................Private.
66. Sullivan, James..........................Private.
67. Styles, S. B..............................Private.
68. Staggs, Enoch............................Private.
69. Tisdall, John B...........................Private.
70. Thomas, Henry...........................Private.
71. Todd, Jarrett.............................Private.
72. Tritcher, John............................Private.
73. Vivian, George W........................Private.
74. Waddell, John C.........................Private.
75. Waddell, Joseph H.......................Private.
76. White, Coleman..........................Private.
77. Williams, Lemuel.........................Private.
78. Weaver, Joseph..........................Private.
79. Windsor, Upton..........................Private.
80. Yeager, John.............................Private.
81. Young, James B..........................Private.
82. Young, Thomas..........................Private.
83. Kirkpatrick, A. A.........................Sgt.
84. Donovan, Leonidas......................Private.
85. Dyer, John C.............................Private.
86. Jones, Charles A.........................Private.
87. Inman, Asa...............................Private.
88. Ridge, Jacob.............................Private.
89. Leechman, William H....................Private.

OFFICIAL ROSTERS AND RECORDS. 537

90. King, George S..........................Private.
91. Spears, Robert M.......................1st Lieut.
92. Stewart, James.........................Private.
93. Cook, William H........................Private.
94. Goshen, Marshall C.....................Private.
95. Whitsett, Thomas M.....................Private.
96. Merchant, William......................Private.
97. Ward, Thomas...........................Private.
98. Butler, George M.......................1st Lieut.
99. Ritchie, Franklin......................Private.

IDENTIFICATION OF COMPANY B.

The following information concerning Company B, First Regiment Missouri Volunteers, Mexican War, was furnished me by J. Hale, Esq., one of the oldest and most respected residents of Lexington, Missouri. It is of much value.

First Lieutenant James Lea was born in Maryland; came to Lexington, Mo., about 1842. Subsequent to the Mexican War he went to California. He returned, and he died in Baltimore in 1858. He was appointed quartermaster of the regiment, and served in that capacity throughout the campaign. He was a bookkeeper and accountant.

Second Lieutenant Robert I. Barnett was born in Madison county, Kentucky; came to Lafayette county, Mo., in 1844; served gallantly in the campaign. After being discharged was Lieutenant of Dragoons, Regular Army; resigned, and died at San José, California, about 1890.

Ensign William P. Tyree was born in Sumner county, Tennessee. Came to Missouri in 1843. Was Associate Judge of the Lafayette County Court. Was a farmer. Of good family. Died in 1874.

First Sergeant Thomas Hinkle was born in Maryland. Subsequent to Mexican War served four years in the Confederate Army. Died at Linden, Texas, in 1880.

Corporal William B. Hale was born in Bedford county, Virginia. Came to Lafayette county, Missouri, in 1835. Was a lumber merchant. Died at Lexington, Mo., in 1903.

Hiram M. Bledsoe was born in Fayette county, Kentucky, and came to Lafayette county, Missouri, in 1839. Served gallantly in Company B in the Mexican War. Was conspicuous on the Pro-Slavery side in the war in Kansas in 1856. Commanded the battery in the Missouri State Guards under General Sterling Price in 1861, and after the Missouri Army was mustered into the Confederate service in the spring of 1862 he served with great credit to himself and profit to his cause in the armies of General Beauregard and General Joseph E. Johnston, in command of Bledsoe's famous Missouri Battalion of Artillery, in the States of Tennessee, Mississippi, Georgia, and Alabama. He died on his farm in Cass county, Missouri, early in February, 1899. He was of a fine family, was a farmer, and was one of Missouri's most noted men.

Robert P. Burton, private, was born in Virginia. Came to Lafayette county, Mo., in 1838. Was a steamboat captain. Died in Ripley county, Mo., about 1880.

William A. Chanster, private, was born in Kentucky. Came to Lafayette county, Mo., in 1840. Was a hemp- and grain-dealer. Died at Lexington, Mo. in 1894.

John S. Mosby, private, was born in Fayette county, Kentucky. Was a farmer. Came to Lafayette county in 1835. Died in Johnson county, Mo., about 1875.

Chatham Renick was born in Missouri. Killed in Kentucky in 1864, while serving as a Lieutenant in Colonel Quantrill's command. Farmer. [Name not found on Roll.—W. E. C.]

Philip Gau, private; native State not known. Farmer. Died in Lafayette county, Mo. [Name not found on Roll.—W. E. C.]

Joseph Curry, private; place of birth not known; died in New Mexico; date of death not known.

Reuben P. Letton, private, born in Maryland. Came to Missouri about 1840. Farmer. Died in New Mexico about 1890.

W. V. Cromwell, private, was born in Kentucky; came to Missouri about 1842; died in Texas, but place and date unknown to writer.

William Nelson, private, was born in Lafayette county, Mo., and died in Ray county, Mo., in 1902.

Upton B. Winsor, private, was born in Maryland. Came to Missouri in 1844. Was Provost Marshal General, Trans-Mississippi Department, C. S. A. Died at Lexington, Mo., in 1882.

Isaac Braden, private, died in Lafayette county, Mo., in 1895; was a farmer.

Henry J. McIlvrain, private, was born in Kentucky. Farmer. Died in Lafayette county, Mo., about 1880.

Asa Inman, private, was a merchant. Drowned in the Missouri river at Fort Leavenworth, in June, 1846.

Joseph Pearson, private, was born in Missouri. Died in New Orleans in 1847.

William J. Ferguson, private, was born in Kentucky. Returned to Kentucky and died there; place and date not known to writer.

Thomas Young, private, was born in Tennessee. Came to Missouri in 1831. Farmer. Died in Lafayette county soon after Mexican War.

George W. Vivian, private, was born in Kentucky. Died at Higginsville, Mo., in 1901.

John Hickland, private, was born in Lafayette county, Mo. Died in Colorado, in 1900.

Palestine Hall, private, was born in Missouri. Farmer. Died in Lafayette county, Mo., in 1867.

William F. Chinn, private, was born in Lexington, Kentucky, and came to Lexington, Mo., in 1843, where he died in 1854.

Joseph G. Chinn, private, was born in Lexington, Kentucky, and came to Lexington, Mo., in 1843. Is the only member of Company B now in Lexington, Mo., where he is Judge of the Police Court.

John C. Waddell, private, born in Kentucky. Came to Missouri in 1837. Steamboat captain. Died in Nebraska, about 1895.

Joseph H. Waddell, private, born in Kentucky. Came to Missouri in 1837. Farmer. Died in Lafayette county, Mo., about 1875.

James Peacock, private, born in Madison county, Kentucky. Is now Police Judge of Independence, Mo.

Wiley Aiken, private, born in Tennessee; died at Independence, Mo., about 1895. Was a tailor. [Name not found on Roll.—W. E. C.]

John S. MacGruder, private, was born in Virginia; was of a distinguished family. Died at Lexington, Mo., in 1848, of a wound received at the battle of Sacramento.

A. A. Kirkpatrick, private, was born in Tennessee. Came to Missouri about 1843. Lawyer. Died in Chihuahua of a wound received at the battle of Sacramento. Was Sergeant at the time.

George S. King, private, was born in Lafayette county, Mo., and died in New Mexico in 1846.

Robert M. Spears, First Lieutenant, was killed by Indians in New Mexico, in 1846.

Jeremiah Bair, [Bear on Roll.—W. E. C.] private, was a contractor; died at Kansas City, 1890.

B. F. Gordon, Bugler, was born in Lafayette county, Mo., and was a farmer. Was a Colonel in the Confederate Army. Died about 1890.

Sherman Eddy, private, was born in New York. Lawyer. Died in Sacramento, California, in 1850. [I do not find his name on the Roll.—W. E. C.]

Charles C. Bays, private, was born in Missouri. When last heard from was in Mexico.

Gabriel F. Brown, private, was born in Kentucky. Was a live-stock trader. Died in California, in 1898.

Thomas H. Bradford, private, was born in Tennessee.

Desha B. Graves, Second Lieutenant, was first a private. Born in Fayette county, Kentucky. Came to Missouri in 1839—to Lafayette county. When First Lieutenant James Lea was appointed Quartermaster, Second Lieutenant Robert I. Barnett was promoted to be First Lieutenant and Desha B. Graves was elected Second Lieutenant. He was a grand-nephew of Governor Desha, of Kentucky. Was a farmer. Died in Lafayette county, Mo., in 1850.

Company B was composed of as noble men as ever carried muskets.

George M. Butler, First Lieutenant, an educated gentleman, was made Adjutant of the Regiment, but died, and was succeeded by De Courcy.

I insert the following letter in regard to the life of Colonel Hiram Bledsoe:

OLATHE, KANSAS, January 4, 1907.

WILLIAM E. CONNELLEY—*My Dear Sir*: Your letter asking about events in the life of Col. Hiram Bledsoe (deceased) was given to me by my son. I will try to give you a short sketch of his life. When eighteen he joined Capt. Walton's Company at Lexington, Mo., in 1846, which was a part of Col. Doniphan's Regiment. He served through the campaign.

In 1856, I believe, he engaged in the Kansas troubles, to make it a slave State; was at the battle of Osawatomie, and, I think, in charge of the Missouri forces.

In the War of the Rebellion he raised the first Missouri Battery, in which Old Sacramento figured so conspicuously in the early part of the war. This gun was condemned at Memphis, Tennessee, and was stored there. Parties have tried to find it, but failed to do so. There is a little incident that has never been made public, that might do to tell in regard to the battle of Springfield. The battle was opened by General Lyon in front, and Sigel attacked in the rear where Bledsoe's Battery was stationed; Sigel opened fire; Bledsoe responded; but after a few shots he received orders to cease firing, as it was then supposed it was friends firing upon him. He continued to respond, when General McCulloch rode up in haste and ordered the firing stopped, telling Bledsoe they were Confederates he was firing on. Bledsoe replied: "General, I don't give a d——n who they are; they are shooting at me and I am going to shoot at them." If he had obeyed orders the whole Confederate Army

Col. Hiram Bledsoe.
[Courtesy of Lafayette County Historical Society, Lexington, Missouri.]

would have been captured or routed, and the war would have been practically over in Missouri.

At the battle of Carthage he received a severe wound, really a dangerous wound; but he remained with the army, and came back, and was in the battle of Lexington, Mo. He was made a Colonel, and fought in the battle of Pea Ridge, where his horse was killed under him and he was again dangerously wounded.

Afterward he was Colonel of Artillery, with Johnston and Hood, in front of Sherman. He covered Hood's retreat from Franklin with artillery alone, without orders and without any support from infantry, and he never lost a gun, though often charged by cavalry.

He surrendered at New Orleans, returned to Lexington, Mo., and settled on a farm. Afterwards he moved to Cass county, Mo., where he was elected to the State Senate, but refused to accept another term.

He died in Cass county about seven years ago.

Respectfully, R. D. BLEDSOE.

The following clipping was taken from the *Kansas City Journal*, date not known, but it was early in February, 1899:

HIRAM BLEDSOE DEAD.

WAS IN COMMAND OF THE FAMOUS "BLEDSOE BATTERY."

ONE OF THE MOST WIDELY KNOWN EX-CONFEDERATES IN THE STATE PASSES AWAY AT HIS HOME NEAR PLEASANT HILL.

Colonel Hiram Bledsoe, one of the most widely known men in the State, died at his home near Pleasant Hill yesterday. The news of his death was a great surprise to the many friends of Colonel Bledsoe, as it was thought he was enjoying unusually good health. He was about 75 years old, and had been a resident of the State during almost his entire life. He was born in Kentucky, but removed to this State at an early age, and spent his early life on a farm in Lafayette county with his father. He served through the Mexican War, and rendered distinguished services.

At the beginning of the Civil War Colonel Bledsoe enlisted in the Confederate army, and within a very short time was promoted to a colonelcy. Although occupying various positions, he commanded a battery which was known as "Bledsoe's Battery" throughout the war. This battery became famous for its gallantry, and distinguished itself particularly at Missionary Ridge and during the two-days fighting at Chickamauga. Shortly after this the battery was ordered to join the army then operating in Virginia. It has been said of Colonel Bledsoe that he participated in all the most important engagements of the Civil War.

The Confederate Congress, then in session at Richmond, Va., presented the battery with a very expensive cannon, decorated with solid silver.

After the close of the war Colonel Bledsoe returned to Missouri and settled down on his farm in Cass county, where he remained until his death. He was twice elected to the office of county judge of Cass county, and served in the State senate. His friends urged him to make the race for the gubernatorial nomination, but he refused.

There are but two near relatives of Colonel Bledsoe living. They are a sister and one brother, Robert Bledsoe, who lives at 2524 Troost avenue, in this city.

Colonel Bledsoe frequently came to Kansas City, and was on terms of intimacy with all the prominent ex-Confederates and ex-Union soldiers in the city. Captain S. C. Roger, who served with him, and Major Warner expressed themselves feelingly last night when they learned of his death.

Hon. Milton Moore, of Kansas City, Mo., was well acquainted with Hiram Bledsoe. In a conversation between them about the battle of Sacramento, Bledsoe said that just before the charge there was much confusion, and that some one gave the order to charge, when the men rushed forward in the great charge that overwhelmed the Mexicans. He did not say who gave the order to charge.

OFFICIAL ROSTERS AND RECORDS.   541

Mr. Moore believed that Bledsoe himself had given the order, and said, "I presume I know who gave the order to charge," to which Bledsoe made no reply. Mr. Moore repeated his remark, but Bledsoe remained silent. There is little doubt that he gave an order to charge, and there is no doubt whatever that he did heroic service in the charge. But he was a very modest man, and said little of his services to his country.

This is perhaps a good place to settle the discussion about the guns captured by Colonel Doniphan at the battle of Sacramento. In the letter quoted above, Mr. Bledsoe says the gun known as "Old Sacramento" was condemned and stored at Memphis, Tenn. This is probably correct. It was afterward sent to Selma, Alabama, where it was melted and recast into other guns. The following extract from the *Jefferson City Tribune*, May 12, 1906, may be regarded as absolutely reliable and conclusive as to the disposition of the famous cannon:

"OLD SACRAMENTO."

INTERESTING HISTORY OF A GUN FAMOUS IN MILITARY HISTORY OF MISSOURI.

WAS ORIGINALLY CAST FROM CHURCH-BELLS BY MEXICANS—WAS CAPTURED BY GENERAL DONIPHAN AND BROUGHT TO THIS STATE FROM MEXICAN WAR—RECAST AT SELMA, ALABAMA.

In a scrap-book, once the property of the late General James Harding of this city, a piece of manuscript was recently found by his son-in-law, A. S. Ferguson, bearing a heading: "The Fate of Old Sacramento." The author of the manuscript is not known, but it refers to a field-piece known to every soldier of the Civil War who served west of the Mississippi river, and also to Confederate soldiers generally all over the country. The manuscript purports to give General Harding's account of this gun in the following language:

"In the spring of 1861 Captain Hiram Bledsoe came to Jefferson City looking for a carriage on which to mount a gun he had in Lexington (Mo.). I showed him the only one in store, and which was the self-same carriage not considered worthy a place in the battery of the Southwest Expedition. Bledsoe looked at it; thought it would suit his purpose, and took it home with him. On that carriage, "Old Sacramento," a name which became as a household word in the Missouri State Guards, appeared. This gun was originally a long nine-pounder, cast from church-bells by the Mexicans, and with other guns was captured by General Doniphan's regiment (Missourians) in Chihuahua, and brought back from the Mexican War by them.

"Bledsoe had the gun bored out to a 12-pounder at a machine-shop in Lexington, and mounted, as stated. It went through the campaigns of the State Guards, firing its last round at Elk Horn. The gun was afterwards condemned, and recast at Selma, Ala. I saw it there in the early part of 1863."

At the breaking out of the Civil War General Harding was connected with the Adjutant-General's office in this city, under Judge Warwick Hough, now of the Circuit Court of St. Louis, but at that time Adjutant General of Missouri. General Harding enlisted in the Confederate service, and rose to the rank of the title here given him. During his lifetime he was considered excellent authority on matters pertaining to the Civil War. His home was in this city, where he died several years ago.

The other guns brought home by the First Regiment Missouri Mounted Volunteers as trophies of the victory at Sacramento were melted and recast. The number of guns recast I have not ascertained. But two of these recast guns stand on the terrace of the State Capitol at Jefferson City, Mo. One stands on the southeast corner of the terrace, and the other on the southwest corner. They measure seventy inches in length, thirty-two and three-fourth inches in circumference at largest part, and twenty-one inches at the muzzle. They have a bore of four inches in diameter. Each gun has the following inscription engraved upon it:

"This Gun was recast from Guns Captured by Missouri Soldiers in the Mexican War."

Photographs of these guns were furnished me by Mr. E. S. Link, of Jefferson City, and they are reproduced here.

There is in the Collection of the Kansas State Historical Society a cannon known as "Old Kickapoo." The history of this gun is not clear. But it was used by the Kickapoo Rangers, a pro-slavery organization in the early border troubles in Kansas. It is said to have been taken from the arsenal at Liberty, Mo., and carried into Kansas by the Missourians. It is of Mexican pattern, and there is little doubt that it was captured at the battle of Sacramento and brought to some of the western Missouri towns as a trophy. In the border troubles it was seized by the Kickapoo Rangers. It has remained in Kansas since the border troubles.

COMPANY C.
[CLAY COUNTY.]

Captain O. P. Moss's Company C, First Regiment Missouri Mounted Volunteers, Mexican War.

Muster-in Roll dated June 7, 1846.

This company came from Liberty, Clay county, Mo., distant from Fort Leavenworth 32 miles.

Roll signed by O. P. Moss, Captain. The following certificate appears on the Roll:

I certify that the above is a true copy of the Muster Roll of this Company as mustered by Captain Allen, First Dragoons, June 7, 1846, except English W. Burton and Balor Jacobs, who were mustered into the service by Captain McKissick, Q. M. Dept., June 25, 1846.
(Signed) O. P. Moss,
Captain Commanding Company.

Muster Roll, June 7, 1846, to June 21, 1847, shows company at New Orleans, La.

OFFICIAL ROSTERS AND RECORDS. 543

This company was organized and marched from Liberty to Fort Leavenworth, June 4, and arrived there June 6, O. P. Moss commanding Company.

Company mustered for discharge at New Orleans, La., June 21, 1847, and honorably discharged, by S. Churchill, Insp. Gen., Mustering Officer.

ROSTER.

1. O. P. Moss..................................Captain.
1. L. B. Sublette..............................1st Lieut.
1. James H. Moss.............................2nd Lieut.
2. Henry T. Ogden............................2nd Lieut.
1. James H. Long.............................1st Sgt.
2. Thomas McCarty...........................Sgt.
3. William Wallace............................Sgt.
4. A. K. McClintock..........................Sgt.
1. William C. Scaggs..........................Corp.
2. George H. Wallace.........................Corp.
3. John S. Grooms............................Corp.
4. Benjamin W. Marsh........................Corp.
1. Abraham Estes.............................Bugler.
1. James T. Barnes............................Farrier.

    1. Ammons, Henry B......................Private.
    2. Briscoe, John...........................Private.
    3. Beale, William..........................Private.
    4. Burns, James...........................Private.
    5. Bell, George W.........................Private.
    6. Burton, E. W...........................Private.
    7. Cooper, James P........................Private.
    8. Cummins, Smith........................Private.
    9. Crowley, George W.....................Private.
    10. Christy, John G........................Private.
    11. Chorn, James..........................Private.
    12. Crapster, Edmon W....................Private.
    13. Campbell, William C...................Private.
    14. Chaney, Hiram........................Private.
    15. Carpenter, Noah P.....................Private.
    16. Clayton, Simon H......................Private.
    17. Drew, Washington.....................Private.
    18. Darneal, James H......................Private.
    19. Duncan, Theodore.....................Private.
    20. Duncan, Matthew......................Private.
    21. Everett, Benjamin R...................Private.
    22. Ellis, Henry...........................Private.

23. English, H. W..........................Private.
24. Faubion, Spencer......................Private.
25. Franklin, Levi.........................Private.
26. Franklin, William R...................Private.
27. Fielding, Thomas I....................Private.
28. Fleming, Robert W....................Private.
29. Fleming, George.......................Private.
30. Gunter, William C....................Private.
31. Green, Hiram..........................Private.
32. Human, Charles........................Private.
33. Holt, John D..........................Private.
34. Hughes, Francis C....................Private.
35. Hughes, John T.......................Private.
36. Hall, Alexander........................Private.
37. Hall, Willard P........................Private.
38. Jacobs, Newton........................Private.
39. Jacobs, Baylor.........................Private.
40. Job, Andrew...........................Private.
41. Letchworth, Joseph M.................Private.
42. Lard, William T......................Private.
43. Lamar, James..........................Private.
44. Long, Southey.........................Private.
45. Long, Richardson......................Private.
46. McNeese, Solomon......................Private.
47. McQuiddy, Albert [McQuidley?]..........Private.
48. Martin, Westley.......................Private.
49. Murray, Eli............................Private.
50. Mosely, De Wilton.....................Private.
51. McGee, James..........................Private.
52. Miller, Abraham.......................Private.
53. Moore, John J.........................Private.
54. Nealey, Richard A.....................Private.
55. Nash, John............................Private.
56. Neale, John...........................Private.
57. Owens, Edward P......................Private.
58. Price, Jesse L........................Private.
59. Pence, Josiah..........................Private.
60. Pence, William H......................Private.
61. Pixlee, Peter C........................Private.
62. Patterson, William C..................Private.
63. Pendleton, Benjamin...................Private.
64. Pendergrass, Nimrod...................Private.
65. Rollins, John K.......................Private.
66. Russell, William H....................Private.

67. Ringo, Martin..........................Private.
68. Rudd, O. F............................Private.
69. Shearer, Robert.......................Private.
70. Shouse, John W........................Private.
71. Sullivan, Obadiah.....................Private.
72. Story, John S.........................Private.
73. Sites, James R........................Private.
74. Scott, Alexander C....................Private.
75. Sanders, James........................Private.
76. Stephenson, Robert T..................Private.
77. Sanderson, Joseph.....................Private.
78. Smith, Joseph A.......................Private.
79. Samuel, Chilton B.....................Private.
80. Snowdon, W. P. A......................Private.
81. Tillery, Joshua.......................Private.
82. Tillery, Henry........................Private.
83. Tracy, Andrew W.......................Private.
84. Thompson, William A...................Private.
85. Waller, Thomas........................Private.
86. Wells, William........................Private.
87. Warren, Hardin........................Private.
88. Warren, John..........................Private.
89. Wood, Gideon..........................Private.
90. York, James N.........................Private.
91. York, John............................Private.
    Coe, Allen............................Private.
    Duncan, William.......................Private.
    Finley, James M.......................Private.
    Hall, James...........................Private.
    Lard, John D..........................Private.
    Wills, James A........................Private.
    Cox, Russell R........................Private.
    Morton, James T.......................Private.
    Benthal, Parker.......................Private.
    Ogden, Henry T........................Private.
    Patterson, William C..................Private.
    Rawlins, John K.......................Private.
    Fleming, R. W.........................Private.
    Ruff, C. F............................Private.
    Doniphan, A. W........................Private.

IDENTIFICATION OF COMPANY C.

This identification is principally from information given me by John Smith Story, a private in the company, who lives now at Liberty, Clay county, Missouri.

546   DONIPHAN'S EXPEDITION.

He was born at Versailles, Woodford county, Kentucky, July 24, 1826; son of Smith Story and Elizabeth Ferguson Story, his wife. His father was born in Woodford county; his mother was born in Indiana. Story's father moved from Kentucky to Clay county when Story was but four weeks old; Story has lived in Clay county from that time. He was one of the detachment sent out to overtake the traders.

Privates are referred to by their number on the Roster; officers are named.

Henry T. Ogden, 2d Lieutenant. A man of wonderful energy; full of life; nervous; had to be doing something; always playing pranks. Came to Clay county before the Mexican War; as a joke pretended for a day or two to be deaf and dumb; a bright man, and well educated; could quote from Shakespeare by the hour; often harangued the troops in a humorous vein; a favorite of officers and men; was a lawyer; lives now in Cincinnati, Ohio.

No. 1. From one of the Carolinas; a tailor.
No. 3. A Virginian; farmer; killed two deer at one shot in the north part of Clay county.
No. 4. Irishman; died in Clay county.
No. 5. Kentuckian; born in Mason county.
No. 8. Kentuckian; farmer; died in Arkansas.
No. 10. Merchant in Liberty; went to St. Louis; killed in southern Missouri in the Civil War.
No. 11. Virginian; farmer.
No. 13. Raised in Clay county; married a Miss Evans, whose father owned 240 acres of land now in heart of Kansas City.
No. 14. Virginian; raised in Clay county.
No. 15. From Woodford county, Kentucky; John T. Hughes married his sister.
No. 18. Kentuckian; cousin to wife of John T. Hughes and Noah P. Carpenter.
No. 19. Reared in Clay county; brother to No. 20.
No. 20. Reared in Clay county.
No. 21. Reared in Clay county; family came to Missouri in 1821; his father was a minister (Disciple or Christian); Everett was a devout Christian, and carried his religion clear through the term of his service; did not backslide, and had the respect of all the soldiers; read his Bible constantly.
No. 22. Died in Clinton county, Missouri.
No. 23. Went to Congress from Nebraska.
No. 24. From Tennessee; died in Clay county.
No. 36. Father a Kentuckian; went to California in 1849; became reckless there; killed two or three men; was killed; no relation to Willard P. Hall.
No. 38. Brother to No. 39; from Ray county, Missouri.
No. 41. Father a Kentuckian.
No. 44. Brother to James Long, 1st Sgt.; father a Kentuckian; came from Woodford county with Story's father; James Long was a merchant at Plattsburg; died at Missouri City.
No. 45. Kentuckian; cousin to the other Longs.
No. 47. Father from Woodford county, Kentucky; died two months after he got home from the army.
No. 49. Kentuckian.
No. 50. Father a Kentuckian.
No. 52. Tennesseean.
No. 53. Tennesseean.
No. 54. Tennesseean.
No. 58. Son of Ebenezer Price, of Clay county; cousin to John T. Hughes; his uncle was a candidate for Colonel against Doniphan.
No. 59. Kentuckian; married a daughter of Richard M. Johnson, of Kentucky.
No. 60. Kentuckian; lives on a farm near Kearny, Clay county, now (1906).
No. 61. Kentuckian.
No. 66. Kentuckian.

No. 70. Kentuckian.
No. 71. Kentuckian; had been five years in the regular army; knew how to forage for food; would aid his starving comrades to steal food from the commissary with great pleasure.
No. 74. Kentuckian; big man; was called "Frosty" White, because he was old and his hair and beard were white.
No. 76. Living yet in Clay county.
No. 81. Kentuckian.
No. 82. Kentuckian; brother to No. 81.
No. 84. Tennesseean.
No. 85. Kentuckian.
No. 90. New-Yorker; brother to No. 91.

William Wallace, Sgt., and George H. Wallace, Corp., were brothers; sons of a noted character, who was an Indian fighter and freighter across the plains.

John Grooms, Corp., was born in Clay county; his father was a Tennessean, and came to Clay county about 1818.

Benjamin Marsh, Corp., reared in Clay county.

James Barnes, Farrier, came to Clay county from Maysville, Kentucky.

COMPANY D.
[SALINE COUNTY.]

Captain John W. Reid's Company D, First Regiment Missouri Mounted Volunteers, Mexican War.

Company Muster Roll, June 10, 1846, shows station of Company at Fort Leavenworth.

This Company joined at Fort Leavenworth from the town of Marshall, Saline county, Missouri; distant from Fort Leavenworth 150 miles.

Roll signed by John W. Reid, Capt. Company D, Mo. Vols.

Company Muster Roll for June 10, 1846, to June 21, 1847, shows station of Company at New Orleans, La.

This company was organized and marched from Marshall, Mo., on the 4th day of June, 1846, to Fort Leavenworth, and arrived there on the 9th day of the same month.

Company was mustered for discharge at New Orleans, La., June 21, 1847, and honorably discharged, by S. Churchill, Insp. Gen., Mustering Officer.

ROSTER.

1. John W. Reid .... Captain.
1. C. I. Miller .... 1st Lieut.
1. F. A. Boush .... 2nd Lieut.
2. W. P. Hicklin .... Asd. 2nd Lieut.
1. William M. Lewis .... 1st Sgt.
2. Thomas E. Staples .... Sgt.
3. Thomas I. Edwards .... Sgt.
4. Andrew W. Cain .... Sgt.

1. Lachlin A. Maclean...................................Corp.
2. James A. Gaines..................................Corp.
3. Isaac Hays..Corp.
4. Robert P. Payne..................................Corp.
    1. Alder, Conrad B.........................Private.
    2. Albertson, Jesse B......................Private.
    3. Beattie, William E......................Private.
    4. Brown, Benjamin F......................Private.
    5. Brown, John B..........................Private.
    6. Berry, Robert H........................Private.
    7. Campbell, Andrew.......................Private.
    8. Clarkin, Christopher...................Private.
    9. Coffey, Benjamin F.....................Private.
  10. Craig, Harvey H........................Private.
  11. Dille, Stephen H.......................Private.
  12. Dille, Squire..........................Private.
  13. Dresslor, George W.....................Private.
  14. Durrett, Benjamin B....................Private.
  15. Edwards, Marcellus B...................Private.
  16. Ferril, John...........................Private.
  17. Fizer, Joseph..........................Private.
  18. Garrett, Chris K.......................Private.
  19. Garrett, James M.......................Private.
  20. Gilmore, Campbell......................Private.
  21. Green, Alexander.......................Private.
  22. Green, William M.......................Private.
  23. Hays, Isaac............................Private.
  24. Harrison, Daniel P.....................Private.
  25. Hentow, Andrew.........................Private.
  26. Jackson, Alfred........................Private.
  27. Johnston, Edward I.....................Private.
  28. Jones, John S..........................Private.
  29. Kile, William..........................Private.
  30. Kile, Joseph...........................Private.
  31. Langford, Thomas.......................Private.
  32. Lansdell, William......................Private.
  33. Lewis, John A..........................Private.
  34. Lewis, John S..........................Private.
  35. Linch, Andrew W........................Private.
  36. Lysle, William.........................Private.
  37. Long, Isaiah...........................Private.
  38. Martin, John...........................Private.
  39. Marshall, Joseph.......................Private.
  40. Morris, Matthew........................Private.

OFFICIAL ROSTERS AND RECORDS.

41. Neff, Henry W..........................Private.
42. Nichols, James..........................Private.
43. O'Bannon, Thomas H....................Private.
44. Osborne, William N.....................Private.
45. Obushon, Basil..........................Private.
46. Patterson, George W....................Private.
47. Pemberton, John T......................Private.
48. Reed, James............................Private.
49. Reese, Bradford........................Private.
50. Robinson, Jacob........................Private.
51. Shannon, James D......................Private.
52. Sheridan, John..........................Private.
53. Steele, James...........................Private.
54. Smith, Samuel F........................Private.
55. Smith, Benjamin F......................Private.
56. Smith, Frederic.........................Private.
57. Smith, Bartholemew.....................Private.
58. Stephenson, Charles....................Private.
59. Stewart, Alexander......................Private.
60. Vaughan, Joseph P......................Private.
61. Wall, John..............................Private.
62. Wallace, Reuben M......................Private.
63. Walker, Isaiah P., [Wyandot Indian]......Private.
64. Waugh, Thomas.........................Private.
65. Wayne, Joshua T........................Private.
66. Weffley, Redman........................Private.
67. Winkle, Adam...........................Private.
68. Whitson, Tipton.........................Private.
69. Ritchie, Franklin........................Private.
70. Durrett, James M.......................Private.
71. Gwinn, Bartlett.........................Private.
72. Moore, Henry W........................Private.
73. Wheeler, Thomas.......................Private.
74. Ferguson, Isaac L.......................Private.
75. Smith, Samuel..........................Private.
76. Corwin, Andrew........................Private.
77. Farris, Warren..........................Private.
78. Haynie, Alfred..........................Private.
79. Hays, Joshua C.........................Private.
80. Lemon, Scott...........................Private.
81. Sullivan, William........................Private.
82. Strother, William.......................Private.
83. Hurkins, John...........................Private.
84. Farris, Franklin.........................Private.

550 DONIPHAN'S EXPEDITION.

COMPANY E.
[FRANKLIN COUNTY.]

Captain John D. Stephenson's Company E, First Regiment Missouri Mounted Volunteers, Mexican War.

No Record of Events given.

Roll signed by John D. Stephenson, Captain.

Mustered in by Captain William D. McKissack, U. S. Army, June 27, 1846.

Memo.: Private Elias Tourgate, on the 28th of March, at Chihuahua, was convicted by Regimental Court-Martial, on charge preferred by Captain Stephenson, of having stolen eight guns and selling them to Mexicans.

Company mustered for discharge at New Orleans, La., June 24, 1847, and honorably discharged, by S. Churchill, Insp. Gen., Mustering Officer.

ROSTER.

1. John D. Stephenson..................Captain.
1. Fenton G. McDonald..................1st Lieut.
1. Scott Richardson.....................2nd Lieut.
2. John Campbell.......................2nd Lieut.
1. Patton, Robert A....................1st Sgt.
2. Cooper, Barnett H...................Sgt.
3. Jones, Stephen M....................Sgt.
4.. McCallister, John....................Sgt.
1. Ramsey, James......................Corp.
2. Bell, I. Russell......................Corp.
3. Evans, Isaac........................Corp.
4. Davidson, Ansolm L.................Corp.
1. King, Clark M......................Bugler.
2. Hemdhauson, Julius.................Bugler.
1. Rinehart, William....................Farrier and Blacksmith.

    1. Alexander, Lemuel......................Private.
    2. Armstrong, James......................Private.
    3. Anderson, George......................Private.
    4. Arbuckle, Matthew.....................Private.
    5. Bassett, Thomas........................Private.
    6. Bell, James A..........................Private.
    7. Bell, William..........................Private.
    8. Brown, William D......................Private.
    9. Brant, Jacob L........................Private.
    10. Brown, Benjamin......................Private.

OFFICIAL ROSTERS AND RECORDS. 551

11. Bryant, William......Private.
12. Butler, Thomas......Private.
13. Caldwell, Nelson D......Private.
14. Campbell, Moore M......Private.
15. Canetey, Samuel......Private.
16. Casper, John......Private.
17. Chunning, Richard......Private.
18. Doggett, Jesse......Private.
19. Dollarhide, Henderson......Private.
20. Duncan, Henry......Private.
21. Duncan, William B......Private.
22. Frickey, John F......Private.
23. Forsythe, Thomas......Private.
24. Franklin, William......Private.
25. French, Josiah......Private.
26. French, Aaron......Private.
27. Gaines, Congrave I......Private.
28. Groff, James S......Private.
29. Hammock, Andrew......Private.
30. Hart, Epenetus......Private.
31. Hausst, Gustavus......Private.
32. Heatherly, James......Private.
33. Heneke, Frederick......Private.
34. Hendrick, Enos......Private.
35. Hensley, Erwin H......Private.
36. Hettenhouse, David......Private.
37. Hite, Stuart......Private.
38. Hite, John S......Private.
39. Hodge, Wilson......Private.
40. Hull, Laban......Private.
41. Hemdhausen, Robert......Private.
42. Jones, William......Private.
43. Jones, Richard......Private.
44. Jump, John R......Private.
45. Kelly, Morgan......Private.
46. Lane, Hugh I......Private.
47. Lane, Simeon......Private.
48. Lemons, Isaac......Private.
49. Marsh, Charles......Private.
50. May, Robert H......Private.
51. Matthews, Andrew......Private.
52. Massie, John......Private.
53. McDonald, William P......Private.
54. McIntire, Robert......Private.

55. McIntire, Williamson....................Private.
56. Miller, James F.........................Private.
57. Mitchell, John..........................Private.
58. Mitchell, Volney........................Private.
59. Montray, Joseph.........................Private.
60. Murphy, James M........................Private.
61. Ohl, Theodore...........................Private.
62. Pearce, George M.......................Private.
63. Phillips, Richard.......................Private.
64. Piper, Alexander........................Private.
65. Pope, Hezekiah..........................Private.
66. Pohlig, William.........................Private.
67. Perkins, John D.........................Private.
68. Ramsbottom, Abner.......................Private.
69. Reed, Zachariah S.......................Private.
70. Roach, John W...........................Private.
71. Robertson, John R.......................Private.
72. Rule, Preston G.........................Private.
73. Shelton, John...........................Private.
74. Shelton, James H........................Private.
75. Shelton, Leroy C........................Private.
76. Shoakman, George W......................Private.
77. Smith, Thomas...........................Private.
78. Smith, Solomon..........................Private.
79. Tourgate, William.......................Private.
80. Tourgate, Elias.........................Private.
81. Valentine, James........................Private.
82. Veeman, Jacob...........................Private.
83. Vliet, George...........................Private.
84. Ware, Mark..............................Private.
85. White, James............................Private.
86. Withington, Thomas......................Private.
87. Woodland, Robert........................Private.
88. Whitemire, Isaac........................Private.
89. Bray, William...........................Private.
90. Campbell, Sutton F......................Private.
91. Carr, Garland O.........................Private.
92. Clark, John.............................Private.
93. Jett, James.............................Private.
94. McClure, Andrew T.......................Private.
95. Roach, Rufus............................Private.
96. Schwallenberg, Stephen..................Private.
97. Salling, Ferdinand......................Private.
98. Musick, Abraham.........................Private.
99. Todd, John A............................Private.

COMPANY F.
[COLE COUNTY.]

Captain M. M. Parsons' Company F, First Regiment Missouri Mounted Volunteers, Mexican War.

Copy of Muster-in Roll dated June 20, 1846, shows company at Fort Leavenworth.

This company comes from Jefferson City, Cole county, Missouri, distant from Fort Leavenworth, 190 miles.

ROSTER.

1. Adams, William P..........................Private.
2. Allen, Joseph..............................Private.
3. Allen, Samuel.............................Private.
4. Adams, John Q. C.........................Private.
5. Bolton, George W.........................Private.
6. Bible, Adam...............................Private.
7. Boone, George L..........................Private.
8. Baber, Albert G...........................Private.
9. Bridgeman, James.........................Private.
10. Cogburn, Green B........................Private.
11. Chandler, Timothy.......................Private.
12. Coffee, Chesley..........................Private.
13. Criner, Christopher......................Private.
14. Dyer, R. Harrison........................Private.
15. Evans, Joseph............................Private.
16. Fant, Hamilton G........................Private.
17. Fant, Joseph L...........................Private.
18. Fisher, Fenwick..........................Private.
19. Gordon, William.........................Private.
20. Green, Andrew...........................Private.
21. Greenup, Thomas W.....................Private.
22. Gouge, Martin............................Private.
23. Grigsby, A. Jackson......................Private.
24. Harris, John..............................Private.
25. Harrison, Samuel.........................Private.
26. Hill, James M............................Private.
27. Hamlet, Archibald........................Private.
28. Hanson, Hugh............................Private.
29. Hudson, G. R............................Private.
30. Hudson, Isaac............................Private.
31. Horn Christopher........................Private.
32. Harrison, William I......................Private.
33. Jefferson, Thomas........................Private.
34. Johnson, James M........................Private.

35. Johnson, James Y.........................Private.
36. Lane, Martin R...........................Private.
37. Lack, Berryman..........................Private.
38. Longun, Jacob C., [On Roll as Langdon]....Private.
39. Lundy, Paschall F........................Private.
40. Leintz, Montgomery P....................Private.
41. Lewis, Hunter N..........................Private.
42. Mahan, Thomas W........................Private.
43. Martin, Charles..........................Private.
44. McAfee, John.............................Private.
45. Moad, William E.........................Private.
46. Moad, Granville L........................Private.
47. Moad, Sterling...........................Private.
48. Miller, Edward...........................Private.
49. Martin, James............................Private.
50. Morgan, John.............................Private.
51. Merodeth, Charles H......................Private.
52. Moore, Meredith T........................Private.
53. Martin, Henderson C......................Private.
54. Meadows, Joel............................Private.
55. Rogers, Thomas...........................Private.
56. Rice, John I..............................Private.
57. Riggins, George W........................Private.
58. Reirson, Winston.........................Private.
59. Radford, Jackson.........................Private.
60. Sanford, Frederick W.....................Private.
61. Skidmore, James W.......................Private.
62. Smith, Phillips...........................Private.
63. Smith, Canimillius D.....................Private.
64. Spaulding, Reuben........................Private.
65. Sone, G. Washington.....................Private.
66. Sone, La Fayette.........................Private.
67. Swan, David..............................Private.
68. Tipton, John I............................Private.
69. Taylor, William..........................Private.
70. Vanover, William R.......................Private.
71. Wray, Tandy A...........................Private.
72. Wamsley, Nathan.........................Private.
73. Winston, Benjamin W....................Private.
74. Wiley, James A..........................Private.
75. Wyatt, Eli................................Private.
76. Yount, Joseph............................Private.
77. Bacon, Thomas...........................Private.
78. Cogburn, Samuel.........................Private.

OFFICIAL ROSTERS AND RECORDS. 555

79. Henkle, William........................Private.
80. Leslie, A..............................Sgt.
81. Maxwell, Samuel.......................Blacksmith.
82. Lockett, Thomas.......................Sgt.
83. Paulsel, Henry R......................Private.
84. Rierson, G. W.........................Private.
85. Wade, Johnson.........................2nd Sgt.
86. Francis, Andros.......................Private.
87. Moore, B. N...........................Private.
88. Snyder, Nicholas......................Bugler.
89. Ray, T. A.............................Private.
90. Sharp, John...........................Private.

IDENTIFICATION OF COMPANY F.

This identification is from information given me by Meredith T. Moore, who was a private in the company, and who lives now (1906) at Cedar City, Missouri, just across the river from Jefferson City.

No. 3. Father of No. 2.
No. 6. Pennsylvania Dutchman; repeated every word or sentence he uttered—said it twice; had violated the rules of "bundling," common among the Pennsylvania Germans, and ruined a girl; had to leave; came to Missouri; went from Missouri to Texas, and in 1873 Moore found him living at Bastrop, in that State. Soon after he went there the girl with whom he had bundled in Pennsylvania appeared there also, accompanied by a daughter, the result of Bible's infraction of the rule. He admitted that he was the father of the daughter, and he then married the mother, and when Moore saw them they were well-to-do and respected by all who knew them.
No. 10. The owner of the mare which died near Cebolleta, and which the Indian carried to his lodge, dividing liberally of her flesh with Moore and Yount when they were returning starving from the Navajo expedition under Captain Reid, as told in a note, *ante.*
No. 11. Always carried his gun cocked; could not be prevailed upon to carry it otherwise; wanted to be ready to fight instantly; died recently in Lafayette county.
No. 14. Moore's messmate; was left at Santa Fé.
No. 19. Shot through the shoulder; died from the wound fifty years afterward.
No. 20. School teacher.
No. 23. Brigadier-General in Confederate Army in Civil War.
No. 29 and 30. Brothers; so careful of their horses that they would often walk and lead them; Isaac had a fiery little mare that would throw him frequently; just below Bent's Fort she left the ranks, "cavorting" and rearing, and all knew he would be thrown, and greeted him with many sorts of advice. Above the din was heard a stentorian voice, that of Ed. Miller, No. 48, saying, "Cast anchor, Ike! Cast anchor, Ike!" But Ike could not cast anchor. He was thrown on his head in the sand. It was thought his neck would be broken, but the only damage he sustained was the loss of his plug hat. His head had been rammed through it by the fall in the sand, and he got up with it around his neck.
No. 32. Wrote poetry.
No. 38. Son of a minister; always preaching his father's sermons to his comrades; did not do much at the battle of Sacramento; said his legs would not carry him forward very rapidly.
No. 45. Cousin to No. 46 and No. 47.

No. 46. Carried his religion through his term of service; became one of the greatest Presbyterians ministers in Missouri. Kept up prayer-meetings in the army.
No. 47. Cousin to No. 45 and No. 46.
No. 48. The man who advised "Ike" Hudson to cast anchor; a wit and joker.
No. 50. Was called "Morgan the Rattler"; disliked Lieutenant Wells; was continually threatening to write a history of the company and use only a dot or fly-speck to designate Wells.
No. 51. Always mad; nothing in the whole war suited him.
No. 56. The man who split the Mexican with his sword at Sacramento; foamed at the mouth in battle; the man to whom a comrade in after years drank the following toast: "Here's to John Rice, the only man who ever cut a Mexican in two twice with one saber-stroke!"
No. 60. Red-headed Dutchman; fine mathematician; good soldier.
No. 62. The only man who got scared and ran in battle.
No. 63. Everything was always wrong with him; nothing ever right; found fault with everything and everybody.
No. 64. Always claimed that his liver crawled up out of place and grew fast there, and that he ought to have a pension because of it.
No. 67. Shot on the belt-buckle at the battle of Brazito; had a black eye and a blue one.
No. 71. Smallest man in the company.
No. 72. Cold reduced him from 190 pounds to 90 pounds; died from effects of it fifty years later.
No. 73. Took No. 67 to the river to wash after he was wounded.
No. 74. Blacksmith.
No. 75. Brother-in-law to No. 42.
No. 76. Now blind; lives at San Bernardino, California.
No. 77. Moore rode his horse at the battle of Sacramento.
No. 78. Had measles at El Paso; fever made him crazy; went out and ate ice, which killed him.
No. 79. Shot through the knee, and died from it; German.
No. 80. Died of consumption just beyond Pawnee Fork.
No. 81. Talked himself to death because he thought the move from El Paso to Chihuahua was a dangerous one.
No. 82. Went no farther than Fort Leavenworth; Baptist preacher.
No. 83. Colonel Doniphan sent him back with mail from Pawnee Fork; Moore bought his horse for George L. Boone; he never returned to the company.
No. 86. Deserted; had deserted before from regular army; Moore afterward found him running a boat on the Bay of San Francisco.
No. 90. Turned back at Lexington, Missouri; Moore does not know why he returned.

COMPANY G.
[HOWARD COUNTY.]

Captain Horatio H. Hughes's Company G, First Regiment Missouri Mounted Volunteers, Mexican War.

This company had two Captains during its service, Congreve Jackson and Horatio H. Hughes; Jackson was made Lieutenant-Colonel of the Regiment. Hughes succeeded him as Captain.

Muster-in Roll does not show when nor where the company was mustered into the service of the United States.

This company was organized in Fayette, Howard county, Mo.,

OFFICIAL ROSTERS AND RECORDS. 557

on the 5th day of June, 1846, under a requisition from the Governor on said county for a company of mounted men for the service of the United States. The following certificate appears on the Roll:

I certify on honor that the above is a correct copy of the Muster Roll of Company G, Mo. Volunteers.

(Signed) CONGREVE JACKSON, Captain.

The last named eight men were mustered into the service of the United States by Captain W. M. D. McKissack. Their names do not appear on the original Roll.

(Signed) CONGREVE JACKSON, Captain.

The company was organized at and marched from Fayette, Howard county, Mo., on the 5th day of June, 1846, to Fort Leavenworth, and arrived there on the 16th of June. Roll signed: H. H. Hughes, Captain.

Company mustered for discharge at New Orleans, La., on the 21st day of June, 1847, and honorably discharged by S. Churchill, Insp. Gen., Mustering Officer.

ROSTER.

1. Hughes, Horatio H.............................Captain.
1. Hinton, John..................................1st Lieut.
1. Wright, Nicholas B...........................2nd Lieut.
1. Saffarrans, Isaac.............................1st Sgt.
2. Barthalon, Thomas J..........................Sgt.
3. Smith, Stephen...............................Sgt.
4. Taylor, Townsend.............................Sgt.
1. Bouldin, Joseph..............................Corp.
2. Humphrey, Daniel E...........................Corp.
3. Maupin, Garland M............................Corp.
4. McCully, William.............................Corp.
1. Frant, Phillip...............................Bugler.
2. Hackley, George W............................Bugler.
1. Browning, John T.............................Farrier.
  1. Arnold, Finis..............................Private.
  2. Browning, Robert H.........................Private.
  3. Basket, James P............................Private.
  4. Brown, John S..............................Private.
  5. Bouldin, Daniel W..........................Private.
  6. Bailey, Samuel G...........................Private.
  7. Clock, James G.............................Private.
  8. Cooper, Joseph D...........................Private.
  9. Cooper, Dudley H...........................Private.

10. Cunningham, William F................Private.
11. Cooper, Sarshel F......................Private.
12. Calloway, Stephen.....................Private.
13. Calloway, James.......................Private.
14. Collins, James........................Private.
15. Crems, James W........................Private.
16. Campbell, James H.....................Private.
17. Creson, Joshua........................Private.
18. Carson, George H......................Private.
19. Day, James............................Private.
20. Davis, Andrew S.......................Private.
21. Donehae, Thomas S.....................Private.
22. Denney, Alexander.....................Private.
23. Davis, Talbot J.......................Private.
24. Fugate, Royal S.......................Private.
25. Fristoe, Richard M....................Private.
26. Gibbs, Talton T.......................Private.
27. Graham, James R.......................Private.
28. George, William.......................Private.
29. Hovey, Oliver P.......................Private.
30. Hackley, John F.......................Private.
31. Hall, Jonathan W......................Private.
32. Halstead, Benjamin....................Private.
33. Hughes, William M.....................Private.
34. Hughes, Ami F.........................Private.
35. Haston, William A.....................Private.
36. Harvey, Thomas J......................Private.
37. Horsley, Walter J.....................Private.
38. Hayter, William S.....................Private.
39. Jackson, John H.......................Private.
40. Jackson, William P....................Private.
41. Jacks, Milton.........................Private.
42. Jones, Jonathan.......................Private.
43. Jackson, Alel R.......................Private.
44. Kennerly, Shelton.....................Private.
45. Lockridge, Andrew D...................Private.
46. McKehan, John.........................Private.
47. McDonald, William A...................Private.
48. Maupin, Cornelius.....................Private.
49. Marr, John T..........................Private.
50. Means, Thomas I.......................Private.
51. Morrisson, William J..................Private.
52. Mastin, Lewis.........................Private.
53. Mahone, John R. T.....................Private.

54. McCrary, Absalom.......................Private.
55. Morin, John.............................Private.
56. Miller, John............................Private.
57. Price, John W..........................Private.
58. Powell, Ransom.........................Private.
59. Quiro, Henry W.........................Private.
60. Rains, John Riley......................Private.
61. Rupe, David O..........................Private.
62. Reid, James B..........................Private.
63. Reynolds, Andrew.......................Private.
64. Reynolds, Thomas.......................Private.
65. Stokeley, Henry........................Private.
66. Schmidt, Jacob.........................Private.
67. Smith, William.........................Private.
68. Thorpe, William........................Private.
69. Thrash, Richard........................Private.
70. Turner, Henry A........................Private.
71. Wright, Thomas.........................Private.
72. Williams, Wesley.......................Private.
73. Williams, John S.......................Private.
74. Witt, Elisha B.........................Private.
75. Walker, Robert D.......................Private.
76. Ware, George...........................Private.
77. Wolfkill, Sarshel C....................Private.

1. Jackson, Stephen........................2nd Lieut.

1. Browning, John T........................Farrier.
2. Swain, James H.........................Farrier.

1. Carson, Nehemiah........................Private.
2. Enyart, Silas, Jr.......................Private.
3. Hopper, Clifton T.......................Private.
4. Hackley, George I.......................Private.
5. Leland, John D..........................Private.
6. Roberts, Marion.........................Private.
7. Smith, Christian........................Private.
8. Sterns, William.........................Private.
9. Stout, Steven B.........................Private.
10. Emerson, Tilley........................Sgt.
11. Simmons, William.......................Private.
12. Jackson, Congreve......................Captain.
13. De Courcy, James A.....................1st Lieut.
14. Hastings, William A....................Private.
15. Hughes, Harrison.......................Private.

COMPANY H.
[CALLAWAY COUNTY.]

Captain Charles B. Rodgers's Company H, First Regiment Missouri Mounted Volunteers, Mexican War.

Muster-in Roll dated June 24, 1846.

The following certificate appears on the Roll:

I hereby certify that the above is a true copy of the Muster Roll of this Company as mustered into the service of the United States by Captain W. M. McKissack, U. S. Army, from June 24, 1846.

(Signed) CHARLES B. RODGERS,
Commanding the Company.

This company was organized and marched from Fulton, Mo., June 14, to Fort Leavenworth, and arrived there June 23.

The company was mustered for discharge at New Orleans, La., June 21, 1847, and honorably discharged by S. Churchill, Insp. Gen., Mustering Officer.

ROSTER.

1. Charles B. Rodgers....................Captain.
1. Duncan, John B......................1st Lieut.
1. Harrison, Crockett...................2nd Lieut.
2. Murray, Benjamin F..................2nd Lieut.
1. Letcher, Fountain F..................1st Sgt.
2. Jameson, Thomas....................Sgt.
3. Blattenburgh, Phillip.................Sgt.
4. Jones, Benjamin.....................Sgt.
1. Harrison, Thomas...................Corp.
2. Van Bibber, Ewing A................Corp.
3. Rodgers, Charles A..................Sgt.
4. Thompson, Joseph D. N.............Corp.
1. Frank, Levi.........................Bugler.
1. Peyton, William....................Farrier and Blacksmith.
   1. Adcock, Joseph Q.......................Private.
   2. Annett, John...........................Private.
   3. Andrews, James M.....................Private.
   4. Bagley, Waddy C......................Private.
   5. Brodwater, William....................Private.
   6. Berry, Francis.........................Private.
   7. Berry, Robert..........................Private.
   8. Bullard, Cubman.......................Private.
   9. Bailey, John...........................Private.
  10. Bailey, Benjamin F....................Private.

11. Bowles, Stephen........................Private.
12. Beeding, James.........................Private.
13. Bean, Benjamin........................Private.
14. Baker, William F.......................Private.
15. Baker, William T.......................Private.
16. Blunt, Levi..............................Private.
17. Brown, William........................Private.
18. Craig, David............................Private.
19. Collier, William B......................Private.
20. Collins, Samuel G......................Private.
21. Carter, Andrew B.......................Private.
22. Curran, David..........................Private.
23. Dickerson, Andrew W..................Private.
24. Davis, William F.......................Private.
25. Davis, Francis..........................Private.
26. Davis, Alexander.......................Private.
27. Davis, Phillip..........................Private.
28. Duley, Paul H..........................Private.
29. Duley, William M......................Private.
30. Dunlap, Robert.........................Private.
31. Elliott, William.........................Private.
32. Ficklin, William T......................Private.
33. French, William........................Private.
34. French, Bryant.........................Private.
35. George, James..........................Private.
36. Guitar, Odon...........................Private.
37. Glover, Robert..........................Private.
38. Hill, Charles............................Private.
39. Hunter, Henry T........................Private.
40. Harper, John N.........................Private.
41. Habernicht, Herman....................Private.
42. Johnston, James........................Private.
43. Kelsoe, John M.........................Private.
44. Love, Smoloff...........................Private.
45. McCray, James..........................Private.
46. McKinney, Francis S...................Private.
47. Maddox, Uriah..........................Private.
48. Morris, William.........................Private.
49. Malone, James..........................Private.
50. McClure, John..........................Private.
51. Northcut, William H...................Private.
52. Null, Henry.............................Private.
53. Overton, Dudley H.....................Private.
54. Oldham, Richard S.....................Private.

55. Overfelt, Elijah..........................Private.
56. Price, James.............................Private.
57. Reed, Alexander.........................Private.
58. Robards, John M.........................Private.
59. Ryan, Joel...............................Private.
60. Ridgeway, Jefferson.....................Private.
61. Sharp, Samuel............................Private.
62. Swan, John...............................Private.
63. Stewart, C. W............................Private.
64. Trimble, John............................Private.
65. Trimble, William.........................Private.
66. Trimble, Mountain M.....................Private.
67. Tureman, Thomas..........................Private.
68. Terrell, James...........................Private.
69. Thompson, David..........................Private.
70. Wells, Elijah H..........................Private.
71. Ward, John M.............................Private.
72. Wilkerson, Hall L........................Private.
73. Williamson, Robert.......................Private.
74. Wright, Charles..........................Private.
75. Yancy, Romulus...........................Private.
1. Cockrel, Benjamin.........................Private.
2. Darinx, Lewis.............................Private.
3. Jones, Lewis..............................Private.
4. Leopard, William..........................Private.
5. Maddox, John..............................Private.
6. Owen, John T..............................Private.
7. Smart, Albert T...........................Private.
8. Snell, James C............................2nd Lieut.
9. Stultz, James C...........................Private.
10. Thompson, James M........................Private.
11. Tharp, Joel..............................2nd Bugler.
12. Humphrey, William........................Private.
1. Fleming, James P..........................Private.
2. Silton, Felix G...........................Private.
1. Beattie, Z. C.............................Private.
2. Jacobs, Ballor............................Private.
3. King, Walter..............................Private.
4. Lucas, O. H. P............................Private.
5. Witchum, James............................Private.
   Ficklin, Thompson......................Private.
   Murray, Benjamin F.....................Private.
   Mitchum, James.........................Private.

LACLEDE RANGERS.
[St. Louis.]

Captain Thomas B. Hudson's Company E, First Regiment Missouri Mounted Volunteers, Mexican War.

Muster Roll, June 11, 1846, to June 24, 1847.

This company was organized at St. Louis, Mo., and marched from St. Louis, June 7th, to Fort Leavenworth, and arrived there on June 10, 1846.

Roll signed by Thomas B. Hudson, Captain.

Company was mustered for discharge at New Orleans, La., June 24, 1847, and honorably discharged by S. Churchill, Insp. Gen., Mustering Officer.

NOTE.—It appears from Record of Events of Clark's Battalion, that this was an independent company of riflemen, known as Laclede Rangers, until September 15, 1846, when it was attached to Clark's Battalion by Brig. Gen. Kearny per Gen. Order No. 23, as Company C. The same authority claims it as of said Battalion until date of Muster-out Roll, although the Muster-out Roll of the Company designates it as "Company E, First Regiment Missouri Mounted Volunteers, commanded by Col. Doniphan."

ROSTER.

1. Thomas B. Hudson.................................Captain.
1. Richard S. Elliott...................................1st Lieut.
1. Louis T. Lebaurne................................2nd Lieut.
1. Henry D. Evans..................................2nd Lieut.
1. Alexander Patterson..............................1st Sgt.
2. John Campbell...................................Sgt.
3. James E. Darst..................................Sgt.
4. Ira I. Drake.....................................Sgt.
1. Thomas Hart....................................Corpl.
2. John W. Work..................................Corpl.
3. Phillip B. Riley..................................Corpl.
4. Edgar L. Hinton.................................Corpl.
1. Morrell, Lorenzo D..............................Bugler.
2. Allington, James B..............................Farrier.

    1. Ashley, Joseph...........................Private.
    2. Anderson, Alexander C...................Private.
    3. Block, Hymen...........................Private.
    4. Barbier, Charles.........................Private.

5. Bombury, Joseph........................Private.
6. Brittell, John K..........................Private.
7. Bradley, Patrick.........................Private.
8. Barr, John...............................Private.
9. Coulter, George W.......................Private.
10. Collier, Valentine S.....................Private.
11. Carey, Robert...........................Private.
12. Cameron, William C.....................Private.
13. Chrisley, James.........................Private.
14. Cruso, William..........................Private.
15. Charleville, Lewis H.....................Private.
16. Clark, George R.........................Private.
17. Chadbourne, Joseph.....................Private.
18. Dougherty, Benjamin....................Private.
19. Decatur, Stephen........................Private.
20. Dessallum, Joseph......................Private.
21. Dinan, Joseph W........................Private.
22. Eoff, George............................Private.
23. Eldridge, John..........................Private.
24. Finch, William..........................Private.
25. Gould, John.............................Private.
26. Goodwin, Asa...........................Private.
27. Griswold, Isaiah A......................Private.
28. Getzendinar, George James..............Private.
29. Harding, Walter D......................Private.
30. Hinton, Thomas.........................Private.
31. Haggerty, Charles......................Private.
32. Howard, James..........................Private.
33. Hope, Alexander W......................Private.
34. Hardigan, Victor........................Private.
35. Jarrott, Thomas, Jr.....................Private.
36. Jamison, George W......................Private.
37. Jamison, William T......................Private.
38. Jefferson, Alexander....................Private.
39. Klinge, John............................Private.
40. Lahey, Timothy.........................Private.
41. Lynch, James...........................Private.
42. Livingston, Federal.....................Private.
43. Martin, George W.......................Private.
44. Murphy, Michael W......................Private.
45. McEnnis, Michael.......................Private.
46. McKinney, Jeremiah G..................Private.
47. McClure, Francis.......................Private.
48. McSorly, Bernard.......................Private.

OFFICIAL ROSTERS AND RECORDS.

49. McDade, John..........................Private.
50. Miller, Merriday........................Private.
51. McDowell, Thomas.....................Private.
52. McLane, Daniel.........................Private.
53. Neal, John T............................Private.
54. Towell, James...........................Private.
55. Quinette, John A.......................Private.
56. Rice, Andrew J.........................Private.
57. Richardson, James W..................Private.
58. Rhodes, John...........................Private.
59. Raney, William.........................Private.
60. Rose, Lewis.............................Private.
61. Rose, Francis E. L.....................Private.
62. Strangman, Samuel....................Private.
63. Smelly, John R.........................Private.
64. Smith, Isaac............................Private.
65. Schiffler, Christopher..................Private.
66. Spands, Edward W....................Private.
67. Taylor, Henry P........................Private.
68. Twombly, Benjamin....................Private.
69. Triplett, John W........................Private.
70. Tons, Henry............................Private.
71. Wilner, Pere............................Private.
72. Wiseman, Alexander...................Private.
73. Williams, Hubbard.....................Private.
74. Williams, William......................Private.
75. Wash, Martin W........................Private.
76. Wise, Franklin..........................Private.
77. Valdego, John B........................Private.
78. James W. Lenle........................Private.
79. Arther E. Hughes......................Private.
80. Larkin Prewett.........................Private.
81. Veary Price.............................Private.
82. James Blair.............................Private.
83. Eli Dana.................................Private.
84. Nicholet Augustus......................Private.
85. Gerry, Oliver...........................Private.
86. Wheeling, James.......................Private.
87. William A. Jones.......................Private.
88. McKenzie, Wallace.....................Private.
89. Larkin, William T......................Private.
90. Roberts, L. L...........................Private.
91. Whitson, William S....................Private.

INFANTRY.
[COLE COUNTY.]

Captain W. Z. Angney's Company A, Battalion Infantry, Missouri Volunteers, Mexican War.

Muster-in Roll, dated June 17, 1846, shows company at Fort Leavenworth.

The following appears on the Roll:

I do certify that the foregoing is a true copy of the Roll of the persons inspected and mustered into service of the United States (except the names of Joseph E. Owing, Wm. G. Meade, Peter Seely and William H. Armstrong, inspected and mustered in by Captain McKissack) by Captain Allen at the time and place in the said Roll mentioned; that the persons in this certificate named were mustered into the service of the United States at the time and place in the Roll mentioned.

(Signed) WM. Z. ANGNEY,
Capt. Commanding Inf. Co. A, Mo. Vols.

Muster Roll, June 15, 1846, to Feb. 28, 1847, shows company at San Fernando de Taos.

Muster Roll, Mch. 1 to May 1, 1847, shows company at Fort Leavenworth.

Company mustered for discharge at Fort Leavenworth July 31, 1847, and honorably discharged by C. Wharton, Lt. Colonel First Dragoons, Mustering Officer.

ROSTER.

1. Lucian J. Eastin................................2nd Lieut.
2. Charles R. Moller...............................2nd Lieut.
    1. Armstrong, William H....................Private.
    2. Bennch, John...........................Private.
    3. Epperson, Jesse........................Private.
    4. Faulkner, Josiah.......................Private.
    5. Glenn, Robert..........................Private.
    6. Hecht, Joseph..........................Private.
    7. Haga, Bernard H........................Private.
    8. Mack, William..........................Private.
    9. Poston, William L......................Private.
    10. Redding, Gerrard......................Private.
    11. Summers, Phillip......................Private.
    12. Walters, John B.......................Private.
    13. Winslow, Nicholas.....................Private.
    14. Angney, W. Z..........................Captain.
    15. Irvine, Alexander.....................1st Lieut.

OFFICIAL ROSTERS AND RECORDS.

16. Hudson, Leroy C...........................1st Sgt.
17. Ferguson, William H.....................2nd Sgt.
18. Wright, John J............................3rd Sgt.
19. Brookshire, Joseph B....................4th Sgt.
20. Brown, John L............................1st Corpl.
21. Bradley, Lewis............................2nd Corpl.
22. Francis, William I........................3rd Corpl.
23. Armitage, Fletcher T....................Private.
24. Clark, Benjamin..........................Private.
25. Coffelt, David............................Private.
26. Clendenin, John I........................Private.
27. Curry, William A.........................Private.
28. Fitzgerald, Silas..........................Private.
29. Freely, Henry.............................Private.
30. Francis, Henry............................Private.
31. Harrison, James L........................Private.
32. Kenser, Ambrose.........................Private.
33. Legg, James M............................Private.
34. McCook, Timothy........................Private.
35. Pace, John W.............................Private.
36. Payne, Charles............................Private.
37. Phillips, John C...........................Private.
38. Phillips, William C.......................Private.
39. Ritchey, John.............................Private.
40. Roy, James M.............................Private.
41. Tooms, John...............................Private.
42. Tooms, William M........................Private.
43. Tyns, Lewis................................Private.
44. Wade, William............................Private.
45. Weaver, John..............................Private.
46. Wells, Reuben L..........................Private.
47. Williams, John............................Private.
48. Williams, Barnet C.......................Private.
49. Whitley, W. F.............................Private.
50. Whitley, John.............................Private.
51. Wayne, William...........................Private.
52. Hix, A. W. G..............................1st Sgt.
53. Hart, John B...............................Private.
54. Hogan, William G........................Private.
55. Owings, Joseph...........................Private.
56. Matthews, Edward.......................Private.
57. Robeson, Josiah..........................Private.
58. Seely, Peter................................Private.
59. Walkin, John A...........................Private.

60. Yukeman, Bernard......................Private.
61. Butt, William............................1st Sgt.
62. Miller, Charles R........................Sgt.
63. Connell, Pierce..........................Private.
64. Francis, William J......................Private.
65. Hudson, Leroy C........................Private.
66. Rightenour, Elenier....................Private.
67. Sloan, Levi.............................Private.
68. Tudor, Franklin........................Private.
69. Williams, Edward......................Private.

INFANTRY.
[PLATTE COUNTY.]

Captain W. S. Murphy's Company B, Battalion Infantry, Missouri Volunteers, Mexican War.

Muster-in Roll, dated June 27, 1846, shows company at Fort Leavenworth.

The following certificate appears on the Roll:

I certify that the above is a true copy from the Muster Roll of my Company as mustered into the service of the United States by Capt. W. M. D. McKissack, U. S. Army, June 27, 1846.

(Signed) W. S. MURPHY, Captain.

Muster Roll, June 27, 1846, to February 28, 1847, shows company at San Fernando de Taos, New Mexico.

Muster Roll, May 30, 1847, to August 18, 1847, accompanys Pay Roll for period from February 28, 1847, to August 18, 1847, and shows company at Fort Leavenworth.

Company mustered for discharge at Fort Leavenworth August 18, 1847, and honorably discharged by C. Wharton, Lt. Colonel First Dragoons, Mustering Officer.

ROSTER.

1. Jonas S. Woods................................Captain.
2. Franklin Finch................................2nd Lieut.
1. Leroy Snodderly..............................Sgt.
2. Samuel Doyle..................................Sgt.
3. John Doyle....................................Sgt.
4. John Hearpst..................................Sgt.
1. McFarland, Alexander.........................Corpl.
2. Campbell, Hugh L.............................Corpl.
   1. Alcorn, Bransford........................Private.

OFFICIAL ROSTERS AND RECORDS. 569

    2. Benijher, Frederick......................Private.
    3. Campbell, Charles E....................Private.
    4. Chambers, John.........................Private.
    5. Carter, James..........................Private.
    6. Curry, John............................Private.
    7. Drummend, William P....................Private.
    8. Funderburgh, Bluford...................Private.
    9. Grooms, Robert.........................Private.
   10. Griffith, William......................Private.
   11. Gladden, Green.........................Private.
   12. Hubble, Ezra...........................Private.
   13. Isaac, Reileigh........................Private.
   14. Isaac, Amos............................Private.
   15. Larrisen, Ezekiel......................Private.
   16. McCormack, Andrew......................Private.
   17. McGuire, John..........................Private.
   18. Morgan, Samuel.........................Private.
   19. Morgan, Jonathan.......................Private.
   20. Pearce, Andrew.........................Private.
   21. Pearce, Elijah.........................Privote.
   22. Riley, James B.........................Private.
   23. Riley, George W........................Private.
   24. Ramey, William.........................Private.
   25. Sharp, William.........................Private.
   26. Sharp, Jacob...........................Private.
   27. Shearer, Joel..........................Private.
   28. Surratt, James H.......................Private.
   29. Swan, Israel...........................Private.
   30. Skaggs, William........................Private.
   31. Thurman, John..........................Private.
   32. Usserry, John..........................Private.
   33. Wooden, Ward...........................Private.
   34. Wilcoxen, Isaac N......................Private.
   35. West, Henry............................Private.
   36. Wiley, John............................Private.
   37. Wiley, Edward..........................Private.
   38. Wells, John............................Private.
   39. Hartwell, Benjamin B...................Private.
1. William S. Murphy..........................Captain.
1. George R. Gibson...........................2nd Lieut.
1. John W. Gibbons............................1st Lieut.
1. Aull, A. B.................................1st Sgt.
    1. Cowan, James...........................Private.
    2. Fox, John S............................Private.

3. Haddock, Lewis..........................Private.
 4. Learia, Henry A........................Private.
 5. Patten, Joseph..........................Private.
 6. Walden, Robert.........................Private.
 7. Short, Addison..........................Private.
 8. Brooker, Martin D.....................Private.
 9. Ellison, John............................Private.
10. Clarke, William........................Private.
11. Jenkins, Richard H....................Private.
 1. Hardin M. L............................Sgt.
 1. Sephert, Gustevous.....................Private.
 1. Drummond, L. D.......................Corpl.
 1. Katchenthal, Albert....................Corp.
 1. Vincent Van Valkenburgh...............1st Lieut.
 1. Easthorne, Thomas.....................Drummer.
 1. Dogherty, James........................Sgt.
 1. Graham, John B........................Private.
 2. Hargis, Richard........................Private.
 3. Richardson, Samuel....................Private.
 4. Dawson, Francis M....................Private.
 5. Grooms, John...........................Private.
 6. Mulkey, Thomas........................Private.
 7. Peery, Robert...........................Private.
 8. Smith, James............................Private.
    S. T. Woods............................4th Corpl.
    Clark, William N.......................Private.
    Campbell, Hugh L......................Private.

The Roll bears the following endorsement, in red ink:

Roster of Co. "B" (Angney's) Battalion Missouri Volunteers Mexican War.

ARTILLERY.

Battalion Missouri Light Artillery, Mexican War.

Muster Roll, August 31 to October 31, 1846, shows station at Santa Fé, N. M.

Record of Events:

The Battery arrived at Santa Fé, N. M. Ty., Aug. 18, 1846, and encamped near city until Sept. 2, 1846, when it accompanied Brig. Gen. Kearny on his march to the southern part of the Territory and proceeded to the town of Tomé, 93 miles south of Santa Fé. Returned to the latter place and went into quarters, Sept. 12, 1846. On Sept.

16, Capt. Fischer, with det. of 50 men of the command, proceeded under S. O. No. 7 to the Apache country to recover property stolen by those Indians, and returned after several days' march into the mountains, bringing in some of the Chiefs of that Nation. Sept. 29, Lieut. Kribben was detached in command of a party of 25 men under G. O. No. 33 and proceeded to Pecos and other points in this territory, to secure arms and ammunition reported to be in possession of traders and intended for the enemy's forces. Since the arrival of Battn. at this city a detachment commanded by a comd. officer has been constantly stationed within 25 miles of this Capital for the purpose of guarding the horses of the command while grazing on the public commons, as well as the horses and mules & cattle belonging to the Q. M. & Comy. Dept. On the 30th inst. this detachment was withdrawn, the public horses, mules and cattle turned over to the departments, and the horses of the command (in default of forage which ought to have been furnished by the Govt.) sent in different directions into the mountains from 75 to 120 miles from Santa Fé to winter upon grass or cottonwood or otherwise maintain their existence. They are herded by Mexican herdsmen at the individual expense of the men of the command, guarded by small detachments from three companies of the Battn. With this exception the whole command is now in quarters in Santa Fé, occupied (besides the regular duties of the garrison) in completing the fortifications at Fort Marcy and in the repairs of arms and preparing the armament for that fort when completed.

On Sept. 15, 1846, the Laclede Rangers, a volunteer company under command of Capt. T. B. Hudson, as riflemen from St. Louis, Mo., was attached to the Battalion by Brig. Gen. Kearny per Gen. Order, No. 23, as Co. C.

Roll signed: M. Lewis Clark, Major Comdg.

MUSTER ROLL, OCTOBER 31 TO DECEMBER 31, 1846.

Since last Muster, Battn. has been in quarters in Santa Fé with exception of 10 men from each of the 3 companies, detached as a guard to the horses of the command grazing in the mountains, and of 29 men from the 3 companies under command of Captain Hudson and Lieut. Krebbin detached under Gen. Order No. 71 of Nov. 17, 1846, and per B. O. No. 35 and 41 of Nov. 20 and Dec. 1, 1846, as an escort to Lt. Col. Mitchell, 2nd Regt. Mo. Mtd. Vols., under orders for opening a communication between Santa Fé and Chihuahua. On Dec. 25, Lts. Garnier and Evans with 16 mounted men were detached under orders to proceed to the towns of Placera and San Miguel to apprehend Damacio Salezar and other persons engaged in a conspiracy against the Govt. On Dec. 14, orders were received from Col. Doniphan for Major Clark with 100 men and a battery of artillery to march towards Chihuahua and join his headquarters. Preparations were immediately made, but in consequence of the revolutionary movements in this territory and of the orders of the Col. commanding this post, of Dec. 30, 1846, this march is postponed until further orders and the Battn. is now in readiness to move whenever circumstances shall render it proper.

Roll signed: M. Lewis Clark, Major Commanding.

Muster Roll, March 7th to June 24, 1847, shows station at New Orleans, La.

This battalion consists of two original companies of horse artillery from St. Louis and two companies of cavalry from Mo. as follows: Co. A, under the command of Capt. Weightman, headqrs. being in New Orleans and a detachment at Santa Fé, N. M. Co. B, commanded by Capt. W. Fischer, headqrs. at Santa Fé and a small detachment in New Orleans. Co. C, commanded by Lieut. L. T. Labeuner, originally the Laclede Rangers, attached to the Battn. by Gen. Kearny at Santa Fé, Hd. Qrs. in New Orleans, a detachment at Santa Fé; and Co. D, commanded by Capt. Hudson of the Laclede Rangers, now commanding detachments of Co. B, of this Battn. and other companies of the 2nd Regt. Mo. Mtd. Vols., stationed at Santa Fé, under command of Col. Price.

Roll signed: M. Lewis Clark, Major Commanding.

Field and Staff mustered for discharge at New Orleans, La., June 24, 1847, and honorably discharged by S. Churchill, Gen. Inspector, Mustering Officer, "except R. F. Richardson, Surgeon, who by G. O. No. 22 is to be discharged the 30th of June."

Card filed with Field and Staff.

Capt. Thos. E. Hudson's Laclede Rangers, (also known as Co. C, Artillery Battalion) Battalion Light Artillery, Mo. Vols. Mexican War. Company Muster Rolls for June 20, 1846, to June 24, 1847.

OFFICIAL ROSTERS AND RECORDS.   573

NOTE.—It appears from Record of Events of Clark's Battn. that Capt. Hudson's Co. was an independent Co. of Riflemen known as Laclede Rangers, until Sept. 15, 1846, when it was attached to Clark's Battn. Light Artillery, by Brig. Gen. Kearny's G. O. No. 23, as Co. C. The same authority claims it of said Battn. until date of Muster-out, although the Muster-out Roll of the Co. designates it as "Co. E, 1st Regt. Mo. Mtd. Vols., commanded by Col. Doniphan."

It was "carded" as of the latter Regt. and this slip is filed with Field and Staff of Battn. Light Arty. to account for the company.

Card filed with Field and Staff.

Capt. Thos. B. Hudson's Detachment (also known as Co. D, Artillery Battn.) Battalion Light Artillery Mo. Vols., Mexican War. (Major M. L. Clark).

Det. Muster Roll for June 11, 1846, to June 24, 1847, shows station of Det., New Orleans, La.

Roll signed: Thos. B. Hudson, Capt. Laclede Rangers, Mo. Vols.

Detachment mustered for discharge at New Orleans, La., June 24, 1847, and honorably discharged by S. Churchill, Insp. Gen., Mustering Officer.

This Detachment is composed of men detailed from Laclede Rangers (Co. E, 1st Mo. Mtd. Vols.), Cos. A, D, K, L, and O, 2nd Regt. Mo. Mtd. Vols., Cos. C. G, & H, separate Battn. Mo. Mtd. Riflemen, and Co. B, Light Artillery, Battn. Mo. Vols. No cards were made from this Roll, but proper entries were made on cards in the several companies. This slip is filed with "Field and Staff" of Battn. Light Artillery to account for the Detachment.

FIELD AND STAFF OF

Major M. Lewis Clark's Battalion Missouri Light Artillery, Mexican War.

1. M. Lewis Clark...........................Major.
2. Robert F. Richardson......................Surgeon.
3. Christian Kribben........................Adjutant.
4. Lea D. Walhn............................Adjutant.
1. John Mudgett............................Sgt. Major.
2. Henry Hancock..........................Q. M. Sgt.
3. John Mossa..............................Chief Bugler.
4. Joseph W. Smith.........................Hospital Steward.

ARTILLERY COMPANY A.
[ST. LOUIS.]

Captain R. H. Weightman's Company A, Battalion Light Artillery, Missouri Volunteers, Mexican War.

Muster-in Rolls, dated June 19, 1846, shows company at Fort Leavenworth. Roll signed: R. H. Weightman, Captain.

CERTIFICATE: I certify that the above is a true copy of the original Muster Roll signed by Captain James Allen, First Dragoons, mustering this company into the service of the United States, with the exception of the two last names, Nos. 100 and 101, who were mustered into the service by Captain McKissack, June 25, 1846.

(Signed) R. H. WEIGHTMAN,
Captain Co. A, Horse Artillery, Mo. Vols.

Roll from October 31, to December 31, 1846, shows company at Santa Fé, N. M.

Muster Roll for December 31, 1846, to June 24, 1847, shows company at New Orleans, La.

The company was organized at St. Louis, and marched from St. Louis on June 13, 1846, to Fort Leavenworth, and arrived there on June 18, 1846.

Company mustered for discharge at New Orleans, La., on the 24th of June, 1847, and honorably discharged by S. Churchill, Inspector General, Mustering Officer.

ROSTER.

1. R. H. Weightman.................................Captain.
1. Andrew J. Dorn..................................1st Lieut.
2. Edmond F. Chouteau.............................1st Lieut.
1. John O. Simpson.................................2nd Lieut.
2. John R. Gratiot..................................2nd Lieut.
1. Robert T. Jenkins................................Sgt.
2. Davis Moore.....................................Sgt.
3. Alfred V. Wilson.................................Sgt.
4. William C. Kennerly..............................Sgt.
1. Clay Taylor......................................Corp.
2. George A. Shinston...............................Corp.
3. William N. Chambers.............................Corp.
1. Alexander Houston...............................Bugler.
2. Frank Rath......................................Bugler.
1. Miles Nesmith...................................F. and B.

   1. Allison, Lewis H............................Private.

OFFICIAL ROSTERS AND RECORDS.

2. Burgess, John T..........................Private.
3. Bishop, Nelson............................Private.
4. Ballard, George W.......................Private.
5. Baker, Thomas...........................Private.
6. Bryan, Morrison..........................Private.
7. Beideman, Jacob C......................Private.
8. Cameron, Monroe......................Private.
9. Coote, George T.........................Private.
10. Chapin, Samuel W.....................Private.
11. Compayuette, Oliver....................Private.
12. Calladay, John............................Private.
13. Cross, George............................Private.
14. Coffee, W. A..............................Private.
15. Chaplin, James H.......................Private.
16. Claimonb, Antoine......................Private.
17. Correll, John C...........................Private.
18. Clary, John................................Private.
19. Dourty, James...........................Private.
20. Edwards, Francis S.....................Private.
21. Evans, Jason.............................Private.
22. Edgell, Frederick M....................Private.
23. Foley, Patrick............................Private.
24. Fish, Moses G............................Private.
25. Ferrill, Charles J.........................Private.
26. Fay, Edward.............................Private.
27. Fox, John H..............................Private.
28. Gratoit, Theodore.......................Private.
29. Garland, R. Rice.........................Private.
30. Goodfellow, John T.....................Private.
31. Geissant, George........................Private.
32. Grey, Nathan M.........................Private.
33. Grey, Edward C.........................Private.
34. Hastings, Daniel H......................Private.
35. Hayward, George A....................Private.
36. Halstead, Thomas G...................Private.
37. Hooper, George T.......................Private.
38. Heguembourg, George W.............Private.
39. Heguembourg, Alexander G.........Private.
40. Hansell, Lewellen.......................Private.
41. Johnson, Charles T....................Private.
42. James, Thomas.........................Private.
43. Kavenaugh, Thomas W..............Private.
44. King, Franklin S........................Private.
45. Loque, John L...........................Private.

46. Malloy, James....................Private.
47. Massey, Nelson W................Private.
48. McLane, Charles.................Private.
49. KcKee, John.....................Private.
50. Mitchell, Henry D...............Private.
51. Piper, William A................Private.
52. Platt, Anson B..................Private.
53. Quinn, James H..................Private.
54. Rankin, William G...............Private.
55. Roussin, Carpenter B............Private.
56. Ryan, Cornelias.................Private.
57. Richardson, Samuel..............Private.
58. Smith, Joseph W.................Private.
59. Smith, William L................Private.
60. Smith, James....................Private.
61. Smith, Bernard..................Private.
62. Skinner, William C..............Private.
63. Shivers, Edgar..................Private.
64. Scott, Thomas B.................Private.
65. Thomas, Elihu B.................Private.
66. Vose, William...................Private.
67. Van Martin, Dwight W............Private.
68. Williamson, William.............Private.
69. Wolf, Joshua B..................Private.
70. White, John.....................Private.
71. White, Harrison.................Private.
72. White, Martin P.................Private.
73. Warnock, Francis W..............Private.
74. Wade, Thomas B..................Private.
75. Yealton, Oliver C...............Private.
76. Crummey, Arthur.................Driver.
77. Craig, E. Lyman.................Driver.
78. Dewhurst, George................Driver.
79. Hudson, James...................Driver.
80. Luther, Caleb C.................Driver.
81. McLane, Chs.....................Driver.
82. Malone, Charles P...............Driver.
83. Power, David....................Driver.
84. Pottinger, James................Driver.
85. Pierce, Silas...................Driver.
86. Rogers, Patrick.................Driver.
87. Rice, Omri B....................Driver.
88. Shannahan, William..............Driver.
89. Thompson Wm. G..................Driver.

OFFICIAL ROSTERS AND RECORDS.

90. White, John R..........................Corp.
91. Hodgman, H. C..........................Private.
92. Nunis, H. S.............................Private.
93. Tabor, D. B.............................Private.
94. Connery, Thomas.......................Private.
95. Morton, Peter G........................Private.
96. Owens, William T......................Private.
97. Ryan, John C...........................Private.
98. Richardson, R. F.......................Private.
99. Mudgett, John..........................Private.
100. Hancock, Henry........................Private.
101. Powers, Daniel.........................Private.
102. Edwards, Francis......................Private.

ARTILLERY COMPANY B.
[St. Louis.]

Captain Woldemar Fischer's Company B, Battalion Light Artillery, Missouri Volunteers, Mexican War.

Muster-in Roll, dated June 21, 1846, shows company at Fort Leavenworth. Roll signed: Woldemar Fischer, Captain.

Company accepted into the service of the United States, for term of 12 months from June 21, 1846, by Captain W. M. D. McKissack, Mustering Officer.

Muster Roll from October 31, 1846, to December 31, 1846, accompanies Pay Roll for period from June 21 to December 31, 1846.

Muster Roll, October 31, to December 31, 1846, shows Company at Santa Fé, N. M. Roll signed: Woldemar Fischer, Captain.

Muster Roll from April 30 to August 19, 1847, accompanies Pay Roll for period from December 31, 1846, to August 19, 1847.

Muster Roll, April 30 to August 19, 1847, shows Company at Fort Leavenworth. Roll signed: Woldemar Fischer, Captain.

Company mustered for discharge at Fort Leavenworth, August 19, 1847, and honorably discharged by C. Wharton, Lieut. Col. First Dragoons, Mustering Officer.

ROSTER.

1. Fischer, Woldemar...............................Captain.
1. Garnier, Lewis C................................1st Lieut.
2. Kribbin, Christian...............................1st Lieut.
1. Seiffarth, Martin................................1st Sgt.
2. Gochrisch, Christian............................2nd Sgt.

578 DONIPHAN'S EXPEDITION.

3. Genz, Henry..3rd Sgt.
1. Wessel, Henry...1st Corp.
2. Homan, Frederick..................................2nd Corp.
3. Lamsbach, Chr. Aug.............................3rd Corp.
1. Kohlhauff, Phillip...................................Artificer.
2. Schubert, George...................................Artificer.
1. Lauzberger, Mechail..............................F. and B.

    1. Aulman, Adam.........................Private.
    2. Balmer, Christian......................Private.
    3. Biehl, Christian Frederick.........Private.
    4. Bruner, Lorenz.........................Private.
    5. Behringer, Jacob.......................Private.
    6. Bruzmann, John H....................Private.
    7. Bauer, George...........................Private.
    8. Buchel, Julius...........................Private.
    9. Berch, Casper...........................Private.
    10. Braun, John.............................Private.
    11. Cayon, Louis............................Private.
    12. Dresseng, Henry.......................Private.
    13. Doarre, Henry..........................Private.
    14. Evers, Gerhart.........................Private.
    15. Elend, Louis............................Private.
    16. Friburg, Christian...................Private.
    17. Frick, Henry............................Private.
    18. Fischer, Theodore....................Private.
    19. Garlesch, John.........................Private.
    20. Gross, Ernest...........................Private.
    21. Gilbert, Christian....................Private.
    22. Gehb, John..............................Private.
    23. Helmbold, Charles...................Private.
    24. Hermann, John........................Private.
    25. Helmring, Christian................Private.
    26. Hartmann, John......................Private.
    27. Jod, Michael............................Private.
    28. Kuntz, William........................Private.
    29. Krentzbauer, Edmond.............Private.
    30. Karta, Henry...........................Private.
    31. Lang, Conrad...........................Private.
    32. Loeshonkohl, John...................Private.
    33. Luthy, John..............................Private.
    34. Meyer Samuel..........................Private.
    35. Meyer, Peter............................Private.
    36. Meyer, Conrad.........................Private.
    37. Moeller, Henry........................Private.

OFFICIAL ROSTERS AND RECORDS.

38. Neimeyer, Henry..........................Private.
39. Nock, Nicholas............................Private.
40. Reinking, Conrad..........................Private.
41. Reinking, Frederick.......................Private.
42. Rechlind, Sebastian.......................Private.
43. Reimenschneider, John.....................Private.
44. Sieling, Henry............................Private.
45. Schreiber, Frederick......................Private.
46. Schmidt, Frederick........................Private.
47. Schnebel, Henry...........................Private.
48. Scheilberg, George........................Private.
49. Schulthies, Christian.....................Private.
50. Scheifly, Francis.........................Private.
51. Vogt, Lewis...............................Private.
52. Wolkenhauer, John.........................Private.
53. Wessling, Henry...........................Private.
54. Wolf, George..............................Private.
55. Wood, John................................Private.
56. Masse, John...............................Bugler.
57. Roth, Francis.............................Bugler.
58. Schlumpf, Casper..........................Bugler.
59. Biedman, J................................Private.
60. Hassendrubel, Francis.....................2nd Lieut.
61. De Marla, August..........................2nd Lieut.
62. Webber, Charles...........................1st Sgt.
63. Casper, Henry.............................4th Sgt.
64. Hartz, Frederick von......................1st Corp.
65. Homberg, Sigosmund........................2nd Corp.
66. Oberhoff, William.........................4th Corp.
67. Gebhart, August...........................Bugler.
68. Bortling, William.........................Private.
69. Brieg, Charles............................Private.
70. Deuss, Charles............................Private.
71. Damurt, William...........................Private.
72. Elend, William............................Private.
73. Eberle, Daniel............................Private.
74. Egert, Christian..........................Private.
75. Flohr, August William.....................Private.
76. Frederick, Conrad.........................Private.
77. Fritz, Lewis..............................Private.
78. Goester, Frederick........................Private.
79. Hatzer, Lewis.............................Private.
80. Henz, Henry...............................Private.
81. Kruse, Harman.............................Private.

82. Keller, Frederick..........................Private.
 83. Knapp, Erhard............................Private.
 84. Koehn, Henry.............................Private.
 85. Loesch, William..........................Private.
 86. Lipharrt, Peter...........................Private.
 87. Meyer, Frederick.........................Private.
 88. Mild, Christian...........................Private.
 89. Mink, John Henry........................Private.
 90. Marty, Benedict..........................Private.
 91. Metzger, Godfreid........................Private.
 92. Plate, George.............................Private.
 93. Pertenson, Peter..........................Private.
 94. Pross, Hubert.............................Private.
 95. Ricker, Christian.........................Private.
 96. Ritter, Gottfried..........................Private.
 97. Rogers, Albert............................Private.
 98. Sachteleben, Henry.......................Private.
 99. Schoehar, Valentine......................Private.
100. Schalyly, Charles.........................Private.
101. Striberg, Henry...........................Private.
102. Steinberg, Henry.........................Private.
103. Seibel, Morritz...........................Private.
104. Stendeman, Lewis........................Private.
105. Singer, John..............................Private.
106. Bogel, Peter...............................Private.
107. Wagner, John.............................Private.
108. Wilkes, Henry............................Private.
109. Walder, Frederick........................Private.
110. Egelhaaf, William.........................Private.
111. Beilefeld, Frederick U....................Private.
112. Muller, John..............................Private.
113. Johanning, Lewis.........................2nd Lieut.
114. Schuhle, Jacob............................Private.
115. Leobbes, Herman.........................Private.

FIELD AND STAFF OF

Second Regiment, Missouri Mounted Volunteers, Mexican War.
1. Sterling Price...............................Colonel.
1. D. D. Mitchell.............................Lieut. Colonel.
1. Robert Walker............................Adjutant.
2. John J. Tisdale............................Adjutant.
1. Benjamin G. Edmondson..................Major.
1. W. S. May.................................Surgeon.

OFFICIAL ROSTERS AND RECORDS. 581

1. R. S. Edmonson..........................Assistant Surgeon.
1. Lucien Stewart..........................Sgt. Major.

There are no Field and Staff cards from the United States on file in the office of the Adjutant General, State of Missouri.

FIELD AND STAFF OF

Santa Fé Battalion, United States Mounted Volunteers, Mexican War.

1. Robert Walker..........................Major.
1. William B. Royall.....................1st Lt. & Adjt.
1. Eliathal S. Gale........................Asst. Surgeon.
1. Louis Slendiman........................Sgt. Major.
2. Randolph H. Dyer......................Sgt. Major.
3. Caleb I. Church........................Sgt. Major.
1. Marcell Neale...........................Q. M. Sgt.
2. William P. Smith.......................Q. M. Sgt.
1. Augustine Gebhard.....................Chief Bugler.
2. John Hughes............................Chief Bugler.

This Battalion was recruited at Santa Fé, and was composed chiefly of Missourians.

FIELD AND STAFF OF

The Separate Battalion, Missouri Mounted Volunteers, Mexican War.

1. David Willock..........................Lieut. Colonel.
1. Robert P. Clark........................Adjutant.
2. Samuel Shepherd.......................Adjutant.
1. William C. Remington..................Sgt. Major.
2. Robert P. Clark........................Sgt. Major.
1. E. S. Gale..............................Asst. Surgeon.
1. William R. Pye.........................Q. M. Sgt.

No Field and Staff cards, Company Rolls, or Rosters found in office of the Adjutant General, State of Missouri.

WILLARD P. HALL.

APPENDICES.

APPENDIX A.

INTERVIEW WITH ALEXANDER W. DONIPHAN, WHILE ON A VISIT TO SANTA FE, NEW MEXICO, AUGUST 5, 1880.

GENERAL ALEXANDER W. DONIPHAN.

HIS HISTORICAL CAMPAIGN—6,000 MILES IN THIRTEEN MONTHS—3,000 MILES THROUGH AN ENEMY'S COUNTRY WITH 900 MEN—TWO DECISIVE ENGAGEMENTS AGAINST GREAT ODDS.

[This writer made the visit of Gen. Doniphan the occasion for an interview with this distinguished man, for the *Era Southwestern* a weekly newspaper then published in Santa Fé, which interview describes one of the most brilliant chapters in the history of New Mexico.— MAX FROST.]

Thursday's train from the East brought with it to Santa Fé Alexander W. Doniphan, from Liberty, State of Missouri. Gen. Doniphan was accompanied by Mr. and Mrs. Lawson, of the same place, and came confessedly to visit once more some of the scenes of his early life, when he crossed the Great Plains and marched into Santa Fé in 1846, with Gen. Stephen W. Kearny, at the head of the Army of the West,—from which event dated the American occupation of New Mexico, then taking in the largest part of Spanish United States, and now covered by the States of California and Nevada and most of Colorado and the Territories of Utah, Arizona, and New Mexico. Col. Doniphan, of the Army of the West of the Mexican War, ranked second, and was immediately in command of the First Missouri Mounted Infantry. He is the hero of the grandest march of either ancient or modern times, considering numbers and opportunity, and is fairly entitled to rank among the first men of the nation, although his illustrious deeds have in a great measure been for the time forgotten.

The distinguished visitor remained at Santa Fé on Friday, and on Saturday departed north, going to Manitou. He has given some encouragement that he will again honor Santa Fé with his presence before returning to his home. The civil officers, generally, from Governor down, took an early opportunity to call upon Gen. Doniphan, as also did old residents, and prominent citizens.

[Here follows a short biographical sketch of Doniphan.]

With the breaking-out of the Mexican War in 1846, and the organization of the Army of the West under Col. Stephen Watts Kearny, constituting the right wing of the advance on Mexico territory from Fort Leavenworth across the Plains,— Gen. Taylor advancing on the extreme left from the Rio Nueces, while Gen. Wool advanced from the center. Gen. Doniphan was largely instrumental, through his eloquence and personal influence, in recruiting the First Missouri Mounted Volunteers, himself enlisting as a private. The regiment rendezvoused at Fort

Leavenworth on the 5th of June, 1846, and was composed of eight companies, aggregating 856 men. On the 18th of June he was elected Colonel of the regiment over Gen. J. W. Price. The wisdom of the choice was amply verified. For twenty days only were the men subjected to discipline and drill. On the 26th, Col. Doniphan with his regiment took the advance; and thus began the great march and campaign which afterwards was made known to fame in the great reception speech of Hon. Thomas H. Benton at St. Louis, is inseparable from the good history of the Southwest, and will live in history as greater than that familiar march in classic history of Cyrus and Xenophon.

Col. Kearny followed on the 29th with 300 men of the First U. S. Dragoons, two companies of light artillery of 250 men and two battalions of volunteers. Col. Kearny's army numbered all told 1658 men, and of ordnance twelve six-pounders and four twelve-pound howitzers. Without considering the details of the march, the command arrived on the 1st day of August at Bent's Fort, near Las Animas, now a station on the railroad on the north side of the Arkansas river; at Raton Pass on the 7th; at Las Vegas on the 15th; passed Apache Cañon on the 18th, and occupied Santa Fé on the evening of the same day. At Las Vegas, Col. Kearny received his commission as Brigadier-General through a messenger. At Cañoncito or Puertocito, five miles south of Las Vegas, on the old stage-road, Gen. Armijo, with a force of 2000 men, was occupying a strong position, where it was confidently believed by the Mexican people he would make a stand and resist the invading foe. This was very natural, as the advantage lay with him, both as to numbers and to strength of position, besides being at home and thoroughly familiar with the country. with its trails and short-cuts and mountain fastnesses. Such hostile opposition, however, did not appear upon the arrival of the American forces, and this very strong natural position of the enemy's own selection in a gorge at the foot of the hills was safely passed. It lent encouragement to the rank and file, and they pushed on by rapid marches fifty miles farther, to Apache Cañon, a still stronger position in the mountains, about twenty miles southeast of Santa Fé. This pass had been occupied by Gen. Armijo with a force, according to a proclamation of the latter, of 7000 men and a battery of three pieces of artillery. As in the cañon near Las Vegas, the Army of the West, arriving at this point, found no obstacles to the march, Armijo having withdrawn, and passed rapidly forward the same day to Santa Fé, occupying and taking possession of the Ancient City of the Holy Faith on the 18th day of August, 1846, without bloodshed or opposition.

It is due to the New Mexico people to state in this connection that 500 of the prominent people of the Territory entered their solemn protest in a written statement over their signatures, to the supreme government of Mexico, repudiating in emphatic terms any responsibility or necessity for the retreat which was ordered by Armijo, the Governor, and Commander-in-Chief of the Mexican forces; that Armijo had given positive assurance up to almost the last moment that he would give battle at Apache Cañon; that they were patriotically ready, anxious and able to give battle with success; that they had so answered Armijo repeatedly, and had every reason to believe that the latter would carry out his expressed intention to give battle; that his order for retreat at the last moment took them wholly by surprise, and that in the confusion and disorder following the weak or wicked abandonment by their leader in the face of the American army, there was no other alternative but retreat. The same statement numbers the force of Ar-

INTERVIEW WITH ALEXANDER W. DONIPHAN. 587

mijo at 4000, including a small detachment of Mexican dragoons. Of the 4000, one-half were armed with muskets and the balance with pikes or otherwise indifferently armed. How much James Magoffin—an old resident of El Paso and the retained secret agent of the American government—and diplomacy had to do with Armijo's abandonment of strong positions and retreat, never yet has been very clearly made known to the general reader. It is a well-known fact, however, that Senator Benton recommended a compensation to this secret agent of $50,000; that President Taylor, among his first acts, recommended its payment, and that it was subsequently settled by the Secretary of War, by paying $30,000 to Mr. Magoffin, as sufficient to cover his expenses and the amount by him paid out. In the retreat, Armijo, accompanied by the dragoons and artillery, made a precipitate escape down the Rio Grande and on to Mexico, while the volunteer forces returned to Santa Fé and to their homes, disheartened and discouraged. Under the influence of Captain Donacio Vigil (afterward respectively Secretary and Governor of the Territory) and others of the more wise and influential, encouraged by a judicious proclamation of Gen. Kearny, the people and local authorities, including the Secretary and acting Governor, Alarid, submitted without opposition to what was then inevitable.

The headquarters of the Army of the West was at once established in the Governor's Palace, and the construction of Fort Marcy ordered. While Gen. Kearny with a considerable force marched south as far as Tomé and returned, Gen. Doniphan was in command at Santa Fé, attending to the administration of civil and military authority, as Military Governor and Commandant, the construction of the fort, and last but not least, the drafting of the "Kearny Code," so called, for the future government and guidance of civil authority.

In a conversation of the Chief Justice with Gen. Doniphan during this visit to Santa Fé, Col. Doniphan credited Willard P. Hall, a private soldier of his regiment, with material assistance in this work, and that the Code was based upon the statutes of Missouri, as far as applicable, and with respect to acequias and kindred topics peculiar to the country, upon the statutes of Texas and the Mexican State of California. The drafting of a code for the government of a people speaking a foreign language and familiar only with foreign customs and laws and practically adapting it to the people in their new relations, will be recognized as a work of no small moment. Col. Doniphan's thorough knowledge of the law and large experience eminently qualified him. The wisdom of his work in this respect is well exemplified in the fact that the Kearny Code remained the law of the Territory in its scope for five years, and while it has been superseded from time to time in sections or titles, as circumstances seemed to require, portions of it are to some extent still among the laws of the Territory.

Willard P. Hall has been referred to. It will be of interest, as an illustration of the strictly republican character of the United States Government, to learn that he was nominated and elected Representative in Congress, over Col. Doniphan, the Whig candidate, while both were serving their country in the field. The news was received by Col. Doniphan and communicated in person to Private Hall with congratulations.

The Code, upon being presented by Col. Doniphan for examination and approval, was accepted by Gen. Kearny and proclaimed as the law of the Territory, with the remark that it was a subject about which he knew little or nothing, and as it came from thoroughly competent hands, he adopted it without examination. On the 22d of September the Kearny Code was formally proclaimed and civil officers appointed—Charles Bent, an old American resident, being named for Governor, and Donaciano Vigil, a Mexican, for Secretary.

After issuing orders directory of Col. Doniphan's movements, but leaving him in command until such time as he could be succeeded by Col. Sterling Price, then *en route* for Santa Fé with the Second Missouri Volunteers, Gen. Kearny, on the 25th of September, with a command of about three hundred, started for California. Col. Doniphan's orders contemplated his reporting at Chihuahua to Gen. Wool, commanding, as before noted, the center of operations. In consequence of the depredations of the Navajo Indians reported to Gen. Kearny at La Joya, under date of October 2d, the latter issued another order to Col. Doniphan, modifying his first by ordering him to proceed to the Navajo country to recapture and restore stolen stock so far as possible, and effect a treaty for the future. For the more effective carrying out of this order, Col. Doniphan at once ordered Major Gilpin (afterwards Governor of Colorado), then stationed at Abiquiu, and Lt. Col. Jackson, stationed at Cibolleta, to take the advance, and each proceed without delay to the Navajo country, advise the Indians of what was wanted, and that he would follow in a few days; Sho-shi-pee, or Bear Springs, now Fort Wingate, being designated as the rendezvous. Col. Price and command having arrived, Col. Doniphan with a small command left Santa Fé on the 26th of October, first ordering Captain Walton with the balance of his regiment to proceed to Valverde, in company with a merchant train *en route* for Chihuahua, and there await his return from the Navajo country. Proceeding on his expedition, he arrived at Cuvero on the 2d of November, and at Bear Springs on the 21st, finding the chief men of the Navajos and the advance, as anticipated. A treaty—the first made with Indians in New Mexico by the United States—was here consummated on the following day, to the apparent satisfaction of the Indians. All stolen stock was to be surrendered to the owners, and the rights of the Indians on their reservations were guaranteed. As a diplomat among Indians, Col. Doniphan showed the same tact and ability which characterized him in every other relation of life.

While a portion of the force returned direct to Valverde, Col. Doniphan, with a portion of the command, took in the Zuni pueblo on the return, here effecting a treaty between the latter and the Navajos, and made an impression that was favorable to the "Americanos," the good effect of which is apparent among the Zuni Indians to this day. The latter have ever remained friendly.

Col. Doniphan and force arrived at Valverde on or about the 12th of December. The long march was made pluckily and rapidly, amid much hardship, on short rations, over a barren country, in light clothing in winter-time, with little sickness and few deaths. No pay had been received by the men since entering the service, seven months previous. Amid natural murmurings of discontent, Col. Doniphan's tact and good-nature and electric presence never forsook him, and by discarding any better mess or lodging than his men, complaints were anticipated, and the maximum of cheerfulness in trying times was the result.

First dispatching Lieut. Hinton back with orders to Col. Price to send forward ten pieces of artillery and 125 men, and a special request that Capt. Weightman and his battery be included in the detail, Col. Doniphan ordered a forward movement from Valverde, which, for greater convenience in crossing the Jornada del Muerto, a distance of 96 miles, then without water, was made in three divisions, Major Gilpin taking the advance on the 14th of December with 300 men; Lieut.

Col. Jackson following on the 16th with 200 men, and Col. Doniphan bringing up the rear with the balance of the forces on the 19th, the total number of the command being Doniphan's regiment, 800 strong, and the teamsters and employés of the merchant train, organized into two companies. Crossing the Jornada in midwinter, facing its fierce winds, without wood or water and with poor rations, was attended with much fatigue and suffering, but was accomplished without loss. On reaching the Rio Grande at Dona Ana, forage and supplies were found in abundance and purchased, and, with brief rest, privations were forgotten.

The advance, numbering about 500 men under Lieut. Col. Jackson, reached an arm of the river known as Bracito, thirty-five miles north of El Paso, on Christmas day, 1846, Col. Doniphan and staff immediately following. The latter had been in camp only a short time, when his attention was called to a rising dust in the distance, which was thought to indicate the enemy. The Colonel and Judge Caldwell, his interpreter, now living in Kansas and recently a visitor at Santa Fé, and others were engaged at the time of the announcement, in a game of "three-trick-loo." The cards were laid upon the ground as in hand; the Colonel, nothing daunted, ordered the bugle sounded, mounted his horse, which happened to be at hand, and the boys fell into as good order as possible, which proved none too soon. In less than five minutes the Mexican troops, 1300 strong, under Gen. Ponce de Leon, were in sight. A lieutenant made a demand for surrender, with a black flag in hand, which being declined, the rejoinder came, "Curses be upon you; prepare for a charge; we neither ask nor give quarter," and the lieutenant, waving his black flag, galloped back to the Mexican lines. The Vera Cruz dragoons, who occupied the right of the enemy's lines, then made a bold charge upon the Americans' left. The latter, as with the whole command, under special orders from Col. Doniphan, reserved their fire until the enemy was within rifle range, and received them at close quarters with a deadly fire, which had the effect to break and disorganize the Mexican lines. This was followed by a charge of a few mounted men led by Captain Reid, which resulted in irretrievable demoralization to the Mexican right. The Mexican left, composed of Chihuahua infantry and cavalry, advanced under cover of the chaparral, and delivered three rounds before the fire was returned. Col. Doniphan was personally in command of the American right, and had ordered his men to lie down on their faces. The enemy came boldly up within sixty paces; the latter, supposing from appearances they had worked fearful execution, were received with a galling fire. This caused them to retreat in utter confusion. Consternation thus became general and the repulse complete. The battle lasted thirty minutes. Upon the command first falling into line of battle, Col. Doniphan had addressed the soldiers briefly in words of encouragement, reminding them of the disgraceful retreat of the Missouri volunteers in the Florida Indian war nine years previously, by the memorable words, "Remember Okechobee." And right well did the First Missouri Mounted Infantry remember the words at Bracito. The Mexican forces retreated as rapidly as possible to El Paso, the regulars not stopping, save for a trifle of supplies, and continued their retreat to Chihuahua. The Americans had eight wounded, none killed. The Mexican loss was 71 killed, five prisoners and 151 wounded, among them Gen. Ponce de Leon. The Mexican dead were buried and the wounded all properly cared for. All the Mexican baggage and supplies, with numerous hampers of El Paso wine, fell into the American hands. The march to El Paso was properly guarded, and elicited no incidents beyond a couple of false alarms and running upon the abandoned accoutrements and supplies thrown away by the fleeing enemy. The capture of El Paso on the 27th followed, and, like that of Santa Fé, was bloodless. There the troops enjoyed rest and repose. In reply to a commission of the citizens of El Paso appointed to make terms of capitulation, Col. Doniphan's reply was: "Publish to the inhabitants that we did not come to plunder and ravage, but to offer liberty and protection, except when we find them taking up or instigating others to take up arms against the Americans. These will be punished as they deserve." A good understanding was established with the citizens, and all moved smoothly along. In the meantime, Col. Doniphan made preparations and gathered supplies for the coming advance upon Chihuahua.

The artillery battalion ordered from Santa Fé arrived on the 18th of January, 1847, under Major Clark, accompanied by Captain Weightman; and on the 8th of February the whole command, with army and merchant trains, baggage and camp-followers, cheerful and hopeful, took the line of march for Chihuahua, the command to report, as will be remembered, to Gen. Wool, who, with 3500 men, had or was to operate against that point, although nothing definite could be learned as to the fact. Col. Doniphan obeyed orders, and advanced on trust over an arid and inhospitable waste of three hundred miles. What opportunities for consternation, if, upon arriving within twenty miles of Chihuahua, cut off by a broad desert from additional supplies, to find the whole country in arms to meet him and him alone! And still such was the fact. Upon arriving at Sacramento, Feb. 28th, Col. Doniphan's command, including organized teamsters, and additional volunteers, numbering less than 1200 men, confronted by over four thousand Mexican troops, under Gov. Trias and experienced officers, including Major Gen. José A. Heredia, Gens. Conde and Ugarte, and entrenched behind earthworks in a strong position. As at Bracito, Col. Doniphan and his officers and men were as cool and undismayed as the "Old Guard." There was but one thing to be done, and that was to drive out the Mexican troops and take the position. Had Doniphan approached the Mexican fortifications as had been marked out for him, defeat would have been inevitable; as it was, he chose his own line of advance, which was from the west. Moving thus as an onward, determined and irresistible force, the enemy were routed with consternation and dismay, and the breastworks occupied with small loss to this Spartan band,—capturing baggage, camp equipage, cattle, sheep and military stores in quantity. The battle lasted three hours and a half, with losses to the American forces of Major Owens killed, and eleven men wounded, of whom three died. The Mexican loss was 304 killed, a large number wounded, and over 500 prisoners, among them a Brigadier-General. Col. Doniphan immediately followed up the advantage, and on the 2d of March entered and took possession of Chihuahua, the band playing "Yankee Doodle" and "Hail Columbia," and confirming it with a national salute of 28 guns, fired upon the public square, and the floating of the stars and stripes from the cathedral. Among names of volunteers familiar to old residents of New Mexico, and with Doniphan, were James L. Collins, Captain Skillman, Major Campbell, and James Stewart.

Col. Doniphan gave assurance by proclamation, similar to those given at El Paso. As he had anticipated, he did not find General Wool and his command, but he had gained one of the most remarkable victories in the entire history of the Mexican War. Gen. Wool, according to Young's History, was encamped at Monclova, and found the route to Chihuahua impracticable. After receiving the news from Buena Vista and much waiting and voluminous correspondence, Col. Doniphan evacuated Chihuahua on the 26th of April, first stipulating for the protection of American merchants and residents, and formally turning the government over to Mexican authorities. Going via Durango, Saltillo and Monterey, and, after a march of 900 miles, Col. Doniphan's regiment reached the Rio Grande near Matamoras with not only his whole regiment, but their horses and seventeen pieces of artillery, eleven of which had been captured at Bracito and Sacramento. After making provision for returning horses overland, and the preliminary steps for embarkation, Col. Doniphan with 700 men sailed on the 9th of June, in the ship Republic, from the mouth of the Rio Grande for New Orleans, arriving safely at the latter post on the 15th of June, 1847. Ragged, footsore, and without pay since leaving Fort Leavenworth on the 28th of June the year before, received their pay at New Orleans and were there honorably discharged. And thence departed each to his liking, for their homes, arriving generally at St. Louis on the 1st day of July, having been absent thirteen months, traveling by land nearly 4000 miles, and by water about 2500 miles, and gaining grand victories with the loss of less than 100 of their original number. They brought with them their trophies, including the cannon, numerous standards and the "black flag" with which they were confronted at Bracito. A formal reception was given to Col. Doniphan and his officers and men at St. Louis on the 4th of July, and a public dinner at Independence on the 29th of July. At St. Louis Hon. Thomas H. Benton, U. S. Senator, and a particular friend of Col. Doniphan, although opposed to politics, made the reception speech. Senator Benton related in terse phrases the deeds of Col. Doniphan and command as a most wonderful campaign, which it truly was.

[Here follows quotation from Benton's speech, about "The President made it a question," etc.]

An additional item in conclusion. In reply to a question 'from Governor Lew Wallace when calling last Friday, as to how he subsisted his men on such a campaign in such a country, General Doniphan replied that he had no quartermaster (which then included the commissary), nor army chest; he acted as his own quartermaster and used his personal credit, operating through traders and sutlers; that his men were without money save what they brought with them, and that much of the time his men were ill-clad and upon half-rations, and at no time supplied with pickles, and such vegetables as were essential to the good health of a command. For ready cash he had discounted his own checks drawn upon the Government. He could hardly understand how he brought his command through as well as he did.

After the Mexican War he was repeatedly chosen to represent his district in the Legislature of his State, although never seeking office, and evincing a preference for his legal profession. He was a member with General Sterling Price of the State Convention to consider the secession of Missouri in 1860. Doniphan and Price each worked in opposition to secession, and were largely instrumental in defeating the same. The difference afterward was that Gen. Doniphan remained quietly at home, a friend to the Union, while Gen. Price went into the rebellion.

Gen. Doniphan is still active and vigorous for one of his age, and gives promise of usefulness for the next ten years or more.

APPENDIX B.

REMARKS OF MAJOR GILPIN, AT THE BARBECUE GIVEN THE COLE INFANTRY, AT JEFFERSON CITY, AUGUST 10, 1847.

Happy are those who, after hopes long suspended and harassing anxieties long and doubtingly endured, come to find their hopes consummated by brilliant successes, their anxieties relieved by enthusiastic praises and the shouts of triumph.

Such are the soldiers who, their trials ended and their long and exhausting services at an end, are here assembled to receive the greetings of their kindred, and listen to their flattering praises and their shouts of victory and welcome.

During thirty-two years of peace—a long period, which includes the birth of nine-tenths of us—our own State has joined the confederacy. War came suddenly. With the same pen which signed the declaration of hostilities between Mexico and the United States the President directed to Missouri the first requisition for the war.

It asked a slender force of 1500 men—all volunteers but 300 dragoons—to cross the Great Plains and penetrate Mexico by the north.

Bounding forth at the sound of the war-bugle, in one month were assembled at Fort Leavenworth, beyond the western verge of our Union, the First Regiment of Missouri cavalry, the battalion of artillery from St. Louis, the battalion of Cole Infantry, and the Laclede Rangers,—1200 in all; and forth they marched.

Wars had occupied mankind for one hundred centuries, but they had been wars between adjacent nations—marches had been confined to inhabited countries, where provisions abounded on the routes.

Here was a wilderness of a thousand miles to be traversed, and the enemy to be encountered at home, in great strength, and abounding in resources. A failure to transport with us complete supplies was certain disaster and starvation—a check received from the enemy at their threshold would eventuate the same. This enemy was the people of Mexico, a sister republic.

Years had been exhausted in ingenious devices on our part to avoid this conflict. Our citizens had been massacred in Texas amidst the very orgies of barbarism; our merchants had been plundered and imprisoned; our flag insulted in their metropolis; our citizens murdered, maltreated, and scoffed for their religion; debts accumulating during thirty years unpaid; treaties contemptuously violated; more than all, an attempt to imitate our republican system, productive only of anarchy, stood as a burlesque beside us on our own continent, furnishing to the malevolent food for satires upon popular freedom in the New World.

Forth, then, into the wilderness plunged the little army of Missouri, to encounter these enemies of their country,—their country to them always right.

AN ADDRESS BY MAJOR GILPIN. 593

The plains were passed, and the rugged mountains which, dividing from the Rocky Mountains, encircle New Mexico, were reached. Their rapid progress had outstripped the provision trains. Amidst fatiguing marches, dust, solstitial heats, and scanty water, subsisting on one quarter of the ordinary ration, they rushed onward to Santa Fé.

The army of New Mexico, in numbers three to one of our force, occupying the impregnable gorge of Galisteo, which covers the approach to Santa Fé, dispersed in dismay. On the 18th of August, three months from the proclamation of war, made at Washington City, 2300 miles distant, the State of New Mexico lay conquered, and the American flag floated over the capitol at Santa Fé.

Occupied until the middle of September in securing the subjugation of the country, the First Regiment descended the Del Norte to the lower settlements, receiving the submission of the towns and people, and returned to Santa Fé.

New Mexico contains 100,000 inhabitants, vast resources, and by its basin-like configuration is easily defensible and difficult to be conquered or long held in subjection.

New Mexico is surrounded by powerful tribes of hostile Indians: the Comanches, toward Texas, the Yutas and Navajos in the Rocky Mountains and on their slope toward the Pacific.

Issuing from the surrounding mountains, these warlike Indians strike down the people, devastate the banks of the Del Norte, and drive forth the stock. In years past they have plundered from Mexicans many millions of sheep and cattle. By the submission of New Mexico we had become the guardians of her people and territory. The pious duty remained to tame her savage foes.

The infantry, artillery, and dragoons remained to garrison Santa Fé; a fort was built to command its approaches; a treaty was asked for and made by the Comanches. The First Regiment, in three detachments, departed for the recesses of the Rocky Mountains late in September: the one penetrating toward the northwest by Canada and the Chamas against the Yutas and Navajos; another, southwest by Albuquerque and Cibolera; a third descended by the Del Norte, covering the American traders bound eventually to Chihuahua.

The northern column passed out through a denuded country and devastated villages, to which the fugitive Mexicans returned under its protection, and, reaching the recesses of the Rocky Mountains by the sources of the River Chamas, in one month delivered to the authorities in Santa Fé sixty-five Yutas, including their chiefs and chief warriors.

With them was formed a treaty of peace, since faithfully observed by those Indians. This restored many thousand families of Mexicans to their farms and firesides, and gave quiet to the northern frontier.

Supplies having been with great difficulty collected, this same column prepared to pass the eternal barrier of the Rocky Mountains, and scare up the Navajos, reposing in security on their western slope.

On the 2d of November—in this climate the depth of winter, indicated by the snows which enwrapped the surrounding mountains—this little force, 300 strong, abandoning their tents and wagons, entered the gorges that led up to the pass of the San Juan, the head of this great river, which flows to the Pacific.

With us were 70 Mexican allies, and 100 pack-mules transporting provisions. In seven days, contending against snow-storms and ice at an altitude of 10,000 feet in midwinter, and unpalatable water, the passage of the great mother mountain of the continent was accomplished. The measles scourged our camp. The brave boys Foster and Bryant fell a prey to its ravages.

Following for some days the great San Juan, leaving its banks swarming with the sheep and horses of the Navajos, and crossing toward the south the impracticable mountain of Tunicha—never before trodden by white men—we descended into the cavernous region of Challa, amidst the seclusion of which are the forts and fastnesses of the Navajos.

Astounded at the appearance of an American force where they had trusted it could never penetrate, the chiefs tendered presents, restored the horses which had been stolen from New Mexico, and promised abject submission.

Taking with us nine chiefs commissioned to bind the nation, we hastened toward the snowy peaks, which rose 200 miles to the east and barred our return to New Mexico. At the western base of these, in the territory of the Zunis, we awaited the arrival of the colonel commanding, to whom the Navajos' chiefs swore eternal friendship to the white man.

Marching hence under the western edge of the mountain-crest, we visited and smoked the pipe in the city of the Zunis. This people, many of them albinos, one of the lost specks of the antique Aztec race, inhabit a solitary city in the center of the immense plain traversed by a northern branch of the Gila river.

Hence, recrossing the great mother mountain by the Zuni Pass on the first four days of December, we descended to the Del Norte. Joyously did we meet again our fellow-soldiers, and soon the First Regiment found itself reunited at Valverde, 250 miles below Santa Fé, about to pass onward to the conquest of El Paso and Chihuahua.

Thus, since our departure from Santa Fé, had our little force under my command reduced to peace the Yuta and Navajo nations, 40,000 strong, accomplished a march of 750 miles, crossed and recrossed the Sierra Madre, passed the Tunicha and Chiuska mountains, and many rivers.

During many successive nights the cold descended to the freezing-point of mercury; the streams were frozen solid; the pasture scanty; and of fuel there was but a stingy handful of evergreen weeds; two brave men and many horses had perished; for the rest, their health was good, and their spirits always gay and undaunted.

This is the first military force of our nation which, crossing the Rocky Mountains and unfurling the national standard upon the waters of the Pacific, has received for it the submission of a hostile people; and this was accomplished in the depth of winter.

A portion of our little army, the artillery and infantry, remained to occupy New Mexico; another, accompanying General Kearny, had gone to secure the conquest of California. The Indians having been subdued, the First Regiment was now concentrated at Valverde, on the lower edge of New Mexico, meditating the conquest of the rich and populous State of Chihuahua.

This was the 12th of December. Our regiment mustered 760 men. The weather was intensely cold, the river ran with ice; we had no tents, and our animals starved upon the harsh, dry grass. In El Paso, 200 miles below, are comfort and plenty, wine and corn, and houses, and a delicious climate; but there, too, are a regular force of 1500 Mexicans and five pieces of artillery. Between the armies is the Jornada, or Journey of the Dead, a dreary stretch of 100 miles, without wood or water.

AN ADDRESS BY MAJOR GILPIN. 595

At the entrance of the Jornada, awaiting our advance, were the American merchants, having 300 wagons, charged with $1,000,000 worth of merchandise. One hundred men under Captain Hudson subsequently came to us from Santa Fé, called the Chihuahua Rangers; they were drawn from the Second Regiment, Colonel Price's. An express was sent back to Santa Fé for one company of artillery, commanded by Captain Weightman. This company overtook us afterwards in El Paso, about the 1st of February.

On the 12th, a forlorn hope of 300 passed onward to open the passage through the Jornada; with this were Captains Parsons, Waldo, Reid, and Rodgers. We expected to meet the enemy as we should pass onward from its jaws.

The passage was accomplished; no enemy obstructed our exit at the farther end; we descended to the river and quenched our thirst, continued during through three days and nights. Robledo is the name given to the lower mouth of the Jornada. Twelve miles below is the little town of Dona Ana; it has plenty of corn, and 600 people.

This is the only settlement above El Paso, which is 80 miles distant. On the morrow we entered Dona Ana, and there learned that the Mexican army would advance to meet us as we should descend to El Paso.

On the 23d, our whole force, having successfully passed the Jornada, reunited at Dona Ana.

On the 24th, our march was 18 miles. On the 25th, advancing rapidly ahead of the wagon-train, we encamped at Brazito, 19 miles, about one o'clock. The camp-guard, 60 strong, the wagon-guards, and many men with jaded horses, were in the rear. This was Christmas day.

At two o'clock the approaching cloud of dust revealed the advance of the Mexicans. The bugles sounding to arms, our force was deployed in a single line on foot upon the prairie in front, and enveloping the wagons; we numbered 424.

The Mexicans deployed immediately on our front in gallant style, and rapidly; they numbered 1250. The veteran Vera Cruz dragoons were on the right; the Chihuahua cavalry on the left; in the center, infantry. Now it was that a black flag was flapped in our eyes from the center of the Mexican line. It was defied; the shock of battle followed.

The Mexicans charged upon our line, their cavalry converging to our front, their infantry advancing. Our men, sitting down and receiving many volleys from their artillery, musketry, and escopetas, decoyed them close, when, suddenly rising and pouring in a lurid sheet of fire, the enemy, riddled everywhere, fled howling.

Their artillery was taken, 63 were killed, and a vast quantity of arms taken from them. Those who escaped deserted from the Mexican army.

This was Christmas day, the ninth anniversary of Okechobee. Thus did the Missouri volunteers confirm upon him the great lie uttered against them by their commander on that former day.

Victory hastened our marches. On the morning of the 27th we entered El Paso. Awaiting our arrival of artillery, we lingered six weeks in the delicious settlements of El Paso. About 20,000 Mexicans here cultivate the grape, and enjoy much prosperity and a delicious climate.

On the 9th of February we moved on to Chihuahua. The interval, 280 miles, if seen by you who inhabit this, our verdant land, would be pronounced a howling desert, such is its austere and forbidding aridity; Sahara does not exceed it; jornadas of 75 miles, without water, wood, or grass; gravel, sand, and rocks possess it merely; benumbing cold at night, at midday, heat and dust.

On the 27th we reached Sous, 40 miles from Chihuahua. Midway between Sous and Chihuahua is Sacramento; here is the only water in that whole distance, and between us and the opportunity to slack our thirst was intrenched the Mexican army.

On the afternoon of the 28th was gained the marvelous victory of Sacramento, in which your soldiers covered themselves with imperishable glory. On the following and succeeding days our whole column entered Chihuahua.

At Chihuahua we heard with exultation of the gallant conduct of the Cole infantry and Fisher's artillery at Canada and Taos—of their good discipline and gallant bearing whilst in garrison at Santa Fé. These were soldiers of the first requisition, and tried with us the opening campaign of the prairies. Let us here, then, as at Chihuahua, crown with the same chaplet the soldiers of Brazito, Sacramento, Canada, Taos, and El Paso, sharing alike the honors won by all.

During two months did the Missouri column hold undisturbed possession of the metropolis of Chihuahua and control its dependencies. Insurrections planned both here and at El Paso were anticipated and nipped in the germ. American traders and messengers traversed the State unharmed. It had been said that so small a force could not hold Chihuahua. It was done, and that with a firm and tranquil grasp.

But the period of our service neared its close. From our own Government not a whisper had reached us from the outstart; no pay, no ammunition, our cartridges were made of powder taken at Brazito, no reinforcements, no money, no reminiscence of our own existence was discernible.

General Wool had deflected from his intentions, and never appeared at Chihuahua. On the 28th of April Chihuahua was evacuated, in obedience to an order from General Taylor that we should join his column at Buena Vista and Monterey.

The march to Monterey, 650 miles, was accomplished in 29 days; 17 pieces of artillery, with their caissons, and a train of 200 heavy wagons, accompanied us. It was upon this descent from the table-lands to the maritime region that our sufferings, from brackish water, suffocating dust, night marches rendered necessary by long stretches and heat, were most excessive.

Here, too, at El Paso, near the city of Parras, was won a glorious victory over the Comanches, by a small handful of our gallant men, led by Captain Reid; 17 Indians bit the dust.

From the outposts of the southern army, beyond Buena Vista, we reached Camargo, on the Rio del Norte, in nine days, passing through the cities of Saltillo, Monterey, and through Ceralvo.

Since the departure of the Missouri column from the western border up to our return to our homes by the eastern border of our State, we have traversed the full distance of 7500 miles.

No position of equal importance to that of Chihuahua has ever yet been held by the United States in Mexico, nor anywhere, by so small a force. One thousand Missourians, occupying Chihuahua, were cut off from Mexico, New Mexico, and the two Californias in their rear.

Fearing perpetually to be invaded, the States of Durango and Sonora withheld from the Mexican Government all men, military supplies, or financial aid. The ample wealth, resources, mints, cannon, foundries, and *materiel* of Chihuahua were converted to our uses.

Thus, then, by this central position, were held in check and severed from the enemy three-fifths of the territorial soil of the Republic of Mexico and 500,000 of her population.

The position, too, commands the great and magnificent road which leads down the central table-lands, through the capitals of Durango, Zacatecas, Aguas Calientes, Leon, Guanaxuato, and Queretaro, to the city of Mexico. This route is unobstructed by mountains, and leads to Mexico through a prolific and very healthy region. It is the one by which the traders from Missouri annually visit the great fair of San Juan and the City of Mexico.

It appears to me that the column of Missouri is the only one which has made war with effect and obtained from it worthy results. To be sure, our Government has thrown them away, as unworthy of notice, and worthless; but this does not lessen our merits.

In June, 1846, when the Missouri column left Fort Leavenworth, General Taylor's column was at Camargo, ready to march on Mexico by the route of San Luis Potosi. In June, 1847, the Missouri column, returning by the gulf, found General Taylor's advance posts at Buena Vista, only nine days' march in advance of that same Camargo.

To be sure, Taylor's column had won great victories; but so, also, has the column of Missouri, against a variety of enemies.

The southern army lay helpless upon an unimportant edge of Mexico, hemmed in by guerrillas,—such as we found it. Its expenses amounted to $1,000,000 per week. Seventy-five thousand American soldiers had been sent in and out of Mexico in a single year in this direction.

The numbers of soldiers had borne a small ratio to those employed in men-of-war, in fleets of transports and steamers, at the depots, and with wagon-trains. Four months had been consumed in advancing from the Del Norte to Monterey, 280 miles; five months from Monterey to Saltillo, 80 miles. Henceforward all has been complete stagnation.

The possessions of the southern army are strictly confined to the cities of Monterey and Saltillo. A whole army is consumed in guarding from massacre and destruction the trains passing along the road that connects them with the Del Norte, only 300 miles.

The column of Missouri supported itself from the Mexican purse. After fulfilling its orders completely, by the conquest of the States of New Mexico, Chihuahua, the two Californias, and punishing many Indian nations, closing its onward progress at Chihuahua, we have marched 600 miles from the heart of the Mexican territory, coming out to Generals Taylor and Wool.

Finally, one great result is proved by these various campaigns: it is by the route of the plains and the table-lands of Mexico only that the Mexican nation can be conquered and held in subjection by the Americans.

The configuration of the country, the health, the supplies upon the route, its shortness, and the extraordinary results accomplished by the Missouri column, demonstrate this. The slender means and small cost of our campaign add more strong proof of this.

Fellow-countrymen and ladies: The soldiers of the first requisition from Missouri, excepting those who sleep forever beneath the shadows of the Sierra Madre, have returned to receive the greetings of their friends and kindred. We bring with us the spoil of the enemy as trophies of our victories.

These assemblies, these crowds of fair women and brave men, these complimentary festivals and flattering words resounding in our ears from every village and from every cabin, are the gratifying rewards of our efforts and our deeds.

Thus are our long-suspended hopes and painful anxieties consummated by a deep and gratifying sense of triumph. So have we performed our task, and such is our munificent reward.

Suffer me to say, as one elevated by their own suffrages to an important command among them, as well to my fellow-soldiers as to those here present who have sons or brothers or friends among them, that I found among the men at all times the most admirable discipline, the most prompt and spontaneous obedience; at all times a modest, unassuming bravery, which met thirst and cold and starvation and exhausting night marches with songs and gayety and merriment.

They displayed on the field and in the hour of battle a quiet anxiety for the charge, and then plunged down upon the enemy with a fiery fury which overwhelmed them with defeat and stung them with despair. These qualities they adorned with moderation after victory and clemency to the vanquished.

But the career of your soldiers, so happily begun, closes not here. May they not yet devote their young energies to a country which they ardently love and which thus generously illustrates its love for them?

War has been to our progressive nation the fruitful season of generating new offspring, to our confederation.

During the Revolution, little armies, issuing from the Alleghanies, passed over Kentucky, the Northwest Territory, and Tennessee. These new countries had been reconnoitered and admired. With hardy frames, confirmed health, and recruited by a year or two of peace, these soldiers returned to occupy the choice spots which had been their bivouac and camping-grounds. From the campaigns of war grew the settlements of peace, and populous States displaced the wilderness. Another war came with another generation; armies penetrated Michigan, upper Illinois, and into Mississippi. The great Mississippi, crossed at many points, ceased to be a barrier, and the steamboat appeared, plowing its yellow flow. Five great States and 2,000,000 of people emblazon its western bank.

And now, again, have come another generation and another war. Your little armies have scaled the eternal barriers of the mother mountain of the New World, and, buried for a time in the mazes of its manifold peaks and ridges, have debouched at many points upon the briny beach of the Pacific.

Passing round by the great oceans, a military marine simultaneously strikes the shore and lends them aid. Thus is the wilderness reconnoitered in war, its geography illustrated and its conquerors disciplined.

Your soldiers, resting for a time at home, will sally forth again, and, wielding the weapons of husbandry, give to you roads that will nurture commerce and a sisterhood of maritime States on the new-found ocean.

We return, then, to the bosom of our glorious State, to bury our bounding hearts in the joys of responsive gratulations. Coming from arid wastes and the unrelieved sterility of mountains and plains to scan again the verdant fields and mantling forests of our mother-land, which of us all does not apostrophize, with glowing hearts, our native scenes? Hail to Columbia, land of our birth; hail to her magnificent domain, hail to her generous people; hail to her matrons and her maidens; hail to her victorious soldiers; all hail to her as she is; hail to the sublime destiny which bears her on through peace and war, to make the limits of the continent her own, and to endure forever!

APPENDIX C.

Charles R. Morehead was born at Richmond, Missouri, in 1838. Son of Charles R. Morehead, senior, and Fanny Warder, his wife, both natives of Virginia. Their

CHARLES R. MOREHEAD.

parents, Turner Morehead,* a Revolutionary hero, and John Warder, emigrated

---

*TURNER MOREHEAD, soldier, was born in Fauquier county, Va., Jan. 7, 1757, son of Charles and Mary (Turner) Morehead. His father, Charles Morehead, was a captain in the colonial army. His grandfather was John Morehead, whose father, Charles, was a native of Scotland, whence he emigrated to Virginia in 1630. He enlisted at an early age in the Revolutionary army, the records showing that he served as sergeant of Capt. James Scott's company of Virginia troops in 1777. On May 25, 1778, he was appointed captain, and later became a colonel. He served with distinction throughout the Revolution, participating in the various battles in which the Virginia troops were engaged, and was twice bayoneted in the breast. Col. Morehead was a man of great physical courage and moral bravery, flinching at nothing, and upholding the colonial cause with the foremost of Virginia patriots. He was married to Polly A. Hove, and had several sons and daughters. In 1811 he removed from Virginia to Kentucky, where his death occurred.—*National Cyclopædia of American Biography.*

(600)

from Virginia to Kentucky in 1811 and 1807, respectively. Charles R. Morehead, senior, moved from Bowling Green, Kentucky, to Lafayette county, Missouri, in 1826. Charles R. Morehead married Miss Lemire Morris of Mason county, Kentucky, in 1862. She was a daughter of Colonel William V. Morris, who served in the War of 1812 and was with General Andrew Jackson at the battle of New Orleans. Her grandfather, David Morris, of Essex county, New Jersey, served in the Revolutionary War, and emigrated from that State to Kentucky in 1788.

Mr. Morehead was for some years in the service of Russell, Majors & Waddell, and was at the meeting in Washington where the Pony Express was planned and organized. In the service of this great firm Mr. Morehead spent much time on the Great Plains, and met with numerous adventures in the discharge of his duties. At my request he prepared a brief sketch of his life on the plains for this work, and it is here inserted, for the reason that it contains material vital to the history of several of the Western States. It is a matter of regret that lack of space compels me to omit the interesting narratives of his associates, Captain John I. Ginn, Captain J. W. Brady, and Parker Burnham, Esq., all residents of El Paso, Texas.

PERSONAL RECOLLECTIONS OF CHARLES R. MOREHEAD.

William H. Russell* took the first contract let by the United States Govern-

* Concerning William H. Russell and his freighting business Mr. Morehead writes me as follows:

William H. Russell was born in Vermont, in 1812; died at Palmyra, Mo., in 1870. He was a merchant in Lexington, Mo., and he also engaged in the freighting business and in the Santa Fé trade. In this business his partner was a Mr. Bullard, the firm being Bullard & Russell. Mr. Bullard went to Santa Fé to conduct the business there. The firm was afterwards changed to that of Russell, Majors & Waddell. Mr. Majors was an old-time Jackson county, Mo., freighter, and Mr. Waddell was a merchant in Lexington, Mo. At the time Mr. Russell arranged to take the contract for the transportation of all the army supplies across the Plains he had about three trains of wagons and teams, and Mr. Majors had about the same number. Russell and Majors were among the most prominent freighters in business on the Plains. Mr. Waddell was taken in because of his financial ability and credit. Major Ogden, Assistant Quartermaster U. S. A., had been long in that capacity on the frontiers, in which he exhibited superior ability. Prior to 1855 it was the custom for the Quartermaster at Fort Leavenworth to engage transportation from time to time at rates agreed upon by him and the freighters, when such service was required for the various forts in the West. The fact that Mr. Russell took the first contract is evidence that he originated it. Major Ogden recommended it on the ground that it made the contractor responsible for the prompt performance of any requisition which might be made upon him at any time for the transportation of supplies in any direction.

WILLIAM H. RUSSELL.

[Of the great Freighting-and-Express Firm of Russell, Majors & Waddell. From a photograph furnished by C. R. Morehead, El Paso, Texas.]

The first contract was let to Mr. Russell at a price which was the average of the prevailing prices or rates before that date, but after two years it was let to the lowest bidder. In the transportation of supplies for the army to Utah in 1858 the contract was extended at a higher rate, and there was some change in the contractors.

ment for the transportation of all army supplies for all of the military posts west of Fort Leavenworth, Kansas, in the early part of the year 1855. He formed a copartnership with Alexander Majors, of Jackson county, Mo., and W. B. Waddell, of Lexington, Mo., under the firm-name of Russell, Majors & Waddell. They established headquarters two and a half miles south of Fort Leavenworth, at which point a town was laid off and called Leavenworth City. They established there a large store for outfitting trains, warehouses, blacksmith and wagon shops, corrals, etc. His son, John W. Russell, George Shields, myself and others embarked at Lexington on a steamboat about the first of April, 1855, for the above-named place. There was a great deal of cholera on the Missouri river and the plains that year, and thirteen cases broke out on the boat we were on, among the afflicted being a young carpenter from Lexington, who was going to work on the various buildings the company was then erecting. He died the night we reached Leavenworth, and we buried him the next night on Pilot Knob, just west of the townsite. We all went to work in the store, except John W. Russell, who took a position as bookkeeper in the office.

About the middle of November, 1856, the outfitting business being about over for the season, I was sent out to Fort Kearny as one of the assistant wagon-masters, with a large train consisting of thirty-five wagons loaded with corn, which was to complete a contract the transportation company had with the Government to furnish corn to Forts Kearny and Laramie. As there had been in previous deliveries to the posts a considerable shortage in weights, an agreement had been made between the company and the quartermaster at Fort Leavenworth to the effect that if this train-load held out it should be counted as if all had been delivered as weighed at Fort Leavenworth. Consequently a pair of new Fairbanks scales was sent along, and I was to make the delivery, which was made about the first of December, and proved satisfactory.

Nothing unusual happened on the trip out, except that we were "held up" by a band of Indians just after crossing the Big Blue river. They demanded some flour, sugar and coffee, which was given them, and they moved on.

As we were passing up the Little Blue river, one afternoon about dusk, I was riding ahead of the train to a place where we were to camp, when suddenly my mule began to turn back. Looking ahead a short distance I saw something in the grass that looked like a wild animal. I waited awhile until the wagon-master came up, when we cautiously approached the object and found it to be an old, decrepit Indian squaw, crawling around in the grass. She had been left on the river-bank to die. She had some dried buffalo-meat in her hand, and we found some more on the bank of the river, together with an old buffalo-robe which had been left for her bed. As soon as we made camp we took her bread, bacon, cooked meat and other articles, which was all we could do for her, and for which she seemed very grateful. On our return trip we saw no signs of her. We afterward learned that it was the custom of the Indians to leave the old ones in this way when they got so old and feeble they could not travel.

We completed the corn delivery, and left Fort Kearny early in December. About this time we had the first snow-storm, and we encountered these with more or less frequency all the way home.

Passing through the Pawnee Indian country we encountered a large camp, and were greatly annoyed by them. They exacted food, of which we had but little to spare, and drove off and slaughtered the loose cattle with impunity in our presence. They would crawl into the wagons and help themselves. The boys would climb upon the wagon-tongues and jump on the backs of the wheel cattle in crossing a creek, scare and tangle up the cattle, while the bucks would rob the wagons.

We had a daredevil young fellow named Tobe Edgar, from Lexington, Mo., driving the rear team, and he resolved to punish a big buck Indian who had climbed into his wagon and was helping himself to its contents. Tobe told him all right, gave him tobacco and other articles valued by the Indian, invited him to ride on the wagon-tongue with him, and made him so welcome that the buck went with him some miles beyond his own camp. The wagonmaster and myself were behind, bringing up the loose cattle, and before we caught up with the rear team we heard an awful yelling ahead. We hurried on, to find that Tobe and another one of the men had tied the Indian to the hind wheel of the wagon, and were standing off taking a whack about at him with their ox-whips. The fellow's back was bleeding, and he was terribly punished otherwise. The wagonmaster, Mr. Foster, put a stop to it, and we concluded not to turn the Indian loose, but to carry him on that night and next day in the wagon, for fear that he would return and bring some warriors with him to attack our camp. So he was doctored up and treated kindly; we fed him well, and guarded him that night. We did not go into camp until midnight, and got an early start the next morning and traveled about ten miles before we turned him loose, well clad and in good humor. This was my first experience with wild Indians, and I concluded that the saying I had often heard from the plainsmen that there were "no good Indians except dead ones" was about correct.

We arrived safely at Fort Leavenworth about December 20th, and the work-cattle were sent to Missouri to be fed up, ready for the spring freighting.

Early the next spring (1857) the Cheyenne Indians, a numerous and warlike tribe of the plains, went on the war-path, as did the Mormons. As shown by the report of the Secretary of War, for reasons given by him the Government determined to establish a military post in Salt Lake valley to protect emigration to California, which was on the increase, and the contractors for the transportation of army supplies were called upon for almost double the quantity of wagons and teams that had ever been necessary before. Consequently transportation had to be provided for—two regiments of infantry, six companies of cavalry and two batteries of artillery in addition to what had theretofore been required. So every available wagon, yoke of cattle and teamster was called for and were promptly provided by the transportation company.

Captain James Rupe, the most experienced plainsman then to be had, was appointed general agent of the company, and myself as his assistant and clerk. Captain Rupe had been a soldier in Colonel Sterling Price's cavalry regiment of Missouri volunteers in the Mexican War, and since that time had been a conductor on the Santa Fé mail line, and also a wagonmaster from the time he left that service until the present. So his experience in the management of freight trains and Indian warfare was successful up to that time.

We left Fort Leavenworth about the first of May, 1857, in a two-mule spring wagon. Some of the trains and 800 head of loose beef cattle had preceded us, the company having contracted to furnish the army two thousand head of beef cattle in Utah, 800 head of which were to be driven on foot from the States and the balance after the work cattle were fattened after arrival in that territory.

We expected to overtake the beef cattle and travel with them through the Cheyenne country, or until we reached Fort Laramie, 640 miles out; but at Soldier creek, this side of the Big Blue river, we overtook a train the teamsters of which had mutinied against the wagonmaster. We had to send back for another wagonmaster and settle the mutiny before we could go on, which required several days. We then resumed our journey, passing another train at Big Blue, and pressed on to overtake the beef cattle, when we heard the Cheyennes were infesting the country west of us.

At the point where we first struck the Little Blue our mules began to prick up their ears and act a little strange. Captain Rupe stopped to look around for the cause, when he discerned what appeared to be eight or ten Indians on the opposite side of the river among the trees. He handed me the reins, took up his breech-loading rifle and said:

"You turn around and drive as fast as you can; if they pursue us I will hold them back."

As soon as we made this move the Indians broke for a point up the river to find a crossing, the banks being very steep opposite our position. By the time they got over the river and on the road we were a considerable distance ahead, and as soon as Rupe saw they were gaining on us and that they were near enough for a shot he opened fire on them. After five or six shots they slackened up, returning the shots. We went on to the train we had left behind us and remained with it that night.

The next evening about dusk we left the train, traveled all night, and reached Fort Kearny about noon the following day. The small band of Indians alluded to were Cheyennes, scouting around to see what was on the road.

At Fort Kearny we met a party of packers, ten in number, from California, who told us they had met our beef cattle between that post and Plum creek; that they had seen Indians popping their heads up from behind the sandhills all the way down the Platte river, and thought the cattle were in danger. So we waited until dark and left to overtake the cattle. By the time we got to the big bend of the Platte, where the road left the river, it began to rain so hard that we had to stop. It was not long before we discerned, by the vivid flashes of lightning, a party of men and one mule with a rider coming down the river-bank. We at once concluded that it was our own men, which proved to be the case. They told us the Indians had come down Plum creek into their camp, one at a time, and professed friendship and begged for something to eat, which was given them. After fifteen or twenty had assembled in camp, and while they were eating, a large band of Indians on horseback charged among the cattle and stampeded them. One of the Indians started to get into one of the wagons and a man named Sanborn resisted him, when the Indian stepped back and shot Sanborn dead. The Indians then retreated to a ravine close to the corral, from which they opened fire upon the other herders, numbering thirteen, who had by that time gathered about the wagons. The fight was kept up until the herders retreated to the river-bank. Sanborn was killed outright, and a man named Robb was shot through the thigh and severely wounded. The herders managed to get one mule, upon which they placed Robb, and he made the journey to a meeting with us. We then put Robb in the wagon with myself, and Captain Rupe got on the mule and led the way back to Fort Kearny, where we put Robb in the hospital under the care of the post surgeon. Robb afterward recovered and returned to Kentucky.

The following morning we applied to the captain commanding the post for an escort, to try to recover the lost cattle, as we had a right to do under the contract. We were informed that there were but fifty soldiers at the post, all infantry, and that the best he could do was to give us ten men and one six-mule team to carry them. We managed to get ten mules and ponies from the sutler and others about the post, and upon these mounted our men, who were provided with army muskets. We then started for the camp where the cattle were stampeded, under the direction of Captain Rupe. We found the body of poor Sanborn terribly mutilated, and we proceeded to bury it. While doing so Magraw's Pacific Wagon Road expedition passed us, and camped at or near Plum creek. Some of his men stopped and viewed the remains and battle-ground, where were found evidences that several Indians had been wounded or killed. The wagons, minus the sheets, yokes, chains, medicine-chests and Bibles, were all that was left of the equipment.

We then started in the direction in which the cattle had been driven, their trail having been almost entirely obliterated by the previous night's rain-storm. After getting a short distance up in the sandhills we found, scattered about, sixty-five head of the cattle. The mounted men were ahead of the wagon carrying the soldiers and our wagon, in which were a young man named Doolittle and myself. When we were on a table-land, skirted by a long cañon, suddenly there appeared, coming down the cañon, a band of mounted Indians, about one hundred and fifty in number, dashing toward us. The sergeant in charge ordered the men to dismount and tie the mules to the wheels, which was instantly done, myself and Doolittle following suit. A gun was fired to attract the attention of our mounted men, who soon came to us. Captain Rupe ordered all of us to repair to a side cañon near by, and as soon as the Indians came within safe range all present (twenty-two in number) were ordered to fire at the line as we stood, our first man aiming at the head of the band, and so on down the line, which was done with good effect. The charge was checked, and by the time we were ready and delivered our second fire they were in flight. They did not locate us until after our first fire, and fired only a few shots in return. They left no dead on the field, but it was believed that eight or ten of them were killed or mortally wounded.

We then gathered the cattle and returned to Fort Kearny. We left the men there to take care of the cattle until some company train should come along, and themselves to be returned to the States, unless they found other employment.

Captain Rupe and myself remained at the post that night and next day until nightfall, when we left for Fort Laramie. We traveled at night to the crossing of the South Platte river, and crossed that stream late one afternoon, drove down the river about one mile, got supper, grazed our mules, and got ready at dark to go through Ash Hollow. When a little way out we heard a terrible splashing in the river above us, dogs barking, and other evidences of a large band of Indians on our course. So we moved cautiously from them, waited about an hour, and when all seemed quiet we went on to Ash Hollow, and passed through in safety. This was considered one of the most dangerous places on the road, it being mountainous and timbered and forming a gorge putting down between the North and South Platte rivers.

When we reached the valley of the North Platte we drove off from the road and hid ourselves as well as we could, and remained there until dark. We then traveled on up the river to Fort Laramie, passing, a short distance east of that post, the graveyard of Lieutenant Gratton and 28 soldiers, who had been killed by Sioux Indians in 1854.

At Fort Laramie we rested a few days, gathering data about the road beyond, from trappers and traders, for the information of ourselves and the trains to follow. There was no military post beyond Fort Laramie, and there had been no travel except California emigrants and such trains as the merchants in Salt Lake employed to haul their goods. This post, situated in the eastern part of what is now Wyoming, on the Laramie river, close to its confluence with the North Platte, was founded in 1834, by William L. Sublett and Robert Campbell of St. Louis, well-known fur-traders of that time. It was purchased by the Government in 1849, and was garrisoned many years as a protection to emigrants passing through that region. Just above the post, on the Laramie river, at the time I saw it, there was an Indian burial-place. The bodies were sewed up in elk- or buffalo-skins and lashed to poles laid across the limbs of the trees. There was quite a cluster of trees along the river, and a number of Indian bodies so laid to rest. This famous fort has long since dropped out, along with the Indians and buffalo.

While at Laramie a party of Indians came into the post with a lot of gold-dust and nuggets to trade for such articles as they wanted; and this was not the first time they had done so. They had refused to tell where they got it; but this time it attracted more attention than usual, and great inducements were offered them if they would pilot a party to the place. They demanded ponies, sugar, coffee, flour, tobacco, and blankets. A bargain was arrived at finally, and a party was made up and started westward, when the place was found to be Pike's Peak; and in the spring of 1859, after I returned to the States, there was a great rush to Pike's Peak, and thus Colorado has become a great State, and no doubt still greater development of the precious metals will take place in that region.

From Fort Laramie we started out up the North Platte river, with no one ahead of us. The only Indians we met on this branch of the Platte was a band of Arapahoes on a hunt. Captain Rupe could communicate with them enough to give them to understand that we were soldiers and that other soldiers were coming behind us, and as they were not at war they did not molest us, except to try to bulldoze us into trading them our guns, but these we kept close in hand.

We kept on traveling at night until we reached the Sweet Water, near the three crossings, when we hid away among the willows along that stream, where we found good grass, water, and plenty of mountain trout, upon which we fed sumptuously.

One morning early I was on a little prominence near our camp, taking my turn on guard watching the road, and saw in the distance a lone man coming on a mule. We supposed it was some trapper, but it proved to be Jesse Jones, who had also been a noted conductor of the mails on the Santa Fé route—a brave and fearless fellow—who had come alone from Fort Leavenworth with a letter from the contractors instructing us to buy all the cattle we could in that country to fill the contract that the cattle captured by the Cheyennes were intended to fill, and to advise us that Captain Stewart Van Vliet, U. S. Quartermaster, was on his way to great Salt Lake Valley to locate a military post, and for us to be governed by his instructions as to the disposition of trains, etc. We also received other letters from friends in the States.

Jones remained with us two days. We compared notes and made out memoranda of the road for the benefit of the trains behind us, and sent him back to meet Captain Van Vliet and the trains and guide them on, advising Captain Van Vliet that we would await his arrival at Green river, where we had been informed there was an Indian trading-post, owned by a Frenchman named Baptiste (pronounced Batïce').

The day after Jones left we made ready to start that evening. Captain Rupe went up on the hillside to look the field over, and discerned in the distance behind us a band of Indians, about fifty in number. The bucks were on ponies and the squaws were driving ponies with the lodge-poles, plunder and children attached to them. They seemed to leave the road and go into camp on the river below, and were soon out of sight. Then we hitched up and left for Independence Rock, which stands out some distance from the main mountain range. It seemed, as I recall it, about fifty feet high and one hundred feet long and probably as wide. It leaned toward the west, making quite a shelter under it, upon which many names were painted and carved. Not far from this was the Devil's Gate, which is a square, vertical cut through the Rocky Mountains, probably fifty feet wide in places, and through which the Sweet Water river flows. The road passed west of it, over the mountain, and then wound down into the valley again.

From the last crossing of the Sweet Water, at the eastern base of Frémont's Peak (13,470 feet above sea-level), we turned southwest up through the famous South Pass of the Rocky Mountains, the gateway to the Pacific slope, the dividing-line between the waters of the Atlantic and Pacific. On the Pacific side we came to the famous camping-place known as Pacific Springs, where the Mormons stampeded the mules of the Tenth Infantry sometime later, a splendid description of which is given by Captain Ginn, who was with the regiment at that time. This was the alarm that saved the army from possible starvation that winter, because it hurried Colonel Alexander on to our rescue, which will be more fully set forth hereafter.

We now felt that we were in but little danger from Indians, and we pressed on to the Little Sandy, and then to the Big Sandy, where Simpson's train belonging to the contractors was afterwards burned by the Mormons. Next we came to the beautiful Green river, the valley of which we could not see until we got to the very edge of it, and as we did so and looked down into the valley we could see the trading-post, consisting of a long mud house with dirt roof, in which was a store and other rooms for the family of Baptiste, the trader, consisting of a Shoshone squaw and his children.

For a considerable distance, up and down the river, under the trees, there was a large number of lodges and what appeared to be two or three thousand Shoshone Indians, men, women and children. At first sight we were greatly surprised and alarmed, but there was no turning back, and we went on down to the river, where we were met by a number of Indians on foot and were followed to the house where we met Baptiste. He presented us to Chief Washakie, to whom we made a present of a pair of blankets bought of and as advised by Baptiste, and all was well.

We told Baptiste who we were and where we were going and all about the army coming, which he interpreted to the chief, and we told him that we would stay until Captain Van Vliet came up, which would be in a few days. We made arrangements with him to care for our mules. The trading was about over, and we witnessed some Indian games,—riding and arrow-shooting by the men and boys, which were a sight worth seeing. Two days after our arrival the Indians left, and we were then left free to listen to the wonderfully interesting stories of the Western wilds as related by old Baptiste.

In the meantime Captain Van Vliet arrived, with an escort of fifty soldiers under command of Lieutenant Deshler. The following day Captain Van Vliet moved on to Ham's Fork of Green river, and the next day to Fort Bridger, which was the headquarters of the Mormon army. He was there informed that he would not be allowed to proceed further with his escort, but that he would be sent in under a Mormon escort in his own ambulance to have a conference with Brigham Young. He accepted the proposition, and Lieutenant Deshler was ordered back to Ham's Fork and to camp until Captain Van Vliet returned.

We joined Lieutenant Deshler at Ham's Fork, and awaited the return of Captain Van Vliet. The latter was gone about ten days, and reported that the army could not get into Salt Lake valley that winter. He left Lieutenant Deshler with forty soldiers at Ham's Fork, and ordered us to halt all trains at that point and await orders from the commander of the army for Utah. As the trains arrived there they were corraled and the cattle moved on up the river (as it was necessary, to get grass), until seven trains had come up. By that time the cattle herds had moved some miles up the river, until one day William McCarty came down from the cattle camp and told us that an Indian who belonged to the family of old Jack Robinson and a Mexican named Mariano, who had married Shoshone squaws, and who had a herd of ponies near the cattle camp, had come from Fort Bridger and notified them that the Mormons were preparing to take the cattle the next day. The cattle were brought down that night, double corrals were made, and our camp put in the best possible condition for defense.

The teamsters got their guns in order, and all the ammunition they had in hand. Lieutenant Deshler inspected the guns, and then mounted a wagon-wheel and called the soldiers and teamsters around him and told them he was bound to defend the camp until every man among them was killed, which was necessary to save the army from starvation, and to make up their minds to that end; adding that any man who failed or refused to fight would be shot down by the soldiers. He did this because a rumor had gotten out among the teamsters that if they did not resist the Mormons they would not be hurt. In the meantime Lieutenant Deshler, as soon as he received word of the intentions of the Mormons, had dispatched a man on a mule with a note to Colonel Alexander of the Tenth Infantry, which was the advance regiment, advising him of the situation, and, owing to the attempt of the Mormons to stampede his mules at Pacific Springs, he had been hurrying on. The message reached him at Green river, and he made a forced march that night to our camp, reaching us just before sunrise.

Lieutenant Deshler, Captain Rupe and myself, after getting all in readiness and after a mounted guard was placed in all directions around the camp, went up on a butte near camp and remained there during the night, and by the time we could see in the morning we discerned the Mormons, six hundred strong, mounted, marching toward us from the direction of Fort Bridger; and on the other hand we could see the soldiers coming, which meant we were saved from a bloody battle and certain capture. It was the plan of the Mormons to cripple and delay the army and capture our supply trains with their contents and cattle and take them into Salt Lake.

During our stay at Ham's Fork we wrote Captain Wm. H. Hooper, Secretary *pro tem.* under Governor Brigham Young, who had gone to Great Salt Lake City in the employment of Livingston, Kincade & Co., merchants of that city, who had afterward become a Mormon, having married a Mormon woman, that we held a claim against him due the firm of Russell, Majors & Waddell for several thousand dollars, and we would be glad to take flour or anything in the way of provisions, in any quantity, as a payment on the debt. In response to this he sent us several wagon-loads of flour and other provisions. It was through this means that the teamsters received the word that if they did not fight they would not be molested; but they refused to eat the flour until Captain Rupe and myself did so for a day or two, so they could see whether or not it was poisoned.

There was a settlement of Mormons near Fort Bridger called Camp Supply, and we on several occasions bought vegetables from them, and on the day before we received word that we would be attacked we sent Jesse Jones up after vegetables. He was made a prisoner, and we never saw him afterwards. Captain Ginn was also taken prisoner at Fort Bridger and sent over to Camp Supply to work, and later on was taken to Great Salt Lake City, but says he never heard of Jones either about Bridger or Supply or in the city.

It was on the 28th of September that the Tenth Infantry arrived at Ham's Fork, Phelps's battery arrived on the 29th, and the Fifth Infantry and Reno's battery on the 4th of October. Soon after the arrival of the Tenth Infantry news reached us of the burning of three supply trains by the Mormons—two at Green river and one at the Big Sandy. Simpson, wagonmaster of the Big Sandy train, showed fight, but seeing there was no use of resistance, he compromised by getting one wagon and team and enough provisions to last him to the States, and made his way back.

Captain R. B. Marcy of the Fifth Infantry, with four companies of troops, was sent to Green river with us to protect the men while gathering up the cattle belonging to the trains destroyed, which we did without molestation. We had in the mean time bought a lot of cattle from Jack Robinson and others in the vicinity, which gave us a herd of about 1200 head of cattle and thirty mules.

On the day after Colonel Alexander arrived at Ham's Fork he received a letter from Brigham Young ordering him to return by the route he had come— or he could give up his arms and remain on Black's Fork or Green river unmolested that winter.

Colonel Alexander, after we gathered up the cattle, marched up Ham's Fork, thus carrying out his plan as set forth in his letter of October 9th. A few days later, as we marched up the river, we camped about 4 o'clock P. M., the army in advance, the supply train next, and the loose cattle in the rear. The army tents had been set up and the wagons corraled when the alarm of "Grass on fire!" was heard all down through the camp, and the order was given to the soldiers and teamsters to come with gunny-sacks and blankets to put out the fire. The grass was then drying up, the wind was favorable to the enemy, and it was with great difficulty that the fire was arrested before it reached the tents and wagons.

In the meantime there were left with the cattle only the herders. By the time the fire was checked we saw our stampeded cattle, under an escort of about one hundred and fifty Mormon cavalry commanded by Lot Smith, (who was killed by the Navajo Indians near Tuba, Arizona, June 30, 1892,) speeding over the table-land toward Fort Bridger. Smith was one of the most daring of the Mormon Danites. There being no cavalry in camp, they could not be pursued, and the cattle were driven on into Salt Lake City.

Here arose a real dilemma, which was soon solved by an order from Colonel Albert Sidney Johnston to move back to Black's Fork, which we did without delay. We then joined Colonel Johnston and the balance of the army at Black's Fork of the Green river.

On the 2d of November Colonel Johnston called the quartermaster, Captain Rupe and myself to his tent, overhauled the bills of lading, which gave the number of the wagon and the number and contents of each package, so that we had no trouble or delay in finding the clothing and other articles wanted, and issued winter clothing to the soldiers. This being done, on the 6th of November he began his march to Fort Bridger. The weather was cold but clear, but clouded up about noon and began to snow very fast. It was a wet snow, but began to freeze late in the afternoon. The snow fell so thick and fast that a teamster could scarcely see his lead yoke of oxen. Night come on before we could corral the trains.

The order was for the supply trains to follow the army wagons, and the sutlers' last. That night it turned bitterly cold, and the next morning it was found that more than half of our cattle had frozen to death, as also a large number of the Government mules.

The army moved on to Fort Bridger, which was an old rock fort, built of cobble-stones in the shape of a square, taken from the bed of Black's Fork, upon which river it was situated. It was constructed by old Jim Bridger in 1842 for a trading-post. It is now in the western part of Wyoming, a region then known as Green river county, Utah. The Mormons had vacated this post and Camp Supply, near by, and destroyed everything except the rock walls of the post. This was made use of for the storage of supplies, which were piled round on the inside of the walls and shed-roofed with wagon-beds and sheets. The stores were hauled up as fast as we could do it with the remaining poor cattle, and the quartermaster's clerk and myself checked in every package as it arrived. The delivery was completed on the 25th of December. Some of the supplies had been damaged in crossing the high streams, and some had been taken out by the army, receipts for which had been given, and when the quartermaster began to check up and receipt the bills of lading he found a rather complicated job.

At the quartermaster's suggestion, we repaired to Colonel Johnston's tent to consult with the commander on the subject. The quartermaster proposed that we be heard upon the subject of getting a clean receipt for the bills of lading, on account of the terrible losses and long delays. Captain Rupe made a statement, recounting our strict obedience to all his orders, our assistance in getting the teamsters to volunteer as soldiers, and their organization into companies, which were placed under command of Major B. E. Bee; stating also the great necessity of our getting the receipted bills back to the contracting company as soon as possible.

Colonel Johnston thought the matter over for a moment, and then told the quartermaster to receipt the bills. He then asked: "How do you propose to get these bills back to the contractors?" Captain Rupe replied: "We propose to carry them back ourselves, as there is no other way." We explained that a camp had been established by us on Henry's Fork, and all the cattle had been sent there except a few which would be left at headquarters for slaughter, and that one of the wagonmasters, Dudley Harper, had charge, and would deliver the cattle to the quartermaster as called for, and that we had picked out three of the best mules we had and would return to the States over the South Pass route.

Colonel Johnston discouraged our going that route, saying we could never get through the snow on the South Pass, as the snow was unusually heavy that winter and the pass was over nine thousand feet above sea-level. Captain Rupe explained that he knew that route and was used to exposure and winter travel on the plains, and thought we could successfully make the trip. The Colonel then said we must be the judges, and asked if there was anything he could do for us. We asked for a ham and some hard-bread, which he granted. He then stepped to his table and handed me a large package of prairie (wind-proof) matches, which he said we would need, and requested me to write him from Fort Laramie and Fort Kearny, and if we met any messengers coming with mail to advise him through them, saying he would feel interested to know how we got along,—all of which I did.

We were now all ready to start except to get the bills and pack our mules, which we did that night and went over to Green river. We found the snow very deep, but part of the time, on the high plateau between Green river and the Big and Little Sandy, it was frozen hard enough to bear our mules up much of the time; and to save our mules we walked where the snow would not bear them up. We worked, turn about, to break the snow, and the mules would trail after us. We kept the mules blanketed all the time they were not traveling, and had leggings made of elk-skin for their fore-legs, to keep the snow-crust from cutting them when they would break through. Our plan was to spare and feed our mules in every possible way, and not to remain in camp all night anywhere, but stop when they were tired and where we could see any grass cropping out of the snow. We would stop and kick the snow off enough to start them, when they would paw the snow off themselves, and eat enough of it with the grass to answer for water. A mule is the next thing to a watchdog. He will always give the alarm when a wolf or any other animal is near. When they became restless we would pack up and travel. In this way we were enabled to make good time.

After passing the Sandys we came to Pacific Springs, where we found grass and water, and started over the South Pass in the morning. The wind was blowing steadily from the west almost at our backs, and the snow was flying in the air so thick that we could scarcely see the sun. It took hard work all day to get over, and at the foot of the rocky ridge, which was on the east side, about dark we saw in a small cañon to our right a sheltered place with plenty of dead quaking-asp trees and tops of bunch-grass protruding through the snow. Here we concluded to make camp and remain until morning. We kicked the snow off a camping-place, started a big fire, put our mules to feeding, made some coffee, and had a good meal of hard-bread and bacon. Our mules had a good feed, and all were resting comfortably until about midnight, when it began to snow and drift very fast; so Captain Rupe said if we remained there we might get snowed under so deep that we could not get out. We concluded to pack up and get out on the road. After we got a little way up our pack-mule broke through into a hollow about ten feet deep and could not move. We got down, unpacked him, and tramped the snow down hard enough to get him out. We then packed up again, but remained in that place, fighting the snow in order to keep uncovered until daylight, when we proceeded down the slope, on to Devil's Gate, Independence

Rock and to the Sweet Water, where we found a sheltered spot near our old camp. Here we had two good meals, took a snow bath, rested our mules, and took the road again and traveled on as usual until we came to the North Platte.

One night about 9 o'clock, as we were nearing the Red Buttes, thinking of another sheltered spot where we would get a rest for our weary mules, all at once we heard the barking of dogs. We stopped to consider the situation. The dogs kept up still louder barking. About that time a trail of buck Indians appeared, and we prepared to receive them, when a voice among them called out: "Hello!" Captain Rupe answered: "Friends. Who are you?" We thought some white man was among them, but when they came up we found that it was an Arapahoe Indian called Friday, who had been educated in St. Louis by Captain Bent. It was a great relief when he told us it was a camp of Arapaho Indians and that there was no danger. He invited us to the lodge of the chief, which was about a mile away. We explained that we were officers of the army, and, having soldier overcoats, it looked that way to them. He said the chief would be glad to hear from the army, and that when we got to the lodge he assured us our mules would be safe, and to trust that to him. We did so, and entered the lodge, where we were cordially received. The fire was renewed and the pipe of peace lit, when Captain Rupe told the chief, through Friday, all about the army and the Mormons. He invited us to remain overnight, but we declined. He then complimented us on our trip, saying "Brave men!" and advised us not to go through Ash Hollow, as there was a big camp of Cheyennes there, but to keep on down on the north side of the North Platte to its junction with the South Platte, and cross there. He gave us some dry buffalo-meat and we gave him some tobacco. When we were ready to go he stepped out and looked at our mules and then at our guns, and said he would like to have a gun like ours. Captain Rupe told him he would like to give him one, but we might need them very much when we got to the Cheyenne country. We shook hands with him and about twenty bucks, and departed, —glad to get off so easy.

We pushed on down the North Platte to Fort Laramie, where we expected to get fresh mules, but found none belonging to the company, nor any for sale. We learned here that the John Bartletson party, which left Fort Bridger on the 1st of December, through the Bridger Pass, had arrived on the 21st of December, being twenty-one days out. This proved the wisdom of Captain Rupe in taking the South Pass route, as we had been less than fifteen days in making the trip. We did not delay here, only long enough to get some provisions.

We crossed the Platte river one morning early, and passed on down the river three or four miles and camped on the bank of the stream opposite a little island. By this time it was sunrise, and, looking to the west, we saw a small herd of buffalo bulls, and also coming toward us at full speed about fifteen mounted Indians. When they got within hearing distance they set up an awful yelling. We immediately got our mules and baggage down behind the river-bank, our rifles in hand and our navy six-shooters belted on, and stood upon the bank with drawn guns. When they got within easy gunshot Captain Rupe motioned them to stop, which they did. They immediately made signs professing friendship. Captain Rupe then made signs for one of them to come to us, when one of them threw his lariat to another of the party and came up on foot. Captain Rupe asked him, "What tribe?" He said, "Arapahoes." Rupe shook his head and said: "No; Cheyennes." The Indian replied, partly by signs and partly in broken English, that they were friendly and were hungry and wanted something to eat. Rupe gave him to understand that we had not enough for all, and pointed to the buffalo bulls, not far away. At this the Indian gave an angry scowl, and, pointing to his band, motioned that they would come and take it, and give us fresh ponies for our poor mules and our guns. But as Rupe refused he grew more saucy; Rupe caught him by the arm, with the navy pistol in the other hand, and started him to his party, and said to me: "You saddle and pack our mules, and I will stand guard; if they attempt to close in on us I will drop down behind the bank of the river, and we will stand them off or kill as many as we can." I did as requested,—and did not take long to do it, either. In the meantime they plunged around, coming pretty close, then circling around again and again. After they had done this three times, Rupe said: "They are doing this to see if we are weakening; but with thirty-eight ready shots I think we are safe. They have but two old rifles and the balance of them have long spears, with which they kill buffalo."

As soon as we were ready I started ahead, Rupe behind, urging the mules on as fast as we could go, keeping close to the river-bank, being prepared any moment to fire and get behind the bank to make a fight. They followed us for two hours, yelling and dashing around in the same way, until finally they left, going toward the buffalo.

We then traveled on, keeping along the river, until about 4 P. M., when we discovered that the Indians had crossed the river and were keeping along down as we were, on the other side. We took a good rest, grazed our mules, and at dark we left the river and made the best time we could to Plum creek. We traveled all night as fast as we could, except to rest and graze our mules, and kept this up until we reached Fort Kearny.

On our way we were attacked near Plum creek by a pack of prairie wolves, which were, on account of the deep snow and scarcity of game, unusually fierce and ravenous. They followed us so closely that one of them bit our pack-mule. They were so bold that they would get close enough for us to almost put our navy pistol to their heads—so close, that every shot we fired brought down a wolf. This would check them until they could devour the dead ones, and then they would come at us again. This fight was kept up until daylight. These wolves, when they are very hungry, will run down and hamstring a buffalo, kill and eat him.

When we reached Fort Kearny we found the post almost snowed under. The soldiers had dug paths through the snow to the sutler's store, the stables and other parts of the post. The snow was so deep that you could only see the top of a man's head as he walked along one of the trails. We were here told that the night before the wolves had broken into the stables and eaten up twelve large post mules, and that the Cheyennes had killed two herders, almost in sight of the post, and stolen some cows they were herding on the day we arrived.

At Fort Kearny we again failed to get a change of animals, and remained there part of the day and left at dark. We met with no more Indians, except the Pawnees, with whom we had no serious difficulty; but had another attack from the wolves, and fought them off as before.

We now passed through Nebraska and Kansas Territories, and arrived at Fort Leavenworth on the 26th of January, 1858, which was thirty days out from Bridger.

William H. Russell, head of the contracting firm, wired us to come on to Washington. We took stage to Jefferson City, Mo., and there took the Missouri Pacific Railroad to St. Louis and the Baltimore & Ohio Railroad to Washington.

In the estimation of all we had made a splendid trip, and we felt very proud of it. We had traveled about 1200 miles, as the road then ran, in thirty days, in the dead of a severe winter, through hostile Indians and ravenous wolves, in snow every foot of the way, without a change of animals and without grain,—indeed, we walked at least two-thirds of the way.

After we completed our report, accounting, as we did, for the loss of every wagon, ox, yoke, mule, log-chain, and everything pertaining to the expedition, Mr. Russell took us to see the President, some Senators and members of Congress, and also the Secretary of War and Quartermaster-General. With Mr. Floyd, Secretary of War, the question of the feasibility of a pony express across the continent was presented by Mr. Russell, and fully discussed. Captain Rupe's views were called for, and he expressed the opinion that it was entirely practicable at all seasons on this route, all the way to California.

I will here state that the Mormons had the contract for the transportation of the mails previous to that year, but broke up and destroyed such stations as they had as soon as the Utah expedition was determined upon by the Government. Consequently there were no mail facilities, and for that reason we made this trip, to take back the bills of lading for supplies delivered to the army. While the Pony Express was conceived at that time by Mr. Russell, which was suggested to his mind by the success and circumstances of our trip in midwinter, 1200 miles without change of animals in thirty days, it was not put into operation by him and his associates until 1860, when the first overland or Pony Express mail was carried from Washington and the East over the various railroads, the last being the Hannibal & St. Joseph Railroad, which terminated at St. Joseph, Mo. Mr. Hale, who was afterwards superintendent of the Missouri Pacific Railroad, took an engine from Quincy, Ill., to St. Joseph, met the pony and rider at the depot and threw the mail to the rider; the ferry-boat was in waiting on the Missouri river, which took him on and moved across the river immediately, and the last that was seen of the pony and rider they were flying over the prairies. This was on April 3, 1860, at 5 o'clock P. M. The Pony Express was met at Sacramento, Cal., by a great concourse of people with bonfires on the streets and huzzas for the rider and pony. The last rider on the line, which terminated at the Sacramento river, was made by Jimmy Monahan, a Sacramento boy sixteen years old, on a fleet-footed little pony; and no sooner had the rider delivered his mail on the waiting San Francisco steamboat and remounted his pony than he was seized by the rejoicing multitude and carried through the streets on men's shoulders and his pony was soon decorated from foretop to tail with fancy ribbons and flowers.

The Pony Express, though a daring and hazardous undertaking, proved a success at the start, and became famous. It also blazed the way for the overland stage-coach and railway. Stations, with a change of rider and pony, were established every twenty-five miles, or as nearly so as it was found practicable. Its operation was punctuated with many interesting and thrilling incidents. The famous Buffalo Bill was one of the first riders on the line.

This great enterprise was, later on, followed up by the same man of nerve and genius, W. H. Russell, then known as the Napoleon of the Plains, as he was indeed the greatest moving spirit of the Western world. He was the first man to contract to transport the Government supplies across the plains. He inaugurated and put in operation the overland passenger, mail and express coaches, which remained in operation until the steam horse took their places. And now, when we ride in Pullman cars over these great plains and mountains and behold the beautiful towns and settlements along the railroad all the way to the Pacific coast, it does indeed seem like a fairy dream to those of us who encountered the hardships and dangers from the various tribes of savages, snow and wolves, and some of whom beheld the countless herds of buffalo, deer, antelope and elk roaming over the plains and the grizzly bears, mountain sheep, jack-rabbits, sage-hens and other wild game in the mountain regions.

While in Washington we were shown all the sights of the capital. Captain Rupe's arrival, the news by letters we brought, and our report of the expedition created considerable excitement about the Mormons and the Indians, and it was determined to send out reinforcements as early as possible in the spring. The contract with the old company was renewed, and Mr. Russell was anxious to have Captain Rupe return as general agent, and so was I, as I was to go back; but he declined, stating that he was getting along in years, had experienced little but hardship since and during the Mexican War; that he had a good farm and a growing family, and was well enough fixed to afford to stay at home the remainder of his days. He said:

"I do not wish to discourage you, but my advice is not to undertake the same kind of a trip again. Several times when I told you there was no danger, I had but little hope for our safety."

To me this was a sad parting, as we had been long acquainted, had spent about a year together in a way that tried the temper and souls of men, and we had never had a cross word or the slightest difference about anything.

I remained in Washington for a month or more, visited Baltimore, Philadelphia, and New York, aided Mr. Russell in the purchase of various outfitting goods, and then went West with him, stopping at Pittsburg, where he purchased a large amount of log-chains and other train equipments, and thence to Fort Leavenworth.

His company having renewed their contract for the transportation of army supplies, and the amount of freight being largely increased, two shipping points were established: one at Fort Leavenworth, and one at Nebraska City, Nebraska. Mr. Majors took up his headquarters at Nebraska City and Mr. Russell at Fort Leavenworth, and then began the great bustle and stir of outfitting and shipping.

General Harney, in command of large reinforcements for the army in Utah, left Fort Leavenworth early in the spring, but when he reached Cottonwood Springs, about ninety miles west of Fort Kearny, he was ordered back, on account of the fact that General Johnston had entered Great Salt Lake City and Governor Alfred Cumming and Peace Commissioners Governor L. W. Powell and General Ben McCulloch, who had been appointed by President Buchanan to confer with the Mormons, had settled the trouble. Therefore there was no necessity for reinforcements, and this of course cut down the transportation to the extent of supplies for the reinforcing army.

Still the business on the Plains in 1858 was larger than for the preceding year, owing to the merchants' and sutlers' trains of merchandise in addition to the army supplies, and a heavy California and Mormon emigration.

I left Fort Leavenworth in company with Hiram Lightner, who had been appointed agent for the company at Fort Laramie, the former agent there having been drowned in the Laramie river a short time before. Our means of travel was a light spring wagon and a pair of mules. We traveled without fear or molestation to the Big Blue. Here we met quite a large band of Otoe Indians. Among them was a trader, who explained to them where we were going, and we passed on undisturbed. From the Big Blue we, as formerly, traveled at night, and met only the Pawnees, this side of Fort Kearny. They had not yet recovered from a terrible scourge of smallpox, that had broken out among them the fall before and raged all winter. We also passed General Harney's command of reinforcements.

Next we reached Fort Kearny, and had the pleasure of listening, at Harry Dyer's sutler store, to many exaggerated stories about the Indian depredations out west, which greatly disturbed Lightner's peace of mind, as he had never crossed the plains before. On this trip I was the guide, and it became my duty to quiet his fears by telling him it was the delight of these old plainsmen to relate such stories as would disturb the tenderfoot. We remained one day, laid in some supplies, and left for Fort Laramie. We stopped at the Plum creek camping-ground of the party in charge of the beef cattle stampeded there the year before, to look at the grave of young Sanborn, who was killed by the Cheyennes at that time. We passed one company of Mormon emigrants, numbering 600, consisting of men, women, young boys and girls, all of whom were foreigners, and another not far distant, of 700. The only means of transportation they had was handcarts. Many of these emigrants were frozen to death before they reached Great Salt Lake City that winter, and others were frost-bitten and maimed for life. It was a strange and pitiful sight to see them trudging along, poorly shod and clothed.

We passed on to the crossing of the South Platte river, which was very high. Here we found Irving's train, laden with merchandise for Livingston, Kincade & Co., of Great Salt Lake City. It had been there for several days, unable to cross, and we found it impossible to cross, except by abandoning our wagon and swimming our mules over. Irving finally concluded, on the next day after our arrival, to unload his train, place yokes and goods that could not be damaged by water in the bottom of the wagon-beds, then place the other goods on top of these, and cross one wagon at a time by putting on about twenty yokes of cattle, so that while some were swimming others would have a footing on the bed of the stream so that they could pull the wagon along. The river at no place came more than one-third of the way up the side of the wagon-bed. In this way he was enabled to cross the whole train in about five days. We tied our small wagon onto the back part of the first wagon, put our provisions in the top of the big wagon, and mounted our mules and swam the river alongside of the cattle, aiding the other mounted men of the train to keep the cattle in line, as the current was very swift. We did not have to swim all the way thus, to enable the train to cross. After getting over we remained another day with Mr. Irving, in order to repay him for his kindness to us, and would have remained longer, but by that time everything was going well and Mr. Irving excused us.

We crossed Ash Hollow that night, and as we passed into the valley of the North Platte the next morning we were astonished at the sight of about four hundred lodges of Indians. We stopped to talk and think. Lightner insisted on turning back. I then told him what Captain had so often said to me: "An Indian is sure to get you if you show the white feather." So we stood our ground until a small band approached us on ponies, in a run, but not yelling. While we felt uncomfortable, still we thought they were friendly. We could not understand them, and they motioned to the chief's tent and beckoned us to follow. As we approached the lodge it seemed to us that there were a thousand Indians around our wagon. By means of an interpreter, who was a French trader, we were told that they were Sioux, who had come to meet General Harney, who had given them an awful whipping near Ash Hollow two years before, in 1856. They called him the Great Wasp, and respected him on account of his fighting qualities. They were greatly disappointed upon learning that General Harney had been ordered back.

After some further inquiries and answers about the army that had passed the year before, we presented the chief with some tobacco, and he, with a great deal of flourish, assured us of our safe passage to Fort Laramie. A way was opened for us to pass out to the road, and, while driving along through the great throng, we could and did complacently look upon the faces of some of their beautiful young squaws, some of whom were tall and comely, and after we were composed we were pleased to have had the experience, because it proved to be a tonic to our nervous systems.

This was not far from the burial-ground of Lieutenant Gratton and his thirty soldiers, who had been killed by these same Indians four years before, in 1854. It was said at this time, however, that the Sioux had never committed any depredations on the whites since the chastisement given them by General Harney. We passed on to Fort Laramie without any unusual incident. On arriving there we took up our quarters in the adobe houses on the west side of the Laramie river, opposite the fort, which belonged to Ward & Igarie. This firm were post sutlers and Indian traders—the former conducting the sutler business and the Indian trading. The latter had been to Salt Lake City and had only three good-looking squaws for wives and a plentiful supply of children in his commodious quarters. He was a good story-teller, and highly entertained us every evening by relating events and experiences in the Indian country.

A few days after our arrival, one morning early we heard a great commotion among the Indian campers on the river just above us, when we rushed out to ascertain the cause. On a little hill just west of us we saw a splendid-looking Indian standing behind his horse with a strong bow and arrows flying at some object below him. Advancing a little further we saw three more buck Indians ready for attack upon the Indian on the hill, and the fight was opened at once. The pony of the Indian on the hill was shot full of arrows and managed to get away, when the three closed in on the other, downed him and scalped him. The others were also badly wounded, but mounted and escaped to their camp. The dead Indian was removed by the camp Indians and buried. We learned afterward that the Indian killed and scalped had followed the Indians we met down the river from the Missouri river country and killed one of their number who had run away with his squaw, and that the three who had just killed him were relatives of the one killed in camp. So it seems that the savages as well as white men are sometimes engaged in eloping affairs.

Under the 1858 contract for the transportation of army supplies it was stipulated that all trains should be inspected and bills of lading be checked by the quartermaster at Fort Laramie and returned, upon receipt of which the freight to that point should be paid, so that the contractors should not wait for the whole amount until the delivery in Salt Lake valley.

After the trains passed Laramie I started west on my saddle-mules, which I had left with one of the trains. I passed on my way out and made my way from train to train until I reached the front train, and traveled with that until we got within a day's ride of Great Salt Lake City, and then to Camp Floyd, the army post, which was fifty-two miles southwest. On the way we crossed the river Jordan and passed little Utah Lake. The peculiarity of the river and lake is that when the wind is blowing from a certain direction it forces the water from the lake through the river, which empties into the Great Salt Lake, and when not blowing in this direction the water remains only in holes here and there along the river-bed.

We next arrived at Camp Floyd, when I called on General Johnston, who thanked me for the safe delivery of letters sent by us to the States, acknowledged the receipt of letters I had written at Forts Laramie, Kearny and Leavenworth, and congratulated me on our successful trip over the mountains and plains the winter before.

I remained in Great Salt Lake City and vicinity until January, 1859, attending to the business entrusted to me. I made one trip to Fort Bridger, distant 125 miles from Salt Lake City, upon muleback, and one to Laramie in a stage, the only stopping-place on the road being the ranch of Ephe Hanks, a Mormon Danite, whose acquaintance I had made on my way into the valley, and with whom I remained one night going and coming on my return from Bridger.

After crossing Bear river on my return from Bridger I stopped in an open space in the willow bushes to feed my mule some barley I had with me. I poured the barley on the grass, and sat down in reach of her. While she was eating I devoured my lunch, and when I got ready to start my mule shied away from me, at the same time looking to the left side. I also turned in that direction, to behold a huge grizzly bear within twenty steps of us, standing still. He certainly was as surprised as we were. I got on my mule as soon as possible and left, the bear following close by. As soon as I got into the road I drew out my navy pistol and fired; I suppose I missed him, as he did not slacken his pace. As soon as I saw I was gaining ground and could slacken my speed I turned and fired again, which shot must have taken effect in one of his shoulders, as he began to limp, and stopped. I was content to part company with the bear, and without further incident of note I arrived at Great Salt Lake City.

In the meantime Mr. Majors arrived, and after all the trains got in and were disposed of he returned to the States with a light covered spring wagon and three men. He left about the middle of December.

Before leaving he had occasion to go to see Brigham Young, to buy some mules for his homeward trip. I was invited to go along. After the trade was concluded Mr. Majors asked him if he had any objection to talking on Mormon church matters a little, to which Mr. Young readily consented. Mr. Majors was a frank kind of man, and made some pertinent inquiries about the management of the plurality system. The Bible was largely quoted, and to those who would like to believe as they did and practice what they did it all seemed plausible enough. I could not with propriety repeat here all the questions asked and answers given.

On the first day of January I left Great Salt Lake City with Edward Rollins.

Before going I went to see Mr. Young, who persuaded me that mountain horses were best for such a trip. So I bought a pony-built roan horse for a pack-animal and a stout, bay saddle-horse for Rollins from him. I took the same mule I brought from the States. Ephe Hanks volunteered to help us over the mountain to his ranch. We accepted, and camped the first night in his cabin, made a big fire, had a good supper and a good night's rest on the floor.

The next morning it was cloudy and threatening snow. We got breakfast, packed up and bade good-by to our friend, who said: "If it begins to snow you had better go into camp and wait until it is over;" but we did not heed his advice. It did begin to snow about midday, but we kept on and got off the road. Night came on and we camped in a big grove of sage-brush, some of it ten to fifteen feet tall and a good deal of it dead. We made up a big fire and remained all night.

The next day in looking about we found we were lost. I had a small pocket compass, through which means we could tell pretty well the direction of Fort Bridger, and struck straight across the country to it. Both ourselves and animals were a day without anything to eat, because we started with only enough to last until we got to Bridger. Here we outfitted for Fort Laramie, and lost no time in getting there.

The snow that winter was not so deep, and the only trouble we had was in crossing the South Pass.

At the Red Buttes we found a camp of Arapaho Indians, but not our man Friday nor the old chief; but we were not molested, and traveled on as Captain Rupe and myself had done the winter before.

We overtook Mr. Majors at Fort Laramie, in the company's quarters, about midnight. He was surprised, and would not believe us as to the time we left Great Salt Lake City until we showed him the dates of letters and papers we had with us. We then traveled with him to Nebraska City, being out twenty-seven days from the City of the Saints. With great regret I turned my faithful little mule into the company's corral, and left on the stage on the north side, through Iowa, to St. Joseph, Fort Leavenworth, and Lexington, Mo., where I was married.

I took my wife to see her old home and friends in Maysville, Kentucky, and then returned to Leavenworth and engaged in the mercantile business on my own account, and remained in it for a number of years.

In 1861 my partner, Mathew Ryan (who was also engaged in the cattle business), and myself took a contract to deliver three hundred head of beef cattle to the new forts, Larned and Lyon, just then established on the Santa Fé route. We bought Texas cattle and some few other cattle on our way through the Kansas river country. We drove them by way of Fort Riley, crossed the river there, and camped one night at Diamond Springs, out on the Santa Fé road. We went into camp about dark. Our cattle grazed a while and then laid down to sleep around our wagons. A storm of hail and rain came up in the night and our cattle stampeded. We followed them as long as we could stand it, but they got away. We returned to await daylight, and went into the little store at the Springs and sat up until daylight, lamenting our bad luck. The rainfall had stopped, and at the break of day we went out to get our mules and start for the cattle, and found all of the Texas cattle lying down around the wagons, and the others missing. We started two men out to find them, and they returned that night with the missing cattle.

We then went on without further trouble, except from the innumerable buffalo on the Arkansas river, which made it necessary to closely guard our cattle at night. We made the deliveries all right.

I had a fleet, hardy pony, and at Larned I decided to go on ahead of the men and take the stage from Fort Riley to Leavenworth, and thus save several days' time. All went well until I got to a small adobe house at the Big Bend of the Arkansas river. I stopped to stay all night, but found the owner had nothing to eat except wild grape-juice and slapjacks, and no place to sleep except on a dirt floor. He said he had been afraid to go out and kill any buffalo on account of some Indians who had been around that part of the country hunting buffalo. I fed my horse, made my supper on grape-juice and slapjacks, and left about dusk for Turkey Creek ranch. He told me to take a trail not far off, which would shorten the distance. I did so, but just before I reached the trail I saw several Indians with ponies loaded with buffalo-meat coming to the road. As soon as they saw me they unloaded the meat from two of the ponies, mounted them and started to head me off, beckoning me to stop. Instead I put spurs to my horse and reached the trail ahead of them. They followed close behind me for two miles or more, and then gave up the chase. But I kept going, and the truth is I did not linger in that country any longer than I could help, but made my way to Fort Riley and then to Leavenworth in the stage.

Again, in November, 1863, I made a trip to New Mexico on the stage line. They then had a change of animals at Fort Larned and Fort Lyon. Conductors, drivers and passengers camped out every night and did their own cooking. At Larned we encountered a heavy snow-storm and had to abandon our coach and had to take a light, canvas-covered spring wagon. We were nine days going 240 miles, the distance between Fort Larned and Fort Lyon. Then again we encountered deep snow in crossing the Raton Mountains, between Bent's old fort and Fort Union, and thence to Santa Fé. Here the stage line ended, and I had to make a canvass of New Mexico towns in private conveyances, such as I could get.

I reached Las Vegas on my return trip on the 25th of December. On that night there was a terrific snow-storm. The next day another traveler and myself engaged an open buggy and two mules of Charles Kitchen and went over to Moro. Here I saw the house where Captain Hendley, of the Ray County company belonging to Colonel Price's regiment during the Mexican War of 1846, was killed in a battle during that war. My brother William belonged to his company, and was with him at the time he was killed. After the war Captain Hendley's remains were taken back to Richmond, Mo., and buried.

We returned to Vegas and then took the stage over the Raton Mountains to Bent's old fort on the Arkansas river, and from there up the river via Pueblo to Denver, which was then a mining town built mostly of boards and logs.

From Denver we took the stage to Atchison, Kansas, and thence home.

February 5, 1880, the late O. T. Bassett and myself took passage on the Southern Overland Stage coach at Fort Worth for El Paso. We arrived at Comanche on the 6th, left on the 7th, and arrived at Brownwood that day. We arrived at Walthal on the 8th and Fort Concho on the 9th, where we spent the day with Lieutenant L. P. Hunt, and left there at 9 P. M. for Fort Stockton. Among the passengers was Mr. Corbett, sutler at Fort Stockton, a fine talker, who told many Indian stories calculated to disturb a tenderfoot. Every passenger in those days carried a Winchester rifle as well as pistols. We arrived at Fort Stockton on the

11th, and left Mr. Corbett and one other passenger, thus leaving Mr. Bassett and myself alone in the stage. Arrived at Fort Davis at 1: 30 A. M. on the 12th, where we found that nothing was talked of but Victoria, the great leader of the Mescalera Apache Indians. The drivers pointed out many graves along the road, the occupants having been victims of the Indian raids. We arrived at old Fort Quitman the night of the 13th. At the stage station we found two Mexican herders who had been robbed of their sheep that day by a band of Indians, which they supposed was Victoria's band. We partook of some black coffee, bacon and hardbread for supper. By this time the driver called out "All aboard," and advised us to get our guns in order and keep them on our laps. The curtains were rolled up so that we could be ready to jump out in case of an attack and take to the tornillo bushes. It was understood that we would stick together and make the best fight we could in case of an attack. The driver was also provided with a Winchester rifle. We had been on the road about an hour when the driver stopped and pointed to a camp-fire almost out, among some bushes near the road. He got down and went to the place, lighted a match, and looked around the camp, then came back, bounded into his seat, and said: "Moccasin-tracks, gentlemen," and put whip to his horses. We encountered no Indians, however, and arrived in El Paso at 8 o'clock P. M.—one hundred miles, with one change of horses.

A short time after this the eastbound stage, with General Burns as the only passenger, left Quitman Station, and had not gone far when the driver discovered Victoria's band of raiders in the road ahead of him. The driver turned his team to go back to the station. As he turned the Indians opened fire on them and shot one of the horses through the top of the mane. General Burns, with a Winchester, opened fire on them from the rear of the coach. The Indians also fired upon him and shot him through the chest. He lived three hours after they reached the station. He stated that he saw two Indians fall, and supposed that put a stop to the chase.

On reaching El Paso on the night of the 14th we put up at Mrs. Roman's hotel, an old adobe on the plaza, where there now stands a fine brick building. I had one acquaintance in El Paso, Judge Allen Blacker, then Judge of the El Paso District Court, and a letter to Judge Joseph Magoffin, with whom we took dinner on Sunday, the 15th of February. We spent six days in El Paso, and were royally entertained by Charles Richardson at El Paso del Norte, just across the Rio Grande river, in Mexico.

We purchased four hundred acres of land from Judge Magoffin in the suburbs of El Paso, made some investigations for the Texas & Pacific Railroad Company (which was a part of my mission), and left on the stage on the evening of the 19th of February for Mesilla, New Mexico, where we arrived at 6 A. M. on the 20th, took breakfast and left for Silver City, where we arrived at 8 A. M. on the 21st. We reached Euell's Springs on the 22d, Tucson on the 23d, Florence on the 24th, and the Silver King mine on the same day. On the way we cut a huge cactus which measured thirty-eight feet in length.

We remained all night at the Silver King and left the next day for Globe City on pack-animals. We passed over a mountain trail and through the Devil's Cañon to Globe, a distance of twenty-eight miles, which took all day. We remained at Globe until the 3d of March.

We returned via the Silver King to Florence, and then to a station called Pecats, where we intercepted the regular stage-coach line operated from the terminus of the Southern Pacific Railroad to Fort Worth. We arrived at Pecats at 10 P. M., sat up on a chair until the stage came along, and were unable to get in or on top of it, owing to it being already overcrowded with passengers. We waited there until daylight, when a man who had been sleeping on the dirt floor of the station told us he had been waiting two days to get a seat in the stage; and the station-keeper said it was that way every day.

We then tried to get passage on some private wagons that were camped there, and which were hauling freight from the railroad to Tucson, but the best we could do was to get our valises hauled to the next station, twenty-seven miles off. We walked all the way from there to the next station. I knew the keeper at the next station, Charles Labadeau, where I expected to get some conveyance to Tucson, but next morning we were able to crowd into the stage, and arrived in Tucson on the 6th of March.

On the 9th we staged to Tombstone, returned to Tucson on the 14th, and left on the 15th for Casa Grande, the then terminus of the Southern Pacific Railroad.

We took the caboose on a construction train on the Southern Pacific, and arrived in Los Angeles on the 17th.

At that time the citizens of Los Angeles claimed a population of 25,000. Business was dull, and the merchants were complaining.

We arrived at San Francisco on the night of the 18th, and left on the 21st via the Central Pacific Railroad for home. Count De Lesseps and party were on the same train. We arrived at Ogden on the 23d; at Omaha on the 25th, and at St. Louis on the 27th, of March, where I remained until the 1st of April, when I left for Fort Worth, Texas, arriving there on the 3d.

On the 16th of January, 1881, I left Fort Worth with my wife and daughter for St. Louis, where we met Mr. Bassett, and were introduced by Charles Music to Juan, Luis and Alberto Terrazas, sons of Governor Terrazas of Chihuahua, Mexico. We all left St. Louis for El Paso via the Missouri Pacific Railroad to Kansas City and the Atchison, Topeka & Santa Fe to Rincon, N. M. At the depot at San Marcial, N. M., where we left the sleeping-car, there were eight dead Mexicans, who had been killed that day near the town by Indians. From San Marcial to Rincon we traveled on a construction train. From Rincon we took the stage for El Paso, where we arrived on the first day of February, 1881.

This trip ended my travels on the Plains and through the Wild West. There is no such thing any more as the Wild West, except in the deep recesses of the great Rocky Mountain range.

CHARLES R. MOREHEAD.

APPENDIX D.

THOMAS HART BENTON.

Thomas Hart Benton was born at Hillsboro, North Carolina, March 14, 1782; died at Washington, D. C., April 9, 1858. His father was Jesse Benton, a lawyer of ability and good character. His mother was Ann Gooch, a niece of Governor Gooch of Virginia and of Colonel Thomas Hart of Kentucky, and a cousin to the wife of Henry Clay. He was the eldest son. His father died in 1790, leaving, among other possessions, a tract of land containing some twenty thousand acres. This land was about twenty-five miles south of Nashville, in middle Tennessee. His widowed mother moved upon this tract of land. She sent Thomas to Chapel Hill University, in North Carolina, where he was educated. After his return from school he taught for a time in the schools of his locality, and studied law. He was admitted to the bar in 1808, and opened an office at Franklin, where he practiced for a short time, moving later to Nashville. In 1811 he was elected to the Legislature, where he made a good record. In 1812 he joined the army under General Andrew Jackson, whom he served as aide-de-camp. He was made Lieutenant-Colonel of the Thirty-ninth Regiment, infantry. Trouble arose between General Jackson and Colonel Benton in 1813, and this trouble resulted in a clash of arms in Nashville, September 4, 1813, between the parties and their friends. In one party were General Jackson, Alexander Donaldson, Colonel Coffey, Stockley Hays, and Captain Hammond; in the other, Colonel Benton and his brother Jesse. Several pistols were discharged by each party. General Jackson and both Bentons were wounded. The difficulty was the result of personal trouble between General Jackson and Jesse Benton. It made enemies of General Jackson and Colonel Benton until the policy of Jackson in relation to the United States Bank and Nullification, which Benton supported, brought about a reconciliation.

Colonel Benton settled at St. Louis about 1815, and began there the practice of law. He also established a newspaper in opposition to the *Missouri Gazette*. He was soon prominent and widely known as a lawyer, editor, and politician. In 1817 he fought two duels with Charles Lucas, who was slain in the second. Benton fought only because it was a custom sanctioned at the time by public opinion, and to have refused would have ruined him; he regretted the result as long as he lived.

In 1820 Benton was elected United States Senator and held the place for thirty years without a break. In the Senate he rose to greatness. His influence was powerful in the councils of the country. As a persistent advocate of the use of gold and silver for money he earned the sobriquet of "Old Bullion." He became the successor of Jefferson in the advocacy of the exploration and settlement of the West as the means to a large commerce with Asia. He was related by marriage to General William Clark, Indian Agent for all the West, by whose aid he was

(623)

enabled to inform himself of the conditions, geography, resources, and possibilities of the West. He became the champion of the fur companies operating from St. Louis. His interest in that country grew as his knowledge increased, and one can scarcely understand our claims to the Northwest without a careful study of his speeches on the Oregon boundary question. It was through his influence that explorations were made under Frémont.

In the Mexican War Senator Benton was in favor of a vigorous policy, and he was one of the earnest supporters of President Polk, who at one time desired to make him Lieutenant-General and put him in command of all the American forces in Mexico. He welcomed, in an eloquent and patriotic address at St. Louis, the discharged soldiers of Colonel Doniphan's regiment upon their return from service in Mexico.

The views of Benton on the slavery question were at variance with those held by a majority of the people of Missouri. He was uncompromising in his opposition to the resolutions introduced in 1849 by Claiborne F. Jackson and passed by the Legislature. They were known as the "Jackson Resolutions," and Benton denounced them as tending to nullification and a disruption of the Union. He fought for his position with all the resources of his greatness; but he was overthrown, being defeated for reëlection to the Senate by Henry S. Geyer in 1851. In 1852 he was elected a member of the House of Representatives from the St. Louis District, and served one term, which completed his public services.

Benton wrote the *Thirty Years' View*, a very valuable historical work; and he was the author of the *Abridgment of the Debates of Congress from 1789 to 1856*, fifteen volumes, a work of the greatest public utility.

For many years Senator Benton was earnest in his efforts for the construction of a railroad from St. Louis to the Bay of San Francisco. It is said that, standing on the bluff overlooking the mouth of the Kansas river, he pointed up that stream and said "There lies the way to India." A mighty commerce now flows over the way indicated by Senator Benton.

Thomas H. Benton was another of those pioneers who attained marvelous fame in Missouri. He left the impress of his genius upon the institutions of our country. He was the strength and support of those who blazed the way from the Missouri river to the Pacific ocean. He believed in the country they explored. He helped subdue it and enlarge its borders. Every State carved from it recognizes his services and claims a share in his glory. The West and its possibilities he proclaimed to the world, and his monument is the greatness of that magnificent land which stretches westward from the Mississippi to the sea.

APPENDIX E.

MICHAEL McENNIS.

Michael McEnnis was in Company B, Laclede Rangers. He lives now at Kirkwood, St. Louis county, Mo. He was born at Baltimore, Maryland, April 28, 1826. He is of the ninth generation of his family in America. Some of his ancestors settled in Maryland in 1650, and others settled in Virginia in 1680. Another ancestor, Thomas McNeir, settled at Annapolis, Md., in 1720, and was the first man wounded at Annapolis in resisting the landing of the British tax collector in 1765; two of his sons served in the armies of the Revolution, one of whom, George McNeir, being a Lieutenant afterwards at Fort McHenry when Francis Key wrote the "Star-Spangled Banner." George McNeir was the grandfather of Mr. McEnnis. Joseph Robert McNeir was under Jefferson Davis at the battle of Buena Vista, and was publicly complimented and promoted on the battle-field for gallantry in action. In the St. Louis *Globe-Democrat*, July 2, 1905, there is an account of the services of Michael McEnnis in the expedition under Kearny and Doniphan, from which we make the following extract:

MICHAEL McENNIS.
[At the age of 81.]

"Company B, Laclede Rangers of St. Louis, of which I was a member, under Capt. Thomas B. Hudson, furnished their own horses, saddles, bridles, spurs, saddle-blankets, etc.; chartered the steamer Pride of the West at their own expense, went up the Missouri river to Fort Leavenworth, and offered their services to Gen. Stephen Kearny. There they were mustered into the battalion of light infantry under Maj. M. Lewis Clark, son of the celebrated Clark of the Lewis and Clark expedition. A few days later Capt. Waldemar Fisher arrived with a company of Germans from St. Louis. Capt. Fisher being an accomplished Prussian artillery officer of rare ability, his services were in demand, and to secure them our company was changed to mounted volunteers and became Company E of the First Regiment, mounted volunteers, under Col. A. W. Doniphan, Fisher's company taking our place in the light artillery. Col. Doniphan commanded the chivalric and historical march from New Mexico to the Gulf of Mexico, with 1000 men through the heart of Mexico.

"We were nearly all mere boys when we marched to the levee to start for New Mexico. Out of more than a hundred, of whom I alone am now left, over eighty were under twenty years old. The enthusiasm was immense, and crowds of ladies followed us to the steamer, where we fired a parting salute from an old cannon. At every town along the river we had the same sort of welcome and had to respond with a salute from the old cannon, until, at Jefferson City, it burst and came near wrecking the boat.

"We left Fort Leavenworth June 15 to cross the prairie and the desert for Santa Fé. The march under the sun peeled the skin from our faces and necks in strips. The country was burned dry and bare and I had no idea that anything along the old Santa Fé trail would ever be worth having or settling. The two thousand men under Kearny camped at Fort Bent, on the Arkansas, for drill; and from the Arkansas, instead of following the usual trail where Mexican resistance might be massed, we turned through the mountains and took Santa Fé as it were on the flank. The Mexicans knew of our coming, and they had planted a battery of cannon at the bottom of a long and deep defile through which we had to pass. They might have held it against any number of men, but when the order was given to charge through the cañon, our boys went through it at top speed, and the Mexicans did not wait to use their battery. They spiked their guns and ran, after our bugle had sounded the charge and they heard us coming. This was at what is now called Kearny's Gap, near San Miguel. We captured the seventeen guns with which they had fortified the gap. They were all antique and looked useless after we had captured them, but we were glad enough the Mexicans did not stop to use them while we were running up to take them, with the queer feeling that comes along with that sort of thing when it is tried for the first time.

MICHAEL McENNIS.
[At the age of 30.]

"I remember now how the word 'forever' took hold on me as I heard Kearny use it, when, after we had reached Pecos, the Mexican officials in their tall hats came out to protest officially against our presence in Mexican territory. When I enlisted it was not known generally that the purpose of the expedition was to annex New Mexico, and the first I knew of it was when Kearny used the word 'forever' in telling the Mexican officials that he had come to 'take possession of the territory forever in the name of the United States.' As the St. Louis boys were unusually well educated, we were often on detail service, and I happened to be so that day, so that I was in the party around Gen. Kearny when the conference with the Mexican officials took place, and heard it all. Joseph Roubidoux, the founder of St. Joseph, Mo., acted as interpreter. When he had translated the Mexican protest into English for Gen. Kearny, he translated Kearny's reply into Spanish for the Mexicans. Thus I learned that the purpose of the expedition was to annex the territory at the same time they did. When we entered Santa Fé under arms there were few men in sight, but the streets were lined on each side with their women, whose faces were all powdered white,—I suppose as part of some ceremony whose meaning I never knew. Perhaps it was a result of some Aztec custom.

"From Santa Fé I was one of the party detailed as escort for a surgeon returning to Fort Leavenworth on Government business in the management of the

Indians, then many of them hostile, and most of them in a starving condition. On the Cimarron the sixteen men in our party were surrounded by a war party of hostile Navajos, who made it more interesting for us than the Mexicans had done. After surrounding us and closing in to discharge their arrows, they broke under our fire and took to cover in the grass around us. Dr. Penn, who was in charge of the expedition, turned over the command to an experienced Indian-fighter named Ward, who told us the Indians feared the saber much more than they did musket-fire. He ordered us to charge the tall grass with the saber, and we did it. The Indians ran from the swords when we began to get close to the grass in which they were hidden, and we were too glad to see them run to follow far.

"I made the journey back to Fort Leavenworth in the worst cold of winter, with the plains covered with snow, after having crossed them in the midsummer drought. All the members of the company who came back to St. Louis received from the Government a bronze medal of honor, such as the one I still keep as a souvenir, but I am the last of them. If there is one other of the 103 left it is one who went from St. Louis to New York years ago and did well there as a confectioner. But I do not know that he is still living."

APPENDIX F.

FRANCIS XAVIER AUBREY.

Francis Xavier Aubrey was a French-Canadian. Very little is known of him until he became identified with the West. He is spoken of as a "famous freighter." (R. M. Wright, in *Kansas Historical Collections*, Vol. 7, p. 51.) He explored and marked a route from the Arkansas river to Santa Fé, which became known as the "Aubrey Route." It left the Arkansas a few miles west of the "Gold Banks" and followed a middle course between the "Raton" and "Cimarron" routes. Mr. Wright says it "was less dangerous because less subject to Indian attacks, and water was more plentiful."

Aubrey became famous on account of the short time in which he made the journey from Santa Fé to Independence, Missouri, on horseback. His first trip was made in eight days, on a wager, in 1850. Of the time stipulated in the wager he had several hours to spare when he arrived at his destination. In 1852 he made a wager of $1000 that he could make the journey in five days. He won the wager, but reached his destination in an exhausted condition and had to be lifted from his saddle. In making these wonderful rides he had fresh horses awaiting him with each of his freight trains on the trail from the frontiers of Missouri to Santa Fé.

It is said that Aubrey drove a large flock of sheep from New Mexico to California, and that the venture was a success financially. He may have made more than one trip to California, for he gained a very comprehensive knowledge of the topography of the country lying between Santa Fé and southern California. He believed it possible to discover a much better route through that country than those in use at the time, and accordingly set about this purpose with a single companion,—an Indian, in whose hardihood, intelligence and fidelity he had perfect confidence. He was successful in finding a new route that was much better than those in use. Beyond the Colorado river the country is devoid of water, but Aubrey skirted the mountains and located his route along their southern base. He discovered a pass through the mountains into southern California which made his route shorter and better than those previously known. He discovered several passes in the ranges in what is now Arizona. The hardships he endured are indescribable. He discovered rich mines of gold and carried back with him nuggets and samples of quartz. (See statements of R. M. Wright, *Kansas Historical Collections*, Vol. 7, p. 51.)

It seems that another man knew of the necessity of a new route to California, and not having the ability to seek and locate for himself, followed Aubrey, and, returning to Santa Fé ahead of him, had certain portions of Aubrey's route and certain passes in the mountains described and their discovery and exploation credited to himself. Major R. H. Weightman was the editor and proprietor of the paper in which the account was printed. Aubrey heard of this publication before his return to Santa Fé. He believed that Weightman had published the story for the purpose of discrediting him. He was the more indignant because he had supposed that Weightman was his friend, as he had always professed to be. And he was confirmed in his belief in the treachery of Weightman by the fact that he had forwarded to him a description of the route he had located, and no part of Aubrey's account appeared in the paper. These circumstances made Aubrey furious. He returned to Santa Fé, and, dismounting, entered the Fonda Hotel. He was instantly recognized and made the center of a crowd of admirers, who became enthusiastic in their demonstrations in his honor. Major Weightman entered the hotel, and the crowd moved towards the bar as congratulations were exchanged. Aubrey and Weightman each ordered brandy. An eye-witness described the scene which followed: "Aubrey raised his glass to his lips, and then putting it down said: 'What has become of your paper?' Weightman answered, 'Dead.' 'What killed it?' asked the other. 'Lack of support,' was the answer. 'The lie it told on me killed it,' said Aubrey. Without a word Weightman threw a glass of brandy into his opponent's face, and, while blinded by its effects, stabbed him to death."

Weightman denied having received the account sent him by Aubrey, and claimed that he had not played falsely as charged. It is known that Weightman said years afterward that he saw always Aubrey before him—saw him dying in defense of what he believed his rights and his honor, and that he regretted that he had not allowed Aubrey to kill him.

The account of the killing of Aubrey is taken mainly from an article prepared by William R. Bernard for the Kansas State Historical Society, and published in the ninth volume of the *Collections* of the Society. Mr. Bernard further says: "Aubrey was an honest, simple-minded man, true to friends, but ever ready to resent any imputation against his honor. Aubrey was the first man to take a loaded train from the Missouri river to New Mexico in winter. He was the discoverer of a third route to Santa Fé, about 1849–'50. Before this there were but two, namely, that by way of the Cimarron, and the other by way of the mountains, which was at a later date followed by the Santa Fé Railroad. Aubrey's route crossed the Arkansas river below the mouth of the Big Sandy, not far from Big Timbers. The greatest distance without water on this route was thirty miles, while on the Cimarron road the greatest distance without water was sixty miles."

APPENDIX G.

THE SANTA FÉ TRAIL.

Gregg tells us that the Santa Fé trade had no very definite origin. Captain Pike found James Pursley, a Kentuckian, at Santa Fé, where he had arrived in June, 1805. A merchant named Morrison, of Kaskaskia, Ill., had conceived the idea of trading with the northern provinces of Mexico, and had sent one LeLande, a French Creole, to Santa Fé by way of the Platte. The agent was successful in his efforts to reach Santa Fé, but he failed to return, and lived out his days in New Mexico. The account published by Captain Pike upon his return to the United States must be held as the primary cause of the large proportions attained by the Santa Fé trade. The disastrous termination of the expedition fitted out by McKnight and others in 1812 prevented further ventures in that direction for full ten years. The expeditions made by Glenn, Colonel Cooper and his sons, and Captain Becknell may be considered as preliminary tours demonstrating that there was profit in the trade with northern Mexico. A number of cargoes went out in 1822, and the profits were so great that enterprising merchants sought a better means of transportation than pack-horses for their goods. It is recorded that about eighty traders crossed the Plains to Santa Fé in 1824, among them M. M. Marmaduke, afterwards Governor of Missouri, and that in the caravan there were "twenty-five wheeled vehicles, of which one or two were stout road-wagons, two were carts, and the rest Dearborn carriages." To the surprise of all concerned, few obstacles to wagons were encountered. Indeed, the discouragements of the trade with Santa Fé lay not in the road over which it was carried, so much as with the Indian tribes which beset it. In 1829 it became necessary to send an escort of troops with the caravan of traders. Another escort was necessary in 1834, and still another in 1843. One of the causes for the establishment of Fort Leavenworth was the necessity for protecting the Santa Fé trade.

The town of Franklin, Missouri, (Howard county,) is credited with furnishing the first traders to Santa Fé. Lexington, Missouri, was an outfitting point for this trade for some time. But the great bulk of the Santa Fé trade was carried on from Independence, Missouri. The trappers starting for the Rocky Mountains, the emigrants to settle in Oregon, and expeditions to explore the West or any part of the Great Plains, outfitted at Independence. Westport afterwards supplanted Independence.

The wagons employed in the Santa Fé trade were of the old Conestoga pattern, with sail-cloth covers stretched on bows, manufactured at Pittsburg, Pennsylvania. In the beginning they were drawn by mules, the teams consisting of six, eight, or even ten of these animals. Oxen were not used until after the year 1829, when they were employed by Major Riley in transporting his baggage-wagons. It was found that they did their work well, even possessing some advantages over mules.

The journey to Council Grove was an individual matter. At that point the caravan was organized, whence it proceeded with order and regularity to Santa Fé. The organization was something after the military order. Camps were selected in advance, water and grass looked out for, indications of Indians sought, and every precaution taken to guarantee the safety and expedite the objects of the caravan. At night the wagons were so disposed as to form a tolerable fort, and, in case of danger, the cattle, horses and mules were brought into this inclosure. Watches and guards were set and relieved as in the march of an army. The larger caravans had cooks, herders, hunters, and scouts. Not infrequently did travelers go out with them, or, having made the rounds of the Mountains and Plains, returned with them to the confines of civilization.

As the trade increased the caravans sought other ports than Santa Fé. As early as 1828 traders carried their cargoes to Chihuahua. These ventures proved profitable, and in the later stages of the trade most of the larger caravans went to Chihuahua or other towns in that part of Mexico. Many Americans established large mercantile houses in Chihuahua and other towns in northern Mexico and carried out their goods over the Santa Fé trail. Some of these did not transport their goods in trains owned by them, and this developed a class of freighters who had no interest in the goods beyond seeing that thay arrived at their destination in good condition. The Mexicans came to engage in the trade, and some of them did business on a large scale. They were encouraged in this course by the American merchants who wholesaled the goods for the trade. And following in the wake of this commerce there arose an Indian trade, a sort of barter on a small scale with Indians encountered on the journey across the Plains. This did not reach any considerable proportions, the Indians generally preferring to trade at forts erected in their country with a view to securing their trade.

The route over which this trade was carried on was known as the Santa Fé Trail. It was so called because it was the road from western Missouri to Santa Fé, the capital of New Mexico. The physical features of a country always determine the routes of travel and commerce. The Santa Fé Trail followed a natural commercial highway. By the conformation of the country we know that this trail or route or road was the great way of communication between the Great Plains and that rolling plateau on the south flank of the Rocky Mountains drained by the Canadian and the Rio Grande. This old road was a commercial highway ages before Coronado toiled over its stretches of desert and sand and plain covered with grass and black with buffalo. Nature made it a way to be followed by men, and modern transportation methods recognize the fact. One of the greatest railroads in the world not only follows the old route almost exactly, but has appropriated a portion of the ancient name.

The Missourians who marched over this old trail in 1846 believed they were traversing a new country. But it was not so. Armies of painted and plumed denizens of desert and plain had marched up and down this hoary road thousands of years before. Could we penetrate the veil which shuts out the past in the history of aboriginal America, we might see hordes of conquest going out and coming in over this ancient way.

Dr. Elliott Coues, in his edition of the account of the Expeditions of Captain Zebulon M. Pike, has identified the old Santa Fé Trail from Independence, Mo., to Great Bend, Kansas, with the names found in our modern geography. His account is quoted below:

"It will be interesting to go over this road, and identify the camping-grounds of those hardy pioneers by the modern names of the places on and near their route; especially as no railroad now follows this primitive trace exactly. It held a pretty straight westward course, bearing all the while southward; the distance from the usual starting-place (Independence, Mo.) was called 300 miles roundly, but is somewhat less than this. The most noted place on the route was Council Grove, so called since 1825, when the U. S. Commissioners Reeves, Sibley, and Mathers, who there treated with the Osages, gave the place its present name. In the most general terms, the road followed the divide between Kansas waters on the north or right hand going west, and on the other, first those of the Osage (a branch of the Missouri), then those of the Neosho (a branch of the Arkansaw), and finally those of the Arkansaw itself. But the route was nearly everywhere in the latter water-shed; after the first few miles, every stream crossed ran to the left. In some places, the divide between the two sets of streams had little breadth; one place was called the Narrows, the approximation was so close. The wagon-train that started from Independence usually left 'the States' the first day out, and entered 'the Indian territory,'—that is, it went from the present State of Missouri into the present State of Kansas; and all the rest of the way to Great Bend was through the latter. Let us look up some maps and itineraries of half a century ago—say Gregg's, published in 1844; Wislizenus', of 1846; and Beckwith's, 1853—to see what sign-posts they set up. These point to such places as the following, in regular order from east to west: Independence and Westport, Mo.—Big Blue camp—Round Grove, Lone Elm, The Glen—Bull creek, Black Jack creek and point, Willow Springs, and The Narrows—two Rock creeks in succession—One Hundred and Ten Mile creek—Bridge creek—Dwissler's or Switzler's creek—five creeks to which the names First Dragoon, Second Dragoon, Soldier, Prairie Chicken, Elm, and One Hundred and Forty-two Mile attach in some itineraries and are to be collated with Fish and Pool, or Fish and Pleasant Valley, of others—Bluff creek—Big Rock creek—Big John spring and creek—Lost Spring and Lost or Willow creek—Cottonwood creek—two or three Turkey creeks in succession—Little Arkansaw river—several Little Cow creeks, among them one called Chavez or Charez and Owl—Big Cow Creek—approach to the Arkansaw river at Camp Osage—up the Arkansaw to Walnut creek, and thus to Great Bend. From such *indicia* as these it may not be difficult to reopen the road in terms of modern geography.

"1. Independence maintains its independence as the seat of Jackson county, Mo., two or three miles south of the Missouri river, and about the same east of Big Blue creek; but Westport is practically absorbed in the suburbs of Kansas City, Mo. Starting from Independence, the first halt on the prairie, after crossing Big Blue river, was likely to be 'Big Blue camp.' This was about the heads of Brush creek, a small tributary of the Big Blue from the west, and the vicinity of present Glen. Being nearly on the present inter-State boundary, it was the 'jumping-off place' from 'the States,' where the traveler entered 'the Indian territory.' The military road between Forts Towson (on Red river) and Leavenworth passed by. A little to the northwest was the Shawnee agency and mission, on a branch of Turkey creek, the first tributary of the Kansas from the south; Shawnee is there now, and other places on Turkey creek are called Merriam, South Park, and Rosedale; the Kansas City, Fort Scott & Gulf Railroad meanders Turkey creek into Kansas City. The position is about lat. 38° 59' north and long. 94° 35' west.

"2. About five miles further southwest the road passed by Lenexa, Johnson county, and a camp could be made on a head of Indian creek, which is a small stream joined by Tomahawk creek before it reaches the Big Blue. The road continued southwest, approximately by the present Southern Kansas Railroad, and thus past Olathe, now seat of Johnson county, where six tracks diverge in various directions. This is the center of the county, near the head of Indian creek, on the head of Mill creek, a tributary of the Kansas, and near the head of a branch of Cedar creek, another Kansas affluent.

"3. 'Round Grove,' 'Lone Elm,' or 'The Glen' was a camping-place on one of the heads of Cedar creek, between Olathe and the village of Gardner; it was reckoned fifteen miles from Big Blue camp, and twenty-two from Westport. Thus far the Santa Fé route coincided with the even more celebrated 'Oregon trail.' But at a point beyond Gardner, in the direction of Edgerton, and six or eight miles from Round Grove, the road forked,—that is, the Oregon trail struck off to the right in the northwest direction of the Kansas, while the Santa Fé trail kept on the left-hand fork westward.

"4. Bull creek is still so called, or specified as Big Bull creek to distinguish it from Little Bull creek, which, with other tributaries, such as Rock, Ten Mile, and Wea, it receives before it falls into Marais des Cygnes (main Osage) river. This is the creek on which is Paola, seat of Miami county, near the junction of Wea creek, and it was the first of the Osage waters which the road crossed. The crossing was high upon its main course, between Gardner and Edgerton, whence the road continued west from Johnson into Douglas county.

"5. From the crossing of Bull creek it is nine miles to Black Jack creek and point, so called from the kind of oak (*Quercus nigra*) which grows there. Black Jack is still the name of a place between the heads of Captain creek (tributary of the Kansas) and Rock creek (a branch of Bull creek); it is three miles due east of Baldwin city.

"6. 'Willow Springs' was a noted camping-place west of Baldwin City, on one of the heads of Ottawa creek, which flows southward into the Marais des Cygnes river, a little below Ottawa, county seat of Franklin. The distance of Willow Springs from the crossing of Black Jack creek is ten and one-half miles. Willow Springs seems to be the same place that was called Wakarusa Point, or was at any rate very near it. Here the approximation of Kansas and Osage waters is very close, and this is the place which consequently became known as 'The Narrows.' The interlocking is between several heads of the Ottawa creek just said and some tributaries of Coal creek, a branch of the Wakarusa. Camp could also be made at a place called Hickory Point, short of Willow Springs by three or four miles.

"7. Two 'Rock' creeks were passed at distances given as nine and twelve miles from Willow Springs by some writers, and quite differently by others; some also mention but one 'Rock' creek. Eight Mile creek was headed if not crossed by the road; and beyond this the road crossed one or both heads of Appanoose creek. These creeks are tributaries of the Marais des Cygnes, falling in a mile apart at Ottawa and just beyond. Part of the uncertainty about these 'Rock' creeks arose from the fact that they often ran dry, were woodless, and thus ineligible for camping-grounds; hence they would often be passed without remark. The names seem to me to apply rather to the two forks of the Appanoose than to the main fork of the latter and to Eight Mile creek.

"8. One Hundred and Ten Mile creek, which still floats its long name, was so called because it was taken to be 110 miles from Fort Osage, our earliest establishment of the kind on the Missouri. This was built in September, 1808, at Fort Point (present Sibley), and was sometimes called Fort Clark. The creek in mention was crossed at a point taken to be twenty-four miles from Willow Springs, and thus in the vicinity of present Scranton, Osage county. It is a branch of the Dragoon creek we have next to consider.

"9. Continuing nearly due west, the road crossed several heads of present Dragoon creek, in the vicinity of Burlingame, Osage county. This is a comparatively large creek, which runs southeastward to fall into the Marais des Cygnes near Quenemo. That one of the several heads of Dragoon creek on which Burlingame is situated is now called Switzler's creek,; the next beyond is the main source of Dragoon creek, into which a branch called Soldier's creek falls, about two miles west of Burlingame. But none of the other itineraries I have consulted speak of either 'Dragoon' or 'Soldier's' creek; instead of which, they give a certain Bridge creek, as crossed eight miles west of One Hundred and Ten Mile creek. This is precisely the distance given by Beckwith for his 'Dwissler's' creek. No doubt 'Switzler' and 'Dwissler' are the same person's names; but whether this has always been applied to the same creek may well be doubted. The 'First

Dragoon' creek is now Dragoon creek; the 'Second Dragoon' creek is now Soldier's creek; these were passed near their confluence.

"10. In the next few miles the road crossed in rapid succession several heads of the Marais des Cygnes itself, thus finishing with the Osage water-shed. Three of these are now known as Onion, Chicken or Prairie Chicken, and Elm; the latter is the main head, and seems to be the one which appears as 'Fish' creek in the early narratives—the name by which it is mapped both by Gregg and Wislizenus. A fourth head of the Marais des Cygnes which the road crossed is that now known as One Hundred and Forty-two Mile creek, which joins the main stream much lower down than the other three. This is mapped by Gregg as Pool creek and by Wislizenus as Pleasant Valley creek. All four, of these streams are crossed in Lyon county, the boundary between this and Osage county having been passed at long. 95° 50′ 57″ west nearly.

"11. The road continued across Big Rock creek, having first passed its branch, Bluff creek. This is a tributary of the Neosho. It is probable that the Bluff creek of early writers refers to the main Big Rock rather than to the branch now called Bluff, as it is the last one they give before coming to—

"12. Big John Creek, another tributary of the Neosho, which was crossed immediately before Council Grove was reached; on which account, as well as for its beautiful spring and eligible camping-ground, it early became noted under the name it still bears.

"13. Council Grove, now the seat of Morris county. This was always the most marked place on the route—a sort of halfway station between the Missouri settlements and the great bend of the Arkansaw. Its area was indefinitely extensive along the wooded bottom-land of the Neosho, or, as it was called here, Council Grove creek; but as the situation became peopled, settlement was made chiefly on the west or right bank of the stream, at the mouth of Elm creek, a tributary from the west. This is not far from the center of a tract about forty-five miles square known as the Trust Lands, of which the Kansas Diminished Reserve is a southwestern portion. Council Grove is only some eight miles from the boundary between Lyon and Morris counties, which runs on a meridian close by the course of Big Rock creek.

"14. The road continued west up the left or north bank of Elm creek for about eight miles, crossed it at or near present station Milton of the Topeka, Salina & Western Railroad, and went on southwest to Diamond Spring, about eight miles further. This was a camping-place high up on the waters of Diamond, or, as it is also called, Six Mile creek, a branch of the Cottonwood.

"15. Hence west about sixteen miles to Lost Spring, on Lost or Clear creek,—that branch of the Cottonwood which falls in at Marion. This place is a little over the border of Marion county, and a town or station Lost Spring perpetuates the name, at the point where the Chicago, Kansas & Nebraska Railroad crosses a branch of the Atchison, Topeka & Santa Fe Railroad.

"16. From Lost Spring the route turned southwest seventeen miles to the Cottonwood, approximately by the present railroad line, and struck that river at or near Durham, Marion county.

"17. Continuing southwest and then bearing more nearly west, the road passed by or near Canton and thence to McPherson, both in the county of the latter name. Both are situated among the heads of Turkey creek, a branch of the Little Arkansaw; two or three of these were crossed. When two were noted, it used to be by the names of Little and Big Turkey creeks; map names are now Running Turkey, Turkey, and West Turkey; McPherson is on the last of these, some twenty-five miles from the crossing of the Cottonwood. The Turkey creeks vary very much in character with season and the weather.

"18. The road continued about twenty miles to the crossing of the Little Arkansaw, in the vicinity of the place now called Little River.

"19. In ten miles the road reached one of the tributaries of Cow creek, and it was ten more before all of these were passed; there are five or six of them, and some hardly ever run water. One of them is now called 'Jarvis' creek. Another is known as Long Branch; between this and Little Cow creek is Lyons, seat of Rice county, and beyond this Big Cow creek is crossed.

"20. The road now makes for the Arkansaw on a due west course, and comes

THE SANTA FÉ TRAIL. 635

to that river at a place which was known as Camp Osage, in the vicinity of present Ellinwood, Barton county. This town is only three miles from the mouth of Walnut creek, and the city of Great Bend is a mile or two beyond that."

From Great Bend to Santa Fé the old trail was followed almost exactly by the Atchison, Topeka & Santa Fé Railroad, maps of which are plentiful and always easily accessible.

APPENDIX H.

GENERAL STEPHEN WATTS KEARNY.

[From a miniature in possession of his son, Colonel Henry S. Kearny, of New York City.]

It was never the design to have any extensive biography of General Stephen Watts Kearny set out in this work. This conclusion was the result of the intention to confine its scope largely to the movements of Colonel Doniphan. I did not secure the address of Judge Joseph Magoffin until the work was in press. Judge Magoffin furnished material for a short sketch of his father, the late James Magoffin. Some reference in that sketch made it necessary to quote the views of Senator Benton on the Conquest of New Mexico. I immediately notified the descendants of General Kearny, and requested them to furnish me any facts in their possession bearing on that subject. It developed that little could be furnished by them. Colonel Henry S. Kearny, son of General Kearny, sent me the photograph from which was made the splendid portrait at the head of this short biography.

I wish to avoid doing any man, living or dead, the least injustice. Senator Benton developed an enmity towards General Kearny such as he, only, could hold. No more uncompromising man ever lived than Benton. No man ever in American public life was more intolerant, and often he was, despite his greatness, rash and unreasonable. Colonel John C. Frémont was the son-in-law of Senator Benton. In the unfortunate controversy which arose in California between General Kearny and Commodore Stockton, Colonel Frémont was involved. General Kearny deemed it his duty to arrest Colonel Frémont and prefer charges against him, which he did, the result of which was the court-martial which tried and convicted Colonel Frémont. That was the cause of the hatred which Senator Benton bore General Kearny. No one can read the correspondence (much of it published in this work) between General Kearny, Commodore Stockton and Colonel Frémont without a feeling that General Kearny maintained his position very ably. That the controversy was distasteful to him, we know. But he believed the instructions delivered to him placed upon him a great responsibility. In assuming this responsibility and acting under it he believed himself the personal representative of the President. He would not surrender any part of the prerogatives committed to his care. He acted solely from a sense of duty. A number of the friends of General Kearny have expressed to me the opinion that because of the statements made by Senator Benton concerning the conquest of New Mexico, the causes responsible for his bitterness towards General Kearny should be mentioned in this work. Believing them right, I have briefly alluded to them here.

I had hoped to be able to publish the documents filed with the War Department by James Magoffin in support of his claim for the services rendered the United States in the Mexican War, but the department refused my request made through the usual channels for copies of them. It is more than probable that the documents so filed would have settled all these matters, could they have been printed for general perusal. It is not certainly known that Mr. Magoffin ever claimed the honors ascribed to him by Senator Benton, though it is possible that he may with justice have done so. Should it prove to be true, even then the services of General Kearny can never be considered the less efficient and valuable. He was the commander of "The Army of the West" until he turned it over to Colonel Doniphan and departed from New Mexico for California, and even then it followed orders formulated for it by him. He acted in the conquest of New Mexico with promptness, energy, firmness, and intelligence.

Some information of General Kearny's ancestry, additional to that found in the sketch at page 225, this work, is given here. Stephen Watts Kearny was descended from chivalric ancestors. He was the son of Philip Kearny and Lady Barney Dexter (Ravaud) Kearny, his wife. The founder of the family in America was Michael Kearny, who came from Ireland and settled in Monmouth county, N. J., prior to 1716. The family were always particular as to the spelling of the name, writing it uniformly *Kearny*, never *Kearney*. Among his ancestors were the De Lanceys, glorious soldiers for ages. John Watts,

Senior, married Anne, the second daughter of Stephen De Lancey, who immigrated to New York in 1686. They were the grandparents of General Stephen Watts Kearny, and the great-grandparents of Major-General Philip Kearny. Their second son, John Watts, served in the wars against the French, under Sir William Johnson. Their youngest son, Stephen, commanded the First Battalion New York Volunteers during the War of the Revolution.

The following is taken from the *Biography of Major-General. Philip Kearny:*

"Stephen Watts Kearny was a student of Columbia College, in the City of New York, in 1812, and would have graduated in the summer of that year. As soon, however, as it became a certainty that war must ensue between the United States and Great Britain, he applied for and obtained a commission in the U. S. Army. On the 12th of March, 1812, while still in his eighteenth year, he was appointed from New York First Lieutenant in the Thirteenth U. S. Infantry. He distinguished himself particularly in storming a British battery, and throughout the assault on Queenstown Heights, 13th October, 1812. Lieutenant-Colonel Christie, commanding his regiment, himself wounded in this action, presented young Kearny with his sword on the field of battle for the cool and determined manner with which he executed the command which devolved upon him. A companion in arms states that as 'First Lieutenant of Captain Ogilvie's company, he [S. W. K.] enjoyed at an early age the character of high promise his after years developed. He was made prisoner on this occasion, and sent to Quebec,' and was long detained in captivity. He became Captain in April, 1813, Brevet-Major in April, 1823, and Major in May, 1829. Upon the organization of the first U. S. Dragoons, he was appointed their Lieutenant-Colonel, 4th March, 1833, and Colonel, 4th July, 1836. On the 30th June, 1846, he was commissioned Brigadier-General, was placed in command of the Army of the West, and made the conquest of the Province of New Mexico. He received the Brevet of Major-General, United States Army, for gallant and meritorious conduct in New Mexico and California, to date from the battle of San Pascual, 6th December, 1846, in which he was twice wounded. He commanded the combined force, consisting of detachments of sailors and of marines and of dragoons, in the battles of San Gabriel and Plains of Mesa, 8th and 9th of January, 1847, and was Governor of California from the date of his proclamation, 1st March, 1847, down to June of the same year. On the 31st October, 1848, he fell a victim at Vera Cruz to illness contracted in the course of his arduous service during the Mexican War. Like his nephew, Major-General Philip Kearny, he died for his country."

'One who knew him well, being competent to judge, said: "If ever there was a man whom I considered really chivalrous, in fact, a *man* in all that that noble term conveys, that natural soldier and gentleman was Stephen Watts Kearny."

Following the *History of Saint Louis*, by J. Thomas Scharf, I stated in the sketch of General Kearny, page 225, that he attended Princeton College,—an error which is corrected above.

APPENDIX I.

MEREDITH T. MOORE.

President Missouri Mexican Veterans' Association. Private in Company F, First Regiment Missouri Mounted Volunteers, Mexican War. Was in all the expeditions and battles. Crossed the Plains to California in 1849 and in 1852. Helped much with this book. Born in Callaway County, Missouri, May 25, 1827. Lives at Cedar City, Missouri.

Meredith Tarlton Moore was born at Ham's Prairie, Callaway county, Missouri, May 25, 1827. He is the son of Samuel Turner Moore and Emily Tarlton Moore, his wife. In 1816 Samuel Turner Moore came from his home in Fayette county,

Kentucky, (where he was born,) to Callaway county, and selected a place for his future home; he returned and married Emily Tarlton, and in 1818 moved to Callaway county and settled at the place which he had selected, where he lived the remainder of his life. He was of sturdy Scotch-Irish stock, and always a self-reliant and good citizen. By his first marriage his children were: (1) William T.; (2) Alfred Jeremiah; (3) John Hendley; (4) Meredith Tarlton. His wife died, and he went to Kentucky and married her sister, Catherine Tarlton. Children by the second marriage were: (1) Emily Amanda; (2) Samuel, who died when four years old. Emily Amanda married Benjamin Lawrence Locke, of Oldham county, Kentucky, who moved to Audrain county, Mo., where he now lives.

Meredith Tarlton Moore married Martha Hannah Ramsay, daughter of Allan Ramsay, son of General Jonathan Ramsay, of Kentucky. General Ramsay was in the War of 1812, and was a soldier in many campaigns against the Southern Indians. He was a member of the Kentucky Legislature. He moved to Missouri at an early day; settled in Callaway county; was a member of the Constitutional Convention and of the Legislature. He is said to have been the ablest man in the convention. He was a stern and uncompromising man, and but for this severity of disposition, it is said, he would have been made Governor of Missouri. Meredith Tarlton Moore was married June 26, 1856, at Jefferson City. Children: (1) Allan, died when two years old; (2) Kate, died unmarried; (3) Leulah, married George Carlton, Callaway county; (4) G. Ewing, died in infancy; (5) William Alfred, married Nellie McHenry, lives in Jefferson City; (6) Hendley H., married Bessie Gundlefinger, lives in St. Louis. Moore's first wife died, and he married Eliza Ramsay, her sister; no children by second marriage. He lives now (1906) in Cedar City, Callaway county, just across the river from Jefferson City. He was in the First Regiment Missouri Mounted Volunteers, (Company F), and participated in all the hardships and glorious achievements of that immortal band. In 1849 he went across the Plains to California, and was a miner at Rough and Ready. He returned to Missouri, and in 1852 he again crossed the Plains to California, driving a large number of cattle. At one time he was in partnership with William Waldo, at Sacramento. He was in the mercantile business at Alviso. He dealt largely in cattle and sheep. In 1849 he started with a large saw-mill, intending to haul it overland to the Sacramento Valley. At Fort Kearny, on the Platte, the army officers offered him such a profit on his venture that he sold them the mill, but always regretted that he did so, for he would have taken it safely to California, where he saw one just like it sold for fifty thousand dollars.

Mr. Moore has had adventures on the Plains and in the Rocky Mountains, by sea and by land. These adventures would fill a volume. His memory is marvelous, and he has told me the story of his life; it is my intention to write and publish it, with other pioneer biographies. Mr. Moore is hearty and vigorous, and has the appearance of a man under sixty. He is an excellent citizen, respected by all, and is keenly interested in all the affairs of the day. On the next page will be found the genealogical record of Mr. Moore.

THE COURTS FAMILY OF MARYLAND.

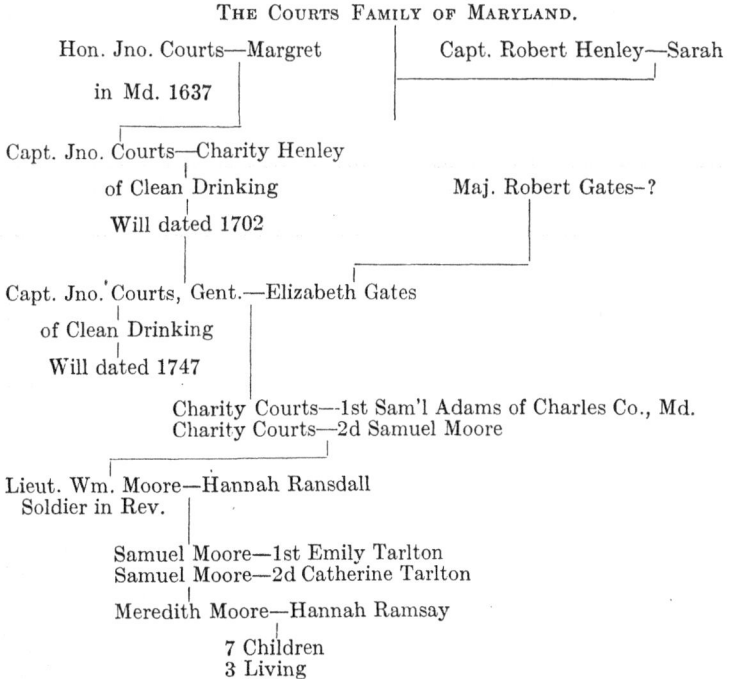

Lyman C. Draper, Secretary of the Wisconsin Historical Society, made the following notes from an interview with General Jonathan Ramsay. It contains the early history of the family:

FROM GEN'L JONATHAN RAMSAY, OF CALLAWAY COUNTY, MISSOURI, (HIBERNIA P. O.)—BORN ON THE HEAD OF HOLSTON, NOV. 23b, 1775. (Interview had Oct. 21st and 22d, 1851.)

In 1757, in Culpeper county, Va., were captured Stephen Holston and Josiah Ramsay, youths (perhaps half a dozen or more years old, Holston a year or so older); were out in a mulberry tree, gathering fruit, and were captured by Indians. Holston got back—perhaps surrendered at Bouquet's Treaty. The prisoners brought in at Bouquet's Treaty belonging to Virginia, were sent to Abm. Buford's (afterwards Colonel), and settled in Kentucky. Thomas Ramsay went there to see if he could find among them his lost son, seven years gone, and, unable to recognize him certainly, finally concluded a certain lad was the one; took him, and reared him as his son, never doubting the fact. He ever after bore the name of Josiah Ramsay. But the youth as he grew up doubted this view of his paternity. He had no recollection whatever of his captivity, which, if old enough to have been in the mulberry tree, he should have had. His earliest recollection was the French abandoning Fort DuQuesne, throwing flour and other articles into the river, and the Indians getting them.

On the Virginia frontiers was taken by the Indians a man named George Coon (or Kuhn) and his family—the youngest child a boy; and the mother enciente, which retarded her march, and an Indian stayed behind with her, and soon overtook the others without her—he had killed her. The children were scattered among the Shawnee Indians. Ramsay's Indian father used to tell him that he ought to be grateful to him; that when he first captured him he was very young, and he had to go and get a cow to furnish milk for him; that when his mother was killed, his father, who could speak French, ran away from the Indians. George Coon could speak French, and did run away. Mr. Ramsay also recollected, while quite small, with the Indians, a white girl coming from another Indian town, and taking him up, caressing and crying over him—whom, he thought, must have been his sister. George Coon subsequently settled and died in Tennessee. (Probably Abraham Kuhn, the white Wyandott war chief, was one of his children.—D.)

Josiah Ramsay was at Point Pleasant Battle—(though he was born in 1755 —and if a Coon, was probably taken in 1756 or '57)—and used to say that during the battle, both whites and Indians indulged mutually in blackguarding each other—the whites calling the Indians squaws, and the Indians returning the compliment by courteously saluting them as "sons of bitches." On the return, Ramsay and one other came through the mountains and laurel to Holston settlements—very rugged [ragged?—W. E. C.] and nearly starved—little or no game —found only one turkey, and that just gone to roost and very poor. He considered Cornstalk a great warrior and commander. No recollection by Gen. Ramsay. of hearing his father speak of the Crooked Creek Movement.

1776—Long Island Battle of Holston—Josiah Ramsay, Thomas Price and Ezekiel Smith, were spies—were rising, somewhat separated, to the summit of a ridge—and there Ramsay discovered an Indian on one knee, his gun leveled, resting it on the side of a sapling, aiming at Price, some forty yards off to one side. Ramsay instantly shot and killed the Indian, who proved to be a principal man among his people. Other Indian spies near by, ran, dropping some match-coats, a string of conjuring conch-shells, and some other articles, accidentally. The firing attracted the attention of a few of the nearest of the troops, who ran up to see, and were near enough to see the match-coats; and among those who thus ran forward, was John Sicks. But without venturing further, returned to the whites down the hill. Here a sort of council was held, and had resolved to return to Eaton's Fort, when Price and the spy party came. Cocke said, "We've got their conjuring tools—they ain't going to come any more—this will satisfy our wives and children." Sicks and others said they had seen the match-coats, and would go and get them; that the Indians were coming. The result was, they returned and fought the battle.

CHRISTIAN'S CAMPAIGN AND LONG ISLAND TREATY.—Thomas Price and Josiah Ramsay were sent to bring in some Indians to the treaty. Price had lived with the Indians, and could speak their language. They came to an Indian town, and saw a squad of fifteen or twenty Indians—told them about the treaty. They appeared sullen. Price had his rifle cocked lying across the pommel of his saddle, ready for use, if necessary. Happening to cast his eye around, Price discovered several horses near by, and among them recognized a horse of his own, which the Indians had stolen from him. He at once jumped off and went and boldly took the horse, saying he was his property, and had been stolen from him. "No," said an Indian—"didn't steal him—only took him for make haste." Price took him off unmolested.

In the fall of 1780 Josiah Ramsay and family, accompanied by six or eight young men going to see the country, removed to Kentucky, and settled at Mason's Station on Dick's river. When at Cumberland Gap, on the journey, one bright moonlight night, Indians attempted to steal their horses, but Ramsay and one John Cowdry out with their rifles. Ramsay made a loud yell, and the Indians, probably seeing their guns by the glittering reflection from the moon's rays, fled. Going on the Kentucky, they found, in three or four different places, persons killed at their camps and unburied.

In the fall of 1781 Mr. Ramsay and family removed to Eaton's Station, two miles from Nashville, and reached there Christmas night, and frolicking and dancing was going on in different cabins.

Renfro's Station broke up, and going to Eaton's Station, at Battle Ground Creek, near Sycamore Creek, Indians came upon them, and killed fourteen of the party. Gen. Ramsay has seen the bones loosely buried at an uprooted tree. Old Mr. Johns, Mr. Renfro and old Mr. Coultney were among the unfortunate slain. Renfro's negro "Bob" escaped, and afterwards became free and kept tavern in Nashville in early times, when Gen. Ramsay was residing in that region of country, and long after.

Josiah Ramsay was in Cold Water campaign—was not at Nickojack—and was major of militia when residing in Tennessee county (now Robertson county), before Tennessee became a State; was nearly always out in spying and scouting service. Got a pension just before he died, through the perseverance of Colonel Richard M. Johnson, and perhaps got one payment after, and died about 1834 or '35 at his son Gen. Ramsay's, in Callaway county, Missouri. Gen. Ramsay has somewhere a copy of his father's pension declaration.

APPENDIX J.

GENERAL ODON GUITAR.

GENERAL ODON GUITAR.
[From photograph in the collection of William E. Connelley.]

General Odon Guitar was born in Madison county, Kentucky, August 31, 1825. His father, John Guitar, was born in Agen, France, came to America, settled at Richmond, Madison county, Ky., married there Emily, the daughter of David Gordon, and moved to Columbia, Mo., in 1827.

Odon Guitar was of an adventurous spirit, and in 1843 he ran off from home and joined the freighting caravan of Amos Marney, who was engaged in carrying goods from Missouri to Chihuahua for Dr. Henry Connelly. At Coon Creek, on the Santa Fé Trail, he met with an accident in which his leg was broken, and he was sent back to Fort Leavenworth by Colonel Philip St. George Cooke.

There was no company recruited in Boone county, Mo., for the First Regiment Missouri Mounted Volunteers, but as the company from Callaway county passed through Columbia on its way to Leavenworth it halted there to secure some additional men. The men who enlisted at Columbia were Odon Guitar, Jefferson B. Ridgeway, William H. Northcutt, Elijah H. Wells, John M. Robards, and James P. Fleming. Fleming was a young lawyer recently arrived at Columbia from Pennsylvania. The company was the last to arrive at Fort Leavenworth, as General Guitar believes, and was denominated Company H. Guitar served through the campaign, and was discharged at New Orleans with his company. Numerous notes appear in this volume, based on information given by General Guitar.

In the Civil War Guitar recruited a regiment and did good service for the Union cause, and was made a Brigadier-General.

General Guitar married, December 25, 1865, Miss Kate Leonard, daughter of Judge Abiel Leonard, of Howard county, Mo. Of this union were born four sons and three daughters.

By profession General Guitar is a lawyer, and in the days of his strength had as large a practice as any lawyer in Missouri. He has always lived at Columbia, Missouri, having a magnificent home and grounds there.

(644)

APPENDIX K.

EDWARD JAMES GLASGOW.

EDWARD JAMES GLASGOW.
[From a painting made in 1840, in Philadelphia, while on his way to Mazatlan, Mexico, via Vera Cruz, by Mrs. Staughton, daughter of the artist Peele.]

Edward James Glasgow is one of the few survivors of that heroic age when the sons of Old Missouri made conquest of the Plains and Rocky Mountains and carried American trade overland far into Mexico and out to the Pacific Ocean. He was always a man of fine judgment, high character, and undaunted courage. He was ever a keen observer of events, bold in the execution of enterprises determined upon, a merchant by instinct, of a retiring disposition, and so modest that he can see nothing unusual in his numberless journeys over mountain and plain through wild lands overflowing with wild beasts and savage men, and by frail barks that sailed tediously down to the extremities of the earth. Such men become the moral force of the nation and the conservators of our institutions.

Mr. Glasgow aided me greatly with this book. I constantly appealed to him for material for an extended sketch of his life, but this he could not be prevailed upon to furnish, seeing nothing in his adventures upon the "American Desert" but duty and fidelity to the trust given into his charge by his business associates. Only through the kindness and courtesy of his niece, Miss Eleanor Glasgow Voorhis, of New York city, did I secure the following facts in addition to those set down in another part of this work. Miss Voorhis appreciates fully the value of the record of the life of a man of such sterling worth as Mr. Glasgow. She is a great-granddaughter of General William Clark, and has preserved in the collections of the private library belonging to her and her mother, Mrs. Julia Clark Voorhis, the priceless original records of the Lewis and Clark Exploring Expedition, recently edited by Dr. R. G. Thwaites and published by Dodd, Mead & Company.

Edward J. Glasgow's father, William Glasgow, was born at Christiana, Delaware, October 4, 1787, and was of Scottish descent. William Glasgow married Sarah Mitchell, who was born at Fincastle, Virginia, June 16, 1801. She was a descendant of Sir Humphrey Forester, of Aldermaston, England. Her father was Edward Mitchell, who served in the War of the Revolution. Mr. Glasgow gave Miss Voorhis the following information concerning his grandfather Mitchell:

"When it was learned in Virginia that Lord Dunmore, acting as Governor and commanding the British forces there, was shipping away the artillery and other armaments from that province, a company of militia or minute-men was raised and sent to capture him. But he had escaped and was gone when they reached the capital, and the company raised for this purpose was disbanded. Our grandfather, Edward Mitchell, was a member of that company, and it was his first service in the War of the Revolution. He married Anne Haley,* also of Virginia, and he was later for many years a minister, greatly beloved by his people."

Before William Glasgow's marriage to Sarah Mitchell, in 1818, he had spent several years in Spain, as the Secretary of the American Consul at Cadiz. That was in the times of the great Peninsular Campaign, during which the Duke of Wellington won brilliant victories for the English. Mr. Glasgow sometimes attended church-services in the camp of the Duke. Returning to America through France, William Glasgow witnessed at Bordeaux the wild enthusiasm of the people on the return of Napoleon from his exile, preceding the campaign which ended at Waterloo. After his return to America he foresaw the great possibilities of the West, and moved to Belleville, Illinois, in 1816. There his son, Edward James Glasgow, was born, June 7, 1820. In 1827 he moved with his family to St. Louis, Missouri.

Edward J. Glasgow was educated at the St. Louis University and St. Charles College, St. Charles, Mo. In August, 1840, he sailed from New York for Vera Cruz, Mexico, to engage in business on the Pacific Coast, having dispatched the goods by sailing-vessel around Cape Horn. When he started he expected to locate at Guaymas, Sonora, but on arriving there decided to change to Mazatlan, Sinaloa, where he remained two and one-half years, and disposed of the cargoes of three vessels. Before leaving home he had been appointed U. S. Consul for Guaymas by President Van Buren, but as he did not remain at that seaport he resigned his commission. In reaching the Pacific coast he proceeded from Vera Cruz to the City of Mexico by stage-coach, thence to Durango in private carriage, and from thence over the mountains on mules. The ships which carried out his merchandise from New York returned laden with dyewoods and mother-of-pearl shells from the fisheries in the Gulf of California.

When he closed up his business in Mazatlan he returned to New York in the firm's vessel, sailing around Cape Horn. He returned to Mazatlan by way of New York and Vera Cruz to close up the old business, and then proceeded on horseback to Chihuahua, where he had formed a partnership with Dr. Henry Connelly. He continued in the overland trade five years, making many trips over the old Santa Fé Trail to Independence, Missouri, and return. When leaving Independence on the last expedition, war was declared between the United States and Mexico. The traders were put under control of the army by General Kearny, with whom they entered Santa Fé. From that point to Chihuahua they were under command of Colonel Doniphan. At El Paso the traders and their assistants were by Colonel Doniphan organized into a battalion of two companies, of one of which

---

*She was a granddaughter of the Rev. George W. Forester, who was a younger son of Sir Humphrey Forester. He, her grandfather, a clergyman of the Church of England, came to this country in 1733, and was for more than thirty-seven years rector of his parish in Georgetown, Maryland.

companies Mr. Glasgow was elected captain. He was in the battle of Sacramento with his company, and entered Chihuahua with the American army. He remained there until the city was again occupied by the American troops under General Sterling Price, after his defeat of the Mexicans at Santa Cruz, sixty miles to the south. At the close of the war he returned to St. Louis, where he was in the mercantile business nearly thirty years. He says that the uniform hospitality, courtesy and honesty of the Mexicans made his sojourn in their country very agreeable, and that he continued to deal on a large scale with the Mexican merchants of New Mexico for many years after engaging in business in St. Louis.

The voyage around Cape Horn was a monotonous one of five and a half months, but Mr. Glasgow found the trips across the Plains interesting and pleasant. The buffalo and antelope supplied the means for gratifying his fondness for hunting, while the excitement from danger of Indians was sufficient to make the journey agreeable and enjoyable. He thinks the danger from Indians was more from their disposition to rob the trains and stampede the stock than from their liability to take human life. The Plains tribes were then principally armed with bows and lances, while the wagoners and hunters were frontiersmen expert with the rifle. One white man was supposed to be the equal of ten Indians in a battle.

On one occasion Mr. Glasgow crossed the Plains with seventy thousand dollars in silver, in wagons guarded by seventeen men. The caravan passed through a band of Comanches numbering two hundred. This band was encountered on the Cimarron. It required firmness and a perfect knowledge of the Indian character to escape without molestation. A village of Arapahoes was found below Bent's Fort, and a stop was made for the purpose of exchanging tobacco and sugar for buffalo-robes. Camp was made a few miles below at noon, and the mules were sent out a quarter of a mile to grass in charge of a single Mexican herder. Suddenly a band of the Indians came over the sandhills, firing their guns at the traders and yelling, stampeding the whole herd of mules. The herder hastily mounted the old bell-mare and made for camp, and the traders seized their arms and sallied forth. The mules were driven a little way, discovered the loss of the old mare, listened a moment, heard the bell, wheeled about and broke away from the Indians and returned to camp and the old mare. The traders lost a horse which had a lariat about his neck, by which he was led away. There were no killed or wounded on either side. Three of the Indians soon came into camp and told the traders the attacking party were Comanches, and that they had come down to inform them that the traders were friends and must not be attacked. The merchants pretended to believe the Indians, though they knew there was not a Comanche within a hundred miles.

Edward J. Glasgow married Harriet Kennerly, October 27, 1856, a beautiful and lovely woman. Of this union there are two sons, Julian Kennerly Glasgow and William Jefferson Glasgow, the latter a graduate of West Point and a Captain in the United States Army. Edward J. Glasgow and Meriwether Lewis Clark served in the Mexican War under General Kearny and Colonel Doniphan. A picturesque incident exists in the fact that the two sisters of the former married each a brother of the latter, sons of the famous explorer, General William Clark, of the Lewis and Clark Expedition, Eleanor A. Glasgow being the wife of George Rogers Hancock Clark, and Mary Susan Glasgow later having married Jefferson Kearny Clark. He was named for President Jefferson and for his brother-in-law, General Stephen Watts Kearny. A brother of Edward J. Glasgow also served with him in the Mexican War, namely, William H. Glasgow, a prominent citizen of St. Louis, Missouri.

EXTRACTS FROM LETTERS WRITTEN BY MR. WILLIAM E. CONNELLEY,
AUTHOR OF THIS WORK, TO MR. GLASGOW'S GREAT-NIECE, MISS ELEANOR GLASGOW VOORHIS, OF NEW YORK CITY.

From the letter dated Topeka, Kansas, January 28, 1907, in writing of Edward J. Glasgow, Mr. Connelley says: "I find his name all through the Congressional documents of that time as a merchant and civil officer. He was a great merchant, and the unparalleled victory of Colonel Doniphan was but the culmination of the conquest commenced by your Uncle and his brother traders twenty years before."

In the letter of March 22, 1907, Mr. Connelley writes: "I know that he [Mr. Glasgow] has had a life full of stirring incidents, and these incidents are a part of the history of the country and ought to be preserved. He has been blessed with long life and placed in the fields where history was made. There are now living very few men indeed who have had the experiences he has passed through. He has been a great merchant and a successful man. He has faced death for his country, and there may have been other times when he took his life in his hands for the sake of his native land."

From letter dated in April, 1907: "I consider your Uncle a remarkable man. Such men have been empire-builders in America, and he should have an adequate mention in history."

Edward J. Glasgow is a man of strong personality. He is in full mental vigor at nearly eighty-seven years of age. He speaks several languages, reads without glasses, and still takes journeys of more than a thousand miles, spending much time in New York. Mr. Glasgow is a quiet man, devoting many hours to reading, but on any subject which interests him his conversation becomes brilliant, possessing the two-fold quality of the rich and varied experiences of so many years that are told, together with a wide knowledge of the progressive thought of modern times. He is a modest man, caring little for general society. At a dinner, however, he is the life of the company, with his amusing stories and glowing anecdotes, told with a serious face while his keen, dark-brown eyes gleam with merriment. He can quote at great length from the various poets of different periods. His knowledge of the Bible is unusual, and he has a deep reverence for religion and the things of Eternal Truth.

Mr. Glasgow and his associates laid deep and well the foundations of empire in the great Southwest. Trade is the civilizer and commerce the conqueror. War is an incident of the progress of the human race, and when it loomed across the trail of these traders they seized the sword and did heroic service in that Spartan band led by Colonel Doniphan. Honor and glory to them now and evermore. May we, their successors, emulate their illustrious deeds and follow in the glorious course marked out by them for the guidance of posterity.

COMPANY F.

[COLE COUNTY.]

ROSTER OF OFFICERS.

[The author very much regrets that in the "make-up" the printer left out the Roster of the Officers of Company F. This Roster should precede the Roster of the Privates of the Company, at page 553.]

1. M. M. Parsons.....................................Captain.
1. Rich A. Wells.....................................1st Lieut.
1. George Pope Gordon............................2nd Lieut.
2. George B. Winston..............................2nd Lieut.
1. Fountain McKenzie..............................1st Sgt.
2. William W. Bolton...............................Sgt.
3. Robert A. Raphael...............................Sgt.
4. Absalom Hughes..................................Sgt.
1. William Rogers....................................Corp.
2. James H. McKenzie.............................Corp.
3. G. Burr Gordon...................................Corp.
4. Thomas L. Anderson...........................Corp.
1. James Henley.....................................Farrier.
1. Nicholas Snyder..................................Bugler.

INDEX.

A.

Abert, Lieut. J. W., returns by way of the Canadian, 86; account of crossing the Kansas river at mouth of the Wakarusa by Gen. Kearny and his army, 142; returns from California, 352; lost some of his men,—robbed by the Pawnees.... 353

Abiquiu, location of,—wagons of Major Gilpin sent to..................... 268

Albuquerque, southern expedition at,—description of country surrounding, 68; Americans camped at, 78; southern expedition at, 230; view of Plaza in,—Armijo lived in the vicinity of........ 231

Alexandro, signed treaty with Navajos.. 307

Alguein, Callisto, priest, — entertained John T. Hughes.................... 96

Algodones, southern expedition at..... 229

Allen, D. C., obligations of author to, viii; biographical sketch of, 15; portrait of. 17

Allen, Captain J., of the First Dragoons, mustered into service companies of Colonel Doniphan's Regiment, 132; recruited the Mormon Battalion, 258; death of........................... 259

Ammunition, discovery of, at El Paso.... 384

Angney, Captain W. Z., member of company of, died, 186; biographical sketch of, 514; Roster of company of........ 566

Annals of Platte County, (Mo.,) by W. M. Paxton, referred to................ 165

Antelopes, a herd of, killed by the army of Col. Doniphan................... 403

Apaches, Chief of, holds council with Gen. Kearny, 73; join Armijo in capturing sheep, 231; speech of, at council with Gen. Kearny, 252; some account of, 325, *et seq.*; historical note of family of, 330; robbers in El Paso............ 394

Appendices......................... 583

Arapahoes, mention of, 73; sometimes spent the winter at Big Timbers, 180; chief of, visits Gen. Kearny on the Arkansas........................... 181

Archulette, signed treaty with the Navajos............................... 307

Archulette, Gen., stirs up insurrection in New Mexico, 391; plans for insurrection in New Mexico................ 512

Arkansas, The, arrival of "The Army of the West" at....................... 161

Arkansas, The Little, account of, — "Army of the West" at.............. 158

Armijo, Governor, disputes with Gen. Salazar, 60; left his camp for El Paso, 61; feared assassination by his own people, 62; where gone to, 67; interested in cargo of Speyers, trader, 139; forming plans to resist the entrance of Gen. Kearny into Santa Fé, 177; text of letter of Gen. Kearny to, 181; course of, predicted by Captain Cooke, 184; fortified pass to oppose Americans, 190; preparations for the defense of New Mexico,—biography of, by Kendall,—in the sheep business, 195; escape of, from New Mexico,—quarreled with officers, 196; had 4000 troops with which to oppose the Americans, 201; how he became Governor of New Mexico, 213; visited Taos to induce the Pueblos to join him, 218; where he went to, 230; early life of,—a lover of sheep, 231; met by Ruxton in Mexico, 461; failure of, to oppose the Americans............................. 586

"Army of the West," amusements of members of, on the march across the Great Plains, 155; arrival of, at the Arkansas, 161; arrival of, at Pawnee Rock, 162; hardships of, on the march over the Old Santa Fé Trail, 168; arrival of, at the "Crossing of the Arkansas," 170; march of, up the Timpa, 182; insufficient rations of.......... 186

Artillery, arrival of the, at El Paso, 395; account of organization and service of .... 570, *et seq.*

Ashley, Gen. William.................. 135

Atchison, D. R., tribute of, to the eloquence of Col. Doniphan............. 37

Aubrey, F. X., killed by Capt. R. H. Weightman, 362, *et seq.*; biographical sketch of, 628; death of, at the hands of Capt. Weightman................ 629

Aull, James, partner of Samuel C. Owens, 468

Austin, W., killed in the insurrection.... 514

B.

Bancroft, H. H., sneering reference of, to actions of Gen. Kearny.............. 200

Baptiste, the French Trader in the valley of Green River..................... 607

Barnes, J., wounded at the battle of Sacramento 416

Barnett, Lieut. Robert, stabbed Lieut. Wells, 97; another account.......... 387

Barnett, ——, Indian in charge of Fish's Ferry............................ 143

Battery, Totten's, at the battle of Wilson Creek............................ 54

Bates, James, heard Gen. Wool relate how a young Missourian told him of his mistake at Buena Vista........... 483

Battle of Sacramento, account of, by James Peacock, 414; account of, by Meredith T. Moore,—positions of companies and battalions of troops at..... 416

(651)

Baubein, N., killed in the insurrection... 514
Baubien, Charles, appointed Judge of the Superior Court of New Mexico........ 243
Bear Flag, The, raised by Gen. Ide and Capt. Grigsby..................... 341
Bear Spring, reached by the expedition against the Navajos................ 301
Bent, Gov. Charles, mention of, 73; assassination of, heard of in El Paso, 97; appointed Governor of New Mexico, 243; murdered by insurgents, 514; mention of 588
Bent, William, founder of Bent's Fort, 179; married to a Cheyenne woman... 180
Bent Family, historical account of...... 179
Bent's Fort, location of, 178; history of, 179; various names and locations of, 180; Gen. Kearny remained at, for three days, 181; illustration of...... 206
Benton, Senator Thomas H., mention of, 3; the friend of William Gilpin, 146; claims that conquest of New Mexico was secured by James Magoffin, 197, *et seq.;* speech of, at reception in honor of Col. Doniphan and men at St. Louis, 502; the speech in full, 591; biographical sketch of 623
Bernalillo, southern expedition arrives at 230
Bernard, William R., gives account of F. X. Aubrey..................... 362
Bible, Adam, some account of,—"bundling" adventure of................ 555
Biddle, Commodore, assumes command of naval forces in California............ 358
Big Timbers, location of, on Santa Fé Trail 179
Birch, James H., conversation of Col. Doniphan with; 48; characterization of John T. Hughes, 51; visited by Col. Doniphan 55
Blair, Francis Preston, sr., the friend of President Jackson.................. 245
Blair, Francis Preston, jr., mention of, 3; appointed United District Attorney for New Mexico, 243; biographical sketch of, 244, *et seq.;* on the stump in Missouri, 247; statue of, in National Hall of Statuary,—tribute of Gen. W. T. Sherman to..................... 248
Blair, Rev. John, emigrates from Ireland to America......................... 244
Blair, Montgomery, one of the instructors of William Gilpin, at West Point, 145; lawyer in St. Louis.................. 245
Blair, Rev. Samuel, Principal of Fagg's Manor........................... 244
Black flag, The, at the battle of Brazito.. 373
Bledsoe, Capt. Hiram M., gave an order to charge at the battle of Sacramento, 418; some account of,—portrait of, 537; biographical sketch of....539, *et seq.*
Bledsoe, R. D., letter of, to the author... 539
Blummer, Charles, appointed Treasurer of New Mexico..................... 243
Bolton, William, at the battle of Sacramento............................. 419
Boone, George L., obligations of author to, viii; horse of, drowned by Meredith T. Moore, 159; learned tailor trade with George Wilburn, 364; at the battle of Sacramento, 417; made buckskin suits for himself and Moore...... 493

Bowers, Joe, not a real character, 5; portrait of, 6; origin of the song about, 8, *et seq.;* words of song, 10; music to song of............................ 12
Bradford, T., mentioned............... 405
Branham, Manlius, a trader............ 80
Bray, William, of Franklin Company, killed by Capt. Stephenson, 70; another account, 136; still another..... 249
Bray, W. N. V., elected to Congress..... 136
Brazito, Battle of, 88; another account, 370; James Peacock's account of the battle of, 371; Richardson's account of the battle of, 372; George R. Gibson's account of the battle of, 373; the black flag at battle of, 373; plan of the battle of, 376; Col. Doniphan's official report of battle of, 377; battle of, described, 589
Bridger, Fort, headquarters of Mormon army............................. 608
Brown, Clark, publisher *Franklin County Tribune,* obligations of author to, ix; letter of....................... 136
Brown, John, condemned at Harper's Ferry............................ 58
Brown, William, journey of, down the Rio Grande....................... 380
Bryant, William Cullen, compares Col. Doniphan to Xenophon............. 438
Buel, Col. James T., at the battle of Independence........................ 57
Buffalo, The, numbers of, to be seen from Pawnee Rock, 140; herds of, seen by the "Army of the West," 161; Dr. Josiah Gregg first to notice the decrease of, 170; soldiers hunt on the Arkansas 171
Buffalo chips, used for fuel by the "Army of the West"................ 158
Burch, John C., member of Congress from California.......................... 364
Burgwin, Captain, mentioned, 74; also at 78; killed Navajos, 80; sent to overhaul the traders, 139; mentioned, 160; rejoined "Army of the West," 179; in southern expedition, 221; sent to Valverde, 270; marched to Albuquerque, 273; set out with Gen. Kearny for California, 317; killed at Taos, 516; buried at Fort Leavenworth............................ 517
Burr, Miss Mary E., mentioned......... 58
Butler, Adjutant G. M., died Nov. 26, 1846, 85; died at Cuvero.........271, 363
Burton, Lieutenant-Colonel, command of, to garrison Santa Barbara........... 358
Burrows, Captain, defeats Californians at Salinas........................... 351
Burnett, Peter H., Governor of California, 279

C.

Caballada, De Mucho, signed treaty with the Navajos...................... 307
Cabeza de Vaca, remarkable adventures of,—not established that he was in New Mexico........................... 211
Caldwell, Thomas, interpreter, starts for Santa Fé and Independence, 89; mention of, 91; at battle of Brazito....... 373
California, emigrants to, in 1849, addressed by Major Gilpin, 151; Commodore Stockton's express stating conditions in........................... 263

INDEX. 653

California Rangers, raised and disbanded, 265
Campaign in New Mexico with Colonel Doniphan, by Edwards, referred to... 361
Campaign in Mexico with Colonel Doniphan, by Wislizenus, referred to...... 490
Campbell, Major John P., has cattle on the Mora, 77; mention of, 96; embargo laid on operations of,—left Chihuahua for U. S., 107; army contractor (with Thompson), 260; mentioned, 405; starts home from Chihuahua,—biography of............................ 451
Canadian, The, descended by the Santa Fé Trace Battalion................. 150
Cannon, that of the Texans secured by Gen. Kearny...................... 209
Cannon, pictures of those at Jefferson City, 542
Carpenter, Mary Lucinda, marriage of, to John T. Hughes.................. 51
Carpenter, Noah Paley, mention of...... 51
Carpenter, Thomas Dudley, mention of.. 51
Carrillo, J. A., one of the Commissioners to settle terms..................... 349
Carson, Christopher, mentioned, 3; biography of, 262, *et seq.*; met by Gen. Kearny,—ordered to return to California, 320; in the country of the Apaches.............................. 329
Carson, N., buried near Pawnee Rock... 165
Carthage, Battle of.................. 54
Castro, Gen., proclamation of, to the Californians............................. 342
Centropolis, city in Missouri at the mouth of the Kansas so designated by William Gilpin............................... 146
Chavez, Angel, interpreter for Major Gilpin.................................. 299
Chavez, Bonifacio, stepson of Dr. Henry Connelly............................. 281
Chavez, Mrs. Dolores Perea, marriage of, to Dr. Henry Connelly............. 281
Chavez, Don Antonio José, murderers of, brought to justice, 146; robbed and murdered............................. 160
Chavez, Don, a friend to the Americans.. 285
Chavez, Francisco, sheep of, stolen by Armijo............................... 195
Chavez, family of, lived at Peralta...... 233
Chapin, Mr. ——, discharged at the Presidio............................. 96
Cheyennes, The, legends of, concerning Pawnee Rock, 163; battle with Pawnees at Pawnee Rock, 172; sometimes wintered at the Big Timbers, 180; woman of, married to William Bent, 180, 181; on the war-path in 1857, 603; battle with, at Plum Creek...... 604
Chihuahua Rangers, organization of, 365, *et seq.*
Chihuahua, City of, in possession of the Americans........................... 444
Chorn, James, mentioned, 61; one of captors of son of Salezar................ 193
Chouteau, Lieut. Edmond F., sent to bring in trains of Harmony & Poras, 99; pays lady $5 damages, 110; supported Captain Reid at Sacramento... 411
Chronicles of the Builders of the Commonwealth, by Bancroft, quoted.......... 147
Cimarron, The, main road to Santa Fé followed in 1846.................... 171
Cimarron Peak, height of............. 185

Clark, Champ, obligations of the author to, x; on Joe Bowers................ 9
Clark, John, death of, at El Paso.....97, 392
Clark, Major Meriwether Lewis, sent for by Colonel Doniphan, 85; presents the camp guidons, 97; ordered to not proceed with artillery, 98; sketch of,—in southern expedition, 221; secures black flag carried by Mexicans at Brazito, 375; arrived with artillery at El Paso, 395; artillery of, at battle of Sacramento, 409, *et seq.;* official report of, on battle of Sacramento, 433; to provide transportation for his batteries, 490; Roster of Battalion of.... 573
Clarkin, ——, found sleeping at his post, 391
Clarkin, C., mentioned................ 405
Clay, Cassius M., one of guard of the White House in 1861................ 152
Clay, Col. E. F., in battles at Paintsville, Ky., in Civil War.................. vii
Clay County, Mo., organized in 1822, 23; sources of early population of, 23, *et seq.;* Roster of Company of......... 543
Clemens, S. L., (Mark Twain,) could not have written the Joe Bowers Song.... 9
Coco-Maricopas, some account of....... 330
Code, the Kearny, of New Mexico, preparation of, 65; source of 587
Cogburn, Green B., mare of, used for food, 296; dead mare of, eaten by Indians.. 555
College, The Log, founded by the Blair Family............................... 244
College, The William Jewell, mentioned, 52; further mention of.............. 135
Collins, James L., interpreter,—sketch of, 91; interpreter to Col. Doniphan, 99; acted as spy, 103; started from Chihuahua to Saltillo with express, 108; with Kirker's scouting party, 400; difficulty of, with James Kirker, 416; reckless charge of, at battle of Sacramento, 418; carried letter of Col. Doniphan to Gen. Wool, 455; resident of New Mexico... 590
Collins, Captain John C., obligations of author to........................... vii
Colorado, The Rio, head branch of the Canadian........................... 186
Colorado, William Gilpin Governor of... 152
Colston, Edward, Second Lieutenant Santa Fé Trace Battalion........... 149
Comanches, The, mentioned, 73; fought by Santa Fé Trace Battalion, 151; infested the Santa Fé Trail............ 522
Commerce of the Prairies, by Dr. Josiah Gregg, referred to, 144, 157, 162, 168, 169 170, 389
Company F, (Cole County,) identification of members of, 555; Roster of Company of.............................. 553
Company F, Roster of Officers of, (by typographical error, omitted from head of Roster of the Company at page 553.)
1. M. M. Parsons............Captain.
1. Richard A. Wells.........1st Lieut.
2. George B. Winston........2d Lieut.
1. George Pope Gordon.......2d Lieut.
1. Fountain McKenzie.......1st Sgt.
2. William W. Bolton......Sgt.
3. Robert A. Raphael.......Sgt.
4. Absalom Hughes........Sgt.
1. William Rogers..........Corp.
2. James H. McKenzie......Corp.

3. G. Burr Gordon..........Corp.
4. Thomas L. Anderson......Corp.
1. James Henley............Farrier.
Conklin, Santiago, interpreter for Major Gilpin.................................... 299
Conley, Constantine, carried lists of relatives in the Civil War............... 278
Connelly, family of, various forms of names of members of,—origin of, in America, 276, et seq.; members of, fought in the American Revolution... 278
Connelly, Miss Gertrude, daughter of Peter..................................... 280
Connelly, Captain Henry, in the Revolution, in North Carolina and Virginia, —settled in Kentucky,—descendants number many...................... 278
Connelly, Dr. Henry, mentioned, 3; partner of E. J. Glasgow, 100; returned from effort to redeem James Magoffin, 107; mentioned, 139; Amos Marney a freighter for, 142; visited Gen. Kearny at the instance of Gov. Armijo with Captain Cooke, 183; biographical sketch of, 276, et seq.; born in Kentucky,—portrait of, 277; engaged in mercantile business in New Mexico, 281; instrumental in saving New Mexico to the Union in Civil War,—appointed Governor of New Mexico by President Lincoln,— fought for the Union in the Civil War,—a pioneer of a family of pioneers,—a patriot, made himself a great name,—death of, 282; goes to El Paso,—arrested by Mexicans 365; sent to Parral to invite Gov. Trias back to Chihuahua, 450; spent winter at Fort Towson.............. 452
Connelly, John Donaldson, probable birthplace of,—in the War of the Revolution,—moved to Kentucky,—married Frances Brent,—father of Dr. Henry Connelly..................... 279
Connelly, Miss Judith Wakefield, daughter of Peter........................... 280
Connelly, Joseph, son of Dr. Henry..... 280
Connelly, Henry, son of Peter......... 280
Connelly, Peter, obligations of the author to, ix; portrait of Dr. Henry Connelly made from photograph in possession of, 277; son of Dr. Henry,—biographical sketch of...................... 280
Connelly, Sanford Ramey, birthplace of,—was in the War of the Revolution, —moved to Kentucky,—married a Miss Edwards..................... 279
Connelley, Miss Edith, music to Joe Bowers song arranged by............ 12
Conde, Gen. Garcia, one of the Mexican commanders at the battle of Sacramento............................ 408
Conquest of New Mexico and California, by Philip St. George Cooke, referred to, 183
Conron, Col. A. H., one of party of Capt. Parsons murdered by Mexicans....... 137
Cook, ——, shot by accident........... 74
Cooke, Capt. Philip St. George, mentioned, 74; disarmed the Texans, 143; sent by Gen. Kearny to Santa Fé,— arrived there, and met Gov. Armijo,— returned,—conclusions of, 183, 184; general remarks upon the expedition to conquer New Mexico, 186, 187; biography of,—to conduct the Mormon Battalion, 264; marched to California, 317; opening roads for Gen. Kearny's march, 322; arrival of. in California, 352; some account of his march, 353; found faithful Indian................ 354
Cooper, A., killed in insurrection....... 514
Cooper, Benjamin, builder of Cooper's Fort.................................. 164
Cooper's Fort, the Gregg family inmates of.................................... 163
Cooper, J., mentioned................ 405
Copper Mines, The, account of.......... 324
Coronado, expedition of............... 211
Cottonwood, The, arrival of the "Army of the West" at................... 158
Council Grove, historical sketch of...... 157
Coues, Dr. Elliott, edition of the Expedition of Zebulon Montgomery Pike prepared by, referred to, 143; tribute of, to map made by Dr. Josiah Gregg.. 170
Covero, (Cuvarro and Cuvaro,) Americans return to, from Navajo Expedition............................. 295
Cow Creek, Col. Doniphan at,—Chavez murdered at........................ 160
Cox, A., of Company C, died........... 93
Cox, Jesse, moved to Illinois and to Missouri,—inmate of Cooper's Fort...... 164
Cox's Bottom, settlers of, mostly Tennesseans............................ 164
Crenshaw, John T., appointed Sergt.- Major........................91, 392
Crittenden, Senator John J., mentioned.. 135
Culver, R., killed in insurrection........ 514
Cunningham, Mrs. ——, delivers address to Clay County Company............ 137
Cunningham, Watt, crossed the Plains... 364
Curry, Dr. W. A., obligations of author to, ix
Cutler's History of Kansas, known as the Kansas "Herd Book"............... 157

D.

Dale, Miss Paulina, mentioned......... 51
Dale, Timothy Redding, mentioned..... 52
Dallan, Richard, appointed Marshal of New Mexico........................ 243
Dalton, Miss Mary Louise, obligations of author to, ix; furnished the author with incident of Dr. Gregg and the clock.............................. 176
"D—mn a mule, anyhow," portrait of, 471; circumstances of.............. 472
Davy, Cornelius, Peter Connelly married daughter of....................... 280
De Armond, General, Adjutant-General of Missouri, obligations of author to... viii
DeCamp, Surgeon, to be left at Santa Fé, 237
DeCourcy, Lieut. James A., mentioned, 66, 72, 85; sent through the mountains to Taos, 179; had his men transport flour in their clothing, 180; returns from Taos with prisoners, 187; in southern expedition, 222; in Navajo Expedition, 288, 303; returned to Covero, 309; some account of,—appointed Adjutant, 363; effort of, to deprive Odon Guitar of the leathern case in which was carried the rosters of the Mexican army, 408; drunk, and halted the charge at battle of Sacramento, 415; insane action of, at battle of Sacramento................... 418

INDEX. 655

Delawares, six of, with Kit Carson, 320; employed to kill Apaches, 330; with James Kirker...................... 388
Deserters, six of, at Santa Fé.......... 217
Diamond Springs, "Army of the West" at, 157
Diary, that of John T. Hughes....60, et seq.
Dick, one of the slaves of Dr. Josiah Gregg............................. 171
Dickerson, Mrs. Julia Pratt, marriage of, to William Gilpin.................. 152
Dodge, Henry S., appointed Treasurer of Santa Fé......................... 220
Doniphan, Colonel Alexander William, biography of, 15, et seq.; born in Mason county, Ky., July 9, 1808, 15; portrait of, 16; origin of the family name of, —a typical Celt, 18; attended college at Augusta, Ky., 20; influences that affected his life, 21; licensed to practice law,—came to Missouri in 1830,—settled at Lexington,—moved to Liberty in 1833, 22; retained in famous law suits, 25; oratory of, 26; attorney in the famous "Harper case," 27; a Whig in politics, 28; his great speech in the "Harper case,"—ovation to, —marriage to Elizabeth Jane Thornton, 29; description and portrait of monument to, 30; volunteers as private in Clay County Company,—elected Colonel First Missouri Mounted Volunteers, 32; ordered into Navajo country,—invasion of Chihuahua,—Expedition of, defined,—distance marched in Expedition of, 33; member of Peace Congress,—removed to St. Louis,—location of residence and offices in St. Louis,—partner of,—removed to Richmond, Mo., 34; character of, 36; tribute of D. R. Atchison to, 37; noble appearance of,—President Lincoln's tribute to, 39; urged for United States Senator, 52; prevented invasion of North Missouri by Col. John T. Hughes, 55; at Santa Fé, 63; left as Governor of New Mexico by Gen. Kearny, 65; mention of, 76; departs for Cebolleta, 78; mentioned, 79; fixes rendezvous at "Ruins of Valverde,"—ordered Maj. Clark to report with artillery from Santa Fé, 85; begins march on Jornada del Muerto, 86; moved camp below Table Mountain, 87; enters El Paso, 88; to push on to Chihuahua, 89; collects ammunition at El Paso,—repairs Mexican mills, 90; secured money for support of his army from Samuel C. Owens, — prohibits gambling at El Paso, 92; visited by priests, —receives letter from Major Clark, 93; prohibits horse-racing, 95; order of march of army of from El Paso,—sets out from El Paso for Chihuahua, 97; organizes the traders into a battalion, —advised to arrest Ortiz, 98; issues proclamation at Chihuahua, 107; refuses offer of Mexicans, 108; leaves Chihuahua, 109; portrait of, 112; Memoir of, 123; directed to march upon Chihuahua, 130; elected Colonel First Regiment,—to command the Expedition in case of the death of Gen. Kearny, 133; brought up the rear of Gen. Kearny's march across the Plains, 144; troops of, in need of food, 159; came up with the advance at Cow Creek, 160; junction formed with Gen. Kearny, 166; reproves his men for wasting ammunition, 189; guard of, captured son of Salezar, 192; acting Governor of New Mexico,—superintends construction of Fort Marcy,— with Willard P. Hall, completes "Organic Laws and Constitution" of New Mexico, 238; official copy of order directing him to report to Gen. Wool,— notifies Willard P. Hall of his election to Congress, 251; in active preparation for march to Chihuahua, 253; disposition of troops made by, 261; holds council with Indian tribes,—Military Governor of New Mexico, 265; directed to delay his march to join Gen. Wool and to march against the Navajo Indians,—order in full, 266; determines to execute the order with haste,—arrangements for invading Indian country,—no means to sustain his army, 267; marched to Cuvarro, 270; route of, on march to country of Navajos, 271; expedition of, into the Navajo country, 300, et seq.; sends troops to Valverde to protect the traders, 302; receives express from Major Gilpin,— march of, on Navajo expedition, 303; treaty of, with the Navajos, 307; given blankets by the Navajos, 308; marched from Ojo Oso to Zuni, 309; makes treaty with the Zunis, 311; joins Major Gilpin at Laguna,—discovers ancient city, 313; concentrates his forces at Valverde, 314; orders Colonel Price to send him artillery,— reports of his Navajo campaign, 360; fights battle of Brazito, 372, et seq.; marches from Brazito to El Paso, 379; enters El Paso, 382; humane rule of, at El Paso, 383; action of, on false alarm at El Paso,—borrowed money from traders,—had Mexican mills repaired and wheat ground, 386; prohibits gambling at El Paso, 387; awaits artillery at El Paso, 395; decides to march deeper into Mexico,—leaves El Paso, 396; organized the Traders' Battalion, 397; horrors of the march, 401; army of, has terrible experience with prairie-fire, 404; calls council of officers, 406; interviews Ortiz night before battle of Sacramento, 406; number of men he had at battle of Sacramento,—order of march on day of battle,—eagle's flight over and among the troops, 407; arrangement of his men at the battle of Sacramento, 409; loss of, at battle of Sacramento, 416; abrupt reply of, to the Mexicans at Sacramento, 417; conversation with Ortiz about battle of Sacramento, 420; sends troops to occupy Chihuahua, 421; enters Chihuahua, 422; official report of, on battle of Sacramento, 423; transmits reports of officers on battle of Sacramento, 427; exclamation of, as his men charged at battle of Sacramento, 427; praised by the Secretary of War, 437; compared to Xenophon by William Cullen Bryant, 438; proclamation of, to citizens of Chihuahua, 444; writes Major Ryland, 450; writes Gen. Wool for orders, 454; determines to go to Saltillo, 463; refuses to advance farther into Mexico, 464; says he is going home to his wife,— evacuates Chihuahua, 466; communication of Gen. Wool to, at Parras, 481; complimentary order of Gen. Wool, 482; army of, reviewed by Gen. Wool, 482; sought by Lem White, who wanted to give him a drink of whisky,

485; takes his sick to mouth of the Rio Grande, 490; embarks his men on the Republic, 492; arrives at New Orleans, 493; reception of, at St. Louis, 496, *et seq.;* crowned with wreath at Independence, 498; expedition of, described, 507; portrait of, 526; interview with Max Frost, 584, *et seq.;* marches against the Navajos, 588; part taken by, in making the "Kearny Code," 587; expedition of, summed up, 591; expedition of, reviewed by Major Gilpin...........................592, *et seq.*
Doniphan, A. W., jr., tragic fate of...... vii
Doniphan, George, killed at battle of Brandywine.......................... 19
Doniphan, Joseph, with Washington at Yorktown,—moved to Kentucky prior to 1779; died in 1813................. 19
Doniphan's Expedition, reprint of the account of, by John T. Hughes.....129, *et seq.*
Doran, Patrick, Peter Connelly marries daughter of....................... 280
Douglas, Stephen A., carried Missouri in 1860............................. 53
Douglas, Judge Walter B., obligations of author to......................... ix
Dozier, James I., instructor of Dr. Henry Connelly.......................... 279
Drake, Charles D., U. S. Senator from Missouri.......................... 247
Draper, Lyman C., interview of, with General Jonathan Ramsay......641, *et seq.*
Duncan, William, died near Bent's Fort, 181
Dunlap, Robert, had his cap shot away by cannon-shot at battle of Sacramento............................ 417
Dyer, John C., died................. 94
Dyer, W. F., did not write Constitution for Nebraska Territory............. 151
Dyer, Mr., died at El Paso............ 392

E.

Eagle, The American, pictured on the setting sun on the Great Plains in 1846, 154; flight of one, over and among the American troops on the day of the battle of Sacramento................. 407
Early Western Travels, edited by Dr. R. G. Thwaites, referred to, 144, 157, 168, 389
Easton, Colonel, commander of "Saint Louis Legion," 131; raised a battalion of troops........................ 523
Edgar, Tobe, punishes Indian warrior... 603
Edmonson, Major Benjamin G., arrival of, at Santa Fé, 74; chosen Major of Second Regiment, 257; detachment of, attacked at Red River Cañon by Indians, 519; marches to Las Vegas.... 521
Edwards, Frank S., describes battle of Sacramento....................... 424
Edwards, Governor John E., requisition upon, for troops, 131; visits Gilpin to induce him to raise battalion to protect Santa Fé Trail.................... 148
El Paso, entered by Col. Doniphan, 88; note upon, 379; entered by Col. Doniphan, 382; conduct of American troops at, 383; described to the War Department by John T. Hughes, 392; Col. Doniphan remained forty-two days at, 395; capture of, by the Americans.... 590
El Pozo, battle at.................... 476

Emory, Lieut. W. H., work of, referred to, 143; account of American occupancy of Las Vegas, 191; meets party of Californians, 332; carries dispatches to Washington for Gen. Kearny......................... 352

F.

F, Company of, Roster of Officers, (omitted by typographical error from head of Roster of the Company at page 553.)
1. M. M. Parsons............Captain.
1. Richard A. Wells.........1st Lieut.
1. George Pope Gordon......2d Lieut.
2. George B. Winston........2d Lieut.
1. Fountain McKenzie.......1st Sgt.
2. William Bolton...........Sgt.
3. Robert A. Raphael........Sgt.
4. Absalom Hughes..........Sgt.
1. William Rogers..........Corp.
2. James H. McKenzie.......Corp.
3. G. Burr Gordon..........Corp.
4. Thomas L. Anderson......Corp.
1. James Henley............Farrier.
Fagg, Thomas J. C., obligations of author to, ix; on origin of the Joe Bowers song........................... 9
Fagg's Manor, Rev. Samuel Blair the Principal of.................... 244
Fannin, Col., of Texas, murdered by Mexicans............................ 130
Fant, Hamilton, clerk to G. Pope Gordon, 364
Ferguson, ——, of Company D, died.... 110
Ferry, Fish's, on the Kansas river at the mouth of the Wakarusa,—Gen. Kearny and army crossed at............... 142
Finley, James M., died at El Paso Jan. 21, 1847......................94, 392
Fire, terrible one threatens the American army............................. 405
Fish, Paschal, Shawnee Indian,—owned Fish's Ferry over the Kansas river,—lived near present town of Eudora.... 142
Fish's Ferry, on the Kansas river at the mouth of the Wakarusa,—owned by Paschal Fish, a Shawnee Indian,—Gen. Kearny and army crossed at......... 142
Fischer, Captain Woldemar, Roster of Artillery Company of............... 577
Fitzpatrick, the Mountaineer, met on the Arkansas, 176; guide brought express to Santa Fé, 262; sent to Fort Leavenworth with Carson's express......... 322
Flag, The black, at battle of Brazito.... 373
Fleming, J. B., wounded at the battle of Sacramento..................... 416
Fleming, R. W., mentioned, 64,—and others, adventure of............... 184
Flores, revolution of, in California...... 350
Folque, L., killed in insurrection........ 514
Forsythe, Thomas, mentioned, 94; trapper and hunter, in charge of hunters for Gen. Kearny's army,—estimate of number of buffalo to be seen from Pawnee Rock, 140; fought at battle of Brazito,—wounded Col. Ponce de Leon, 374; mentioned, 405; returns home with Major John P. Campbell......... 451
Fort Bent, distance of, from Independence, 147; Santa Fé Trace Battalion at, 150
Fort Leavenworth, mentioned, 76; history of, 131; mentioned.............. 141
Fort Lyon, successor to Fort Bent, 180; Kit Carson died at................ 264

INDEX. 657

Fort Mann, location of, 149, 151; Santa Fé Trace Battalion stationed at...... 150
Fort Marcy, at Santa Fé, when erected and named, 237; designed by Lieut. Gilmer and L. A. MacLean......... 245
Fort Towson, location of............. 280
Fort Wise, a successor to Fort Bent.... 180
Forty-niners, five thousand of, addressed by Major Gilpin................... 151
Foster, William, died................ 86
Franklin, John, mentioned........... 74
Fray Cristobal, note concerning....... 367
Frazier, ——, wagoner............... 65
Frémont, John Charles, reported as Governor of California, 76; Gilpin a member of the party of, 147; sketch of, 341; orders a cessation of hostilities, 349; trial of, at Washington.............. 358
Frost, Max, obligations of author to, viii; interview of, with Colonel Doniphan, 584, *et seq.*
Fugate, Francis, died near Bent's Fort.. 181

G.

Galesteo, mentioned, 66, 75; account of, 217; duties for fixed for collection.... 220
Gallatin, Albert, appointed Silas Bent to office........................... 179
Gamble, Hamilton R., Governor of Provisional Government of Missouri...54, 241
Gambling, engaged in at El Paso, 90; prohibited by Col. Doniphan........ 92
Garcia, José suspended as Collector at Santa Fé......................... 220
Garcia, Nicholas, name of the guerrilla executed by the Texans............. 490
Garcia, Savoietta, signed treaty with the Navajos.......................... 307
Garrard, Lewis H., at Fort Bent....... 180
Gazetteer of Missouri, Campbell's, referred to............................... 163
Gentry, trader, train of............... 81
Gentry, Major Richard, in Florida war.. 250
Gibson, Lieut. George R., in Chihuahua Rangers, 366; describes battle of Brazito, 372; description of the battle of Sacramento.................... 440
Giddings, Captain, mentioned......... 75
Gila, The, note concerning............ 326
Gillespie, Captain, wounded in battle with Californians, 335; capitulates, and returns to San Pedro................. 343
Gilmer, Lieut., and others, overtake Gen. Kearny at Las Vegas............... 191
Gilpin, Henry, brother to Major William 145
Gilpin, Major William, mentioned, 3; left in command at Galesteo,—candidate for Lieut.-Colonel,—men not in favor of, because he was West-Pointer, 70; defeated for Lieut.-Colonel,—goes to Abiquiu, 72; mentioned, 78, 84; express from, 86; sent to the Presidio, 89; elected Major First Regiment, 133; biography of, 144, *et seq.*; portrait of, 145; wrote Constitution for Nebraska Territory,—addressed five thousand Forty-niners at site of Lawrence, Kan., 151; in southern expedition, 222; left with a detachment at Del Gardo, 236; defeated for Lieut.-Colonel,—ordered to Abiquiu, 250; brought in Utahs,
251; directed to march into the Navajo country, 267; sends his wagons to Abiquiu, 268; recovered horses and mules from Navajos, 297; sent to Abiquiu, 298; marches against the Navajos, 299; expedition of, into Navajo country, 300, *et seq.*; signed treaty with Navajos, 307; marches for the Del Norte, 313; character of march of, 314; sent to Presidio, 384; position of, at battle of Sacramento, 410; report on battle of Sacramento, 428; mentioned in Col. Doniphan's official report, 436; urges further invasion of Mexico, 464; to provide transportation for his battalion, 490; marches against Navajos, 588; address of, delivered at Jefferson City, Aug. 10, 1847.........592, *et seq.*
Gilpintown, location of............... 146
Glasgow, Edward J., obligations of author to, ix; some account of, 79; letter of, to the author, about James L. Collins, 91; elected Captain, 98, 99; portrait of, 100; describes battle of Sacramento, 104; makes map for author, 105; letter of, to the author, 139; describes manner of conducting the business of himself and Dr. Henry Connelly, 280; writes account of Traders' Battalion and battle of Sacramento,—made Captain of Company of Traders, 398; interviewed Col. Doniphan during battle of Sacramento, 420; mentioned in Major M. L. Clark's report of the battle of Sacramento, 435; charged on Mexicans at Sacramento, 440; portrait of,—biographical sketch of.. 645
Globe-Democrat, The St. Louis, obligations of the author to.................... x
Gordon, John C., first lessee of Missouri penitentiary,—settled at Santa Clara, California........................ 364
Gordon, G. Pope, arrived at Santa Fé, 93; buys oxen for the army, 98; appointed Assistant Quartermaster, 264; biographical sketch of, 364; rejoined company at El Paso, 392; action of, at battle of Sacramento,........... 414
Gordon, William, wounded at battle of Sacramento...................416, 419
Graham, the Scotchman, informer, at El Paso.............................. 88
Gray, John, discharged, and sells coat to Odon Guitar...................... 380
Grazing, detachments for, organized.... 207
Green, James A., defeated for U. S. Senator............................... 54
Gregg, David, sr., and family, inmates of Cooper's Fort..................... 163
Gregg, David, son of Harmon, date of birth of,—murdered by Col. Charles R. Jennison, 165; marriage of, 166; written to by Dr. Josiah Gregg.......... 171
Gregg, Harmon, married Susannah Smelser,—settled in Overton county, Tenn., —moved to Illinois,—moved to Missouri Territory,—he and family inmates of Cooper's Fort, 163; father of Dr. Josiah Gregg,—was a wheelwright, 165; dates of birth and marriage of,—moved to Jackson county, Mo., in 1825....................... 166
Gregg, Jacob, (the Senior,) moved to Cane Creek, N. C....................... 163
Gregg, Jacob, (son of Harmon,) date of birth of, 165; marriage of, 166; notice of,—took census for the organization

of Jackson county,—tells how location of Independence was settled.......... 167
Gregg, John, date of birth of, 165; marriage of, 166; living near Shreveport, La., 171; letter of, to Philip Allan Hardwicke on death of Dr. Josiah Gregg........................... 174
Gregg, Dr. Josiah, mentioned, 3; works of, referred to, 144; his description of Pawnee Rock referred to,—portrait of, —biographical sketch of, 162, *et seq.;* date of birth of, 165; never married, 166; home of, in Jackson county, Mo., —a "lost author,"—identification of, —no knowledge of family of, published before, 167; a physician and mathematician, 169; as a writer and explorer, character of, 170; merchant,—intrepidity of,—lived with his brother John at Shreveport, La.,—letter of, to Philip Allan Hardwicke, requesting his slaves to be sent to him,—his description of Louisiana, 171; correspondent for American newspapers in Mexican War, —visited Col. Doniphan at Chihuahua, —incident of the red umbrella on the march from Chihuahua, 172; went to California in 1849,—went on exploring expedition,—left his property and MS. of *Rovings Abroad* with Jesse Sutton,— Philip Allan Hardwicke to meet in California, 173; builds clock for priest at Santa Fé, 176; describes the Moquis, 313; his description of Chihuahua.... 448
Gregg, L. L., mentioned............... 176
Gregg, Margaret, date of birth of, 165; marriage of....................... 166
Gregg, Miss Patsy, capture of, by Sac-and-Fox Indians.................... 164
Gregg, Polly, date of birth of,—marriage of............................ 166
Gregg, Susan, dates of birth and marriage of......................... 166
Gregg, William, ancestor of Gregg family in America...................... 163
Gregg, William, son of Jacob,—inmate of Cooper's Fort, 163,—married daughter of Jesse Cox,—moved to Missouri, —killed by Indians.................. 164
Gregg, Captain William H., obligations of the author to..................... viii
Gregg Family, The, founding of, in America, 162, *et seq.;* partly of German blood, 163; may have aided in building Cooper's Fort, 164; old Bible of, 165; pioneers across the continent........ 168
Grier, Lieut., sent in pursuit of the Navajos............................. 272
Grigsby, Captain, raises "Bear Flag" in California....................... 341
Griffith, Captain John C., of Santa Fé Trace Battalion.................... 149
Guard, Missouri State, mentioned....... 56
Guerrilla Mexican, executed by Texan Rangers,—Odon Guitar's letter concerning execution of, 487; illustration representing execution of, 489; Nicholas Garcia, name of............ 490
Guitar, General Odon, obligations of author, viii; statement to author concerning subsistence train of Gen. Kearny's army, 140; adventure of, on the Plains,—thigh broken,—sent to Fort Leavenworth,—crossed at Fish's Ferry, —got a meal there, 143; account of expedition down the Rio Grande, 380;
guarded Ortiz night before the battle of Sacramento, 406; at battle of Sacramento captured rosters of the Mexican army, 408; at battle of El Pozo, 477; account of execution of Mexican guerrilla by Texan Rangers, 487; portrait of,—biography of.................. 644
Gulley, Ashley G., Second Lieut., Santa Fé Trace Battalion.................. 149
Gunter, W. C., mentioned.............. 64
Gwyn, ——, died..................... 285

H.

Habernicht, Herman, notice of......... 380
Hackley, G. J., (written "Jordan,") died. 94; died at El Paso................ 392
Hale, J., furnished identification of Lafayette County Company, 528, 537, 538, 539
Hall, Mrs. Ella Walton................ 134
Hall, Willard P., mentioned, 3; aids in the preparation of the New-Mexican Code, 65; adventure of, 184; biographical sketch of, 238, *et seq.;* notified by Col. Doniphan of his election to Congress, 251; offers Gen. Kearny his horse, 351; portrait of, 582; part borne in making Kearny Code............. 587
Halleck, Gen. H. M., mentioned........ 55
Ham's Fort, arrival of Tenth Infantry at, 609
Hammond, Lieut., killed in battle with Californians....................... 334
Hanks, Eph, a Mormon Danite aids Morehead............................ 618
Hardwicke, Mrs. Margaret Gregg, funeral-card of........................... 163
Hardwicke, Philip Allan, letter of Dr. Josiah Gregg to, 171; went to California in 1850,—died on return trip, 173; letter of, to his family, about Dr. Josiah Gregg.................... 174
Hardy, Major, forces of, garrison San Francisco.......................... 358
Harfield, W., killed in insurrection..... 514
Harmon, Hannah, mentioned.......... 136
Harmony, Manuel X., a Spaniard, 99; desired to escape from the Americans at El Paso, 398; a trader and merchant............................ 477
Harmony, P., Nephews & Co., some account of............................ 99
Harney, General, ordered to Utah, 615; called "the Great Wasp" by the Sioux, 617
Harper, John H., married Fannie Owens, 26; murdered Meredith,—trial of, 27, *et seq.*
Harte, Bret, on pliocene skull.......... 8
Harvey, Charles M., obligations of author to................................ ix
Harwood, W., killed in insurrection..... 514
Hawthorne, Nathaniel, tutor of William Gilpin............................ 145
Hays, Colonel Upton, mentioned...... 57
Head, M., killed in insurrection........ 514
Henderson, A., mentioned............. 405
Hendley, Captain, takes possession of Las Vegas, 516; killed,—remains of, brought to Richmond, Mo........... 517
Henkle, Sergt. Thomas, defended himself by throwing stones, at the battle of Sacramento........................ 420
Henkey, W., wounded at battle of Sacramento............................. 416

INDEX. 659

Heredia, Gen. José A., commanded the Mexican troops at the battle of Sacramento.......................... 408
Herkins, I., court-martial to try, 64; dismissed the service................. 208
Herman, C., mentioned............... 405
Hicklin, Lieut., in command of Capt. Reid's Company at battle of Sacramento........................... 411
Hinton, Lieut. John, arrives at Santa Fé, 93; mentioned, 94; sent to aid Captain Weightman, 95; marched to Zuni, 309; elected Lieutenant, 364; rejoined company at El Paso................ 392
History of Battery "A" of St. Louis, by Valentine Mott Porter, referred to.... 362
History of California, by H. H. Bancroft, referred to....................... 359
History of Jackson County, Missouri, referred to........................... 167
History of Middle Tennessee, by A. W. Putnam, referred to................ 164
History of the Pacific States, by H. H. Bancroft, referred to..................... 200
History of Saint Louis City and County, by J. Thomas Scharf, referred to...... 496
Hitchcock, E. A., Brevet-Colonel U. S. A., mentioned................149, 150, 151
Holston, Stephen, captured at Culpeper, Va., by Indians, before the Revolution, 641
Holzscheiter, Paul, Captain Company D, Santa Fé Trace Battalion.......... 150
Hooper, William H., Secretary of Utah Territory........................ 608
Hopkins, E. N., obligations of author to, x
Hopper, C. T., death of, 85; died at Covero........................... 309
Hopper, Edmond, died................ 77
Horine, Captain, Company of, near Las Vegas............................ 520
Howard, Major, sent by Gen. Kearny to Santa Fé to ascertain disposition of affairs, 169; report of.............. 170
Howard, George T., written to by Gen. Kearny............................ 139
Houghton, Joel, appointed Judge of the Superior Court of New Mexico..... 243
Houke, S., trader, loses cattle by the Apaches......................... 98
Hudson, ——, released from prison, 88; Col. Doniphan released from Mexican prison............................ 382
Hudson Bay Company, mentioned...... 147
Hudson, Isaac, could not "cast anchor" and was thrown from his mare...... 555
Hudson, Captain Thomas B., mentioned, 66; appointed to command a company to California, 70; mentioned, 74; 85, 90, 91, 93, 94, 96; in southern expedition, 221; resigned as Captain of Laclede Rangers,—recruited California Rangers, 264; position of, at the battle of Sacramento, 410; supported Captain Weightman at battle of Sacramento, 430; Roster of Company of.... 563
Hughes, Sergt. A., had both legs broken at battle of Sacramento............. 416
Hughes, Ab, (probably Sergt. Absalom Hughes,) detailed to go on Navajo expedition........................... 294
Hughes, A. E., drowned in Pawnee Fork, 159
Hughes, Byron Burr, mentioned........ 58

Hughes, C. F., as Q. M. Sergt. had difficulty in getting wagon-trains through the sand-drifts, 399; relieved from further duty with trains............. 402
Hughes, Elizabeth Tarlton, mentioned.. 46
Hughes, Miss Esther Llewellyn, mentioned............................ 59
Hughes, F. C., mentioned............. 405
Hughes, Henry Clay, mentioned....... 59
Hughes, Captain H. H., mentioned, 85; arrives at El Paso, 93; promoted to be Captain,— sent to Cebolleta, 250; sick at Covero, 303; moved to Socorro, 309; re-formed his company at El Paso, 392; actions of, at battle of Sacramento, 414; Roster of Company of................................. 556
Hughes, Miss Inez D., mentioned....... 58
Hughes, James E., mentioned.......... 51
Hughes, John Dudley, mentioned...... 58
Hughes, Colonel John Taylor, mentioned, 3; origin of family of, in America,—biography of, 46, *et seq.;* portrait of, 47; tribute of Colonel Doniphan to,—private in Company C, First Missouri Mounted Volunteers, 48; became the historian of Doniphan's Expedition,—title of book of,—different editions of book of,—book of, published at Cincinnati, 49; photographic reproduction of cover of paper-bound edition of book, 50; lived at Liberty, Mo.,—married Miss Mary Lucinda Carpenter, Aug. 8, 1848,—appointed Receiver of U. S. Land Office at Plattsburg, Mo.,—moved to Plattsburg—manner of conducting his office, 51; a Whig,—elected to Missouri Legislature,—secured establishment of road from Liberty Landing to the Iowa line,—belonged to the Baptist Church,—elected Superintendent of Schools,—favored education of slaves,—property of, 52; published a newspaper,—as Colonel of Militia organized the militia of Clay and other counties, 53; made Colonel in Confederate Army,—at battle of Carthage, at battle of Wilson Creek, 54; foiled in invasion of North Missouri,—at battle of Pea Ridge, 55; movements of, at Pea Ridge,—goes with Price's army to Mississippi,—returned to Missouri to recruit a brigade,—made Brigadier-General,—why he fought the battle of Independence, 56; plans and fights battle of Independence,—killed in battle of Independence,—credit for the victory belongs to him, 57; estate of, involved,—widow and children of, 58; summary of life of,—death of; buried at Independence,—Diary of, 59; sent to aid Captain Weightman, 95; spends night with priest, 96; reprint of work of, 114; reprint of account of Doniphan's Expedition written by, 129, *et seq.;* adventure of, 184; remarks of, on the Mexican character, 187; adventure of, at Peralto, 232; present when Col. Doniphan notified Willard P. Hall of his election to Congress, 251; writes War Department from El Paso, describing the country, 392; went with party to view Mexican forces at Sacramento, 406; wounded at the battle of Sacramento, 416; one of the express to Gen. Wool from Col. Doniphan, 458; the trip described...............459, *et seq.*

Hughes, John Taylor, jr., mentioned.... 59
Hughes, Miss Mary Edna, mentioned.... 58
Hughes, Paley Carpenter, mentioned.... 58
Hughes, Roland, obligations of author to, ix; sketch of life of.............. 58
Hughes, Mrs. Roland, called attention of the author to Diary of Colonel John T. Hughes...................... 60
Hughes, Samuel Swan, mentioned..... 46
Hughes, Stephen, mentioned.......... 46
Hughes, Thomas Edward, mentioned.... 59
Hughes, Tyre, Clifton, mentioned...... 59
Hutchinson, Mr. ——, released from prison, 88; Col. Doniphan releases from Mexican prison.................... 382

I.

Ide, General, raised "Bear Flag,"........ 341
Independence, town of; how site of came to be selected..................... 167
Indians, Pueblo, did not join New-Mexicans to oppose Americans.......... 60
Indian woman, tribe of, left her to die... 602
Infantry, The, of Platte county........ 568
Ingalls, Lieut., arrived with mail for Gen. Kearny........................... 322
Inman, Asa, drowned at Fort Leavenworth........................... 159
Insurgents, those of New Mexico tried and executed...................... 518
Insurrection, one planned in New Mexico, 511
Inyard, Silas, died at Covero.......... 309
Isleta, pueblo of, mentioned........... 271

J.

Jackson, President Andrew, mentioned.. 145
Jackson, Claiborne F., elected Governor of Missouri....................... 53
Jackson, Lieut.-Col. Congreve, candidate, 70; elected Lieut.-Col., 72; mentioned, 85; biography of, 72; had altercation with C. F. Ruff, 159; detailed to attend burial of N. Carson, 164; Company of, lost horses in stampede, 187; ordered to Cebolleta,—elected Lieutenant-Colonel, 250; directed to march into the Navajo country, 267; marched from Santa Fé to Cebolleta,—route of march,—turned back the Pueblos, 284; signed treaty with Navajos, 307; marched to Zuni, 309; actions of, at battle of Sacramento, 411; mentioned in Col. Doniphan's official report of the battle of Sacramento, 436; to provide transportation for his battalion...... 490
Jackson County, Roster of Company of.. 530
Jackson, Captain H., mentioned........ 75
Jackson, Lieutenant S., died, 110; sent forward to halt provision train, 157; rejoined his company at El Paso...... 392
January, Ephraim P., Assistant Surgeon Santa Fé Trace Battalion............. 149
Jennison, Col. Charles R., murdered David Gregg...................... 165
Jett, James, of Company E, died Oct. 29, 1846........................... 93
Jirmia, Mexican, killed in insurrection... 514
Johnson, Waldo P., elected U. S. Senator, 54; elected a member of the Missouri Legislature........................ 363

Johnston, Col. Albert Sidney, at Black's Fork............................ 610
Johnston, Captain, aide to Gen. Kearny, 321; killed in battle with Californians, 334
Jones, (either James or Charles A.,) died Dec. 25, 1846.................... 93
Jones, Jesse, conductor of mails on the Plains, 606; captured by Mormons and never heard of again............ 609
Jones, Thomas, Captain Company B, Santa Fé Trace Battalion............ 150
Jornada del Muerto, illustration of army marching through,—account of crossing over....................... 368
José, Pedro, signed treaty with the Navajos............................ 307
Journal, The Kansas City, obligations of author to........................ x
Journal of William H. Richardson, referred to........................ 365
Juanico, signed the treaty with the Navajos............................ 307
Justiniani, General, one of the Mexican commanders at the battle of Sacramento............................ 408

K.

Kansas City, Mo., Public Library of, contains plan of city of Centropolis as prophesied by William Gilpin........ 146
Kansas River, The, crossed by the "Army of the West" at mouth of the Wakarusa............................ 142
Kansas State Historical Society, The, obligations of the author to.......... ix
Kearny, Col. Henry S., obligations of author to............................ x
Kearny, Gen. Stephen W., the chivalric soldier,—commander of the "Army of the West," 32; entered Santa Fé without firing a gun, Aug. 18, 1846; bribed Spanish spy, 60; enters Santa Fé,—takes up residence in Royal Palace,—raises American flag,—delivers address to Spaniards, 62; the address,—administers oath of office,—takes possession of New Mexico for United States, 63; issues proclamation, 64; interview with Pueblo chief,—abolishes stamped paper,—starts on tour of New Mexico, 65; roster of companies taken on southern tour,—went by Santo Domingo to receive submission of inhabitants, 66; trouble with soldiers about wearing coats, 67; holds council with Apaches, 73; departs from Santa Fé for California, 74; meets express from California, 76; mentioned, 84; disposition of forces of, 130; to command troops in "Army of the West," 131; given discretionary power as to number of troops to be taken in the campaign, 132; named his successor in case of death,—opposed to Gilpin, 133; entire force of "Army of the West," 134; halted the traders on the Arkansas, 139; writes Gov. John E. Edwards from Fish's Ferry, Kansas river, 142; plan of his march across the Plains, 144; unfriendly to Gilpin, 147; said to have desired to turn back from his expedition, 148; precautions taken on his march, 150; troops of, in need of food, 159; formed junction with Col. Doniphan, 166; bridged Pawnee Fork, 167; sends Major Howard to Santa

INDEX. 661

Fé with proposals of peace, 170; receives an express from Fort Bent, 176; captures Mexican spies and liberates them, 177; crossed the Arkansas and entered Mexican territory below Fort Bent, 178; saluted with cannon at Fort Bent, 180; camped near Fort Bent,—proclamation to New-Mexicans, —letter of, to Governor Armijo, 181; informs War Department of conditions in New Mexico, 184; remarks of Captain Cooke upon, 186; takes position on River Mora, 189; appointed Brigadier-General,—forms line of battle to take the Pass,—arrives at Las Vegas, —administers oath of allegiance to officials of Las Vegas, 190; address of, to officers and citizens of Las Vegas,— Mexicans vacate Pass upon the approach of, 191; receives San Miguel into American Union,—camps on the Pecos, 192; allows prisoners to look through his camp and depart, 193; enters Santa Fé,—aided by James Magoffin,—takes possession of New Mexico, 199; takes up residence in Palacio Grande, — selects campingground for his army,—letter of, to Gen. Wool,—issues proclamation taking possession of New Mexico,—letter of, to Department of War, 200; text of address of, to citizens of Santa Fé, 201; administers oath of office to officers of Santa Fé,—form of oath, 202; administers oath to delegations from Pueblos,—army of, not well provisioned,—confidential instructions of War Department to, 203; proclamation of, annexing New Mexico to the United States, 208; secures Gov. Armijo's artillery, 209; sends an express to Washington, 218; abolishes the use of stamped paper, 219; fixes duties for Santa Fé and Galesteo,—appoints civil officers for New Mexico, 220; hears of plans for insurrection,—preparations for expedition down the Rio Grande, 221; departs from Santa Fé on southern expedition, 222; orders troops to put on their coats, 223; portrait of (from old print),—brief biography of, 225; at Santo Domingo, 227; account by Emory of reception at, 228; at San Tome, 234; returns from southern expedition,—arrives at Santa Fé,—report of his tour, 236; appoints officers of New Mexico,—transmits laws of New Mexico to War Department, 243; orders election to fill vacancy, 249; orders Col. Doniphan to report to Gen. Wool,—orders runners sent to Navajos and other tribes, 250; held council with chief of the Apaches,—writes War Department in detail before starting to California,— text of letter,—set out on the 25th of September, 253; sends orders to Sterling Price, 258; meets express from Commodore Stockton,—orders Kit Carson back to California, 263; orders Col. Doniphan to delay his march to join Gen. Wool and to march his regiment into the Navajo country, 266; causes for this change, 267; marches for California, 317; authorizes retaliation against Navajos, 319; meets Kit Carson with express from Monterey, 320; reduces his forces to go on to California,—dispatch of, to War Department, on meeting Kit Carson, 321; inscription of, at grave of Sancho Pedro, 323; description of his trip to California, 325, et seq.; arrives at Warner's Ranch,—writes Commodore Stockton, 333; battle with Californians,—wounded,—report of battle, 334; arrival of, at San Diego,—reports to Department of War, 336, et seq.; orders surgeon to attend other wounded first, 339; in command at San Gabriel, 344; returns to San Diego,— walked 145 miles, 351; sails from San Diego to Monterey, meets Commodore Shubrick,—refuses to organize a civil government,—proclamation of, to people of California, 355; relations of, with Frémont, 357; disposition of forces of, in California,—returns to Fort Leavenworth,—orders Frémont under arrest, —goes to Washington,—trial of Frémont, 358; capture of New Mexico, 586; goes on to California, 588; portrait of,—biographical sketch of, 636; did not attend Princeton............ 638
Kearny, family of,—form of spelling name of....................... 637
Kennerly, Major W. C., owner of the black flag carried by Mexicans at Brazito............................. 375
Kerford & Jenkins, traders, 97, 99; abandon the merchant caravan.......... 398
Kiatanito, signed the treaty with the Navajos.......................... 307
"Kickapoo, Old," famous cannon....... 542
King, James L., Kansas State Librarian, obligations of author to............. ix
King, Mr. ——, of Company B, died.... 110
Kinney, Mrs. R. S., mentioned......... 134
Kiowas, The, sometimes wintered at Big Timbers.......................... 180
Kirker, Captain James, mentioned, 95; brings in six prisoners, 97; sent out to spy, 98; captures Carizal, 99; guide of the expedition, 101; some account of. 102; captures effects of Gen. Heredia, 106; goes on hunting-trip from El Paso, 386; account of, 388; et seq.; scouting party of, 400; at the taking of the hacienda, 405; difficulty of, with James L. Collins, 416; reckless charge of, at battle of Sacramento, 418
Kirkpatrick, A. A., died at Chihuahua, 106; wounded at battle of Sacramento, 416
Koscialowski, Napoleon, Captain Company E, Santa Fé Trace Battalion.... 150
Kraft, Adam, Chief Bugler, Santa Fé Trace Battalion.................... 149
Kribben, Lieut. Christian, fired salute with gun taken at Brazito.......... 95
Kuhlan, William, Q. M. Sergt. Santa Fé Trace Battalion.................. 149
Kuhn, Abraham, Wyandot chief,—perhaps a brother to Josiah Ramsay..... 642

L.

Lack, Berryman, detailed to go on the Navajo expedition.................. 294
Lafayette\County, Roster of Company of, 534; identification of men in........ 537
Lafayette, General, mentioned.......... 145
Lane, Senator James H., guarded the White House in 1861............... 152
Laramie, Fort, founded by William L. Sublette........................... 606

Lard, John D., (perhaps should be Leard,) shot by Marsh, 84; shooting again mentioned..................... 283
Largo, José, signed treaty with Navajos.. 307
Largo, Sarcilla, signed treaty with Navajos............................. 307
Larkin, Lieut., killed................ 521
Lawrence, Kan., five thousand Forty-niners addressed there by William Gilpin.... 151
Las Vegas, surrender of, to Gen. Kearny,—address of Gen. Kearny at........ 191
Lawson, L. M., obligations of author to, x; with Col. Doniphan on his visit to Santa Fé....................... 585
Lea, Lieut. James, appointed Asst. Quartermaster, 264; acting as Asst. Q. M., 364; rejoined company at El Paso, 392; turned over mules and stores at Matamoras....................... 491
Leal, J. W., killed in insurrection...... 514
Lee, S., killed in insurrection......... 514
Leland, John D., died at El Paso....92, 392
Leintz, Montgomery P., at battle of Sacramento..................... 417
Leslie, Augustus, died on the march to Santa Fé....................... 173
Leitrendorfer, Eugene, appointed Auditor of Public Accounts for New Mexico.... 243
Lewis, Mrs. Sallie Stone, obligations of author to......................... ix
Lice, soldiers infested with large, handsome ones..................... 490
Lickenlighter, of the artillery, mobbed by Mexicans...................... 481
Lincoln, President Abraham, received only the vote of William Gilpin in Jackson county, Mo., in 1860, 151; appointed Dr. Henry Connelly Governor of New Mexico................... 282
Link, E. S., obligations of author·to.... ix
Lipans, The, defeated at El Pozo by Americans, 478; sketch of.......... 480
Livingston, Kincade & Co., merchants at Salt Lake City.................... 609
Log College, founded by the Blairs..... 244
Long, Benjamin S., Assistant Surgeon, Santa Fé Trace Battalion.......... 149
Long, Hon. Chester I., obligations of author to........................... vi
Los Angeles, battle and sketch of field of. 346
Loughrey, Mrs. Mary, obligations of author to, viii; has the Gregg family Bible,—daughter of Philip Allan Hardwicke,—lives in Clay county, Mo.,—letter of, to author, 165; recollections of Dr. Josiah Gregg, 169; letter of Dr. Josiah Gregg belongs to, (she has since given it to the author).......... 171, 173
Love, Lieut., attacked by Indians on the Arkansas...................... 522
Lyon, Gen. Nathaniel, at battle of Wilson Creek........................ 54

M.

Maddox, (either John or Uriah,) died Dec. 13, 1846.......................... 93
Magoffin, family of, in America........ 196
Magoffin, Beriah, Governor of Kentucky, 196
Magoffin, James, goes with Captain Cooke to Santa Fé to interview Gov. Armijo, 183; portrait of,—secret history of conquest of New Mexico in biography of,—biography of, 196; narrow escape of, 199; arrested at El Paso, 365; carried as prisoner to Durango, 445; factor in the conquest of New Mexico.......... 587
Magoffin, Judge Joseph, obligations of author to, x; sketch of,—writes the author.... 197
Magraw, M. F., mentioned............ 135
Magraw, Pacific Wagon-Road Expedition of, mentioned..................... 605
Major, W. Boone, obligations of author to viii
Majors, Alexander, one of the partners of Russell, Majors & Waddell.......... 602
Mann, Captain, party of, attacked by Indians............................... 523
Manuelito, signed treaty with Navajos.. 307
Map, of movements of Americans at battle of Sacramento................... 105
Marcy, Hon. W. L., praises Expedition of Col. Doniphan.................. 437
Marmaduke, M. M., a Santa Fé trader... 630
Marney, Amos, freighter for Dr. Henry Connelly......................... 142
Marsh, Benjamin W., shot John D. Lard, 84, 283
Marshall, J., killed in insurrection....... 514
Marshall, Joseph, joined in the reckless charge of Kirker and Collins at battle of Sacramento.................... 418
Mason, W. S., killed.................. 521
Massey, Tom, said to have been "Brother Ike" to Joe Bowers................ 6
Maxwell, ——, (Samuel?) of Company F, died........................... 99
Maxwell, Samuel, "talked himself to death" at El Paso................. 396
Maxwell, ——, died Feb. 14, 1847...... 399
May, Dr. Ware S., married sister of Peter H. Burnett, 279; chosen Surgeon Second Regiment..................... 257
Meade, Gen. George G., instructor of William Gilpin..................... 145
Memoir of Life and Public Services of John Charles Frémont, referred to.......... 359
Memoir of a Tour to Northern Mexico connected with Col. Doniphan's Expedition, by A. Wislizenus, M. D., referred to... 144
Mexicans, remarks upon, by John T. Hughes, 187; character of, as described by John T. Hughes, 194; group of, 212; remarks concerning................ 447
MacGruder, J. L., wounded at battle of Sacramento....................... 416
MacLean, Lachlan Allan, biography and portrait of,—killed in altercation with one of his own men, 118; a volunteer in Captain Reid's Company,—aided in designing Fort Marcy, 245; went on hunting-trip from El Paso, 386; at taking of hacienda, 405; wounded at battle of Sacramento, 416; in Saline County Company.................. 548
McCarty, Thomas, mentioned, 61, 76; elected 2d Sergeant, 78; one of guard to capture son of Salezar............ 193
McCarty, William, on Green river in 1857, 608
McClure, A., died.................... 110

INDEX. 663

McCord, P. B., obligations of author to, ix; portrait of, 13; painter of the Joe Bowers portrait,—sketch of.......... 14
McDaniel, Captain John, and party, murder Chavez....................... 160
McDaniel, W., mentioned.............. 405
McElwee, Abner, said to have been original of Joe Bowers.................. 6
McEnnis, Michael, obligations of author to, x; portraits of, 625, 626; sketch of............................... 625
McKnight, ——, a prisoner in Mexico,—made fortune at the copper mines.... 324
McLane, L., one of the commissioners to settle terms....................... 349
McLoughlin, ——, factor of Hudson Bay Company, friendly to Gilpin......... 147
Military Reconnoissance from Fort Leavenworth to San Diego, etc., by Lieut. W. H. Emory, referred to............... 143
Mission of the North American People, by William Gilpin, referred to....... 151, 152
Missourians, tribute to, 3; to be called "Pikers," 7; achievements of........ 168
Missouri Historical Society, obligations of author to, viii; preserves black flag carried by Mexicans at battle of Brazito............................... 375
Missouri State Guard, mentioned...... 56
Mitchell, Lieut.-Col. D. D., mentioned, 75, 85, 93, 96; chosen Lieutenant-Colonel of Second Regiment, 257; action of, at the battle of Sacramento, 411; report of, on the battle of Sacramento, 427; mentioned in Col. Doniphan's official report of battle of Sacramento............................ 436
Mitchell, R. B., appointed Governor of New Mexico....................... 282
Montezuma, beliefs concerning, 60; palace to, 61; traditions of, in New Mexico,—ruins of temple to............ 193
Moore, Captain B. D., mentioned, 74; sent to overhaul the traders, 138; mentioned, 160; rejoins "Army of the West," 179; marches with Gen. Kearny to California, 317; killed in battle with Californians................... 334
Moore, Henry, died................... 186
Moore, Meredith T., obligations of author to, vi; on origin of Joe Bowers song, 9; visited by John T. Hughes, 49; describes snakes in camp at Stranger Creek, 141; drowns George L. Boone's horse in Pawnee Fork, 159; describes the Navajo expedition, 293, *et seq.*; devours part of Cogburn's mare, 296; acquaintance of, with J. A. DeCourcy, mentioned, 363; gets his money from G. Pope Gordon, 364; describes stabbing of Lieut. Wells at El Paso, 387; account of James Kirker, 388; account of the battle of Sacramento,—wounded by his horse,—sick at battle of Sacramento, but fought all day, 416; *et seq.*; details of actions of, at battle of Sacramento, 419; fired on by Captain Reid's men at battle of Sacramento, 421; battle of El Pozo described by, 478; wore through the war, buckskin suit made by George L. Boone, 493; furnished information for identification of members of Company F, 555; portrait of,—biographical sketch of, 639; intention of author to write life of, 640;
genealogical table of family of,—marriage of, with the Ramsay family..... 641
Moore, Milton, obligations of author to, ix; knew Hiram Bledsoe........... 540
Moore, Dr. ——, promoted to Assistant Surgeon.......................... 364
Moquis, villages of................... 312
Mora, sketch of...................... 189
Morehead, Charles R., obligations of author to, x; narrative of,—sketch of,—portrait of, 600, *et seq.*; sent to Fort Kearny, 602; sent to the Plains in May, 1857, 603; in battle of Plum Creek,—at Ash Hollow,—at Fort Laramie, 605; journey of, to Fort Leavenworth, in winter of 1857-58, 611; leaves Fort Leavenworth for Fort Laramie, 615; trip of, from Salt Lake City,—marriage of,—visits Maysville, Ky., 619; contracts to deliver cattle at Forts Larned and Lyon, 620; buys land at El Paso from Judge Magoffin, 621; travels of,—settles at El Paso........ 622
Morehead, Turner, biographical sketch of, 600
Morin, Captain I., mentioned.......... 76
Mormon Battalion, mention of, 70, 74; arrived at Santa Fé, 75; departed for California, 76; some of, return to Santa Fé, 81; arrived in California, 352; the sick of, sent to Pueblo for the winter, 352-3; left at San Diego........ 355
Mormons, went to war with the United States in 1857..................... 603
Morton, J. F., promoted to Assistant Surgeon.......................... 364
Morton, Dr. T. M., mentioned, 86; promoted to Regimental Surgeon........ 364
Moss, Captain Oliver P., biographical sketch of, 135; mentioned in address of Mrs. Cunningham, 137; sent to Valverde, 270; actions of, at battle of Sacramento, 411; Roster of Company of............................... 542
Mount, Thornton A., murdered........ 111
Murphy, Captain William S., commands Platte County troops, 373; Roster of Company of...................... 568
Music, The, of Joe Bowers song........ 12

N.

Nagle, Captain, forces of, to remain in the Valley of the San Joaquin........ 358
Narbona, Chief of the Navajos, portrait of, 293; some account of,—wife of, speaks in council, 295; signed treaty with the Navajos................... 307
Narrative of the Texan Santa Fé Expedition, by George Wilkins Kendall, referred to.......................... 192
Narrows, the location of, on Santa Fé Trail.............................. 143
National Cemetery, view of that at Santa Fé................................ 71
Navajos, The, mentioned, 74; chiefs of, 76, 78; two of, killed, 80; marched against by Mexicans, 85; country of, to be invaded, 266; difficult for them to understand why they are prohibited by the Americans from making war on the New-Mexicans,—sketch of, 286; account of visit to and council with, 295; drive off mules and horses, 297; treaty with, 305; country of,—remarks upon,

315; expedition into country of, letter of Captain John W. Reid, describing, 293
Navajo Expedition, The, described by Meredith T. Moore.......... 294, et seq.
Nebraska Territory, first constitution for, written by William Gilpin........... 151
New-Mexicans, traits and characteristics of............................... 216
New Mexico, Code for, in preparation, 65; proclamation to citizens of, by Gen. Kearny, 181; conditions in, before entrance of American troops, 184; proclamation of Gen. Kearny annexing to the United States, 208; brief history of, 211, et seq.; account of conquest of, sent to Washington, 218; condition of, reported by Gen. Kearny, 236; Code and Constitution of. compiled by Col. Doniphan and Willard P. Hall, 239; Code printed, 241; officers appointed for by Gen. Kearny, 243; administration of justice in.................. 246
Noah, one of the slaves of Dr. Josiah Gregg........................... 171
Noble, Lieut., mentioned, 74, 78; rejoins the "Army of the West," 179; marches with Gen. Kearny to California........................... 317
Noyes, ——, killed in insurrection...... 514

O.

Ochoa, Governor, proclamation of...... 110
Ogden, Lieut. Henry T., mentioned, 78; ordered to prevent the traders from advancing, 83; reinforced, 84; some account of...................... 546
Ojo Caliente, American army at........ 402
"Old Kickapoo," famous cannon....... 542
"Old Sacramento," some account of the famous cannon.................... 541
Oklahoma, resources of, described by Dr. Josiah Gregg...................... 170
Oldham, Lieut. James S., dismissed from service...................... 64, 217
Olvera, A., one of the commissioners to settle terms...................... 349
Onate, made new conquest of New Mexico............................ 213
Oregon Trail, The, by Francis Parkman, referred to........................ 180
Ortiz, Francisco, superseded as Treasurer of Santa Fé....................... 220
Ortiz, Ramon, captured, 90; taken into custody, 97; charged with stirring up insurrection, 391; carried from El Paso as hostage, 397; kindness of, to Americans, 400; interview with Col. Doniphan the night before battle of Sacramento............................. 406
Otero, Antonio José, appointed Judge of the Superior Court of New Mexico.... 243
Otero, M. A., Secretary of New Mexico.. 282
Owen, Mrs. Rush Campbell, obligations of author to........................ ix
Owens, Major Samuel C., furnishes money to Col. Doniphan, 92; election of, as Major, 99; Major of Traders' Battalion, and killed at battle of Sacramento, 398, 411; joined in the reckless charge of Kirker and Collins at battle of Sacramento, 418; funeral of, 446; partner of James Aull. 468; death of, at Sacramento............................. 590
Owens, W., killed.................... 521

P.

Pacos, (Pecos,) ruins of the village of.... 193
Paintsville, Ky., battles at, in Civil War, vii
Palace, to the Montezumas, description of................................. 61
Palace, Old, at Santa Fé, portrait of.... 2
Palmer, John, removed as Sergt.-Major, 91
Palo Alto, battle of................... 129
Parsons, Miss Mildred, marriage of, to Col. A. M. Standish................. 138
Parsons, Captain M. M., mentioned, 72; biography of, 136; in the southern expedition, 222; sent to Cebolleta, 250; sent in pursuit of the Navajos, 297; in Navajo expedition, 303; returned to Covero, 309; position of, at battle of Sacramento, 410; halted by DeCourcy at battle of Sacramento, 418; supported Captain Weightman at battle of Sacramento, 430; Roster of Company of, 553; Roster of officers of Company of, omitted by typographical error from page 553, but to be found under "F," "Rolls," "Rosters," and at page 649
Pass, The, fortified by Gov. Armijo..... 190
Patton, J. W., portrait of.............. 115
Paulsel, Henry R., sent to Fort Leavenworth with mail.................... 556
Pawnees, The, fought by Santa Fé Trace Battalion, 151; legends of, concerning Pawnee Rock, 163; trains guarded from, 166; battle between and Cheyennes at Pawnee Fort, 172; infested Santa Fé Trail.................... 522
Pawnee Fork, provision train halted at, 157; arrival of "Army of the West" at, 166; bridged by Gen. Kearny.... 167
Pawnee Fort, passed by "Army of the West"............................. 172
Pawnee Rock, number of buffalo to be seen from top of, 140; arrival of "Army of the West" at............. 162
Pea Ridge, Battle of.................. 56
Peacock, James, obligations of author to, viii; describes battle of Brazito, 371; account of James Kirker and the Delawares, 388; story of, about the socks being fired from cannon at El Paso, 395; account of battle of Sacramento, 414; in the portrait of "D—mn a mule, anyhow," 472; relates circumstances of the review of Col. Doniphan's troops by Gen. Wool, 482; tells of Lem White being directed by Gen. Taylor where to get some good whisky, 484; relates incident of large lice................ 490
Pedro, Sancho, Gen. Kearny's hostler,— some account of,—inscription at grave of................................. 323
Pelzer, Capt. William, of Santa Fé Trace Battalion.......................... 149
Penn, William, Gregg ancestor came to America with...................... 163
Penn, ——, Surgeon, resigned......... 364
Peralta, mentioned, 68; residence of the Chavez family..................... 233
Peterson, Hon. Cyrus, President Missouri Historical Society, obligations of author to............................. viii
Pettus, Charles P., Secretary Missouri Historical Society, obligations of author to............................. viii

INDEX. 665

Picayune, The New Orleans, Dr. Josiah Gregg correspondent for............ 172
Pickett, Mr. ——, living at Van Buren, Ark................................ 171
Pico, Andreas, one of the commissioners to settle terms.................... 349
Pike, Captain Zebulon M., in New Mexico................................ 213
Pike, Captain Albert, went in advance of the army......................... 469
Pike's Peak, discovery of gold at........ 606
"Pikers," origin of name for.......... 7
Pimos, The, mention of............... 330
Pino, Manuel, search for.............. 91
Platte County, Annals of, by W. M. Paxton, referred to.................... 165
Platte County, Roster of Company of.... 568
Pollard, ——, arrested by Mexicans, 88; released by Col. Doniphan........... 382
Pomeroy, Mr. ——, aided James L. Collins to escape..................... 92
Ponce de Leon, General, wounded by T. Forsythe at battle of Brazito........ 374
Pony Express, origin of............... 614
Potts, Mr. ——, refuses to open mint at Chihuahua......................... 446
Powell, Lieutenant-Colonel, raised a battalion............................ 523
Prentis, Noble L., on origin of "Pikers".. 7
Price, General Sterling, mentioned, 3; biography of, 40, *et seq.;* portrait of, 41; appearance of, 43; character of army of, 44; love of men for, 45; at battle of Wilson Creek, 54; sent Col. John T. Hughes to invade North Missouri, 55; at battle of Pea Ridge,—at Des Arc, 56; mentioned, 70, 72; arrival of, at Santa Fé, 74; fought last battle of Mexican War, 92; delayed sending artillery to Col. Doniphan on account of insurrection, 93; portrait of, 112; to garrison Santa Fé, 130; no news of, at Santa Fé, 202; organized Second Regiment, 256; originally intended to march to California by way of South Pass,—march of, to Santa Fé, 257; letter of Gen. Kearny to, 258; went by the Cimarron Route,—at Cimarron Springs, sent to Santa Fé for rations,—arrived at Santa Fé in poor health, 260; left in command of forces in New Mexico, 510; fights battle of La Canada, 514; marches to Taos, 515; loss sustained by,—returns to Santa Fé................................. 524
Price, Col. William, mentioned........ 46
Proclamation, text of that issued by Gen. Kearny to citizens of New Mexico.... 181
Proclamation, text of that annexing New Mexico to the United States......... 208
Provisional Government of Nebraska Territory, by William E. Connelley, referred to.................................. 151
Pueblos, The, chief of, visits Gen. Kearny to learn of the conquest of New Mexico, 218; have a war-dance, 272; served under Major Gilpin................. 299
Puerco, The, notice of................ 270
Pursley, Captain James, found by Pike at Santa Fé........................ 630

Q.

Quantrill, W. C., at battle of Independence............................... 57

R.

Radell, Miss Aimee, mentioned....... 59
Railroad, Pacific, advocated by William Gilpin, 151; one to be built around the world, mapped by William Gilpin.... 152
Ralls, Colonel, raised a regiment....... 523
Ramsay, history of family of....641, *et seq.*
Ramsay, Josiah, the many adventures of, 642, *et seq.*
Rangers, The Laclede, Roster of Company of, 563; attached to Major Clark's Battalion of Artillery.,...... 572
Rations, "Army of the West" had insufficient.......................... 186
Reading, P. B., one of the commissioners to settle terms.................... 349
Regimental Field and Staff, First Missouri Mounted Volunteers.......... 529
Red River Cañon, Battle of........... 520
Red Sleeve, Apache Chief, visits Gen: Kearny............................ 324
Reid, Captain John W., mentioned, 66; candidate for Lieutenant-Colonel, 70; mentioned, 72; company of, paid for clothing, 85; commands scouting party, 87; sent to the Presidio, 89; gains information, 90; sent to aid Captain Weightman, 95; starts for Parras, 109; at battle of El Pozo, 111; biography of, 135; sent to overhaul the traders, 138; mentioned, 160; rejoined "Army of the West," 179; in southern expedition, 221; resents Gen. Kearny's order to wear coats, 224; sent to Cebolleta, 250; solicits permission to penetrate Navajo country, 287; permission obtained,—begins the march, — nature of country, — difficulties, 288; went to meet the Navajos, 289; letter of, to John T. Hughes, describing the Navajo expedition, 291; charged at battle of Brazito, 374; sent to the Presidio, 384; takes hacienda 405; position of, at battle of Sacramento, 410; joined in the reckless charge of Kirker and Collins at battle of Sacramento, 418; foolishly attacks Mexican officer who had surrendered, —men of, fired on Meredith T. Moore on battle-field, 421; supported Capt. Weightman at battle of Sacramento, 430; fights battle of El Pozo, 476, *et seq.;* Roster of Company of......... 547
Republic, The St. Louis, obligations of author to........................... x
Resaca de la Palma, Battle of......... 129
Rice, John, as tender-hearted as a woman, —became a demon in battle,—threw away his gun and with sword brandished aloft swept over the field slaying Mexicans,—typographical error in the word *brandished*, 420; toast drunk to, after the Mexican War, 421; mention of................................. 556
Richardson, William H., describes the hardships of the soldiers, 365; describes battle of Brazito............ 372
Riche, ——, sutler to First Dragoons.... 166

666 DONIPHAN'S EXPEDITION.

Riggin, George W., at battle of Sacramento.......................... 419
Ringo, M., and others, adventure of..... 184
Rio Grande, description of valley of, 66, et seq.; valley of, explored by Coronado, 212; remarks concerning, 229; note of........................... 397
Rivera, Tomas, appointed Collector of Santa Fé........................ 220
Robards, Mr. ——, died.............. 403
Robb, Mr. ——, wounded in battle of Plum Creek...................... 604
Roberts, P., killed in insurrection...... 514
Robidoux, Anthony, the interpreter.... 91
Rodgers, Captain Charles B., mentioned, 66; sick, 81; biography of, 138; in southern expedition, 222; sent to Valverde, 270; actions of, at battle of Sacramento, 414; Roster of Company of............................... 560
Rodgers, ——, escaped from Chihuahua and came to Col. Doniphan at El Paso, 391
Rogers, James, arrested.............. 94
Rogers, James R., obligations of author to,—letter on death of A. W. Doniphan, jr................................ vii
Rollins, Edward, left Salt Lake City with Morehead........................ 618
Rolls, official, of troops under Col. Doniphan.......................527, et seq.
Rosters, official, of troops under Col. Doniphan.......................527, et seq.
Roster, that of Officers of Company F, (omitted by typographical error from head of Roster of the Company at page 553.)
1. M. M. Parsons............Captain.
1. Richard A. Wells...........1st Lieut.
1. George Pope Gordon........2d Lieut.
2. George B. Winston.........2d Lieut.
1. Fountain McKenzie.........1st Sgt.
2. William W. Bolton.........Sgt.
3. Robert A. Raphael.........Sgt.
4. Absalom Hughes...........Sgt.
1. William Rogers...........Corp.
2. James H. McKenzie.......Corp.
3. G. Burr Gordon...........Corp.
4. Thomas L. Anderson......Corp.
1. James Henley.............Farrier.
See also page 649 for this omitted list of officers.
Rothwell, Mrs. John H., obligations of author to, viii; of the Gregg family.... 163
Routt, Henry L., Adjutant Santa Fé Trace Battalion,................. 149
Ruff, Lieut.-Col. Charles F., in command of southern expedition, 68; elected Lieutenant-Colonel of First Regiment, —caused arrest of soldiers at Tome, 69; biography of, 133; camped on Stranger creek, 141; another mention of his election, 148; has altercation with Capt. Congreve Jackson, 159; overtaken at Cow creek by Col. Doniphan, 160; popularity of, waning, 175; appointed to command grazing detachment at Galesteo creek, 207; mentioned, 222; resigns his command, 247; subsequent service of, 248; dislike of men for........................ 249
Rupe, Captain James, soldier in Price's Regiment, Mexican War, — superintendent of mail routes on the Plains,—employed by Russell, Majors & Waddell,—left Fort Leavenworth in May,

1857, 603; fights Cheyennes, 604; passes Ash Hollow, 605; with Morehead,—starts back to States........ 610
Russell, John W., clerk for Russell, Majors & Waddell................ 602
Russell, W. H., (not of the great freighting firm,) one of the commissioners to settle terms...................... 349
Russell, William H., the Napoleon of the Plains, biographical sketch of,—portrait of......................... 601
Russell, W., mentioned............... 405
Ruxton's Adventures in Mexico, referred to............................... 461
Ryan, Matthew, partner of Charles R. Morehead........................ 620
Ryland, Major, written to by Colonel Doniphan....................... 450

S.

Sac-and-Fox Indians, killed William Gregg and carried away his daughter.. 164
Sacramento, Battle of, mentioned, 103; description of, 409, et seq.; plans of the battle of, 412; illustration of the charge of Captain Reid at, 413; Americans wounded at, 416; reckless charge of Kirker, Collins and others, at,—confusion in ranks of American army at,—Americans saved by the reckless charge of Kirker, Collins and others, 418; described by William H. Richardson, 422; official report of Col. Doniphan upon, 423; described by Frank S. Edwards, 424; Col. Mitchell's report of, 427; Major Gilpin's report of, 428; Major Clark's report of, 433; Lieut. Gibson's description of.................... 440
"Sacramento, Old," famous cannon, account of........................ 541
Sagundo, signed treaty with Navajos... 307
Salazar, General, mentioned, 60; captures Gen. McClure and men, 64; in insurrection in New Mexico, 93; captures the Texans under Gen. McLeod.. 192
Salazar, General, son of, captured, 61; supposed to be a spy.............. 192
Salazar, Ignacio, guide for Major Gilpin, 299
Saline County, Missouri, history of, referred to........................ 164
Salute, one fired with pair of socks at El Paso............................ 395
Sanborn, ——, killed by Indians at Plum Creek............................ 604
Sandoval, sent to interview his people, 286; guide to Captain Reid in Navajo expedition, 289; true friend of the Americans, 296; signed treaty with Navajos........................ 307
San Filipe, mentioned, 67; priest of, acknowledges authority of U. S., 218; southern expedition at............. 228
San Gabriel, Battle of, 344; sketch of field of.......................... 345
San Miguel, surrenders to Gen. Kearny... 192
Santa Fé, entered by Americans, 62; houses of, 63; view of National Cemetery at, 71; Gen. Kearny expects resistance in entering, 170; visited by Captain Cooke and other Americans, 183; entered by Gen. Kearny with his army, 198; American flag planted in public square of,—entered by Gen.

INDEX.   667

Kearny without opposition, 200; citizens of, assemble to hear address,—text of address, 201; officers of, take oath of allegiance, 202; abuse of American traders and residents in, 207; plan of, 210; description of,—when settled, 215; duties established for, 220; conditions of, in fall of 1846............ 260
Santa Fé Trace Battalion, organization of, by William Gilpin,—various names known by,—officers of,—operations of, —some account of............148, *et seq.*
Santa Fé Trail, "Army of the West" marches over, to Conquest of New Mexico and California, 140, *et seq.;* maps of, referred to,—references to authorities on, 143; where it crossed the Cottonwood and the Little Arkansas, 158; where it crossed Cow creek and the Walnut, 160; hardships of the "Army of the West" in marching over, 168; the main road of, by the Cimarron, in 1846, 171; Bent's Fort an important post on, 179; account of,— identification of route of.......630, *et seq.*
Santo Domingo, mentioned, 66, 77; Gen. Kearny at, 227; sketch of........... 267
Scott, General Winfield, sent to Vera Cruz................................... 130
Shawnees, The, "Army of the West" camped in country of, 142; employed to kill Apaches.................... 330
Sherman, Gen. W. T., tribute of, to Francis P. Blair, jr...................... 248
Sherry, Gen. Byron, mentioned......... 58
Shoshones, met at Green river by Morehead and Rupe.................... 607
Shubrick, Commodore, to blockade Guaymas............................... 358
Sick, The, one hundred in "Army of the West," 172; some of, left at Bent's Fort................................ 181
Sioux, The, marched against by Gen. Kearny, 226; called Gen. Harney "the Great Wasp"..................... 617
Skillman, Captain, election of, 99; spies on Mexico, 103; made a Captain in Traders' Battalion, 398; pursues some of the enemy, 406; charged on Mexicans at battle of Sacramento, 440; resident of New Mexico................ 590
Sloat, Commodore John D., raises American flag at Monterey............... 340
Smelser, Susannah, marriage of, to Harmon Gregg...................... 163
Smith, Frank, of Saline Company, killed two Mexicans at one shot........... 369
Smith, Lot, a Mormon Danite......... 609
Smith & Co., Messrs. Robert, had trading-house in California................. 174
Smith Trading-House, California, letter of Philip Allan Hardwicke written from............................. 174
Snakes, number of, encountered at Stranger creek........................... 141
Snell, Lieut. James G., died, 81; buried at La Joya........................ 273
Socks, pair of, fired from cannon at El Paso............................... 395
Socorro, sick of American army moved to, 309
Southern Expedition, officers and men in, 222
South Pass, Gen. Kearny at, in 1845.... 226
Spears, Robert, killed..............82, 275

Speyers, ——, caravan of, 139; escapes from pursuing detachment, 179; some account of........................ 462
Spies, Mexican, captured in camp of Gen. Kearny............................ 177
Stearne, William, died, 85; sick on Navajo expedition, 296; died at Covero.... 309
Stamped paper, use of, in New Mexico, discontinued by Gen. Kearny........ 219
Stampede, that of horses below Bent's Fort................................ 178
Standish, Col. Austin M., one of party of Captain Parsons murdered by Mexicans in Civil War, 137; biography of.. 138
Standish, Mrs. Mildred P., obligations of author to............................. ix
Star, The Kansas City, obligations of author to.............................. x
St. Louis, reception of Col. Doniphan and men at......................496, *et seq.*
St. Vrain, Cerean, associated in business with the Bents................... 179
Steele, Count Sobieska, mentioned..... 58
Steele, Miss Maud, marriage of, to Roland Hughes............................ 58
Stephenson, Captain John D., killed William Bray, 70; sent to Abiquiu, 72; arrives at El Paso, 90; mentioned, 96; obtains cattle, 97; biography of, 135; in southern expedition, 222; mention of his killing William Bray, 249; ordered to Abiquiu, 250; sent to the Rio de Charxa, 298; actions of, at battle of Sacramento, 414; fine conduct of company of, at battle of Sacramento, 419; Roster of Company of............. 550
Stevenson, Colonel, command of, to garrison Monterey....................... 358
Stewart, James, killed..............82, 275
Stokes, Mr. ——, gives Gen. Kearny information of Commodore Stockton.... 333
Stockton, Commodore Robert Field, mentioned, 76; express from, 262; in command of navy in California, 342; forms junction with Frémont, 343; marches against the insurgents, 344; report of battle of San Gabriel and Los Angeles......................347, *et seq.*
Story, John Smith, obligations of author to, x; identifies members of Clay County Company.................. 545
Sublette, Lieut. L. B., mentioned, 66; officer of the guard at Tome,—arrested a number of soldiers, 69; pursues Indians, 83; takes wagons, 69; sent to halt commissary wagons, 174; sketch of family of,—in southern expedition............................... 221
Sullivan, J., wounded at battle of Sacramento.............................. 416
Sumner, Captain E. V., mentioned, 74; met Gen. Kearny on the Santa Fé Trail, 184; marched to California with Gen. Kearny, 317; returned to Albuquerque................................ 322
Sutton, Jesse, held MSS. and property of Dr. Josiah Gregg................... 173
Switzler, Col. W. F., mentioned, 75; writes of Francis P. Blair, jr........ 247
Swords, Major, overtakes Gen. Kearny at Las Vegas, 191; ordered to arrest rioter, 208; Quartermaster on march to California, 321; sent to Sandwich Islands to buy supplies.............. 355

T.

Taos, Curate of, comes to acknowledge authority of United States, 218; battle at.............................. 516
Tapio, signed treaty with Navajos...... 307
Taylor, Gen. Zachary, as President appointed John T. Hughes Receiver of Land Office, 51; victories over Mexican forces, 129; commander of "Army of Occupation," 130; directs Lem White where to get whisky, 484; poor showing made by................... 597
Tecolate, surrenders to Gen. Kearny.... 192
Tennesseans, settle Cox's Bottom (Saline county, Mo.),—the boast of...... 164
Tennessee, *History of Middle*, by A. W. Putnam, referred to................ 164
Texans, cannon of, secured by Gen. Kearny........................... 209
Texan Rangers, execute a Mexican guerrilla, 487; illustration representing... 489
Texan Santa Fé Expedition, by Kendall, referred to...................... 389
Thirty Years' View, by Thomas H. Benton, referred to..................... 197
Thompson, Col. Gideon W., mentioned... 57
Thompson, Captain, raised the Chihuahua Rangers.......................... 365
Thompson, Captain, defeats Californians at Salinas...................... 351
Thompson, Captain, orders charge at Sacramento....................... 415
Thompson, D. F., obligations of author to............................... vii
Thompson, D. P., obligations of author to............................... viii
Thornton, John..................... 135
Thorpe, T. B., Zuni described to, by Col. Doniphan......................... 312
Thwaites, R. G., editor *Early Western Travels*, 157; reprinted work of Dr. Josiah Gregg,—could obtain no information concerning Gregg.......... 168
Tindall, Jacob T., Sergt.-Major Santa Fé Trace Battalion.................... 149
Tolley, W., died at Laguna de los Patos.. 401
Tome, southern expedition at,—reception of army at,—army returns from, to Santa Fé, 69; Americans encamped near, 79; entertainments at.......... 233
Totten's Battery, at battle of Wilson creek............................. 54
Towson, Fort, on Red river, 280; location and history of..................... 452
Traders, The, encamped near Fray Cristobal, 81; spies in camp of,—dismiss American drivers,—prohibited from advancing, 83; begin journey across Jornada del Muerto, 86; sell goods at El Paso, 89; two of, lost 280 mules by Apaches, 93; organized into a battalion, 99; ten of, remained at Chihuahua, 109; halted by order of Gen. Kearny, 139; annual caravan of, 140; some of, overtaken at Walnut Creek, 161; encamped at Valverde, 270; in fear of attack, 273; formed corral,—spies among, 274; English officer brings proposal of Mexican authorities to, 276; advance money to Col. Doniphan, 386; organized into battalion... 397
Treaty, that of Col. Doniphan with the Navajos........................... 307
Trias, Gov. Angel, proclamation of, 88; proclamation of, against the Americans, 385; one of the Mexican commanders at battle of Sacramento..... 408
Tungitt, ——, found sleeping on picket.. 391
Turkey Creek, "Army of the West" crossed........................... 158
Turley, ——, killed in insurrection...... 514
Turner, Captain, ordered to arrest rioter, 208; aide to Gen. Kearny, 321; sails with Gen. Kearny for Monterey...... 355
Tuttle, Caleb, Captain Company E, Santa Fé Trace Battalion................. 151
"Twain, Mark," did not write Joe Bowers song.............................. 9

U.

Ugarte, General Mauricia, one of the commanders of the Mexicans at battle of Sacramento...................... 408
Utahs, The, chiefs of, call on Gen. Kearny at Santa Fé, 72; chiefs of, mentioned, 76; brought in to hold council........ 251

V.

Valdez, Mary Gertrude, marriage of, to James Magoffin.................... 196
Valverde, concentration of soldiers at, 270; note concerning............... 367
Van Bibber, Ewing, horse of, disabled and killed at battle of Sacramento.... 417
Van Bibber, Sergt., undertakes to drive home mules and horses............. 491
Van Vliet, Stewart, Quartermaster U. S. A.,—detailed to locate a military fort, 606
Vaughan, Dr. I. P., left with 21 sick below Bent's Fort, 181; arrives at Santa Fé, 244; resigns..................... 364
Vaughan, J., mentioned............... 405
Vest, George G., member of Missouri Legislature,—introduced resolution calling convention.................. 53
Vigil, C., killed in insurrection.......... 514
Vigil, Donaiso, appointed Secretary of New Mexico....................... 243
Vigil, Lieut. ——, commanded force that went with Gilpin................... 299
Vilandi, Benezate, guide to Major Gilpin, 299
Voorhis, Miss Eleanor Glasgow, obligations of author to, x; aided author, 645
Voorhis, Mrs. Julia Clark, valuable papers of............................... 645

W.

Waddell, W. B., one of the firm of Russell, Majors & Waddell............. 602
Waldo, Captain David, mentioned, 66; sent to Abiquiu, 72; injured by fall from his horse, 87; mentioned, 95, 96; biography of, 133; sent to overhaul the traders, 138; friend to William Gilpin, 147; mentioned, 160; detailed to guard train at Pawnee Fork, 166; rejoins "Army of the West," 179; sent to Abiquiu, 250; sent to Rio de Chama, 298; on Navajo expedition, 302; translated proclamation of Angel Trias, 385; hunting party of, at El Paso, 386; at battle of Sacramento........ 411
Waldo, L., killed in insurrection......... 514
Wah-to-yah and the Taos Trail, by Lewis H. Garrard, referred to.............. 180

INDEX.   669

Wakarusa Creek, Kansas river crossed by "Army of the West" at mouth of.... 142

Wallace, William, son of Indian trader... 547

Walla Walla, exploring party arrives at, 147

Walker, I., Wyandot Indian in Mexican War.............................. 405

Walker, J. R., sheriff of Jackson county, Mo............................... 167

Walker, Robert, chosen Adjutant Second Regiment...................... 257

Walker, Robert D., told Gen. Wool of the mistake he made at the battle of Buena Vista................................. 484

Walmsley, Nathan, detailed to go on Navajo expedition................. 294

Walnut Creek, notice of,—"Army of the West" at, 160; the traders overtaken at.................................... 161

Walter, Uriah, adventure of........... 380

Walton, Captain William P., mentioned, 66; biography of, 134; in southern expedition, 221; sent to Valverde, 270; action of at battle of Sacramento.... 411

Walton, J. R., Treasurer State Hospital, Nevada, Mo....................... 134

Ward, General ——, of Platte county, Mo., held election for officers of First Regiment.......................... 133

War Department, confidential instructions of, to Gen. Kearny............ 203

Ware, E. F., obligations of author to, x; describes kindness of Gen. Sterling Price to prisoners................. 45

Warner, W. H., wounded............. 335

Warner, Lieut., sails with Gen. Kearny for Monterey...................... 355

Warren, John U., desperate man —shot Sublette.............................. 221

Watts, John S., Delegate in Congress from New Mexico....................... 282

Waugh, T., mentioned................ 405

Webster, Daniel, visits St. Louis in effort to defeat Senator Benton,—opposition of, to the West.................... 146

Weightman, Captain Richard Hanson, mentioned, 66; calls for aid, 95; comes up with Gen. Kearny near Las Vegas,—brings Kearny's commission as Brigadier-General, 191; in southern expedition, 221; services of, specially requested by Col. Doniphan,—portrait of,—biography of, 361; position and services at battle of Sacramento, 411, et seq.; threat to cut down artilleryman at battle of Sacramento, 426; charged with his battery at battle of Sacramento, 430; prepares to shoot down doors of mint at Chihuahua, 446; delivers his battery to Captain Washington, 483; Roster of Company of, 574; presence of, requested by Col. Doniphan, 588; kills F. X. Aubrey.... 629

Wells, Lieut. Richard A., stabbed by Lieut. Barnett, 97; went on Navajo expedition, 288, 294; stabbed in Frenchman's saloon at El Paso....... 387

Wharton, Lieut.-Col. Clifton, enmity of, towards Gilpin, 148; mustering officer, 149

Wheeler, Thomas, Company D, died Oct. 18, 1846............................ 93

White House, The, guarded by Senator James H. Lane and others.......... 152

White, Lem, directed by Gen. Taylor where to get some whisky.......... 484

Whitney, Mrs. Carrie Westlake, obligations of author to.................. ix

Wilburn, Thomas, tailor in Jefferson City, 364

Wilder, D. W., obligations of author to.. x

Willis, ——, died Feb. 14, 1847........ 399

Wilkinson, ——, killed................ 521

Williams, Major S. C., one of the party of Captain Parsons.................... 137

Wills, J. A., died..................... 99

Wilson, Albert, mentioned............ 74

Wilson, A., sutler Second Regiment..... 257

Wilson, John, attorney in the famous "Harper Case"...................... 27

Wilson, Hon. R. P. C., obligations of author to, viii; letter of, to author, describing Col. Doniphan.............. 29

Wilson Creek, Battle of............... 54

Wiltshire, John, foreman of jury which condemned John Brown............. 58

Winston, Dr. George B., Company F, suggests way for Meredith T. Moore to collect his money from G. Pope Gordon... 364

Wislizenus, A., M.D., work of, referred to, 144

Witherspoon, Dr. President Princeton University.......................... 244

Witten, Hon. Thomas A., mentioned.... 58

Wolf, J., wounded at battle of Sacramento............................ 416

Woods, Jonas, Captain Platte County Company........................... 373

Woodson, Samuel H., name of, erroneously written "Silas" H.,—attorney in famous "Harper Case," 27; delivers address at ceremony of crowning Col. Doniphan..................... 499

Woodson, Silas H., no such man,— Samuel H. Woodson erroneously so called, 27

Woodson, W. H., obligations of author to, viii

Woodward, John, probable author of Joe Bowers song....................... 9

Wool, General John E., mentioned, 77; commander of the "Army of the Center," 130; notified by Gen. Kearny that "Army of the West" would be sent to him, 200; supposed destination, Chihuahua, 251; abandons march on Chihuahua, 396; written to by Col. Doniphan, 454; complimentary letter of, to Col. Doniphan and men,—circumstances attending his review of Col. Doniphan's army, 482; endeavors to secure reënlistment of Missourians, 483; told by Robert D. Walker of the mistake he made at the battle of Buena Vista................................ 484

Wright, J. A., killed.................. 521

X.

Xenophon, Col. Doniphan compared to.. 438

Y.

Yount, Joseph, detailed to go on Navajo expedition, 294; devoured part of Cogburn's mare, 296; carries the carcasses of eleven sheep to his quarters,— "could read the Lord's Prayer" through one of them, 390; in battle of Sacramento, 417; missed Mexican at battle of Sacramento................ 419

Z.

Zuni, passed by Coronado, 211; pueblo of, 309; treaty with inhabitants of, 311; city of, described.............. 312

www.ingramcontent.com/pod-product-compliance
Lightning Source LLC
Chambersburg PA
CBHW070904300426
44113CB00008B/927